RW

Rules of Origin
in International Trade

STUDIES IN INTERNATIONAL TRADE POLICY

Studies in International Trade Policy includes works dealing with the theory, empirical analysis, political, economic, legal relations, and evaluations of international trade policies and institutions.

General Editor: Robert M. Stern

Rules of Origin in International Trade

A Comparative Study

**Edited by
Edwin Vermulst,
Paul Waer, and
Jacques Bourgeois**

Ann Arbor
THE UNIVERSITY OF MICHIGAN PRESS

1997   1996   1995   1994   4   3   2   1

A CIP catalogue record for this book is available from the British Library.

Rules of origin in international trade : a comparative study / edited by Edwin Vermulst,
    Paul Waer, and Jacques Bourgeois.
        p.   cm. — (Studies in international trade policy)
    Includes bibliographical references (p.   ) and index.
    ISBN 0-472-10411-X (acid-free paper)
    1. Certificates of origin.   2. Customs administration—Law and legislation.   3.
Customs administration.   I. Vermulst, Edwin A., 1958–   . II. Waer, Paul,
1958–   .   III. Bourgeois, Jacques, 1936–   .   IV. Series.
K4640.O74R85   1994
341.7'54—dc20   93-45611
                                                                       CIP

STUDIES IN INTERNATIONAL TRADE POLICY

Foreword

Professor John H. Jackson

The trade and customs laws of many countries often require identification of the country of origin for imported goods. If true most-favored-nation (MFN) treatment were followed for all goods and all origins, then presumably there would be no need for such rules. In fact, however, there is considerable differentiation in the treatment of imports, depending on their origin. For example, if six countries that are GATT (General Agreement on Tariffs and Trade) members form a customs union to free all trade among them from tariffs, then at least three levels of tariffs may apply to goods imported into one of the six: the GATT-bound tariff level of GATT members who are not in the customs union; tariff-free treatment for customs union goods; and tariffs on goods from other countries that are not GATT members. Thus, when widgets are imported, it may be necessary to determine from which of the three groups of countries the goods originated. In some case, there may be more than three categories, when other special preferential areas exist.

In addition, there are numerous other problems. The increasing recourse to trade restrictive measures, notably antidumping and countervailing duties, voluntary restraint arrangements (VRAs), etc., will normally also need to be supported by rules of origin to prevent the circumvention of such measures.

So let us imagine that producer X in country A, which does not belong to GATT, produces plastic pellets that are shipped to GATT member B. In B these are melted and extruded into combs. Can B ship the combs to GATT member C and claim GATT benefits? The key question is whether the products are those of B. Merely transhipping, or even merely repackaging products X, would probably not obtain for B the GATT treatment for the combs. But when substantial processing occurs, then B can claim the goods are now B's product. But how much processing is necessary?

GATT does not offer a single definitive answer to this question. Instead, each country, within the bounds of reasonableness, has the sovereign right to define its "rules of origin," which will govern the determinations of its customs officials about the "origin" of goods presented for import. Indeed, the same country may have several different rules of origin depending on the purpose of the regulation that governs the particular imports.

Hessel E. Yntema Professor of Law, University of Michigan Law School, Ann Arbor.

A multilateral convention covering rules of origin, called the Kyoto Convention was concluded under the auspices of the Customs Cooperation Council in 1974. However, not all countries have fully adopted the convention, and a number of the substantive rules of the Convention are not clear enough for developing modern commerce.

Rules of origin seem to be increasingly the subject of complaints from exporting countries, which argue that such rules unfairly restrict imports from the complainant. For example, the United States became quite upset about standards for rules of origin in some free trade agreements (FTAs) between the European Community (EC) and other European countries (former European Free Trade Association (EFTA) partners). Allegedly, the rule in question required 95 percent of the value of goods to be attributed to the free trade partner, thus reducing the opportunity for the United States to sell parts or partly completed products to EC countries in competition with favored third-country goods. More recently, the United States found itself sitting on the other side of this argument, with Canada accusing it of abusing rules of origin under the U.S.-Canada FTA in order to levy duties on cars produced by the Japanese producer Honda in Canada.

In the light of these trends, it is not surprising that a number of countries in the Uruguay Round insisted that rules of origin should be subjected to some form of GATT discipline, and a draft agreement on the subject is included in the December 1991 provisional texts of Uruguay Round agreements.

The present comparative study of the rules of origin of the European Communities, the United States, Japan, Australia and Canada is well timed. If the Uruguay Round succeeds, experts on the rules of origin from all over the world will strive to harmonize these rules in the framework of the Customs Cooperation Council, and this book will be an invaluable tool for them. In any event, the myriad rules of origin will likely continue to have great impact, and this book will be an important contribution to analysis and policy development.

This comparative study follows in the footsteps of a book on comparative antidumping law and practice[1] that I co-edited with Edwin Vermulst, a distinguished former student of mine. Dr. Vermulst and his impressive colleagues Jacques Bourgeois and Paul Waer have followed similar working methods as those employed in the antidumping book. Thus, they first selected one author for each key jurisdiction who in each case has had long experience as an attorney working on rules of origin cases, but who also has the scholarly qualities needed for this study. Their contributions, together with the comparative chapter and the chapter on rules of origin in GATT, provide the

---

1. John H. Jackson and Edwin A. Vermulst, eds., ANTIDUMPING LAW AND PRACTICE: A COMPARATIVE STUDY, (ANN ARBOR: THE UNIVERSITY OF MICHIGAN PRESS, 1989).

main chapters of this book. These chapters do not focus on "how to do it" nuts and bolts subjects but rather probe a number of more subtle empirical and policy issues about the substantive rules and the procedures of each jurisdiction and how they may affect trade flows and trade policy in general. To promote uniformity, these authors were provided with a template consisting of what the editors perceived to be the main issues and problems in present rules of origin, although each author has responded to the template in his or her own way. These and other chapters describe developments up to December 1992, with some updating to account for developments until August 1993. The chapters were then distributed to a small number of commentators who were given complete freedom to comment on these chapters or to raise particular issues that they felt were not addressed sufficiently in the rest of the book.

This book is the result of two and a half years of what has obviously been a great deal of work for a small group of dedicated and busy trade lawyer-scholars. I commend them for their diligence and for the high quality of their contributions. They have succeeded in reducing the extreme technicalities inherent in rules of origin to intelligent and concise overviews of the hidden trade-restrictive dangers lurking behind what are supposed to be "technical" applications of "technical" rules. They have put rules of origin in the spotlight in such a manner that they can be more easily subjected to the scrutiny of trade policy makers, academics and practising lawyers. And as rules of origin are an area of law that deserves and needs further study, they have performed a useful service to the world of freer trade and its consequent benefits for humanity.

Acknowledgments

The idea for this comparative trade law project was conceived in 1990 and followed in the aftermath of the publication of a comparable work analyzing the antidumping laws of the EC, the United States, Australia, and Canada.[1] Subsequent preparation and finalization took approximately three years. In the course of that period we benefitted considerably from the help of a number of individuals.

This book would have been impossible without its main contributors David Palmeter, Richard Gottlieb, Keith Steele, Danny Moulis, Ivan Kingston, Norio Komuro, and Edurne Navarro Varona (who also assisted in the early editing process). We thank all of them for their great efforts to explain with such clarity what is by all means a very technical subject. We also thank John Jackson, Ian Forrester, Gary Horlick, Michael Meyer, Jeff Waincymer, and Jochen Matthies for their valuable comments.

Finally, we would like to express our special appreciation to Folkert Graafsma for his invaluable assistance in getting the manuscript ready for publication.

Edwin Vermulst   Paul Waer   Jacques Bourgeois

Brussels, August 1993

---

1.   John H. Jackson and Edwin A. Vermulst, eds., ANTIDUMPING LAW AND PRACTICE: A COMPARATIVE STUDY, (ANN ARBOR: THE UNIVERSITY OF MICHIGAN PRESS, 1989).

Summary Table of Contents

Analytical Table of Contents

Chapter 5   Canadian Rules of Origin
              Richard S. Gottlieb   257

Rules of Origin: An Introduction

Jacques H. J. Bourgeois

1. Their Purpose

At first blush, rules of origin appear as an exclusively technical, albeit practically important, subject matter. In theory if every country were to apply MFN treatment to imported products, the origin of these products would arguably not matter; countries nevertheless do use origin rules, called nonpreferential, to distinguish foreign products from domestic products for a variety of purposes when they do not want to grant national treatment to foreign products. For example, this is the case with respect to government procurement in many countries that exclude foreign products, reserve certain transactions to domestic products, or grant a margin of preference to domestic products. This is also the case where certain countries subject the benefit of government investment subsidies to the condition that the investor acquires machinery or inputs of domestic origin.

Many countries also depart from MFN treatment of imported products. Whenever an importing country wants, for whatever reason, to differentiate between countries from which it imports products, it needs to define the nature of the link between each of these countries and the product that it wants to subject to a different, preferential treatment; such importing country must then define not only the foreign origin of the product but also the conditions under which it will consider that a product originates in the country to which it grants preferential treatment. The rules it adopts to do so are preferential rules of origin; they depart from the normal, general rules of origin in that the preferential country origin of a product, and thus the preferential treatment of the product when imported, will be made dependent on different or additional conditions.

2. Different Methods

There are at least three different theories or methods: the technical test (i.e., the product resulting from a process or operation in the exporting country must have its own specific properties and composition that it did not have

---

Member of the Brussels Bar, Partner of Baker & McKenzie (Brussels); Professor at the College of Europe (Bruges).

before the process or operation), the economic test (i.e., work done, expenditure, or material, added value), and the custom classification test (i.e., the process or operation in the exporting country results in a product that is classified under a different heading of the custom tariff classification than before the process or operation).[1] They may also be applied in combination; for example when applying the technical test, an importing country may well consider that although the process or operation in the exporting country results in a technically different product, the process or operation involves an increase in value or a cost that is too small to justify conferring origin.

These methods may also be applied alternatively in function of specific policy aims in particular in the framework of preferential trade arrangements.

Moreover, there are cases in which administrative agencies will depart from these methods when the origin of a product has to be determined in another framework than that of customs clearance. An obvious example is the origin of semiconductors for the purposes of antidumping measures both in the European Community (see chapter 3, § 3.2.2.2.7.) and in the United States (see chapter 2, § 5).

3. The Legitimacy of Preferential Origin Rules

This discrepancy raises a first issue, which needs to be addressed. The issue is not using the legitimacy of differential rules of origin as such, which is bound up with the legitimacy of the non-MFN trade policy measures that these origin rules serve. It has rather to do with the conditions set out in the origin rules on which preferential treatment is made dependent (see chapter 1). They reflect the intention of the preference-granting country to effectively reserve the benefit of the preference to the economy of the beneficiary country, usually by requiring higher beneficiary country content of the relevant product than is the case under the nonpreferential rules of origin. In some cases, it may work as under the FTAs between the European Community and the States of the European Free Trade Association where — as has been suggested — 75 percent of the trade benefits from the preferential trade regime (see chapter 3, concluding remarks). In other cases, it does not work because the conditions on which the recognition of origin depends cannot be met in the beneficiary country. The Fourth Lomé Convention concluded between the European Community and the so-called African, Caribbean and Pacific (ACP) States contains an interesting example: to benefit from the preferential treatment, fishery products must comply with the

---

1. For more details, see chapter 9, § 2. In addition, in some jurisdictions assembly operations involve an independent intellectual element; this interpretation tends to favor artisanal methods of production.

following origin rules: canning does not confer origin; to have origin of the ACP States the fish must be "taken from the sea by their vessels"; to qualify as "their" (i.e. ACP) vessels, vessels must be registered in an ACP State (or in an EC Member State), sail under the flag of an ACP State (or an EC Member State), must be owned at least 50 percent by nationals of an ACP State (or of an EC Member State) or by a company that has its head office in one of these states, of which the manager or managers, chairman of the board of directors or the supervisory board, and the majority of the members of such boards are nationals of an ACP State (or of an EC Member State) and of which, in addition, in the case of partnerships or limited companies, at least half the capital belongs to ACP States (or to EC Member States) or to public bodies or nationals of such states, and of which at least 50 percent of the crew, master and officers, are nationals of ACP States (or of an EC Member States).[2]

While one can understand the underlying development policy concerns, one wonders how many ACP countries are able to comply with these conditions.

4. Origin Rules Favoring Domestic Producers

The foregoing example of rules of origin for fisheries products under the EC/ACP States agreement raises a second issue. If these rules of origin are designed to encourage the ACP countries into developing a fishing and fish processing industry entirely of their own, it is difficult to understand why fishing vessels may be owned by EC nationals or by EC companies.

This example shows that preferential rules of origin can also be designed to favor the use of parts and components supplied from the country granting the preferential treatment. Where in addition these parts and components are duty free, as would normally be the case in free trade areas, suppliers of these parts and components benefit from a double advantage over suppliers in third countries. This advantage will normally lead to more trade diversion than trade creation.

5. Origin Rules and the International Division of Labor

A third issue arises: the days that the bulk of products traded internationally were wholly obtained in a given country are long gone. To coin the term

---

2. Fourth ACP-EEC Convention signed in Lomé on 15 December 1989. Protocol 1 concerning the definition of the concept of "originating products" and methods of administrative cooperation, Art. 2, § 2, *Official Journal of the European Communities* (1990) L 84/8.

used by two U.S. authors, this is the age of the "Global Factory"[3], characterized by the splitting up of production processes and spreading them over many countries and the sourcing of parts and components in function of the economically most advantages location.

This situation creates three distinct problems. The first one is a matter of policy. As the Commission of the European Communities recognized, the vertical integration required by the preferential rules of origin of the European Communities' Generalized System of Preferences (GSP)[4] with a view to encouraging industrialization in developing countries is at odds with the development of intra-industrial trade. This is also the case for other preferential rules of origin that pursue the same policy aim.

The second problem has legal aspects. The far reaching international division of labor within companies that produce and market globally is both dependent on rules of origin and instrumental in shaping them. This situation carries with it the risk that rules of origin are tailor made or, where they leave discretion to the administrative authorities, are applied in a way that favors domestically based firms or certain international firms over others.

The third problem is the increasing complexity of these rules. The Agreement establishing the European Economic Area between the European Community and the States of the EFTA signed at Oporto on 2 May 1992 comprises a Protocol 4 on rules of origin: it has 38 articles and 8 appendices and covers 211 pages. Press reports suggest that the rules of origin to be inserted in the North American Free Trade Area Agreement (NAFTA) will be no less complex. The emergence of actual codes on origin is probably to be welcomed, as they improve predictability and legal certainty and protect civil servants against the temptation to use administrative discretion to apply rules of origin as an additional nontariff barrier and their political masters against the temptation to instruct their civil servants to do so. Yet, experience in other areas suggests that even fairly detailed rules still leave room for administrative discretion that can be used to protect domestic interests. This opportunity has apparently been understood by negotiators of the draft GATT Origin Agreement: it provides for the review of administrative action by judicial, arbitral or administrative tribunal or procedure in relation to the determination of origin (see chapter 7, § 2.3.1.1.4.).

---

3.   J. Grunwald and K. Flamm, The Global Factory (Washington DC: The Brookings Institution, 1985).

4.   *Generalized System of Preferences: Guidelines for the 1990's* cited by Waer, Ch. 3, text corresponding to fn. 2.

6. This Book

These and many other issues both of law and policy are addressed in this book. They are dealt with in six chapters covering five major jurisdictions and a comparison among them. These reports have been drafted by practising lawyers who could draw on their practical experience but who, as a result of their academic interests, were also able to put the matter in a broader perspective. The necessary economic analysis is provided by a consultant who advises both governments and businesses in trade policy matters and who is thus particularly qualified to explore the economic and policy issues from different angles. The comparative analysis would not be complete without a review of the (few) international rules and the draft Origin Agreement negotiated in the Uruguay Round of Multilateral Trade Negotiations; although this draft agreement covers only nonpreferential rules of origin, it is to be welcomed. GATT Contracting Parties would be wise to enter into this agreement, as it will at least prevent some of the controversies and the disputes to which rules of origin are likely to give rise.

CHAPTER 1

The Economics of Rules of Origin

E. Ivan Kingston

It may be readily seen that the trading community faces serious difficulties with such a wide variety of rules and that no single legal principle tends to be used in the majority of instances. This situation may result in increased costs and delays, higher prices to consumers and other problems. Thus, a reduction in the number of rules and the differences in standards and record keeping requirements would tend to facilitate trade.[1]

1. Origin Rules: Is There an Economic Basis?

It has been argued that all laws, rules, and regulations have an economic basis and hence economic consequences. Origin rules might be considered the exception to this premise. Origin rules, on the whole should not have an economic implication. By themselves their application has a limited purpose other than for routine administrative tasks such as ensuring the correct application of tariffs and the collection of statistical data.

In the last ten years their principal objective has evolved, so that today origin rules are used as the main evidence to support certain other laws and regulations. It is when they are used for such purposes that they become important not only in administering discriminatory policies such as country-specific restrictive trade measures or "buy national" public procurement requirements but also in economic terms.

With increasing trade flows there also developed product- and policy-specific origin rules, so that today there exist various and sometimes conflicting rules that have been used increasingly over the past few years to protect national industries.

Consequently origin rules can have powerful economic implications, not necessarily in themselves, but when they are used to reinforce another trade policy instrument.

---

1. Report to the Committee on Ways and Means, U.S. House of Representatives, Standardization of Rules of Origin, May 1987.

2. Origin of Origin Rules

Origin rules were first introduced to gather statistics, to enable governments to determine the provenance of goods entering and leaving their territory, and to enable the analysis of sources of demand and supply.

However as the major trading nations entered into special arrangements resulting in different tariffs with certain countries, the ability to identify origin became important for other reasons. Once that need had to be met, origin as a concept also had to be defined. Thus origin regulations and definitions ensured that the correct tariffs were applied and that trading partners received treatment in accordance with the treaties and agreements between them. In addition the information thereby obtained provided useful statistics by both industrial sector and for balance of payment purposes. As long as origin rules were applied to this slightly extended use — the distinguishing of trade flows as between preferential and other trading partners — they had little distorting effect on the flow of manufactured goods.

Three types of trading arrangements existed: unilateral, bilateral, and multilateral. These in turn had different bases and can be divided as follows:

1. preferential agreements: these were originally arrangements such as the British Imperial Preferences, those the United States entered into with the Philippines and Cuba, and arrangements between France and its colonies
2. free trade areas that were genuinely considered as customs unions
3. GSP to aid developing countries.

These uncoordinated special arrangements led to many different tariffs and country quotas, and the consequent distortions to trade flows were a principal reason for the United States to press for a world order in trade and the establishment of the GATT. Through GATT it was intended to replace these arbitrary, unilateral systems and to introduce instead a system of MFN treatment for countries who became signatories.

At first it was accepted that existing arrangments could continue as long as signatories undertook not to enter into new arrangements and it was assumed that as tariffs were reduced across the board, the value of preferential arrangements would be eroded and finally disappear. However under Article XXIV of the GATT,[2] it was accepted that GATT rules would not stand in the way of genuine free trade area arrangements. It was further agreed that there could be GSP arrangements for developing countries. As a result, from the beginnings of the GATT there were provisions for exceptions, and once there

---

2. General Agreement on Tariffs and Trade, text of the General Agreement, 1969 (BISD Volume IV).

were differentiations, the need for distinguishing trade flows and the consequent need for origin determinations became accepted.

Such permissable arrangements led, not surprisingly, to institutionalized exceptions: First, nobody abolished existing country or quota arrangements. Second, a special regime was set up in the case of textiles. Third, domestic suppliers were allowed to be favored in the public procurement area (e.g. the Buy American Act). As a result, although the GATT forbade differentiation, this objective was not achieved. In addition there was no mechanism to ensure that the resultant, now necessary, origin rules were used only for essential purposes or that they were uniformly developed. Instead, over the years different rules were introduced by different governments. The situation was further complicated by different rules being designed for different purposes.

Like for any controls and supervisory functions there had to be an administrative body; questions of origin have always been within the prerogative of national customs. The first serious efforts to coordinate origin rules were made within the context of the early GATT meetings but were resisted by national customs bureaus. However the proposals surfacing in the GATT led to the Kyoto Convention in 1975 under the aegis of the Common Customs Council at which some harmonization of principles — even if not rules — was agreed.

Now, forty years after the first discussions on origin in the GATT, it is noteworthy that origin is recognized as a subject that should be covered by GATT rules and is one of the only two areas on which agreement was reached within the original time frame of the Uruguay Round negotiations. Assuming a successful outcome for the round as a whole, rules of origin — although still remaining the responsibility of the Common Customs Council as far as technical questions are concerned — will, in future, operate within GATT disciplines.

3. A Secondary Trade Policy Instrument

Over the last few years, determinations of the country of origin of goods in international trade have gained importance. Additionally, as a result of the inclusion of trade in services in the Uruguay Round GATT negotiations, the concepts enabling nationality determinations within the services sectors will also need to be addressed (see § 5).

During earlier years when the norm was to produce goods in one country and export from there, the use of origin rules to define a product's place of manufacture was simple. Over the past decade the issue has become more complicated.

The advances in the technology of manufacturing processes have resulted in greater specialisation requiring ever-increasing capital investment. This has led to a growth in component suppliers, mostly independent of the manufacturer whose name appears on the final product. In many product areas the manufacturer, after the initial design and development stage, is little more than the much maligned "screwdriver" factory operator. The subcontract manufacturers who supply many of the components need not even be located in the same customs territory as the manufacturer or ultimate exporter but often operate in a country where the required resources, such as labor, are most economically available. This situation brings into question the weighting in relative importance of the factors of production in the drafting of origin regulations (see § 4.3.). It also follows that the need for an origin definition becomes more relevant when, as a result of a great variety of manufacturing procedures, it is increasingly difficult to arrive at simple criteria on which the rules should be based.

This question is further complicated by the variety of situations in which origin needs to be addressed and the consequent potential for abuse. It is therefore useful to identify the different types of discriminatory trade measures where an origin determination is required:

1. measures designed to correct "unfair trade"
2. measures designed to protect local industry
3. measures designed to give preference to
   a. products of developing countries
   b. countries where MFN treatment applies or
   c. customs unions.

In addition, origin rules are employed

4. in administering "buy national" policies;
5. when, as a market opening tool, reciprocity is used for market access; and
6. as an extension of political policy where sanctions are applied.

Consequently, once any of these trade policy instruments is activated, the respective origin rule is an essential component in its administration. The resulting origin decision, in turn, can have significant economic implications.

4. Economic Consequences of Origin Rules

4.1. Distortions to Trade

4.1.1. Safeguard and Protective Measures

In an ideal world it is assumed that by minimizing restrictions free trade will produce an economically efficient allocation of resources. Thus, specialisation in particular activities is determined by resource endowments. Using free trade assumptions it is clear that any protective impediment will produce a less efficient outcome. This, therefore, must be the implication when origin regulations are employed as an instrument by which a protectionist safeguard measure is reinforced.

On the other hand, if one assumes that world trade is imperfectly competitive, then trade restrictive measures may be employed for strategic policy purposes. That is, if industries are generally characterised by economies of scale, strategic protection can be used to help industries gain such economies. In such cases, origin rules can be constructed in a way that the rule is applied to ensure that "helpful" trade policy measures are actually effective.

There are situations — whilst adopting a free trade approach — where protection might not create inefficiency. If unfair trade (e.g. dumped or subsidized goods) is distorting the market so that the result is not an efficient distribution of production and trade according to comparative advantage, then discriminatory counter-action may be justified. In this case strictly defined origin requirements can reinforce the measure designed to correct this market distortion. The need for origin rules is also then extended to ensure the noncircumvention of the measure.

However, in the way they are actually implemented, origin rules even for justified protectionist measures might be doing more than just correcting a distortion. The interpretation of rules has, at times, been in question. A recent European Court judgment[3] involving electronic typewriters from Taiwan made clear that assembly, even if it was of 100 percent imported parts, did not in itself constitute the circumvention of an antidumping duty imposed on the same machines coming from Japan. However, it did not state categorically that pure assembly amounts to substantial transformation and therefore origin. This omission suggests that once an antidumping duty is in place against the products of a specific country, it is then very difficult for a third country with a comparative advantage in labor intensive activities (i.e. assembly) to participate in the manufacture of such products. A case such as this illustrates the difficulty in that it can be argued that although the origin determinations by both the exporting and importing customs authorities were based on quite different criteria, they were both economically justifiable. The origin certificate by Taiwan demonstrated that the amount of activity carried out in the local plant was to the economic interest of Taiwan; whilst for the European Community the rejection of the certificate could also be justified on

---

3. *Brother International GmbH v. Hauptzollamt Giessen*, Case 26/88 (1989) ECR 4253.

economic grounds. Had the European Community accepted without question the Taiwanese certificate, such third country involvement after the adoption of an antidumping measure would negate the purpose intended, not only in the specific case but also as a precedent running counter to the intended objective of an international agreement.[4] Consequently, from the purely economic standpoint, restrictive interpretations of origin rules — in reinforcing justified countervailing measures — might not result in the greatest benefits being gained from comparative advantages.

In addition to problems arising from how origin rules are implemented, there are also distortions created by anticircumvention provisions, which are by definition an origin issue. Depending on the circumstances, different origin regulations or rules relating to free circulation of goods for manufacturers in different locations can seriously distort the incentives to trade. This distortion can be illustrated by the effect of Article 13 (10) of the European Community's Antidumping Regulation.[5] Using this provision, it can be illustrated how a number of rules would apply to a product (subject to an antidumping duty) that is manufactured to identical specifications in the following circumstances and destined for sale in EC markets.

4.1.1.1. Product Manufactured by an Operation Related to the Company Originally Found to be Dumping

If this company sets up a factory in a third country, EC Regulation 802/68 (unless any product specific rules exist) would be used to determine if the product could be deemed to be originating in the third country and if the criteria of 802/68 are met the goods would not be liable to the duty. If the company sets up a factory within the EC, Article 13 (10) of the EC's basic Antidumping Regulation would be used to determine if the product is subject to the duty before being granted free circulation.

The differences in requirements are highlighted in the case of a product manufactured in a subsidiary established in a third country of a company whose products are subject to an antidumping duty when exported from the home country. It is possible that such a product with a 59 percent part content from the county subject to antidumping duties would not be considered to have met EC origin criteria under regulation 802/68 and thus be subject to the anti-dumping duty on imports into the EC. On the other hand, a similar subsidiary established within the EC with an identical parts content

---

4. The GATT Anti-Dumping Code, to which both Japan and the European Community, but not Taiwan, were signatories.

5. Council Regulation (EEC) No 2423/88 of 11 July 1988.

would pass the Article 13 (10) anticircumvention test and be free of antidumping duties.

4.1.1.2. Product Manufactured by an Unrelated Company Not Subject to Antidumping Duties

In the case of an unrelated manufacturer the situation is slightly different. A producer from any third country who produces exactly the same product using identical parts and components to the example in § 4.1.1.1. will face the Regulation 802/68 test when exporting to the European Community. A nonrelated manufacturer would be able to produce within the European Community using parts and components originating from whatever source without any antidumping duties as long as the necessary tariffs on the imported items had been paid.

In the United States the relevant anticircumvention provisions — less restrictive but also less predictable — are covered by Section 1321 of the Omnibus Trade and Competitiveness Act 1988.

Further evidence of this kind of problem arose during the European Community's long deliberations on how to define origin for stuffed boards (a printed circuit board with all other components affixed to it). The U.S. administration put immense pressure on the EC Commission in an effort to influence it not to introduce a specific regulation. The U.S. industry feared that their products would be designed out of stuffed boards as a consequence of such a regulation. At that time EC regulators felt that it was essential, in support of existing safeguard measures, to have Community origin applying to stuffed boards, which could represent a substantial proportion of the total cost when incorporated into a final product.

As a consequence of the problems set out above in the case of manufacturing a protected product, not only may third countries be unable to realise comparative advantages that exist, but their producers will also be reluctant to use components with an origin of the country subject to restriction, for fear that their products may be denied access to the protected markets. Trade in the finished article being manufactured is thereby further distorted in that such producers might be reluctant to use what may be cheaper or higher quality parts and components, making their goods less competitive and desirable in the market place.

In addition to specific origin regulations, local content requirements have been informally used as a method of tightening up EC Regulation 802/68 (see the case of cars produced by Japanese-owned plants in the United Kingdom in § 6). Informal local content agreements again result in producers being deterred from incorporating into the final product what might be the most cost- and quality-effective components. Similarly in the North American free trade talks the question of origin is considered to be one of the most critical areas for agreement. It is of note that in the case of motor vehicles, always a very high profile item in trade negotiations, the regional local contents requirement demanded by U.S. industry is 70-80 percent as against the current 50 percent operative under the U.S.-Canada FTA.

4.1.2.   Preferential Measures

Origin rules are also required in administering preferential trade agreements, to ensure that only the intended countries benefit. Here, although preferential treatment is recognised as a distortion to trade, it is felt to be justified on developmental grounds.

Origin rules in preferential agreements have often been criticised for being more restrictive than general origin rules. This question is specially relevant when we look at preferential agreements with developing countries. The greatest advantage these countries normally have is cheap and abundant labor. Yet the developed countries ensure through the wording of these agreements that the labor content of the production process is hardly ever sufficient to guarantee origin. The origin rules incorporated nearly always close the easiest route, that of simple assembly, as a way for management and labour of underdeveloped countries to learn the skills that will enable them to move first into component production and ultimately to total manufacturing.

Furthermore, producers in countries who, on the surface, are intended to gain benefits from these agreements are restricted in the sourcing of their components. Cumulation makes the problem worse. The origin rules in both the Lomé Convention to which the European Community is the other party and in the Caribbean Basin Initiative initiated by the United States allow for the cumulation of goods in origin determinations from the specific country groupings plus the other party. This situation helps to maintain possibly inefficient industries in some if not all of the countries signatory to the agreements and hinders yet again the developing country producer from sourcing from the cheapest or highest quality supplier.

The economic consequence of these agreements may well be the retardation of the development of these countries and the maintenance of their present levels of underindustrialization. So much for preferential agreements.

4.1.3.   Public Procurement

In many countries and in individual states in cases where a customs union or federal system operates, there are specific rules of origin for public procurement. These create pressures on firms to favour local contractors and even extend to encouraging the employment of local suppliers and subcontractors. The most blatant examples can be found in the construction sector where, in the case of public works, even national firms have been known to lose out to smaller firms located in the region where the project is located. As an example of gross economic inefficiency this approach is even more evident in the area of defence procurement, where national pride often results in maintaining industries that are — in the light of the huge research and development costs and high technology manufacturing facilities required — clearly of an uneconomic scale. The overall result is a bias toward the maintenance of inefficient producers.

4.2. Distortion to Investment

Restrictive origin and anticircumvention regulations can also distort investment flows since they lead to disproportionate amounts of investment entering the territories of major importers such as the United States and the European Community.

Such manufacturing inward investment can, within a short period, become an effective competitor to the established local firm. The inward investment manufacturers usually develop on a greenfield site, introduce the most modern equipment, enter into unfettered labor agreements, and often incur relatively lower social costs (pensions, etc.) than the existing local manufacturer. The beneficial consequence of bringing a competitive product and employment into the market place is often negated in economic terms by driving the traditional local producer out of business. Furthermore, in an effort to meet local content requirements, due either as part of an undertaking to the host government or to meet origin rule definitions, these transplants are often followed by subcontractors' plants, which endanger the local supply industry as well.

Inward investment assistance and other forms of artificial encouragement that lead to import substitution can have further economically inefficient consequences. The resultant lack of competition from more efficiently manufactured imported products and the disappearance of the previous local competitors tend to price these — now locally produced — products out of their export markets.

In addition, by segmenting markets and establishing production capacity in each of them, global capacity can outstrip total demand, and underutilization of individual plants can reduce or even negate the benefits that can be expected from the economic advantages of scale. Local contents and origin requirements can therefore lead to investment that otherwise, on solely commercial grounds, might not have been economically justifiable.

4.3. Distortions to Industrial Structure

In addition to distorting trade and investment, origin rules can affect and possibly even distort a country's industrial structure. In industries that depend on exports and where origin is considered important for the product being manufactured, a bias towards the stage of production that is emphasized in relevant origin rules might develop. Table 1 segregates typical production into four stages and attempts to classify the different types of origin rules that are and could be used, highlighting the stage that each rule might affect.

Current origin rules are predominantly based on the criteria of last substantial transformation. Rules of origin based on this concept have their impact on the third stage (final production) in table 1. The effect of the widespread use of substantial transformation criteria is that in products where origin is important, a bias is created towards the localization of the third stage in the production process.

An important issue is the extent to which the second stage (intermediate production), which essentially represents component production, should be included before an operation can be claimed to be substantial enough to confer origin status. In certain products it might be considered that one key component is so vital to the essential character of the final product that it should provide the key to determining origin. In such products the final production stage, no matter how complex, may be considered little more than simple assembly and thus not regarded as sufficient to determine origin. This situation also raises the problem of difficulties as to the differences between simple and more sophisticated assembly and leaves a grey area regarding the extent to which work covered in stage two should be considered. Where rules based on specific components are used, an incentive to move into the production of such a component is created within countries where restrictive origin regulations, rather than, for example, comparative advantage, would make it advantageous to do so.

As pointed out earlier in the text, however, the use of concepts that preclude pure assembly from determining origin often means that the use of the most economic inputs such as cheap labor or ample availability of raw materials tends to be discouraged.

The activities of the fourth stage — the marketing and distribution stage — are usually disregarded, although these activities can be a substantial proportion of the cost of the final product (e.g. in the case of some chemically based products, the largest cost element after research and development (R & D) is packaging and marketing). The case of Ricoh is a prime example. The European Commission investigated the U.S. production facilities of the company as part of an antidumping circumvention investigation. The company appears to have met the "Buy American" requirements, since those rules allow the inclusion of its sales and marketing costs in the United States. However when the same product was exported in bulk and the local sales and marketing costs were deducted, the percentage of local added value was rumoured to be below an internationally acceptable norm for origin. The issue was resolved by the EC introducing a specific origin rule setting out operations that did not confer origin.[6]

Stage one (R&D) has, to date, not usually been considered in origin determinations, although it can be significant. With the rapid increase in crossborder investment flows, governments are now recognizing that the important elements in the manufacturing process in the case of high technology consumer goods seldom lie in the final production (substantial transformation) stage but rather in the R&D stage and in the capital equipment that is employed in the production stage. It could be argued — although it would add confusion to the debate — that the country of origin of a product should be where the capital equipment for producing the product is made. There is a clear difference between increasing a country's capital stock by installing imported modern equipment and having the technological ability to produce the equipment domestically.[7]

Despite its importance, traditional concepts of origin — such as substantial transformation — do not therefore reflect the origin of the technology. Initial research and development leading to the core (generic) technology is often adapted to a multitude of products. Its use in a particular product, although crucial, might represent only a small proportion of final costs. When considering origin in the production of key components the initial R&D might be slightly more significant. Increasingly technology is built into components rather than being an element in the final manufacturing (substantial transformation) stage; therefore, local content requirements become ever more relevant. Overall, the R&D on which future industrial capabilities rest — which some recent origin rules applied to industrial policy measures appear to wish to protect — is not taken into account in origin decisions. However

---

6.   EC Regulation 2071/89.

7.   An example is an assembly line with 150 workers. If the automation of the plant leads to the installation of 50 robots, the new operation might, with only 25 workers, produce the same amount of goods. Admittedly, some of the 25 workers would now have to handle the robots; the robots need qualified handling, repair, and maintenance; and the labor productivity will increase, but the point is that the local added value in production now crucially depends on the provenance of the robots. If the 50 robots are imported, they can be considered to be foreign cost content replacing 100 workers. This increases the domestic capital stock, and there might be a certain amount of technology transfer in the handling, servicing, and maintaining of the robots, but much of the technology would be embodied in the robots.

there are signs that governments are moving in this direction. In a recent decision in the United States on the standing of a U.S. subsidiary of a Japanese company in an antidumping investigation, the International Trade Administration stated, "The nature of the operation is qualitatively different from the type of operation characterised by design, engineering and the actual manufacturing by some of the essential parts, to which Congress intended to afford a remedy."[8]

When strong industrial lobbies can make what on the surface is a justifiable case, officials try and find solutions without necessarily being in a position to take into account long term economic results. The negative effect of origin rules in such circumstances is emphasized for example by the diffusion rule[9] for semiconductors, despite the fact that the need for a specific origin rule was seen as an essential element in ensuring the effectiveness of the finding in a "justified" antidumping case.[10]

The diffusion rule has resulted in an inflow of investment for building diffusion plants in the European Community, thus putting Member States' existing producers under more competitive pressure than they previously faced from imports.

The current practice of technologically advanced, multinational corporations supports the view that origin determinations based on the second and third stages in table 1 can sometimes be misleading and therefore create possible distortions. The production activities of large multinational firms often consist of R&D, final production, and marketing and distribution, leaving much of the intermediate production process to mainly independent and not necessarily local subcontractors. It is rarer to subcontract R&D, and in the case of branded consumer goods, marketing is also considered as being an important in-house activity. The result is that such firms will wish to own as well as control the first (R&D) and last (sales and marketing) stages of the production process. The intermediate stages, although representing a major cost element, hardly matter as long as the firm can ensure quality control.

If one looks at the different rules of origin currently in use it is doubtful in the changed world in which modern industries operate that any of them fully meet their intended objectives. Some, like the European Community's diffusion rule in the case of semiconductor manufacturing, attempt to meet the

---

8.   Department of Commerce, International Trade Administration, Ref A-559-806, 25 September 1991.

9.   Commission Regulation (EEC) 288/89.

10.   Council Regulation (EEC) No. 2112/90 of 23 July 1990 imposing a definitive antidumping duty on imports of DRAMs from Japan.

high technology criteria. Others, which encourage investment flows, may satisfy the value-added aim. Such attempts may succeed in achieving a fairer representation of origin concepts than rules based on substantial transformation, which would usually apply to the final stage of the manufacturing process. However, there is substantial evidence to show that the use of any particular rule encourages investment flows in such a way that it distorts the effect of the rule by influencing the type of activities undertaken in the country of manufacture. As this influence is not based on purely commercial calculations, the most efficient resource utilization is not necessarily achieved.

5. Beyond Trade in Goods: Services

Most of this chapter up to this point has dealt with origin rules as they currently exist, focusing on goods. In the past most service providers in transport, construction, financial services, telecommunications, etc., were, for cross-frontier trade, subject to individual multilateral or bilateral agreements. The current efforts to incorporate services into the GATT might mean that the origin of services will have to be determined for the first time, and will have economic consequences. The problem in attempting to determine the origin of a service is that it is not possible to simply adopt similar criteria to those used in the case of goods.

In a narrow range of cases in which the service itself can be defined to move internationally (e.g. a computer service, such as a data base, which can be accessed by customers in other countries via telecommunications facilities or the purchase, through the use of communications facilities, of an insurance policy by a customer in one country from an insurance company in another country) one might be able to justify, perhaps with some difficulty, the application of origin concepts analogous to those developed for trade in goods. The rule of substantial transformation, however, could be applied only in very restricted instances, and rules based on added value concepts, which might be easier to determine, might also be only occasionally relevant. In the vast majority of international services transactions, the foreign service provider has a presence in the market of the consumer, either as an individual providing, say, professional advice or as some sort of entity (corporation, agency, branch, etc.) that is owned or controlled abroad, although it might employ local resources (personnel, buildings) to create the service.

If the origin of a service cannot be defined on the basis of transformation and only seldom where value is added, then presumably one needs to seek a rule that is based on the national origin of the provider, or in which signatory country the service providing entity is owned or controlled.

The question of the origin of services, at least when delivered by entities (that is, other than individuals selling their own services), is the question of the nationality of corporations and of the ownership and control of corporations.

The major difficulty determining nationality in services is that most service sectors differ from goods in that one cannot evaluate the different components that make up a service. Many services are based on networks and the question is whether it is possible to determine the value added at each point within the network.

Incorporation might not be considered a useful criteria. Service providers are more likely to use "flags of convenience" thereby making it difficult to point to where control is exercised. In shipping, air transport, banking, and insurance, notional and effective control may well be located in different customs territories.

Where origin can be determined, the following possible criteria, singly or in combination, may apply:

1. ownership and effective control
2. value added
3. intellectual input (control of the essential knowledge without which the service does not exist).

Consequently, the economic implications for rules of origin in the area of services are even less clear than in the case of goods. However, it is possible to presume that with origin being much harder to determine in services, the introduction of a meaningful code in services will be extremely difficult. Thus the impact of a services agreement and any economic effects as a result of the origin determinations of its operation might not be economically significant.

The draft services agreement prepared for the December 1990 Uruguay Round meeting in Brussels defines a service provider of another party as "any natural or juridical person of another (contracting) Party that supplies a service."[11] A natural person is defined as "any natural person who is a national of a Party under the law of that party," while juridical person means (1) "any entity legally constituted under the law applicable in the territory of another party and any partnership or association organized under such law" and (2) "any entity legally constituted or organized under the law applicable in the territory of a Party that is owned or controlled by natural persons . . . or entities identified" in (1) above.[12]

---

11. MTN.TNC/W/35.

12. Ibid.

If an origin rule for services is adopted based on incorporation, ownership, or control, this rule could lead to less trade and investment distortion than the rules that apply to goods. This is because the inputs to the firm, especially labor, will have no bearing on the origin. To this extent it might be possible for service providers to establish in countries with, say, cheap labor, to gain from the cheapest inputs available. Another labor-related aspect is that of the technological input of information providers (computer programmers, designers, engineers, etc.) who might be located outside the territory of the establishment. A loose and possibly ineffective general rule of origin might therefore in these sectors result in a better allocation of resources than attempting to draft more specific rules such as those presently applied to goods.

6. Absence of Uniformity

The Kyoto convention agreed on criteria for products coming from one country and laid down the rules of substantial transformation where two or more countries were involved. Had they adopted a straight percentage rule, matters would have been fairly simple. Unfortunately, by also listing manufacturing or processing operations that in certain cases would denote origin, it opened the door to the introduction of different rules for individual products. This lack of certain, predictable, and transparent criteria also encouraged the proliferation of individual rules based on different percentages usually arbitrarily decided and on the specification of manufacturing and processing operations that were declared to be insufficient to grant origin. The matter was further complicated by individual countries deciding to use different criteria for different purposes in the case of the same product and there being no established institution to agree on internationally acceptable criteria for any one product. This situation has resulted in a plethora of different origin rules depending on the use or the destination of the goods in question.

It is the existence of such variations as well as the provisions of the different bilateral agreements that aggravated economic distortions and resulted in the creation of a jungle of rules through which the imaginative circumventor can move. As an example, an issue that has been subject to bilateral negotiations over many years affecting the United States, the European Community, and Japan — the manufacture of motorcars and the status of the so called transplant factories — origin is determined differently under each of the following agreements selected to illustrate the point.

1. EC/EFTA:

For cars there is a specific percentage origin rule. The value of all nonoriginating materials must not exceed 40 percent of the exworks price.

The cumulation of inputs from any one EFTA country and from EC countries is permitted.[13]

2.   U.S./Canada FTA:

The origin rule for cars is that, in addition to a change in tariff heading, the value of materials originating in the territory of either or both parties plus the direct cost of processing performed in the territory of either or both parties constitute not less than 50 percent of the value of the goods when exported to the territory of the other party.[14]

3.   EC/Eastern Europe Association Agreements:

A specific rule for cars states that the value of nonoriginating materials used must not exceed the value of 40 percent of the exworks price.[15]

4.   EC Member States:

EC Regulation 802/68 is the origin rule that underlies all EC origin issues. This incorporates the Kyoto convention concept of "last substantial transformation" with the additional qualification of "that is economically justifiable."

Toyota, as Nissan previously, has agreed with the United Kingdom government that it will reach initially at least 60 percent local content and eventually 80 percent.[16] The UK government believes that this goes beyond any level that could raise a question about EC origin. On a previous occasion, for Honda motor cars made in the United Kingdom, the UK government, supported by the EC Commission, convinced both the French and Italian governments that a motor car with such a percentage of local content cannot be subject to restrictions.

5.   Caribbean Basin Economic Recovery Act (CBERA) or the Caribbean Basin Initiative (CBI):

The origin rules are similar to those in the U.S. GSP. Origin is conferred when "the sum of A) the cost or value of the materials produced in the beneficiary country or two or more of the beneficiary countries, plus B) the direct costs of processing operations performed in a beneficiary country or countries is not less than 35 per centum of the appraised value of such article

---

13.   Annex 3, Protocol 3 of the Free Trade Agreement between the European Community and EFTA countries, Official Journal (1988) L 49.

14.   U.S.-Canada Free Trade Agreement. Annex 301.2.

15.   Protocol 4 to Association Agreements between the EC and Czechoslovakia, Hungary and Poland.

16.   "The Changing Climate of Investment in Britain: Toyota's Decision to Build Its First European Plant in the U.K.," Financial Times 5 July 1991.

at the time it is entered."[17] The rules in the U.S. GSP are identical, except that cumulation is not allowed.

6.   Lomé Convention:

Origin is conferred by sufficient working or processing. The cumulation of ACP States and EC products is allowed.

Sufficient processing is defined by a change of tariff heading and, in some cases, an additional percentage criteria. For cars, origin is determined by "Manufacture in which the value of all the (non-originating) materials used does not exceed 40 percent of the ex-works price of the product."[18]

7. Conclusion

In spite of attempts to standardize rules and make the results of applying origin determinations more efficient, the opposite has happened as a consequence of attempts to combat the balance of payment divergences between Western and Far Eastern industrialized countries. The impetus behind the increased protectionist use of origin rules has been the surge of exports from the Far East led by Japan and a desire to counter the uneconomic pricing policies of nonmarket economies.

Origin rules used to reinforce protective measures, sometimes even in cases where it might be argued that the measure is justified, merely serve to increase economic inefficiencies in that they help to maintain an industry in a location where perhaps there is no comparative advantage.

Preferential arrangements to assist developing economies often negate the intended effect (i.e. helping the transition to industrialization).   The comparative advantages for these countries in labor-intensive activities are usually specifically excluded.

Local content undertakings have no legal basis but appear frequently to be offered by inward investors.   Such rules can prevent the realization of comparative advantages, in that inefficient industries are sustained through this indirect protection.

The effect of investment projects shifting to where they gain origin advantages can result in damage to existing local industry.   Origin rules can result in an inefficient bias regarding location, industrial sector, or particular stage of production.

Increasing investment from the exporting to the importing countries caused as the result of the enforcement of origin requirements can cause further distortion by creating global overcapacity and damage to the local industry

---

17.   General note 3(c)(v) of the harmonised tariff schedule of the United States.

18.   Annex II, Fourth ACP - EEC Convention, 1989.

due to the consequent inefficient utilization of plants. The ultimate result has on occasions led to the closure of the factories which the rule was intended to protect. This situation is further aggravated by governments who, while trying to protect the existing industries, provide incentives for foreign firms to locate within their territories.

The conclusion is clear. Although the application of origin rules should not have any economic effects, it can be a crucial trade distortion weapon when used in conjunction with a protective measure.

Exporters will always seek to find the most cost-effective solution to counter governments interfering with the economic efficiency of the market. It is an economically justifiable activity in itself to circumvent rules that deter the most efficient methods of satisfying the demand in the market place.

In the final analysis, the consequence of the misuse of origin rules, like with any laws or rules that are overused or stretched, is that they are often negated by counter measures and their effectiveness is greatly reduced. In addition, with investment flows now growing at a far greater rate than trade flows,[19] the question arises to what extent it will be practical to define the origin of goods. Furthermore, it might be questionable whether it will be of any value to do so, with growing multicountry production and the largest producers becoming international corporations through acquisitions as well as the increasing establishment of transplant factories. Therefore origin rules that are so important now in implementing regulations that are introduced to counter the economic consequences of, say, predatory pricing or assistance to those with preferential agreements might well become irrelevant as well as unenforceable in future.

Until that future arrives, some certainty in the determination of origin would make the system and its economic impact more efficient. Whatever the nature of trade policies — tariff concessions, antidumping duties, safeguard actions, investment incentives — the concept of country specificity for individual products should be the same. This would be more helpful to industry since it would make the rules transparent, certain, and predictable whether a given geographical identification of economic activities would be supported, subsidized, or penalized. Industrial managers can cope with even the harshest rules as long as they know what they are. However, as long as discriminatory trade policies prevail, origin rules will continue to have economic consequences.

---

19.   1985-1990 direct investment flows of major Organization of Economic Cooperation and Development (OECD) countries expanded 34 percent against trade flows 9 percent per year. OECD Economic Outlook, December 1991.

TABLE **1.** **Effect of Type of Origin Rule on Production Stages**

	Production Stages			
Basis of Rule	Research & Development	Intermediate Production	Final Production	Marketing & Distribution
Substantial process or operation		Can be relevant when final production is only simple assembly	Usually determined to be during final production process unless this is simple assembly	
Specific process based on high technology component	Origin determined by key process or component in terms of research and development of its relative value			
Origin of capital inputs	Would emphasize technical know-how and research and development embodied in the machines			
Value added	Usually research and development forms small proportion of final value added	Individual components can be crucial in calculating value added	Most value usually will be added at this stage if marketing and distribution is disregarded	In certain cases can constitute a large percentage or even a majority of value added
Negative list	Can exclude any part of production process in origin determination			

CHAPTER 2

Rules of Origin in The United States

N. David Palmeter

1. Introduction

Modern rules of origin law in the United States began more than half a century ago in cases involving the marking of imported goods with the name of their country of origin. The "marking statute," Section 304 of the Tariff Act of 1930, requires that "every article of foreign origin," or its container, be marked in a manner that will inform the "ultimate purchaser" in the United States of its country of origin.[1] The "ultimate purchaser" is the last person in the United States receiving the article in the form in which it was imported. If the article is to be sold at retail in its imported form, the retail customer is the ultimate purchaser, but if it is to undergo further processing in the United States, the question arises, — Is the ultimate purchaser the processor or the customer of the processor? The answer to this question determines whether the article must be labeled "Made in Foreign Country X" or whether it may be marked "Made in the U.S.A." Depending on the product, obvious commercial advantages can flow from one label or the other.

The issue reached a Federal Court of Appeals in 1940. In *United States v. Gibson-Thomsen Co.*, a manufacturer of brushes imported brush handles to which, in a U.S. operation, it attached bristles.[2] At the time of their importation, the handles were clearly marked with the word "Japan," but this word was removed in the process of attaching the bristles. The court held that the attachment of the bristles constituted a manufacturing process in the United States, that the brush manufacturer therefore was the ultimate purchaser of the handles, and accordingly that the finished brushes did not have to be marked with the word "Japan."

---

1.   19 U.S.C.A. § 1304.

2.   *United States v. Gibson-Thomson Co.*, 27 C.C.P.A. 267 (1940).

Section 304 by its terms gave no guidance to the court about how it was to determine who was the ultimate purchaser of the imported product or, to reach the more basic question, how it was to determine whether the finished brushes were articles "of foreign origin." The government attempted to avoid the issue, contending that the handles should have been marked in a manner that would permit the retail purchaser of the brush to determine that they (i.e., the handles) were of foreign origin. The court rejected this argument, holding that the marking statute does not apply to *"imported materials used in the manufacture in the United States of a new article having a new name, character, and use."*[3]

For the substantive law of what constitutes "manufacture," the court reached to the law of duty drawback as it had developed in the United States over many years. Duty drawback permits an importer of raw materials to receive a refund of duties paid on the reexport of those materials if they had been used in the United States to manufacture a new article (see § 6.2). The only case cited by the *Gibson-Thomsen* court, *Tidewater Oil Company v. United States*, was a nineteenth century drawback case.[4] More significantly, however, the *Gibson-Thomsen* court paraphrased the language of the U.S. Supreme Court in *Anheuser-Busch Brewing Assn. v. United States*, another old drawback case, which gave the "substantial transformation" standard to rules of origin law in the United States.[5] The language of the Supreme Court in *Anheuser-Busch* has become the starting point of any discussion of U.S. law concerning origin:

> Manufacture implies a change, but every change is not manufacture, and yet every change in an article is the result of treatment, labor and manipulation. But something more is necessary, as set forth and illustrated in *Hartranft v. Wiegmann*, 121 U.S. 609. There must be a transformation; a new and different article must emerge, 'having a distinctive name, character or use.'[6]

Hartranft v. Wiegmann, cited and partially quoted in *Anheuser-Busch*, involved tariff classification, not drawback. The question there concerned whether imported shells that had been cleaned and polished were, or were not,

---

3. *Gibson-Thomson Co.,* 27 C.C.P.A. at 273 (italics in original).

4. *Tidewater Oil Co. v. United States,* 171 U.S. 210 (1897).

5. *Anheuser Busch Brewing Assn. v. United States,* 207 U.S. 556 (1907).

6. Ibid. at 562.

manufactured shells. The answer to this question determined whether the duty would be 35 percent ad valorem or zero. In holding that the shells were not manufactured, the Supreme Court in 1886 coined the language later adopted by the *Anheuser-Busch* decision that echoes in rules of origin decisions a century later:

> They were still shells. They had not been manufactured into a new and different article, having a distinctive name, character or use from that of a shell. The application of labor to an article, either by hand or by mechanism, does not make the article necessarily a manufactured article, within the meaning of that term as used in the tariff laws.[7]

This nineteenth century language constitutes the basic rule of origin in the United States, the "substantial transformation" test: an article that undergoes processing in two or more countries is the product of the country in which it last underwent a substantial transformation. Despite a proliferation of various rules of origin for preferential purposes, substantial transformation remains the basic rule of origin in the United States, even for imports from countries eligible for preferences. Eligibility for the preference is determined in addition to origin by such factors as value added or change in tariff heading.

The substantial transformation standard has been criticized as too imprecise, too subjective.[8] The alleged imprecision and subjectivity of the test have led to a U.S. proposal to the GATT for an internationally accepted standard based primarily on change in tariff heading.[9] Industry groups have been critical of the substantial transformation standard, though not necessarily because of jurisprudential concerns over imprecision and subjectivity but because existing doctrine often thwarted protectionist schemes. They have not always liked the results. Thus, the lack of restrictiveness in existing rules of origin for textiles and apparel led to an administratively imposed definition of substantial transformation for those products that essentially adopts a specified process

---

7.   121 U.S. at 615.

8.   John Simpson, *Reforming Rules of Origin*, Journal of Commerce, 4 October 1988, at 12A.

9.   This proposal is set forth and discussed in David Palmeter, *The U.S. Rules of Origin Proposal to GATT: Monotheism or Polytheism?* 24 Journal of World Trade No. 2 p. 25 (April 1990).

standard that is far more restrictive than previous case law.[10] It is reflected also in a special origin rule enacted in 1988 for steel products subject to quotas,[11] and in a September 1991 proposal for wholesale change in rules of origin for steel and other base metal products.[12] It is reflected as well in the existence of a separate test to determine whether third country operations circumvent antidumping or countervailing duty orders.[13]

2. General Overview

While substantial transformation is the basic U.S. rule of origin, virtually all varieties of rules of origin play a part in U.S. law. The textiles rules of origin are cast in terms of substantial transformation but use the specified process method to define it; the Canada-U.S. FTA uses change in tariff heading to determine eligibility;[14] the U.S.-Israel Free Trade Area employs a value-

---

10.   The textile rules of origin are set out in Part 12 of the Customs Regulations, 19 C.F.R. § 12.130. Part 12 deals with "Special Classes of Merchandise," such as viruses, toxins, narcotics, immoral articles, merchandise produced by convict labor, counterfeit coins, switchblade knives, and pesticides. This company suggests just how "special" are the textile rules of origin. See generally Craig R. Giesse and Martin J. Lewin, *The Multifiber Arrangement: "Temporary" Protection Run Amuck*, 19 Law & Policy in International Business 51 (1987); David Palmeter, *Rules of Origin or Rules of Restriction? A Commentary on a New Form of Protectionism*, 11 Fordham International Law Journal 1 (1987).

11.   Omnibus Trade and Competitiveness Act of 1988, Pub. L. 100-418, 102 Stat. 1107, § 1322 adding subsection (d) to § 805 of the Trade and Tariff Act of 1984, 19 U.S.C.A. § 2253 note.

12.   Proposed Customs Regulations Amendments Regarding Rules of Origin Applicable to Imported Merchandise, 56 Fed. Reg. 48448 (Sept. 25, 1991).

13.   Omnibus Trade and Competitiveness Act of 1988, *supra* note 11, § 1321 adding § 781 to the Tariff Act of 1930 as amended, 19 U.S.C.A. § 1677j. This is discussed below in § 5.

14.   27 International Legal Materials 281 (1988). Value added also is used in the FTA for specified assembly operations, e.g., Ch. Three, Art. 301:2, Annex 301.2, § VI(2). See generally, David Palmeter, "The FTA Rules of Origin and the Rule of Law," *Proceedings of the Seventh Judicial Conference of the United States Court of Appeals for the Federal Circuit*, 128 F.R.D. 500 (1990).

added test,[15] as do the basic U.S. tariff preference programs, the GSP[16] and the CBI;[17] tariff preferences for the U.S. insular possessions and freely associated states are also based on value added.[18]

3. Nonpreferential Rules of Origin

There is a single nonpreferential rule of origin in the United States: substantial transformation. Perhaps its most pervasive application is in the marking of goods: every imported article or its container, as has been noted, must be marked with the name of its country of origin.[19] Substantial transformation is the rule that determines country of origin for MFN tariff rates.[20] It also is the rule that generally determines origin for quota purposes.

3.1. Procedure

The administrative agency directly concerned with the application of rules of origin is the U.S. Customs Service, an agency under the jurisdiction of the Department of the Treasury. Customs is headed by a commissioner who is appointed by the president and confirmed by the Senate. An assistant secretary of the Treasury for enforcement oversees the Customs Service. The deputy assistant secretary for regulatory, tariff and trade enforcement has overall responsibility for rules of origin policy.

---

15. U.S.-Israel Free Trade Area Implementation Act of 1985, Pub. L. No. 99-47, 99 Stat. 82, *reprinted in* 19 U.S.C.A. § 2112 note.

16. 19 U.S.C.A. §§ 2461-2466.

17. 19 U.S.C.A. §§ 2701-2706.

18. Harmonized Tariff Schedule of the United States, General Headnote 3(a)(iv) (1991).

19. 19 U.S.C.A. § 1304 and *supra* text accompanying note 1.

20. Because MFN rates, which have been established as a result of multilateral trade negotiations, are lower than the prenegotiation statutory rates, MFN rates, in a sense, are preferential. However, because MFN rates are available to the vast majority of nations, to characterize them as preferential would be a distortion. It is more accurate to term the statutory rates discriminatory. Substantial transformation is not the only means by which articles may obtain MFN rates. Through the theory of divestiture an article produced in a non-MFN country, that becomes a bona fide part of the commerce of an MFN country may acquire MFN status. *Ashdown U.S.A., Inc. v. U.S.*, 696 F. Supp. 661 (Ct. Int'l Trade 1988) (printing press manufactured in East Germany imported from West Germany where it was used for nine years prior to import in United States entitled to MFN rate applicable to West Germany).

Rules of origin decisions of the Customs Service and of the Treasury Department may be appealed to the U.S. Court of International Trade (CIT) (formerly the Customs Court), which sits in New York. Decisions of the CIT may be appealed to the U.S. Court of Appeals for the Federal Circuit (CAFC) (formerly the Court of Customs and Patent Appeals), which sits in Washington. Decisions of the CAFC, in turn, may be appealed to the U.S. Supreme Court. Supreme Court review of customs and trade matters is discretionary and is not common.

3.1.1. Administrative

An origin determination is required of Customs on every importation as part of the agency's enforcement of the marking law, Section 304 of the Tariff Act. Frequently the issue is whether the import is "marked in a conspicuous place as legibly, indelibly, and permanently as the nature of the article (or its container) will permit."[21] However, the issue may be whether the correct country has been marked as the country of origin. This decision effectively requires that Customs make an origin determination at the time of entry on every import. If the marking — including the designation of the country of origin — is incorrect, Customs will refuse to release the merchandise.[22] The importer may challenge such a decision through a protest filed with Customs within 90 days after the date of the decision denying the entry of the merchandise.[23] Protests of decisions excluding merchandise from entry or delivery must be acted on within 30 days (unless the person filing the protest requests a delay for the purpose of presenting evidence or argument).[24] A protest not acted on within this time is deemed denied.[25] At that point, the issue may be appealed to the CIT.

Because of the serious economic consequences that flow from an erroneous country of origin mark, it is prudent to obtain a prospective ruling from Customs before importation if there is any question concerning origin. An importer or an exporter with a direct and demonstrable interest in the issue may request a prospective ruling in writing. The request must contain a complete statement of the facts and may (and usually does) contain legal

---

21.   19 U.S.C.A. § 1304(a).

22.   19 U.S.C.A. § 1304(g).

23.   19 U.S.C.A. § 1514; 19 C.F.R. § 174.12.

24.   19 C.F.R. § 174.21(b).

25.   19 U.S.C.A. § 1515.

argument supporting the requesting party's proposed country of origin. Requests should be addressed to the Commissioner of Customs, Office of Regulations and Rulings, Washington, D.C. 20229.[26]

Rulings are generally issued in the form of a letter specifically addressing the facts described in the request. If Customs believes the ruling has broader interest, it may be published in the Customs Bulletin as a Customs Service Decision (CSD). A ruling involving a significant matter of policy is normally the subject of a Federal Register notice before it is issued, inviting comment from interested parties, and is later published, under the aegis of the Treasury Department, as a Treasury Decision (TD).

A separate procedure exists for country of origin rulings relating to government procurement.[27] These rules implement waivers of "Buy American" restrictions for countries that are signatories to the Agreement on Government Procurement.[28] Customs issues advisory rulings as well as final determinations under the government procurement regulations. Advisory rulings do no more than call attention to well-established interpretations or to principles of law relating to country of origin, without applying those interpretations or principles to a particular set of facts.[29] They are of limited use.

Final determinations are both more formal and more reliable. They may be requested by a foreign manufacturer, producer, or exporter; a U.S. importer; a U.S. manufacturer, producer, or wholesaler of a like product; a U.S. labor

---

26. 19 C.F.R. § 177.2(a). It will become apparent in this chapter that the regulations of the Customs Service often are inconsistent or incomplete. This regulation is an example. In fact the Customs regulations contain *no* provision for prospective rulings on country of origin other than for purposes of government procurement. The general ruling regulations deal only with tariff classification, valuation, and matters concerning carriers. Despite this inexplicable oversight, requests directed to the Commissioner of Customs in Washington, complying with the general ruling procedure of 15 C.F.R. Part 177, in fact are processed, albeit most of the time, rather slowly.

27. These are set out at 19 C.F.R. Part 177, Subpart B, §§ 177.21-177.31 (1991).

28. The "Buy American" Act is codified at 41 U.S.C.A. §§ 10a-10d. The Agreement on Government Procurement is published in GATT BISD 26/S 33. It is *reprinted* in Agreements Reached in the Tokyo Round of the Multilateral Trade Negotiations, H.R. Doc. No. 153, 96th Cong., 1st Sess. pt. 1, at 67 (1979). The statutory authority for the waiver was enacted by the Trade Agreements Act of 1979, Pub. L. 96-39, which implemented the various Tokyo Round agreements, including the Agreement on Government Procurement. *See generally* 19 U.S.C.A. §§ 2511-2518. For an authoritative commentary on the Agreement on Government Procurement, see Morton S. Pomeranz, *Toward a New International Order in Government Procurement*, 11 Law & Policy in International Business 1263 (1979).

29. 19 C.F.R. § 177.22(b).

organization whose members are employed in the manufacture, production, or wholesaling of the product; or a U.S. trade association a majority of whose members manufacture, produce, or wholesale a like product in the United States.[30] Requests, in writing, are to be filed with the Director, Office of Regulations and Rulings, Headquarters, U.S. Customs Service, 1301 Constitution Avenue, N.W., Washington, D.C. 20229.[31] Customs considers requests that include the specific procurement for which the final determination is requested before all other requests for advisory rulings and final determinations.[32]

Notice of all final determinations must be published in the Federal Register within 60 days of the date on which they were issued.[33] Any party in interest may appeal a final determination to the CIT within 30 days of its publication.[34]

3.1.2.   Judicial

Importers may challenge an adverse, final decision of the Customs Service by initiating an appeal in the CIT.[35] The importer files a summons with the clerk of the court within 180 days of the denial of the protest.[36] The CIT has held that domestic parties may also challenge enforcement of the marking

---

30.   19 C.F.R. § 177.23. While the Customs regulations define "country of origin," "advisory ruling," "final determination," and "party-at-interest," 19 C.F.R. § 1722(a)-(d), they do not define "like product."

31.   19 C.F.R. § 177.26.

32.   19 C.F.R. § 177.28(c).

33.   19 C.F.R. § 177.29.

34.   19 C.F.R. § 177.30. The definition of "party-at-interest" in 19 C.F.R. § 177.22(d) parallels the delineation of those who may request a final determination. Thus, a party other than the requester — including an adverse party — may appeal a final determination.

35.   The term "importers" is used here as shorthand for a larger list from 19 U.S.C.A. § 1514(c)(1):
    (a)   the importers or consignees shown on the entry papers or their sureties;
    (b)   any person paying any charge or exaction;
    (c)   any person seeking entry or delivery;
    (d)   any person filing claim for drawback; or
    (e)   any authorized agent of any of the persons described in clauses (a) through (d).

36.   28 U.S.C.A. § 2632(b) and § 2636(a)(2).

statute.[37] The CIT has published detailed rules governing the conduct of its proceedings, comparable to the Federal Rules of Civil Procedure. Decisions of the CIT may be appealed to the CAFC.[38] The Supreme Court of the United States may grant petitions to review decisions of the CAFC.[39]

3.2. Substantive Law

3.2.1. Basic Rules

The basic nonpreferential rule of origin — indeed, *the* nonpreferential rule of origin — in the United States is, as has been stated, substantial transformation. This is a judge-made rule, nowhere defined by statutory law. Its basic, most authoritative formulation is that of the Supreme Court in *Anheuser-Busch Brewing Assn. v. United States*: A new and different article with a distinctive name, character, or use must emerge from the manufacturing process.[40] Just what is new and different and what is a distinctive name, character, or use are, of course, difficult questions. The questions are made more difficult because courts have formulated the rule differently from case to case, because the Customs Service itself does not use consistent terminology in its own regulations, and further because Congress has been content to remain silent on the issue.

Consider first the court formulations. In *Anheuser-Busch* the Supreme Court said "There must be transformation; *a new and different article* must emerge 'having a distinctive name, character or use.'"[41] The CIT, in *Uniroyal, Inc. v. United States,* said "[A] substantial transformation' . . . results in an article having a name, character or use differing from that of the imported article."[42] The CIT simply dropped the Supreme Court's requirement that "a new and different article must emerge" and required only the production of an article having a different "name, character or use." By this formulation, the process need change only the name, the character, or the use, not all of them, and the

---

37. *Norcal/Crosetti Foods, Inc. v. U.S.*, 758 F. Supp. 729 (Ct. Int'l Trade 1991).

38. 28 U.S.C.A. § 1295.

39. 28 U.S.C.A. § 1254.

40. *Anheuser-Busch Brewing Association, supra* note 5.

41. *Ibid.* (emphasis added)

42. *Uniroyal Inc. v. United States*, 542 F. Supp. 1026, 1029 (Ct. Int'l Trade 1982), *aff'd*, 702 F.2d 1022 (Fed. Cir. 1983).

article need not be new and different. A mere name change would meet the test articulated in *Uniroyal*, and this is exactly what the CIT said in *Koru North America v. U.S.*: "The article need not experience a change in name, character *and* use to be substantially transformed. Only one of the three prongs needs to be satisfied for a product to achieve substantial transformation."[43]

These statements, however, may be deemed dicta since they clearly were unnecessary to the decisions rendered. In *Uniroyal* the court found that no substantial transformation had occurred, and in *Koru North America* the court found a transformation of both name and character.[44] But the CAFC also has used the CIT's incomplete *Uniroyal* terminology. In *Torrington Co. v. United States*, the appellate court said "[A] substantial transformation occurs when an article emerges from a manufacturing process with a name, character, or use which differs from those of the original material subjected to the process."[45] Despite the inexplicable exclusion of the "new and different" article requirement of *Anheuser-Busch*, the CAFC cites that case as authority for its formulation.

Four years later, however, a different three-judge panel of the CAFC, in an opinion that cited both *Anheuser-Busch* and *Torrington*, rejected that approach "With respect to the third of the *Anheuser-Busch* factors . . . the two products have different names . . . . This is the least persuasive factor *and is insufficient by itself to support a holding that there is a substantial transformation.*"[46]

The verbal confusion is compounded by the Customs Service whose regulations would not always be considered by everyone to be the best example of the draftsman's art. For instance, in its regulations implementing the marking statute, Customs refers to a "process which results in a substantial transformation of the article, *even though the process may not result in a new or different article.*"[47]

Unlike the CIT and the CAFC which, in *Torrington*, simply dropped the Supreme Court's "new and different article" requirement, Customs reformulates it (from "new *and* different" to "new *or* different") and then explicitly

---

43. *Koru North American v. United States*, 701 F. Supp. 229, 234 (Ct. Int'l Trade 1988).

44. Ibid. at 235.

45. *Torrington Co. v. United States*, 764 F.2d 1563, 1568 (Fed. Cir. 1985).

46. *Superior Wire v. U.S.*, 867 F.2d 1409, 1414 (Fed. Cir. 1989).

47. 19 C.F.R. § 134.1(d)(1) (emphasis added).

rejects it. But elsewhere in its regulations dealing with articles assembled abroad with U.S. components, consistent with *Anheuser-Busch*, Customs states:

> Substantial transformation occurs when, as a result of manufacturing processes, *a new and different article emerges, having a distinctive name, character, or use*, which is different from that originally possessed by the article or material before being subject to the manufacturing process.[48]

For purposes of one Customs regulation, therefore, a substantial transformation occurs when "a new and different article emerges," and for purposes of another, a substantial transformation may occur "even though the process may not result in a new or different article." There is no apparent policy reason for this inconsistency; the most likely explanation is simple carelessness in drafting.

3.2.2.   Interpretation by the Administrative Agencies and by the Courts

3.2.2.1.   The Issue of a Different Standard of Origin for Different Purposes

The different formulation of the substantial transformation test in the administrative regulations and in judicial opinions raises the question whether different statutory purposes require different degrees of substantial transformation. Is the test different if the issue is, for example, duty drawback rather than country of origin marking or MFN tariff rates? Both the courts and the Customs Service have been on both sides of this question, and it remains unresolved. The CAFC suggested that different standards might apply depending on statutory purpose in 1984 in *Belcrest Linens v. United States*:

> Although we decline to advance a definition of this term for all purposes, particularly because the implementing regulations under various tariff provisions define the term differently, it is clear that a "substantial transformation" occurs when as a result of a process an article emerges, having a distinctive name, character or use . . . .[49]

---

48.   19 C.F.R. § 10.14(b) (emphasis added).

49.   *Belcrest Linens v. United States*, 741 F.2d 1368, 1372. In a footnote, the court refers to the marking regulations, 19 C.F.R. § 134(d)(1), and to regulations concerning preferences discussed below in part 4.

Two years later, in *National Juice Products Assn. v. United States*, Judge Restani of the CIT noted the different policy purposes underlying tariff preferences, duty drawback, and country origin marking and observed, "although the language of the test applied under the three statutes is similar, the results may differ where differences in statutory language and purpose are pertinent."[50] In *Coastal States Marketing Inc. United States* the following year, Judge Carmen of the CIT elaborated on the point in a case involving MFN rates:

> Tests applied by the courts in determining whether a product has been "substantially transformed" in the course of its progression through intermediate countries such that the country of origin for customs purposes is affected are not necessarily identical within the various contexts.[51]

Less than a year later, in *Ferrostaal Metals Corp. v. United States*, Judge DiCarlo of the CIT took a very different approach.[52] He termed "misplaced" the government's argument that the stringency of the substantial transformation test applied should depend on the context in which the issue arises.[53] None of the cases cited by the government in support of the argument, Judge DiCarlo held, including *National Juice Products*, "even remotely suggests that the Court depart from policy-neutral rules governing substantial transformation in order to achieve wider import restrictions in particular cases."[54]

Ferrostaal dismisses the authority on the point of *National Juice Products* as simply a comment in a footnote; it does not mention *Coastal States Marketing*, and it concludes the topic with a very clear, straight-forward statement:

---

50. *National Juice Products Ass'n v. United States*, 628 F. Supp 978, 988-989 (Ct. Int'l Trade 1986).

51. *Coastal States Marketing Inc. v. United States*, 646 F. Supp 255, 257 (Ct. Int'l Trade 1986), *aff'd* 818 F.2d 860 (Fed. Cir. 1987).

52. *Ferrostaal Metals Corp. v. United States*, 664 F. Supp. 535 (Ct. Int'l Trade 1987). *Ferrostaal* was decided June 26, 1987; *Coastal States*, September 18, 1986; and *National Juice Products*, January 30, 1986.

53. *Ferrostaal*, 664 F. Supp. at 538.

54. Ibid.

As a practical matter, multiple standards in these cases would confuse importers and provide grounds for distinguishing useful precedents. Thus, the Court applies the substantial transformation test using the name, character *and* use criteria in accordance with longstanding precedents and rules.[55]

Two months later, in *Superior Wire, A Div. of Superior Products Co. v. United States*, Judge Restani returned to the issue and seemed to edge somewhat away from her view in *National Juice Products* and toward the view of Judge DiCarlo in *Ferrostaal*.[56] *Superior Wire*, like *Ferrostaal*, presented the question whether a steel product, subject to a VRA, had been substantially transformed in a second country. Judge Restani raised the issue directly. "There is," she wrote, "a preliminary dispute as to whether the court may consider the purpose of the VRA in making its decision as to whether a substantial transformation occurred."[57]

In *National Juice Products*, she continued, the court "indicated" that "differing statutory language or purposes might vary the results."[58] The issue there was marking, and the court "found cases discussing substantial transformation in the context of marking most directly applicable, although the court relied on cases applying similar standards in other cases."[59] No statutory language or legislative purpose was available to "directly guide" the court in the context of a VRA, she wrote.[60] "Thus, to the extent it is possible, the court must seek a neutral standard, unaffected by specialized statutory purpose, to determine the country of origin of the merchandise at issue."[61]

---

55.   Ibid. at 539 (emphasis added).

56.   *Superior Wire, A Div. of Superior Products Co. v. United States*, 669 F. Supp. 472 (Ct. Int'l Trade 1987) (decided 21 August 1987).

57.   Ibid. at 477.

58.   Ibid.

59.   Ibid.

60.   Ibid.

61.   Ibid. This statement was followed immediately by, "*Cf Ferrostaal*, 664 F. Supp. at 539 ('multiple standards in these cases would confuse importers and provide grounds for distinguishing useful precedents')." Subsequently, in *Timex Corp. v. United States*, 691 F. Supp. 1445 (Ct. Int'l Trade 1988), Judge Restani observed, again in a footnote, that Customs regulations define "product of the United States" for purposes of American goods returned

Judges of the CIT are coequal, and while they may be persuaded by each other, they are not bound by the opinions of their colleagues. However, Judge Restani might have been persuaded by Judge DiCarlo. *Superior Wire,* accordingly, both because of its result and because of Judge Restani's language, would seem to strengthen the authority of *Ferrostaal.*

But the issue is complicated by the fact that *Coastal States* was appealed and affirmed, "on the basis of the decision below," a month *before Ferrostaal* was decided.[62] Neither the CIT nor the CAFC opinions in *Coastal States* is mentioned in either *Ferrostaal* or in *Superior Wire.* Moreover, *Superior Wire* itself was appealed, and affirmed, less than two years after the affirmance in *Coastal States,* without mention of the issue.[63]

The issue is complicated even further by a still later decision by yet another CIT judge. In *Koru North America,* decided more than a year after *Ferrostaal,* Judge Tsoucalas stated: "In ascertaining what constitutes the country of origin under the marking statute, a court must look at the sense in which the term is used in the statute, giving reference to the purpose of the particular statute involved."[64] However, this statement was made not in the section of the opinion dealing with substantial transformation but in the previous section entitled "The Law of the Flag," dealing with the country of origin of fish caught by a vessel on the high seas.[65] In the portion of his opinion dealing with substantial transformation, Judge Tsoucalas cites *National Juice, Coastal States,* and *Ferrostaal*[66] for a number of points, but not on the question of the statutory purpose. In fact, other than in the statement quoted, the opinion in *Koru North America* does not address the issue.

If judicial authority is uncertain, the administrative position, at least, should be clear. It was the Customs Service itself, after all, that contended in *Ferrostaal* that changes sufficient to constitute a substantial transformation for one purpose would not be sufficient for another. But principled consistency does not always appear to prevail over short-term expediency at the Customs Service. On the day immediately after the trial was concluded in *Ferrostaal,*

"generally in terms of substantial transformation. The same standard applies for drawback purposes." (*Citing National Juice Products. See* 691 F. Supp. 1445, 1448 n. 6.)

62.　*Coastal States,* 818 F.2d 860 (Fed. Cir. 1987) (decided 26 May 1987).

63.　*Superior Wire, supra* note 46 (decided 15 February 1989).

64.　*Koru North America, supra* note 43, at 233 (decided 23 November 1988).

65.　Ibid. at 231.

66.　Ibid. at 234.

Customs, through the Treasury Department, published a Treasury Decision justifying a change in the country of origin of wool sweaters because there is but one law of substantial transformation "to be applied in all country of origin decisions."[67] Indeed, in an earlier ruling, Customs had been even more explicit:

> Customs believes that Congress, by using similar language in statutes dealing with the origin of merchandise, clearly intended that there should be only one rule for determining the country of origin of merchandise without regard to the particular statute requiring that determination.[68]

Customs made this statement when issuing new rules of origin for textiles and textile products, rules that largely applied a specified-process test to determine substantial transformation for these articles. While the textile rules were issued under the authority of Section 204 of the Agricultural Act, and not under the Tariff Act, Customs expressed its view that "Congress did not intend for Customs to apply one rule of origin for duty and marking purposes and a different rule of origin for the purposes of Section 204."[69] According to Customs, "the principles of origin contained in [the textile rules] are applicable to merchandise for all purposes, including duty and marking."[70]

Yet the following year, in *Yuri Fashions*, Customs unblushingly argued precisely the opposite.[71] The case involved sweaters from an insular possession of the United States, the Commonwealth of the Northern Mariana Islands (CNMI). Customs denied entry to the sweaters, maintaining that, under the textile origin rules, they were a product of Korea and therefore were subject to the quota applicable to sweaters from Korea — even though the sweaters met the criteria necessary for both duty-free treatment and country of origin marking as a product of the CNMI.

It sometimes is difficult to avoid a sense of cynicism concerning the attitude of Customs on this issue. Indeed, soon after *Koru North America* was decided, Customs began quoting from it for the proposition that "a court must look at the sense in which the term is used in the statute, giving reference to

---

67.   T.D. 87-29, 21 Cust. B. & Dec. 37, 45, 52 Fed. Reg. 7825 (13 March 1987). Trial was concluded in *Ferrostaal* on March 12, 1987. 664 F. Supp. at 536.

68.   T.D. 85-38, 19 Cust. B. & Dec. at 64-65, 50 Fed. Reg. at 8713 (1 March 1985).

69.   Ibid. Section 204 of the Agricultural Act is codified at 7 U.S.C.A. § 1854.

70.   T.D. 85-38, *supra* note 68, at 68.

71.   632 F. Supp. 41 (Ct. Int'l Trade 1986).

the purpose of the particular language involved."[72] Customs does not explain whatever happened to its publicly declared policy that "there should be only one rule for determining the country of origin of merchandise without regard to the particular statute requiring that determination."[73]

Presumably it is still good law, for while Customs was citing *Koru North America* for the proposition that the purpose of the statute controls, it published a further rule concerning origin for textiles that explicitly confronted the issue and explicitly reached the opposite conclusion. In a section of its ruling entitled "Uniform Application of Standard," Customs responded to commentators on the rule who "noted that recent court decisions have appeared to hold" that origin "depends on the particular statute under which that determination must be made and the intent of Congress in enacting that statute."[74] Customs disagreed, with a statement that merits extended quotation:

> Although such an inference may be drawn from language contained in some recent judicial decisions, Customs does not agree that the intended purpose of any of the statutes concerned requires standards to be applied which are different from the standard which Customs now seeks to uniformly apply. Customs also believes that application of the various statutes may not result in an article having more than one country of origin (*e.g.*, for marking, duty or textile restraint purposes) unless that result is explicitly directed by statute.
>
> Unless the courts hold that Customs should not apply the uniform standard in interpreting a particular statute, and that an article is to be considered a product of more than one country, Customs intends to continue its application of a unitary origin standard. Such a result is not only administratively expedient, but is legally required.[75]

If this is so, why does Customs continue to cite *Koru North America* for just the opposite proposition?

---

72.   *See, e.g.*, C.S.D. 90-52, 24 Cust. B. & Dec. adv. sheet no. 18, at 32; C.S.D. 90-61, 24 Cust. B. & Dec. adv. sheet no. 21, at 31; C.S.D. 90-64, 24 Cust. B. & Dec. adv. sheet no 21, at 40; C.S.D. 90-68, 24 Cust. B. & Dec. adv. sheet no. 23, at 18; C.S.D. 90-1, 25 Cust. B. & Dec. adv. sheet no. 18, at 1.

73.   T.D. 85-38, *supra* note 68, at 64-65.

74.   T.D. 90-17, 24 Cust. B. & Dec. adv. sheet no. 11, at 3-5 (14 March 1990).

75.   Ibid.

3.2.2.2. Administrative Interpretation

Some of the inconsistencies in the interpretation of the substantial transformation standard by the Customs Service appear to result simply from carelessness. Examples would include the regulations implementing the marking statute, which state that a substantial transformation may occur "even though the process may not result in a new or different article,"[76] and the ruling request procedure itself, which, as a formal matter, does not include a procedure for origin rulings.[77] Most of the other inconsistencies — and all of the major ones — result from the contortions the agency goes through as it attempts to deal with increasing protectionist pressure from the textile and steel industries. Rulings in other product areas generally have not been subject to the controversy surrounding rulings for textiles and steel and therefore have tended not to be particularly inconsistent.

Because issues of origin are very product specific, examples of some rulings may serve to give content to the phrase *substantial transformation*:

— A manufacturer of ceiling fans does not substantially transform components by assembling and combining them into fans.[78]

— Peeling, deveining, cooking, freezing, and repacking does not substantially transform raw shrimp.[79]

— Smoking does not substantially transform raw salmon.[80]

— Assembly into leather harnesses substantially transforms precut leather components.[81]

— Tanning substantially transforms raw skins.[82]

— Silver plating substantially transforms steel cutlery.[83]

---

76. 19 C.F.R. § 134.1(d)(1). See *supra* text accompanying note 47.

77. 19 U.S.C.A. § 1515.

78. C.S.D. 80-111, 14 Cust. B. & Dec. 898 (1979).

79. C.S.D. 89-101, 23 Cust. B. & Dec. 797 (1989).

80. C.S. Priv. Ltr. Rul. 729,256, (23 May 1988).

81. C.S.D. 80-113, 14 Cust. B. & Dec. 904 (1979).

82. C.S.D. 89-120, 23 Cust. B. & Dec. 864 (1989).

83. C.S.D. 80-237, 14 Cust. B. & Dec. 1150 (1980).

- Silk-screening with the cartoon "Snoopy" image does not substantially transform cloth bags.[84]
- The assembly of integrated circuits from semiconductors constitutes a substantial transformation.[85] (This ruling is not followed by the Department of Commerce in antidumping matters, as discussed in § 5 of this chapter.)
- Programming an EPROM (erasable programmable read only memory) semiconductor constitutes a substantial transformation.[86]
- The application of a photosensitive emulsion coating substantially transforms the photographic film base to which it is applied when the resulting bulk photographic film is cut to width and length, inserted into cassettes, and packaged for retail; cutting, inserting into cassettes, and packaging for retail does not, however, substantially transform bulk photographic film.[87]

Most of these rulings have not stirred great controversy. While important to the parties involved, they were not part of major trade controversies of the day. The semiconductor ruling, however, might be different. The industry is important both for the product it manufactures and for the industries it supplies. It is at the center of significant trade disputes. Semiconductors might be candidates for the treatment that befell textiles and, to a lesser extent, steel. A look at administrative interpretation of origin rules in those industries might therefore be both instructive and prophetic.

3.2.2.2.1. Textiles

Trade in textiles and textile products has long been controversial. In recent decades, markets in developed countries have been shielded from imports by a series of international arrangements that authorize importing countries to impose limits on the quantities that may be exported to their markets from particular exporting countries. This regime, which began with the "Short Term" Arrangement Regarding International Trade in Textiles in 1961, has

---

84. C.S.D. 90-52, 24 Cust. B. & Dec. adv. sheet no. 18, at 32 (1990).

85. C.S.D. 80-227, 14 Cust. B. & Dec. 1133 (1980).

86. C.S.D. 84-85, 18 Cust. B. & Dec. 1044 (1984).

87. C.S.D. 90-64, 24 Cust. B. & Dec. adv. sheet no. 21, at 40 (1990).

evolved into the Arrangement Regarding International Trade in Textiles, usually called the Multifiber Arrangement or MFA.[88]

These export limits, or quotas, not surprisingly led exporters and importers to attempt to maximize trade in whatever ways the regime would permit. One way was to ship incomplete products from countries limited by quota to countries not covered by restraints or with quota available. A substantial transformation of the incomplete products in the second country would confer origin on the second country and would free the final product from the limits imposed on the first country.

These developments outraged the industries in importing countries and frustrated the bureaucrats charged by governments to do their bidding. In the United States, the charge of "unfair" by the textile industries was met by exporters and importers with the response that the multicountry production processes conformed to existing rules of origin and that the transformations occurring in the second country were, by definition, substantial. The counter-response of the U.S. government was typical of the child on the playground who owns the ball and is losing the game: change the rules.

Action to change the rules of origin for textiles and textile products began — as many actions that affect these industries begin — in an election year.[89] In response to industry complaints that textiles and textile products were being imported in circumvention of existing quotas,[90] President Reagan, in May 1984, directed the Secretary of the Treasury to issue new country of origin regulations for textiles and apparel.[91] Interim regulations were published in August 1984,[92] and final regulations in March 1985.[93] They provide:

A textile or textile product will be considered to have undergone *a substantial transformation* if it has been transformed *by means of*

---

88. These are analyzed in great detail in Craig R. Giesse and Martin J. Lewin, *The Multifiber Arrangement: 'Temporary' Protection Run Amuck*, 19 Law & Policy in International Business 51 (1987).

89. Ibid. at 93.

90. Ibid. at 129-142.

91. Exec. Order No. 12,475, 3 C.F.R. 203 (1985), reprinted in 7 U.S.C. § 1854 note, at 363-364 (Supp. III 1985).

92. T.D. 84-171, 18 Cust. B. & Dec. 480 (1984).

93. T.D. 85-38, 19 Cust. B. & Dec. 1 (1985); 19 C.F.R. § 12.130 (1987).

substantial manufacturing or processing operations into a new and different article of commerce.[94]

The addition of a "substantial manufacturing" requirement to substantial transformation resulted from dictum of the CIT in a 1982 case, *Uniroyal, Inc. v. United States.*[95] Customs grabbed the opportunity offered by that unfortunate judicial phrase and proceeded to spell out what would — and what would not — be considered a substantial manufacturing operation that would substantially transform textiles and textile products.[96]

The regulation begins with the general criteria that will be used to determine origin for textiles and textile products:

(1)   A new and different article of commerce will usually result from a manufacturing or processing operation if there is a change in:

    (i)   Commercial designation or identity,

    (ii)   Fundamental character or

    (iii) Commercial use.

(2)   In determining whether merchandise has been subjected to substantial manufacturing or processing operations, the following will be considered:

    (i)   The physical change in the material or article as a result of the manufacturing or processing operations in each foreign territory or country, or insular possession of the U.S.

    (ii)   The time involved in the manufacturing or processing operations in each foreign territory or country, or insular possession of the U.S.

    (iii) The complexity of the manufacturing or processing operations in each foreign territory or country, or insular possession of the U.S.

    (iv)   The level or degree of skill and/or technology required in the manufacturing or processing operations in each foreign territory or country, or insular possession of the U.S.

---

94.   19 C.F.R. § 12.130(b) (emphasis added).

95.   See *Uniroyal, supra* note 42.

96.   The case and its "substantial manufacturing" dictum are discussed in the next section.

(v)   The value added to the article or material in each foreign territory or country, or insular possession of the U.S., compared to its value when imported into the U.S.[97]

The regulation then continues with specific examples of operations that usually will, or will not, confer origin.[98]

The textile rules of origin have one purpose and one purpose only: to restrict imports of textiles and textile products. "Because of the nature of textile and apparel products and current conditions of international trade in

---

97.   19 C.F.R. § 12.130(d).

98.   See ibid. § 12.130(e), which reads:
(e) Manufacturing or processing operations.
  (1)   An article or material usually will be a product of a particular foreign territory or country, or insular possession of the U.S., when it has undergone prior to importation into the U.S. in that foreign territory or country, or insular possession any of the following:
    (i)   Dyeing of fabric and printing when accompanied by two or more of the following finishing operations: bleaching, shrinking, fulling, napping, decating, permanent stiffening, weighting, permanent embossing, or moireing:
    (ii)   Spinning fibers into yarn;
    (iii)   Weaving, knitting or otherwise forming fabric;
    (iv)   Cutting of fabric into parts and the assembly of those parts into the completed article; or
    (v)   Substantial assembly by sewing and/or tailoring of all cut pieces of apparel articles which have been cut from fabric in another foreign territory or country, or insular possession, into a completed garment (e.g. the complete assembly and tailoring of all cut pieces of suit-type jackets, suits, and shirts).
  (2)   An article or material usually will not be considered to be a product of a particular foreign territory or country, or insular possession of the U.S. by virtue of merely having undergone any of the following:
    (i)   Simple combining operations, labeling, pressing, cleaning or dry cleaning, or packaging operations, or any combination thereof;
    (ii)   Cutting to length or width and hemming or overlocking fabrics which are readily identifiable as being intended for a particular commercial use;
    (iii)   Trimming and/or joining together by sewing, looping, linking, or other means of attaching otherwise completed knit-to-shape component parts produced in a single country, even when accompanied by other processes (e.g. washing, drying, mending, etc.) normally incident to the assembly process;
    (iv)   One or more finishing operations on yarns, fabrics, or other textile articles, such as showerproofing, superwashing, bleaching, decating, fulling, shrinking, mercerizing, or similar operations; or
    (v)   Dyeing and/or printing of fabrics or yarns.

these products," the U.S. International Trade Commission subsequently reported, "rules of origin have a particularly significant impact."[99] The commission explained that textiles and textile products undergo a sequence of processes, and may be traded at any point along that sequence:

> [A] finished apparel item may be the end result of a process that began with production of the raw fiber and continued through spinning of the yarn, weaving the fabric, dyeing and finishing the fabric, cutting the fabric into pieces according to pattern, sewing or otherwise assembling the pieces, adding buttons, zippers, pockets, linings, and ornamentation, and labeling and packaging the end product. Products in any of these stages may be shipped to another country for further processing.[100]

By changing the rules for established trade patterns for products already governed by country-specific quotas, Customs was able to alter the charging of an imported product from one country quota to another; if the new country of origin has no quota for the product, the import will be excluded. This is precisely what occurred in trade involving China and Hong Kong, two of the largest suppliers to the United States.[101] The commission explained:

> Previously products processed in Hong Kong using intermediate materials from China qualified as products of Hong Kong and entered the U.S. under Hong Kong's quotas. Under the new regulations, some of these products will be classified as products of China rather than of Hong Kong. Since China has fully utilized its quotas in the past, this will have the effect of reducing China's exports of intermediate materials to Hong Kong for reexport to the United States.[102]

---

99. United States International Trade Commission, Pub. No. 1695, The Impact of Rules of Origin on U.S. Imports and Exports 79 (1985).

100. Ibid. The purely protective motivation for the new rules is shown in their different treatment of knit-to-shape and cut-apparel components. Importers tend to use the first, U.S. producers with overseas operations the latter; thus Customs determined that the final assembly of knit-to-shape components would not confer origin but that the final assembly of cut-apparel components would do so. Giesse & Lewin, *supra*, note 88, at 140-141.

101. Giesse & Lewin, *supra* note 88, at 135.

102. U.S. International Trade Commission, *supra,* at 86. But attempts to contort rules of origin for protectionist purposes can have unintended consequences. Customs has been compelled to rule, in conformity with the new rules of origin, that when sweater parts knitted by machine in the United Kingdom are combined and finished in China, the country or origin of the completed sweater is the United Kingdom—a country whose exports of textiles to the

The textile regulations were the occasion of the statement by Customs in 1985 that "there should be only one rule for determining the country of origin of merchandise without regard to the particular statute requiring that determination."[103] This pronouncement was followed, of course, by the *Yuri Fashions* case in which Customs argued the opposite: origin for textile quota purposes is one thing, origin for marking and duty purposes is another.[104]

The issue appears to have been settled in favor of uniformity in 1990 with the publication of a final interpretive rule regarding the origin of imported textiles and textile products.[105] This rule effectively applied the textile quota origin rules to textile products for all purposes. The 1985 quota rules specify five processes that usually will not confer origin.[106] Four of these, Customs noted in the background statement to the 1990 rule, were in conflict with previously announced Customs positions and with existing uniform and established practices.[107]

Because the substantial transformation criteria of the quota rules were derived from court decisions and administrative rulings, Customs said they "should be used in making country of origin determinations for all Customs purposes, including determinations for purposes of country of origin marking and for assessing duty on imported articles."[108] The change, as a legal matter, is described as mere housekeeping. Customs, it says, is simply making its administrative practice consistent, or is simply changing its practices to conform to court decisions. Errors are being corrected, nothing more. They are being corrected, of course, by increasing significantly the degree of substantiality required for a substantial transformation. The substantial manufacturing test is added to the substantial transformation test. With considerably less formality, Customs has extended its more restrictive policy to the other industry that is the special object of Customs (and Congressional) solicitude — the steel industry.

United States were not, at the time of the ruling, subject to quota. C.S. Priv. Ltr. Rul. 079,844 (16 April 1987).

103. *See* T.D. 85-38, *supra* note 68.

104. *See Yuri Fashions*, *supra* note 71 and accompanying text.

105. T.D. 90-17, *supra* note 74.

106. 19 C.F.R. § 12.130(e).

107. T.D. 90-17, *supra* note 74.

108. Ibid.

3.2.2.2.2.   Steel

For decades, trade in steel and steel products has been, together with trade in textiles and textile products, a major trade policy issue in the United States. We have had the "voluntary" steel export restraints of the 1960s, the Trigger Price Mechanism of the 1970s, scores of antidumping and countervailing duty cases in the early 1980s, and, in the late 1980s and early 1990s, a series of bilateral agreements with major steel exporters limiting exports to the United States of steel and steel products.[109] As is the case with textiles, the country-specific import quotas that result from the bilateral steel agreements bring country of origin issues to the fore. And, as is the case with textiles, the response of the Customs Service to this situation has been, on the whole, restrictive. Until September 1991 this response was discernible only from specific rulings because there were no comprehensive rules of origin for steel as there are for textiles. But on 25 September 1991 Customs proposed amendments to its regulations that would define *substantial transformation* for steel and other base metal products in terms of specified changes in tariff headings.[110] The proposal is based on the change in tariff heading standards of the Canada-U.S. FTA (see § 4.2.1.1.). There are a number of differences, most of them involving the elimination of the value added criteria of the FTA. If enacted in its proposed form, the proposed rule would reverse several court rulings adverse to Customs on the issue of substantial transformation.[111] The rationale Customs gave for proposing changes in steel rules of origin at this time is transparently without merit. According to Customs, the proposal is of "particular importance" because of "special legal requirements and restrictions" that apply to steel products.[112] Two examples of these "special legal requirements and restrictions" are given: voluntary steel export restraints and special country of origin marking requirements for certain pipe and pipe fittings.[113] But the steel quotas expired on schedule, six months later in

---

109. The first VRAs covered the 5 years from 1 October 1984 to 30 September 1989. A 2½-year extension occurred in 1989. The VRAs were scheduled to expire on 31 March 1992. U.S. International Trade Commission, Quarterly Report on the Status of the Steel Industry, x-xi, USITC Pub. 2386 (June 1991).

110. Proposed Customs Regulations Amendments Regarding Rules of Origin Applicable to Imported Merchandise, 56 Fed. Reg. 48448.

111. The most prominent, perhaps, is *Ferrostaal, supra.*

112. 56 Fed. Reg. 48450.

113. Ibid.

March 1992.[114] And why do special marking requirements — requirements that deal only with the method of marking — require new rules of origin? One need not be a total cynic to suspect that the reasons for the proposal have more to do with the interests of the steel industry in the United States, and its political power, than they do with expiring quotas and laws concerning how pipes and pipe fittings should be marked.

Some earlier steel rulings offer a perspective that suggest this skeptical outlook is justified. In 1965 Customs ruled that steel plate of U.S. origin, exported for tempering and quenching (heat treatment), was not eligible upon its reimport for favorable duty treatment as returned American goods because the tempering and quenching imparted new characteristics to the steel that went beyond mere alteration.[115] By clear implication, the steel had undergone a substantial transformation because a finished article, advanced in value but not merely altered by the advance, must be transformed; there is no third category in the law. A decade later, Customs ruled that when unmachined castings for hose couplings were machined, drilled, threaded, plated, and assembled, they too were substantially transformed.[116]

Three years later, this ruling was cited as authority for a determination that the simple threading of stainless-steel pipe fittings constitutes a substantial transformation: "The process of threading stainless steel pipe fittings substantially transforms them into new and different articles of commerce so as to make them products of the country in which the threading process is performed."[117]

This is a somewhat surprising ruling because it involved only threading, while the ruling upon which it relied involved machining, drilling, plating, and assembly in addition to threading. To the more cynical, however, the ruling is not totally surprising: its consequence was to confer country of origin status on Japan, not on Taiwan, and thereby to deny the product duty-free treatment under the GSP.[118] A decade later, when it was realized that this ruling could permit the establishment of threading operations in countries without bilateral

---

114. *See Multilateral Steel Trade Break Up With No Agreement, As U.S. VRAs Expire,* 9 Int'l Trade Reporter (BNA) 573 (1 April 1992).

115. T.D. 56,545(1), 100 Treas. Dec. 868 (1965).

116. T.D. 75-199, 9 Cust. B. & Dec. 435 (1975).

117. C.S.D. 79-437, 13 Cust. B. & Dec. 1666, 1662 (1978).

118. The ruling seems particularly unnecessary because the fittings were not, as the GSP statute requires, imported directly from a beneficiary country; their sojourn in Japan, whatever processing took place there, saw to that. 19 U.S.C.A. § 2463(b)(1). See § 4.2.1.1.

restraint agreements, thereby permitting circumvention of the steel quotas, Customs reversed itself: "[T]he threading operation does not so transform the unthreaded fitting as to cause its identity to be lost in the finished product."[119] "The nature of the threading operation," Customs said, "is insubstantial in relation to the nature of the operations required to manufacture the fitting."[120]

This later ruling in fact probably is correct, totally apart from its use of a substantial manufacturing criterion in addition to substantial transformation. The steel fitting remained a steel fitting — it simply had undergone a finishing operation. To paraphrase the Supreme Court in *Anheuser-Busch*: a fitting put through the claimant's process is still a fitting.[121] It is not a new and different article. However, in a yet later ruling, involving steel wire rod, Customs stated "The relative simplicity of the process does not change the fact that the character of the resulting product may be significantly different."[122]

In this ruling, however, Customs stressed the value added by the process and then reverted to a substantial manufacturing standard. Since the transformation of wire rod added only 11 percent to the value of the resulting steel wire, Customs held, the process was not substantial; consequently, neither was the transformation.

If 11 percent will not satisfy the "substantial processing" requirement, perhaps 50 percent will. To the contrary: Customs has ruled that the conversion of black plain-end pipe into electrical conduit by means of cutting, threading, hot-dip galvanizing, chromating, varnishing, and assembling, adding "approximately 50 percent of the value of the completed conduit," is not substantial transformation.[123] In addition to adding 50 percent to the value, the process altered the tariff classification of the article from "Metals, Their Alloys, and Their Basic Shapes and Forms" to "Electrical Machinery and Equipment." Not even the ruling that reversed the previous "threading is substantial transformation" determination would explain this result. Customs' deference to the steel industry and its supporters, however, would explain it.

Yet Customs was not through. As we have noted, it went on to argue, in *Ferrostaal,* that even though annealing and galvanizing normally would substantially transform cold rolled sheet, a different result should be reached

---

119. T.D. 87-46, 21 Cust, B. & Dec. 139, 141.

120. Ibid.

121. "A cork put through the claimant's process is still a cork." 207 U.S. at 562.

122. C.S. Priv. Ltr. Rul. 075,923, at 2 (18 March 1987).

123. C.S. Priv. Ltr. Rul. 076,950 (24 February 1986).

because of the steel VRAs.[124] That argument being unsuccessful, Customs now proposes to overrule *Ferrostaal* by administrative fiat. According to the proposed regulation, a change from cold rolled steel sheet (HTS Item 7208) to galvanized steel sheet (HTS Item 7210) would not constitute a substantial transformation. No changes within the tariff categories encompassing carbon steel flat rolled products (HTS Items 7208-7212) would qualify, according to the proposal. Indeed, conversion of such diverse categories of products as steel bars and rods (HTS Items 7213-7215) and angles, shapes, or sections (HTS Item 7216) into flat rolled products, or vice versa, would not qualify under the proposal, which defines substantial transformation for all of these products as "[a] change to headings 7208-7216 from any heading outside that group."[125] In other words, any change within that group of headings would not constitute a substantial transformation. If the proposal is implemented in its present form, a serious judicial challenge is likely, for the authority of the Customs Service to overrule a court decision in this manner is, to say the least, highly questionable.

3.2.2.3. Judicial Interpretation

Judicial interpretation of the rules of origin, like administrative interpretation, tends to be highly fact specific:

— Sorting, sizing, branding, dating, air-cleaning, steaming, drying, and coating does not substantially transform bottle corks.[126]
— The attachment of bristles substantially transforms wooden blocks into brushes.[127]
— Manufacturing grade orange juice concentrate is not substantially transformed when made into juice.[128]
— The assembly of encapsulated integrated circuits from slices containing integrated circuit chips, wire, frame strips, molding compound, and epoxy substantially transforms those assembled components.[129]

---

124. *Ferrostaal*, supra note 52 and accompanying text.

125. 56 Fed. Reg. at 48452.

126. *Anheuser-Busch*, *supra* note 6.

127. *United States v. Gibson-Thomsen*, *supra* note 2.

128. *National Juice Products*, *supra* note 50.

129. *Texas Instruments Inc. v. United States*, 681 F.2d 778 (Fed. Cir. 1982).

Like most of the administrative interpretations of the substantial transformation test, most of the judicial interpretations involved matters of great interest to the parties but of little interest to those outside the particular trade involved. One notable exception to this generalization is *Uniroyal*.[130] This is the case whose dictum has provided the rationale for Customs' "substantial manufacturing" addition to the substantial transformation test.

The issue presented in *Uniroyal* was whether footwear uppers, consisting of complete shoes except for the outsoles, were substantially transformed by the attachment of the outsoles. The court held that they were not. The imported uppers underwent no physical change whatsoever, being subject only to finishing by the addition of the outsoles. The court drew an analogy to "attaching buttons to a man's dress shirt or attaching handles to a finished piece of luggage."[131] The imported upper, "the very essence of the finished shoe,"[132] retained its identity throughout the process: it was a shoe when the process began, and it was a shoe when the process ended.

There appears to be no reason to quarrel with this holding. However, in reaching it, the court relied in part on a comparison of the process that produced the shoe uppers with the process that attached the outsoles. The court found the process of attaching the outsoles less time consuming and less costly than the process of producing the uppers, and it found that more highly-skilled labor was needed to produce the uppers than to attach the outsoles.[133] The attachment of the outsoles, the court said, "is a minor assembly operation which requires only a small fraction of the time and cost involved in producing the uppers."[134]

Where *Uniroyal* broke new ground — and where it went astray — was not in finding the attachment of the outsoles to be a "minor assembly operation" but in holding relevant the magnitude of this operation as compared to the magnitude of the processes that produced the uppers. A "minor assembly operation" that does not change the identity of a product does not substantially transform that product, regardless of whether it involves a small or a large fraction of the time and the cost involved in producing the original article. On the other hand, a substantial transformation can occur even though the process

---

130. *Uniroyal*, supra note 42.

131. Ibid. at 1030.

132. Ibid.

133. Ibid. at 1028.

134. Ibid at 1030.

that transforms the article is of smaller magnitude than that which produced it.

Whether a substantial transformation has occurred has historically depended upon the nature of the article emerging from a particular process — as compared to the nature of the article that entered the process — and not on the nature of the process itself.[135] To be sure, the process is a relevant factor in the determination, and it is typically set forth in the decisions.[136] But the key question has been whether an article has been substantially transformed — by whatever process — into a new and different article having, in the words of *Anheuser-Busch*, "a distinctive name, character or use."

Substantial transformation can occur — a new and different article can be produced — by an insubstantial process. Congress recognized this point when it enacted, for example, the preferential origin requirements for the CBI.[137] Caribbean Basin Initiative preference requires both origin in the beneficiary country, which is subject to the substantial transformation test, and a contribution, in CBI countries, of at least 35 percent to the value of the article. Implicit in the 35 percent requirement is the fact that a substantial transformation can occur with less than 35 percent. Otherwise, a minimum would not be needed. Origin alone would do. Indeed, the President originally proposed a 25 percent minimum for CBI, thereby recognizing that a process

---

135. "There must be transformation; a new and different article must emerge, 'having a distinctive name, character or use.'" *Anheuser-Busch*, 207 U.S. at 562. "Just how complex the operation was does not appear, but we do not think that is important." *United States v. International Paint Co.*, 35 C.C.P.A. 87, 95 (1948). "Slabs . . . are clearly not the same articles as ingots and differ therefrom in name, value, appearance, size, shape and use." *Burstrom v. United States*, 44 C.C.P.A. 27, 29 (1956). "We do not deem it necessary to determine whether or not the processes employed at the plaintiff's Tube Line plant in the conversion of the imported articles into flanges and fittings are generally prevalent throughout any segment of the industry in the United States . . . [t]he end result of the manufacturing processes to which the imported articles are subject in plaintiff's Tube Line plant is the transformation of such imported articles into different articles having a new name, character and use." *Midwood Industries, Inc. v. United States*, 64 Cust. Ct. 499, 507 (1970). "[W]here, as here, foreign processing of an export article, *to whatever degree*, produces such changes in the performance characteristics of the exported article as to alter its subsequent handling and uses over that which earlier prevailed, the resultant product is of necessity a new and different article." *Dolliff & Co., Inc. v. United States*, 81 Cust. Ct. 1, 5, 455 F. Supp. 618, 622 (1978) (emphasis added), *aff'd*, 599 F.2d 1015 (C.C.P.A. 1979).

136. *Anheuser-Busch*, 207 U.S. at 559 n. 1; *Burstrom*, 44 C.C.P.A. at 29; *International Paint*, 35 C.C.P.A. at 89-90; *Dolliff & Co., Inc.*, 455 F. Supp. at 619; *Midwood Industries*, 64 Cust. Ct. at 504.

137. Caribbean Basin Economic Recovery Act, Pub. L. No. 98-67, tit. III, subtit. A, 97 Stat. 369, 384-395 (codified as amended at 19 U.S.C.A. §§ 2701-2706).

that left untouched as much as 75 percent of the value of an article nevertheless could transform it substantially.[138]

Uniroyal's dictum, that a substantial transformation cannot occur without substantial manufacturing, flies in the face of the Congressional understanding as exemplified by the "substantial transformation plus value added" criteria of the CBI. It flies in the face of the cases from *Anheuser-Busch* forward. It was unnecessary to the result of the *Uniroyal* case itself, which seems correctly decided on its facts. But it offered a straw that has been grasped by the Customs Service to fashion its highly restrictive special rules of origin for textile and apparel imports and to justify an increasingly restrictive series of origin rulings for steel products as well.

Perhaps the most unusual judicial interpretation of the substantial transformation test occurred in *United States v. Murray.*[139] Among the reasons *Murray* is unusual is (1) it was a criminal case; (2) it progressed through the ordinary federal courts (i.e., the District Court for the District of Massachusetts and the Court of Appeals for the First Circuit) rather than through the CIT and the CAFC; (3) it tellingly referred to decisions of the Customs Service as "unprincipled" and compared them to "decisions by a Kadi at the gate";[140] and (4) it amounted to something of a decision by a Kadi at the gate itself.

The defendant in *Murray* was convicted of conspiracy and of knowingly introducing imported glue into the United States by means of false statements concerning country of origin. He claimed the glue originated in Holland and therefore was entitled to MFN rates of duty, rather than in China to which MFN rates did not apply (see § 6.1.) On appeal, he argued inter alia, that the terms "country of origin" and "substantial transformation" are unconstitutionally vague. The conviction was affirmed.

The appellate court, in a decision by District Court Judge Wyzanski sitting by designation, proceeded to construe "country of origin" and "substantial transformation" completely de novo. Not only did the *Murray* court ignore the "unprincipled" administrative decisions of Customs, it ignored all prior judicial decisions as well, even Supreme Court decisions. *Anheuser-Busch*, for example, is nowhere mentioned.

A substantial transformation, the court said, occurs only when the contribution to the product in the second country is "of great significance

---

138. H.R. Rep. No 266, 98th Cong., 1st Sess. 12 (1983).

139. *United States v. Murray*, 621 F.2d 1163 (1st Cir. 1980), *cert den.* 449 U.S. 837.

140. Ibid. at 1169.

compared to the contribution of the first country."[141] The term "great significance" is not defined, except circularly, e.g., "the adjective 'substantial' informs us that the degree of change is to be measured with reference to economic value, and the degree must be very great."[142] Moreover, the court said, the term "transformation," by itself, without the modifier "substantial," means a "fundamental" change. In the context of determining whether MFN rates apply, the court went on, "transformation" alone "means such a change as to move the article either from one to another of the classes established by official tariff schedules, or from one to another of the classes of goods, wares, and merchandise commonly recognized in the commercial markets where such articles are traded."[143] Thus, without so much as a nod to seventy-five years of rules of origin jurisprudence, the court suggests that change in tariff heading may be required for any transformation, to say nothing of a substantial one. In concluding that "substantial transformation" should be read as a unified expression and not as two separate words, the *Murray* court said it means

> a fundamental change in the form, appearance, nature, or character of an article which adds to the value of the article an amount or percentage which is significant in comparison with the value which the article had when exported from the country in which it was first manufactured, produced or grown.[144]

As a statement of what a good rule of origin might be, of how substantial transformation might be defined by a court, legislature, or rule maker starting with a clean slate, this formulation has much to commend it. But as a statement of existing law in 1980 it could hardly provide a sound basis for holding an importer liable for civil penalties. As the basis for sending an individual to prison, the statement of the law stands with the characterization the court itself gave to rulings of the Customs Service: a decision by a Kadi at the gate.

---

141. Ibid. at 1168.

142. Ibid. at 1169.

143. Ibid.

144. Ibid.

4. Preferential Rules of Origin

The United States, strictly speaking, has no preferential rules of origin. The substantial transformation test determines origin for all purposes unless, as discussed above, the statutory purpose is to be taken into account. Even when statutory purpose is considered, however, the test remains substantial transformation. The substantiality of the transformation required would vary to some unspecified degree, depending upon the purpose. Nevertheless, the United States maintains a number of preferential programs that contain criteria, in addition to origin, necessary to obtain the preference. These include the GSP, the CBI, special treatment for products of the insular possessions and freely associated states, and the FTAs with Israel and Canada. Rules of origin — again, really rules of preferential eligibility — play a major role in the trilateral negotiations between Canada, Mexico, and the United States, NAFTA.

4.1. Procedure

The procedures for determining origin for preferential purposes, both administratively and judicially, are the same as for nonpreferential purposes.

4.2. Substantive Law

The substantive law of preference eligibility in the United States generally centers on value added. The Canada-U.S. FTA, however, while using value added in some areas, relies essentially on change in tariff finding.

4.2.1. Basic Rules and their Interpretation by the Administrative Agencies and the Courts

4.2.1.1. The Generalized System of Preferences

The GSP was established in 1974 to provide duty-free treatment to imports of eligible articles from eligible developing countries.[145] To be eligible for duty-free treatment under GSP, an article must originate in, and be imported directly from, the beneficiary developing country (BDC), and the sum of the cost of materials produced in the BDC plus the direct cost of processing there must equal at least 35 percent of the appraised value of the article at the time

---

145. Trade Act of 1974, Pub. L. No. 93-618, tit. V, 88 Stat. 1978, 2066-71 (codified as amended at 19 U.S.C.A. §§ 2461-2466).

of its entry into the United States.[146] This statutory requirement — that the sum of the costs of the materials plus the costs of processing must total at least 35 percent of the article's value — applies in addition to the requirement that the product originate in the BDC.

The requirement that an eligible article originate in the BDC underwent a brief hiatus when the CIT in 1988 held, in *Madison Galleries, Ltd. v. United States*, that the GSP statute demanded only 35 percent value added, not origin.[147] The CAFC affirmed.[148] While the Customs regulations required that an eligible article be produced in the BDC, the statute, by its explicit terms, required only that the article be exported directly from the BDC and that at least 35 percent value be added there. To the argument from Customs that the GSP so interpreted would be inconsistent with the standard of the Caribbean Basin Initiative, and that Congress intended that the GSP and CBI origin tests be uniform, the CAFC replied "If Congress wants uniformity, let it so enact."[149] Congress wanted uniformity, subsequently, it did "so enact." The Customs and Trade Act of 1990 added language to the GSP statute limiting duty free treatment to eligible articles that originate in a BDC.[150]

An important concept in the calculation of value added in the BDC is *dual substantial transformation*, which assists BDCs in reaching the 35 percent requirement for preference eligibility. The term *dual substantial transformation* refers to an intermediate step in the processing of raw material imported into the BDC. If imported raw material is substantially transformed in the BDC into an intermediate product that is itself a new and different article, and if that new article in turn is substantially transformed into an eligible article, the intermediate product becomes a product of the BDC by virtue of its substantial transformation in the BDC — and its total value is counted toward the required 35 percent.[151]

---

146. 19 U.S.C.A. § 2463(b).

147. *Madison Galleries, Ltd. v. United States*, 688 F. Supp. 1544 (Ct Int'l Trade 1988).

148. *Madison Galleries*, 870 F.2d 627 (Fed. Cir. 1989).

149. Ibid at 634.

150. Pub. L. 101-382, 104 Stat. 629, § 226, amending § 503(b) of the Trade Act of 1974, 19 U.S.C.A. § 2463(b).

151. *See* 19 C.F.R. § 10.177(a)(2).

An example will illustrate how dual substantial transformation works. In *Torrington Co. v. United States,*[152] sewing machine needles, an eligible article, were exported to the United States from Portugal, then a BDC. The needles were manufactured in Portugal from imported wire. Therefore, the value of the wire — a non-Portuguese product — could not count toward the 35 percent requirement. The processing operations in Portugal added less than 35 percent to the value of the exported needles. Thus, at first glance, it would seem that the sum of Portuguese materials (zero) plus Portuguese processing totalled less than the required 35 percent.

But GSP eligibility was granted because the court found a dual substantial transformation: the first was the processing of the imported wire into needle blanks; the second was the processing of the needle blanks into needles. Because the needle blanks were produced in Portugal by the substantial transformation of imported wire, they were considered to be Portuguese materials — and the total value of the needle blanks was included in determining the value of the needles produced in Portugal. By this analysis, the sum of the costs of Portuguese materials (needle blanks) plus their Portuguese processing into needles equalled 100 percent of the value of the needles.

Since the courts in *Torrington* in fact found two substantial transformations, their results legally are correct. The major dispute in the case centered on the processes and products themselves and not on the law. However, the opinions of both the CIT and the CAFC contain dicta that are misleading, if not erroneous. They imply that a dual substantial transformation is required in every case if duty free treatment is to be granted. Thus, they would appear to deny eligibility where a single substantial transformation occurs in a process that adds at least 35 percent to the value of the article. In such a case, by definition, the sum of BDC materials (zero) plus processing (35 percent) equals 35 percent. If the process that adds 35 percent to the value of the article also involves a substantial transformation, the statutory requirements for eligibility are met.[153] Dual transformation is needed only if the value of the materials is required to meet the 35 percent test, which was the case in *Torrington.* Yet the CIT stated:

---

152. *Torrington Co. v. United States,* 596 F. Supp. 1083 (Ct. Int'l Trade 1984), *aff'd,* 764 F.2d 1563 (Fed. Cir. 1985).

153. See 19 U.S.C. § 2463(b)(2), which provides, in relevant part, that duty free treatment shall be provided: "If the sum of (A) the cost or value of the materials produced in the beneficiary developing country . . . plus (B) the direct costs of processing operations performed in such beneficiary developing country . . . is not less than 35 percent of the appraised value of such article at the time of its entry into the customs territory of the United States."

[A]bsent such a dual requirement, the GSP's goal of industrialization, diversification, and economic progression for underdeveloped nations could be frustrated. For example, a BDC could import eligible items, merely decorate or assemble these items and thereby satisfy the 35 percent value-added requirement since these direct costs of processing operations would be includable in the calculation. In this manner, BDC's could become mere conduits for the merchandise of developed countries.[154]

In this analysis, the court completely ignored the fact that, in addition to adding at least 35 percent to the value of the article, the processing in the BDC by definition substantially transforms the imported raw materials into a new and different article of commerce. If decoration or assembly does not amount to a substantial transformation, then it would not matter how much value is added by the process. The CAFC, unfortunately, fell into the same trap:

In the absence of a dual transformation requirement, developed countries could establish a BDC as a base to complete manufacture of goods which have already undergone extensive processing. The single substantial transformation would qualify the resulting article for GSP treatment, with the non-BDC country reaping the benefit of duty free treatment for goods which it essentially produced.[155]

Here, too, the court overlooked the fact that so long as imported raw materials are substantially transformed by an operation that adds 35 percent or more to their value, for GSP purposes they no longer are goods "essentially produced" in a non-BDC country. Indeed, the CAFC's reasoning turns the statute's 35 percent requirement into a 100 percent requirement. This follows because all the relevant processing — 100 percent of it — occurs in the BDC. Assuming that this processing effects a substantial transformation, the question is whether it alone amounts to 35 percent of the value of the article. To require in addition that the raw materials be a product of the BDC, either by origin or by substantial transformation, is to require that 100 percent of the article — materials plus processing — be attributable to the BDC. What role then does the 35 percent requirement play?

The dicta of both courts would read the 35 percent requirement out of the law, ignoring the statutory scheme that permits up to 65 percent of the value of an eligible article to be attributable to a non-BDC country. That both courts

---

154. *Torrington*, 596 F. Supp. at 1085.

155. *Torrington*, 764 F.2d at 1568.

misconstrued this point is made clear by the fact that this aspect of the *Torrington* rationale has not been followed. Indeed, the decisions of both the CIT and the CAFC in *Madison Galleries* reached the result posited as a "horror story" by the *Torrington* courts: GSP eligibility without origin and with only 35 percent value added. Nothing could be further from the dicta of the *Torrington* cases. And, based on the statutory language, nothing could have been more correct. The 1990 amendment, reversing *Madison Galleries,* does not restore *Torrington.* Rather, it aligns the standard of GSP with that of the CBI.

4.2.1.2. The Caribbean Basin Initiative

The CBI was implemented by the Caribbean Basin Economic Recovery Act of 1983, which authorized the president to designate twenty-seven Central American and Caribbean nations as eligible to receive duty free treatment for their exports to the United States.[156] The CBI rule of preference is comparable, but not identical, to the GSP rule of origin. However, the differences do not affect the questions of origin or substantial transformation.

Under CBI, as under the GSP, no problem arises when an article is totally the product of a CBI country. Under the CBI, as under the GSP, the 35 percent test is employed when imported raw materials are substantially transformed in the CBI country; however, the 35 percent test for the CBI is slightly different from the 35 percent test for the GSP. While the CBI permits the cumulation of value added among all CBI beneficiary countries to reach the required 35 percent,[157] the GSP permits cumulation only among members of a free trade association such as the Association of South East Asian Nations (ASEAN).[158] Value added in Puerto Rico and in the U.S. Virgin Islands counts as value added by a beneficiary country under the CBI, but not under the GSP.[159] Finally, if U.S. raw materials are substantially transformed in a CBI country, up to 15 percent of their value may be included

---

156. Caribbean Basin Economic Recovery Act, *supra* note 137. This preference, which originally was scheduled to expire on 30 September 1995, has been extended indefinitely by § 211 of the Customs and Trade Act of 1990, *supra* note 152.

157. 19 U.S.C.A. § 2703(a)(1).

158. 19 U.S.C.A. § 2463(b)(2).

159. 19 U.S.C.A. § 2703(a)(1).

in determining whether the 35 percent requirement is met;[160] there is no such provision in the GSP.

Another important difference between the GSP and the CBI is related to the permitted cumulation of value added by eligible countries other than the country from which the product is exported: this is the "direct export" requirement. Under the GSP, to qualify for the preference, the eligible article must be imported directly from the BDC for which the preference is granted.[161] Limited exceptions apply only to well-documented transshipment through third countries and to narrowly defined free trade zone operations.[162] And, of course, the 35 percent value must be satisfied totally from the materials and processing attributable to the single BDC.[163] Under the CBI, the article may be imported directly from *any* beneficiary country, not necessarily the one for which the benefit is granted.[164] This difference facilitates the cumulation of value among countries eligible for CBI benefits.

The CBI regulations explicitly provide — contrary to the dicta of the *Torrington* cases — that a single substantial transformation will suffice if the direct costs attributable to that transformation represent at least 35 percent of the appraised value of the imported article.[165] Moreover, in summarizing the eligibility requirements of the CBI, the House Report leaves no doubt that a

---

160. Ibid.

161. 19 U.S.C.A. § 2463(b)(1)-(2).

162. *See* 19 C.F.R. § 10.175 (1987).

163. 19 U.S.C.A. § 2463(b)(2).

164. 19 U.S.C.A. § 2703(a)(1).

165. 19 C.F.R. § 10.196(a) (1987). Example 2 to this regulation provides: "A raw, perishable skin of an animal grown in a non-beneficiary country is sent to a beneficiary country where it is tanned to create nonperishable "crust leather." The tanned skin is then imported directly into the U.S. Although the tanned skin represents a new or different article of commerce produced in a beneficiary country within the meaning of § 10.195(a), the cost or value of the raw skin may not be counted toward the 35 percent value requirement because (1) the tanned material of which the imported article is composed is not wholly the growth, product, or manufacture of a beneficiary country and (2) the tanning operation creates the imported article itself rather than [an] intermediate article which is then used in the beneficiary country in the production or manufacture of an article imported into the U.S. *The tanned skin would be eligible for duty free treatment only if the direct costs attributable to the tanning operation represent at least 35 percent of the appraised value of the imported article*" (emphasis added).

single substantial transformation that adds at least 35 percent to the value of the transformed article will suffice.[166]

4.2.1.3.   Products of the Insular Possessions

The United States traditionally has granted preferential treatment to articles produced in its insular possessions provided required value was added.[167] This amount was stated in the negative. Prior to the enactment of the CBI, products of the insular possessions were admitted duty free if no more than 50 percent of their value was attributable to foreign content.[168] This amounted to a 50 percent value added requirement.

To maintain a preference for the insular possession, the CBI legislation also modified the preferential rules of origin that apply to the insular possession.[169] First, the CBI legislation provides that articles imported from the insular possessions are afforded duty treatment "no less favorable" than the treatment afforded articles from Caribbean countries under the CBI, thereby placing the insular possessions at least on a par with the CBI countries.[170] Second, the CBI legislation provides that the maximum "50 percent foreign content permitted" rule of origin will be modified to a maximum "70 percent foreign content permitted" rule of origin for articles eligible for duty-free

---

166.   "To be eligible for duty free treatment under CBI, an article must meet three basic tests under the rule-of-origin requirements: (1) direct importation; (2) 35 percent minimum local content; and (3) a product wholly of the country or 'substantially transformed' into a new or different article." H.R. Rep. No. 26612171, 98th Cong., 1st Sess. 12 (1983).

167.   19 U.S.C. § 1202 General Headnote 3(a) (Supp. III 1985). The insular possessions include Guam, Wake Island, Midway Islands, Kingman Reef, Johnston Island, and American Samoa. 19 C.F.R. § 7.8 n. 5 (1987). They also include the Commonwealth of the Northern Mariana Islands. *See supra* note 71 and accompanying text.

168.   Watches and watch movements were admitted duty free if their foreign content did not exceed 70 percent. 19 U.S.C. § 1202 General Headnote 3(a) (Supp. III 1985).

169.   H.R. Rep. No. 266, *supra* note 166, at 22-24; Senate on Finance, 98th Cong., 1st Sess., Explanation of Committee Amendment to H.R. 2973, at 33 (Comm. Print 1983).

170.   General Headnote 3(a) of the Harmonized Tariff Schedule of the United States provides, "(iv) Subject to the provisions in Section 213 of the Caribbean Basin Economic Recovery Act, articles which are imported from insular possessions of the United States shall receive duty treatment no less favorable than the treatment afforded such articles when they are imported from a beneficiary country under such Act." 19 U.S.C. § 1202 General Headnote 3(a)(iv) (Supp. III 1985) (citations omitted). The General Headnotes and Rules of Interpretation of the Harmonized Tariff Schedule are no longer carried in the United States Code Annotated. See 19 U.S.C.A. § 2702(d) (West Supp. 1987).

treatment under the CBI.[171] This rule is the equivalent of a 30 percent value added requirement, which gives the insular possessions a 5 percent advantage over the CBI countries. For articles not eligible for duty free treatment under the CBI, the insular possessions retain their traditional entitlement to duty free treatment under the 50 percent rule.[172] Because the value requirement is phrased in terms of maximum foreign content, the value of U.S. materials is included in the value attributable to the insular possession.

4.2.1.4. Freely Associated States

The Marshall Islands and the Federated States of Micronesia — the Freely Associated States — receive duty-free treatment on most of their exports to the United States.[173] The rule of origin for the Freely Associated States is comparable to the GSP rule as enunciated in *Madison Galleries*: direct importation from the state and a minimum of 35 percent value added in the state.[174] The product need not originate in the state.

4.2.1.5. U.S.-Israel Free Trade Area

In 1985, Congress implemented the U.S.-Israel Free Trade Area, which provides for duty-free treatment in each country for the products of the other.[175] The rules of origin for this duty-free treatment parallel those of the CBI; for the United States to grant duty-free treatment, the sum of the cost of the materials produced in Israel, plus the direct cost of processing operations performed there, may not be less than 35 percent of the appraised value of the

---

171. General Headnote 3(a)(i) of the Harmonized Tariff Schedule of the United States.

172. Ibid.

173. Compact of Free Association Act of 1985, Pub. L. 99-239, 99 Stat 1770, § 401, 99 Stat. 1838, 48 U.S.C. § 1681 note, General Headnote 3 (viii) to the Harmonized Tariff Schedule of the United States.

174. Ibid. There are product and value limitations on the duty free treatment that may be granted. *See generally* General Headnote 3(viii) to the Harmonized Tariff Schedule of the United States.

175. U.S.-Israel Free Trade Area Implementation Act of 1985, Pub. L. No. 99-47, 99 Stat. 82, reprinted in 19 U.S.C.A. § 2112 note. Negotiation of the Free Trade Area was authorized in title IV of the Trade and Tariff Act of 1984, Pub. L. No. 98-573, §§ 401-406, 98 Stat. 2948, 3013-18. The U.S.-Israel FTA origin rules are set out in General Headnote 3(c)(vi) to the Harmonized Tariff Schedule of the United States.

merchandise when it enters in the United States.[176] The cost or value of materials produced in the United States may account for up to 15 percent of the appraised value of the merchandise.[177] To qualify for the duty free preference, articles must be imported directly from Israel.[178]

4.2.1.6.   Canada-U.S. Free Trade Agreement

In the FTA with Canada, the United States adopted for the first time the change in tariff heading system of origin.[179] This marks a sharp departure from previous preference rules and may indeed eventually supplant — or, perhaps more accurately, define — substantial transformation for origin purposes as well.[180]

The FTA provides generally that a product will be deemed to originate in the territory of Canada or of the United States if the production process using third-country materials is sufficient to change their classification under the Harmonized Commodity Description and Coding System, called the Harmonized System.[181]

Chapter Three of the FTA sets out the general rules of origin and the definitions of key terms. The tariff changes needed to confer origin for FTA purposes are in Annex 301.2 to Chapter Three. The twenty pages of the

---

176. General Headnote 3(c)(vi), *supra* note 175.

177. Ibid.

178. Ibid.

179. Free Trade Agreement, Canada-United States, 23 December 1987, 27 International Legal Materials 281 (1988).

180. Change in tariff heading is the essence of the U.S. proposal to GATT for an international code on rules of origin. *See*, N. David Palmeter, *The U.S. Rules of Origin Proposal to GATT: Monotheism or Polytheism?*, *supra* note 9. This is also the basis of the proposed rules of origin for steel and other base metals, see notes 12, 111-114, and 125 and accompanying text. In its announcement of the proposed steel rules, Customs said it intends to incorporate the change in tariff heading system for all products. 56 Fed. Reg. 48450.

181. The FTA rules of origin are discussed in detail in Richard Dearden and David Palmeter, eds., Free Trade Law Reporter (CCH International). The FTA rules are criticized in David Palmeter, *The FTA Rules of Origin and the Rule of Law*, Proceedings of the Seventh Judicial Conference of the United States Court of Appeals for the Federal Circuit, 128 F.R.D. 500 (1990); *The FTA Rules of Origin: Boon or Boondoggle?* in Dearden, Hart & Seger, eds., Living with Free Trade: Canada, the Free Trade Agreement and the GATT (Institute for Research and Public Policy, Ottawa, 1989); *The Canada-U.S. FTA Rule of Origin and a Multilateral Agreement,* 16 Int'l Bus. Lawyer 513 (1988).

annex specify precisely what classification changes must occur in the twenty-one sections that incorporate the ninety-seven chapters of the Harmonized System. Sometimes the change need be only at the two-digit chapter level; at other times, change at the four-digit heading level is required; at still other times, change at the six-digit subheading level is needed; in a few instances change at the eight-digit, statistical level is necessary.

Two of these sections contain simply stated rules. Section I deals with live animals and animal products and encompasses Chapters 1 through 5 of the Harmonized System. Annex 301.2 provides that a change from any one Chapter of Section I to another will confer origin but that changes within Chapters (at the heading or subheading level) will not. This means that the conversion of a live animal, Chapter 1, into meat, Chapter 2, confers origin under the FTA but that the conversion of milk into cheese, both Chapter 4, does not. Section XXI deals with works of art, collectors' pieces and antiques and encompasses the final chapter of the Harmonized System, Chapter 97. A change to that chapter from any other chapter will confer origin.

For the other nineteen sections and ninety-one chapters of the Harmonized System between Sections I and XXI, however, the specific operations that confer origin cannot be articulated as a general rule or principle. Instead, each section must be studied separately to determine what specific operations are required to confer origin on specific products. At this point there is no single rule of origin or preference, but literally hundreds of separate rules.

While change in tariff heading is the fundamental rule of the FTA, value added also plays a part. In twenty-three of the rules set out in annex 301.2, in addition to a required tariff classification change, a 50 percent value added requirement must also be met. Materials originating in either country count toward this 50 percent. For example, one of the fifteen rules that applies to products of the chemical or allied industries, Section VI, Chapters 28-38 of the Harmonized System provides:

A change to any subheading of Chapters 28-38 from any other subheading within those chapters; provided, except for the other rules in this section, that the value of materials originating in the territory of either Party or both Parties plus the direct cost of processing performed in the territory of either Party or both Parties constitute not less than 50 percent of the value of the goods when exported to the territory of the other Party.[182]

Indeed, for all assembled products except apparel and made-up textile articles, the 50 percent standard will confer FTA origin, even without a

---

182. FTA Ch. 3, Annex 301.2, Section VI, para. 2.

change in tariff heading, provided the goods have not undergone third country operations.[183] This provision is most applicable to imported unassembled or disassembled products subsequently assembled in Canada or the United States in a process adding the required value.

4.2.1.6.1.   The Honda Decision

The value-added provision has been the center of the most significant and controversial origin decision under the FTA: the celebrated Honda decision. This decision really is a series of rulings by the U.S. Customs Service in the course of an audit of the firm's North American operations that had the cumulative effect of reducing Honda's claimed North American content from 69 percent to less than 50 percent.[184] Most of the rulings dealt with technical accounting issues, but two in particular, concerning the production of engines at Honda's Anna, Ohio plant, involved significant interpretations of the FTA and its U.S. implementing legislation. These are the "intermediate material" ruling and the "assembling/processing" ruling. The result of these rulings was to exclude much of the value added by Honda at its Ohio plant from the North American value of the engine, thereby reducing the calculated North American content of the finished automobile, as U.S. Customs calculated it, below 50 percent, with the resultant loss of the FTA duty preference when the autos were exported to the United States from Canada.

4.2.1.6.1.1.   The "Intermediate Material" Ruling[185]

Honda produced engines at its Ohio plant from materials produced in Japan and from materials produced in the United States. Honda claimed, and Customs agreed, that for purposes of the FTA the engines originated entirely

---

183. *Erasable Programmable Read Only Memories (EPROMs) From Japan; Final Determination of Sales at Less Than Fair Value, 51 Fed. Reg. 39680, 39692 (1986).*

184. U.S. Customs Internal Advice Rulings HQ 000112 (14 November 1991); HQ 000116 (14 November 1991); HQ 544833 (3 December 1991); HQ 544834 (3 December 1991); HQ 000131 (12 December 1991); HQ 000155 (10 February 1992); HQ 000160 (27 February 1992); HQ 000161 (27 February 1992). Many of the details concerning Honda's operations are not made explicit in the rulings, which are largely cast in hypothetical terms. The many news accounts provide the relevant facts of the Honda operation. *See, e.g., Customs Rules Civic Engines Are 'Foreign,'* Washington Post, 3 March 1992 at D3; *U.S. Tariff Imposed on Hondas,* N.Y. Times, 3 March 1992 at D1; *U.S. Says Canadian-Assembled Hondas Don't Qualify for Duty-Free Treatment,* Wall St. Journal, 3 March 1992 at A2.

185. U.S. Customs Internal Advice Ruling HQ 000131 (12 December 1991).

in North America because the parts imported from Japan were used or consumed in the U.S. production of the engines. The engines were shipped to Canada where they were included in the finished automobiles that were then exported to the United States. When they entered Canada, the engines were treated as products of U.S. origin for purposes of the FTA. Honda therefore claimed 100 percent of their value as "North American content" in asserting that the total North American value of the automobile exceeded 50 percent.

While U.S. Customs agreed that the engines originated in North America despite the inclusion of some Japanese parts, it disagreed with Honda's conclusion that 100 percent of the value of the engines qualified for inclusion in the value-added calculation. Instead, Customs held that *none* of the U.S. value added by Honda in Ohio but *all* of the value of the parts imported from Japan counted as "North American." In other words, if Honda's U.S. operations contributed 90 percent of the value of the materials for the engines, and the parts acquired from Japan contributed 10 percent, Customs concluded that the 10 percent contributed from Japan counted as North American but the 90 percent contributed by Honda's U.S. operations did not.

This result, Customs said, was mandated "by the plain language" of the U.S. statute implementing the FTA, language that tracked the FTA language in relevant part.[186] The FTA provides that, for purposes of calculating North American content, the "value of materials originating" in North America means the aggregate of

the price paid by the producer of an exported good [the automobile] for materials originating in the territory of either Party or both Parties [the engine] or for materials imported from a third country [the Japanese parts] used or consumed in the production of such originating materials [the engine].[187]

A literal reading of this language initially suggests Customs was correct. The producer of the "exported good" — the automobile — was Honda in Canada. The question, therefore, is what would count as the "value of materials originating" in North America in that automobile. According to the FTA, "the price paid" for the engines — "materials originating" in North America — would count.

---

186. United States-Canada Free Trade Agreement Implementation Act of 1988, Pub. L. 100-449, 102 Stat. 1851, as amended by Pub. L. 101-207, §1(b), 101 Stat. 1833, Pub. L. 101-382, Title I §§103(b), 134(b), 104 Stat. 635, 651, 19 U.S.C.A. §2112 note.

187. FTA Art. 304.

But, said Customs, there was no "price paid" by Honda in Canada for the Ohio-built engines. Honda in Ohio simply shipped the engines to Honda in Canada.[188] Since Honda paid no price for the engines, the only other value mentioned in the FTA is the price the company paid "for materials imported from a third country" — the Japanese parts. Thus, Customs reasoned, the FTA explicitly provides that if no price is paid by the producer of the exported goods (automobiles) for "materials originating" in North America (engines), the only other value that may be attributed to those originating materials is the price paid for third country parts used in the production of the "materials originating" in North America. Customs accordingly concluded that Japanese parts contributed North American value but U.S. parts did not.

Customs conceded that "at first blush" the result might seem "incongruous," but, the agency continued, "further analysis demonstrates the appropriateness of this interpretation."[189]

Customs' analysis is less than convincing. First, neither the FTA nor the U.S. implementing legislation, as Customs acknowledged, makes any distinction between producers who are vertically integrated and those who are not.[190] Yet the rationale of Customs leads to one result for a producer that is vertically integrated and a different result for one that is not. Assume, for example, that Honda in Canada had purchased the engines from an unrelated U.S. supplier whose operations exactly duplicated those of Honda in Ohio. The entire price paid to that supplier would be treated as a price paid for North American materials and would include the value added by the seller's U.S. operations as well as the cost to the seller of third-country parts. Yet this U.S. value may be lost, Customs ruled, if the engine manufacturer and the auto producer are vertically integrated.

Customs reaches this result by virtue of imposing a mandatory, irrevocable "election" on the producer of the exported automobile. Once that election is made, Customs concluded, there is no going back. This is an unwarranted conclusion.

---

188. The ruling does not make clear whether Honda in Canada and Honda in Ohio were separate corporate entities or how the two facilities maintained their records for internal accounting as well as taxation purposes. In most such situations, however, an internal transfer price would be used. This transfer price normally would be accepted by Customs authorities for valuation purposes 19 U.S.C.A. § 1401a. Presumably it should be used as the price paid for FTA purposes as well.

189. HQ 000131, *supra* note 185 at 10.

190. HQ 000131, *supra* note 188 at 7 (discussing whether a vertically integrated producer even may claim an intermediate material as an originating material for FTA duty preference purposes).

According to Customs, Honda could have elected to qualify only the automobiles for FTA treatment, or it could have attempted to qualify both the engines and the automobiles. But when, as a vertically-integrated producer, it attempted to qualify both the engines and the automobiles, the value of the North American materials used to produce the engines was lost. This is the "intermediate material" ruling: In the absence of a price paid by the automobile producer for the engines, the only question the FTA asks is what is the price paid for third country materials that went into the production of the engines?

But, says Customs, if Honda had claimed that the North American materials used in the automobiles were not the engines but, for example, the ingots from which they were cast, the result under the FTA would have been different. The amount allowed would have been the aggregate of "the price paid by the producer of the exported good [the automobile] for materials originating in the territory of either Party or both Parties [ingots] . . . ."[191] According to Customs, the choice was Honda's, and once the choice was made, "the statutory rules dictate the consequences of that choice."[192]

Of course the statutory rules dictate what will occur if one course is followed rather than another, but it does not follow that the "choice" is irrevocable. Customs cited no authority for its conclusion that Honda was not free, after disallowance of its claim for 100 percent of the value of the engines, to claim the amount contributed by the U.S. operations. This would have been consistent with the entire purpose of the FTA which is, after all, to give preference based on North American content. To exclude North American value and simultaneously include third-country value, as Customs did, was more than "incongruous." It was absurd.

Almost as absurd was Customs' conclusion that Honda was not entitled to its claim of 100 percent of the value of the engines. When the engines were exported from the United States to Canada, U.S. Customs agreed that they were 100 percent North American. How is it that when the engines simply were attached to the chassis of automobiles and reexported to the United States they lost some of that value? In particular, how is it that they lost their U.S. value? A construction of the FTA and the U.S. implementing legislation that reaches such a result truly is absurd. But how can the language be read to reach a rational result?

One way is to read *and* for *or* so that the relevant phrase refers to the price paid "for materials originating in the territory of either Party or both Parties *and* for materials imported from a third country." *Or* is thus read in the

---

191. FTA Art. 304. Compare *supra* note 187.

192. HQ 000131, *supra* note 185 at 11.

conjunctive rather than in the disjunctive. Such a reading certainly makes more sense in terms of the FTA's purpose. But may *or* be read as *and*? Of course it may, and it frequently is. The U.S. Supreme Court has observed, in the course of reading *or* in the conjunctive, "that the word or is often used as a careless substitute for the word and; that is, it is often used in phrases where and would express the thought with greater clarity."[193]

Reading *or* for *and* would express what must have been the thoughts of the FTA negotiators with greater clarity. Such a reading has the advantage of reaching a rational result, which cannot be said of the reading made by Customs.

4.2.1.6.1.2.   The "Assembling/Processing" Ruling

Custom's "intermediate materials" ruling is a literal reading of the FTA that ignores the purpose of the agreement and reaches an absurd result. Customs' "assembling/processing" ruling, however, is a reading of the FTA that disregards its explicit language, ignores the purpose of the agreement and also reaches an absurd result.

The "assembling/processing" ruling deals with labor contributed in North America to the production of Honda's engines. Both the FTA and the U.S. implementing legislation provide that the "direct cost of assembling the goods" must be added to the cost of materials in calculating North American value.[194] The value of all North American operations devoted to assembly are includable in the North American value regardless of the origin of the materials on which those operations are performed.

Honda claimed the cost of die casting and machining as necessary costs of assembling finished engines. Customs denied the claim, holding that the direct costs of casting and machining are costs of processing, not costs of assembling.[195]

As a lexicographic exercise, Customs might be correct, but as an interpretation of the FTA and the U.S. law, it simply is wrong. In both the FTA and the law the terms "direct cost of processing" and "direct cost of

---

193. *DeSylva v. Ballentine,* 351 U.S. 570, 573 (1956) (Harlan, J.). See also *United States v. Moore,* 613 F.2d 1029, 1040 (D.C. Cir. 1979) (citations omitted), *cert denied,* 446 U.S. 954: "Normally, of course, 'or' is to be accepted for its disjunctive connotation, and not as a word interchangeable with 'and.' But this canon is not inexorable, for sometimes a strict grammatical construction will frustrate legislative intent. That, we are convinced, is precisely what will occur here unless 'or' is read as 'and.'"

194. FTA Annex 301.2:4(a); Act §202(c)(3)(A).

195. U.S. Customs Internal Advice Ruling HQ 000160 (27 February 1992).

assembling" share the same definition: *"direct cost of processing or direct cost of assembling means* the costs directly incurred in, or that can reasonably be allocated to, the production of the goods . . . ."[196] These specifically include the cost of all labor as well as the cost of dies and molds.[197] Even design and engineering costs are within the definition of "assembling."[198] Customs' attempt to squirm out of this definitional box is startling.[199] According to Customs, the FTA defined only the phrase "direct cost of assembling." It did not separately define the word "assembling" standing alone. Thus, Customs reasoned, the operations listed as includable as "direct cost of assembling" are not the same as those includable as "assembling" when that word is unpreceded by the phrase "direct cost of." And thus, Customs concluded, the value of labor performed in North America is not part of the North American value added.

The Honda decision is an excellent example of the shortcomings of value added as a standard for determining origin. It is widely recognized that the standard is uncertain because fluctuations in materials prices and exchange rates can upset the most careful calculations.[200] Apart from these uncertainties, the decision also demonstrates that lengthy and expensive audits are a normal part of the process. And, most important, the decision demonstrates that whatever else the value added standard may be, efficient, predictable, and nonpolitical it is not.

5. Rules of Origin in the Context of Antidumping Proceedings

Antidumping investigations in the United States, and any antidumping duty order that might result from an investigation, are directed at specified products from specified countries. Origin accordingly is an inherent element of any antidumping proceeding. In the United States the uncertainties that may be attendant to origin determinations are generally compounded by the asserted authority of the Department of Commerce to determine origin for antidumping purposes and are compounded further by an anticircumvention provision in the antidumping law. The result is an increased likelihood that a product will be

---

196. FTA Art. 304 and Act §202(f)(3) (emphasis added).

197. Ibid.

198. Ibid.

199. HQ 00160 *supra* note 26, at 5.

200. *See, e.g.,* U.S. International Trade Commission, Standardization of Rules of Origin 17, USITC Pub. 1976 (May 1987).

included within an antidumping duty order. The Commerce policy and the anticircumvention provision stack the antidumping deck against exporters by giving origin issues in antidumping proceedings a "heads-we-win, tails-you-lose" aspect.

Here is how it works: To enforce an antidumping order against, for example, semiconductors from Japan, Customs must determine whether an imported semiconductor in fact is from Japan. If so, it is included automatically within the order; if not, it normally would be excluded. But if the semiconductor had been assembled and tested in Hong Kong using processed wafers or dice fabricated in Japan, then the views of Customs concerning origin would become irrelevant for antidumping purposes. Customs has concluded that assembly and testing confer origin on a semiconductor.[201] Commerce has decided that for antidumping purposes they do not,[202] and this position has been sustained on appeal.[203] Thus, for Customs purposes — marking, rate of duty, and quota if any — the semiconductor is a product of Hong Kong. For antidumping purposes, it is a product of Japan.

The process is furthered by the addition, in 1988, of an anticircumvention provision to the antidumping law.[204] This provision states that articles completed or assembled in the United States or in third countries, which are of the same class or kind as those covered by an antidumping duty order may be included within the order if (1) the components or materials used in the United States or third countries are themselves subject to the order, or if they are produced in the country subject to the order; (2) the difference between the value of the completed product and the components or materials is

---

201. C.S.D. 80-227, 14 Cust. B. & Dec. 1133 (1980).

202. *Erasable Programmable Read Only Memories (EPROMs) From Japan; Final Determination of Sales at Less Than Fair Value*, 51 Fed. Reg. 39680, 39692 (1986).

203. *American NTN Bearing Mfg. Corp. v. United States*, 739 F. Supp. 1555, 1565 (Ct Int'l Trade 1990) (citations omitted): "[T]he concept of 'substantial transformation' is used for identifying the country of origin of imported merchandise for purposes of determining the dutiable status of that merchandise. The term is of primary importance in cases involving country of origin markings. In the context of determining the scope of an antidumping order, 'substantial transformation' has little significance."

204. Pub. L. No. 100-418, § 1321, 102 Stat. 1192, adding § 781 to the Tariff Act of 1930, as amended, 19 U.S.C.A § 1677j.

"small"; and (3) Commerce considers inclusion "appropriate" to "prevent evasion" of the antidumping order.[205]

This brings us back to the "heads-we-win, tails-you-lose" aspect of origin in antidumping proceedings. If Customs decides that the Hong Kong operations do not substantially transform the components and materials from Japan, then the semiconductor remains a product of Japan and is subject to the order.[206] Heads, we win. But if the transformation, in the view of Customs, is substantial enough to confer origin on Hong Kong, Commerce may disagree and term the transformation insubstantial for antidumping purposes, or it may term it *shall* and find circumvention. Tails, you lose.[207]

6. Rules of Origin in Other Contexts

6.1. Most-Favored-Nation Tariff Rates

The determination of the country of origin of an article imported into the United States is necessary to determine the applicable rate of duty. The Harmonized Tariff Schedules of the United States provide for two rates of duty, the Column 1 and the Column 2 rates. Column 1 rates are applied generally to imports from countries that receive MFN treatment from the United States, while Column 2 rates are extended to countries that do not receive MFN treatment.[208] Column 2 represents the statutory rate enacted by

---

205. It is worth noting that origin is treated slightly differently in U.S. countervailing duty law. All of the above analysis applies to countervailing duty law, but in addition, Section 771(12) of the Tariff Act, 19 U.S.C.A. § 1677(12), applies explicitly in countervailing duty proceedings, but not in antidumping: "For purposes of part I of this subtitle [i.e., Imposition of Countervailing Duties], merchandise shall be treated as the product of the country in which it was manufactured or produced without regard to whether it is imported directly from that country and without regard to whether it is imported in the same condition as when exported from that country or in a changed condition by reason of remanufacture or otherwise."

206. Rule 2(a) of the General Rules of Interpretation, Harmonized Tariff Schedule, provides: "Any reference in a heading to an article shall be taken to include a reference to that article incomplete or unfinished, provided that, as entered, the incomplete or unfinished article has the essential character of the finished article. It shall also include a reference to that article complete or finished (or failing to be classified as complete or finished by virtue of this rule) entered unassembled or disassembled."

207. *Supra* note 205.

208. General Headnote 3(a) to the Harmonized Tariff Schedule of the United States.

the Smoot-Hawley Tariff of 1930,[209] the highest in the history of the United States.[210] The rate in Column 1 reflects the reductions in the Column 2 rates that have resulted from various rounds of tariff-cutting trade negotiations.[211]

Once again, the origin situation is clear when an article is totally the product of a single country, and once again, the test should be "substantial transformation" when more than one country is involved. But this situation has been confused by the Customs Service. In one ruling, Customs posed the issue in these unsurprising terms: "whether the cutting process producing the instant merchandise constitutes a substantial transformation thereby entitling the merchandise to entry . . . under Column 1 . . . [I]f the merchandise has not been substantially transformed, it is dutiable under Column 2."[212] But this ruling does not even mention a highly relevant prior decision by the Treasury Department.[213] Probably this omission is just as well.

The question answered by Treasury in that prior decision was whether linen piece goods manufactured in Czechoslovakia, further processed in Belgium or West Germany, and then exported to the United States, were dutiable as the product of Czechoslovakia or as the product of Belgium or West Germany. Treasury stated "[T]he term 'substantial transformation' has no direct applicability to the determination required."[214] This puzzling statement is followed by one that approaches the amazing:

> [T]his issue is to be determined not on the question of whether the "loomstate" linen piece goods underwent a "substantial transformation" in either Belgium or West Germany, but rather whether the printing and finishing operations accomplished in these countries result in a new and different article possessing a distinctive name, character, or use

---

209. Act of June 17, 1930, ch. 497, 46 Stat. 590 (codified as amended in scattered sections of 18 U.S.C., 19 U.S.C., and 28 U.S.C.).

210. *See generally* House Committee On Ways and Means, 100th Cong., 1st Sess., Overview and Compilation of U.S. Trade Statutes 4-5 (Comm. Print 1987); *see also* J. Dobson, Two Centuries of Tariffs 34 (1976).

211. Ibid.

212. C.S.D. 84-17, 18 Cust. B. & Dec. 433 (1983).

213. T.D. 78-202, 12 Cust. B. & Dec. 433 (1977).

214. Ibid.

substantially different from that which it possessed before printing and finishing.[215]

Perhaps Treasury was attempting to deal with the "some substantial transformations are more 'substantial' than others" problem, as it stated that "each situation must be determined on a case-by-case basis and cases involving 'substantial transformation' for other purposes under the tariff laws (e.g., marking, drawback . . .) are valuable only as extrinsic aids in making such determinations."[216] But even this possibility is far from clear for Treasury states that the issue is not substantial transformation, but whether the process results "in a new and different article processing a distinctive name, character or use substantially different from that which it possessed before." What is the difference? And why does Treasury cite *Anheuser-Busch* as its only authority for this remarkable statement? *Anheuser-Busch* defines the required transformation as one in which "a new and different article must emerge, 'having a distinctive name, character or use.'"[217] How is it authority for the proposition that this is not substantial transformation? Moreover, *Anheuser-Busch* is a drawback case, precisely the kind of case, according to the same ruling, that is "valuable only" as an "extrinsic" aid in making determinations. Why, then, is it the only authority cited in this ruling? Fortunately, this particular ruling seems to have been given a well-deserved burial. Substantial transformation is the test for MFN rates.

6.2.   Drawback

Drawback is the refund of duties paid on imported merchandise that has been used in the production of an article that is later exported.[218] "The theory underlying the granting of drawback . . . is and always has been that it would encourage the development in the United States of the making of articles for

---

215.   Ibid., (citing *Anheuser-Busch, supra* note 5).

216.   Ibid.

217.   *Anheuser-Busch, supra* note 5, at 562.

218.   19 U.S.C.A. § 1313(a): "Upon the exportation of *articles manufactured or produced in the United States* with the use of imported merchandise, the full amount of the duties paid upon the merchandise so used shall be refunded as drawback, less 1 per centum of such duties."

export, thus increasing our foreign commerce and aiding domestic industry and labor."[219]

Although the substantial transformation test derives from the *Anheuser-Busch* drawback case, the term itself is absent from both the drawback law and the drawback regulations. The latter simply define a "drawback product" as "a finished or partially finished product manufactured in the United States under a drawback contract."[220] Given the export-promotion theory underlying the granting of drawback, it might make sense for the law and the regulations not to require a substantial transformation to determine whether an article is "manufactured or produced" in the United States for drawback purposes. Yet there is the *Anheuser-Busch* language and its requirement that "a new and different article must emerge", a requirement that, as noted, is absent from the country of origin marking regulation implementing a law intended to inform consumers of the origin of their purchases.[221] Comparing the language of the *Anheuser-Busch* test with that of the marking regulation, a greater degree of transformation seems to be required before drawback will be granted than is required before a consumer no longer need be notified of the origin of an article. Given the purposes of the two laws, this seems to be the reverse of the way it should be.

6.3. Tariff Provisions

6.3.1. Goods Returned

When United States merchandise is exported and is subsequently reimported, it is fully dutiable, as if it were a totally foreign product, unless it falls into one of four specified exemptions.[222] Products of the United States exported and returned without having been advanced in value or improved in condition

---

219. *International Paint Co.*, *supra* note 135, at 90.

220. 19 C.F.R. § 191.2(g).

221. See 19 C.F.R. § 134.1(d)(1) and *supra* note 47 accompanying text.

222. The basic exemptions are set out in the Tariff Schedules:
   — Products of the United States exported and returned without having been advanced in value or improved in condition abroad. HTS Item 9801.00.10.
   — Articles exported for repairs or alterations and returned. HTS Item 9801.00.10.
   — Articles of metal (except precious metal) manufactured in the United States, or subject to a process of manufacture in the United States, exported for processing and returned for further processing. HTS Item 9802.00.60.
   — Articles assembled abroad from components produced in the United States. HTS Item 9802.00.80.

are free of duty. In the case of articles returned after repair, alteration, or processing, only the value added by the foreign operation is subject to duty. For articles returned after assembly, the value of the U.S. components is deducted from the total value to arrive at dutiable value. Country of origin issues arise in connection with these tariff items regarding both the U.S. origin of the product returned and the extent to which foreign operations substantially — or otherwise — transform the article.

6.3.2.   Goods not Advanced in Value

This item has commercial significance because limited processes may be applied to articles in another country without advancing their value or improving their condition.[223] To be eligible for duty-free treatment, the returned article must be a product of the United States.[224] The substantial transformation test is used to make this determination.[225] Previously imported articles, on which duty has been paid, also may receive duty free treatment on reimportation, but with limitations that do not apply to products of the United States.[226]

6.3.3.   Goods Repaired or Altered Abroad

Substantial transformation is the key issue here. Articles exported for repair or alteration are dutiable only on the value of the repair or alteration.[227] But

---

223. For example, fishhooks exported in bulk, assembled and placed in retail packages abroad, were held not to be advanced in value or improved in condition abroad and were therefore entitled to duty-free entry. *United States v. John V. Carr & Sons, Inc.*, 496 F.2d 1225 (C.C.P.A. 1974). Similarly, tomatoes grown in the United States, exported for sorting, grading, and retail packaging, were eligible for duty-free treatment on their return. *Border Brokerage Co. v. United States*, 65 Cust. Ct. 50, 314 F. Supp. 788 (1970).

224. HTS Item 9801.00.10 provides, in part, "Products of the United States when returned after having been exported."

225. *See* United States International Trade Commission, Pub. No. 1695, The Impact of Rules of Origin on U.S. Imports and Exports 34 (1985).

226. *See* HTS Item 9801.00.25.

227. HTS Item 9802.00.40; *see* 19 C.F.R. § 10.8.

if the foreign processing goes beyond repair or alteration, a substantial transformation occurs, and the article is dutiable on its full value.[228]

Repairs and alterations are distinguished from finishing operations because they are made to completed articles. Thus, the coating of glass beads for costume jewelry was held to be an alteration of the completed uncoated beads with which they were used interchangeably,[229] but the cutting of nonwoven fabrics to customer specifications constituted not an alteration but the final step in the manufacturing process.[230] Similarly, the redyeing of an already dyed fabric is an alteration,[231] but the dyeing and finishing of greige goods is not.[232] The latter, in fact, was held to produce a "new and different article."[233]

And then there is the saga of the dogs exported to Canada to be trained as hunting dogs and reimported. "Because such training constitutes an alteration which advances the value and improves the condition of the exported animals," the Customs Service ruled, "the dogs are dutiable only on the value of their training."[234] Not every alteration of a canine is a substantial transformation.

6.3.4. Metal Articles Processed Abroad

A special rule exists for a metal article that is exported for processing and then returned.[235] It must be "manufactured in the United States or subject to a process of manufacture in the United States" if it is to be dutiable only

---

228. Conversion of steel ingots into steel slabs was found to be more than an alteration. *Burstrom v. United States*, 44 C.C.P.A. 27 (1956). So too was the tempering of annealed glass for use in patio doors, which was held to transform the product into a new and different commercial article. *Guardian Indus. Corp. v. United States*, 3 Ct. Int'l Trade 9 (1982).

229. See *Royal Bead Novelty Co. v. United States*, 342 F. Supp. 1394, 1400 (1972).

230. U.S. Customs Internal Advice Ruling 40/85, CLA-2 CO:R:VC:G 076861 JAS (October 31, 1986).

231. *Amity Fabrics, Inc. v. United States*, 43 Cust. Ct. 64 (1959).

232. *Dolliff & Co. v. United States*, 455 F. Supp. 618 (1978), *aff'd* 599 F.2d 1015 (C.C.P.A. 1979).

233. *Dolliff*, 455 F. Supp. at 622.

234. T.D. 66-7(1), 101 Treas. Dec. 12, 13 (1966).

235. HTS Item 9802.00.60.

on the foreign value added.[236] An important requirement is that the exported article that is processed outside the United States or that results from that processing must be subject to still further processing after its return to the United States.[237]

6.3.5.   Components Assembled Abroad

The value of components that are the product of the United States may be deducted from the dutiable value of qualified imported articles.[238] A "product of the United States," according to the regulations of the Customs Service, is an article manufactured within the Customs territory of the United States. It may consist wholly of United States components or materials, of United States and foreign components or materials, or wholly of foreign components or materials. "If the article consists wholly or partially of foreign components or materials, the manufacturing process must be such that the foreign components or materials have been *substantially transformed into a new and different article,* or have been merged into a new and different article."[239]

In addition to the requirement that the components assembled abroad be products of the United States, eligibility for U.S. component treatment depends on whether the components were exported in a condition ready for assembly without further fabrication; whether they lost their physical identity in the assembled article by a change in form, shape, or otherwise; and whether they were advanced in value or improved in condition while abroad. Assembly and operations incidental to the assembly process such as cleaning, lubricating, and painting are not counted in the calculation of improved condition.[240]

---

236. Ibid.

237. Ibid.; see 19 C.F.R. § 10.9(a).

238. HTS Item 9802.00.80 provides for "[a] duty upon the full value of the imported article, less the cost or value of such products of the United States."

239. 19 C.F.R. § 10.12(e) (emphasis added).

240. HTS Item 9802.00.80.

6.4.   Government Procurement

The "Buy American" Act requires the federal government to give preference to American-made goods in its purchases.[241] A country of origin determination is required to determine what is and what is not American for purposes of the "Buy American" Act.[242] Unfortunately, the "Buy American" Act employs terminology to define U.S. merchandise that differs from that used in the customs context. The Act refers to

> only such unmanufactured articles, materials, and supplies as have been mined or produced in the United States, and only such manufactured articles, materials, and supplies as have been manufactured in the United States substantially all from articles, materials, or supplies mined, produced, or manufactured, as the case may be, in the United States.[243]

The Federal Acquisition Regulations refer to a "domestic end product" which "means (a) an unmanufactured end product mined or produced in the United States, or (b) an end product manufactured in the United States, if the cost of its components mined, produced, or manufactured in the United States exceeds 50 percent of the cost of all its components."[244]

A second country of origin determination is required to learn whether the "Buy American" preference may be waived in accordance with the terms of the international Agreement on Government Procurement, which provides for nondiscriminatory treatment for products of signatory countries.[245] To determine if a product originates in a country that is a signatory to the agreement, and is therefore eligible for waiver of the "Buy American" preference, the substantial transformation test is used.[246]

---

241.   41 U.S.C. §§ 10a-d (1982).

242.   41 U.S.C. § 10a.

243.   Ibid.

244.   48 C.F.R. § 25.101.

245.   See *supra* note 28.

246.   "An article is a product of a country or instrumentality only if (i) it is wholly the growth, product, or manufacture of that country or instrumentality, or (ii) in the case of an article which consists in whole or in part of materials from another country or instrumentality, it has been substantially transformed into a new and different article of commerce with a name, character, or use distinct from that of the article or articles from which it was so transformed." 19 U.S.C.A. § 2518(4)(B).

6.5.   Process Patents

The Omnibus Trade and Competitiveness Act of 1988 added a section to the U.S. patent law providing that the importation, sale, or use within the United States of a product made by a process patented in the United States shall constitute infringement.[247] The amendment further provides that a product made by a patented process shall no longer be considered to be so made after "(1) it is materially changed by subsequent processes; or (2) it becomes a trivial or nonessential component of another product".[248]

Could an article undergo a substantial transformation but not a material change or vice versa? Perhaps, and perhaps not. Did the Congress even consider the issue? Perhaps, and perhaps not. There is no evidence that it did.

7. Conclusion and Recommendations

The law of origin in the United States is highly confused. Congress could and, perhaps, should resolve matters by specifying what it means in the numerous laws in which origin issues arise. However, Customs, which is primarily responsible for the confusion, could improve matters greatly by acting within its administrative authority. The following would be a good start:

1.   Customs should determine just what its policy is on the question whether the test for origin should vary depending on the purpose of the statute involved and apply the position consistently.

2.   Customs should rewrite its regulations concerning origin, making them consistent with the standard of *Anheuser-Busch* and with each other. If the agency intends to vary the standard based on statutory purpose, make that clear in the regulations. For the reasons given by the CIT in *Ferrostaal,* the sounder policy would appear to be one in which a single standard of substantial transformation applies, regardless of statutory purpose. The alternative only seems likely to promote further confusion.

3.   If Congress disagrees, then it should do so legislatively using different language when it means different things and making clear what it means. While Congress is at it, it should take the opportunity to eliminate the anticircumvention provision of the antidumping law; ordinary rules of origin should be used to determine origin and origin-related issues in antidumping proceedings. The process patent

---

247. Omnibus Trade and Competitiveness Act, *supra* note 11, § 903, 35 U.S.C.A. § 271(g).

248. Ibid.

amendment should be clarified either to align it with the rules of origin or, if the policy is to the contrary, to specify in what way it is to differ. Finally, Congress should authorize steps to align the rule of origin in the GATT Government Procurement Code to ordinary rules of origin. There is no reason why origin for government procurement should differ from origin generally.

4. Customs should refrain from announcing new rules based on change in tariff heading until the international situation with regard to rules of origin is clear. The proposed steel rules differ slightly from the FTA rules with Canada; they might differ further from any North American Free Trade Area rules that might be negotiated with Canada and Mexico; and they might differ still further from any GATT Rules of Origin Code that emerges from the Uruguay Round. Unilateral action at this time serves merely to further complexity and confusion. More complexity and more confusion are the last things U.S. law on rules of origin needs.

CHAPTER 3

European Community
Rules of Origin

Paul Waer

1. Introduction

The first act of the European Economic Community (EEC) authorities in the area of origin was Council Regulation (EEC) No 802/68 on the common definition of the concept of the origin of goods.[1] With this framework regulation, the EEC authorities set a first step towards the harmonization of the nonpreferential origin rules, which thus far had been subject to diverging legislation in the different EC Member States.

In principle, the EC applies MFN status to all imported products.[2] As such, nonpreferential rules of origin in the EC have mainly played a role as a criterion for the application of trade protective measures such as the Common Agricultural Policy, quantitative restrictions, and antidumping measures.

The application of nonpreferential origin rules has, since the early years, given rise to controversy on occasion. In recent years the impact of the nonpreferential origin rules has been especially visible in defining the scope of antidumping measures. The product-specific origin rules concerning integrated circuits and photocopiers and the proposals for the adoption of a product-specific origin rule on printed circuit boards had a direct impact on the scope of application of antidumping measures and stirred a debate on the alleged protectionist effect of nonpreferential origin rules. Nonpreferential origin rules have an impact not only on the scope of antidumping measures but equally on the application of quantitative restrictions. The most notable example in the EC was the interesting episode of heated discussions in the car

---

1.   Council Regulation (EEC) No 802/68 on the common definition of the concept of the origin of goods, O.J. (1968) L 148/165 [Regulation 802/68 or Basic Origin Regulation].

2.   *See* Commission Regulation (EEC) No 2587/91 of 26 July 1991 amending Annex I to Council Regulation (EEC) No 2658/87 on the tariff and statistical nomenclature and on the Common Customs Tariff, published in O.J. (1991) L 259 at 11.

industry concerning the treatment of transplant cars within the framework of national quantitative restrictions on imports of Japanese cars within certain EC Member States.

More recently, origin rules also started to play a role in the EC in nontraditional areas, for example, as a result of the new EC rules on government procurement in the excluded sectors.

A new area of development of origin rules is the service sector, as can be exemplified by the EC Directive on television broadcasting services.

In the preferential area, the EC has concluded a considerable number of preferential trade agreements and has implemented several unilateral preferential trading schemes. Two of the major preferential trade arrangements, the GSP scheme and the EFTA agreement are currently being revised. Especially the growing complexity of the preferential origin rules has caused the EC authorities to critically reexamine their practicability and suitability to achieve the aims of these preferential trade schemes.

These recent developments have drawn more attention in the EC to the importance of origin rules and their impact on trade flows and have caused a debate on what was traditionally regarded as a technical customs matter of lesser importance.

2. General Overview

In the nonpreferential area, the EC authorities have shown a clear preference for using technical criterions. Value-added tests have only been used as the second best alternative.

In the preferential area the basic rule is the change of tariff heading approach, although this rule is adjusted for a great number of products with value-added tests and technical tests, or a combination.

3. Nonpreferential Rules of Origin

3.1. Procedure

3.1.1. Administrative Procedure

The procedural rules are provided for in Articles 12 to 14 of the Basic Origin Regulation.[3]

Article 12 of the Basic Origin Regulation provides for the establishment of a Committee on Origin (the Origin Committee). The Origin Committee

---

3. Regulation 802/68, *supra* note 1.

consists of representatives of the Member States,[4] with a representative of the Commission[5] acting as chair.[6]

According to Article 13: "The Committee may examine *all questions* relating to the application of this Regulation referred to it by its Chairman, either on his own initiative or at the request of a representative of a Member State."[7]

Article 14 provides for a special decision-making procedure that must be followed for adopting provisions required for applying Articles 4 to 7,[8] 9, and 10[9] of the regulation. In this procedure, the Commission has the dominant role.[10]

The procedure consists out of the following steps:

1. The Commission representative presents drafts of the provisions to be adopted.[11]

2. The Origin Committee must issue an opinion on such drafts within a time limit set by the chair, having regard to the urgency of the

---

4.   They are public officials from the respective national ministries of the Member States.

5.   The EC Commission is currently located in Brussels. Within Directorate General XXI of the EC Commission, responsible for Customs, there is an Origin Division, currently staffed with nine officials. The division consists of a chef of the division, three officials in charge of nonpreferential origin rules and five officials in charge of preferential origin rules. The meetings of the Origin Committee take place at the EC Commission's offices in Brussels.

6.   Regulation 802/68, *supra* note 1. Article 12(2) provides that the Committee shall draw up its own rules of procedure. The procedural rules as currently drawn up would seem to provide for an oral proceeding. In view of the difficulties sometimes encountered in scheduling timely meetings, it would seem that the introduction of a written procedure is currently being considered.

7.   Ibid., at 167. (emphasis added)

8.   Articles 4 to 7 of the Basic Origin Regulation contain the substantive rules on origin, which will be discussed later. *See* § 3.2.

9.   Articles 9 and 10 of the Basic Origin Regulation contain the requirements and format for the certificates of origin.

10.   This type of decision-making procedure is called the "regulatory committee procedure". *See* KAPTEYN, VERLOREN VAN THEMAAT, INTRODUCTION TO THE LAW OF THE EUROPEAN COMMUNITIES, 241-242 (ED. GORMLEY, 2d ed. 1989).

11.   Article 14(2).

matter. Decisions are taken by a majority of *fifty-four*[12] out of *seventy-six* votes, the votes of the Member States being weighted as provided for in Article 148(2) of the EEC Treaty.[13]

3. If such a majority can be reached in favor of the Commission proposal, the Commission shall adopt the provisions.[14] If the opinion of the Committee is not in agreement with the Commission draft or if no opinion is delivered, the Commission shall submit a proposal to the Council.[15] In practice, the Commission will generally only continue the procedure if at least a simple majority in the Committee is in favor of the Commission's proposal.

4. The Council must decide on the Commission proposal within three months by a qualified majority.[16] Votes are weighted again on the basis of Article 148(2) of the treaty, with a qualified majority needing at least *fifty-four* votes.[17]

5. If the Council does not act within three months, the Commission shall adopt the provisions.[18]

At the moment of writing, this procedure has been used seventeen times to enact provisions relating to Articles 4 to 7 of the Basic Origin Regulation (see

---

12. *Ibid.*, last amended by Treaty (signed on 12 June 1985) between the Member States of the European Communities and the Kingdom of Spain and the Portuguese Republic concerning the accession of the Kingdom of Spain and the Portuguese Republic to the European Economic Community and to the European Atomic Energy Community, O.J. (1985) L 302/9, at 139. The (Commission) Chairman does not have the right to vote.

13. Article 148(2) EEC Treaty weighs the votes of the Member States as follows: Belgium: 5; Denmark: 3; Germany: 10; Greece: 5; Spain: 8; France: 10; Ireland: 3; Italy: 10; Luxembourg: 2; Netherlands: 5; Portugal: 5; United Kingdom: 10.

14. The Commission acts by a majority of the numbers of members (Article 163 of the EEC treaty). The Commission consists of seventeen members (Article 157 of the EEC treaty). This means that nine votes are required. *See* KAPTEYN, *supra* note 10, 170.

15. Article 14(3)(b).

16. Ibid. A qualified majority in the Council could decide to adopt the Commission proposal by Council Regulation. However, this has never happened, which is not surprising since the same Member States that vote in the Council are represented in the Origin Committee.

17. *See* Article 148(2) EEC Treaty providing that acts of the Council require at least fifty-four votes in favor when the treaty requires them to be adopted on a proposal from the Commission.

18. Article 14(3)(c).

annex). The procedure has been used three times to adopt measures relating to Article 9 and 10 of the Basic Origin Regulation.[19]

An overview of the twenty instances in which the Article 14 procedure has been used shows that in three cases the Origin Committee did not deliver an opinion[20] and in two cases the Origin Committee did not deliver a concurring opinion.[21] In the remaining cases the Commission adopted the provisions after a concurring opinion of the Origin Committee.

This indicates that in a majority of cases the EC Commission and Origin Committee were in agreement and that the Commission could adopt the proposals without a proposal to the Council.

It should be noted that Article 14 does not oblige the Commission to hear interested parties before submitting a draft proposal to the Origin Committee. It would appear that in practice the EC Commission has sometimes heard the arguments of producers while formulating a proposal that directly concerned them[22] and has, in other instances, visited (EC) producers[23] to familiarize

---

19.   (1) Reglement (CEE) No 3103/73 de la commission du 14 Novembre 1973 portant sur le certificat d'origine et la demande y relative dans les echanges intracommunautaires O.J. (1973) L 315/34; (2) Commission Regulation (EEC) No 553/81 of 12 February 1981 on certificates of origin and application for such certificates, O.J. (1981) L 59/1; and (3) Commission Regulation (EEC) No 3850/89 of 15 December 1989 laying down provisions for the implementation of Regulation 802/68 in respect of certain agricultural products subject to special import arrangements, O.J. (1989) L 374/8.

20.   Commission Regulation (EEC) No 1480/77 on the determination of the origin of certain knitted and crocheted articles, certain articles of apparel, and footwear, falling within Chapter 60 and heading Nos ex 42.03, 61.02, 61.03, 61.04 of the Common Customs Tariff, O.J. (1977) L 164/16; Commission Regulation (EEC) No 2067/77 concerning the determination of the origin of slide fasteners, O.J. (1977) L 242/5 (In this case the Commission's proposal could not be approved nor rejected with a qualified majority, hence no opinion was delivered, *Yoshida Nederland B.V. v. Kamer van Koophandel en Fabrieken voor Friesland* Case 34/78 (1979) ECR 115, at 125 [*Yoshida I*]); Commission Regulation (EEC) No 749/78 on the determination of the origin of textile products falling within Chapters 51 and 53 to 62 of the Common Customs Tariff, O.J. (1978) L 101/7.

21.   Commission Regulation (EEC) No 964/71 on determining the origin of the meat and offals, fresh, chilled or frozen, of certain domestic animals, O.J. (1971) L 104/12; Commission Regulation (EEC) No 749/78 on the determination of the origin of certain textile products, O.J. (1978) L 101/7.

22.   See *Gesellschaft für Überseehandel v. Handelskammer Kassel* Case 49/76 (1977) ECR 41 [*Überseehandel*]. In this case, which was an informal procedure, the observations of the producer-plaintiff were considered by the Origin Committee. *Ibid.*, at 48; compare with *Yoshida GmbH. v. Industrie- und Handelskammer Kassel* Case 114/78 (1979) ECR 151 [*Yoshida II*]. In this case, concerning the adoption of a product specific origin rule concerning slide fasteners, the Commission acknowledged that the plaintiff had not been heard, but stated

itself with the production processes before proposing product-specific origin rules.

It should be noted that apart from the formal procedure of Article 14 of the Basic Origin Regulation, the Commission and Origin Committee also developed an informal practice.

As recorded in *Überseehandel*:

[i]n practice a Regulation under Article 14 is adopted only where there is doubt or disagreement within the Committee on Origin as to the answer to a particular problem. In the absence of any such doubt or disagreement, it is considered sufficient to record the opinion of the Committee. This has been done, so far, in three cases . . . . In the first case the Committee held that the sterilization of medical instruments was not a process or operation important enough to "confer origin" under Article 5. In the second case, it held on the other hand that the production of corned beef from imported fresh beef was such an operation.[24]

The third case concerned the cleaning, grinding, grading, and packaging of casein, which was not considered sufficient to confer origin.[25]

In *Überseehandel*, the Commission requested the court to express its views on the legal status of these opinions of the Origin Committee taken in the informal procedure.[26]

---

that this is usual in a legislative procedure because there have been guarantees provided in the form of the participation of national experts (the Origin Committee) in the procedure according to Article 14 of the Basic Origin Regulation. The Commission noted that the plaintiff producer did not deny that this, in fact, had not prevented him from making his point of view known to the Commission and the Member States. *Ibid.*, at 159.

23.   *See, e.g., Yoshida I, supra* note 20, at 115. In that case concerning the adoption of a product specific origin rule for slide fasteners, it is stated, "As a result of a question put by five Members of the European Parliament to the Commission, the latter was prompted to carry out an investigation of the technical aspects of the manufacture of slide fasteners, in particular by visiting a factory manufacturing those fasteners chosen in agreement with the trade organization representing the European slide fastener industry (Organisme de liaison des industries métallurgiques européennes)." Ibid., at 124.

24.   Opinion of Advocate General Warner, *Überseehandel, supra* note 22, at 57.

25.   Ibid.

26.   The Commission argued that:

Such an opinion although it does not have direct legal effect, constitutes an important factor in interpreting the provisions of Regulation No 802/68 on the origin of goods. By

The court considered the Commission's request favorably and ruled that:

Although opinions expressed by the Committee are not binding, except in so far as the Commission has adopted implementing provisions in application of Article 14(3)(a) of Regulation No 802/68, nevertheless, until such time as the Commission adopts contrary provisions under subparagraphs (b) and (c) of the said Article 14(3), they constitute an important criterion for interpreting Article 5 of the said regulation, the scope of which they define in respect of specific cases.[27]

The court thus recognized the validity of the informal practice and adopted a practically oriented reading of the procedural requirements set forth in Article 14 of the Basic Origin Regulation.[28]

---

reason of its purpose, its constitution, its composition, and its method of working, the Committee on Origin is in every way similar to the Committee on Common Customs Tariff Nomenclature. The wording of the provisions setting up the two committees and defining their tasks is identical. From this it may be concluded that the opinions submitted by the two bodies have the same legal status. In its case-law, the Court has considered the opinions submitted on tariff matters by the Committee on Common Customs Tariff Nomenclature as an important factor to be taken into account in interpreting the tariff. In the light of these considerations and having regard to the subject-matter of the question referred to the Court, it would therefore be useful if the Court could also express its view in this case on the status of the opinions of the Committee on Origin.

Ibid., at 47.

27.   Ibid., at 54.

28.   Indeed, one could also make an argument that on the basis of a narrow reading of Article 14, the informal procedure would not be allowed. Namely, Article 14 provides:

1. The provisions required for applying Articles 4 to 7, 9 and 10 *shall* be adopted in accordance with the procedure laid down in paragraphs 2 and 3 of this Article.
. . .
3. (a) The Commission *shall* adopt the envisaged provisions if they are in accordance with the Opinion of the Committee. (Emphasis added.)

This reading could be construed as meaning that the Commission is under a duty to adopt the provisions. Obviously, from a practical point of view, it can be argued that such a narrow interpretation would mean that all matters which are discussed in the Origin Committee with regard to the Articles 4 to 7, 9 and 10 and which meet the required majority, even if of trivial importance, would necessarily be recorded as Commission Regulations. The court probably considered that the wording of Article 14 *in initio* (Namely: "The provisions *required* for applying . . . " (emphasis added)) left the Commission and Origin Committee with some discretion as regards the need to adopt provisions in the formal procedure.

It should be noted that the informal proceeding has not been limited to in camera discussions about whether certain processing operations confer origin to a particular product resulting in an opinion of the Origin Committee being put on record. In certain cases, the EC Commission, with the cooperation of the exporter concerned, has investigated the origin of particular products of the exporter (producer-specific investigations). These investigations included on the spot verifications at the producer's production facilities in third countries and its part suppliers and subcontractors.[29] The role of the Commission in these types of informal procedures thus also included substantial fact-finding to assist national customs authorities, rather than its role being limited to questions of interpretation of the Articles 4 to 7 of the Basic Origin Regulation.

3.1.2. Judicial Review

A Member State, the Council, or the Commission may challenge the legality of acts of the Council or Commission before the Court of Justice under Article 173(1) of the EEC treaty.

A natural or legal person may not directly challenge the legality of the Basic Origin Regulation or implementing regulations enacted according to Article 14 of the Basic Origin Regulation before the Court of Justice under Article 173(2), because the court considers neither the Basic Origin Regulation nor its implementing Regulations to be decisions addressed to individual persons or decisions which, although in the form of regulations or decisions addressed to other persons, are of direct and individual concern to individual persons.[30]

The drawback of the court's interpretation might be a lack of transparency of the Origin Committee's practice. As illustrated by the *Überseehandel* case, *supra* note 22, it will not always be that obvious when certain opinions of the Origin Committee deserve to be adopted in the formal procedure to clarify specific interpretations of the Basic Origin Regulation. The Opinions of the Origin Committee in the informal procedure are not recorded in a public record.

29. For example, in 1988 the Commission conducted an investigation into the origin of certain photocopiers produced by a Japanese producer in Hong Kong. The Commission found that the processing operations carried out in Hong Kong were sufficient to confer origin. The Origin Committee delivered a concurring opinion on the findings of the Commission. The Commission then informed national customs authorities who had questioned the origin of the photocopiers of its findings and the Opinion of the Origin Committee. Strictly speaking, it would seem that this Opinion of the Origin Committee was not put on record.

30. *See, e.g.,* Kapteyn, *supra* note 10, at 202.

Producers who wish to challenge the legality of such regulations must therefore initiate a proceeding in the national courts; the national courts may then refer the matter to the European Court of Justice for a preliminary ruling according to Article 177 of the EEC Treaty. This can be done, for example, by contesting the refusal to provide a certificate of origin before the national courts[31] or by contesting the imposition of antidumping duties by local customs.[32]

It seems clear from the Court's dictum in *Überseehandel* that opinions of the Origin Committee put on record in the informal proceeding are not legally binding and cannot be directly attacked.[33]

Similarly, the telexes or memoranda the Commission sends to the Member States may not be challenged before the court. In the *Brother* case, Brother challenged a memorandum that had been sent to all Member States and had been signed on behalf of the Director-General for External Relations of the Commission of the European Communities after the Commission decided to terminate the antidumping proceeding concerning typewriters originating in Taiwan.[34]

The memorandum in question stated that the antidumping proceeding concerning imports of electronic typewriters originating in Taiwan was terminated on the basis of the fact that the imported products actually originated in Japan and further that there were reasons to assume that the imports from Taiwan were a deliberate attempt to evade the antidumping duties imposed on electronic typewriters originating in Japan. The memorandum finally suggested that the national authorities should investigate the case, taking the necessary measures in accordance with their own customs legislation, and, after six months, report to the Commission on the result of their investigation.[35]

In its order, the court stated:

While drawing the attention of the Member States to the seriousness of the

---

31. *See, e.g.*, *Yoshida v. Industrie- und Handelskammer Kassel* Case 114/78 (1979) ECR 151.

32. *See, e.g.*, *Brother International GmbH v. Hauptzollamt Giessen* Case 26/88 (1989) ECR 4253 [*Brother II*].

33. *Überseehandel*, *supra* note 22, at 54.

34. *Typewriters* (Taiwan), O.J. (1986) L 140/52 (Termination).

35. *Brother Industries Limited et al. v. Commission* Case 229/86 (1987) ECR 3758 at 3760 [*Brother I*].

matter, the memorandum does not, however, ask the national authorities to make any specific decision on the origin of the products in question but merely asks them to reach a decision on the basis of their own national legislation. Indeed, the position could not be otherwise having regard to the fact that an obligation on the Member States to adopt specific measures cannot be created by a Commission memorandum in the absence of a particular provision in the Treaty or in binding acts adopted by the institutions. The Member States' general obligation to 'facilitate the achievement of the Community's tasks' laid down in Article 5 of the EEC Treaty cannot be relied upon in this case because no common definition of the origin of the goods has been provided under Regulation 802/78 [*sic*] and consequently the interests of the Community continue to be protected through independent assessments made by the national customs authorities for which the Commission's findings may be a source of guidance but have no binding force.[36]

Therefore, the court decided that the Commission Decision to terminate the anti-dumping proceeding even in conjunction with this memorandum did not constitute an act which may adversely affect the legal position of the producer/exporter concerned and accordingly declared the action inadmissible.[37]

It is interesting to note that in this case, the memorandum emanated from Directorate General I and not Directorate General XXI. However, the case also seems to have repercussions for the informal investigations conducted by the EC Commission and Origin Committee into the origin of certain products of specific producers. In those cases, when the Commission adopted no formal measures, it would seem equally impossible for a producer to directly attack the findings of the Commission and opinions of the Origin Committee as communicated by telex or fax to the national customs authorities.

3.1.3.   Concluding Remarks

The major problem to be noted with regard to the current procedural rules of the Basic Origin Regulation is the lack of transparency of the EC Commission and Origin Committee's practice both as regards the formal and informal procedure.

With regard to the formal procedure, in current practice, it would appear that the EC Commission usually consults with the EC producers before

---

36.   Ibid., at 3763.

37.   Ibid.

making any proposals to the Origin Committee for product-specific origin rules. European Community producers may also express their views through the representatives of their Member State who sit in the Origin Committee. However, it can be questioned whether the existence of the Origin Committee by itself is a sufficient guarantee to ensure a fair and fully informed legislative process.

From the producers' point of view, there is no way of knowing when the Commission is considering adopting, for example, a product-specific origin rule that might affect their business, unless the Commission or their Member State representative informs them of it or they have an ear in Brussels that picks up the information from the grapevine. Moreover, product-specific origin rules not only can affect EC producers but, as practice has shown, have been enacted frequently to clarify the origin of imported products. Therefore, they can also seriously affect foreign exporters to the European Community. The Commission's practice to only consult with the EC industry when adopting product specific origin rules might have the result that these rules might become biased to favor all, or some, EC producers who can make their views known and present the information to the EC Commission in a way to suit their business interests.

The transparency of the legislative process could be considerably improved if the Commission were to publish a notice of its intention to adopt a certain implementing measure concerning the Basic Origin Regulation and invite all interested parties to make their views known to the Commission within a certain deadline. Interested parties could also be given an opportunity to present their arguments orally at a hearing.

This minor procedural improvement would have the advantage of officially informing producers of what is happening with regard to the legislative work undertaken by the Commission and Origin Committee. It also would give the producers a fair chance to make their views known, if they wish to do so. For the Commission and Origin Committee, this approach would have the advantage that the fact-finding concerning the adoption of specific measures could be facilitated and that they would most likely get a better and more diverse picture of the technical arguments pro and contra certain approaches and of the different interests involved of EC and foreign producers. This would allow them to make a more informed and objective decision.

With regard to the informal procedure as described in *Überseehandel*, it should be noted that it might not always be that obvious when a certain opinion of the Origin Committee deserves to be formally adopted to provide guidance on the interpretation of the Basic Origin Regulation, or when it will be sufficient to put the opinion informally on record. Indeed, there is no public record of the opinions informally adopted by the Origin Committee. As will be shown further on in this chapter, the EC rules of origin are unfortunately rather vague so that every piece of information on its interpretation can be valuable information to the producers concerned. Formal adoption of the even rather obvious interpretations by the Origin Committee might still provide useful guidance on the interpretation of the Basic Origin Regulation to the producers concerned and the authorities in charge of applying origin rules.

With regard to the producer-specific origin investigations, it should be noted that there is an obvious need for this type of procedure. The fact that the EC Commission conducts such investigations can be helpful to national customs authorities who might not have the means or expertise to conduct thorough investigations, including eventually on the spot verifications in third countries. For producers — EC and foreign producers — these investigations might have the benefit of providing clarity and legal certainty about the origin of their products under EC rules, especially if these investigations can also take place *before* exports or imports actually start. If these investigations would result in a formal and legally binding ruling by the EC Commission and Origin Committee, this will also ensure a harmonized treatment by all Member States on the export or import of the product and prevent forum shopping by producers in different Member States making different determinations of origin for the same products.

Currently, the EC Commission conducts these "informal" investigations in the twilight zone of its powers under the procedural rules of the Basic Origin Regulation. It is highly desirable that the EC Commission and Origin Committee be given clear powers to conduct producer-specific investigations resulting in legally binding decisions, which should be published with a detailed statement of reasons. At the same time, procedural rules should be provided to ensure a fair hearing of the producer concerned. Decisions should be taken in a form open to direct judicial review.

3.2.   Substantive Rules

The substantive EC rules on origin are provided in the Basic Origin Regulation and in Annex D.1 of the Kyoto Convention.

3.2.1. The Basic Origin Regulation

3.2.1.1. Scope of the Basic Origin Regulation

Article 1 of the Basic Origin Regulation[38] provides:

> This Regulation defines the concept of the origin of goods for purposes of:
> (a) the uniform application of the Common Customs Tariff, of quantitative restrictions, and of all other measures adopted, in relation to the importation of goods, by the Community or by Member States;
> (b) the uniform application of all measures adopted, in relation to the exportation of goods, by the Community or by Member States;
> (c) the preparation and issue of certificates of origin.

The scope of application of the Basic Origin Regulation would appear to be very broadly defined. As is more clearly stated in the preamble, the rules of origin are intended to apply to both commercial policy with regard to third countries and to free movements of goods within the Community.[39] They apply equally to import and export regimes instituted by the Community or the Member States.

It should be noted that the Basic Origin Regulation limits itself to providing rules on the common definition of the origin of goods. The regulation does not provide a definition of the term *goods* and therefore the distinction between *goods* and *services* is necessarily provided by the rules on customs classification. This issue is relevant because the distinction between what is a service and what is a good is not always that obvious, for example, in the case of software.

It should also be mentioned that originally, the Basic Origin Regulation Article 3 excluded petroleum products listed in Annex 1 to the Basic Origin

---

38.   Regulation 802/68, *supra* note 1.

39.   Ibid. Article 2, as amended by Article 1 of Council Regulation (EEC) No 1318/71 of 21 June 1971 amending Regulation 802/68, however specifies that: "This Regulation shall be without prejudice to the special rules concerning: trade between the Community or Member States and the countries to which the Community or Member States are bound by agreements which derogate from the most-favoured-nation clause, and in particular those establishing a customs union or a free-trade area; trade to which preferences granted by the Community unilaterally in derogation from the most-favoured-nation clause are applicable."

Regulation from the scope of application of the regulation.[40] This was because apparently there were significant differences between Member States with regard to the determination of the origin of petroleum products. Only recently the Basic Origin Regulation was amended to include these products within its scope of application.[41] While bringing these products within the scope of the application of the Basic Origin Regulation might be a first step toward the harmonization of origin determinations in the Member States, it can be expected that in view of the previous existing differences in treatment, implementing measures might be required to provide clarity on the application of the general substantive rules laid down in the Basic Origin Regulation with regard to these petroleum products.[42]

3.2.1.2. Basic Origin Rules

The substantive origin rules provided in Articles 4 to 7 of the Basic Origin Regulation are extremely succinct and vague.

Article 4(1) of the Basic Origin Regulation provides that goods wholly obtained or produced in one country shall be considered as originating in that country.

Article 4(2) specifies that:

The expression 'goods wholly obtained or produced in one country' means:

(a) mineral products extracted within its territory;

---

40. Ibid., at 166 and 168. Annex 1 was later amended by Commission Regulation (EEC) No 3860/87 of 22 December 1987 replacing Annex 1 of Regulation 802/68, O.J. (1987) L 363/30 to conform to the new combined nomenclature. The Commission amended the Council Regulation based on its powers to amend Community acts that include the tariff or statistical nomenclature, provided for in Article 15 of the Council Regulation (EEC) No 2658/87 of 23 July 1987 on the tariff and statistical nomenclature and on the Common Customs Tariff, O.J. (1987) L 256/1, at 5.

41. Council Regulation (EEC) No 456/91 of 25 February 1991 amending Regulation 802/68, O.J. (1991) L 54/4.

42. The preamble to the amendment merely noted that: "Whereas, in the absence of a common definition of the origin of petroleum products, Member States apply the provisions of their national law; whereas these provisions differ from one another and may give rise to differing results with regard to the application of customs duties or measures and instruments of commercial policy; Whereas, with a view to the completion of the internal market on 31 December 1992, it would appear essential that such provisions be harmonized; Whereas the most appropriate way to harmonize the said provisions is to make Regulation (EEC) No 802/68 applicable to the petroleum products in question." Ibid.

(b)   vegetable products harvested therein;

(c)   live animals born and raised therein;

(d)   products derived from live animals raised therein;

(e)   products of hunting or fishing carried on therein;

(f)   products of sea-fishing and other products taken from the sea by vessels registered or recorded in that country and flying its flag;

(g)   goods obtained on board factory ships from the products referred to in (f) originating in that country, if such factory ships are registered or recorded in that country and flying its flag;

(h)   products taken from the sea-bed outside territorial waters, if that country has, for the purposes of exploitation, exclusive rights to such soil or subsoil;

(i)   waste and scrap products derived from manufacturing operations and used articles, if they were collected therein and are only fit for the recovery of raw materials;

(j)   goods which are produced therein exclusively from goods referred to in subparagraphs (a) to (i) or from their derivates, at any stage of production.

Article 5 addresses the determination of origin in case two or more countries are involved in the production process and provides that:

[a] product in the production of which two or more countries were concerned shall be regarded as originating in the country in which the last substantial process or operation that is economically justified was performed, having been carried out in an undertaking equipped for the purpose, and resulting in the manufacture of a new product or representing an important stage of manufacture.

The Basic Origin Regulation also attaches to Article 5 an anticircumvention provision in Article 6 stipulating that:

[a]ny process or work in respect of which it is established, or in respect of which the facts as ascertained justify the presumption, that its sole object was to circumvent the provisions applicable in the Community or the Member States to goods from specific countries shall in no case be considered, under Article 5, as conferring on the goods thus produced the origin of the country where it is carried out.

Article 7 provides for a presumption of origin for accessories, spare parts, or tools:

Accessories, spare parts or tools delivered with any piece of equipment, machine, apparatus or vehicle which form part of its standard equipment shall be deemed to have the same origin as that piece of equipment, machine, apparatus or vehicle.

This provision is clearly inspired by administrative convenience.

3.2.1.3. Evidence of Origin: The Origin Certificate

Evidence of the origin of a product will be provided by an origin certificate. Article 9 of the Basic Origin Regulation provides the requirements relating to certificates of origin presented on importation, while Article 10 regulates the issuance of EC certificates of origin for export.

Article 9(1) requires that when the origin of a product has to be proved on importation by the production of a certificate of origin, that certificate shall fulfil three basic conditions:

1. It must be prepared by a reliable authority or agency duly authorized for that purpose by the country of issue,
2. It must contain all the particulars necessary for identifying the product to which it relates,[43]
3. It must certify unambiguously that the product to which it relates originated in a specific country.

Article 9(2) further specifies that the production of this certificate of origin does not necessarily constitute conclusive evidence and provides:

Notwithstanding the production of a certificate of origin which fulfils the

---

43. These particulars are

- the number of packages, their nature, and the marks and numbers they bear,
- the kind of product,
- the gross and net weight of the product; these particulars may, however, be replaced by others, such as the number or volume, when the product is subject to appreciable changes in weight during carriage or when its weight cannot be ascertained or when it is normally identified by such other particulars,
- the name of the consignor.

Council Regulation (EEC) No 1318/71 of 21 June 1971 amending Regulation 802/68, O.J. (1971) L 139/6 (this amendment relaxed the requirement in Article 9 of the Basic Origin Regulation that the gross and net weight be mentioned, by adding a number of acceptable exceptions to this rule).

conditions prescribed by paragraph 1, the competent authorities may, if there is cause for serious doubt, demand any additional proof with the object of ensuring that the indication of origin conforms to the rules laid down in this Regulation and to the provisions adopted for its implementation.

Article 9(2) would seem to address the fundamental problem of the lack of harmonization of origin rules on a worldwide basis. In practice, authorities in third countries are not always familiar with the EC origin rules or only have competence to issue certificates of origin based on the origin rules applicable in their jurisdiction.[44] Therefore, it is sometimes necessary to verify whether the indications of origin on the origin certificates also conform to EC origin rules.

Article 9(2) provides that the competent authorities may demand "any additional proof." It does not specify in detail an investigation procedure nor the sanctions for, for example, submitting false declarations of origin. These matters have thus far not been harmonized by EC law and remain subject to legislation in the Member States.[45]

It should also be noted that special provisions have been adopted according to Article 14 of the Basic Origin Regulation concerning certificates of origin to be presented on the importation of certain agricultural products benefitting from special nonpreferential import arrangements in the EC.[46]

Article 10 regulates the issue of certificates of origin in the EC for export. These certificates are basically subject to the same requirements as certificates required on importation.[47] The difference is that these certificates should not unambiguously state that the products relate *in a specific country* but shall

---

44. It seems to follow from Article 1(c) of the Basic Origin Regulation that also the competent authorities in the EC Member States can only issue certificates of origin based on EC rules of origin.

45. For an example of a procedure relating to allegedly false declarations of origin, *see Criminal proceedings against Paul Cousin and others* Case 162/82 (1983) ECR 1101 [*Cousin*].

46. Commission Regulation (EEC) No 3850/89 of 15 December 1989 laying down provisions for the implementation of Regulation 802/68 in respect of certain agricultural products subject to special import arrangements, O.J. (1989) L 374/8. The regulation provides for a special format of these certificates and establishes an administrative cooperation procedure.

47. Article 10(1) provides that certificates of origin of goods originating in and exported from the Community must comply with the conditions prescribed by Article 9(1)(a) and (b).

certify that the goods originate *in the Community*. Article 10(2), however, specifies that when the needs of the export trade require, the export certificates may certify that the goods originated in a particular Member State.[48] In Annex II to the Basic Origin Regulation, requirements are set forth to achieve uniformity in the origin certificates issued by the Member States.[49]

3.2.2. The Kyoto Convention[50]

By Council Decision of 18 March 1975, the Community concluded and accepted the International Convention on the simplification and harmonization of customs procedures (the Kyoto Convention).[51] The Kyoto Convention, negotiated under the auspices of and administered by the Customs Cooperation Council in Brussels, aims at simplifying and harmonizing customs procedures. To achieve this, Contracting Parties undertake to conform to the standards and recommended practices in the Annexes to the convention.[52] By Council

---

48. Article 10(2), however, further clarifies that "If the conditions of Article 5 are fulfilled only as a result of a series of operations or processes carried out in different Member States, the goods may only be certified as being of Community origin."

49. Annex II was amended by Article 3 of Council Regulation (EEC) No 1318/71 of 21 June 1971 amending Regulation 802/68, O.J. (1971) L 139/6 (making it possible to use air mail paper for preparing the certificates and altering its size to conform to the relevant international standards); in Commission Regulation (EEC) No 582/69, O.J. (1969) L 79/1, the Commission laid down the forms of certificates of origin and application for such certificates; these forms were later modified by Commission Regulation (EEC) No 518/72, O.J. (1972) L 67/25; both implementing Commission regulations were subsequently repealed and replaced by Commission Regulation (EEC) No 553/81 of 12 February 1981 on certificates of origin and applications for such certificates, O.J. (1981) L 59/1.

It should be noted that this format is not compulsory. According to Article 10 (3) Member States should ensure that this format is followed "in so far as the needs of the export trade do not otherwise require."

50. For the text of the Kyoto Convention and all its Annexes, *see* Compendium of Community Customs Legislation, Chapter X.C (1989).

51. Council Decision of 18 March 1975 concluding an international convention on the simplification and harmonization of customs procedures and accepting the Annex thereto concerning customs warehouses, O.J. (1975) L 100/1. Convention of 18 May 1973, signed in Kyoto. The English and French texts of the Convention are authentic.

52. Kyoto Convention, *supra* note 50, Article 2, provides, "Each Contracting Party undertakes to promote the simplification and harmonization of customs procedures and, to that end, to conform, in accordance with the provisions of this convention, to the standards and recommended practices in the Annexes to this convention. However, nothing shall prevent a

Decision of 3 June 1977, the Community accepted Annex D.1. of the Kyoto Convention concerning rules of origin.[53]

The relevance of Annex D.1. of the Kyoto Convention for the interpretation of the EC rules of origin was first recognized by the European Court of Justice in the *Brother* case.[54]

In the first place, Annex D.1 sets forth a number of general procedural standards. It notes that the same origin rules should be used for import and exports[55] and provides for general transparency and predictability standards.[56]

The substantive standards in Annex D.1. broadly correspond to the principles laid down in the Basic Origin Regulation.

The Second Standard concerns the goods "wholly obtained" in one country and parallels Article 4 of the Basic Origin Regulation. A significant difference is that according to the Second Standard of the Kyoto Convention "products obtained from live animals in that country" are also considered to be wholly obtained in that country,[57] whereas Article 4 the Basic Origin Regulation limits this to "products derived from live animals *raised therein.*"[58]

Contracting Party from granting facilities greater than those provided therein, and each Contracting Party is recommended to grant such greater facilities as extensively as possible." The possible practical impact of the Kyoto convention, however, is to a great extent neutralized by Article 3, which provides, "The provisions of this convention shall not preclude the application of prohibitions or restrictions imposed under national legislation."

53.   Council Decision of 3 June 1977 accepting on behalf of the Community several Annexes to the international convention on the simplification and harmonization of customs procedures, O.J. (1977) L 166/1.

54.   *Brother II, supra* note 32.

55.   Ibid. the First Standard.

56.   The Thirteenth Standard provides, "The competent authorities shall ensure that the rules of origin, including any changes and interpretative information, are readily available to any person interested." The Fourteenth Standard provides: "Changes in the rules of origin or in the procedures for their application shall enter into force only after sufficient notice has been given to enable the interested persons, both in export markets and in supplying countries, to take account of the new provisions."

57.   Second Standard (d). A note thereto specifies, "[w]hether these animals are raised in that country or not. Any Contracting Parties imposing special conditions on the application of this subparagraph would have to make them known by entering reservations." Perhaps surprisingly, the European Community did not enter any reservations with regard to this provision.

58.   Regulation 802/68, *supra* note 1.

Of particular interest is the third standard, which parallels Article 5 of Regulation 802/68: "Where two or more countries have taken part in the production of the goods, the origin of the goods shall be determined according to the substantial transformation criterion."

The "Text and Commentary" Section of the Annex specifies under the heading "Definitions" that

[f]or the purposes of this Annex . . . the term "substantial transformation criterion" means the criterion according to which origin is determined by regarding as the country of origin the country in which the last substantial manufacturing or processing, deemed sufficient to give the commodity its essential character, has been carried out.

Contrary to Article 5 of the Basic Origin Regulation, the Third Standard does not require that the last substantial process or operation is "economically justified" and takes place in an "undertaking equipped for the purpose."[59] The Third Standard of the Kyoto Convention also defines the last substantial transformation as the transformation deemed sufficient "to give the commodity its essential character." Article 5 of the Basic Origin Regulation would seem to adopt a somewhat broader definition by requiring that the last substantial transformation results in the manufacture of a new product *or* represents an important stage of manufacture.[60]

The Annex notes that the substantial transformation criterion can be expressed in three ways: (1) by a rule requiring a change of tariff heading in a specified nomenclature, with lists of exceptions; (2) by a list of manufacturing or processing operations that do or do not confer on the goods the origin of the country in which those operations were carried out; or (3) by an ad valorem percentage rule, where either the percentage value of the materials used or the percentage of the value added reaches a specific level.

In the Text and Commentary Section, the Annex notes the advantages and disadvantages of the three different techniques but does not express a clear preference.

The Sixth Standard provides a listing of "minimal operations" that do not confer origin:

---

59. Since these two conditions have played a limited role in EC practice, this contrast would appear to be of minor importance.

60. The relevance of this distinction would seem to have to a great extent diminished after the judgment of the European Court of Justice in *Überseehandel, supra* note 22. *See* the discussion below.

[o]perations which do not contribute or which contribute to only a small extent to the essential characteristics or properties of the goods, and in particular operations confined to one or more of those listed below, shall not be regarded as constituting substantial manufacturing or processing:

(a) operations necessary for the preservation of goods during transportation or storage;

(b) operations to improve the packaging or marketable quality of the goods or to prepare them for shipment, such as breaking bulk, grouping of packages, sorting and grading, repacking;

(c) simple assembly operations;

(d) mixing of goods of different origin, provided that the characteristics of the resulting product are not essentially different from the characteristics of the goods which have been mixed."

The Seventh Standard provides substantive rules concerning the origin of accessories, spare parts, and tools:

Accessories, spare parts and tools for use with a machine, appliance, apparatus or vehicle shall be deemed to have the same origin as the machine, appliance, apparatus or vehicle, provided that they are imported and normally sold therewith and correspond, in kind and number, to the normal equipment thereof.

In a commentary attached thereto it is noted:

In other words, the accessories, spare parts, etc. referred to in this provision should be disregarded when determining the origin of the machine, appliance, etc.; hence their value should not be taken into consideration, especially under the "ad valorem" percentage rule.

Although the language of the Seventh Standard of Annex D.1 of the Kyoto Convention would seem to be close to Article 7 of the Basic Origin Regulation, the European Community entered a reservation aimed at the commentary to the Seventh Standard. The European Community stated:

The relevant Community provisions are based on the notion that the origin of the accessories, spare parts, etc. is determined not by considering the accessories, spare parts, etc., in isolation but by considering the entity formed by the machine, appliance, etc., and its accessories, spare parts, etc.

It follows that when the percentage rule is applied, it is necessary to determine the aggregate value of all non-originating parts (including any accessories or parts thereof), and that this value must not exceed the allowable percentage of the value of the entity formed by the machine, appliance, etc., and its accessories, spare parts, etc.

The Eight Standard provides a special rule for partial shipments of unassembled or disassembled articles[61] and the Ninth Standard introduces a presumption of origin for packings.[62]

Finally the Eleventh Standard should be noted: "For the purpose of determining the origin of goods, no account shall be taken of the origin of the energy, plant, machinery and tools used in the manufacturing or processing of the goods."

This Eleventh Standard would seem to suggest that in an added-value calculation, depreciation, lease and rental payments and royalties relating to nonoriginating plant, machinery, and tools should also be counted as local added value.[63]

While Annex D.1 of the Kyoto Convention would seem to provide more detail and reasons than the Basic Origin Regulation, the crucial substantive standards, such as the Third Standard, nevertheless remain too vague and uncommitted to provide more clarity.

A proposal of the Customs Cooperation Council (CCC) Secretariat to adopt substantive rules that go further was rejected by the Contracting Parties

---

61.   "An unassembled or disassembled article which is imported in more than one consignment because it is not feasible, for transport or production reasons, to import it in a single consignment shall, if the importer so requests, be treated as one article for the purpose of determining origin."   The European Community also entered a reservation with regard to this standard simply stating that the Community's own rules do not contain any provision of this kind.

62.   "For the purpose of determining origin, packings shall be deemed to have the same origin as the goods they contain unless the national legislation of the country of importation requires them to be declared separately for tariff purposes, in which case their origin shall be determined separately from that of the goods." Although the EC origin rules would not seem to provide an explicit rule to this effect, the European Community did not enter any reservations with regard to this Standard. However, the European Community entered a reservation with regard to the Recommended Practice 10 attached to it that provides, "For the purpose of determining the origin of goods, where packings are deemed to have the same origin as the goods account should be taken, in particular where a percentage method is applied, only of packings in which the goods are ordinarily sold by retail." The European Community simply noted that there is no provision of this kind in Community legislation.

63.   Which makes sense since these are costs locally incurred. It might moreover in practice be a nearly impossible task to go through the list of all buildings, machinery, and tools, to determine the origin of each item. In some factories, machinery and tool depreciation lists may include, for example, up to 20,000 items.

because it was considered to be too political for the technically oriented CCC.[64] The Contracting Parties apparently considered that rules of origin were part of commercial policy rather than of their customs law and that accordingly, international supervision within the CCC was not desirable.[65]

Since then, the CCC Secretariat has focused its efforts on compiling a compendium of rules of origin that is designed to provide descriptions of the rules of origin of its Contracting Parties.[66] Even this more modest effort seems not to have found much support.[67]

The current institutional framework of the CCC in the area of origin might not be effective for international supervision over national rules of origin.

Both the Council and the Technical Committee meet only once a year for a week at the level of Director-Generals of the national ministries. During such meetings, not only rules of origin but all matters resorting under the jurisdiction of the CCC are discussed. All decisions are taken by consensus.

Working parties or expert groups may be established on request, but in the field of rules of origin, no such request has ever been made.[68]

It should be noted that Article 10 of the Kyoto Convention provides for a dispute settlement procedure. Contracting Parties may refer any dispute between them to the Permanent Technical Committee.[69] However, thus far

---

64. Interview with Mr. Gervais Farines, CCC (2 March 1990).

65. Ibid.

66. Compendium of Rules of Origin of Goods, CCC (1st ed. 1986).

67. The compendium presently covers twenty countries, including Japan. It would seem that the United States and the European Communities are in the process of finalizing their submissions.

68. Interview with Mr. Gervais Farines, CCC (12 March 1990).

69. Article 10 of the Kyoto Convention, *supra* note 50, provides:

1. Any dispute between two or more Contracting Parties concerning the interpretation or application of this convention shall so far as possible be settled by negotiation between them.

2. Any dispute which is not settled by negotiation shall be referred by the Contracting parties in dispute to the Permanent Technical Committee which shall thereupon consider the dispute and make recommendations for its settlement.

3. If the Permanent Technical Committee is unable to settle the dispute, it shall refer the matter to the Council, which shall make recommendations in accordance with Article III(e) of the convention establishing the Council.

4. The Contracting Parties in dispute may agree in advance to accept the recommendations of the Permanent Technical Committee or Council as binding.

this dispute settlement procedure has never been used with regard to origin or any other matter relating to the Kyoto Convention.[70]

3.3. Interpretation by the European Court of Justice, the Origin Committee, and the Commission

3.3.1. The Case Law of the European Court of Justice

3.3.1.1. Introduction

Thus far, the Court of Justice has rendered five judgments on the interpretation of the Basic Origin Regulation: *Überseehandel*,[71] *Yoshida*,[72] *Cousin*,[73] *Zentrag*,[74] and *Brother*.[75] Perhaps not surprisingly, these judgments all related to the interpretation of Article 5 of the Basic Origin Regulation.

Article 5 of Council Regulation 802/68 essentially lays down four substantive criteria for the determination of the origin of products in the production of which two or more countries are involved. Origin will be obtained in the country

1. where the last substantial process or operation is performed
2. that is economically justified
3. in an undertaking equipped for the purpose and
4. resulting in the manufacture of a new product or representing an important stage of manufacture.

In these five judgments, the court to some extent clarified the general interpretation of these vague criteria and has not hesitated to scrutinize the application of these criteria by the Commission in the cases at hand, rather than allowing the Commission extensive discretionary powers.

---

70.   Interview with Mr. Gervais Farines, CCC (28 March 1990).

71.   *Supra* note 22.

72.   *Yoshida I, supra* note 20; and *Yoshida II, supra* note 22.

73.   *Cousin, supra* note 45.

74.   *Zentralgenossenschaft des Fleischergewerbes e.G. v. Hauptzollamt Bochum* Case 93/83 (1984) ECR 1095 [*Zentrag*].

75.   *Brother II, supra* note 32.

3.3.1.2. Überseehandel

In *Überseehandel*, the question before the Court was whether untreated casein, imported from the Soviet Union and Poland, but cleaned, grinded, graded, and packaged in Germany, had acquired EC origin.[76] From the facts of the case, it is clear that the Origin Committee had concluded that these processes were insufficient to confer origin.[77] The question before the court concerned only the interpretation of the first and the fourth condition of Article 5 of the Basic Origin Regulation because the parties seemed to agree that the processes were "economically justified" (second criterion) and were "performed in an undertaking equipped for that purpose" (third criterion).[78]

The main line of the plaintiff's argument was to link the first criterion to the second criterion by stating that the word *substantial* is semantically similar to the words *economically justified* because the question whether an operation is substantial can only be determined in economic terms. Since it was not contested that the processes were economically justified, these should also be considered as substantial. With regard to the fourth criterion, the plaintiff argued that untreated casein is not soluble in water and cannot be used. The grinding of the casein is essential if the product is to be used, which shows that the processes represent an "important stage of manufacture" and meet the fourth criterion.[79]

The court held that the determination of the origin of goods must be based on a "[r]eal and objective distinction between raw material and processed product, depending fundamentally on the specific material qualities of each of those products."[80]

The last process or operation can only be considered substantial for purposes of Article 5 (first condition) if "[t]he product resulting therefrom has its own properties and a composition of its own, which it did not possess

---

76. From the facts of the case as recorded in the judgment, it is not perfectly clear what exactly the material benefit for the plaintiff was in obtaining EC origin. In the Advocate General's opinion, it is simply noted that, "Many of the plaintiff's customers are in third countries . . . For its exports to them it is to the advantage of the plaintiff to have certificates showing the origin of its ground casein as being the Federal Republic of Germany." *Überseehandel, supra* note 22, at 58.

77. Ibid., at 48.

78. Ibid., at 52.

79. Ibid., at 45.

80. Ibid., at 53.

before that operation or process."[81]

The Court then in effect linked the first and the fourth condition by holding that

[i]n providing that the said process or operation must, in order to confer a particular origin, result in the manufacture of a new product or represent an important stage of manufacture . . . Article 5 shows in fact that activities affecting the presentation of the product for the purposes of its use, but which do not bring about a significant qualitative change in its properties, are not of such a nature as to determine the origin of the said product.[82]

The court ruled that the grinding of the casein only changed "[t]he consistency of the product and its presentation for the purpose of its later use; it does not bring about a significant qualitative change in the raw material."[83]

The court further held that "the quality *control by grading* to which the ground product is subjected and the manner in which it is *packaged* relate only to the requirements for marketing the product and do not affect its substantial properties."[84]

The court decided that the grinding together with the grading and the packaging of casein could not be considered a substantial process or operation for the purposes of Article 5.[85]

It should be noted that the court in its judgment cut through the sophisticated semantic distinctions drawn by the plaintiffs and the Commission between the meaning of the word "substantial" in the first criterion and the fourth criterion[86] by effectively linking both criteria. A manufacturing

---

81. Ibid.

82. Ibid.

83. Ibid.

84. Ibid.

85. Ibid., at 54.

86. It is worth noting that in its arguments in this case the Commission tried to provide a theoretical distinction between the first criterion, "substantial process or operation," and the fourth criterion "manufacture of a new product or important stage of manufacture." According to the Commission, the criterion "substantial process or operation" expresses a "dynamic" point of view, because it necessitates an examination whether that activity as such plays an important part in the production as a whole. Regarding this, the question whether such an activity is indispensable to putting the product to its final economic use is not decisive. The

process would seem to be substantial for purposes of the first criterion if it satisfies the fourth criterion, namely, if the process results in the manufacture of a new product or represents an important stage in the manufacture.[87]

With regard to the fourth criterion, the court also seemed to blur the distinction that the process or operation must result in the manufacture of a new product, or represent an important stage of manufacture.[88] By requiring that the process should bring about a significant qualitative change in the properties of the product — which would seem to mean essentially the manufacture of a (new) distinct product — the court, within the limits of the facts of this case, would seem to deny a distinct alternative meaning to the criterion "important stage of manufacture." An alternative meaning of "important stage of manufacture" could consist of operations that do not bring about a significant qualitative change in the product but represent nevertheless a considerable value added.[89] This could have been the case if the value of the untreated casein would have been very low, but the cleaning, grinding, grading, and packing operations, for example, being the most machine and labor intensive, would be the most expensive production processes in the production of ready-for-use casein. In other words, this interpretation would confer origin in the country where (expensive) processing operations are performed on (cheap) raw materials but do not bring about a significant

---

Commission argued that, on the other hand, the criteria "manufacture of a new product" or "important stage of manufacture" express more of a "static" point of view since they involve making some sort of comparison between the product as it was before the process and the one obtained after it, in particular to establish whether there is a significant qualitative change which would mean that the process represents an "important stage of manufacture." Ibid., at 49.

In the opinion of Advocate General Warner this distinction was given short thrift. The Advocate General stated, "It seems to me that this is pushing semantic analysis too far. To my mind a process or operation is 'substantial' if it is the opposite of insubstantial, *i.e.*, if it is not negligible or not trivial. Indeed I think that the phrase 'the last substantial process or operation' in Article 5 is to be interpreted as a single phrase, in which the emphasis is on 'last'." Ibid., at 59.

87. The court on this point did not follow the Advocate General's Opinion. In the Advocate General's opinion, the first condition was satisfied in this case, but the difficult question was only whether the fourth condition was satisfied. Ibid., at 59.

88. This distinction had been maintained by the Advocate General in its Opinion. *See ibid.*, at 59, *in fine*.

89. This would seem to some extent have been the reasoning of Advocate General Warner, who considered the value added and the comparative importance of the processes in determining the quality level of the finished casein to arrive at the conclusion that the processes in the case at hand were not an important stage in the manufacture. Ibid., at 61-62.

qualitative change in the product.

It may be noted that, although not discussed by the court, the value added by the processes in the case before the court would appear to have been rather small.[90] Although the choice between an economic and technical approach of the origin determination would not seem to have been a material issue with regard to the facts of the case as presented to the court, the court in *Überseehandel* would seem to have chosen a technical and qualitative approach.

The court also denied relevance to the use of the customs tariff classification of processed products as a criterion in the origin determination because the Common Customs Tariff has been "conceived to fulfil special purposes and not in relation to the determination of the origin of products."[91]

Finally, the court followed the invitation of the Commission[92] to give prominence to the opinions of the Origin Committee. The court stated:

> Although opinions expressed by the Committee are not binding, except in so far as the Commission has adopted implementing provisions in application of Article 14(3)(a) of regulation No 802/68, nevertheless, until such time as the Commission adopts contrary provisions under subparagraphs (b) and (c) of the said Article 14(3), they constitute an important criterion for interpreting Article 5 of the said regulation, the scope of which they define in respect of specific cases.[93]

3.3.1.3. Yoshida

In the *Yoshida* cases, the court had to judge the validity of the product-specific origin rule on slide fasteners that the Commission had adopted in 1977 and which provided in Article 1 that slide fasteners originated in the country of "assembly including placing of the scoops or other interlocking elements onto the tapes accompanied by the manufacture of the slider and the

---

90.   As is apparent from the Advocate General's Opinion, customers estimated the value added to range mainly between 5 and 20 percent. Ibid., at 62.

91.   Ibid., at 52.

92.   In its arguments the Commission had requested the court to express its view on the status of the opinions of the Origin Committee, which the Commission argued should — similar to the case law of the Court on the opinions of the Committee on Common Customs Tariff Nomenclature — be considered to be an important factor for the interpretation of the Basic Origin Regulation. Ibid., at 47.

93.   Ibid., at 54.

forming of the scoops or other interlocking elements."[94]

This specific origin rule was the result of a long history going back to an antidumping proceeding that the Commission had initiated in 1973 against slide fasteners from Japan.[95] The proceeding had been terminated two years later "having regard to the development of the situation,"[96] in particular the assurances the Japanese company Yoshida Kogyo gave to the Commission to raise its export prices and not to exceed a certain ceiling of exports to Italy.[97] In 1975 the Commission introduced a Community surveillance system with regard to imports of slide fasteners[98] because it had found that Community imports of slide fasteners, particularly from Japan, had increased considerably and thereby threatened to cause injury to the EC industry of slide fasteners. Yoshida Kogyo furthermore negotiated a voluntary export restraint with the Italian government. Nonetheless, Italian imports of Yoshida zippers kept increasing. When the Italian government discovered that the zippers produced by Yoshida Kogyo in its Dutch and German factories included Japanese parts, it addressed the Origin Committee.[99] This action eventually led to the adoption of the specific origin rule, which had the effect that the zippers produced by Yoshida Kogyo in its Dutch and German factory could no longer obtain EC origin. It should also be noted that the product specific origin rule, in the absence of a qualified majority in the Origin Committee and action being taken by the Council, was promulgated by the EC Commission in accordance with Article 14(3)(c) of the Basic Origin Regulation.[100]

Both Yoshida's Dutch and German subsidiaries challenged the validity of this product specific origin rule in two separate national proceedings, which both culminated in requests for a preliminary ruling by the court.[101]

The court held that the examination whether the operations required by the

---

94. Regulation (EEC) No 2067/77 of the Commission of 20 September 1977 concerning the determination of the origin of slide fasteners, O.J. (1977) L 242/5.

95. O.J. (1973) C 51/2.

96. O.J. (1975) C 63/1.

97. *Yoshida II, supra* note 22, at 163.

98. Commission Regulation (EEC) No 646/75, O.J. (1975) L 67/21.

99. Opinion of the Advocate General Capotorti in *Yoshida I*, Case 34/78 (1979) ECR 146.

100. Ibid., at 138.

101. *Yoshida I, supra* note 20; *Yoshida II, supra* note 22.

product-specific origin rule correspond to the requirements laid down in Article 5 of the Basic Origin Regulation was a "question of a technical nature which must be examined having regard to the definition of a slide fastener and of the various operations resulting in its formation."[102]

On the basis of an analysis of the production processes of zippers, the court determined — contrary to the opinion of Advocate General Capotorti[103] — that the combination of the processes of

the attaching of the metal scoops or nylon spirals to the tapes and the subsequent joining of the tapes

the attaching of bottom stops and top stops;

the insertion and where necessary the colouring of the sliders; and

the drying and cleaning of the slide fasteners followed by the cutting of them to make individual slide fasteners;

must be considered as constituting the "last substantial process or operation" conferring origin because they resulted in "a new and original product which, in contrast to each of the basic products, is a linking element which can be separated over and over again and is used to join objects, in particular pieces of fabric."[104]

The Court then declared the specific origin rule not valid because

The slider constitutes merely a particular part of the whole, the price of

---

102. *Yoshida I, supra* note 20, at 135.

103. In his opinion Advocate General Capotorti essentially stated that for the origin determination a technical criterion should be preferred over an economic criterion because there are serious objections against the use of economic criterion. The differences in production costs — among others dependent on salary levels, interest rates, and other factors differing from country to country — fluctuations in certain cost factors, the difficulties that arise from determining whether the costs of different processes have been accurately assessed, etc., make the use of an economic criterion problematic. Therefore, according to the Advocate General, the Commission was right in using a technical criterion with a high degree of objectivity. With regard to the origin determination of the slide fasteners, the Advocate General stated that basically the alternative was, on the one hand, to consider the assembly (the attachment of the scoops and the slider) as the last substantial transformation or, on the other hand, to go one step further back to the manufacture of both parts that are the typical components of a slide fastener, namely the scoops and the slider. According to the Advocate General, the Commission was right in considering the "assembly" process as such as not decisive. Otherwise every product assembled in the Community would achieve Community origin even if all parts are manufactured elsewhere. Since the production of either the scoop or the glider in itself cannot be considered as a "substantial transformation," the Commission correctly considered that the manufacture of both elements together with the assembly constituted the last substantial transformation. Ibid. at 141, 143, 144.

104. Ibid.

which cannot moreover have an appreciable influence on the final cost of a slide fastener and which, although it is a characteristic feature thereof, is however of no use unless it is combined in a harmoniously assembled whole.

The Commission, in taking the view that it had to go back beyond the last process to the process of the manufacture of the glider and make that a binding condition for the grant of a certificate of origin, relied upon an operation which is extraneous to the objectives of Regulation No 802/68 which requires a real and objective distinction between raw material and processed product depending fundamentally on the specific material qualities of each of those products.

The requirement that virtually all components of a product must be of Community origin, even those of little value which are of no use in themselves unless they are incorporated into a whole, would amount to a repudiation of the very objective of the rules on the determination of origin. The Commission has therefore by that very fact exceeded its power under Article 14(3) of Regulation No 802/68.[105]

The court here for the first time set limits to the powers of interpretation of the Commission under the Basic Origin Regulation.

In its reasoning the court would seem to have emphasized that it should be the *last* substantial transformation that confers origin. The court further — in rather strong terms — rejected the use of rules of origin for the imposition of excessive local content conditions.[106]

3.3.1.4. Cousin

The *Cousin* case involved the interpretation of the specific origin regulation on certain textile products.[107] Unbleached cotton yarn imported from Egypt

---

105. Ibid., at 136 (emphasis added).

106. It may be noted that in the arguments of the plaintiffs in this case, it was put to the forefront that the product-specific origin rules should be neutral and cannot be used for commercial policy purposes. The plaintiffs exposed the trade restrictive character of the product specific origin rule aimed at Yoshida, which had been using gliders of Japanese origin in its production of slide fasteners in the European Community. *Yoshida II, supra* note 22, at 155. *See* Opinion of the Advocate General Capotorti, who essentially argued that no rule will ever be neutral since every rule will always be beneficial for some companies and work to the disadvantage of others and further challenged Yoshida's assertions on the facts. Ibid., at 145 ff.

107. Commission Regulation (EEC) No 749/78, O.J. (1978) L 101/7.

and the United States was processed into ready-to-use yarn through the processes of gassing,[108] mercerizing,[109] dyeing, spooling and respooling in Germany.[110] The products thus processed had been declared to French customs by the parties concerned as being of German origin. French customs challenged the origin declarations on the basis of the application of the criteria laid down in the product specific origin regulation.[111]

The product-specific origin regulation essentially relied on a combined change in tariff heading and technical description approach. The principal rule was that a change in tariff heading conferred origin with the exceptions of, on the one hand, certain processing operations that resulted in a change of tariff heading but did not confer origin or conferred origin only subject to certain conditions (list A) and, on the other hand, certain processing operations that did not result in a change of tariff heading but that nevertheless did confer origin (list B).[112] The processes carried out in Germany did not result in a change of tariff heading, and as the cotton yarn concerned did not appear in list B, the application of the product-specific origin regulation led to the conclusion that no German origin had been acquired.[113]

In addressing the issue of the validity of the product specific origin rule,

---

108. In this process fluff and small fibres are burnt off the thread with the aid of electric burners. The yarn is passed over the burners at a speed sufficient to ensure that the protruding material is burnt away without scorching or burning the yarn. The effect of the process is that the yarn is lighter in weight, smoother and softer to the touch. Its commercial value and usefulness is increased. Opinion of Advocate General Sir Gordon Slynn, *Cousin, supra* note 45, at 1,124.

109. In this process the yarn is impregnated under tension with caustic soda. This increases its strength by between 30 and 40 percent and gives it a silky sheen after drying. Ibid., at 1125.

110. *Cousin, supra* note 45, at 1,105.

111. It is interesting to note that the material issue in the case only concerned the criminal sanctions for incorrect origin declarations under French law. Imports into France of cotton yarn not put up for retail sale, in free circulation in Germany but originating in the United States or Egypt, were free at the time and not subject to restrictions, since France had not introduced protective measures based on Article 115 of the EEC Treaty with regard to this product. Ibid., at 1,113.

112. Commission Regulation (EEC) No 749/78 on the determination of textile products falling within Chapters 51 and 53 to 62 of the Common Customs Tariff, O.J. (1978) L 101/7.

113. The product in issue, cotton yarn not put up for retail sale, falling under heading 55.05 of the CCT, appeared only in List A with the additional requirement of "manufacture from products falling within Heading No 55.01 or 55.03," namely cotton or cotton waste, not carded or combed. *Cousin, supra* note 45, at 1,118.

the court first recalled the principle set forth in the *Yoshida* judgments

> that in adopting implementing provisions pursuant to Article 14 of Council
> Regulation (EEC) No 802/68, the Commission is obliged not to exceed the
> powers which the Council has conferred upon it for the implementation of
> the rules which it has promulgated in that regulation and, more precisely,
> that it must define specific criteria of origin which comply with the
> objective criteria of Article 5 of Regulation (EEC) No 802/68 of the
> Council which is the legal basis of the implementing regulation and the
> source of the powers which the Commission exercises in adopting it.[114]

The court also reiterated its dictum in *Überseehandel* that for the purposes
of the application of Regulation 802/68 it was not sufficient to seek criteria
for defining origin in the tariff classification of processed products and that
the determination of origin had to be based on a real and objective distinction
between raw material and processed product, depending fundamentally on the
specific material qualities of each of those products.[115]

The court then stated:

> However, those principles do not prevent the Commission, in exercising the
> power conferred upon it by the Council for the implementation of Article
> 5 of Regulation No 802/68, from having a *margin of discretion* which
> allows it to define the abstracts concepts of that provision with reference
> to specific working or processing operations.[116]

The court held that the product specific origin rule on textiles had not
breached the principle set forth in *Überseehandel*, because it had only taken
tariff classification as a basic rule and had adapted and supplemented that rule
by lists A and B to take account of the particular features of specific working
or processing operations.[117]

The court objected, however, to the fact that under the regulation the
processes of dyeing, accompanied where appropriate by mercerizing and
gassing, are not to confer on unbleached cotton yarn the status of product
originating in the country where those processes took place, while dyeing

---

114. Ibid., at 1,119.

115. Ibid., at 1120

116. Ibid.

117. Ibid.

accompanied by finishing operations is sufficient to confer that status on knitted and crocheted fabrics.[118] The court noted that the Commission had provided no explanation relating to the nature of the products and the processes in question that might justify such a difference in treatment between the process of dyeing and other finishing operations carried out on cloth and fabrics on the one hand and on cotton yarn on the other.

The court held that:

> In these circumstances, it appears contradictory and discriminatory for Regulation No 749/78 to provide substantially more severe criteria for the determination of the origin of cotton yarn than for the determination of the origin of cloths and fabrics. Although the Commission possesses a discretionary power for the application of the general criteria contained in Article 5 of Regulation No 802/68 to specific working or processing operations it cannot however, in the absence of objective justification, adopt entirely different solutions for similar working or processing operations.[119]

Notwithstanding the fact that the court would seem to recognize a certain discretionary power for the Commission in the application of the Basic Origin Regulation, it nevertheless invalidated the product-specific origin regulation basically on the ground of its contradictory and discriminatory character.

Although the court did not invoke this ground, it is clear from the opinion of Advocate General Sir Gordon Slynn, that the processes of dyeing, eventually accompanied by mercerizing and gassing, bring about a substantial qualitative change and a very substantial value added.[120] It is interesting to

---

118. In addition the court noted, "In fact, not only does cotton yarn not appear in List B, but it is mentioned in List A in such a way that, to enable it to be regarded as originating in a country, it must even have been made there from cotton or cotton waste which has not been carded or combed." Ibid., at 1,121.

119. Ibid., at 1,121.

120. In his opinion Advocate General Gordon Slynn stated, "In my opinion, the processes involved in this case, with the exception of spooling, do satisfy the test laid down in Article 5; gassing reduces the weight of the yarn and makes it smoother, with consequent effects on the fabric woven from the yarn; the increase in strength resulting from mercerizing, which is of the order of 30 to 40%, is in my view a significant qualitative change; dyeing was accepted by the Commission as an operation which would affect origin in both Regulation No 1039/71 and Regulation No 749/78 in the case of woven fabrics (where accompanied by finishing operations such as mercerizing." Ibid., at 1,128, 1,129, and further, "[t]hese processes increase the commercial value by 159%. even if certain processes such as gassing and mercerizing . . . [are not performed] . . . the increase in value attributable to dyeing alone

note that the court in *Cousin* did not go as far as in *Yoshida*, by stating that the processes of dyeing, eventually accompanied by mercerizing and gassing, would be sufficient to confer origin.[121]

3.3.1.5. Zentrag

In *Zentrag*,[122] the court confirmed its judgment in *Überseehandel*. Zentrag imported meat from Austria. The meat originated from animals slaughtered and cut in beef quarters in Hungary. Zentrag's Austrian supplier had the meat boned, trimmed and the sinews drawn, cut in pieces and vacuum packed in a processing plant in Austria. It was in Zentrag's interest to have the meat considered as originating in Austria because then it would be subjected to substantially lower import levies in the context of the Common Agricultural Policy.[123]

The court first had to interpret the applicability of the Meat and Offals Origin Regulation[124] to the facts at hand. The court noted that this regulation provides that slaughter confers on the meat the origin of the country where it takes place if the slaughtered animals were previously fattened for a certain period in that country. The court further noted that the statement of the reasons for this regulation showed that the Commission did not wish to adopt a position on the matter of what subsequent processing operations may be capable of conferring a new origin on the meat.[125] Hence, this regulation was not conclusive for determining whether the subsequent processing operations performed by Zentrag's Austrian supplier did confer origin.

With regard to this question, the court referred to *Überseehandel* and reiterated that activities that alter the presentation of a product for the

---

is 99%." Ibid., at 1,125.

121. As was suggested by Advocate General Sir Gordon Slynn, ibid., at 1,129. This origin rule was finally amended nine years later by Commission Regulation (EEC) No 1364/91 of 24 May 1991 determining the origin of textiles and textile articles falling within Section XI of the combined nomenclature, O.J. (1991) L 130/18.

122. *Supra* note 74.

123. By considering the meat as originating in Hungary, rather than in Austria, to which the lower levy applied, the Hauptzollamt Bochum claimed the difference which amounted to DM 1,918,709. Ibid., at 1,098.

124. Commission Regulation (EEC) No 964/71 on determining the origin of the meat and offals, fresh, chilled or frozen, of certain domestic animals, O.J. (1971) L 104/12.

125. *Zentrag, supra* note 74, at 1,105.

purposes of its use but that do not bring about a significant qualitative change in its properties do not determine the origin of the product.[126]

The court stated:

> In the present case, it may be accepted that the operations in question facilitate the marketing of the meat by enabling it to be sold to the consumer through commercial undertakings which do not have their own butcher. However, these operations do not produce any substantial change in the properties and the composition of the meat, and their main effect is to divide up the different parts of a carcase according to their quality and pre-existing characteristics and to alter their presentation for the purposes of sale. A certain increase in the time for which the meat will keep and a slowing down in the maturing process do not constitute a sufficiently pronounced qualitative change in substance to satisfy the requirements mentioned above.[127]

The court also noted that:

> Finally, while the market value of a whole beef quarter which undergoes the operations at issue is increased, according to the calculations supplied by Zentrag at the hearing, by 22%, that fact is not in itself of such a nature as to enable those operations to be regarded as constituting the manufacture of a new product or even an important stage of manufacture.[128]

In this case, the court thus for the first time explicitly addressed the value added criterion. It held that a 22 percent added value in itself would not seem to lead to any conclusions about whether the process constitutes the manufacture of a new product or represents an important stage of manufacture.

---

126. Ibid., at 1,106.

127. Ibid., at 1,106. The court seems to have followed the arguments of the Commission in this case. The Commission had argued that "Those operations can be carried out with expert knowledge alone and do not require the use of any special machines or implements . . . marketability is not the decisive criterion. The operations described do not bring about any change in the essential properties of the product or enhance its value appreciably . . . Admittedly, those processes also improve the quality of the product to a very slight extent, but they do not add to its properties unlike the case where a processed product such as corned beef or sausage is manufactured from beef." Ibid., at 1,101.

128. Ibid.

3.3.1.6. Brother

This case followed a 1986 Commission decision to terminate the antidumping proceeding concerning typewriters from Taiwan, because "the cost of these (Taiwanese) operations was found to be less than that which would constitute the last major transformation required by Regulation 802/68 to confer Taiwanese origin on the goods in question."[129]

Brother Ltd., Brother Taiwan and Brother UK had first brought a direct action against this decision and a subsequent memorandum sent to all Member States signed on behalf of the Director-General for External Relations of the EC Commission. The court had declared this direct appeal inadmissible because the court held that the decision, even considered in conjunction with the memorandum, did not constitute an act that might adversely affect the legal position of Brother: the actual determination with regard to the origin of the typewriters produced by Brother in Taiwan was to be made by the Member States.[130]

The customs authorities in Germany verified Brother in September 1986 and determined that the typewriters imported from Taiwan originated in Japan and the antidumping duty for typewriters originating in Japan[131] was retroactively applied to the typewriters exported from Taiwan. The consequence was that the Hauptzollamt Giessen ordered Brother to pay 3,210,277.83 DM in antidumping duties.[132] Brother appealed against this decision on the ground that the typewriters produced in Taiwan should be considered as originating in Taiwan on the basis of the application of Regulation 802/68: while most of the parts came from Japan, they were mounted and assembled in Taiwan in a fully equipped factory into ready-for-use typewriters. In the opinion of Brother, this was furthermore not a case of circumvention because the factory had existed for a long time and typewriters produced there had been exported to Germany since 1982.[133]

In the questions submitted for a preliminary ruling by the Hessische Finanzgericht, the European Court of Justice was requested to apply the principles of Article 5 and 6 of Regulation 802/68 to the situation at hand.

With regard to the application of Article 5 to assembly operations, the court

---

129. *Electronic Typewriters* (Taiwan), O.J. (1986) L 140/52.

130. Order of the Court, *Brother I, supra* note 35, at 3,763.

131. *Typewriters* (Japan), O.J. (1985) L 163/1 (definitive).

132. *Brother II, supra* note 32, at paras. 5, 6.

133. Ibid., at para. 7.

first noted the basic arguments submitted by the parties involved.

Brother's view was that the conditions in Article 5 were technical and that assembly constituted a classical operation of transformation within the meaning of this provision to the extent that it consists of the assembly of a great number of parts to form a new coherent whole.[134]

The Commission argued that the mere assembly of previously manufactured parts should not be regarded as a substantial process or operation within the meaning of Article 5 where, in view of the work involved and the expenditure on materials on the one hand and the value added on the other, the operation is clearly less important than other processes or operations in another country or countries.[135]

In this case, the court for the first time recognized the relevance of the Kyoto Convention for the interpretation of the Basic Origin Regulation.

In its reasoning, the court referred to the sixth standard of Annex D.1. of the Kyoto Convention to distinguish "simple" assembly operations from other types of assembly operations. It defined a simple assembly operation as an operation that does not require a specially qualified labor force, precision machinery, or a specially equipped factory. Such an operation could not be considered to confer on a product its essential characteristics or properties.[136]

Other types of assembly could confer origin. The court stated that an assembly process could confer origin if it represents, from a technical point of view and having regard to the definition of the assembled product, the decisive stage of production during which the use to which the component parts are to be put becomes definite and the goods in question are given their specific qualities.[137]

However, the court noted that in view of the variety of assembly operations there might be situations in which an examination on the basis of technical criteria might not be decisive for determining the origin of a product. In those cases it is necessary to take account of the value added as an ancillary criterion.[138]

The court did not specify the value added required but limited itself to providing some guidelines, which in view of the practical importance of this

---

134. Ibid., at 13.

135. Ibid., at para. 15.

136. Ibid., at paras. 16 to 19.

137. Ibid., at para. 19. The court referred here to its judgment in *Yoshida I, see supra* note 20.

138. Ibid., at para. 20.

matter deserve to be quoted in full:

> As regards the application and in particular the question of the amount of value added which is necessary to determine the origin of the goods in question, the basis should be that the assembly operations as a whole must involve an appreciable increase in the commercial value of the finished product at the exfactory stage. In that respect it is necessary to consider in each particular case whether the amount of the value added in that country of assembly in comparison with the value added in other countries justifies conferring the origin of the country of assembly.
>
> Where only two countries are concerned in the production of goods and examination of technical criteria proves insufficient to determine the origin, the mere assembly of those goods in one country from previously manufactured parts originating in the other is not sufficient to confer on the resulting product the origin of the country of assembly if the value added there is appreciably less than the value imparted in the other country. It should be stated that in such a situation value added of less than 10%, which corresponds to the estimate put forward by the Commission in its observations, cannot in any event be regarded as sufficient to confer on the finished product the origin of the country of assembly.[139]

It should be noted that the court in these paragraphs suggests that the value added in the country of assembly should be important as compared to the value added in other countries but is not necessarily the most important. The court seems to suggest that it is sufficient that the value added should "not be appreciably less" than the value imparted in other countries.[140] On this important point the court seems to have followed in its judgment the reasoning suggested in the Advocate General's Opinion.

Advocate General Van Gerven stated:

> That criterion is also consistent with the wording of Article 5 in so far as it mentions the "last" substantial process or operation and not "the most" substantial process or operation; in many circumstances differing from

---

139. Ibid., at paras. 22 and 23.

140. The importance of this point can be illustrated with an example in which the value added in Taiwan (country of assembly) was 47 percent and the value added of imported parts with Japanese origin was 53 percent.

If it is required that the value added in the country of assembly is the highest (most important), the product would have Japanese origin. According to the court's requirement in the *Brother II* case that the value should not be "appreciably less," the product would have Taiwanese origin.

those in the present case it is possible that three or four successive operations carried out in three or four different countries each make a not inconsiderable economic contribution. However, it is only the last, which from an economic point of view need not necessarily be the most important of the three or four operations, which confers origin.[141]

The court also added that it is not necessary to examine whether the assembly includes a proper intellectual contribution, because this criterion is not provided for in Article 5.[142]

Finally with regard to the interpretation of Article 6, the court stated that

the transfer of assembly from the country in which the parts were manufactured to another country in which use is made of existing factories does not in itself justify the presumption that the sole object of the transfer was to circumvent the applicable provisions unless the transfer of assembly coincides with the entry into force of the relevant regulations. In that case, the manufacturer concerned must prove that there were reasonable grounds, other than avoiding the consequences of the provisions in question, for carrying out the assembly operations in the country from which the goods were exported.[143]

3.3.1.7. Concluding Remarks

The main principles adopted by the European Court of Justice in its case law concerning the interpretation of the Basic Origin Regulation can be summarized as follows.

---

141. Opinion of Advocate General Van Gerven, *Brother II, supra* note 32, at para. 14. According to the report of the hearing, the Commission's position was that "Only assembly entailing considerable technical or time-consuming work can constitute a substantial process or operation within the meaning of Article 5 in which case two closely linked criteria must be applied, namely the input in labour and materials and the added value. Consequently, an assembly may determine origin when it is practically as costly as the production of the other components in a different country or when its significance is not appreciably less than that of the other manufacturing processes. Any other interpretation of Article 5 *would remove the point of the link between measures of commercial policy and origin.* Ibid., Report for the Hearing, at 6 (emphasis added).

142. Ibid., at para. 24.

143. Ibid., at para. 29. It can be noted that according to the Report for the Hearing, "The Commission favours a narrow interpretation of article 6, namely that the circumvention of the applicable provisions must be the exclusive purpose of the process or operation in another country, not just one reason amongst many." Ibid., Report for the Hearing, at 8.

First, it should be noted that the court has not hesitated to scrutinize the interpretations adopted by the EC Commission. While the court in *Cousin* seemed to allow the Commission a margin of discretion, it is clear from *Yoshida* and *Cousin* that this is a narrow margin. The court seems to have established a satisfying level of judicial review and has shown its intent to guard the conformity of the Commission's interpretations with the basic principles laid down in the Basic Origin Regulation.

Since *Überseehandel*, the court has consistently shown a clear preference for a technical assessment of the determination of origin. In *Brother*, the court for the first time acknowledged the relevance of the value-added test, but only as an ancillary criterion where a technical test cannot provide a conclusive answer.

In *Überseehandel* and *Zentrag* the court stressed the need for a qualitative change in the properties of product. Processing operations that only enhance the marketability of a product without bringing about a significant qualitative change of its properties will not be sufficient to confer origin. In those cases, the Commission has emphasized the fourth criterion requiring the creation of a "new product." The concept "important stage of manufacture" in the fourth criterion was not developed as an alternative criterion.

While assembly operations would seem to lead to the creation of a new product, the court made it clear in *Brother* that further qualifications may be required in the form of a comparative economic test where a technical test is not conclusive. In *Yoshida*, the court itself set an example of a conclusive technical test with regard to assembly operations without the necessity for the use of a value-added test as ancillary criterion. In *Yoshida*, the court also set out a clear warning for excessive local content requirements.

In *Yoshida* and, most clearly, in *Brother* the court also reinstated the importance of determining the *last* substantial transformation, as opposed to the *most* substantial transformation, a distinction that had somewhat been blurred in *Überseehandel* and *Zentrag*, undoubtedly because of the relatively simple fact pattern in those cases.

Finally, it should be noted that the court introduced the nondiscrimination principle in *Cousin*. The importance of that principle may not be limited to the application of identical technical processing operations to different products as were the facts in *Cousin*, but, for example, might also be extrapolated to the application of value-added tests. In this respect one can think of the application of the 45 percent value-added test adopted in the product specific origin rule concerning the assembly of Radio and Television

Receivers[144] to assembly operations of other electronic products.

3.3.2. Interpretation by the Origin Committee and the Commission

3.3.2.1. Introduction

In this section an overview will be provided of the EC Commission's and Origin Committee's interpretations as apparent from the product-specific origin rules adopted.

The product-specific origin rules adopted under the Article 14 procedure of the Basic Origin Regulation are designed to provide clarity about the application of the substantive rules of the Basic Origin Regulation in concrete cases to ensure uniform application of the rules of origin by the EC Member States customs authorities.

The following list in chronological order provides a list of the product-specific origin rules and the nature of the criterion used (see Annex).

1.	Eggs:	Technical
2.	Spare parts:	Technical
3.	Radio/television:	Value-added
4.	Vermouth:	Technical
5.	Tape recorders:	Value-added
6.	Meat/offals:	Technical
7.	Woven textiles:	Technical
8.	Ceramics:	Technical
9.	Grape juice:	Technical
10.	Knitwear:	Technical
11.	Slide fasteners:	Technical
12.	Textiles:	Technical
13.	Ball bearings:	Technical
14.	Integrated circuits:	Technical
15.	Photocopiers:	Technical
16.	Eggs:	Technical
17.	Textiles XI:	Technical/value-added

The Commission's first choice seems to be to have a technical test as opposed to a value-added test for the purposes of adopting product-specific

---

144. Commission Regulation (EEC) No 2632/70 of 23 December 1970 on determining the origin of radio and television receivers, O.J. (1970) L 279/35.

origin rules. In two cases, radio and television receivers[145] and tape recorders,[146] a (45 percent) value-added test was utilized. In textiles within Section XI of the combined nomenclature,[147] the Commission used value-added requirements of 60 percent, 52 percent, and 50 percent.

It should further be noted that the Commission adopted a technical test that was essentially based on the change in tariff heading approach in three cases[148] and a negative technical test (defining operations that do not confer origin) also in three cases.[149]

The substantive rules adopted in these product specific origin regulations, discussed by product category, are as follows:

3.3.2.2. Essential Spare Parts

Article 7(1) of the Basic Origin Regulation provides that accessories, spare parts, or tools delivered with any equipment, machine, apparatus, or vehicle that form part of its standard equipment shall be deemed to have the same origin as that equipment, machine, apparatus, or vehicle.[150]

---

145. *Supra* note 144.

146. Commission Regulation (EEC) No 861/71 of 27 April 1971 on determining the origin of tape recorders, O.J. (1971) L 95/11. But even in those two cases, one could argue that the Commission effectively adopted a technical test in holding that *assembly* constitutes the last substantial process or operation *provided that* at least 45 percent value is added in the assembly process.

147. *Supra* note 121.

148. With regard to ceramics (*infra* note 185), grape juice (*infra* note 159), and Textiles within Section XI (*supra* note 121).

149. With regard to basic wines in the vermouth regulation (*infra* note 156), grape juice (*infra* note 159), and photocopiers (*infra* note 195).

150. As mentioned before, the EEC entered a reservation with regard to the Seventh Standard of the Annex D.1. of the Kyoto Convention concerning the calculation methods for determining the origin of the machine together with which accessories, spare parts, or tools have been imported, for purposes of applying the presumption of origin.
A commentary to the Seventh Standard provided, "[t]he accessories, spare parts, etc. referred to in this provision should be disregarded when determining the origin of the machine, appliance, etc.; hence their value should not be taken into consideration, especially under the "ad valorem" percentage rule."
In its reservations, the European Community made it clear that its provisions do not conform to this Standard: "The relevant Community provisions are based on the notion that the origin of the accessories, spare parts, etc., is determined not by considering the accessories, spare parts, etc., in isolation but by considering the entity formed by the machine,

Article 7(2) provides that the conditions under which this presumption also apply to essential spare parts shall be determined by an implementing regulation taken under the Article 14 procedure.

The origin regulation concerning essential spare parts[151] was taken in execution of this Article 7(2) of the Basic Origin Regulation and basically lays down the conditions under which the presumption of same origin shall apply to essential spare parts[152] that have not been shipped together with the equipment, machine, apparatus, or vehicle but have been shipped subsequently.

The regulation provides that the presumption of (same) origin shall only be accepted:

if it is *necessary* for importation into the country of destination and if the use of the essential spare parts at the production stage of the piece of equipment, machine, apparatus, or vehicle would not have prevented that piece of equipment, machine, apparatus, or vehicle from having Community origin or that of the country of manufacture. In other words, if the essential spare part is actually of a different origin, its inclusion in the product should not alter the origin of the product.

The application of this rule can cause considerable problems in practice. First of all, it can be difficult to establish the linkage between the essential spare parts and the equipment, machine, apparatus, or vehicle dispatched beforehand. This can especially be the case when the manufacturer has shipped equipment, a machine, etc., from different origins and the spare parts, also being of a different origin — the only hypothesis where the rule really

---

appliance, etc., and its accessories, spare parts, etc. It follows that when the percentage rule is applied, it is necessary to determine the aggregate value of all non-originating parts (including any accessories or parts thereof), and that this value must not exceed the allowable percentage of the value of the entity formed by the machine, appliance, etc., and its accessories, spare parts, etc."

151. Commission Regulation (EEC) No 37/70 of 9 January 1970 on determining the origin of essential spare parts for use with any piece of equipment, machine, apparatus or vehicle dispatched beforehand, O.J. (1970) L 7/6.

152. Article 2 defines essential spare parts as being parts which at the same time "are components without which the proper operation of the goods referred to in (a) which have been dispatched beforehand cannot be ensured; are characteristic of those goods; are intended for their normal maintenance and to replace parts of the same kind which are damaged or have become unserviceable."

matters — can be used for all these machines.[153] Moreover, the second condition for the application of the presumption of origin, namely whether the inclusion of the essential spare part would alter the origin of the equipment, machine, etc., can also cause considerable practicable problems. For example, if the equipment, machine, etc., is subject to a value-added rule, besides the linkage problem mentioned above, it will also be difficult to ascertain the breakdown of the value added to the equipment, machine, etc., previously dispatched, because there might be a considerable time lag between the dispatch of the equipment, machines, etc., and the dispatch of the essential spare parts.[154]

3.3.2.3. Agricultural Products

The need for clarifications on the application of origin rules concerning agricultural products arises especially in connection with application of measures under the EC's Common Agricultural Policy. The following product specific origin rules have been enacted with regard to agricultural products.

3.3.2.3.1. Certain Goods Produced From Eggs

The Commission considered that the processes for the production of dried egg, dried egg yolk, and dried egg white from eggs in shell or eggs not in shell can only be carried out in an undertaking equipped for that purpose. Those processes constitute a substantial and economically justified operation. Dried egg, dried egg yolk, and dried egg white are products distinct from eggs in shell or eggs not in shell.

Therefore, the Commission concluded that dried egg, dried egg yolk, and dried egg white must be considered as originating in the country where the drying process took place.[155]

---

153. Article 5 gives some indication of the evidence that may be considered sufficient to establish the linkage. It provides, "In order to ensure application of the rules laid down in this Regulation, the competent authorities may require additional proof, in particular production of the invoice or a copy of the invoice relating to the piece of equipment, machine, apparatus or vehicle dispatched beforehand; the contract or a copy of the contract or any other document showing that delivery is being effected as part of the normal maintenance service."

154. It should be noted that the regulation does not provide for any time restrictions in this respect.

155. Commission Regulation (EEC) No 641/69 of 3 April 1969 on determining the origin of certain goods produced from eggs, O.J. (1969) L 83/15; as amended by Commission Regulation (EEC) No 2884/90 of 5 October 1990 on determining the origin of certain goods

3.3.2.3.2. Basic Wines and Vermouth

This product-specific origin rule provides that the processing of wines into basic wines involves chemical or organoleptic analysis and is a substantial and economically justified process. However, it cannot be considered to result in a new product or to represent an important stage in its manufacture and therefore does not confer origin.

On the other hand, the processing of these basic wines into vermouth confers origin because the "organoleptic characteristics of vermouth are so distinct from those of the basic wines that it is changed beyond recognition after processing."[156]

3.3.2.3.3. Meat and Offals

With regard to edible meat and offals, the Commission considered that the slaughter of the animals and related operations such as evisceration, skinning, curting, and refrigeration may not be considered to constitute a substantial process or operation within the meaning of Article 5 of the Basic Origin Regulation.

In the absence of a concurring opinion of the Origin Committee and a decision by the Council, the Commission enacted that origin is conferred in the country of slaughter if the animals are also fattened in that country preceding slaughter for a period of at least three months for horses, asses, mules, and cattle and at least two months in the case of swine, goats, and sheep.

As is clear from the preamble to the regulation, if the slaughter of the animals was not preceded by a fattening period at least equal to the above periods, the meat and offals should be recognized as originating in the country where the animals from which they were obtained were fattened or reared for

---

produced from eggs, O.J. (1990) L 276/14 (the amendment only considered the explicit inclusion of drying processes from egg white in the Annex attached to the regulation to cover all possibilities; it would not seem to have changed the substantive rule in this respect which was already implicit in the recitals to the old Commission Regulation) (emphasis added).

156. Commission Regulation (EEC) No 315/71 of 12 February 1971 on determining the origin of basic wines intended for the preparation of vermouth, and the origin of vermouth, O.J. (1971) L 36/10. For nonconnoisseurs, this distinction may not be so obvious. According to the recitals to the Regulation "[t]he preparation of vermouth from wines generally involves, in the first place, the processing of these wines into basis wines by adding must of fresh grapes, concentrated must or alcohol and, in the second place, the processing of these basic wines into vermouth by flavouring them, with or without the addition of alcohol."

the longest period.[157]

This product-specific origin rule would seem to be a logical extension of the principle laid down in Article 4(d) of the Basic Origin Regulation providing that among the products that will be considered as wholly obtained and originating in a country are "products derived from lived animals raised therein."[158]

3.3.2.3.4. Grape Juice

This negative origin rule provides that processing of grape must into grape juice will not confer origin.[159]

3.3.2.4. Textile Products

The need for clear nonpreferential origin rules in the textile sector arises especially in connection with the application of quantitative restrictions within the framework of the MFA.

The EC Commission recently reorganized and amended the product-specific origin rules concerning textiles in two regulations.

3.3.2.4.1. Textile Products of Section XI

The basic rule is that origin obtains if the products have undergone one complete process of manufacture as a result of which the products obtained receive a classification under a heading of the combined nomenclature other

---

157. Commission Regulation (EEC) No 964/71 of 10 May 1971 on determining the origin of the meat and offals, fresh, chilled or frozen, of certain domestic animals, O.J. (1971) L 104/12.

158. As noted earlier, the rule of Article 4(d) of the Basic Origin Regulation would seem to be stricter than the Second Standard (d) of the Kyoto Convention, which does not require that the live animals are also raised in the country where the products from these animals are obtained. The Second Standard (d) of the Kyoto Convention only mentions "products obtained from live animals in that country."

A note to that standard specifies, "[w]hether these animals are raised in that country or not. Any Contracting Parties imposing special conditions on the application of this subparagraph would have to make them known by entering reservations." Perhaps surprisingly, the EC did not enter any reservations in this respect. The product-specific origin rule concerning meat and offals could be seen as an extension of the stricter EC approach.

159. Commission Regulation (EEC) No 2026/73 of 25 July 1973 on determining the origin of grape juice, O.J. (1973) L 206/33 amended by Commission Regulation (EEC) No 2883/90 of 5 October 1990 on determining the origin of grape juice, O.J. (1990) L 276/13.

than those covering the various nonoriginating materials used.[160]

This basic rule is supplemented by Annex II to the regulation, which provides for specific product processes that confer origin, whether or not they involve a change of heading.[161]

Article 4 provides for a list of minimal operations that are not considered to confer origin irrespective of whether there is a change of heading.[162]

The specific processes conferring origin on products listed in Annex II are in certain cases subject to value added requirements. The value-added required varies from 75 percent,[163] 60 percent,[164] 52 percent[165] to 50 percent.[166]

---

160. Article 2 and Article 3 of Regulation 1364/91, *supra* note 121.

161. Ibid., Article 3.

162. (a)   operations to ensure the preservation of products in good condition during transport and storage (ventilation, spreading out, drying, removal of damaged parts and like operations);

    (b)   simple operations consisting of removal of dust, sifting or screening, sorting, classifying, matching (including the making-up of sets of articles), washing, cutting-up;

    (c)   (i)   changes of packing and breaking-up and assembly of consignments;

        (ii)   simple placing in bags, cases, boxes, fixing on cards or boards, etc., and all other simple packing operations;

    (d)   the affixing of marks, labels or other like distinguishing signs on products or their packaging;

    (e)   simple assembly of parts of products to constitute a complete product;

    (f)   a combination of two or more operations specified in (a) to (e).

163. CN Code 6308, incorporation of non-originating materials in sets consisting of woven fabrics and yarn, whether or not with accessories, for making up into rugs, tapestries, embroidered table cloths or serviettes or similar textile articles, put up in packings for retail sales, in which the total value of all the nonoriginating articles incorporated does not exceed 25% of the ex-works price of the set. Ibid., at 27.

164. For example, CN Code 6213 and 6214, handkerchiefs, shawls, scarves, mufflers, mantillas, veils and the like, embroidered: manufacture from yarn *or* manufacture from unembroidered fabric, provided the value of the unembroidered fabric used does not exceed 40% of the ex-works price of the product. Ibid., at 26.

165. CN Code ex Chapters 50 to 55, printing or dyeing of yarn or monofilaments, unbleached or prebleached, accompanied by preparatory or finishing operations, twisting and texturizing not being considered as such, the value of non-originating material (including yarn), not exceeding 48% of the ex-works price of the product. Ibid., at 22.

With regard to the calculation of the value added, Article 5 specifies that

term value used in Annex II shall mean the customs value at the time of import of the non-originating materials used or, if this is not known and cannot be ascertained, the first ascertainable price for such materials in the country of processing. The term "ex-works" price used in Annex II shall mean the ex-works price of the product obtained, less any internal taxes refunded or refundable, on exportation.[167]

As noted in the preamble to the regulation, the Commission on this occasion also amended the rules concerning the dyeing and printing of yarn, to conform with the judgment of the court in *Cousin*,[168] rendered nine years earlier. In this respect, Annex II now provides that origin will be obtained by

[p]rinting or dyeing of yarn or monofilaments, unbleached or prebleached, accompanied by preparatory or finishing operations, twisting or texturizing not being considered as such, the value of non-originating material (including yarn), not exceeding 48% of the ex-works price of the product.[169]

Interestingly, the Commission and Origin Committee maintained a distinction between the dyeing and printing of yarn and the printing and dyeing of knitted and crocheted fabrics, criticized by the court in *Cousin*.[170] Although the new rule now provides that the printing and dyeing of yarn may confer origin, it requires a minimum value added of 52 percent, which is not required for the printing and dyeing of knitted and crocheted fabrics.[171]

In this respect, the preamble to the regulation merely notes that

---

166. For example CN Code ex 5101, degreasing, respectively carbonizing of wool; ex 5201, manufacture of bleached cotton, not carded or combed from raw cotton. Ibid., at 22.

167. Ibid., at 5.

168. *Supra* note 45.

169. *Supra*, note 121, at 22.

170. *Supra* note 45, at 1,121.

171. For knitted or crocheted fabrics, CN Code Chapter 60, printed or dyed, Annex II mentions as origin conferring processes manufacture from yarn or printing or dyeing of unbleached or prebleached fabrics, accompanied by preparatory or finishing operations. *Supra*. note 121, at 25.

[a] new rule for dyeing and printing of yarn has now been formulated as a result of detailed studies of manufacturing operations and following consultations with the economic sector concerned; this rule closely reflects the manufacturing realities involved in dyeing and printing of yarn and confirms the objective distinction between the nature of such operations carried out on yarn and on fabrics.[172]

It is regrettable that the preamble to this new regulation does not provide more detailed explanations about the reasons underlying the fixing of different value-added requirements for different processing operations, or even different value-added requirements for the same processing operations carried out on different products.

For example, for products CN Code Chapter 58, special woven fabrics; tufted textile fabrics; lace; tapestries; trimmings; embroidery; embroidery in the piece, in strips, or in motifs (CN Code 5810), origin is conferred by manufacture in which the value of the nonoriginating materials used does not exceed 50 percent of the exworks price of the product.[173] On the contrary for products under CN Code 6213 and 6214 — handkerchiefs, shawls, scarves, mufflers, etc., embroidered — origin is conferred by manufacture from unembroidered fabric, provided the value of the nonoriginating unembroidered fabric used does not exceed 40 percent of the exworks price of the product.[174] The objective reason for the difference in value added requirements (50 percent respectively 60 percent) for what would appear to be essentially embroidery processes is not obvious.[175]

Therefore, there might still be some doubt whether certain of the rules in this regulation can withstand the nondiscrimination test set forth in *Cousin*, when strictly applied. It can further be questioned whether the relatively high value-added requirements (75 percent, 60 percent, 52 percent, 50 percent) conforms with the dictum of the court in *Brother* that it is sufficient if the

---

172. Ibid., at 18.

173. Ibid., at 24.

174. Ibid., at 26.

175. It should be noted that these two value-added requirements were taken from the List A to the previous Commission Regulation (EEC) No 749/78 of 10 April 1978 on the determination of the origin of textile products falling within Chapters 51 and 53 to 62 of the Common Customs Tariff, O.J. (1978) L 101/7. Commission Regulation (EEC) No 1039/71 of 24 May 1971 on determining the origin of certain woven textile products O.J. (1971) L 113/13 had provided that embroidery could confer origin if the embroidered area represented at least 5 percent of the total area of the embroidered product.

value added in the country where the last processing operations took place should not be "appreciably less" than the value added in other countries.

3.3.2.4.2. Cotton Linters and Others

Commission Regulation (EEC) No 1365/91 of 24 May 1991 on determining the origin of cotton linters, impregnated felt and nonwovens, articles of apparel of leather, and footwear and watch straps of textiles[176] essentially adapts the products falling within other Sections than Section XI of the combined nomenclature and covered by previous Regulations[177] to the new combined nomenclature.[178]

3.3.2.5. Consumer Electronics

The need for clear origin rules concerning radio and television receivers and tape recorders arose in connection with the quantitative restrictions applicable in certain EC Member States and taken under Article 115 of the EC Treaty.

3.3.2.5.1. Radio and Television Receivers

The product-specific origin rule for radio and television receivers was the first origin rule in which a value-added test was adopted.

In the preamble to the regulation the Commission noted that

at the present stage of technical development in this branch of the industry, the assembly operations do not generally constitute in themselves an important stage of manufacture within the meaning of Article 5 of Regulation (EEC) No 802/68; whereas it may be otherwise in certain cases,

---

176. O.J. (1991) L 130/28.

177. Regulation 1039/71, *supra* note 175; Commission Regulation (EEC) No 1480/77 on determining the origin of certain knitted or crocheted articles and certain articles of apparel and footwear, O.J. (1977) L 164/16 and Commission Regulation (EEC) No 749/78 of 10 April 1978 on determining the origin of certain textile products falling within Chapters 51 and 53 to 62 of the Common Customs Tariff, as amended by Regulation (EEC) No 2747/79, O.J. (1979) L 311/18.

178. It is interesting to note that the three regulations mentioned in the previous footnote are overruled by Article 6 of Regulation 1364/91, *supra* note 121. This Article 6 did not limit the repeal of these regulations to the products currently covered in Section XI of the combined nomenclature, and one could argue that these regulations being repealed, Regulation 1365/91 — not being taken according to the procedure of Article 14 of the Basic Origin Regulation — would be not valid.

for example where high performance apparatus or apparatus requiring strict control of the parts used are concerned or where assembly of all the component parts of the apparatus is involved;

Whereas the variety of operations which come within the scope of "assembly" makes it impossible to establish on the basis of a technical criterion the cases in which those operations represent an important stage of manufacture.[179]

The Commission therefore adopted a two step economic test:

1. Radio and television receivers shall obtain origin in the country in which they are manufactured if the increase in value they acquire through assembly and through the incorporation of parts originating there represents at least 45 percent of the exworks invoice price.
2. If in the country of assembly 45 percent value is not added, a value of parts test is used. The radio and television receivers have the origin of the country in which more than 35 percent of the value of the parts originates. If there are two countries in which more than 35 percent of the value of parts originates, origin obtains in the country in which the highest portion of the parts originates.

The Commission Regulation contains little guidance on the calculation of the added value or value of parts. Article 3 merely provides:

when the ex-works invoice price of the apparatus or parts is unknown, the percentages laid down in the preceding Articles shall be calculated on the basis of the value for customs purposes which the apparatus has or would have on importation into the Community.[180]

This article would seem to cause more confusion rather than providing more clarity. A literal reading leaves in the dark what will happen if the exworks price of the parts is unknown[181] for the application of the value of parts test. Furthermore, the essential meaning of this article would seem to be that if the product is bought on a cost, insurance, freight (CIF) EC basis and the CIF costs are unknown (the exworks price being unknown), the percentage

---

179. Regulation 2632/70, *supra* note 144.

180. Ibid.

181. Resorting to the value for customs valuation purposes of the *apparatus* on importation into the Community would seem to provide little answer to this question.

of value added can be calculated on the basis of the CIF EC invoice price (the value for customs purposes on importation into the Community). This means that in such a case, the CIF costs are effectively included in the value added in the country of assembly for the purpose of calculating of the first 45 percent added-value test.

An opinion of the Origin Committee recorded in the informal procedure provides some more meaningful clarifications. It states that

[t]o calculate the percentage referred to in Article 1 of the Regulation (the 45% added value test) account should be taken of the increase in value resulting from assembly, finishing and control operations and, if it applies, the incorporation of parts originating in the country concerned or in the Community — wherever the operations in question were carried out — including the profit made and the general costs borne in the country or in the Community as a result of the said operations[182]

and

[t]he "parts" referred to in the Regulation are to be understood to be all the components, of whatever nature, used in the manufacture of the apparatus

---

182. Undated, as recorded in the EC Compendium of customs legislation. The opinion further provides that for purposes of the application of the 45 percent value-added test,

[t]he *Community origin* of apparatus manufactured by firms in the EEC and *intended for export* may be determined in accordance with the following detailed rules:

(a)   in order to calculate whether the value acquired in the Community as a result of assembly operations and, if it applies, the use of parts originating in the Community accounts for at least 45% of the ex-works invoice price of the apparatus, an overall calculation shall be made covering the whole of the production exported to third countries by each firm concerned in the specific period, which may not exceed one year.

(b)   in making this calculation it shall be admitted, given the relative homogeneity within the Community of the industry in question, that the cost of assembly, finishing and control plus profit and general costs are to be estimated as representing an aggregate of 40% of the ex-works invoice price of radio receivers and 35% of the ex-works invoice price of television receivers.

If the actual sum of the above factors represents a higher percentage than those indicated, this higher percentage shall be taken into account, provided that the party concerned can produce evidence to justify it. (emphasis added)

The same lenient rules thus do not apply concerning apparatus imported into the Community or intended for intra-Community sale.

in question.[183]

In practice, especially under the second value of parts test, the origin of the television receivers will hinge on the origin of the picture tube, which is by far the most expensive component.

3.3.2.5.2. Tape Recorders

The product-specific origin rule for tape recorders is identical to the one for radio and television receivers.[184]

3.3.2.6. Ceramic Products

This negative origin rule provides that the decoration of ceramic products is not a substantial operation and will not confer origin if this decoration does not result in a change of tariff heading of the goods.[185]

3.3.2.7. Ball Bearings

The product specific origin rule for ball bearings seems to have been enacted following the first antidumping case brought against ball bearings from Japan.[186]

The product-specific origin rule provides that origin will be conferred by assembly preceded by heat treatment, grinding, and polishing of the inner and outer rings.[187]

---

183. Ibid.

184. *Supra* note 146.

185. Commission Regulation (EEC) No 2025/73 of 25 July 1973 on the determination of the origin of ceramic products falling under heading Nos. 69.11, 69.12 and 69.13 of the Common Customs Tariff, O.J. (1973) L 206/32; as amended to conform to the new combined nomenclature by Commission Regulation (EEC) No 3561/90 of 11 December 1990 on determining the origin of certain ceramic products, O.J. (1990) L 347/10.

186. *Ballbearings* (Japan), O.J. (1976) C 268/2 (initiation); O.J. (1977) L 196/1 (definitive duties).

187. Commission Regulation (EEC) No 1836/78 of 27 July 1978 concerning the determination of the origin of ball, roller or needle roller bearings, O.J. (1978) L 210/49; as amended to conform to the new combined nomenclature by Commission regulation (EEC) No 3672/90 of 18 December 1990 on determining the origin of ball, roller or needle roller bearings, O.J. (1990) L 356/30.

This product-specific origin rule is an interesting one because rather than defining the required operations as assembly entailing a certain added value, it defines the last substantial process conferring origin as assembly in combination with a technical preparatory process.[188]

3.3.2.8. Integrated Circuits

This product specific origin rule provides that diffusion rather than assembly and testing is the last substantial process or operation for purposes of Article 5 of the Basic Origin Regulation.[189]

In the preamble to the regulation, this rule is motivated as follows:

Whereas the diffusion stage of manufacture is technically highly sophisticated, requires great precision and presupposes a large research investment; whereas, in the context of the totality of the operations necessary for the manufacture of integrated circuits, it is considered that the manufacturing operations following diffusion (such as assembly and testing) are so significantly less important than diffusion that they cannot individually or collectively constitute a substantial operation and thus cannot meet the requirement of being the last substantial operation in the manufacture of integrated circuits; whereas diffusion by means of which the intelligent contribution to the integrated circuit is completed and the integrated circuit is given all its functional capabilities has to be designated . . . as the last substantial operation in the manufacture of integrated

---

188. The reasoning underlying this approach is recorded in detail in the preamble of the regulation. After noting that bearings consist essentially of an outer ring; an inner ring; balls, rollers, or needle rollers; and cages, it is stated that the manufacture of balls, rollers, or needle rollers and cages are of minor importance compared with the manufacture of the inner and outer rings. Neither the assembly of a roller bearing from its constituent parts nor the grinding and polishing of the inner and outer rings of such bearings can be considered a substantial process. The regulation then states, "whereas the process of heat treatment to which the inner and outer rings in their unhardened state are subjected results in a product which has its own properties and a composition of its own which it did not previously possess; whereas nevertheless having regard to the manufacturing process as a whole which results in the production of rolling bearings the process of heat treatment cannot be regarded as being substantial; Whereas in the case of rolling bearings, the processes or operations which may together be considered as the last substantial process or operation and which result in the manufacture of a new product or represent an important stage of manufacture, consist of the heat treatment of the rings, their grinding and polishing and the assembly of the rolling bearings." O.J. (1978) L 210/49.

189. Commission Regulation (EEC) No 288/89 of 3 February 1989 on determining the origin of integrated circuits, O.J. (1989) L 33/23.

circuits.[190]

This origin rule emerged during the course of the anti-dumping proceeding concerning erasable program read only memories (EPROMs)[191] and dynamic random access memories (DRAMs)[192] originating in Japan. It had the interesting side effect of conferring EC origin on the DRAMs manufactured by Siemens, one of the complainants in the antidumping proceeding, which, at the time, performed diffusion in Germany but assembly and testing in Austria. It also had the effect to confer Japanese origin on DRAMs assembled by Japanese companies in third countries, like Malaysia, and thus include these products within the scope of the antidumping measures. Some Japanese manufacturers which had, at the time, assembly and testing operations in the European Community could no longer obtain EC origin for the integrated circuits manufactured there. The product-specific origin rule thus was controversial in view of its alleged protectionist effects.

It should be noted that the value added in the assembly and testing process, being the most labor intensive, is considerable and in certain cases even exceeds the value added in the diffusion process.

3.3.2.9. Photocopiers

The product-specific origin rule concerning photocopiers was equally controversial because it was essentially aimed at the photocopier production facilities of the Japanese company Ricoh in California.

Following the imposition of definitive duties in the antidumping proceeding concerning photocopiers from Japan,[193] Directorate-General XXI of the Commission decided to investigate Ricoh's Californian production facilities and determined that photocopiers made in the United States by Ricoh should actually be considered of Japanese origin because the operations effected in the United States were not sufficient to confer origin.

The Commission proposal to adopt a negative specific origin rule was opposed in the Origin Committee by the Netherlands, the United Kingdom, Ireland, Germany, and Denmark. The Netherlands was of the opinion that the photocopiers *did* have U.S. origin while the other four Member States

---

190. Ibid.

191. *EPROMs* (Japan), O.J. (1987) C 101/10 (Initiation).

192. *DRAMs* (Japan), O.J. (1987) C 181/3 (Initiation).

193. *Photocopiers from Japan*, O.J. (1987) L 54/12 (definitive).

disagreed with the adoption of a negative origin test.[194] Faced with a blocking minority vote in the Origin Committee, the Commission adopted its proposal autonomously.

The Photocopiers regulation as finally adopted provides that the assembly of photocopying apparatus accompanied by the manufacture of the harness, drum, rollers, side plates, roller bearings, screws, and nuts does not confer origin.[195]

3.3.2.10. Other Opinions of the Origin Committee

Finally, it should be noted that there is a record on two opinions of the Origin Committee that did not result in product-specific origin rules. In the first opinion the Committee held that the sterilization of medical instruments was not a process or operation important enough to "confer origin" under Article 5. In the second opinion, it held that the production of corned beef from imported fresh beef confers origin.[196]

3.3.2.11. Concluding Remarks

First of all it should be noted that the Commission and Origin Committee would seem to have clearly favored a technical test above the use of a value-added criterion.

In a 1987 written answer[197] to Mr. Stephen Hughes of the European Parliament, then-Commissioner Cockfield explained the reasons for this preference as follows:

These [Article 5] provisions do not contain the criterion of added value.

---

194. *See* 1513 European Report, at 10 (15 July 1989).

195. Commission Regulation (EEC) No 2071/89 of 11 July 1989 on determining the origin of photocopying apparatus, incorporating an optical system or a system of the contact type, O.J. (1989) L 196/24. The Commission motivated this decision by stating that: "[t]he assembly operations in question accompanied by the manufacture of the above mentioned components are, with regard to the totality of the operations necessary for the production of the photocopy machines concerned so significantly less important than the other operations (manufacture of complicated or technically sophisticated components such as the various printed circuit boards, lenses, various motors and high-voltage generators) that they cannot be considered being, whether individually or collectively the last substantial operation."

196. Opinion of Advocate General Warner, *Überseehandel, supra* note 22, at 57. Also in the EC Compendium of customs legislation.

197. O.J. (1987) C 270/7.

In those cases where the multiplicity of the operations to be carried out makes it difficult to determine the origin on the basis of a technical test, the added-value concept has to be used instead . . . .

The added-value criteria and the percentage laid down on the said Regulations do not constitute a general rule, but apply only to the products specifically concerned. If the adoption of an added-value rule seems necessary for other goods the individual circumstances of each case would need to be taken into account and therefore any statement as to a general percentage level is not possible.[198]

It is interesting to contrast this statement with a later statement of the Commissioner Scrivener in answer to a question of Mrs. Ewing of the European Parliament concerning the origin of cars. Commissioner Scrivener stated:

The notion of the last substantial process or operation mentioned in Article 5 above is fulfilled when a considerable added value is achieved. In order to take into account the technological realities of the sector in question and to add a technical element to the economic test, it is also necessary that not all the essential parts originate from outside the Community.[199]

In this statement Commissioner Scrivener would seem to reverse the order of preference, which shows that the Commission's position has not always been unequivocal.

With regard to the application of the value-added criterion, there is a lack of clarity on how the value added should be calculated. This is even more the case for the application of the value of parts test, such as used in the product-specific origin rule for radio and television receivers, in particular with regard to the level of breakdown of the parts and subparts. For example, it is not clear whether subassemblies originating in a certain country should be further broken down into their smallest parts by origin. This approach might have the effect that a large portion of manufacturing costs are excluded in the evaluation of origin. In its extreme form, the total breakdown approach ends

---

198. O.J. (1987) C 270/7. Compare with the written observations of the Commission in *Yoshida I, supra* note 20, at 115: "However, that 'percentage rule" cannot, according to the Commission, be taken into consideration unless it is impossible to determine what the last substantial process or operation is; this was possible in the present case because the manufacture of the slider constitutes such an important stage that in comparison with it all the other processes or operations are of much less importance."

199. O.J. (1989) C 255/13.

up in an origin of raw materials test, for example, if for determining the origin of plastic parts one would also look at the origin of the resin, and in turn at the origin of the chemicals used to make the resin and in turn to the origin of the petroleum from which these chemicals were produced, etc. It is clear that reasonable and practical limits have to be found. The EC Commission's practice in this respect is still developing.

Another open question is whether special rules should be adopted to assess the added value in case of nonmarket economies.

The Commission and Origin Committee's approach toward assembly operations also seems to have evolved. For television and radio receivers the Commission adopted a 45 percent value added test. For ballbearings the Commission required assembly in combination with crucial preparatory operations. For integrated circuits the Commission dismissed assembly and testing and, arguably, looked at the "most important" process rather than at the "last substantial" process. The photocopiers regulation, together with the statement of Commissioner Scrivener concerning the origin of cars, would suggest that there would also be a requirement of manufacture of the technically most sophisticated components in combination with the assembly. Taking these different approaches case by case risks infringing on the nondiscrimination principle laid down in *Cousin.*

More residual rules are also needed to deal with the problem of dual origin or nonorigin. This is the case when a product, according to a positive product-specific origin rule, may be considered as originating in more than one country or fails to obtain origin in any country. The product-specific origin rule for radio and television receivers is the only one that provides some rules in this respect. These rules, even applied by analogy, do not provide a conclusive answer to all questions. For example, a compact disc player consists of 27.7 percent Japanese parts, 27 percent Singapore parts, and 21 percent Taiwanese parts and subassembly fee, and 24.3 percent value is added in Hong Kong where the final assembly takes place. In this type of case, which tends to occur more frequently in practice, the tests of the radio and television receivers regulation do not provide an answer as to the origin of the product. This could, for example, have Japanese origin (the highest value added, the highest value of parts) or Hong Kong origin (the *Brother* test, namely the value added in the last operation is not considerably less than the value added in other countries). The problem can also arise in connection with other product specific origin rules. For example, if the diffusion process of integrated circuits, which consists of different production steps, is performed in more than one country, the product will, depending on the interpretation given to the specific origin rule, have a potential dual origin, no origin in either country where the diffusion is performed, origin in the country where most of the diffusion process took place, or origin in the country where most value is added in the production of the integrated circuit as a whole.

The negative product-specific origin rules enacted have only a limited informative value and do not answer the crucial question, namely, which operations will be considered to confer origin. While the adoption of negative origin rules might be an easy way out to settle individual cases without having to make difficult choices of principle, the Commission and Origin Committee by doing so would seem to dodge the tasks entrusted to them by the Basic Origin Regulation to provide clarity concerning the application of the origin rules.

4. Preferential Rules of Origin[200]

Preferential rules of origin set forth the requirements for products to be considered as *originating products* for the application of preferential trade agreements between the European Community and third countries.

The European Community currently has the following preferential trade agreements in which tariff preferences are conditional on origin requirements (for the complete references see Annex):

1. members of the EFTA (Austria, Sweden, Switzerland, Iceland, Norway, Finland)
2. ACP Countries
3. Mashreq countries (Syria, Jordan, Lebanon, and Egypt)
4. Magreb countries (Tunisia, Morocco, and Algeria)
5. Cyprus
6. Israel
7. Malta
8. Yugoslavia

The European Community also unilaterally applies tariff preferences to

1. overseas countries and territories (OCTs);
2. Faroe Islands;
3. Ceuta, Melilla, and the Canary Islands;
4. territories occupied by Israel; and
5. developing countries within the framework of the GSP.

The preferential origin rules in the different preferential schemes are

---

200. For a discussion of preferential rules of origin, *see* Forrester, *EEC Customs Law: Rules of Origin and Preferential Duty Treatment*, European Law Review 167 (Part I), 257 (Part II) (1980).

broadly similar, although there are differences in product scope, direct shipment requirements, cumulation rules, and some special origin rules. Within the framework of this contribution it is not possible to provide a detailed analysis of each of these preferential trade schemes.

4.1.   Procedure

4.1.1.   Administrative

In the reciprocal preferential trade agreements, the origin rules are of course subject to negotiation with the trading partners. In this respect, for example, the EFTA treaties provide for the establishment of a Joint Committee. Article 28 of Protocol 3 concerning the definition of the concept of originating products and methods of administrative cooperation confers on this Joint Committee the power to amend the origin rules.[201] The preparation of the decisions of the Joint Committee take place in a Customs Committee in which the EC is represented by members of the EC Commission Origin Division and representatives of the Member States, who are in practice the same persons as the members of the Origin Committee. Since the changes to the origin rules are generally the same for all EFTA countries, the real prenegotiations take place in an informal "Group of 18," in which the EC Member States and all EFTA countries are represented. Decisions taken by the Joint Committee are adopted into Community legislation by Council regulations.[202]

In the case of the unilateral preferential trade regimes, for example, with regard to the GSP[203] the implementing measures concerning the preferential origin rules are taken by the Commission and Origin Committee in accordance with Article 14 of the Basic Origin Regulation.[204]

---

201. *See e.g.*, the agreement with Sweden, O.J. (1972) L 300/137.

202. *See, e.g.*, Council Regulation (EEC) No 4271/88 of 21 December 1988 on the application of Decision No 5/88 of the EEC-Austria Joint Committee modifying Protocol 3 concerning the definition of the concept of 'originating products' and methods of administrative cooperation in order to simplify the cumulation rules, O.J. (1988) L 381/1.

203. *See e.g.*, Article 1(4) of Council Regulation (EEC) No 3635/87 of 17 November 1987 applying generalized tariff preferences for 1988 in respect of certain industrial products originating in developing countries, O.J. (1987) L 350/1, at 5.

204. Regulation 802/68, *supra* note 1. See the discussion in § 3.1.1.

4.1.2. Judicial

The same principles apply as those concerning nonpreferential rules of origin (see § 3.1.2.).

4.2. Substantive Law

4.2.1. Basic Rules

The preferential rules of origin used under the different preferential trade schemes are identical or broadly similar. In this contribution we will take the European Community's GSP rules of origin as an example, which appear most interesting for comparison purposes.[205]

4.2.1.1. The General System of Preferences Rules of Origin

The currently applicable GSP rules of origin are provided for in Commission Regulation (EEC) No 693/88 of 4 March 1988 on the definition of the concept of originating products for purposes of the application of tariff preferences granted by the EEC in respect of certain products from developing countries.[206]

The basic rule is that products will be considered *originating products* in beneficiary countries if the products have been "wholly obtained" in that country or if they have undergone "sufficient working or processing" and have been transported direct to the Community.[207]

---

205. For a comparative study, *see* Generalized System of Preferences, Digest of Rules of Origin, UNCTAD/TAP/133/Rev.5 (May 1982).

206. O.J. (1988) L 77/1.

207. Ibid., Article 1, at 2. The direct transport is defined in Article 6 as meaning: "(a) products transported without passing through the territory of another country; "(b) products transported through the territories of countries other than the exporting beneficiary country, with or without transhipment or temporary warehousing within those countries, provided that transport through those countries is justified for geographical reasons or exclusively on account of transport requirements and that the products have remained under the surveillance of the customs authorities of the country of transit or warehousing, and have not entered into commerce or been delivered for home use there, and have not undergone operations other than unloading, reloading and any operation intended to keep them in good conditions; (c) products transported through the territory of Austria, Finland, Norway, Sweden or Switzerland and which are subsequently re-exported in full or in part to the Community, provided that the products have remained under the surveillance of the customs authorities of the country of transit or warehousing and have not been delivered for home use and have not

Article 2 defines that the following shall be considered as products being "wholly obtained":

(a)   mineral products extracted from its soil or from its sea bed;

(b)   vegetable products harvested there;

(c)   live animals born and raised there;

(d)   products obtained there from live animals;

(e)   products obtained by hunting or fishing conducted there;

(f)   products of seafishing and other products taken from the sea by its vessels;

(g)   products made on board its factory ships exclusively from the products referred to in (f);

(h)   used articles collected there fit only for the recovery of raw materials;

(i)   waste and scrap resulting from manufacturing operations conducted there;

(j)   products produced there exclusively from products specified in (a) to (i).[208]

With regard to the definition of *sufficient processing or working*, Article 3 specifies that as a basic rule this will be the case when the product obtained is classified in a heading[209] that is different from those in which all the nonoriginating materials used in its manufacture are classified (change of tariff heading).

This rule applies except for the products listed in Annex III (and this list is very substantial),[210] for which the processing specified product by product is required.

Article 3(4) further lists of minimal processing operations that shall be considered insufficient working or processing, regardless of whether they

---

undergone operations other than unloading, reloading and any operation intended to keep them in good condition there." Ibid., at 4.

208. Ibid., Article 2. When compared with the similar provision for nonpreferential origin rules, Article 4 of Regulation No 802/68, *supra* note 1 the rule is almost identical in meaning except for item (d). The preferential rule does not require that the live animals are also raised in the country where the products from live animals are obtained and therefore would appear less strict.

209. Four digit code of the Harmonized commodity description and coding system. Ibid., Article 3(1).

210. About forty pages.

result in a change of tariff heading.[211]

Article 7 provides special rules for dismantled or nonassembled articles;[212] accessories, spare parts, and tools;[213] and sets.[214]

Annex II lists products that are temporarily excluded from GSP treatment.[215]

---

211. (a) operations to ensure the preservation of products in good condition during transport and storage (ventilation, spreading out, drying, chilling, placing in salt, sulphur dioxide or other aqueous solutions, removal of damaged parts, and like operations);

(b) simple operations consisting of removal of dust, sifting or screening, sorting, classifying, matching (including the making-up of sets of articles), washing, painting, cutting up;

(c) (i) changes of packing and breaking up and assembly of consignments,

(ii) simple placing in bottles, flasks, bags, cases, boxes, fixing on cards or boards, etc., and all other simple packing operations;

(d) the affixing of marks, labels or other like distinguishing signs on products or their packaging;

(e) simple mixing of products, whether or not of different kinds, where one or more components of the mixture do not meet the conditions laid down in this Regulation to enable them to be considered as originating products;

(f) simple assembly of parts of products to constitute a complete product;

(g) a combination of two or more operations specified in (a) to (f);

(h) slaughter of animals.

212. Article 7(4) provides: "without prejudice to Article 3(4) where, at the *request of the person declaring the goods* at the customs, a dismantled or non-assembled article falling within Chapter 84 or 85 of the harmonized system is imported by instalments on the conditions laid down by the appropriate authorities, it shall be *considered to be a single article* and a certificate of origin Form A may be submitted for the whole article upon importation of the first instalment." Ibid., at 5 (emphasis added).

213. Article 7(5) provides: "Accessories, spare parts and tools dispatched with a piece of equipment, machine, apparatus or vehicle which are part of the normal equipment and included in the price thereof or are not separately invoiced shall be regarded as one with the piece of equipment, machine, apparatus or vehicle in question."

214. Article 7(6) provides: "Sets in sense of the general rule 3 of the harmonized system shall be regarded as originating when all component articles are originating products. Nevertheless, when a set is composed of originating and non-originating articles, the set as a whole shall be regarded as originating provided that the value of the non-originating articles does not exceed 15% of the value of the set."

215. Mainly petroleum derivates. *Supra* note 206, at 14.

4.2.1.2. Specific Processing Requirements

The specific processing requirements set forth in Annex III concerning a substantial list of products are expressed in variety of forms: as purely technical requirements, general value-added tests, value-added test combined with additional restrictions and obligatory inputs, specific input restrictions on certain nonoriginating ingredients or requirements of specific originating inputs, change of heading tests with the possibility to use a limited amount of materials from the same heading, etc.

The following are examples of simple technical tests: ex 4102 raw skins of sheep or lambs, without wool on: removal of wool from sheep or lamb skins, with wool on;[216] ex 9614 smoking pipes or pipe bowls: manufacture from roughly shaped blocks.[217]

The simple value added tests do not require a uniform percentage of value added. For some products, the value added required is 50 percent, for example, ex 2520 plasters specially prepared for dentistry[218] and ex 4820 letter pads:[219] manufacture in which the value of all the (nonoriginating) materials used does not exceed 50 percent of the exworks price of the product.

For other products the value added required is 60 percent, for example, 8408 compression-ignition internal combustion piston engines (diesel or semidiesel engines)[220] and 8469 to 8472 office machines (for example, typewriters, calculating machines, automatic data processing machines, duplicating machines, and stapling machines):[221] manufacture in which the value added of all the (nonoriginating) materials used does not exceed 40 percent of the exworks price of the product.

For certain products, a value-added test with additional restrictions applies. This test can be a value added test combined with a value of parts test and obligatory inputs. For example, 8520 magnetic tape recorders and other sound recording apparatus, whether or not incorporating a sound reproducing device: manufacture in which the value of all the materials used does not exceed 40 percent of the exworks price of the product, where the value of all the

---

216. Ibid., at 31.

217. Ibid., at 58.

218. Ibid., at 24.

219. Ibid., at 33.

220. Ibid., at 45.

221. Ibid., at 47.

nonoriginating materials used does not exceed the value of the originating materials used and all the transistors of heading No 8541 used are originating products.[222]

For some products specific restrictions on certain nonoriginating inputs apply, or specific requirements for originating inputs are provided. For example, ex 2208 whiskies of an alcoholic strength by volume of less than 50 percent volume: manufacture in which the value of any (nonoriginating) cereal based spirits used does not exceed 15 percent of the exworks price of the product[223] and, for example, 2402 cigars, cheroots, cigarillos, and cigarettes of tobacco or tobacco substitutes: manufacture in which at least 70 percent by weight of the unmanufactured tobacco or tobacco refuse of heading No 2401 used must already be originating.[224]

For some products a more lenient change of tariff heading test applies. For example, the change of tariff heading test is softened by allowing limited use of materials of the same heading, as for example Chapter 34, soap, organic surface-active agents, washing preparations, etc.: manufacture in which all the materials used are classified within a heading other than that of the product. However, materials classified within the same heading may be used provided their value does not exceed 20 percent of the exworks price of the product.[225]

With regard to the calculation of the value of nonoriginating materials as required in some of the tests used in Annex III, Article 4(1) specifies that the term *value* in the List in Annex III shall mean the customs value at the time of the import of the nonoriginating materials used or, if this is not known and cannot be ascertained, the first ascertainable price paid for the materials in the country concerned.[226] However, as is clear from the introductory notes to Annex III, this principle is not absolute in that it does not exclude operations performed in the country of import that might have already conferred a different origin to some of the materials or parts used in the production of the

---

222. Ibid., at 48.

223. Ibid., at 24.

224. Ibid., at 24.

225. Ibid., at 28.

226. Ibid., at 3.

product.[227] To illustrate this important principle, one can refer to the example given in Note 3.4. of the introductory notes to Annex III:

For example, an engine of heading No 8407, for which the rule states that the value of the non-originating materials which may be incorporated may not exceed 40% of the ex-works price, is made from "other alloy steel roughly shaped by forging" of heading No 7224. If this forging has been forged in the country concerned from a non-originating ingot then the forging has already acquired origin by virtue of the rule for heading No ex 7224 in the list. It can then count as originating in the value calculation for the engine regardless of whether it was produced in the same factory or another. The value of the non-originating ingot is thus not taken into account when adding up the value of the non-originating materials used.[228]

This principle has the advantage that a certain portion of nonoriginating material value — the materials having undergone sufficient processing to change their origin — may already be fully counted as originating value.

4.2.1.3. Origin Certificates and Administrative Cooperation

Articles 7, 8, 9, 12, 13, and 15 to 32 relate to the use of origin certificates and establish a procedure of administrative cooperation with the authorities of the exporting countries.

The basic outline of the system is as follows. To benefit from GSP treatment an origin certificate (form A or form APR)[229] has to be presented issued by the customs authorities or other governmental authorities of the

---

227. It would seem that this is a difference with the practice of the EC Commission in nonpreferential origin determinations, where the percentage of value added is typically calculated as exworks price minus the value of nonoriginating (imported) parts and materials divided by the exworks price and multiplied by 100. This approach ignores possible changes in the origin of processed parts and materials in the country where the last processing operations take place.

228. *Supra* note 206, at 16.

229. The requirements concerning form A are laid down in Articles 16 to 24. Ibid., 6 to 8. The requirements concerning form APR (used for smaller consignments sent by post, Article 7(2)) are provided for in Article 25.

exporting beneficiary country.[230]

The customs authorities in the Community can request verifications with regard to the authenticity or accuracy of these forms from the issuing authorities in the beneficiary exporting countries.[231] The authorities in the beneficiary country shall communicate the results of these verifications within a maximum of six months.[232] If, in case of reasonable doubt, there is no reply or if the reply does not contain sufficient information to determine the authenticity of the document in question or the real origin of the products, a second communication shall be sent to the authorities. If a negative answer or no satisfactory answer is received at the latest within four months, the Communities' customs authorities shall refuse, except in the case of force majeure or exceptional circumstances, any benefit from the generalized preferences.[233]

---

230. "The beneficiary countries shall send the Commission the names and addresses of the governmental authorities who may issue certificates of origin together with specimens of stamps used by these authorities. The Commission then forwards these to the Member States." Ibid., Article 26, at 8. Article 27(3) specifies that "For purposes of subsequent verification of certificates of origin Form A, copies of the certificates as well as any export documents referring to them shall be kept for at least two years by the appropriate governmental authority in the exporting beneficiary country."

231. Article 13 provides: "1. Subsequent verifications of certificates Form A and Form APR shall be carried out at random or whenever the customs authorities in the Community have reasonable doubt as to the authenticity to [sic] the document or as to the accuracy of the information regarding the true origin of the products in question. 2. [For this purpose] the customs authorities in the Community shall return the certificate Form A or the Form APR to the appropriate governmental authority in the exporting beneficiary country, giving where appropriate the reasons to form or substance for an inquiry. If the invoice has been submitted, such invoice or a copy thereof shall be attached to Form APR. The customs authorities shall also forward any information that has been obtained suggesting that the particulars given on the said certificate are inaccurate." Ibid., at 6.

232. Article 27, which further specifies that "the results must be such as to establish whether the certificate of origin Form A or the Form APR in question applies to the products actually exported and whether these products were in fact eligible to benefit from the tariff preferences specified in Article 1."

233. Article 27(2). Ibid., at 8, 9.

4.3. Interpretation by the European Court of Justice, the Origin Committee, and the Commission

4.3.1. Interpretation by the European Court of Justice

In *Amministrazione delle Finanze*[234] the court was requested to rule on the validity of the recovery of duties following a verification procedure under the GSP scheme.

The defendant had imported various lots of transistor radios from Hong Kong, stated to be originating products according to a GSP certificate of origin (Form A), and obtained customs clearance of these goods based on the GSP scheme. A subsequent verification procedure by the Italian authorities with the Hong Kong authorities under the Article 13 procedure of the GSP rules of origin regulation[235] revealed that these products were not originating products, and the Italian authorities required the importer to pay the appropriate duties unpaid on importation.[236]

The question before the court was whether according to Article 13, this verification could be undertaken by the customs authorities of an importing Member State after having permitted without reserve the final importation of goods and the application of the preferential tariff treatment.

The court held that the subsequent verification at random[237] provided for in Article 13 can only take place after the production of the certificate of origin and customs clearance, which according to article 6 automatically

---

234. *Amministrazione delle Finanze v. Ciro Acampora* Case 827/79 (1980) ECR 3,731.

235. At that time Commission Regulation No 1371/71 of 30 June 1971 on the definition of the concept of originating products for the purpose of the tariff preferences granted by the EEC to certain products of developing countries O.J. (1971) L 146/1. The language of Article 13 remained unchanged in the currently applicable Commission Regulation (EEC) No 693/88 of 4 March 1988 on the definition of the concept of originating products for purposes of the application of tariff preferences granted by the European Economic Community in respect of certain products from developing countries, O.J. (1988) L 77/1.

236. *Amministrazione delle Finanze, supra* note 234, at 3,742, 3,743.

237. The court distinguished between two types of verifications provided for by Article 13. "Verifications at random" and verifications when the customs authorities have reasonable doubt about the authenticity of the documents or the accuracy of the information regarding the true origin of the goods in question or their components. In the latter case, article 13(2) provides that if the customs authorities decide, in case of doubt, to *suspend* the application of the provisions on tariff preferences while awaiting the results of the verification, they "shall offer to release the goods to the importer subject to any *precautionary measures* judged necessary." Ibid., at 3,744. The court would seem to have concluded that the case brought before it, concerned a "verification at random."

follows the production of the certificate when there has been nothing to cast initial doubt on the authenticity of the certificate. The court further noted:

> Moreover, for the purpose of subsequent verification of the certificates of origin of Form A, Article 30 of the regulation provides that "the competent governmental authorities of the exporting country must keep the export documents, or copies of certificates used in place thereof, for two years", which necessarily implies the possibility of effective verification during that time.[238]

Hence the court confirmed that verification could take place after final importation of the goods without reserve and that if the verification is negative, payment of duties could be demanded.

The case *Rapides Savoyards*[239] concerned the use of exchanges rates for the calculation of value-added requirements in the EFTA preferential origin rules.

The plaintiff had imported a consignment of ballpoint pens from Switzerland that had the required certificate of Swiss origin issued by the Swiss authorities for obtaining EFTA preferential duty treatment. The ballpoint pens had been manufactured in Switzerland of components of U.S. origin. The applicable preferential origin rule provided for a maximum of 5 percent of nonoriginating components for products to obtain Swiss origin. The French customs analyzed the value of the product on importation to France and according to their calculations the value of nonoriginating components

---

238. Ibid., at 3,745. According to the defendant, the case raised a question of a moral nature: the irregularity was committed "in a country some thousands kilometres from the importer's place of business" and the official responsible for checking the regularity of certificates had certified the transaction. Thus the Italian importer, who had neither power, duty, or opportunity to check the regularity of the certificates, was "just a victim of possible duplicity committed in Hong Kong." Ibid., at 3,734. To this the court replied, "It must be recognized that the possibility of checking after importation without the importer's having been previously warned may cause him difficulties when in good faith he has thought he was importing goods benefitting from tariff preferences in reliance on certificates which, unbeknown to him, were incorrect or falsified. It must however be pointed out that in the first place the Community does not have to bear the adverse consequences of the wrongful acts of suppliers of its nationals, in the second place the importer can attempt to obtain compensation from the perpetrator of the fraud and in the third place, in calculating the benefits from trade in goods likely to enjoy tariff preferences, a prudent trader aware of the rules must be able to assess the risks inherent in the market which he is considering and accept them as normal trade risks." Ibid., at 3,745.

239. *Les rapides Savoyards Sàrl and others v. Directeur Général des Douanes et Droits Indirects* Case 218/83 (1984) ECR 3,105.

exceeded 5 percent.[240]

The dispute between the parties concerned the calculation of the value of these nonoriginating components and in particular the use of the exchange rate to convert the value in U.S. dollars of the imported U.S. components. The French customs authorities took the position that according to French customs law the exchange rate on the day of the importation of the finished product into France had to be used. The plaintiffs argued that the exchange rate on the day the components were imported should have been used.[241]

The court ruled that

[s]ince the goods in question were assembled in Switzerland, it is for the Swiss authorities, in accordance with Protocol No 3, to establish the origin of products intended to be exported to the Community. In consequence, the customs rules and the exchange rules of the Swiss Confederation applied to the determination of the elements involved in the calculation of the values used to establish whether or not the product in question could be considered to be a product originating in Switzerland. In particular, it was for those authorities to determine the customs value of components imported from a third country, at the time referred to in the first indent of Article 6(1) of Protocol No 3, namely the *time of the importation of those components* into Switzerland and, at the same time, to carry out the exchange operations in accordance with their national rules.[242]

On the basis of an analysis of the agreement between the EEC and the Swiss confederation, the court considered that the assessment of the elements used in determining the origin of a product and, accordingly, in determining whether it is eligible for the preferential treatment provided for by the agreement, is the responsibility of the customs authorities of the state exporting the finished product and should not be challenged by the customs authorities of the importing country.[243]

---

240. Ibid., at 3,116, 3,117.

241. Ibid., at 3,118.

242. Ibid., at 3,124, 3,125. (emphasis added)

243. The Court stated that "It follows from all the provisions that the determination of the origin of goods according to Protocol No 3 is based on a division of powers between the customs authorities of the parties to the free-trade Agreement inasmuch as origin is established by the authorities of the exporting country and the proper working of that system is monitored jointly by the authorities concerned on both sides. That system is justified by the fact that the authorities of the exporting Sate are in the best position to verify directly the facts which

In *S.R. Industries*[244] the question before the court essentially was whether preferential rules of origin for GSP purposes could be more strict than nonpreferential rules of origin.

S.R. Industries had imported sails from Hong Kong that had been manufactured in Hong Kong from fabric imported from Japan. According to nonpreferential origin rules, the sails were considered of Hong Kong origin.[245] The preferential rule of origin for GSP purposes, however, required "manufacture from single unbleached yarn," which meant that the sails in question could not be considered to have originated in Hong Kong for GSP purposes.[246]

S.R. Industries essentially argued that the preferential rules of origin for products from developing countries must be established in favor of those countries in derogation of the nonpreferential origin rules and hence could not be more strict than nonpreferential origin rules.[247]

The court, however, stated that the Commission may

[a]pply the concept of the origin of goods in a different and stricter manner in the field of generalized tariff preferences than in the framework of the common rules drawn up by Regulation No 802/68. Such an application may, in fact, be necessary to attain the objective of the generalized tariff preferences of ensuring that the preferences benefit only industries which are established in developing countries and which carry out the main

---

determine origin; moreover, it has the advantage of producing certain and uniform results regarding the identification of the origin of goods and of thereby avoiding deflections of trade and distortions of competition in trade. However, that mechanism can function only if the customs authorities of the importing country accept the determination legally made by the authorities of the exporting country." Ibid., at 3,123, 3,124.

244. *S.R. Industries v. Administration des douanes* Case 385/85 (1986) ECR 2,929.

245. The nonpreferential product-specific rule at that time, Commission Regulation (EEC) No 1520/79 of 20 july 1979 amending in respect of sails and tents Regulation (EEC) No 749/78, O.J. (1979) L 185/16, provided that in the case of the manufacture of sails and tents by cutting and making up from fabric, it is considered that such products have undergone one complete process and accordingly had acquired origin.

246. *S.R. Industries, supra* note 244, at 2,940.

247. Ibid., at 2,932. In the opinion of Advocate General Sir Gordon Slynn it was also noted that "It is suggested on behalf of the company that it has not been shown that any industry in the Community needs protection in respect of these sails and it is said, also, that the Commission was not sufficiently generous in the approach it adopted in Regulation 3749/83. Those seem to me to be entirely matters for the Commission and within its discretion."

manufacturing processes in those countries. In laying down the relevant definition of the concept of the origin of goods, the Commission has consequently not exceeded the limits of [its] discretion.[248]

4.3.2.   Interpretation by Administrative Agencies

The substantive rules adopted by the Commission in accordance with the opinion of the Origin Committee, for example, in the area of GSP rules of origin have already been discussed above.

The EC authorities are currently considering a major review of the EC GSP system. In a communication to the Council called "Generalized System of Preferences: guidelines for the 1990s,"[249] the EC Commission analyzed the deficiencies of the current EC system.[250] With regard to the rules of origin the document states:

Originally intended to encourage greater industrialization in developing countries, the origin rules define the substantial processing necessary for the acquisition of originating status. Most beneficiary countries have been unable to achieve the degree of processing required for certain products and have accordingly been unable to benefit from the preferences. This is particularly true for the least developed countries and in the textiles and electronics sectors. The particularly rapid development of intra-industrial trade, as opposed to inter-industrial trade, signals a trend for the production to be spread over several countries which runs counter to the vertical integration required by certain origin rules. It is therefore essential to adapt the rules to modern international trade practice, without forgetting the need to reserve preferential treatment for those countries which need it and for which it is intended.[251]

In the GSP scheme announced for 1992, the changes proposed by the

---

248. Ibid., at 2,942.

249. COM (90) 329 final.

250. Among others, diversity in the level of the development of beneficiary countries, the unpredictability of the preferences that are annually renewed, unsatisfactory operation of the quota and fixed ceiling systems, etc.

251. *See supra* note 249. *See also* Report of the Committee on Development and Cooperation on the Communication from the Commission to the Council concerning the Generalized System of Preferences: Guidelines for the 1990s, 29 November 1990, European Parliament, Session Documents, DOC EN\RR\100266.

Commission were not yet implemented.

Another major EC preferential trade scheme, namely the agreement with the EFTA countries, is currently also subject to a major overhaul in the context of the negotiations on the European Economic Space.

4.4. Concluding Remarks

The EC preferential rules of origin are fairly complex. While contrary to the nonpreferential rules of origin, they have the advantage of being rather precise; grasping the applicable rules, including cumulation rules, may mean quite an effort for exporters and certifying authorities in third countries. A simplification of the scheme is desirable.

Second, the preferential origin rules in respect of certain products are clearly too demanding. In view of the general lowering of tariff levels following the successive GATT Rounds, the benefit conferred by the preferential schemes in certain cases becomes marginal in comparison with the administrative workload and cost to plan the product mix to comply with the preferential origin rules.

For example, a study in connection with the EC EFTA agreement suggest that the cost of the border formalities to determine the origin of products amounts to at least 3 percent of the value of the goods concerned.[252] Although the same study would seem to suggest that about 75 percent of EC EFTA trade benefits from the preferential trade regime,[253] the use of tariff preferences under other schemes such as the GSP scheme would appear to remain at an unsatisfactory low level. Only 21 percent of the eligible imports from GSP beneficiary countries into the European Community actually benefit from GSP tariff preferences.[254]

The preferential rules of origin are clearly lacking uniformity in standards

---

252. J. Herin, Rules of origin and differences between tariff levels in EFTA and in the EC, Occasional paper No. 13, European Free Trade Association, 10 February 1986, at 16.

253. Ibid., at 6.

254. Report of the Committee on Development and Cooperation on the communication from the Commission to the Council concerning the Generalized system of preferences: guidelines for the 1990s, 29 November 1990, European Parliament Session Documents, DOC\EN\RR\100266, at 8 (30 percent of 70 percent of imports from eligible countries that qualify in principle for GSP treatment); *see also* R. Langhammer & A. Sapir, Economic Impact of Generalized Tariff Preferences (1987).

and are considerably more strict for certain products than for others.[255] Since they are the result of negotiated or unilaterally extended tariff preferences, a protectionist approach for sensitive products seems hardly avoidable, be it to the detriment of the consistency of the schemes.

5. Origin Rules and Antidumping[256]

In the EC, origin rules have played an important role in antidumping proceedings in defining the scope of antidumping duties, anticircumvention measures and the delineation of the domestic industry.

5.1. Origin Rules and the Scope of Antidumping Duties

The currently applicable Council Regulation (EEC) No. 2423/88[257] (the EC Antidumping Regulation) would seem to provide that both the country of export and the country of origin can be used as a yardstick in applying antidumping measures.[258]

---

255. For example, Annex III of Regulation 693/88, *supra* note 235, provides for 8469 to 8472, Office machines (for example, typewriters, calculating machines, automatic data processing machines, duplicating machines, stapling machines): manufacture in which the value of all the materials used does not exceed 40% of the ex-works price of the product at 47. Considerably more strict is the requirement for 8528 Television receivers: manufacture in which the value of all the materials used does not exceed 40% of the ex-works price of the product, where within the above limit, the (non-originating) materials classified within heading No 8529 are only used up to a value of 5% of the ex-works price of the product, where the value of all the non-originating materials used does not exceed the value of the originating materials used, and all the transistors of heading No 8541 used are originating products, at 50.

256. For a general discussion *see* Waer, *Multinational enterprises and the European Communities' External Commercial Policy*, 32 Journal of Behavioral and Social Sciences, 12 (1990); Vermulst and Waer, *European Community Rules of Origin as Commercial Policy Instruments?*, 24:3 Journal of World Trade 54, at 74 (1990); Vermulst and Waer, *Anti-diversion Rules in Anti-dumping Proceedings: Interface or Shortcircuit for the Management of Interdependence*, 11 Michigan Journal of International Law 1,119 (1990).

257. Council Regulation (EEC) No. 2423/88 of 11 July 1988 on protection against dumped or subsidized imports from countries not members of the European Economic Community, O.J. (1988) L 209/1.

258. With regard to the definition of dumping, in particular the determination of normal value, Article 6 of the EC Anti-dumping Regulation incorporates the transshipment provision of Article 2:3 of the GATT Anti-dumping Code. It should be noted that the EC Anti-dumping Regulation is not always carefully drafted to maintain the distinction between the country of export and the country of origin. For example, Article 13 (10) containing the

The EC Antidumping Regulation is somewhat vague regarding the scope of antidumping investigations. With regard to the initiation of an antidumping proceeding, the regulation requires that the official notice of initiation "shall indicate the product and countries concerned."

Although in the early stages of EC antidumping enforcement some cases appear to have been initiated against products "exported from" certain countries,[259] it has been the consistent practice of the EC authorities to always initiate cases against products "originating" in certain countries.

One notable exception was the *Video Recorder* case, which was only initiated against two Japanese producers, Funai and Orion, and not against all products originating from Japan. The Commission justified its approach with the following reasoning:

> The Commission is not legally required to always initiate anti-dumping proceedings against all exporters in a country concerned. There is nothing in Community law that requires the Commission to extend the scope of the investigation to all imports from a given country.

> It is the Commission's practice to open investigations against all imports from a given country because, in most cases, the evidence available suggests that all imports from a certain country are dumped and are causing material injury. In the present case, not only did the evidence available not show this to be the case, but the complainant had expressly limited the complaint to certain exporters.[260]

---

anticircumvention provision for assembly operations within the European Community, refers with regard to the value of parts test to value of parts *"originating in the country of exportation* of the product subject to the anti-dumping duty" (emphasis added). Article 3(1) concerning subsidies provides that: "A countervailing duty may be imposed for the purpose of offsetting any subsidy bestowed, directly or indirectly, in the *country of origin or export,* upon the manufacture, production, export or transport of any product whose release for free circulation in the Community causes injury" (emphasis added). However, further in the Regulation concerning the right to disclosure, Article 7(4)(b) provides that: "Exporters and importers of the product subject to investigation and, *in the case of subsidization, the representatives of the country of origin,* may request to be informed of the essential facts and considerations on the basis of which it is intended to recommend the imposition of definitive duties or the definitive collection of amounts secured by way of a provisional duty" (emphasis added).

259. This was done most likely inadvertently. *See Sisal Cords* (Cuba), O.J. (1970), C 133/23; *Ammonium Nitrate Fertilizer* (Yugoslavia), O.J. (1971), C 103/6; and the ambiguous wordings in *Stockings* (Korea), O.J. (1974), C 25/2; *Stockings* (Taiwan), O.J. (1974), C 25/3.

260. *Video Cassette Recorders* (Japan, Korea), O.J. (1988), L 40/5 (provisional duties).

Article 13 (2) provides that regulations imposing provisional or definitive duties "shall indicate in particular the amount and type of duty imposed, the product covered, *the country of origin or export*, the name of the supplier, if practicable, and the reasons on which the Regulation is based."

Article 13 (7) further provides:

In the absence of any special provisions to the contrary adopted when a definitive or provisional anti-dumping or countervailing duty was imposed, *the rules on the common definition of the concept of origin and the relevant common implementing provisions shall apply.*

This article empowers the EC authorities to apply antidumping duties while derogating from the common rules of origin and its implementing provisions.

In EC antidumping practice, origin issues were dealt with in the following cases. In *Phenol*, one U.S. exporter claimed that its phenol exports to the Community were outside the scope of the antidumping investigation against imports of Phenol originating in the United States because they were manufactured from cumene of Community origin, which, in view of the small value added to it in the United States, *retained its Community origin*. The Commission considered that

[i]n accordance with Article 5 of Council Regulation (EEC) No. 802/68 of 27 June 1968 on the common definition of the concept of the origin of goods, the phenol exported by the company is of American origin because the last process by which it becomes a new product takes place in the USA; whereas, moreover, upon entering the products for consumption in the Community the company itself declares the products to be of American origin.[261]

In *Ballbearings*, the Commission terminated the proceeding initiated against products originating in Thailand, on a finding that the products produced there were not of Thai origin. The Commission stated:

The investigation has established that, during the period investigated, imports of the product in question were declared, for customs purposes, as being of Thai origin and were sold in the Community on this basis.
Pursuant to Commission regulation (EEC) No 1836/78 (the product

---

261. *Phenol* (U.S.), O.J. (1982) L 12/1. Although not extensively discussed in the regulation, it is interesting to note that the Commission apparently disregarded the argument that the value added was small and applied a technical origin test.

specific origin rule for ballbearings), these ball bearings originate in the country in which assembly preceded by heat treatment, grinding and polishing of the inner and outer rings takes place.

Although the ball bearings referred to above were shipped from Thailand to the Community, it was ascertained during the investigation that the operations carried out in Thailand were not sufficient to confer Thai origin on the products within the meaning of Commission Regulation (EEC) No 1836/78.[262]

Also in *Typewriters*, the Commission terminated the proceeding opened against products originating in Taiwan on a finding that the production activities carried out by Brother in Taiwan were not sufficient to confer Taiwanese origin on the products.[263]

As a result of these findings the products assembled in Thailand and Taiwan by Japanese manufacturers were considered to be of Japanese origin and therefore de facto subjected to the antidumping duties imposed with respect to such products originating in Japan.

In the proceeding on small screen color televisions the Commission first initiated an antidumping proceeding with regard to televisions originating in South Korea.[264] The Commission decided nine months later to extend the proceeding to small screen color televisions originating in Hong Kong and China.[265] By the time the Commission had completed its provisional investigation and was ready to publish its provisional results in the Korean proceeding, it had become apparent that some of the Hong Kong manufacturers in fact procured color picture tubes and other important components from Korea for their production of color televisions in Hong Kong. Consequently, there was a risk that such Hong Kong products might be treated by the customs authorities in the EC Member States as being of Korean origin and be subjected to the residual duty of 19.6 percent to be imposed in the Korean provisional determination.

It was argued that this result would effectively have penalized the Hong Kong producers concerned for the dumping of their Korean exporters. It would also have deprived such producers (who had already decided to

---

262. *Ballbearings* (Thailand), O.J. (1985) L 59/30.

263. *Typewriters* (Taiwan), O.J. (1986) L 140/52; which later resulted in the *Brother* case, extensively discussed *supra*.

264. *Small screen colour televisions* (Korea), O.J. C 44/2 (notice of initiation) (1988).

265. *Small screen colour televisions* (Hong Kong and China), O.J.(1988) C 288/13.

cooperate in the *Hong Kong* proceeding and incurred significant costs in the process) of the opportunity to have their own dumping and injury margins, based on an investigation into *their* pricing policies and costs. Finally, it inadvertently would have discriminated such producers vis-à-vis other Hong Kong and Chinese producers who had sourced their color picture tubes from other countries such as Japan.

The Commission took the remarkable step in the regulation imposing provisional duties on Korean exports of excluding from the scope of the application of the Korean determination SCTV exports of — specifically mentioned — Hong Kong producers who had decided to cooperate in the Hong Kong and China proceeding, irrespective of the origin of such products:

[A] supplementary proceeding has been opened in respect of SCTVs from Hong Kong and from the People's Republic of China. During the investigation doubts have been raised as to the origin for Community customs purposes of this product when manufactured and exported by Hong Kong companies. In response to requests by certain exporters and their representatives, and in view of the fact that the above-mentioned proceeding is still open and findings are not complete, the Commission has decided that the Hong Kong exporters currently cooperating with its investigation should — in the event that Korean origin should be attributed to any of their exports of SCTVs to the Community — be excluded from the application of the present provisional duty. It is emphasized that this exclusion is strictly temporary and provisional, and without prejudice to any determination of the origin for customs purposes of SCTVs manufactured in Hong Kong. The scope of this exclusion is subject to revision in the light of the outcome of the investigation at present being carried out or in any other procedure which may be undertaken relevant to this question.[266]

The Commission however came back on its steps in its proposal to the Council for the regulation imposing definitive duties. There it was stated:

[t]he Commission . . . had decided to exclude on a strictly temporary basis, certain Hong Kong exporters from the scope of the provisional duty, in the event that Korean origin should be attributed to any of their exports of SCTVs to the Community. This provision was made at the request of Hong Kong exporters and their representatives. It has been challenged by the complainants, and by a Korean producer, who argued that the derogation

---

266. O.J. (1989) L 314/16.

from the normal application of origin rules that the provision implies is incorrect and discriminatory towards Korean exporters. The Commission considers, in the light of the facts now available to it, that this derogation is not justified and should not be prolonged beyond the period of provisional duty on SCTVs originating in Korea.[267]

The SCTV case is remarkable in that it effectively is a story of certain Hong Kong producers cooperating in the wrong procedure. Indeed, the Hong Kong producers manufacturing televisions of Korean origin should have participated in the case against products originating in Korea and then would have obtained their own dumping duty for Korean origin products rather than falling under the residual duty.

In the regulation imposing provisional duties on products originating in Hong Kong, the Commission moreover clearly expressed its doubts about the correctness of the origin declarations made by certain Hong Kong producers and stated:

[I]t was found that there was no production in Hong Kong of the major components used in SCTV manufacturing, such as colour picture tubes, fly back transformers, etc. Components were imported from several sources, among which figured Korea principally, and to a lesser extent, Japan. Given the above, and the fact that it has not been possible for the Commission to verify the correctness or otherwise of the claimed origin during the course of the proceedings, it cannot be excluded that customs authorities, in the event of a check carried out on the basis of the abovementioned Community origin rules, may determine an origin which differs from that which is declared.[268]

In DRAMs from Japan,[269] the Commission decided to treat wafers and dice as "like products" to assembled DRAMs. This technical "like product" definition allowed the Commission to bring processed wafers and dice within the scope of the proceeding of the finished product, (i.e. the DRAM). The question then arose what to do with DRAMs assembled in third countries from processed wafers and dice produced in Japan:

---

267. *Small Screen Colour Television Receivers* (Korea), O.J. (1990), L 107/56.

268. Ibid., at 33.

269. *Certain types of electronic microcircuits known as DRAMs (dynamic random access memories)* (Japan), O.J. (1990) L 20/5.

The Commission also requested information in respect of DRAMs assembled in third countries from processed wafers and dice produced in Japan for subsequent importation into the Community EC [*sic*]. The information gathered revealed that the quantities of such products imported into the Community at the time were relatively small. The Commission decided, therefore, for the purpose of its preliminary findings, not to investigate the assembly operations of such imports.[270]

As the proceeding had been opened[271] with respect to Japan only, this request for information could be construed as an implicit decision by the Commission that DRAMs assembled in third countries from processed wafers and dice in Japan are to be considered as originating in Japan. The preliminary decision not to further investigate such third country production operations, on the other hand, seemed more based on practical considerations.

Finally it is interesting to note that for potassium permanganate[272] the Commission decided not to take into account exports from Taiwan and Hong Kong in its injury analysis because there were indications that such imports did not have Taiwanese respectively Hong Kong origin as "potassium permanganate is not likely to be produced in these countries."

5.2. Origin Rules and Anticircumvention Measures

5.2.1. Article 13 (10) of Regulation 2423/88

When an anti-dumping duty is imposed on a finished product, but not on its parts and components,[273] a producer could try to avoid paying antidumping

---

270. Ibid., at 6-7.

271. It should be noted that when the antidumping proceeding was initiated (9 July 1987), it was not clear how the origin of DRAMs was to be determined. In the meantime (on 3 February 1989), the Commission adopted a regulation on the origin of integrated circuits, ibid., which holds that determinative for the origin of integrated circuits is the process of diffusion (i.e., "the process whereby integrated circuits are formed on a semiconductors substrate by the selective introduction of an appropriate dopant").

272. *Potassium Permanganate* (Czechoslovakia), O.J. (1990) L 42/1.

273. Of course, EC industry is free to bring simultaneous complaints against a finished products and its inputs, see, for example, *Video cassettes* (Hong Kong and Korea), O.J. (1989) L 174/9 (definitive duties), where the case was brought against video cassettes, pancakes, and jumbos, and *Audio cassettes* (Japan, Hong Kong and Korea), O.J. (1989) C 11/9 (notice of initiation), where the case was brought against audio cassettes, pancakes, and jumbos. However, on a determination that jumbos and pancakes and finished cassettes are not "like

duties by importing parts and components and assembling them into the finished product within the Common Market.

Article 2 (a) of the General Rules for the Interpretation of the Combined Nomenclature provides that

> Any reference in a heading to an article shall be taken to include a reference to that article incomplete or unfinished, provided that, as presented, the incomplete or unfinished article has the essential character of the complete or finished article. It shall also be taken to include a reference to that article complete or finished (or falling to be classified as complete or finished by virtue of this rule), presented unassembled or disassembled.[274]

In other words, the EC customs classification rules provide that when a product is imported in an unassembled form and when all or all essential parts for the finished product are imported, these parts fall under the same customs classification heading as the finished product. Subsequently, any antidumping duty imposed on the finished product would then also apply to the parts. "Normal" customs classification rules therefore already seem to contain an anticircumvention provision.

However, it must be admitted that the anticircumvention provision in the customs classification rules has its limits. From a practical point of view, circumvention can be difficult for the national customs administrations to detect if essential parts were shipped separately and entered the Community in different Member States.

In June 1987, the European Community, as the first active user of antidumping laws, introduced a specific anticircumvention provision covering assembly operations in the European Community of products subject to antidumping duties.[275]

---

products," the EC authorities must find that there is dumping and resulting injury on both the finished product and its inputs.

274. Commission Regulation (EEC) No. 2886/89 of 2 October 1989, amending Annex 1 to Council Regulation (EEC) No. 2658/87 on the tariff and statistical nomenclature and on the Common Customs Tariff, O.J. (1989) L 282/1.

275. Council Regulation (EEC) No. 1761/87, O.J. (1987) L 167/9. The amendment was incorporated in the new antidumping Regulation (EEC) No. 2423/88, O.J. (1988) L 209/1. *See* Bellis, Vermulst, and Waer, *Further Changes in the EEC Anti-Dumping Regulation: A Codification of Controversial Methodologies*, 23:2 J.W.T., 21-34 (1989). It should be noted that a similar provision is lacking in the Commission decision No. 2424/88/ECSC of 29 July 1988 on protection against dumped or subsidized imports from countries not members of the

This provision was subsequently attacked by Japan in GATT. A GATT panel held in 1990 that the measures taken by the European Community pursuant to this provision (duties and undertakings) infringed on GATT.[276] Since the GATT panel ruling, the EC anticircumvention provision has remained on the books but is no longer applied. Although the application of this provision now seems to belong to legal history, in the seven proceedings that have been initiated under this provision[277] interesting issues of origin determination have arisen and the solutions adopted might be relevant for future anticircumvention provisions.

Article 13 (10) of the European Community's Anti-Dumping Regulation provided that antidumping duties may also be levied on products assembled within the European Community, provided that the following three — cumulative — conditions have been fulfilled:

1. The producer in the European Community must have a relationship[278] or association[279] with an exporter of the like

---

European Coal and Steel Community, O.J. (1988) L 209/18.

276. For a detailed discussion of the GATT panel report *see* Vermulst and Waer, *Anti-diversion Rules in Anti-dumping Procedures*, supra note 256, at 1,177.

277. In chronological order from the date of initiation: (1) *Electronic typewriters* (assembly operations of Brother, Canon, Matsushita, TEC, Sharp and Silver Seiko), O.J. (1987) C 235/2; (2) *Electronic scales* (assembly operations of TEC Keylard and TEC U.K.), O.J. (1987) C 235/3; (3) *Hydraulic excavators* (assembly operation of Komatsu), O.J. (1987) C 285/4; (4) *Photocopiers* (assembly operations of Canon, Konishiroku, Matsushita, Minolta, Ricoh, Sharp and Toshiba), O.J. (1988) C 44/3; (5) *Ballbearings* (assembly operations of Nippon Seiko and NTN Toyo Bearing), O.J. (1988) C 150/4; (6) *Serial impact dot matrix printers* (assembly operations of Brother, Citizen, Fujitsu, Juki, Matsushita, NEC, OKI, Seiko Epson, Seikosha, Star Micronics and TEC) 0.J. (1988) C 327/8; (7) *Video cassette recorders* (assembly operation of Orion), O.J. (1989) C 172/2.

278. In *Electronic scales*, O.J. (1988) L 101/1 (1988), TEC-Keylard was deemed to be related to TEC because it had substantial capital links and close economic and commercial relations with TEC Japan. In *Photocopiers*, O.J. (1988) L 284/36; L 284/60, a 50 percent shareholding was considered sufficient.

279. Although in *Electronic typewriters*, O.J. (1988) L 101/4, at 5, assembly operations were in one case carried out by an independent company, the Council determined that this did not preclude the application of the parts amendment: "One company, namely Silver Reed International (Europe) Ltd, claimed that it should not be included in this investigation because the assembly operation was not carried out by Silver Reed but by Astec Europe Ltd. However, the investigation revealed that Astec's activities in this context were limited to the mere assembly of all parts of electronic typewriters which were imported and delivered to it at its premises by Silver Reed. These assembled electronic typewriters were then exclusively

product subject to duties,[280]

2. The producer in the European Community must have commenced or substantially increased[281] its production after the commencement of an antidumping proceeding,

3. more than 60 percent of the value[282] of parts or materials used in the EC manufacturing operation must originate in the exporting country subject to antidumping duties.[283]

Besides these three basic conditions, "other circumstances" such as the variable costs incurred in the assembly or production operation, the research and development carried out, and the technology applied within the Community should be considered.[284] In practice, this "other circumstances" criterion has not played a significant role.[285] Investigations have focused on

---

sold on the Community market by the Silver Reed Group. This group bore all costs between importation of the parts and the sale of the finished products. An assembly fee was paid to Astec by the Silver Reed Group but this fee constituted only a small percentage of Silver Reed's total costs of sale. In these circumstances, this assembly operation should be considered as having been carried out by Silver Reed."

280. Since antidumping duties are imposed on products originating in certain countries, EC production facilities of companies that never exported the product concerned to the European Community from the foreign country, can nevertheless be covered by a parts proceeding. *See Electronic typewriters*, O.J. (1988) L 101/4, at 7, where typewriters produced by Matsushita in the United Kingdom were subjected to antidumping duties under the parts amendment even though Matsushita had never exported typewriters from Japan.

281. In *Ballbearings*, O.J. (1989) L 25/90, it was held that increases of respectively 24 percent in one year and 40 percent in two years were substantial, in particular because they had followed a period of stability.

282. Value of parts and materials from the country of export is determined on an "into-EC-factory" basis. This includes cost items such as freight in the exporting country, ocean freight and insurance, customs duties at the EC border, customs clearance costs, and freight in the European Community (from the border to the factory). In addition, as products shipped from the exporting country to the EC production facility involve transactions between related parties, the Commission will want to see evidence that the prices of such products are at arm's length, in other words, cover the cost of manufacture, Selling, General and Administrative Expenses (SGA), and a reasonable profit.

283. Article 13 (10) (a).

284. Ibid.

285. Of course, this might have been so because the Commission found during its investigation that there was little more than simple assembly operations.

the hard and fast 60/40 percent rule.

The application of this value-of-parts rule entailed crucial determinations about the origin of such parts. Problems emerged especially for parts assembled in the European Community (or a third country) from subparts. The question then arose whether such parts must be treated as single parts or whether they must be broken down into subparts. The answer to this question was important because if they are treated as single parts, the value added in the EC production process could perhaps be included in the value of the parts and counted as nonexporting country content. In certain cases, this could decide the origin of the whole parts. Origin of the whole parts depends on where the last substantial transformation or process took place.

Over the seven proceedings initiated, the European Community practice in determining origin, especially of parts or subassemblies manufactured in the EC changed considerably. In the first three cases, i.e., typewriters, scales and excavators, the Commission determined origin on different bases depending on the status of the manufacturer of the parts or subassemblies. Thus, if the parts or subassemblies were manufactured in the European Community by the producer under investigation or by a party related to the producer, the parts or subassemblies were broken down into their subparts (the molecular approach) and subassembly costs were always excluded.[286] If the parts or subassemblies were manufactured in the European Community by an independent producer, a further distinction was made: If the parts or subassemblies as assembled had acquired European origin, the whole parts or subassemblies would be treated as European even though they might have contained subparts from other countries.[287] If, on the other hand, the parts or subassemblies had not acquired European origin in the production process, the Commission adopted a case-by-case approach whereby it sometimes broke

---

286. For example, in *Electronic scales*, O.J. (1988) L 101/29: "TEC-Keylard requested that the 'transformation costs' of some subassemblies incurred in its own factory should be included in the value of EEC parts. This request, however, cannot be granted because the 'transformation costs' are part of the total costs of assembly or production, they cannot be included in the value of parts or materials used in the assembly or production operation, but constitute a value added to these parts or materials in the assembly or production process."

287. Ibid, at 29: "TEC-Keylard claimed that some subassembled items used for some models were of Community origin. It was found that these items were assembled in the Community, from parts imported from Japan and from parts purchased in the Community, by an independent Community producer. On the basis of information received from two sources, one being the complainants carrying out virtually identical assembly operations themselves and the other being the company referred to above, it was concluded that these subassemblies did constitute a substantial transformation as required by Article 5 of council Regulation (EEC) No. 802/68. The assembly operation and the manufacture of the components carried out in the Community was of a substantial nature. The item was thus of Community origin."

down the subassemblies into subparts (the molecular approach).[288]

These rules were revised in the photocopiers determinations. In these determinations, the Community institutions focused on the nature of the manufacturing process rather than on that of the producer. Specifically, the authorities distinguished between subassemblies and parts, based on the rule of thumb destruction theory. If a part could be taken apart without destroying any of the subparts (in other words, if the part typically was merely screwed together), it was considered to be a subassembly. Subassemblies were treated in the same way as before, with a distinction being made between subassembly in house[289] or by a related supplier and subassembly by an independent supplier.[290]

If, however, in disassembling a part, one or more of its sub parts would be destroyed, it was treated as a single part, whether it was produced in house, by a related producer, or by an independent producer. The EC authorities determined that with respect to single parts it was appropriate to include subassembly costs in the value of nonexporting country parts to the extent that

288. *Electronic typewriters*, O.J.(1988) L 101/5: Canon claimed that one sub-assembled item which was the most costly individual one used for some models was of Community origin. It was found, however, that this item was assembled in the Community, entirely from parts imported from Japan, by a subsidiary company of a Japanese producer which normally manufactures these products in Japan and supplies Canon's mother company there. On the basis of information received from two other sources, one being an electronic typewriter producer carrying out a virtually identical assembly operation itself and the other being the company referred to above, it was concluded that this sub-assembly did not constitute a substantial process or operation as required by Article 5 of Regulation (EEC) 802/68. The simple assembly operation carried out in the Community was of a basic and unsubstantial nature compared with the manufacture of the components which was performed in Japan. The item was thus not of Community origin."

289. *Photocopiers*, O.J. (1988) L 284/38: "A number of companies requested that the assembly costs of certain subassemblies, incurred in their own factory, should be included in the value of Community parts. This request, however, cannot be granted because the cost of assembly cannot be included in the value of parts or materials used in the assembly or production operations under Article 13 (10) . . . ."

290. Ibid.: "Several companies concerned claimed that certain subassembled items were of Community origin and that, in addition, they should be treated as parts within the meaning of Article 13 (10) . . . . It was found, however, that these items were merely assembled in the Community, mainly from parts imported from Japan, by independent suppliers. On the basis of information obtained from the companies making the claim, it was concluded that this assembly did not constitute a substantial process or operation as required by Article 5 . . . . The simple assembly operation carried out in the Community was of a basic and unsubstantial nature and was not sufficient to confer Community origin."

the whole single part had acquired Community origin.[291] This approach was also followed in the Ball bearings[292] and the Printers[293] proceedings.

In the Printers[294] proceeding, the Community institutions stated explicitly that printed circuit boards constituted single parts,[295] because some companies had argued that printed circuit boards be treated as subassemblies[296] while others had requested that they be treated as single parts.[297] The institutions added that the origin of single parts was determined on the basis of the nonpreferential origin rules of Regulation 802/68. In practice the Commission — by analogy to the specific origin rules adopted radio and television receivers[298] and tape recorders[299] — considers a PCB

---

291. Ibid. It is not completely clear how Community origin is determined. The regulations typically state that such origin is determined on the basis of Regulation 802/68, *supra* note 1. However, the investigation is conducted by officials of Directorate General I, who, with one exception, are not origin experts. In concrete investigations, the Commission has sometimes indicated that it will challenge the European origin of parts if they contain less than 45 percent EC value added. If more than 45 percent EC value is added and the assembly operation is complex, the Commission will normally accept EC origin. EC certificates of origin are not decisive, as the Commission conducts its own investigation in the context of parts proceedings. This is perhaps understandable: in the EC Member States certificates of origin are issued either by customs authorities or (in most cases) by chambers of commerce. Apparently, especially the latter tend to issue certificates of origin rather freely, without always checking whether the substantive conditions for origin have been complied with.

292. *Ball bearings*, O.J. (1989) L 25/90, at 91.

293. *Printers*, O.J. (1989) L 291/52, at 53; L 291/57, at 58.

294. Ibid.

295. *See also Photocopiers*, O.J. (1990) L 34/28 (termination Ricoh Industrie France), where the Commission determined again that printed circuit boards constitute single parts in view of "the nature of their structure."

296. Presumably those companies that overall did not add enough EC value. As a result of the treatment of printed circuit boards as a single part, such companies would lose the value of EC and other nonexporting country components assuming that the Japanese subparts represented the single highest value.

297. Presumably those companies that overall added enough EC value in the EC assembly of printed circuit boards. As a result of the treatment of printed circuit boards as one single part, such companies' printed circuit boards produced in the European Community would be counted as 100 percent European even though they might have contained exporting country subparts.

298. Commission Regulation (EEC) No. 2632/70 on determining the origin of radio and television receivers, *supra* note 144.

to be of EC origin if at least 45 percent value is added in the assembly process in the EC.[299]

While the abolition of the discriminatory treatment of single parts depending on the nature of the assembler was a step in the right direction, the approach with regard to subassemblies produced in house remained bizarre: If the same subassembly processes are performed in house in the exporting country factory, subassembly costs are included in the value of exporting country parts because the value of parts and materials is determined on an into-EC-factory basis.

5.2.2. Third-Country Production

Production migrations to avoid antidumping duties can also be directed towards third countries not (or not yet) covered by antidumping measures for the product.

Circumvention in this context can be countered in two ways. The complaining EC industry can lodge a new antidumping complaint against products originating in third countries. If a proceeding is opened, the EC Commission (Anti-Dumping Division) normally determines whether the products exported from the third countries actually originated in that country. If not, like with ballbearings from Thailand and electronic typewriters from

---

299. Commission Regulation (EEC) No. 861/71 on determining the origin of tape recorders, *supra* note 146.

300. This is one of the sources of friction with the United States. While the assembly or "stuffing" of printed circuit boards is very labor- or capital intensive, it does not in most cases add enough value. Companies that are likely to be the target of a parts investigation therefore scramble to source EC subparts, notably integrated circuits. This development has apparently led to a decrease in American (Texas Instruments) exports of integrated circuits to the European Community. Thus, while the application of the origin rules with respect to printed circuit boards on its face is not discriminatory, in practice it stimulates EC sourcing because a company needs to have the "last substantial process or operation" take place in one country other than the exporting country. As many integrated circuits are manufactured exclusively in Japan, the sourcing of the remaining integrated circuits becomes even more important. Of course, if a company were to decide to stuff its printed circuit boards in the United States and use U.S. integrated circuits, the resulting printed circuit board would be likely to have U.S. origin. For an excellent discussion of these problems, *see EC Sends Conflicting Signals on Clarifying Technical Rules for Circuit Boards*, Inside U.S. Trade, at 3-4 27 October 1989; *see also EC 1992 : An Update on U.S. Views*, Testimony of Peter Allgeier, Assistant USTR for Europe and the Mediterranean, Before the House Foreign Affairs Committee (20 February 1990); Testimony of Eugene MCallister, Assistant Secretary of State for Economic and Business Affairs, Before the Subcommittee on Europe and the Middle East, and Subcommittee on International Economic Policy and Trade, Committee on Foreign Affairs, U.S. House of Representatives (20 February 1990).

Taiwan, the proceeding is terminated and the products may de facto fall under the scope of already existing antidumping measures.

However, the origin of products may also be disputed before the EC Commission (Origin Division). For example, after the imposition of definitive antidumping duties on photocopiers originating in Japan,[301] the origin of photocopiers produced by Ricoh in the United States and by Mita in Hong Kong was challenged.

Following an on-the-spot investigation in California by officials of (Division B.2. of) Directorate-General XXI, the Commission took the view that the photocopiers produced by Ricoh in the United States should be denied U.S. origin. In the absence of a qualified majority on this matter within the Origin Committee and the Council, the Commission enacted Regulation (EEC) No. 207/89 on the origin of photocopiers, which, although couched in general terms, was essentially tailor-made for the Ricoh situation. This regulation provides that the manufacture of photocopiers accompanied by the manufacture of the harness, drums, rollers, side plates, roller bearings, screws, and nuts shall not confer origin.[302]

On the basis of an origin investigation conducted at Mita's Hong Kong premises, the Commission arrived at the conclusion that the photocopiers made by Mita in Hong Kong had Hong Kong origin and advised the members of the Origin Committee accordingly. As the members of the Origin Committee unanimously agreed with the conclusions of the Commission, the case was dealt with informally.

One difficulty with the application of origin rules to determine whether third-country circumvention occurs — besides questions about its GATT legality — is that it does not allow the administering authorities to measure the nature and the level of the relief to the circumstances of the case. Thus, for example, the finding that the photocopiers manufactured by Ricoh in the United States had not acquired U.S. origin — and continued to be of Japanese origin — meant that Ricoh's exports to the EC from its California plant could be subjected to the full Japanese antidumping duty imposed in 1987 in the photocopiers proceeding despite the fact that such photocopiers presumably included a substantial U.S. value added. In other words, antidumping duties were in part levied on U.S. parts, materials, and overheads.

It should be noted that the decision which procedure to apply very much

---

301. O.J. (1987) L 54/12.

302. Commission Regulation (EEC) No. 2971/89 of 11 July 1989 on determining the origin of photocopying apparatus, *supra* note 195. For background information, *see* 1499 European Report, at 19 (27 May 1989); 1513 European Report, at 10 (15 July 1989); 5057 Agence Europe, (14 July 1989); 5058 Agence Europe (15 July 1989).

depends on factual circumstances over which the Commission has little control. If an EC industry brings an antidumping complaint against the product now coming from a third country and the complaint contains sufficient evidence of dumping and resulting injury, (the Anti-Dumping Division in Directorate-General I of) the Commission may open an antidumping proceeding against products originating in that third country. From the point of view of the domestic industry, starting a new antidumping proceeding has the advantage of providing for a "double shot." If in the course of the new antidumping proceeding it is established that the manufacturing operations in the third country are not sufficient to confer origin, the products can effectively fall under the scope of existing measures. If the Commission establishes that the manufacturing operations in the third country do confer origin, an investigation of dumping and injury is also carried out.

Origin investigations, on the other hand, may start as a result of identical products being subjected to different treatment by the EC Member States customs authorities, or as a result of complaints or requests by producers concerned, or for a variety of other reasons the issue may be brought up in the Origin Committee.

Finally it should be noted that the Basic Origin Regulation incorporates a special anticircumvention provision in Article 6 which provides:

Any process or work in respect of which it is established, or in respect of which the facts as ascertained justify the presumption, that its sole object was to circumvent the provisions applicable in the Community or the Member States to goods from specific countries shall in no case be considered, under Article 5, as conferring on the goods thus produced the origin of the country where it is carried out.

In the *Brother* case, the court interpreted this provision as meaning that

[t]he transfer of assembly from the country in which the parts were manufactured to another country in which use is made of existing factories does not in itself justify the presumption that the sole object of the transfer was to circumvent the applicable provisions unless the transfer of assembly coincides with the entry into force of the relevant regulations. In that case, the manufacturer concerned must prove that there were reasonable grounds, other than avoiding the consequences of the provisions in question, for carrying out the assembly operations in the country from which the goods

were exported.[303]

A first point to note is of course that the court left open what can constitute "reasonable grounds" other than the avoidance of the measures in question.[304]

Second, it can be questioned whether Article 6 does not surpass the borderline between circumvention and legitimate avoidance of restrictions. Indeed, the application of Article 6 to de facto apply antidumping duties on products that, according to the Basic Origin Regulation, would otherwise obtain origin in a third country not subject to antidumping duties — without a separate finding of dumping and injury — is a likely violation of GATT.

5.3. The Definition of the Domestic Industry

The GATT Anti-Dumping Code[305] and the EC Anti-Dumping Regulation contain only cryptic requirements concerning the "domestic industry."

Article 4 (5) of the EC Anti-Dumping Regulation provides:

The term "Community industry" shall be interpreted as referring to the Community producers as a whole of the like product or to those of them whose collective output of the products constitutes a major proportion of the total Community production of those products . . . .

Hence, the EC Anti-Dumping Regulation does not provide for a clear requirement that Community production should be determined by the use of the EC rules of origin.

The matter has come up in a number of cases, with respect to the position of certain EC producers or the position of manufacturing bases in the Common Market owned by or having links with producers under investigation for injurious dumping.

---

303. *Brother II, supra* note 32 at para 29. It may be noted that according to the report for the hearing, "The Commission favours a narrow interpretation of Article 6, namely that the circumvention of the applicable provisions must be the exclusive purpose of the process or operation in another country, not just one reason amongst many." Ibid., Report for the Hearing, at 8.

304. *See* Waer and Vermulst, *De toepassing van algemene oorsprongsregels in de Europese Gemeenschap: Een probleemschets naar aanleiding van het Brother arrest,* 38 S.E.W. 435, at 451 (1990).

305. *See* Article 3, Article 4, GATT, Agreement on the Implementation of Article VI of the General Agreement on Tariffs and Trade (1979), BISD, 26 Supp. 171 (1980).

In outboard motors proceeding, several of the Japanese producers accused of dumping questioned whether the major EC complainant, Outboard Marine Belgium, qualified as a European producer. The Commission concluded that under Regulation 802/68 the outboard motors produced by Outboard Marine originated in the Community[306].

In the photocopiers proceeding, the Community institutions had to determine in particular whether Rank Xerox's EC production facilities should be included in the domestic industry.

This case is the only one thus far in which the Community institutions discussed in detail the issue of "domestic production":

In the Netherlands it was found that integrated manufacturing operations were carried out by, or on behalf of, Rank Xerox in the Community. The value added within the Community in these manufacturing operations exceeds 70%. The photocopiers produced by Rank Xerox in the Netherlands have Community origin.

In the United Kingdom, Rank Xerox's products were manufactured on the basis of parts originating predominantly in Japan and to a lesser degree in the Community. However, Rank Xerox had already set in motion concrete plans to replace certain key components of Japanese origin with parts produced in the Community. These plans have materialized in the meantime, leading to a substantial increase in value added within the Community for these low-volume products.

As regards the type of operations carried out in the United Kingdom, these consist of the construction of sub-assemblies for the production line, including the fusers, modules, develop boxes, cassettes, semi-automatic document handlers, optics and other minor assemblies. These operations are completed by the frame assembly and the final mainline assembly of sub-assemblies and components by testing and packing of the photocopiers. Overall, in the reference period, the value added in the Community in the production of Rank Xerox's low-volume photocopiers was between 20% and 35%.

The Commission has examined whether, in view of these facts, Rank Xerox can be considered as a Community producer of segment 1 and 2 copiers within the meaning of Article 4 (5) of Regulation (EEC) 2176/84. The Commission has noted that the Regulation does not lay down precise guidelines in this context. In particular, no threshold has been specified in either Community legislation or in previous cases for the minimum value added that must be respected in order for a producer to qualify as part of

---

306. Outboard motors (Japan), O.J. (1983) L 152/18.

Community industry. Therefore the Commission has been obliged to look at the particularities of the present case.

The first point to note is that the company is a manufacturer of photocopiers in the Community of long standing and one of the largest companies in the market.

Whilst the production operations of Rank Xerox in the United Kingdom were more limited than the activities undertaken at its plant in the Netherlands during the reference period, the company did nonetheless undertake a multiplicity of manufacturing operations necessary in order to produce copiers for the market. In addition, Rank Xerox has been actively engaged in the process of replacing parts from Japan with other key components either of its own manufacture or from subcontractors within the Community.

The investigation showed that, if no protective measures covering segment 1/2 copiers were taken, then the process actively engaged in by Rank Xerox of replacing key parts sourced from Japan with Community-produced supplies would be jeopardized. Article 4 (1) of Regulation (EEC) No. 2176/84 authorizes protective measures in the case of the retardation of the establishment of an industry. If no anti-dumping measures were to be taken in this case, there would be a setback not only to Rank Xerox's future plans on sourcing products from the Community, but also a threat to the process already begun in this area. This might lead to a rupture in the process of building up Rank Xerox's production of low-volume copiers based on parts manufactured in the Community.

In any event, since the like product in the proceeding has been defined to be all photocopiers from personal photocopiers up to and including machines clarified in Dataquest segment 5, it would be inappropriate to analyze whether a Community producer should be part of Community industry just in terms of its production of one model or a limited range of models. This is the case even if, looked at in isolation, there were doubts as to whether Rank Xerox's manufacturing operations in the United Kingdom were sufficient to confer upon it the status of a Community producer in the sense of Article 4 (5) of Regulation (EEC) No. 2176/84, for segment 1/2 copiers. The weighted average value added in the Community for all PPCs manufactured by Rank Xerox in the range segment 1 to segment 4 was in excess of 50% in the reference period. Also the company has a policy of obtaining an increasing proportion of its components from within the Community.[307]

---

307. *Photocopiers* (Japan), O.J. (1987) L 54/22.

For VCRs, the Commission distinguished four groupings of companies producing or assembling VCRs in the Community:

1. fully Community-owned producers
2. joint ventures between European and Japanese companies
3. fully Japanese-owned European production facilities, not targeted by the complaint
4. European production facilities owned by the producers under investigation (Samsung, Goldstar, Funai, and Orion)

The Commission concluded that the second category could definitely be identified as EC producers "given the high level of local content in their products and their long-term commitment to investment and employment in the Community"[308] and left open the question whether the third category constituted part of the Community industry or whether it was merely assembling the products in the Community.[309] The Council essentially sustained by the Commission's conclusions.[310]

If one compares the outboard motors case on the one hand and the photocopiers and VCRs cases on the other hand, there seems to be a clear change in the Commission's methodology. In the former, the Commission essentially applied a strict origin test based on Regulation 802/68. In the latter two cases, however, the Commission appeared to move away from such a test and relied rather on soft criteria such as long-term commitment to investment and employment in the European Community.

For SCTVs[311] the Commission distinguished complainant Community producers who represented some 50 percent of total Community SCTV output (for purposes of the antidumping law "clearly a major proportion of Community production") and "non-Community, mainly Japanese, controlled production which has moved into the Community . . . ."[312]

The Commission did not find it necessary to inquire into the value added in the European Community of such Japanese-owned EC production, which could not be excluded by the related party provision since products originating in Japan were not covered by the proceeding. This was presumably because the complaining EC producers represented 50 percent in any event. It would

---

308. *Video cassette recorders* (Korea, Japan), O.J. (1988) L 240/5.

309. The fourth category was excluded because it embodied related parties. This was therefore an application of the related-party provision of Article 4 (5), first indent.

310. *Video cassette recorders* (Japan and Korea), O.J. (1989) L 57/55 (definitive duties).

311. *Small screen colour televisions* (Korea), O.J. (1989) L 31/1.

312. Ibid., at 8.

have been interesting to see what the European Communities would have done if the Japanese-owned EC production facilities had participated in the proceeding and these would, for example, have shown no signs of injury.

Lastly, the discussion about the definition of the domestic industry in the DRAMs proceeding[313] should be mentioned. The Commission first of all analyzed the manufacturing processes of DRAM production and separated the production of wafer diffusion and sorting (front-end operations) and assembly and testing (back-end operations). The issue was important because at the time, the EC producer (Siemens) intended to perform only the front-end operation in the European Community and the back-end operations would be performed in third countries.

The Commission noted that although "wafer diffusion is from a technological and capital investment point of view more significant than the assembly and testing operations . . . assembly and testing operations can account for a significant part of cost of manufacture."[314] The Commission had even found that "as a ratio of total cost of production, assembly costs are generally significant, and may even exceed in some cases wafer diffusion costs."[315] In the end the Commission avoided making onerous determinations by leaving it open whether there was an established Community industry because in the alternative, there would have been injury through material retardation. The product-specific origin rule for integrated circuits had in the meantime cleared the path for the Community industry to perform testing and assembly operations in third countries while retaining EC origin for their products.

6. Other Problems

6.1. Origin Rules and Quantitative Restrictions

The principle of free movement of goods between EC Member States is one of the pillars of the EEC Treaty.

Article 30 of the EEC Treaty provides as a general rule that "quantitative restrictions on imports and all measures having equivalent effect shall, without prejudice to the following provisions, be prohibited between Member States."

In *Commission v. Italian Republic* the court applied this principle on the import registration requirements for foreign motor vehicles in Italy. The

---

313. *DRAMs* (Japan), O.J. (1990) L 20/5, at 9-10, 16-18.

314. Ibid.

315. Ibid.

registration of a new foreign vehicle was made subject to the production of a certificate of origin of the vehicle issued by the manufacturer and a document indicating the technical specifications of the vehicle. After an Italian court proceeding, this practice continued but only for vehicles from the EEC. As a result, parallel imports were completely paralysed because no certificates of origin had been issued by manufacturers or by the representatives of foreign makes established in Italy. In its order, the president of the court held that this practice constituted a measure that had an effect equivalent to that of quantitative restrictions within the meaning of Article 30 of the EEC Treaty in view of the apparently excessive length of time required for the registration of vehicles imported outside the official distribution networks and from the additional expense resulting from the requirement of a certificate of origin.[316]

The principle of freedom of movement of goods between Member States applies equally to goods originating in the EC Member States and to goods coming from third countries and in free circulation in other Member States (i.e., being imported in other Member States).[317]

An exception to this rule can be found in Article 115 of the EEC Treaty, which provides that the Commission can authorize Member States to take (national) protective measures, including quantitative restrictions.[318] Obviously, for these quantitative restrictions to be effective they need to apply not only to direct imports but also to indirect imports through other EC Member States.

Article 115 authorizations for national quantitative restrictions have been given, among others, to maintain bilateral agreements or practices in place prior to EEC Membership.[319] Most prominent are the measures in the textile

---

316. *Commission v. Italian Republic*, Case 154/85, (1985) ECR 1,753.

317. Article 9 (2) EEC Treaty.

318. *See* Bourgeois, "The Common Commercial Policy — Scope and Nature of the Powers," in Protectionism and the European Community 1, at 8 (1987); Cremona, *The Completion of the Internal Market and the Incomplete Commercial Policy of the European Community* 15 European Law Review, 283 (1990).

319. For example, in the first months of 1990, sixty-four applications for Article 115 authorizations were accepted. The main beneficiaries were France (thirty-six), Spain (twelve) and Italy (eleven). *See* Written question No 2133/90, answer given by Mr. Andriessen on behalf of the Commission, O.J. (1991) C 85/29.

sector[320], cars[321], motor cycles[322] and radios.[323]

In *Donckerwolke v. Procureur de la République*, the court had to judge the compatibility of the French practice of requiring a declaration of origin and import license for goods imported into France from other Member States where these goods had been in free circulation. France argued that the measure was intended as a surveillance measure for a possible application for an authorization of national measures under Article 115. The court held that without an Article 115 authorization in place, these measures contravened Article 30.[324]

The court further outlined the requirements concerning origin declarations that may be acceptable if Article 115 measures have been authorized:

In these circumstances, it may be admitted that knowledge of that origin is necessary both for the Member State concerned, so that it may determine the scope of commercial policy measures which it is authorized to adopt pursuant to the Treaty, and for the Commission, for the purpose of exercising the right of supervision and decision conferred on it by Article 115.

Nevertheless the Member States may not require from the importer more in this respect than an indication of the origin of the products in so far as he knows it or may reasonable be expected to know it.

In addition the fact that the importer did not comply with the obligation to declare the real origin of goods cannot give rise to the application of penalties which are disproportionate taking account of the purely administrative nature of the contravention.

In this respect seizure of the goods or any pecuniary penalty fixed according to the value of the goods would certainly be incompatible with

---

320. *See, e.g.*, Shirts, T-shirts, lightweight fine knit roll, polo or turtle-necked jumpers and pullovers, undervests and the like, knitted or crocheted (category 4) originating in China, imports into France, O.J. (1991) C 100/18.

321. *See, e.g.*, Cars originating in Japan, imports into Spain and Italy, O.J. (1991) C 192/2.

322. *See, e.g.*, Motorcycles originating in Japan, imports into Italy, O.J. (1991) C 44/3.

323. *See, e.g.*, Radios originating in China and South Korea, imports into France, O.J. (1991) C 194/3.

324. *Suzanne Criel, née Donckerwolke and Henri Schou v. Procureur de la République au Tribunal de Grande Instance, Lille and Director General of Customs*, Case 41/76, (1976) ECR 1,921 (the case concerned imports of cloth of synthetic fibres and packing sacks coming from Lebanon and Syria).

the provisions of the Treaty as being equivalent to an obstacle to the free movement of goods.

In general terms any administrative or penal measure which goes beyond what is strictly necessary for the purpose of enabling the importing Member State to obtain reasonably complete and accurate information on the movement of goods within specific measures of commercial policy must be regarded as a measure having effect equivalent to a quantitative restriction prohibited by the Treaty.[325]

The court confirmed these principles in *Cayrol v. Riviora & Figli*,[326] *Commission v. Ireland*,[327] and *Tezi Textiel BV v. Commission*.[328]

Despite the clear case law of the Court of Justice, origin questions have also arisen concerning intra-Community trade even in the absence of Article 115 authorizations.

One notable example was the *Yoshida* case (discussed in detail in § 3.2.2.1.3.), where the product specific origin rule had basically been enacted in connection with the application of VRAs negotiated between Yoshida and the Italian government concerning slide fasteners originating in Japan, although the VRA as such did not become an issue in the case.

Another much publicized origin rule dispute relating to national quantitative restrictions was the Nissan U.K. case of 1988. At that time, imports into France of Japanese cars were restricted to a 3 percent market share. In 1988, when Nissan started producing cars in the United Kingdom and intended to export these to France, France took the position that it would consider these cars of Japanese origin and included in the quota unless the U.K. local content reached 80 percent.[329]

From a legal point of view, this dispute was peculiar because the French quota was not formally based on Article 115 of the EEC Treaty and the exact

---

325. Ibid., at 1938.

326. *Leonce Cayrol v. Giovanni Riviora & Figli*, Case 52/77, (1977)ECR 2,261 (concerning the imports of grapes from Spain into France).

327. *Commission v. Ireland*, Case 288/83, (1985) ECR 1,761 (concerning the import from the United Kingdom into Ireland of potatoes originating in Cyprus).

328. *Tezi Textiel BV v. Commission*, Case 59/84, (1986) ECR, 887 (dealing in particular with the national quotas in the context of the MFA).

329. *See France Likely to Resist Exports of Nissan's British Built Cars*, Financial Times, 19 July 1988; *Car Makers Dispute Local Content*, Financial Times, 27 February 1989; *UK Appeals for Resolution of Nissan Deadlock*, Financial Times, 9 March 1989; *Confused EC Drives into Impasse on Nissan*, Financial Times, 10 March 1989.

legal nature of the quota seemed unclear.[330] In view of the high political sensitivity of the dispute, the matter was finally settled behind closed doors. The exact terms of the agreement that was finally reached were not made public.[331] Hence, this dispute provided little guidance to the public on the Commission's approach to this problem.[332]

However, in an answer to a written question in the EC Parliament, EC Commissioner Scrivener stated:

> From a legal point of view, the basis for the determination of the origin of cars sent from one Member State to another where quantitative restrictions or similar measures exist, is Article 5 of Council Regulation (EEC) No 802/68 . . .

> The notion of the last substantial process or operation mentioned in Article 5 above is fulfilled when a considerable added value is achieved. In order to take into account the technological realities of the sector in question and to add a technical element to the economic test, it is also necessary that not all essential parts originate from outside the Community.[333]

In its single market drive, the Commission has set the ambitious goal to gradually eliminate national quotas and replace them by Community measures. To what extent all political hurdles can be cleared to achieve this goal remains to be seen.[334] If this goal is achieved, origin would become irrelevant for

---

330. *See* Bronckers, "A Legal Analysis of Protectionist Measures affecting Japanese Imports into the European Community — Revisited", in Protectionism and the European Community 57, at 78 and 85 (1987); Action brought on 4 February 1992 by Asia Motor France and others against the Commission, O.J. (1992) C 61/8.

331. The press release of the European Commission of 18 April 1989 simply stated that "In reply to a request by Vice-President Bangemann, the French authorities have indicated that the administrative measures required to ensure free access to the French market for Nissan UK Bluebird vehicles, starting at the end of 1988, have been taken. The French Government has confirmed that these imports from the UK will not affect the traditional imports of Nissan vehicles from Japan."

332. It should be noted that in the Nissan dispute also Italy took the position that the U.K. Nissan Bluebird cars should be included within the Italian quota. *See Italy Urges EC to Rule on UK Nissan Bluebird*, Financial Times, 4 November 1988; *Italy Rules out Free Access for UK Nissan Cars*, Financial Times, 19 April 1989.

333. Written question No 1818/88, answer given by Mrs Scrivener on behalf of the Commission, O.J. (1989) C 255/13.

334. In the Treaty on European Union, Article 115 was basically maintained.

intra-Community trade but nevertheless remain an issue for quantitative restrictions in extra-Community trade, in particular VRAs and selective (Community wide) safeguards.[335]

6.2. Origin Rules and Public Procurement

Origin rules are also to be used as a criterion in procurement procedures in the excluded sectors. Article 29 of Council Directive of 17 September 1990 on the procurement procedures of entities operating in the water, energy, transport, and telecommunications sectors[336] provides for discriminatory treatment of tenders depending on the origin of the products that they comprise.

Article 29 applies to tenders comprising products originating in third countries with which the Community has not concluded, multilaterally or bilaterally, an agreement ensuring comparable and effective access for Community undertakings to markets of those third countries.

Article 29 provides:

2. Any tender made for the award of a supply contract may be rejected where the portion of the products originating in third countries, as determined in accordance with Council Regulation (EEC) No 802/68 of 27 June 1968 on the common definition of the concept of the origin of goods, as last amended by Regulation (EEC) No 3860/87, exceeds 50% of the total value of the products constituting the tender . . .

3. Subject to paragraph 4, where two or more tenders are equivalent in the light of the award criteria defined in Article 27, preference shall be given to the tenders which may not be rejected pursuant to paragraph 2. The prices of tenders shall be considered equivalent for the purposes of this Article, if the price difference does not exceed 3%.

In other words, Article 29 leaves the option to reject tenders containing more than 50 percent value of third country products and contains the obligation to give preference to tenders containing less than 50 percent value of third country products if the price difference does not exceed 3 percent.

---

335. The EEC Safeguard Regulation 288/82, O.J. (1982) L 35/1, in principle, authorizes the adoption of any type of measures, which may include (and have included) quantitative restrictions. In addition, the European Community has sometimes acted against specific countries only. See, for example, the footwear cases, O.J. (1988) L 54/59 (imports into Italy of footwear originating in South Korea and Taiwan) and L 166/6 (imports into France of footwear originating in South Korea or Taiwan).

336. O.J. (1990) L 297/1.

Article 29 (5) specifies that products originating in third countries with which the Community has concluded agreements ensuring comparable and effective market access for Community undertakings shall not be taken into account for calculating the value of third country products mentioned in Article 29 (2).[337]

Member States shall adopt the measures necessary to comply with the Directive by 1 July 1992.[338]

An interesting point is that Article 29 (2), *in fine*, provides that "software used in the equipment of telecommunication networks shall be considered as products."[339] Discussions about the adoption of a product specific origin rule for telecommunications software are currently ongoing.

6.3. The Broadcasting Directive

A new development is the emergence of origin rules in service-related sectors.

An example is the Council Directive of 3 October 1989 on the coordination of certain provisions laid down by law, regulation, or administrative action in Member States concerning the pursuit of television broadcasting activities.[340]

Article 4 of this Directive essentially sets forth that Member States shall ensure, where practicable and by appropriate means, that broadcasters reserve for "European works" a majority proportion of their transmission time, excluding the time appointed to news, sports events, games, advertising, and teletext services.[341]

Article 5 further provides that Member States shall ensure, where practicable and by appropriate means, that broadcasters reserve at least 10%

---

337. An interesting point is how the phrase "shall not be taken into account" will be interpreted. The 50 percent value of third-country parts is to be calculated on the total value of products constituting the tender. A restrictive interpretation could be that the value of third country parts would be calculated on the total value of products constituting the tender less the value of products from third countries with which the European Community has agreements in place. This restrictive interpretation, although somewhat nonsensical, would obviously have the effect of inflating the percentage of value of third country parts.

338. O.J. (1990) L 297/1, Article 37.

339. The question whether software is a product or a service is not that obvious. *See, e.g.,* Council Regulation (EEC) No 1055/85 of 23 April 1985, amending Regulation (EEC) No 1224/80 on the valuation of goods for customs purposes, O.J. (1985) L 112/50.

340. O.J. (1989) L 298/23.

341. It should be noted that Article 4 is phrased in such a way that makes this a soft target rather than a hard legal obligation. *See* Article 4(2)-(4).

of their transmission time, excluding the time appointed to news, sports events, games, advertising, and teletext services, or, alternatively at the discretion of the Member State, at least 10 percent of their programming budget for "European works" created by producers who are independent of broadcasters.

"European works" are defined in Article 6 of the Directive as works originating from Member States of the Community or from European third states party to the European Convention on Transfrontier Television of the Council of Europe and mainly made with authors and workers residing in these states, provided that they comply with one of the following three conditions:

1. They are made by one or more producers established in one or more of those states,
2. The production of the works is supervised and actually controlled by one or more producers established in one or more of those states,
3. The contribution of coproducers of those states to the total coproduction costs is preponderant and the coproduction is not controlled by one or more producers established outside those states.

Also considered as "European works" are the works originating from other European third countries made exclusively or in coproduction with producers established in one or more Member State by producers established in one or more European third countries with which the Community will conclude agreements in accordance with the procedures of the Treaty, if those works are mainly made with authors and workers residing in one or more European States.

Article 6(4) finally provides that works that are not European works within the meaning of the above, but made mainly with authors and workers residing in one or more Member States, shall be considered to be European works to an extent corresponding to the proportion of the contribution of Community coproducers to the total production costs.

Thus far there has been little experience with the practice under the national legislation implementing this directive.

7. Conclusions and Recommendations

First, reference should be made to the conclusions and recommendations already made earlier in this chapter concerning the need for major procedural improvements (see § 3.1.3.), the case law of the EC Court of Justice (see § 3.3.1.7.) and the Commission's practice (see § 3.3.2.11.) in the nonpreferential area as well as the concluding remarks concerning the EC's preferential origin rules (see § 4.4.).

The concept of "origin of goods" is esoteric and unnecessary but for the purpose of delineating of the scope of application of discriminatory measures in international trade.

In defining substantial rules two basic approaches are possible. A first approach is the strict economic approach that translates itself into exclusive use of value-added tests. A justification for this approach could be that the function of origin rules is exactly to define trade discriminatory measures and that therefore the value added in the countries concerned is necessarily the appropriate yardstick. Indeed, the economic interest of a country in international trade of certain goods is necessarily a measure of the value added in that country in production and trade of the goods in question.

For example, a car is assembled in Indonesia from parts coming from Japan. The value added in Indonesia is 40 percent and the value of the Japanese parts is 60 percent. If a tariff, quantitative restriction, or dumping measure is aimed at Japan, the conclusion will be that on the basis of the value-added analysis of the car, the car should be of Japanese origin for purposes of applying the trade discriminatory measures. These will then mainly affect the Japanese economic interests, which clearly have the most money at stake in the production of the car. As a result of this analysis, the origin rule for cars could require, for example, 60 percent value added.

However, this reasoning is simplistic to some extent. By looking at figures without regard to the size of the economies of the countries involved, it ignores the proportionality factor. Indeed, the 40 percent value added in Indonesia may be, in relative terms, more important to the Indonesian economy than the 60 percent value of the Japanese parts is to the Japanese economy. Moreover, if the same operations performed in Indonesia were performed in Germany, they might perhaps result in 60 percent value-added and the car would be considered of German origin. Accordingly, value-added tests can have the side effect of discriminating against low-cost or cost-efficient countries. Therefore, from a strict economic point of view, value-added tests that only look at figures relative to the total production cost of the product and not relative to the economies of the producing countries involved might not produce adequate results in a world trade order that is currently characterized by countries with widely different production costs and levels of economic development.

A second approach is the conceptual approach, which defines origin by operations resulting in the creation of a "new product," This approach can be translated in change of tariff heading tests or technical tests. To the extent that this approach takes no account of the economic importance of the operations performed, it becomes too abstract and dissociated with the function that origin rules are deemed to fulfil in international trade.

The best approach is probably a balancing act between both extreme approaches, which seems to some extent the road taken by the European

Community and the suggested guidelines for the harmonization of the origin rules in GATT by not making any exclusive a priori choices for the formulation of substantial rules.

Besides the harmonization of origin rules to prevent protectionist bias in the formulation of substantive rules in importing countries — which has been a problem in the European Community — a major issue which remains to be addressed is the scope for the use of origin rules in applying trade discriminatory measures. A problem area in this respect in EC practice is the questionable use of origin rules in defining the scope of the application of antidumping measures. Clear parameters in the GATT Anti-Dumping Code on the use of origin rules would be a significant step forward.

After the finalization of this chapter, the European Communities adopted a new Common Customs Code. The new code repeals the Basic Origin Regulation but would not seem to introduce any significant changes to the former provisions of the Basic EC Origin Regulation. With regard to the substantive rules, the new Article 23 (2), which replaces the former Article 5 of the Basic Origin Regulation, contains a slightly changed wording that would not seem to change the basic meaning of the text. The provisions concerning accessories, spare parts, or tools (the former Article 7) have been deleted. With regard to products wholly obtained in a country, the new Article 24 now specifies that this comprises products from sea fishing and other products taken from the sea outside the territorial waters of any coastal state by vessels registered or recorded in the country concerned and flying the flag of that country.

Article 247 establishes a Customs Code Committee that replaces the Origin Committee. The rules of procedure for the Customs Code Committee are similar to the procedural provisions in the former Basic Origin Regulation.[342] It can also be expected that in practice the same representatives who now sit in the Origin Committee will sit in the Customs Code Committee as far as it deals with origin issues.

---

342. *See* Article 247-249. It is interesting to note that Article 255 of the original proposal for the Common Customs Code provided for new procedural rules that significantly differed from existing rules. *See* O.J. (1990) C 128/51. However, this Article 255 was changed in the final text.

ANNEX

NONPREFERENTIAL RULES OF ORIGIN

1. Commission Regulation (EEC) No 641/69 of 3 April 1969 on determining the origin of certain goods produced from eggs, O.J. (1969) L 83/15 (replaced by Commission Regulation (EEC) No 2884/90 of 5 October 1990 on determining the origin of certain goods produced from eggs, O.J. (1990) L 276/14);

2. Commission Regulation (EEC) No 37/70 of 9 January 1970 on determining the origin of essential spare parts for use with any piece of equipment, machine, apparatus or vehicle dispatched beforehand, O.J. (1970) L 7/6;

3. Commission Regulation (EEC) No 2632/70 of 23 December 1970 on determining the origin of radio and television receivers, O.J. (1970) L 279/35;

4. Commission Regulation (EEC) No 315/71 of 12 February 1971 on determining the origin of basic wines intended for the preparation of vermouth, and the origin of vermouth, O.J. (1971) L 36/10;

5. Commission Regulation (EEC) No 861/71 of 27 April 1971 on determining the origin of tape recorders, O.J. (1971) L 95/11;

6. Commission Regulation (EEC) No 964/71 of 10 May 1971 on determining the origin of the meat and offals, fresh, chilled or frozen, of certain domestic animals, O.J. (1971) L 104/12;

7. Commission Regulation (EEC) No 1039/71 of 24 May 1971 on determining the origin of certain woven textile products, O.J. (1971) L 113/13 (replaced by Commission Regulation (EEC) No 1364/91 of 24 May 1991 determining the origin of textiles and textile articles falling within Section XI of the combined nomenclature, O.J. (1991) L 130/18; amended by the Commission on the basis of Article 15 of Council Regulation (EEC) No 2658/87 of 23 July 1987 on the tariff and statistical nomenclature and on the Common Customs Tariff, O.J. (1987) L 256/1, at 4, giving the Commission the powers to amend Community acts which include the tariff or statistical nomenclature to conform to the new combined nomenclature);

8. Commission Regulation (EEC) No 2025/73 of 25 July 1973 on the determination of the origin of certain ceramic products, O.J. (1973) L 206/32 (amended by Commission Regulation (EEC) No 3561/90 of 11 December 1990 on determining the origin of certain ceramic products, O.J. (1990) L 347/10. The amendments concern only changes to combined nomenclature. These amendments were therefore not based on the procedure of Article 14 of the Basic Origin Regulation procedure but on the powers given to the Commission under Article 15 of Council Regulation (EEC) No 2658/87 of 23 July 1987 on the tariff and statistical nomenclature and on the Common Customs Tariff to amend Community acts which include the tariff or statistical nomenclature, O.J. (1987) L 256/1, at 5);

9. Commission Regulation (EEC) No 2026/73 of 25 July 1973 on determining the origin of grape juice, O.J. L 206/33 (1973) (amended by the Commission on the basis of Article 15 of Council Regulation (EEC) No 2658/87 (see previous footnote) in Commission Regulation (EEC) No 2883/90 of 5 October 1990 on determining the origin of grape juice, O.J. (1990) L 276/13);

10. Commission Regulation (EEC) No 1480/77 of 24 June 1977 on the determination of the origin of certain knitted and crocheted articles, certain articles of apparel, and footwear, O.J. (1977) L 164/16 (replaced by Commission Regulation (EEC) No 1364/91 of 24 May 1991 determining the origin of textiles and textile articles falling within Section XI of the combined nomenclature, O.J. (1991) L 130/18; amended by the Commission on the basis of Article 15 of Council Regulation (EEC) No 2658/87 in Commission Regulation (EEC) No 1365/91 of 24 May 1991 on determining the origin of cotton linters, impregnated felt and nonwovens, articles of apparel of leather, footwear and watch straps of textiles, O.J. (1991) L 130/28);

11. Commission Regulation (EEC) No 2067/77 of 20 September 1977 concerning the determination of the origin of slide fasteners, O.J. (1977) L 242/5;

12. Commission Regulation (EEC) No 749/78 of 10 April 1978 on the determination of the origin of certain textile products, O.J. (1978) L 101/7 (replaced by Commission Regulation (EEC) No 1364/91 of 24 May 1991 determining the origin of textiles and textile articles falling within Section XI of the combined nomenclature, O.J. (1991) L

130/18; amended by the Commission on the basis of Article 15 of Council regulation (EEC) No 2658/87 in Commission Regulation (EEC) No 1365/91 of 24 May 1991 on determining the origin of cotton linters, impregnated felt and nonwovens, articles of apparel of leather, footwear and watch straps of textiles, O.J. (1991) L 130/28);

13. Commission Regulation (EEC) No 1836/78 of 27 July 1978 concerning the determination of the origin of ball, roller or needle roller bearings, O.J. (1978) L 210/49 (amended by the Commission based on its powers set forth in Article 15 of Council Regulation (EEC) No 2658/87 in Commission Regulation (EEC) No 3672/90 of 18 December 1990 on determining the origin of ball, roller or needle roller bearings, O.J. (1990) L 356/30);

14. Commission Regulation (EEC) No 288/89 of 3 February 1989 on determining the origin of integrated circuits, O.J. (1989) L 33/23;

15. Commission Regulation (EEC) No 2071/89 of 11 July 1989 on determining the origin of photocopying apparatus, incorporating an optical system or a system of the contact type, O.J. (1989) L 196/24;

16. Commission Regulation (EEC) No 2884/90 of 5 October 1990 on determining the origin of certain goods produced from eggs O.J. (1990) L 276/14;

17. Commission Regulation (EEC) No 1364/91 of 24 May 1991 determining the origin of textiles and textile articles falling within Section XI of the combined nomenclature, O.J. (1991) L 130/18.

PREFERENTIAL RULES OF ORIGIN

1. Agreement between the European Economic Community and the Republic of Austria, Protocol No 3 concerning the definition of the concept of 'originating products' and methods of administrative cooperation, O.J. (1972) L 300/38.

2. Agreement between the European Community and the Kingdom of Sweden Protocol 3, O.J. (1972) L 300/131.

3. Agreement between the European Communities and the Swiss Confederation, Protocol 3, O.J. (1972) L 300/224.

4. Agreement between the European Communities and the Republic of Iceland, O.J. (1972) L 301/106.

5. Agreement between the European Economic Community and the Kingdom of Norway, O.J. (1973) L 171/45.

6. Agreement between the European Economic Community and the Republic of Finland, O.J. (1973) L 328/49.

7. Fourth ACP-EEC Convention, Protocol No 1 concerning the definition of the concept of 'originating products' and methods of administrative cooperation, O.J. (1990) L 84/8.

8. Council Regulation (EEC) No 2216/78 of 26 September 1978 concerning the conclusion of the Cooperation Agreement between the European Economic Community and the Syrian Arab Republic, Protocol 2 concerning the definition of the concept of 'originating products' and methods of administrative cooperation, O.J. (1978) L 269/22.

9. Council Regulation (EEC) No 2215/78 of 26 September 1978 concerning the conclusion of the Cooperation Agreement between the European Economic Community and the Hashemite Kingdom of Jordan, Protocol 2 concerning the definition of the concept of 'originating products' and methods of administrative cooperation, O.J. (1978) L 268/24.

10. Council Regulation (EEC) No 2214/78 of 26 September 1978 concerning the conclusion of the Cooperation Agreement between the

European Economic Community and the Lebanese Republic, Protocol 2 concerning the definition of the concept of 'originating products' and methods of administrative cooperation, O.J. (1978) L 267/24.

11. Council Regulation (EEC) No 2213/78 of 26 September 1978 on the conclusion of the Cooperation Agreement between the European Economic Community and the Arab Republic of Egypt, Protocol 2 concerning the definition of the concept of 'originating products' and methods of administrative cooperation, O.J. (1978) L 266/30.

12. Council Regulation (EEC) No 2212/78 of 26 September 1978 concerning conclusion of the Cooperation Agreement between the European Economic Community and the Republic of Tunisia, Protocol 2 concerning the definition of the concept of 'originating products' and methods of administrative cooperation, O.J. (1978) L 265/38.

13. Council Regulation (EEC) No 2211/78 of 26 September 1978 concerning the conclusion of the Cooperation Agreement between the European Economic Community and the Kingdom of Morocco, Protocol 2 concerning the definition of the concept of 'originating products' and methods of administrative cooperation, O.J. (1978) L 264/38.

14. Council Regulation (EEC) No 2210/78 of 26 September 1978 concerning the conclusion of the Cooperation Agreement between the European Economic Community and the People's Democratic Republic of Algeria, Protocol 2 concerning the definition of the concept of 'originating products' and methods of administrative cooperation, O.J. (1978) L 263/40.

15. Council Regulation (EEC) No 2907/77 of 20 December 1977 on the conclusion of the Additional Protocol to the Agreement establishing an association between the European Community and the Republic of Cyprus, Annex: protocol concerning the definition of the concept of 'originating products' and methods of administrative cooperation, O.J. (1977) L 339/19.

16. Council Regulation (EEC) No 1274/75 of 20 May 1975 concluding the Agreement between the European Economic Community and the State of Israel, Protocol 3 concerning the application of Article 2(3), O.J. (1975) L 136/126.

17. Council Regulation (EEC) No 939/76 of 23 April 1976 concluding the Financial Protocol and the Protocol laying down provisions relating to the Agreement establishing an association between the European Economic Community and Malta, Annex: Protocol concerning the definition of the concept of 'originating products' and methods of administrative cooperation, O.J. (1976) L 111/11.

18. Protocol 3 of the Cooperation Agreement between the European Economic Community and the Socialist Federal Republic of Yugoslavia concerning the definition of the concept of 'originating products' and methods of administrative cooperation, O.J. (1983) L 41/39.

19. Council Decision of 25 July 1991 on the association of the overseas countries and territories with the European Economic Community, O.J. (1991) L 263/67.

20. Commission Regulation (EEC) No 3184/74 of 6 December 1974 concerning the definition of the concept of 'originating products' and methods of administrative cooperation for the application of the customs procedure applicable to certain products originating in and coming from the Faroe Islands, O.J. (1974) L 344/1.

21. Council Regulation (EEC) No 1135/88 of 7 March 1988 concerning the definition of the concept of 'originating products' and methods of administrative cooperation in the trade between the customs territory of the Community, Ceuta and Melilla and the Canary Islands, O.J. (1988) L 114/1.

22. Commission Regulation (EEC) No 809/88 of 14 March 1988 on the definition of the concept of 'originating products' and methods of administrative cooperation applicable to imports into the Community of products originating in the Occupied Territories, O.J. (1988) L 86/1.

23. Commission Regulation (EEC) No 693/88 of 4 March 1988 on the definition of the concept of originating products for purposes of the application of tariff preferences granted by the European Economic Community in respect of certain products from developing countries O.J. (1988) L 77/1.

CHAPTER 4

Country of Origin:
The Australian Experience

Keith Steele and Daniel Moulis

1. Introduction and Historical Background

1.1. Introduction

An almost ludicrous state of affairs has arisen. Textile goods manufactured entirely on the Continent of Europe have been sent to England, and there dyed, measured, and wrapped, and have then come to this country under the terms of British preference. Machines in parts have been made on the Continent, and assembled and packed in England, and have come here under the terms of British preference. I am sorry to say that there is in England a type of Anglo-continental manufacturer, and he should be prevented from doing this sort of thing.[1]

In his address to the Australian Parliament in 1925 containing these words, the then Minister for Trade and Customs focused attention on the concerns of Australian industry about a claimed abuse of a tariff preference and proposed a legislative remedy. So began Australia's journey down the road of "origin" definition of imported goods. Preference has always been the driving force behind country of origin rules as those rules are in the majority of cases only relevant where a differential tariff exists in respect of an imported good and a commercial advantage may be gained by compliance with or, in some cases,

---

Keith Steele and Daniel Moulis are partners of the Australian law firm Freehill Hollingdale & Page. The authors wish to thank John Burke (Chief Inspector, Valuation and Preference Branch, Australian Customs Service, Canberra) and Robert Walsh (Government Relations Coordinator, Freehill Hollingdale & Page, Canberra) for their valuable assistance in compiling information and discussing aspects of this chapter with the authors. Without derogating from the importance of the contribution of Messrs Burke and Walsh, the content of the chapter, however, is solely the responsibility of the authors.

1. The Honourable Mr. M. Pratten, Minister for Trade and Customs, in his Second Reading Speech when introducing the Customs Bill 1925 (Australia, House of Representatives 1925, Debates, Vol. 111, at 1,649).

the manipulation of those rules. Australia's approach to determining the origin of goods has been influenced by a mix of policy and bilateralism, rather than a desire for multilateral consistency, and that theme is evident in this chapter.

1.2. Historical Background

On the Federation of Australia in 1901, the process by which the six States of New South Wales, Victoria, Tasmania, South Australia, Western Australia, and Queensland were joined in a sort of sovereign matrimony, the colonial period of Australia's development formally ended and a fledgling independent nation came into being. But the enactment of the Australian Constitution did not remove the strong residual links with Britain, recognized by the very fact that the enactment of that Constitution was itself an act of the British Parliament.

One of the important areas in which the residual link was maintained was in relation to trade. The first preference accorded under Australian legislation was to goods that were the produce or manufacture of the United Kingdom. Under the Customs Tariff Act 1908, the British preference accorded to goods was said to apply only:

[t]o goods the produce or manufacture of the United Kingdom which are shipped in the United Kingdom to Australia and not transhipped or if transhipped then only if it is proved to the satisfaction of the Collector that the goods have not, since they were shipped in the United Kingdom, been subjected to any process of manufacture.[2]

This unsophisticated definition clearly left much room to the imagination of the mercantilists of the day. The provision was simply a place of export rule, rather than a country of origin rule in the sense we would describe one today.

The Australian authorities were alive to the potential for abuse of the British preferential tariff rate. In the House of Representatives debate on the introduction of the 1925 amendments to the Customs Act 1901,[3] the value

---

2.   Section 6.

3.   The Customs Act 1901, although extensively amended on a continual basis since its inception in 1901, is still the principal act dealing with customs issues in general today. It is referred to as the Customs Act in this chapter. In an annotated version of the Customs Act published in 1904, the author H. N. P. Wollaston was moved to write, "As the result of so much labour and professional skill a statute was produced which has been acknowledged by experts in the legal profession as well as by those having special knowledge of the subject of which it treats, in England, Canada and Australia, to be a model of drafting." It is widely

of the preference was quantified at £8,000,000 per year in terms of lost tariff revenue. Even if the legislators did not move quickly to amend the way in which the section in the original Customs Tariff Act operated, the Customs administration[4] soon imposed a 75 percent labor and materials requirement which overlaid the legislative provision quite arbitrarily, and without legislative warrant. The 1925 amendments validated the Customs Service approach that had been in place since 1907. The essential determining factors for country of origin embodied in the 1925 amendments, namely the last process of manufacture teamed with a proportional requirement, has continued in various manifestations to this day.

1.2.1.   Prefederation and the Constitution

Before Federation, the Australian States levied duties amongst each other on goods passing across their boundaries. The inefficiencies and dislocation that such a system caused, amplified in a remote country with a small population, was instrumental to the push for free intercourse in trade between the states, which was embodied from 1901 in Section 92 of the Australian Constitution. In one of the earliest recorded cases involving a question of the origin of goods in Australia, it was decided that cattle imported into Victoria from the adjoining northerly state of New South Wales were not the produce of Victoria unless it was proved they were bred there.[5] The case is indicative of the commercial impediment to the development of Australia caused by internal levies. It placed a grazier running cattle in pastures on each side of a state boundary in the unfortunate position of paying a duty each time it was necessary to drove the herd into the other jurisdiction.

Under Section 90 of the Constitution, the exclusive power to "impose duties of customs and excise, and to grant bounties on the production or export of goods" was bestowed on the federal parliament. So ended the "barbarism of borderism"[6] within Australia.

---

acknowledged that the Customs Act has not maintained these lofty standards over the ensuing eighty-seven years, and efforts to redraft the act, including its origin provisions, are now underway. See note 32.

4.   The Australian Customs Service, referred to as the Customs Service in this chapter.

5.   *Mitchell v. Curlewis*, xv. ALT 143 (1893).

6.   *Peanut Board v. Rockhampton Harbour Board*, 48 CLR 266, 298 (1933).

1.2.2. Early Legislative History

In the original Customs Act, the sixth law passed by the fledgling federal parliament, there was no definition of the origin of goods. Its companion law, the Customs Tariff Act 1901,[7] which listed the classifications of imported goods and the duties payable on them, contained no preferential duties for any country. Although the place of export was required to be stipulated in entry documentation, the question of origin was commercially irrelevant.[8]

It first became necessary to define the place of the origin of goods in 1906, when tariff preferences were exchanged with British South African colonies and protectorates on certain goods. Section 2 of the Customs Tariff (South African Preference) Act 1906 referred to a preference for the goods specified in the Schedule to the Act "when those goods are imported from and are the produce or manufacture of any of the British South African Colonies or Protectorates which are included within the South African Customs Union." The next preference law was Section 6 of the Customs Tariff Act 1908, which has been referred to in § 1.2.

The "themes" of Australian origin rules were established by these early laws. "Produce or manufacture," "process of manufacture," and direct importation and transhipment were already the guiding considerations by 1908. The emphasis in Australian law on the last process of manufacture was first incorporated in the 1925 amendments preceded by the parliamentary debates that described the alleged contrivances whereby anglo-continental manufacturers gained British preferential tariff advantages (see § 1.1.). The genesis of this "last process" rule is important, but it is difficult to provide any firm explanation for it. The importance derives from the apparent divergence from current international practice in the implementation of "substantial transformation" principles under Australian law. The question that is posed is why add a "last process" requirement if 75 percent of manufacture in terms of factory or works cost must take place in the originating country? One possible explanation is the unilateral nature of the preference originally accorded to British goods and a desire to limit the preference as much as possible. The hope that the preference would elicit reciprocal treatment for Australian goods had grown dim in the seventeen years since the 1908

---

7.   Under Section 55 of the Constitution, laws imposing duties of customs may deal only with such imposition. This explains the distinction between the Customs Act and the Customs Tariff Acts, which deal separately with the laws of customs and the imposition of duties respectively.

8.   The first Commerce (Trade Descriptions) Act, which created offences for false descriptions applied to goods, was not enacted until 1905.

preference was instituted. The £8,000,000 per year in foregone tariffs represented a serious revenue deficiency for the Australian economy, one that could not be maintained indefinitely without justification. The free trade attitude of the British Government continued until 1932, bearing out the Australian fear that a liberal rule of origin was not in Australia's continued best interests.

1.2.3.   Bilateral Preference Agreements

Bilateral agreements led to the institution of preferences for goods imported into Australia from New Zealand from 1922, from Canada from 1925, from Papua New Guinea from 1926, and from Rhodesia from 1941. These were renegotiated from time to time. A preferential treaty with Newfoundland in 1939 lapsed in 1949 when that country became a province of Canada. Over this period, Australia's "rule" of customs origin continued to be driven by the policy of preference. The Customs Act was amended piecemeal from time to time, leading to the lengthy and difficult provision that today deals with the origin of goods.[9]

1.3.   Comments

It is technically incorrect to speak of a rule of origin under Australian legislation, because *origin* is not referred to in the relevant Section of the Customs Act,[10] and also because the Section quite evidently does not ascribe an origin to all goods entered at the customs barrier (see § 2.2.). The concern in the legislation has always been to describe conditions that attract the advantages of preferential treatment, rather than to attempt to cover the field with some general statement applicable in all cases. Apart from where preference is involved, the origin of goods imported into Australia has been of little interest to the Australian customs authorities. Customs offences relating to the avoidance of duty have traditionally been expressed as being subject to penalties equal to the amount of duty short paid and, more recently, to a multiplication of the amount of duty short paid. Customs offences where preference is involved have been restricted to cases where importers have benefitted from a preferential rate of duty. Other than in preference cases, no duty is short paid if an inaccurate statement of the country of origin of the goods is set out in the relevant entry documentation. Even in preference cases,

---

9.   Section 151, see Appendix 1 to this chapter.

10.   "Origin" is referred to in several places in that part of the Customs Act dealing with countervailing and antidumping duties. These other references are considered in §5.

the importance of origin, and its ability to generate judicial precedent, will become less as Australia continues to reduce the degree of difference between general rates and preferential rates of duty.[11]

The new area of importance for Australian origin rules will be the area of antidumping law and administration. To offset reduced tariff protection, and as a response to depressed economic conditions, there is mounting pressure for stricter laws designed to counter perceived unfair trading such as dumping. The first signs of movement in this area are evident with the introduction of reduced time limits for antidumping and countervailing investigations and an extension of the grounds for antidumping complaints to so-called upstream industries. More vigorous implementation of antidumping measures is likely to lead to the restructuring of exporters' sourcing practices, place of manufacture, and supply lines to Australia and to renewed calls from Australian industry for more extensive protection by way of origin rules that pursue that result.

2. General Overview of Rules of Origin

As noted in the introductory remarks, Australian rules of origin did not develop from a need to define the countries from which all goods originated. Rather, the rules embodied in the relevant legislation defined the conditions under which preference would be accorded to particular goods. However, the need for preference rules has been the driving force behind the need to define an origin for goods; therefore a general overview of the rules must start with an analysis of the existing arrangements that bestow preferential treatment on the goods of certain countries and groups of countries.

2.1. International Agreements and Arrangements

Australia is a party to a number of international treaties that attempt to define rules of origin that apply between the parties to those treaties. Those treaties do not apply as part of the domestic law of Australia unless specifically enacted in Australian legislation. However, as treaties impose international obligations, it is the expectation of the parties who have entered into those agreements that they will adapt and administer their internal laws and practices to conform with the treaties.

---

11.   On 12 March 1991 the Australian government announced the progressive reduction of Australian tariff protection. In most areas (except when sectoral policy applies, such as motor vehicles and textiles, clothing, and footwear) tariff rates of 15 percent and 10 percent are to be cut to 5 percent by 1 July 1996.

The treaties to which Australia is a party that deal with rules of origin are the Canada Australia Trade Agreement (CANATA);[12] Annex D1 to the International Convention on the Simplification and Harmonization of Customs Procedures (the Kyoto Convention);[13] the Agreement on Trade and Commercial Relations between Australia and Papua New Guinea;[14] the South Pacific Regional Trade and Economic Co-operation Agreement (SPARTECA);[15] and the Australia New Zealand Closer Economic Relations Trade Agreement (ANZCERTA).[16] As a contracting party to the GATT, Australia also recognizes the waiver to Article I to the GATT[17] which underpins the GSP initiated by the United Nations Conference on Trade and Development (UNCTAD).[18] The origin requirements of each of those treaties, and of the GSP, are intended to be reflected in the provisions of Section 151 of the Customs Act, which is the Section dealing with the rules of origin for goods imported into Australia (this lengthy section is set out in full in Appendix 1 to this chapter).

2.1.1.   Canada Australia Trade Agreement

Neither the CANATA, nor the 1973 Exchange of Notes[19] which affected the operation of the original 1960 CANATA, contain a specific rule for determining the rule of origin that applies between the two countries. The preferences accorded are to goods that are "the growth, produce or manufacture" of the two countries. CANATA preserves the operation of the customs laws and regulations of the importing country, except as otherwise provided in CANATA; accordingly, the 75 percent factory or works cost test in place in Australia in 1960 was assumed to be appropriate for the purposes

12.   ATS 1960, No 5; UNTS 369 at 89.

13.   ATS 1975, No 12; UNTS 950 at 269.

14.   ATS 1977, No 7; UNTS 1216 at 183.

15.   ATS 1982, No 31; UNTS 1240 at 65.

16.   ATS 1960, No 5; UNTS 369 at 89.

17.   GATT Doc. (L/3545); GATT, 18th Supp. BISD 24 (1972).

18.   UNCTAD II, 1968, Resolution 21 (II).

19.   Exchange of Notes between Australia and Canada constituting an agreement concerning the future operation of the Trade Agreement of 12 February 1960, ATS 1973, No 28.

of CANATA. The test for Canadian preference is now embodied in Section 151(12) of the Customs Act.[20] A direct shipment requirement also applies.[21]

2.1.2. International Convention on the Simplification and Harmonization of Customs Procedures

This convention, known as the Kyoto Convention, sets out standards and recommended practices to be observed by the signatory countries. Annex D1 to the Kyoto Convention, concerning rules of origin, entered into force for Australia on 5 June 1984, with reservations to the Recommended Practices set out in Provisions 5 and 12. Provision 3 of the Kyoto Convention is important for present purposes as it seeks to deal with one of the currently contentious issues facing the international community, namely the production of goods in more than one country. That provision states, "Where two or more countries have taken part in the production of the goods, the origin of the goods shall be determined according to the substantial transformation criterion." The notes to Provision 3 state that in practice the substantial transformation criterion can be expressed by a contracting party in either of three ways:

– by a rule requiring a change of tariff heading in a specified nomenclature with list of exceptions, and/or
– by a list of manufacturing or processing operations which confer, or do not confer, upon the goods the origin of the country in which those operations were carried out, and/or
– by the ad valorem percentage rule, where either the percentage value of the materials utilized or the percentage of the value added reaches a specified level.

Australia has two reservations to the Kyoto Convention. The first of these distinguishes Australia's practice of isolating the factory or works cost of finished goods, not the ex-works or exportation price as referred to in the Kyoto Convention, as the basis for assessing preference eligibility. The second reservation states that Australia must be the intended destination of the goods when shipped from the country of production or manufacture. The latter reservation has been superseded by legislative change in Australia since 1984.

---

20. See the authors' Rule 6 in §2.2. The Canadian preference is a lasting remnant of the preferential tariff arrangements put in place between the United Kingdom and other Commonwealth countries at Ottawa in 1932.

21. Customs Act, Section 151(4) (see Appendix 1).

Direct shipment requirements now apply only to goods claimed to be entitled to preferential treatment as the produce or manufacture of Canada or New Zealand.[22] Under Sections 151(3) and (4) of the Customs Act (see Appendix 1), goods are not the produce or manufacture of New Zealand or Canada unless they are shipped from the country concerned to Australia and not transhipped (or, if transhipped, the intended destination of the goods was Australia when they were shipped from the country concerned).

The major Australian departure from Provision 3 of the Kyoto Convention, and one in respect of which Australia has no stated reservation, is the "last process of manufacture" requirement, which is repeated in every subsection of Section 151 of the Customs Act when setting out the rules of origin that apply to particular countries. The Kyoto Convention seeks to establish a general test, that does not involve a technical "last process" requirement, for determining the origin of goods. The legacy of the "last process" requirement, originally introduced (as postulated by the authors) to limit the ability of products to qualify for preference in 1925, has been a lasting one.[23]

2.1.3. Agreement on Trade and Commercial Relations between Australia and Papua New Guinea

This agreement, done at Port Moresby on 6 November 1976, entered into force between the two countries on 1 February 1977. Article 3.1 of the agreement states that a free trade area is established between Papua New Guinea and Australia. Article 3.3 provides that the article applies only to trade in goods that originate in a Member State. Article 4 then sets out the rule of origin for determining whether goods originate in either Australia or Papua New Guinea. The article states:

1. Goods shall be treated as originating in a Member State if those goods are:

    (a) the unmanufactured raw products of that Member State, or

---

22. The original reason for these direct shipment requirements is unclear. It has been suggested to the authors that the rule was simply a mechanism to allow the authorities to determine the country of origin of goods with greater ease: others have said shipping union demands were involved. It is more likely another example of the policy that demanded that strict rules be put in place to qualify for the privilege of preference.

23. See § 4.3. Australia can also be accused of not implementing the convention as part of its local law outside the preferential goods origin context. See note 31.

(b) manufactured goods in relation to which
    (i)   the process last performed in the manufacture was performed in that Member State; and
    (ii) the expenditure
        (A)   on material that is of Member State origin,
        (B)   on labour, factory overheads and inner containers that are of Member State origin, or
        (C)   partly on such material and partly on such other items of factory cost,
        is not less than one-half of the factory or works costs at the time of exportation.

2.   Notwithstanding the provisions of paragraph 1 of this Article, the Member States may agree to treat particular goods or classes of goods as originating in a Member State provided that, in the case of manufactured goods, the process last performed in the manufacture was performed in the territory of the exporting Member State.

Section 151(8) of the Customs Act (see Appendix 1) does not faithfully carry out the Article 4(1)(b)(ii)(B) obligation, as it does not refer to the inclusion of "factory overheads" and "inner containers" in the calculation of "expenditure" required. Instead, the section calls for a calculation that expresses the value of labor and materials of Australia or Papua New Guinea as a percentage of the "factory or works cost" of the goods concerned. On a literal interpretation of Section 151(8), the ability to qualify for preference is made more difficult because there is no reference in the Section to permit factory overheads or inner containers to be included as part of the content of Papua New Guinea. This is contrary to the terms of the article. This shortcoming of the Section has been remedied by the Gazettal of notices by the Comptroller pursuant to the Comptroller's power under Section 151(13) to "specify the manner in which the factory or work cost" and "value of . . . labour and materials is to be determined." The notices provide that "factory overhead expenses" and "the cost of inside containers" are to be included in the value of labour and materials of goods when deciding whether goods are the produce or manufacture of a country.[24] It could be suggested that the inclusion of "factory overheads" is beyond the power bestowed under Section 151(13), which only empowers the Comptroller to specify a particular manner of valuation of labor and materials and not what may or may not form part

---

24.   See *infra* note 37.

of the value of labor and materials.[25] "Factory overhead" is not accurately described as either "labour" or "materials." The legality of the notices in this respect has not been tested in a court of law.

2.1.4. South Pacific Regional Trade and Economic Co-operation Agreement

This agreement was done at Tarawa, Kiribati on 14 July 1980 and entered into force for Australia on 30 June 1982. SPARTECA defines certain countries as Forum Island countries (FICs) and Smaller Forum Island countries. The list of countries entitled to preferential treatment pursuant to SPARTECA are all referred to as FICs in the Customs Tariff Act 1987. The current list of countries is set out in Schedule 1 to that Act (See Appendix 2). Article III of SPARTECA states:

Subject to the provisions of this Agreement the Government of Australia shall:
(a) permit the duty free and unrestricted entry of goods listed in Schedule 1 to this Agreement that originate in and are imported from Forum Island countries; and
(b) permit the entry of goods listed in Schedule 2 to this Agreement that originate in and are imported from Forum Island countries, subject to the duties and quantitative limits specified in that Schedule.

Article V then sets out the rule of origin to be observed by Australia in determining whether the goods have originated in the territory of a FIC. It provides as follows:

Goods shall be treated by the Government of Australia as originating in the territory of a Forum Island country if those goods are:
(a) the unmanufactured raw products of a Forum Island country; or
(b) manufactured goods, in relation to which:
    (i) the process last performed in the manufacture of the goods was performed in a Forum Island country; and
    (ii) not less than 50 percent of the factory or works cost of the goods is represented by the value of labour or materials, or both, of:
        (A) a Forum Island country; or

---

25. See the discussion of *Re Gaylor Jewellery Sales and the Collector of Customs* in § 4.2.2.2., where a similar conclusion was reached by the Administrative Appeals Tribunal on the facts of that case.

(B)   a Forum Island country and one or more other Forum Island countries; or

(C)   one or more Forum Island countries and Australia.

Section 151(8) faithfully represents the intended effect of Article V of SPARTECA.[26]

2.1.5.   Australia New Zealand Closer Economic Relations Trade Agreement

The Australia New Zealand Closer Economic Relations Trade Agreement, or ANZCERTA, done at Canberra on 28 March 1983, had as one of its original objectives: "to develop closer economic relations between the Member States through a mutually beneficial expansion of free trade between New Zealand and Australia."[27]

On the occasion of the 1988 Review of ANZCERTA, that objective was effectively met by a further agreement between the two countries to eliminate all tariffs on goods originating in the territory of the other by 1 July 1990.[28] The "partial manufacture" rule of origin under Article 3 of ANZCERTA provides as follows:

1. Goods exported from the territory of a Member State directly into the territory of the other Member State or which, if not exported directly, were at the time of their export from the territory of a Member State destined for the territory of the other Member State and were subsequently imported into the territory of that other Member State, shall be treated as goods originating in the territory of the first Member State if those goods are:

. . .

(c)   partly manufactured in the territory of that Member State, subject to the following conditions:

(i)   the process last performed in the manufacture of the goods was performed in the territory of that Member State; and

---

26.   It is interesting to note that Papua New Guinea is a party to SPARTECA and that Article V of SPARTECA does not refer to "factory overheads" and "inner containers" as does Australia's earlier agreement with Papua New Guinea. See § 2.1.3 for reference to the Gazetted notices that specifically include "factory overheads" and "inner containers" in the definition of "factory or works cost."

27.   Article 1(b).

28.   Article 1(1), Protocol on Acceleration of Free Trade in Goods (ATS 1988 No 18; not yet published in UNTS).

(ii) the expenditure on one or more of the items set out below is not less than one-half of the factory or works cost of such goods in their finished state:

A. material that originates in the territory of one or both Member States;

B. labour and factory overheads incurred in the territory of one or both Member States;

C. inner containers that originate in the territory of one or both Member States.

2. The factory or works cost referenced to in paragraph 1(c)(ii) of this Article shall be the sum of costs of materials (excluding customs, excise or other duties), labour, factory overheads, and inner containers.

Section 151(7) of the Customs Act fails to literally carry out the intention of Article 3, because it refers to "materials" and "labour" but fails to refer to "factory overheads" and "inner containers." This shortcoming has been remedied by a notice issued by the Comptroller under Section 151(13) of the Customs Act that attempts to include into the value of labor and materials "factory overhead expenses" and "the cost of inside containers of the manufacture of New Zealand or of Australia, or of New Zealand and Australia."[29]

2.1.6.   Generalized System of Preferences

Australia claims to be the first country that introduced a system of tariff preferences for developing countries. Australia's GSP predates by two years the 1968 UNCTAD Resolution that formally recognized the appropriateness of preferential treatment. The waiver to Article I of the GATT that legally underpins the GSP refers to the ability of developed contracting parties "to accord preferential tariff treatment to products originating in developing countries." There is no definition in the waiver nor in the UNCTAD Resolution of the required attributes of origin. Those matters have been taken forward by the international practice and general rules concerning origin in the Kyoto Convention.

The Australian rule of origin concerning GSP countries (referred to as Developing Countries under the Customs Tariff Act 1987) is in Section 151(10) of the Customs Act. It specifies 50 percent content, coupled with a last process requirement (see the authors' rule 5 in § 2.2.).

---

29.   Commonwealth of Australia Gazette, No GN45, 30 November 1988, Notice No 88/14.

2.2. The Australian Statutory Rules of Origin

Section 151 of the Customs Act contains the Australian legislative rule of origin regime. The section is lengthy, and is set out in Appendix 1 to this chapter.

The Customs Tariff Act 1987 (the Customs Tariff Act), which sets out the Australian Tariff (based on the Harmonized System) and the applicable rates of duty, provides that goods are the produce or manufacture of a country according to the rules set out in Section 151 of the Customs Act. As will be seen from the analysis which follows, Section 151 refers to countries and to groups of countries to which the rules of origin apply.

Under the Customs Tariff Act, individual rates, which are lower than the normal rate of duty (the general rate), apply to preference countries. A Preference Country is defined under the Customs Tariff Act as New Zealand, Papua New Guinea, a FIC, a developing country, or Canada. FICs and developing countries are specified in Schedule 1 of the Customs Tariff Act, and the current lists of countries are set out in Appendix 2 to this chapter. It is to be noted that the list of developing countries is divided into countries that are developing countries and places that are treated as developing countries. Both of these categories come within the definition of developing country for the purposes of the Customs Act.

It is difficult to appreciate the effect of provisions such as those included in Section 151 on a first reading of the Section. The following guide condenses and simplifies the Section and is provided to assist with an easier familiarity with the operation of the provisions:

Rule 1 - Unmanufactured Raw Products
Unmanufactured raw products originate in the country from which they were extracted or harvested.

Exception
New Zealand and Canadian products do not fall into this category unless they are directly shipped to Australia or, if transhipped, the Comptroller is satisfied that their intended destination was Australia.

Rule 2 - Wholly Manufactured Goods
Goods wholly manufactured in a country other than a FIC or developing country originate in the country in which they were wholly manufactured if they were manufactured from unmanufactured raw products, materials

wholly manufactured in one or both of Australia and the country, or any combination of these materials.[30]

Exceptions
1. New Zealand and Canadian products do not fall into this category unless they are directly shipped to Australia or, if transhipped, a Collector is satisfied that their intended destination was Australia.
2. The Comptroller may determine goods imported into the country to be manufactured raw materials of that country for the purposes of this rule.

Rule 3 - Special Rule for New Zealand
Goods are the manufacture of New Zealand if the last process in their manufacture was performed in New Zealand and not less than 50 percent of their factory or works cost is represented by the value of labor or materials or of labor and materials of New Zealand or of Australia and New Zealand.

Exceptions
1. New Zealand goods do not fall into this category unless they are directly shipped to Australia or, if transhipped, the Comptroller is satisfied that their intended destination is Australia.
2. The Comptroller may determine that a percentage other than 50 percent of factory or works costs for classes of goods is appropriate.

Rule 3 - Special Rule for Papua New Guinea and Forum Island Countries
Goods are the manufacture of Papua New Guinea or a FIC if the last process in their manufacture was performed in Papua New Guinea or a FIC and not less than 50 percent of their factory or works cost is represented by the value of labor or materials or of labor and materials of one or more of Australia, Papua New Guinea, and a FIC.

Exception
The Comptroller may determine a lesser percentage than 50 percent of factory or works cost for classes of goods is appropriate.

---

30.   There is an anomaly in Section 151(6) of the *Customs Act* in the application of this rule to New Zealand, Papua New Guinea, and Canada. Paraphrased, the Section provides that goods wholly manufactured in any one of those countries, from unmanufactured raw products (regardless of origin) are to be treated as the manufacture of the country in which the manufacture took place. *"Customs has confirmed that this appears to be an anomaly and is studying the question further"*: ALRC Report No. 60, *Customs and Excise*, Vol. 3 at 370.

Rule 4 - Special Rule for Papua New Guinea and Forum Island Countries Involving a New Zealand Preference
Goods are the manufacture of Papua New Guinea or a FIC if the last process in their manufacture was performed in Papua New Guinea or a FIC; they were partly manufactured of New Zealand materials not prohibited from importation into Australia (either totally or by volume) and if imported from New Zealand into Australia would be entitled to duty-free entry; not less than 50 percent of their factory or works cost is represented by the value of labour or materials, or of labour and materials of one or more of Australia, New Zealand, Papua New Guinea or a FIC; and not less than 25 percent of their factory or works costs is represented by the value of labor or materials, or of labor and materials, of one or more of Papua New Guinea or a FIC.

Exception
The Comptroller may determine a lesser percentage than 50 percent of the factory or works cost for classes goods is appropriate.

Rule 5 - Special Rule for Developing Countries
Goods are the manufacture of a developing country if the last process in their manufacture was performed in the country and not less than 50 percent of their factory or works cost is represented by the value of labor or materials, or of labor and materials, of one or more of Australia, Papua New Guinea, a FIC, or a developing country.

Exception
Goods will still be a product of a developing country if the requirements of the rule are satisfied for the product except that the last process of manufacture took place in Papua New Guinea or a FIC but Papua New Guinea or a FIC are not themselves the country of origin under Rule 3 or 4.

Rule 6 - Goods Manufactured in or Made from Materials of More Than One Country
Goods are the manufacture of the country where the last process of manufacture occurred provided that not less than 75 percent of the factory or works cost of the goods is represented by the value of labor or materials, or of labor and materials, of Australia and that country.

Exception
1.   This rule does not cover New Zealand, Papua New Guinea or FICs.

2. The Comptroller may determine that the 75 percent requirement should be reduced to 25 percent for goods or classes of goods of a kind not commercially manufactured in Australia.

Rule 7 - Special Rule for Christmas Island, Cocos (Keeling) Island, and Norfolk Island

Rule 6 is applied to these countries as if the 75 percent stipulated in Rule 6 was the lesser percentage of 50 percent.

It is to be noted that these rules are the interpretation of the authors based on the various provisions of Section 151 and that they do not appear in the legislation in the form expressed above. It is easy to see from these rules where the important definitional issues are raised in ascertaining the country of origin of any particular product. The words "rules of origin" or "country of origin" do not form any part of Section 151.[31] As has been expressed earlier in this chapter, the genesis of the Australian law has not been directed at defining with legal accuracy the particular origin of every product presented at the customs barrier for classification and duty assessment.[32] The approach has been instead to set out different rules that have the potential to catch goods from certain places to which policy had dictated a preference should be accorded. Importers would claim the benefit of a preference and if challenged would be required to satisfy the Customs that the particular provision applied to the imported goods. Falling outside the terms of preference does not appear

---

31. In the Australian Customs Service Manual, Customs declares, "It should be noted, however, that Section 151 does not refer to 'origin' and the only purpose of the Section is to provide the criteria for preferential rates of duty. The terms of Section 151 do not provide the criteria for determining origin." Public Edition, Vol. 8, at 103. The conclusion reached by the authors in this chapter accords with the above view expressed by the Customs Service (although one might ask why Section 151(12), embodied in the authors' Rule 6, was enacted if the view is a correct one). Australia does not have a comprehensive origin regime able to meet the changing conditions of world manufacture and trade, where nondomestic inputs are now the norm rather than the exception.

32. The Australian Law Reform Commission has issued a report that considers Australia's customs and excise laws in great detail and that makes recommendations for change, including an almost complete redraft of the Customs Act (ALRC Report No. 60, June 1992). The report does not attempt to grapple with difficult origin issues and perpetuates the preference emphasis of Australian origin rules. The Commission explains its approach to the issue in the following terms: "Although these [preference] rules appear to have much in common with a determination of the origin of goods, the issue of origin and the issue of eligibility for preference only have a tenuous relationship. The origin of goods, although a relatively objective matter, is in many cases difficult to establish with great certainty. Goods partly made in several countries may equally be said to have had their origin in each of those countries." ALRC Report No. 60, Vol. 3 at 368.

to have been a concern for the Australian authorities since the one duty (until recently a rather high duty) would apply no matter which non-preference country was claimed as the origin of the goods. Therefore, no critical attention was paid to the question.[33]

One result of this approach, that is not so obvious from a casual reading of the rules as we have stated them above is that Section 151 does not define the country of origin of goods in all cases. For instance, if goods are manufactured in or made from materials of more than one place (Rule 6) but only 50 percent of the factory or works cost of the goods is attributable to the place where the last process of manufacture occurred in relation to those goods, the Customs Act makes no further provision to determine their origin. In that situation, there are no revenue implications, as no differential duty rate would apply in any case. The only significance would be a statistical one. The system is administered on the basis that only those cases with revenue implications are investigated. One good reason for this is that penalties relating to inaccurate statements in entry documentation are defined in terms of the amount of duty short paid. Entry documentation is accepted in the majority of cases in the form lodged, without an origin investigation, if it leads to the payment of duty at the highest rate (regarding false trade descriptions, see § 6.1.).

The irony of the gaps in Section 151 are made more striking by Section 151(2), which states, "Goods are not the produce or manufacture of a country for the purposes of this Act unless they are such produce or manufacture under this section."

If goods fall into the cracks of Section 151, no legislative country of origin scheme applies in Australia to determine where, at law, they have come from.[34]

2.3. Administrative Implementation

How Section 151 of the Customs Act is administered is partly explained in Volume 8 of the Australian Customs Service Manual in the section dealing

---

33. Section 22(a) of the Customs Tariff Act 1987 provides that the general rate set out in the tariff is the applicable rate of duty for goods that are not the produce or manufacture of a preference country.

34. Another illogical aspect of Section 151 is represented by Rule 1 and the exception to it as set out in the text above. A New Zealand or Canadian raw material must come directly from the originating country: if it does not, and if the original intended destination is not shown to have been Australia, the raw material has no legal origin.

with Preference. Aspects of the implementation of Section 151 by the Customs Service are discussed below.

2.3.1.   Unmanufactured Raw Products

The Customs Act defines "unmanufactured raw products" as

[n]atural or primary products that have not been subjected to an industrial process, other than an ordinary process of primary production and, without limiting the generality of the foregoing, includes:
(a)   animals;
(b)   bones, hides, skins and other parts of animals obtained by killing, including such hides and skins that have been sun-dried;
(c)   greasy wool;
(d)   plants and parts of plants, including raw cotton, bark, fruit, nuts, grain, seeds in their natural state and unwrought logs;
(e)   minerals in their natural state and ores; and
(f)   crude petroleum.[35]

Section 151(5), which is the primary provision from which the authors' Rule 1 is derived, does not deal with many difficult origin issues that are raised for these types of products, and it is left to the intuition of the Customs Service and its officers to fill many of the gaps that are left. For instance, no attempt is made in the Customs Act to cover the origin of fish caught either inside or outside territorial waters, nor of scrap or waste materials collected in a particular country. These issues have tested international negotiators and are dealt with under the Kyoto Convention.[36]

---

35.   Customs Act, Section 4(1).

36.   The Kyoto Convention provides that "scrap and waste from manufacturing and processing operations, and used articles, collected in that country and fit only for the recovery of raw materials" are to be treated as produced wholly in a given country. In Australia, the administrative rule applied by the Customs Service is that scrap will be the manufacture of a country if collected or produced in the country. This can be unclear, depending on the view taken on when *scrap* comes into being. Say lead is collected in Japan but processed in South Korea: does the administrative rule lead to the result that either country may have been the origin of the finished product?

2.3.2. Wholly Manufactured Goods

There are two interesting observations about administrative practice in relation to Rule 2 (Section 151(6) of the Customs Act). First, for administrative purposes "wholly manufactured" is interpreted to mean 97% or greater. Secondly, no materials have been determined by the Comptroller under Exception 2 to the Rule (which permits the Comptroller to determine that materials imported into the country of manufacture are nonetheless manufactured raw materials of the country of manufacture) other than for New Zealand and Canada.

2.3.3. Notices Concerning Determination of Costs and Value

The Comptroller has gazetted notices under Section 151(13) of the Customs Act to specify how the "factory or works cost of goods" and the "value of labour and materials" are to be determined.[37]

Notice No 88/10[38] specifies how the "factory or works cost" of goods is to be calculated under the Australian legislation. One of Australia's reservations to Annex D1 to the Kyoto Convention provides that "The Australian Customs uses the factory or works cost of finished goods as the basis for assessing preference eligibility and not the ex-works price or the price at exportation as specified in [Recommended Practice 5]."

The notice states that the factory or works cost of goods, where those words are used in Section 151, is the sum of the following:

(a)   the cost of materials received into factory but not including any duties or other taxes paid or payable in the country of manufacture of the goods in respect of such materials;

(b)   manufacturing wages;

(c)   factory overhead expenses; and

---

37.   Commonwealth of Australia Gazette No GN33, 7 September 1988, Notices Nos 88/10 and 88/12 and Gazette No GN45, 30 November 1988, Notice No 88/14. The first notice specifies how to determine the factory or works costs for goods of any origin; the second specifies how to determine of the value of labor or materials for goods of nonNew Zealand origin; and the latter notice specifies how to determine the value of labor or materials for goods of New Zealand origin only.

38.   See *infra* note 40.

(d)   the cost of inside containers."[39]

Whilst there is significant latitude in Recommended Practice 5 of Annex D1 for countries to determine the price of goods produced "at exportation," there are basic differences between the Australian position and the Convention relating to the allowable extent of local content of a product partly manufactured in a preference country. The objective of a preference country manufacturer will be to maximize the costs able to be included as local content. A price of goods at exportation allows more leeway for local content to be increased. In the administration of Notice No GN 88/10, the Customs Service considers those items able to be included as local content to be those costs incurred during manufacture, and not others. For instance, in the administration of the notice, selling and administrative costs that are not part of factory overheads and profit included as part of the price, are not accepted as part of the factory or works costs of goods. This "factory gate" approach calls for fine judgements to be made for some costs but is considered by the Customs Service to be less open to manipulation.[40]

2.3.4.   Certificates of Origin

Australia is not a signatory to Annex D2 to the Kyoto Convention, which concerns documentary evidence of origin. Notwithstanding the decision not to accede, the Customs Service requirements for establishing origin are relatively transparent and flexible. They are based on the presumption made in favor of the importer at the time of importation that the importer possesses documentary evidence that establishes the origin of goods claimed to have been imported from a preference country. There is no legal requirement, either under the Act or the regulations, for a certificate of any particular type or in

---

39.   The words "factory overhead expenses" have been considered in Federal Court proceedings dealing with the determination of an "Australian industry" for the purposes of establishing the grounds for an antidumping action. In *Marine Power Australia Pty Limited & Anor v. Comptroller-General of Customs & Ors*, (1989) 89 ALR 561, the Court held that the words "factory overhead expenses" as used in Section 269T(2) of the Customs Act do not have a technical sense as an accounting expression and that although it is open to a decision maker to take accounting concepts into consideration when applying the Section, the words have an ordinary and sensible meaning and may be applied within those bounds in the decision maker's discretion.

40.   In § 2.1.3. the authors have suggested that the attempt by the comptroller to include factory overheads as a component part of the value of labor and materials of imported goods for which preference is claimed is beyond the power bestowed under Section 151(13). See also *supra* note 25.

any particular form to be provided as a condition of entry. An entry of goods from a preference country is normally processed electronically. The Customs Service has the right to review the entry concerned and, if the facts stated in the entry are inaccurate, may sue for the recovery of the duty short paid[41] and demand duty short paid at any time within twelve months of the entry.[42] Substantial penalties also exist under the Customs Act for making false or misleading statements[43] or including inaccurate information,[44] in entry documentation.

The Customs Service has issued guidelines to importers on the type of certification of origin which should be retained by them for the purposes of later review by the Customs Service if a review and random inspection of the manufacturer's commercial documents is undertaken. At law, a certification in accordance with Customs Service requirements is not conclusive in any sense, as the question whether a particular entry was entitled to preferential treatment depends in all cases on the proven facts. In any event, the Customs Service has advised importers of suggested formats for certificates of origin and has stipulated that such certificates should be signed by the overseas manufacturer or, in the case of the Peoples' Republic of China and Hong Kong, by certain specified commercial organizations.[45]

The suggested certificates require a declaration to be made by the overseas manufacturer in the form of the words of the relevant part of Section 151 pursuant to which a preference is claimed, a description of the consignment of the goods, and a signature by a person employed by the manufacturing company.[46]

---

41. Customs Act, Section 153.

42. Ibid., Section 165(1).

43. Ibid., Section 234.

44. Ibid., Section 243T.

45. Australian Customs Notice No 91/51, 10 April 1991.

46. The Australian Customs Service Manual states that: "It is no defence against a demand for paying of additional customs duty to rely on a manufacturer's declaration that the goods comply with particular preference conditions." Public Edition, Vol. 8, at 115.

3. Nonpreferential Rules of Origin

For ordinary customs purposes, the origin of goods not entitled to preference is of little significance to the administering authorities.[47] Rules of origin in special areas, other than in relation to preference, are dealt with in §§ 5 and 6 of this chapter.

3.1. Procedure

3.1.1. Administrative

Goods that are imported into Australia are required to be entered. An entry in the prescribed form under the Customs Regulations must be lodged. One of the required particulars in an entry is: "the tariff, statistical, country of origin and value base codes in respect of the goods to which the entry relates, details of any other factors that affect the amount of duty payable and a full description of the goods."[48]

The duty payable for nonpreference sources does not, by definition, vary depending on the country of origin. No import licensing scheme (i.e., quota control) operates under Australian law by reference to country of origin. Once goods are entered and duty paid, they are released to the owner for the purposes of home consumption in accordance with the entry.[49]

Review by the Administrative Appeals Tribunal, an independent quasi-judicial body established to review specified administrative decisions on their merits, in an origin dispute is predicated on the payment of duty demanded by the Customs Service under protest by the owner on the grounds that the owner disagrees with the assessment. That situation does not arise in a nonpreference situation and the Tribunal therefore has no jurisdiction in such cases.

---

47. See Rules 1, 2 and 6 in § 2.2. for the Australian nonpreference rules of origin and Sections 151(5), (6), and (12) of the Customs Act (reproduced in Appendix 1).

48. Customs Regulations, Regulation 37(1)(e). The reference to "country of origin" does not neatly tie in to the words used in the Customs Act itself. Section 151 determines "When goods treated as the produce or manufacture of a country" (as stated in the section heading), and the words "country of origin" are not used in the section.

49. Customs Act, Section 39(1).

3.1.2.   Judicial

In nonpreferential cases, a decision by the Customs Service concerning origin is unlikely to have a prejudicial effect on the owner of the goods in all but exceptional cases (i.e., except in relation to prohibited imports, antidumping, and trade descriptions, which are considered in § 6). Under the Administrative Decisions (Judicial Review) Act 1977 (the ADJR Act), "a person who is aggrieved by a decision to which [the] Act applies"[50] (i.e., "a decision of an administrative character")[51] may apply for an order of review by the Federal Court of Australia. The degree of grief required for standing under the ADJR Act has been interpreted quite liberally and is not necessarily linked to commercial damage. The Act has proved to be a popular and potent avenue of appeal in administrative law disputes (i.e. disputes about an error of law or procedure that has the effect of vitiating the decision made rather than claimed errors of fact by the administrator, which are not reviewable). However, its application to origin disputes is severely limited, if not completely excluded, by paragraph (e) of Schedule 1 to the ADJR Act, which excludes the operation of the Act from the area of "decisions . . . forming part of the process of making assessments of duty" under the Customs Act. However, there are purposes for which an origin decision may be made that are not for the purposes of assessing duty (such as in the areas of prohibited imports and trade descriptions); accordingly, ADJR Act appeal would be available in those areas.

It has always been possible to challenge administrative decisions of Commonwealth officers in customs and other matters by seeking what are known as "prerogative writ remedies" in the High Court of Australia or in one of the State Supreme Courts in the exercise of their federal jurisdiction. This power of review derives from Section 39B of the Judiciary Act 1903. The Federal Court now also exercises the same jurisdiction, and it is to be expected that any matters appealed by an applicant direct to the High Court would be remitted by it to the lower Federal Court. The prerogative relief remedies are the writs of mandamus (an order requiring a Commonwealth officer to do his or her duty according to law), prohibition (an order prohibiting action by a Commonwealth officer), and certiorari (an order quashing a decision of a Commonwealth officer). The remedies are discretionary, and in the circumstances of a nonpreferential origin dispute an issue would be raised whether an applicant had standing to bring an application or might suffer a potential detriment that would be sufficient to

---

50.   ADJR Act, Section 5(1).

51.   Ibid., Section 3(1).

invoke the court's jurisdiction. Like ADJR Act procedures, the prerogative writ remedies are based on "error of law" principles, and a claimed error of fact or opinion in the exercise of the decision maker's discretion, absent an error of law, is not reviewable by the courts.

3.2.   Substantive Law

3.2.1.   Basic Rules

The basic rules for determining the origin of goods from nonpreference countries are in Sections 151(5), (6), and (12) of the Customs Act: see Rules 1, 2 and 6 in § 2.2. above.

3.2.2.   Interpretation by Administrative Agencies

The interpretation of words used in Sections 151(5), (6), and (12) would be no different from the interpretation adopted for the same words used in relation to the parts of Section 151 dealing with preferences: see § 4.2, which deals with interpretation in preference cases.

3.2.3.   Interpretation by Courts

There is only one reported case concerning Section 151. Section 4.2.3 refers to that case, which gives guidance on the interpretation that would be adopted in nonpreference cases.

4. Preferential Rules of Origin

4.1.   Procedure

4.1.1.   Administrative

The entry of goods entitled to preference is no different from the entry of any other goods. An entry setting out the required particulars, including country of origin, must be lodged. For the purposes of electronic entry, special letter codes must be included in documentation to designate the preferential treatment requested.

It is possible for an importer to informally ask the Customs Service for advice on the origin of goods, and accordingly whether or not they are entitled to preference, in advance of deciding whether to import the goods. However, the Customs Service is unlikely to treat any opinion concerning origin as having any binding future effect, both for the general reason that it would not wish to fetter its administrative discretion in future cases and also for the particular reason, in the case of a preference costing exercise, that costs and values that determine preference eligibility are always subject to change.

An appeal to the Administrative Appeals Tribunal is available to an importer who pays duty under protest in accordance with Section 167 of the Customs Act. That section applies when a dispute arises about the amount or rate of duty payable for any goods. A decision by the Customs Service not to accept a claim for preferential treatment will lead to such a dispute. If the importer fails to pay under protest but still wishes to obtain a refund of duty, the Tribunal has jurisdiction to hear the dispute if the duty was paid "through manifest error of fact or patent misconception of law."[52]

The Administrative Appeals Tribunal is not a court, and is unable to exercise the "judicial power of the Commonwealth."[53] Its role is to stand in the shoes of the decision maker and to make the correct or preferable decision according to the merits of the case and its view of the applicable law. Its decisions are not binding on courts of law nor the bodies whose decisions may be referred to it for review. Nevertheless because the Tribunal is a high-level decision-making body, staffed by both judges and persons experienced in the particular areas of the jurisdiction of the Tribunal, its decisions are highly persuasive in the administration of the law by the agencies whose decisions may be appealed to the Tribunal. Appeals to the Federal Court on contested points of law arising from decisions of the Tribunal are available to parties to the Tribunal proceedings.

The Tribunal has been active in three cases that have examined the preferential origin provisions of Section 151 (see § 4.2.).

4.1.2. Judicial

Three judicial avenues are available to an importer aggrieved by a decision on the origin of goods that has led to an alleged overpayment of duty. Under Section 167 of the Customs Act, an owner of goods may "bring an action in any Commonwealth or State Court of competent jurisdiction, for the recovery of the whole or any part" of the duty paid, provided that payment was made under protest in the manner prescribed under Section 167(3) and the action is brought within six months of the date of payment. Unlike an appeal to the Federal Court from the Tribunal on a point of law, or judicial review proceedings (dealt with below), an action under Section 167 empowers the court to review all the facts and the application of the law to those facts.

---

52.   Customs Regulations, Reg 126(1)(e).

53.   Constitution, Section 71.

The second method of judicial review in a rule of origin case is the avenue of appeal to the Federal Court on a "question of law" arising from a decision by the Tribunal.[54]

The operation of the ADJR Act is excluded from the area of "decisions . . . forming part of the process of making . . . assessments of duty" under the Customs Act by paragraph (e) of Schedule 1 to the Act. Resort may be had to the prerogative writs in suitable cases to argue an error of law before the courts in the absence of the availability of the less formal ADJR Act grounds of review and procedures (see § 3.1.2.).

4.2.   Substantive Law

4.2.1.   Basic Rules

Section 151 of the Customs Act sets out the means by which the Australian authorities determine whether goods are the produce of manufacture of any particular country. The section is set out in Appendix 1 to this chapter, and the authors have summarized the effect of the section in § 2.2.

4.2.2.   Interpretation by the Administrative Agencies

The development of Australian origin rules by the administrative agencies and by the courts is indebted to gold chains from New Zealand and alkaline batteries from Singapore. In two cases, *Rubis*[55] and *Gaylor*,[56] gold chains have been the catalyst for the scrutiny of Section 151, and some of the terms used in it, by the Administrative Appeals Tribunal. The other important authority is the case of *Eveready*, a Tribunal decision[57] that was reversed on appeal to a single judge of the Federal Court[58] and then restored on appeal to the Full Court.[59]

---

54.   Administrative Appeals Tribunal Act 1975, Section 44.

55.   *Re Rubis and the Collector of Customs* (1984) 5 ALN N558.

56.   *Re Gaylor Jewellery Sales Pty Limited and the Collector of Customs*, (1990) 12 AAR 86.

57.   *Re Eveready and the Collector of Customs* No N89/906 (15 April 1991) unreported.

58.   No G229 of 1991 (28 August 1991) unreported.

59.   No G521 of 1991 (6 March 1992) unreported.

4.2.2.1. Last Process of Manufacture

This issue first presented itself in *Rubis*. Gold extracted and processed in New Zealand was shipped in its raw state to Italy, where it was mixed with various alloy material, fabricated into gold chains, and returned to New Zealand. In New Zealand, a bolt ring was attached to the end of each chain before the finished product was shipped to Australia. The finished product comprised 80 percent New Zealand gold by value. The Collector challenged the importers' view that the goods were the manufacture of New Zealand, which would have entitled them to duty free entry into Australia, and instead demanded the payment of ad valorem duty calculated at the rate of 27.5 percent. The Tribunal summarized its conclusion in the following way:

In the result, the conclusion appears to us to be inescapable that the process last performed in the manufacture of the jewellery, albeit a relatively minor and inexpensive process, was performed in New Zealand and that the jewellery was, therefore, partly manufactured in that country. There was no tenable basis suggested to us in argument, nor do we see any basis ourselves, upon which to read Section 151(3) as applying only where the last process in the manufacture of the goods is a "substantial" process or is more than a "simple assembly operation."

Accordingly, the Tribunal decided that the imported jewellery was entitled to entry at the New Zealand preferential rate, namely "free." In its reasoning, the Tribunal assumed that the 50 percent New Zealand content requirement was satisfied (notwithstanding the apparent substantial change brought about to the gold in Italy) and instead focussed on the question of whether the assembly work performed in New Zealand could be properly characterized as a process in the manufacture of the gold chains. In so doing, the Tribunal expressed the view that there was no reason in principle why the making of goods by assembling previously manufactured parts could not be characterized as a process of manufacture. The Tribunal relied to some degree on the English Court of Appeal case of *Prestcold (Central) Limited v. Minister of Labour*[60], where that court was called upon to decide whether the assembly of a refrigeration plant from component parts fell within the proper definition of the word "manufacturing." It was determined in that case that the assembly of the refrigeration plant was no less an example of manufacturing than the processes by which the components were brought into being.

---

60. [1969] 1 All ER 69.

However, the road to the conclusion eventually reached by the Tribunal was not as smooth as the authority of Prestcold might suggest. The Collector relied heavily on *Irving*[61], a High Court of Australia decision given without reasons, that a company that reassembled bicycles in Australia after their importation from England was not a manufacturer within the meaning of the Sales Tax Assessment Act (No 1) 1930. Without reasons being expressed, the Tribunal had little guidance in determining the true purport of the *Irving* decision. Remarkably, at least from the point of view of the Collector, the *Irving* decision was distinguished from the facts of the *Rubis* case because of the Tribunal's view of the significance of the point in time at which the High Court had interrupted argument by counsel in *Irving* to give its one sentence decision. Counsel was then emphasizing that the Australian company reassembled goods that had already been fully manufactured and tested in England before importation. The Tribunal therefore felt that *Irving* could be confined as authority for the principle that reassembly is not a process of manufacture and that it could not be authority for the different proposition that the process of placing a bolt ring in the course of manufacturing a finished product was not a process of manufacture itself.[62]

In view of the decision by the Collector since *Rubis* not to attempt to reargue the proposition that a simple process of assembly is nonetheless a process of manufacture toward a finished product, *Rubis* represents the current Australian approach to the interpretation of the important words "last process of manufacture" in Section 151.[63] The Tribunal's decision in *Rubis* also exposes a major difference between the international norms sought to be confirmed by the Kyoto Convention and Australian law. In the definitions to the convention, the "substantial transformation criterion" is referred to as: "the criterion according to which origin is determined by regarding as the country of origin the country in which the last substantial manufacturing or processing, deemed to be sufficient to give the commodity its essential character, has been carried out."

---

61. *Irving v. Munro & Sons Ltd* (1931) 46 CLR 279.

62. The meaning of the expression "partly manufactured" has been considered in a customs context in a New Zealand case. In *Wellington City Council v. Attorney-General*, (1990) 2 NZLR 281, the New Zealand Court of Appeal decided that a second hand road sweeper originally manufactured in the United States but then imported to New Zealand after being dismantled, reconditioned, and repaired in Australia was not "partly manufactured in Australia."

63. This is perhaps unfortunate, as the conclusions that assembly is a process of manufacture (*Rubis*) but that reassembly is not (*Irving*) are difficult to reconcile.

The ad valorem percentage rule is a particular method of applying the criterion. But under Australian law, a "last process" requirement is superadded to, but separate from, an ad valorem percentage rule that, according to the convention, is the means by which the country of last substantial manufacture is determined. Even where the goods qualify in terms of meeting the set percentage, the failure to meet the last process requirement disqualifies the goods from preferential eligibility. This has the potential effect of defeating the purpose of adopting an ad valorem approach in the first place.

The decision in *Rubis*, and the intellectual debate it has generated, owes much to the fact that gold, a valuable metal, constituted a high proportion of the value of the finished product. The pure gold that left New Zealand returned in a form that was substantially different, having been mixed with alloys and fabricated into fine gold chain. In fact, the gold content of the gold chains was less than half (by volume), having been mixed with silver and platinum to form the alloy that was able to be fashioned into chain. If the "change in tariff heading" or "manufacturing or process operations" tests had been adopted under the convention, then it is clear that the gold chain imported into New Zealand would have become of Italian origin. However, the *Rubis* approach to the ad valorem percentage test, which is to assume that the integral parts of a product retain their origin notwithstanding an application of a process to them, has the effect of preserving the home value of the constituent parts of any particular product. This has obvious results when applied to something that has a value in a finished product that is exponentially greater than the value of any other part incorporated in or process applied to the finished product.

The resolution of these issues concerning the valuing of constituent parts of a product manufactured in more than one country, and whether the origin of a constituent part needs to be traced to its source, depends on the interpretation given to the word materials in Section 151. When does something become a material, and from what country has it come when it becomes such a material? This question came under the scrutiny of the · Tribunal in the *Gaylor* and *Eveready* cases.

4.2.2.2. Where Do Materials Come From?

Next in the saga of gold chains from New Zealand was the *Gaylor* case. In *Rubis*, you will remember that the gold in the chains had been extracted from New Zealand and that it represented 80 percent of the value of the chains on their importation into Australia. The assumption the parties in *Rubis* had made when they argued the case was that the gold constituted a material for the purposes of Section 151(7), which set out the rule for goods the produce or manufacture of New Zealand (see rule 3 in § 2.2.). It refers to the factory or works cost of the goods in terms of the value of their labour or materials. In *Gaylor*, the attack that the Collector mounted was that on return from fabrication in Italy, the gold chain had become a material, the origin of which was Italy, and that it could not be counted as part of the value of labor and materials of New Zealand (irrespective of the fact that the gold itself had been extracted from New Zealand). The argument was in part based on the fact that alloys were added to the gold in Italy in the course of its fabrication into the gold chains.

Before embarking on a detailed analysis of the *Gaylor* case, it is worthwhile to briefly examine the developing ANZCERTA relationship between Australia and New Zealand, as changes to that relationship were instrumental to how the *Gaylor* case was argued and decided. Soon after the decision in *Rubis*, in the course of a periodic review of ANZCERTA, an exchange of letters took place between the respective Ministers of Customs of the two countries to which was attached a Joint Understanding on Harmonisation of Customs Policies and Procedures. Under the heading "Rules of Origin" in the joint understanding, the following appeared:

The two Customs agencies have a common view on the technical application of the rules of origin.
A revised Explanatory Note is attached to this joint understanding (Attachment A). This note seeks to simplify arrangements for trans Tasman traders and at the same time minimise economic distortions created by the existence of different tariff regimes on intermediate goods from third countries.

The Explanatory Note, which revoked the previous explanatory notes to Article 3 of ANZCERTA, stated in part as follows:

Materials of mixed origin
In terms of Article 3.1(c)(ii), in calculating the value of an imported component incorporated in a final product for export to the other Member State the value of that imported component will be taken as:
– wholly of qualifying area content provided that in its imported form it qualified under the rules of origin on importation into the Member State which manufactured the final product
– totally without qualifying area content if in its imported form it did not qualify under the rules of origin on importation into the Member State which manufactured the final product.

The effect of this part of the Explanatory Note was to look to the origin rules of the manufacturing country in determining whether materials incorporated into the final product are entitled to be considered as part of the percentage value of the finished product required to be of qualifying content (i.e., Australian or New Zealand content). Taking the example of gold chain in the *Rubis* case, if New Zealand determined that the country of origin of the chain was Italy, then the Explanatory Note would require Australia to also consider the chain as being of Italian origin.

Soon after the Exchange of Letters, the Comptroller issued a notice published in the Government Gazette in the purported exercise of his power under Section 151(13) of the Customs Act.[64] That Section (see Appendix 1) enables the Comptroller to specify how the factory or works costs, the value of labor, the value of materials, or the value of labor and materials is to be determined for the purposes of the Act. The notice provided that the value of labor and materials in regard to New Zealand was to be determined in the manner specified in the schedule to the notice. That schedule read as follows:

The value of labour and materials shall be determined by the sum of the following:

(a) (i) in the case of materials wholly produced or manufactured in New Zealand or in Australia or in New Zealand and in Australia but not including any duties or other taxes paid or payable in the country of manufacture of the goods in respect of such materials — the cost of those materials; or

(ii) in the case of materials partly manufactured and exported from Australia to New Zealand for incorporation in a final product for export to Australia from New Zealand, the cost of those imported materials into New Zealand will be:

A wholly of qualifying area content provided that in their imported form they qualified under the rules of origin on importation into New Zealand for incorporation in the final product;

B totally without qualifying area content if in their imported form they did not qualify under the rules of origin on importation into New Zealand and incorporation in the final product; or

(iii) in the case of materials partly manufactured in New Zealand, the value shall be the proportion of the cost of manufacture of those materials incurred in New Zealand or in New Zealand and Australia, but not including any duties or other taxes paid

---

64.   Commonwealth of Australia Gazette No. GN 33, 7 September 1988, Notice No. 88/11.

or payable in the country of manufacture of the goods in respect of such materials;
(b)   manufacturing wages;
(c)   factory overhead expenses; and
(d)   the cost of inside containers of the manufacture of New Zealand or of Australia, or of New Zealand and Australia.

Paragraph (a)(iii) of the notice did not of itself advance the interpretation of the law in any way differently from the underlying reasoning adopted in *Rubis*. Taking that same example again, namely gold chains fabricated from New Zealand gold in Italy, paragraph (a)(iii) of the schedule would have had no effect on the previous position that applied. This is because the materials that went into the manufacture of the gold chains had been partly manufactured in New Zealand and further because the paragraph merely preserved the position that applied in *Rubis* of valuing the costs of the materials used in the manufacture of the finished product. Since the gold represented 80 percent of the finished product, the position would not have changed. Paragraph (a)(iii) did not invoke the important reference in the Explanatory Note to an "imported component incorporated in a final product."
Perhaps recognizing this shortcoming in the notice, the Comptroller revoked it on 18 November 1988 and issued a new one[65] that was in the same form except for the addition of the following paragraph at the foot of the schedule:

For the purposes of this notice "materials" means those goods which, had they been exported from Australia and were later imported into Australia would have had at the time of such importation the same identity for the purposes of the Customs Tariff Act 1987 as they had at the time of their prior exportation.

Effectively, the paragraph sought to introduce a "change in tariff heading" test in determining the origin of the materials incorporated in a product exported to Australia from New Zealand. Again, taking the example of gold chains, the position which would then have resulted, with the incorporation of the paragraph, is that the gold would have been treated as Italian content because it would have been exported from New Zealand to Italy under a different tariff heading from the gold chain imported into New Zealand from Italy. The paragraph note to the Schedule would therefore have had the effect of transferring the high percentage value of New Zealand gold into part of an

---

65.   Commonwealth of Australia Gazette No. GN 45, 30 November 1988, Notice No. 88/14.

Italian "material".[66] The paragraph note introduced a mini-country of origin rule for materials incorporated into a final product. In Gaylor, the ACS sought to reargue the facts of *Rubis* as a test case for its new administration of Section 151 following publication of the new notice.

The first issue dismissed by the Tribunal in *Gaylor* was the proposition put by the Collector that by reason of the addition of substances to the New Zealand fine gold to produce an alloy, the gold alloy could not be properly regarded as being gold of New Zealand origin.[67] The Tribunal appeared to use a simple market test, asking what a purchaser's perception of the nature of the imported chain would be. The Tribunal thought that such a purchaser would consider the article to be a gold chain, even if not made of pure gold. The conclusion then reached was: "As the gold of which the chain or necklace is comprised is gold of New Zealand origin, we consider that the material of which they are comprised is "material of New Zealand" within the meaning of the legislation."

The somewhat remarkable result of taking the Tribunal's point of view to its literal extreme is that the material of which an imported good is made ought to be considered to be the material of which a purchaser believes it to be made, rather than the material of which it is actually made. The Tribunal

---

66. The Australian authorities continue to be troubled by the results of the *Rubis* and *Gaylor* cases, and continue to seek legal mechanisms to ensure that the same situations do not arise in the future. In ALRC Report No 60 *Customs and Excise*, the latest proposal in this regard is contained as Rule 4.2 (3) of Schedule 4 to a redrafted Customs Act. It provides:

"If goods that are the manufacture or produce of a Preference Country:
(a) are subjected to a process of manufacture or production in a country that is not Australia or a Preference Country; and
(b) are then subjected to a process of manufacture or production in the same or some other Preference Country (the "second Preference Country");
the total value of the goods does not include so much of the total preference value as originated before the goods entered the second Preference Country."

In the *Rubis/Gaylor* cases, application of the proposed Rule to the Italian fabrication of the gold chain would render the raw gold ineligible for consideration as New Zealand content of the finished product.

67. The Tribunal's conclusion on this point is brief and somewhat unsatisfactory, and the point has now been revisited in the third major Australian rule of origin case: *Re Eveready Australia Pty Limited and the Collector of Customs* N89/906 (Administrative Appeals Tribunal 15 April 1991) on appeal from the Tribunal, *Eveready Australia Pty Limited v. Collector of Customs* No. G229 of 1991 (Beaumont, J., Federal Court of Australia), 28 August 1991 (unreported); and on appeal from the single judge, *Collector of Customs v Eveready Australia Pty Limited*, No. G521 of 1991 (Full Court of the Federal Court of Australia), 6 March 1992 (unreported).

went on to say that it was supported in its view by the Macquarie Dictionary definition of material which is as follows: "1. The substance or substances of which a thing is made or composed; 2. Any constituent element of the thing." The link between that dictionary definition and the view that because people think the material is gold, it is gold (notwithstanding that as a matter of fact it is a gold alloy) is not made clear by the Tribunal.

The Tribunal next dealt with the Collector's argument that the paragraph note to the schedule to the notice required the Tribunal to come to the view that the gold chain, being the relevant material used in the manufacture of the gold chain, was not of New Zealand origin. If this argument were to succeed, then the goods would not satisfy the 50 percent New Zealand content test stipulated in Section 151(7). On this point, the Tribunal determined that the paragraph note to the schedule was not authorized by the empowering provision, namely Section 151(13) of the Customs Act. In short, the Tribunal stated that the paragraph note was beyond the power of the Collector, because Section 151(13) did not permit the Collector to "exclude" a certain category of materials from the calculation of what constituted the value of labor and materials in a product imported from New Zealand.[68]

4.2.2.3. What Constitutes *Materials*?

The questions left unanswered by the Tribunal in its treatment of the meaning of the word *materials* were revisited in the recent case of *Eveready* and the two Federal Court appeals that followed the Tribunal's decision. The facts of this case seem to have been purposefully constructed to elicit a substantial legal and philosophical debate on the question of what is considered to be a *material* for the purposes of the Australian legislation. The importer imported batteries for which it was conceded the last process of manufacture had occurred in Singapore. Singapore is entitled to preference as a developing country under the Australian Tariff. The principal components in a battery of the type involved in the facts of *Eveready*[69] are an anode mix and a cathode mix. All the materials that were combined to produce these mixes were imported into Singapore from countries not eligible for preferential status under the tariff (for example, Japan). The importer argued that the mixture of the substances in their particular chemical formulation in Singapore resulted

---

68.   In a joint press statement issued by the Australian Minister for Trade and Overseas Development, Dr. Neal Blewett, and the New Zealand Minister for Trade Negotiations, Mr. Philip Burdon, on 5 July 1991, it was announced that a further review of the ANZCERTA rules of origin would form an agenda item for the 1992 review of the ANZCERTA.

69.   See *supra* note 67.

in a new product that was distinct from any of the chemicals mixed to produce it. The relevant part of the importer's submission was as follows:

The resultant component in each case [i.e., in the production of a cathode and anode mix] is a material which has electrophysical properties which are quite distinct from any of its inputs. Indeed, the resultant material in each case is quite distinct from all of its relevant inputs which have not undergone the specialist manufacturing process.

Both the anode and cathode are manufactured in specially dedicated areas in the plant at Singapore. The manufacture of batteries is not merely the adding of substances such as [main ingredients] in the assembly. Rather the cathode and the anode are separately manufactured, created, tested and stored in Singapore before battery assembly commences, in the same way as the other components of the battery are separately manufactured, created, tested and stored before battery assembly commences.

Both cathode and anode manufacture are regarded as separate cost centres within Eveready Singapore, and accordingly, the administrative and financial treatment of the manufacture of these components is separate from those of battery manufacture itself.

In this case, the tables were effectively turned in favor of the Customs Service. Here, in the view of the Customs Service, was a product manufactured from materials that had been sourced from nonpreference countries to a degree that meant that preference country factory and works cost fell short of the necessary percentage: surely the authorities of *Rubis* and *Gaylor* would apply in favour of the Customs Service? The essential paragraphs of the Collector's written submissions were as follows:

The [Collector] submits that "materials" is to be understood as those goods, whether they be produce (unmanufactured raw products), or manufactured goods, which are received into the factory for the purpose of manufacturing the subject goods. This interpretation accords with normal commercial usage and understanding of "materials" in the context of factory operations. The ingredients of factory manufacturing operations are: a building, plant, labour plus raw materials equals manufactured goods. The materials are what is delivered at the factory door and not other discrete materials which come into being as part of the manufacturing process and which will, with other components, be used in the final assembly operation.

The materials "received into the factory" were the materials combined to produce the anode and cathode mixes, which the Collector argued were sourced from nonpreference countries. But, to add an element of uncertainty to the position of the Collector, and a further degree of difficulty for the Tribunal, the importer argued that it was possible to trace the materials shipped to Singapore, mainly from Japan, to upstream sources, some of which were developing countries.

Starting with the importer's tracing argument first, the Tribunal decided that this was not a correct approach to adopt to the Section 151 use of the word *materials*. It decided that all of the substances were treated in Japan in one way or another to produce something essentially different in character, form, description, and commercial identity from the primary substances that left developing countries before coming to Japan.[70] You will recall that this was almost exactly the argument put by the importer in arguing that the combination of the materials in Singapore lead to the manufacture of a completely different product in that country. But the Tribunal did not agree that the same argument could be applied to show that the cathode and anode mixes were materials of Singapore, coming to the conclusion that the plain dictionary meaning of materials indicates a reference to anything delivered to the factory and intended to be used in the manufacturing process. To the casual observer, this would appear to confuse the question of what is a material with the actual process of manufacture of the finished product. Is it to be suggested that the cathode and anode mixes would become a material of Singapore if a different factory in Singapore were used to produce those mixes?

The Tribunal's final conclusion is contained in the following paragraphs:

I accept the submission of Counsel for [the importer] that the anodes and cathodes are not simple admixtures of known substances. I accept that they are important components of batteries in their own right. I am unable to accept the Applicant's argument, however, that this thereby makes them the "materials" of the battery and that the imported ingredients are merely "substances making up those materials". The sub-section does not qualify "materials" in any way with adjectives such as essential, important, basic or expensive. It refers simply to the totality of the materials used in the manufacture.

It is also not necessary to accept Counsel's argument that a "factory door approach" would require each of the materials of the battery to be traced through each substance of which each material is comprised until it in turn is broken down to its constituent substances. A factory door approach, it seems to mean, is to apply the plain meaning of materials, calling for no

---

70. In so doing, the tribunal must be taken to have drawn a fine distinction of some sort with the *Rubis* and *Gaylor* findings that the transformation of raw gold into a chain of gold alloy did not lead to the production of something "essentially different."

further analysis of the substances prior to their arrival at the starting point of manufacture. Put figuratively, materials are everything that comes into the factory back door. Batteries are what go out through the factory front door.

The Tribunal's decision was first overturned, and then restored, in two successive appeals to the Federal Court of Australia, and those decisions are considered in § 4.2.3 of this chapter.

4.2.3.   Interpretation by the Courts

Eveready, as appealed to a single judge of the Federal Court of Australia and then the Full Court, is the only Australian judicial consideration of the interpretation of Section 151. In the first appeal, the single judge hearing the case went to great lengths to set out the elaborate process of manufacture of the anode and cathode mixes in Singapore. The purpose of this detailed and lengthy treatment of the production process became obvious in the results of the case. Judge Beaumont concluded his reasoning as follows:

As has been said, the instant question concerns the meaning of the composite expression "materials of a Developing Country" in the context of a definition of the location of manufacture of goods. In that context, applying the relevant dictionary definitions already mentioned, I think that the expression is intended to refer to articles of any kind requisite for making the subject goods which articles have a connection or association with the Developing Country. Applying the first of the definitions, the cathode mix and the anode mix were articles requisite for making the batteries. Further, in my view, the mixes had a connection or association with Singapore. The connection or association arose from the circumstance that the substantial processes undertaken to produce the mixes were carried out in Singapore by a company carrying on its manufacturing operations there. This is not to say that any treatment of an article, however insignificant, will suffice to establish a connection or association which would justify the description of materials as "of" a particular country. Questions of degree are involved but, in the present case, the processes undertaken were both significant and substantial, sufficiently so, I think, to warrant the attribution of the mixes to the Republic of Singapore. It follows, in my view, that the mixes were materials "of" Singapore for the purposes of Section 151(10)(b).

The decision introduces a judicial "substantial transformation" test for the purposes of determining the origin of a material incorporated in a manufactured product. In requiring a "connection or association" with the country of manufacture of material, and describing the requisite link in terms of the substantial processes required to produce the material, the judgment would have had the effect of bringing Australian practice, in the limited context of materials, in line with the "substantial transformation" criterion referred to in the second item of Note 1 to Standard 3 of Annex D1 to the Kyoto Convention. Presumably, the courts would then have proceeded to develop, as mandated by Note 1, "[a] list of manufacturing or processing operations which confer, or do not confer, upon the goods the origin of the country in which those operations were carried out." The origin of the raw materials were unimportant to Judge Beaumont in his decision in *Eveready*. He decided that it was not necessary to deal with the tracing argument advanced on behalf of Eveready (i.e., the argument that suggested that raw materials used to make the anode and cathode mixes had been sourced from developing countries before being processed in Japan on their way to Singapore).

The Collector had no option but to appeal the decision of Judge Beaumont to the Full Court. The decision suggested that both *Rubis* and *Gaylor* were incorrectly decided in that they did not carefully consider the substantial transformation that occurred to the New Zealand gold in those cases whereby it was transformed into a chain of gold alloy in Italy. If unchallenged, it would also have caused a divergence between the interpretation of the words of the legislation when dealing with the origin of a finished product and the judicial interpretation when dealing with the origin of a material. In the former case origin would be attracted by both content and a last process of manufacture (not necessarily a substantial one), whereas in the latter case no last process requirement would be superadded.

The Full Federal Court restored the Tribunal's decision. The Court stated, 'the legislation is concerned with the manufacture of goods, not the manufacture of materials then used in another process in manufacture of those goods.'

The Court decided that no separate regard should be given to the intermediate products, the anode and the cathode mixes, in determining whether the preferential rate should apply. The Court's reasoning was expressed in its view that the factory or works cost in the preferential area had to be based on the value of the materials (amongst other things) used in the processes of manufacture and not materials produced in the course of and then consumed by those processes. On this view, the mixes could not be independent starting points for the determination of a material having preferential area status.

The Court did not go so far as to introduce a tracing test to determine the proportions of origin in a finished product. Although it said there was "a logical appeal" to this argument, it believed it could not be supported because the legislation looked to the value of the materials taken up in the process of manufacture of the goods, and not to their value in the condition they existed prior to that process (i.e., "regardless of the anterior transmutations that had taken place") and because it "would pose insurmountable practical difficulties."

The difficult question that might need to be answered in future Australian cases is where to draw the line where the relevant "processes of manufacture" for purposes of bringing a particular product into existence start. What if the anode and the cathode mixes had shelf lives of longer than seven and three days respectively (a point that appeared to have some significance to the Court), had been produced by a separate corporate entity in a separate factory in Singapore, and were purchased from a warehouse to be used in the production processes at the *Eveready* factory? If the latter was the case, then presumably the batteries (in the same other circumstances presented by the *Eveready* case) would have qualified for preferential treatment.

4.3. Australia's Compliance with International Norms

The authors have already touched on the inconsistency with the Kyoto Convention that arises in Australian rules of origin by reason of the superadded requirement of last process of manufacture. The convention states that the "substantial transformation criterion" is designed to determine the last substantial process of manufacture, not that the words "last substantial process" are an additional test once a contracting party has selected a "substantial transformation criterion" test.

The Australian experience has also highlighted a possible shortcoming of the Kyoto Convention in that the suggested substantial transformation tests permitted under the convention can lead to different results. The word *material* is used in the ad valorem percentage test in the Kyoto Convention, but, as is the case with the Customs Act, there is no express treatment of the origin of a material, nor of what a material is. Until the position is clarified, the ad valorem test falls short of its intended target of harmonization.

5. Australian Antidumping and Origin

5.1. Introduction

One of the major commercial pressures for close scrutiny and reform of origin rules on the world scene has been caused by the attempts by manufacturers to avoid or overcome the impact of dumping duties imposed by countries that are signatories to the GATT Anti-Dumping Code.[71] One can try to circumvent intended dumping measures for goods from a certain country by so-called country hopping, either in the form of transhipment through a second country or the application of a simple process of some sort to the goods in the second country. Another type of circumvention is the dumping of componentry in second countries where significant manufacturing processes nonetheless take place. More robust attempts to overcome the impact of dumping measures are the establishment of production facilities in the country that assessed the dumping duties in the first place, where local labor either assembles or manufactures componentry (of mixed origin, but in the classic case mostly componentry sourced from the original dumping country). The pressures caused by this third type of circumvention are generally not present in Australia, as the size and relative isolation of the Australian market and its labor conditions do not justify the capital intensive requirements for the establishment of local facilities, either for local or export sales.

The Australian legislation uses a discrete set of origin rules for the purposes of antidumping proceedings and enforcement. However, this broad statement must be qualified in at least two ways: first, the issue of the origin of dumped goods has not been the subject of any case law and, secondly, the relevant provisions in the Customs Act do not clearly evince an intention to establish separate rules of origin for all antidumping purposes.

5.2.   Antidumping Measures

Under Section 8 of the Customs Tariff (Anti-Dumping) Act 1975, the Australian authorities are able to charge and collect a special duty of customs, known as dumping duty, "by virtue of a declaration under subsection 269TG(1) or (2) of the Customs Act." Those sections of the Customs Act permit the relevant Minister to make a declaration regarding the application of Section 8 if the minister is satisfied that the amount of the export price of certain goods is less than the amount of the normal value of those goods and, because of that, material injury to an Australian industry producing like goods has been or is being caused or is being threatened or the establishment of Australian industry producing like goods has been or might be materially hindered. A full analysis of the way in which these decisions are reached has

---

71.   Agreement on Implementation of Article VI of the General Agreement on Tariffs and Trade, GATT, 26th Supp. BISD 171-88 (1980).

been fully canvassed by one of the authors in another work and is of course beyond the scope of this chapter.[72]

5.3. Rules of Origin for the Purposes of an Investigation

Part XVB of the Customs Act, comprising Sections 269T to 269U, constitutes the Australian legislative code of law and procedures governing the assessment and investigation of alleged dumping. The actual imposition of dumping duty is dealt with under a separate act, the Customs Tariff (Anti-Dumping) Act 1975.[73]

Under those Sections, it is important to determine the "country of export" of goods alleged to be dumped. The point of export is an important factor in considering export price and normal value issues. For instance, Section 269TAC(1) provides that the normal value of any goods exported to Australia

[i]s the price paid for like goods sold in the ordinary course of trade for home consumption in the country of export in sales that are arm's length transactions by the exporter or, if like goods are not so sold by the exporter, by other sellers of like goods.

Difficult questions arise in cases where transhipment occurs or where more than one country is involved in the manufacture of the allegedly dumped goods, and there are provisions in the Act aimed at dealing with these questions in the antidumping context. The country of export is also important in those provisions that set out the considerations that the Comptroller may take into account in determining whether material injury has been caused or is threatened to an Australian industry. For example, Section 269TAE sets out a number of considerations, such as the quantity of goods exported and any increase or likely increase in the quantity goods exported, and each of these considerations require the Comptroller to ascertain what is the relevant country of export. Section 269T of the Customs Act, which is headed "Interpretation," provides in subsection (2B), " For the purposes of this Part, where, during the exportation of goods to Australia, the goods pass in transit from a country through another country, that other country shall be disregarded in ascertaining the country of export of the goods."

---

72.   See Steele, "The Australian Anti-Dumping System," John H. Jackson and Edwin A. Vermulst, eds., ANTIDUMPING LAW AND PRACTICE: A COMPARATIVE STUDY, (ANN ARBOR: THE UNIVERSITY OF MICHIGAN PRESS, 1989) at 223-286.

73.   This is consistent with the constitutional requirement that an Act dealing with the imposition of duty may not deal with any other subject. See *supra* note 7.

Section 269TAC, which is headed "Normal value of goods," contains two important subsections for origin purposes. They are as follows:

(10) Where:

  (a) the actual country of export of goods exported to Australia is not the country of origin of the goods; and

  (b) the Minister is of the opinion that the normal value of the goods should be ascertained for the purposes of this Part as if the country of origin were the country of export; he or she may direct that the normal value of the goods is to be so ascertained.

(11) For the purposes of subsection (10), the country of origin of the goods is:

  (a) in the case of unmanufactured raw products - the country of which they are products; or

  (b) in any other case - the country in which the last significant process in the manufacture or production of the goods was performed."[74]

The sections empower the Minister to direct that a country other than the country of export of the goods is the country of origin of the goods. The test that the Minister is asked to apply in deciding whether to give such a direction is the country in which the "last significant process of manufacture" was performed. The Australian Customs Service Manual interprets subsection 269TAC(11)(b) as requiring "a substantial transformation of the product, or the addition of some essential or vital quality to the goods".[75]

The increasing formality of Australian antidumping procedures, the litigious inclinations of the participants, and the internationalization of the manufacture and supply of imported goods have all combined to produce a notable case study of the problems that might be ahead for the Australian authorities in the area of the origin of goods. In April 1991, the Australian Electrical and Electronic Manufacturer's Association lodged an application for the initiation of an investigation into the alleged dumping of cross-linked polyethylene

---

74. The Anti-Dumping Authority has employed the power to determine the country of origin under Section 269 TAC (11)(b) in only one reported case: *Certain Outboard Motors from Belgium, the United States of America and Japan*, Report No. 10 (September 1989). In that investigation, country hopping of fully assembled motors from Japan and the USA through Belgium was detected. Ibid. at 16 and 19. The degree of further manufacturing or other processes conducted in Belgium is not revealed in the report.

75. Manual, Public Edition, Vol. 22, at 5-86.

aerial bundled electric cable (xlpe cable). The application stated that "The country of origin is believed to be the Republic of Korea but having regard to Section 269T(2B) of the Act, some minor processing is undertaken in Singapore and, therefore, Singapore is the country of export of the goods."

The application was accepted and an investigation initiated on the strength of the allegations made in it. The exporter and importer of the goods, Midland Metals Overseas Limited, immediately took umbrage at the initiation of the investigation and commenced litigation in the Federal Court under the ADJR Act seeking review of the decision to initiate.[76] One of the grounds of the review was to the effect that the Administrative Appeals Tribunal had decided, in other proceedings, that the place of export of the goods was Korea, not Singapore, and that the Customs Service was bound by an "issue estoppel" because of that decision. If that contention proved correct, Midland argued, the Customs Service was not competent to decide differently and initiate an investigation into the goods said to be exported from Singapore.

The claim that some sort of issue estoppel operated foundered on three bases: the fact that the Tribunal is only an administrative decision-making body (see § 4.1.1.); the legal proposition that the Tribunal's previous decision operated in respect of goods being imported at that time and not the ones now being considered by the Customs Service; and the fact that the Tribunal's previous decision involved the interpretation of the words "place of export" in a completely different context under the Customs Act, namely valuation rather than antidumping. For current purposes, the Tribunal's decision in the valuation case referred to is useful as it indicates the company structures and manufacturing and contractual processes that combined to bring the goods to Australia.[77] The company involved, also Midland, was said to be incorporated in Bermuda with a branch in Singapore from which it conducted its Australian operations. It received goods into Singapore from Spain, Malaysia, China, and Korea, where they were not entered but remained in bond in a free trade zone under the auspices of the Port of Singapore Authority. Whilst in bond the cargo was examined, for example to check the drums on which xlpe cable was wound, and any necessary repairs were made. Later, the goods were aggregated with other goods in different sizes and quantities in response to an order from Australia, put in containers and

---

76. *Midland Metals Overseas Limited v. Comptroller-General of Customs* No. G245 (26 June 1991) (unreported).

77. *Re Midland Metals Overseas Limited and Collector of Customs*, No. V90/518 (29 April 1991) (unreported).

shipped. Midland was successful in its claim before the Tribunal, proving that Singapore was not the place of export of the goods under consideration.[78]

In contrast to its success before the Tribunal, Midland lost its legal battle in the Federal Court to prevent the initiation of the dumping investigation. But the proceedings at least had the effect of signalling to the Customs Service the types of issues Midland felt were important to its threshold inquiries concerning the origin of the goods. On 7 August 1991, the Customs Service issued its Preliminary Finding in the investigation. The conclusion was perfunctory and, for the association that had requested initiation, disappointing. The view of the Customs Service was summed up in just two paragraphs:

In the case of the goods transiting Singapore, they are not entered either for home consumption or for transhipment but rather came under the control of the Port of Singapore Authority in a free trade zone. Customs inquiries established that there is no process of manufacture carried out in the free trade zone. The goods are checked for damage and held pending freight consolidation.

In line with sub-section 269T(2B) of the Act Customs concluded that the goods the subject of the inquiry are exported from Korea and not Singapore. Therefore Customs found no case to sustain publishing a dumping duty notice against exports of the goods under inquiry from Singapore.[79]

The case indicates a consistency with international practice on the issue of what constitutes substantial transformation.[80] It is also an interesting study of the problems that result when an imprecisely prepared application (see the quote from the Association's application supra) is treated with the cautious

---

78. In the result of the proceedings before the Tribunal, it was decided that the place of export of the xlpe cable and other goods exported to Australia was the country of their manufacture where they were placed on board a ship for export, and not Singapore, for the purposes of the valuation section of the Customs Act under consideration, namely Section 154. The repairs to the packing of the goods, and other transhipment-type activities in Singapore, did not displace that conclusion. Other reasons affected the Tribunal's decision, such as the nature of the contracts entered into by the relevant parties and the time at which property passed to Midland. It is reiterated that the case concerns valuation, and not origin principles as are considered in this chapter.

79. Australian Customs Notice No. 91/123, 7 August 1991.

80. See Standard 6(b) to Annex D1 to the Kyoto Convention.

and technical mind of an administrator concerned with preserving the legality of its actions.[81]

5.4. Goods Subject to Antidumping Measures

The Customs Service and the Anti-Dumping Authority, which have the responsibility for investigating, in turn, applications by local industry for the imposition of dumping duties on goods claimed to be dumped and causing material injury, are guided by the GATT Anti-Dumping Code in almost all areas where an ambiguity arises under the Australian legislation or where specific matters are not dealt with under the Australian legislation. The identification of the type of goods, and their origin, in respect of which dumping duties are to be collected, is one of those ambiguous matters. Article 8.2 of the GATT Anti-Dumping Code gives guidance to contracting parties on how to impose dumping duties. It states as follows:

When an anti-dumping duty is imposed in respect of any product such anti-dumping duty shall be collected in the appropriate amounts in each case, on a non-discriminatory basis on imports of such products from all sources found to be dumped and causing injury, except as to imports from those sources from which price undertakings under the terms of this Code have been accepted. The authorities shall name the supplier or suppliers of the product concerned. If, however, several suppliers from the same country are involved, and it is impracticable to name all these suppliers, the authorities may name the supplying country concerned. If several suppliers from more than one country are involved, the authorities may name either all the suppliers involved, or, if this is impracticable, all the supplying countries involved.

---

81. The Australian Electrical and Electronic Manufacturer's Association has now relodged an application for an investigation of the alleged dumping of xlpe cable, and the investigation was initiated on 2 September 1991. Needless to say, the goods are referred to as "from Korea," Australian Customs Notice No. 91/136, 2 September 1991.

In the Customs Service Manual, Article 8.2 of the Code is extracted with approval.[82] The Customs Service is guided by the following principles in determining how to express the ambit of a dumping duty notice:

-   if a company is not dumping or not causing material injury, then it should be exempted from any dumping duty notice;
-   a decision on whether to name particular suppliers, or to exempt particular suppliers from a dumping duty notice, is made on a case by case basis;
-   if several suppliers from the same country are found to be dumping and it is impracticable to name them all, then the country can be named;
-   where a country has not been named in a notice and a new exporter from that country commences dumping the goods, another application and investigation must follow before dumping measures may be extended to that exporter; and
-   notices should be worded in a way which prevents diversion of exports from one company to another company (whether or not they are associated).[83]

Although it is not expressly stated in the manual, another factor influencing the decision whether to refer to particular goods from a country as being subject to dumping duties, as opposed to particular goods from a company in a country, relates to the nature of the goods themselves. Commodities such as grains, dairy, and horticultural products, chemicals and the like are more likely to be subject to country-based notices.[84] The reason is that the normal values assessed for different exporting companies vary little if any because of the simple and similar methods of production of what are identical goods. However, for more elaborately manufactured goods, it is much more likely for dumping duty notices to apply to a company. The current Dumping Commodities Register lists, for example, the following types of goods in the different categories:

-   country-based notices — evaporated milk, brandy, sodium cyanide and certain malleable cast iron pipe fittings;

---

82.   Manual Public Edition, Vol. 22, at 5-192.

83.   Ibid., at 5-193.

84.   A notable divergence from this proposition applies for the antidumping measures in place in respect of sorbitol, which are expressed on an exporter basis.

- company-based notices — replacement automotive lead-acid storage batteries, agricultural ground engaging tools and forklift trucks.

Another area where country-based notices are the norm (in fact, there is no alternative) is in the case of measures imposed against goods from nonmarket economies. Current examples of this type of measure are woven worsted fabrics from the People's Republic of China and self-propelled multitired rollers from Czechoslovakia.[85]

New problems need to be publicly addressed by the Australian administering authorities in due course concerning the operation of company-based notices. There are no provisions in the Australian legislation that are directed toward ascertaining a rule of origin for companies as opposed to that which applies for countries. The Australian Customs Service Manual appears to be alive to the prospect that dummy companies, whether or not related, may be interposed between the company manufacturer named in a given dumping duty notice and Australia to avoid the effect of notices published for goods from the manufacturer. However, there is no legislative solution to the problem should it arise. The interposition of trading companies, and contrived company structures, is an area in which the Customs Act is silent.[86]

5.5. Discrete Antidumping Rules of Origin?

Section 269TG of the Customs Act provides that the Minister may declare that dumping duties are to be imposed for "goods" if the Minister is satisfied that the amount of the export price of the "goods" is less than the normal value of those "goods" and material injury has been caused or is threatened by the continued importation of those goods at dumped prices. The references in Section 269TG to the "goods" clearly suggests that it is those particular goods found to have been dumped that are subject to antidumping measures. Those goods are goods whose normal value has been determined under the part. Accordingly, the country of origin rule under Section 269TAC(11) would appear to be the relevant section to deal with origin if any party were to complain that goods were being incorrectly entered and therefore avoiding the scope of a particular notice.

---

85. An interesting situation applies for canned ham, for which antidumping measures have been taken on a company basis; countervailing measures have also been undertaken but on a country basis.

86. Undertakings are offered by exporters, not countries, and therefore also raise this issue.

This conclusion is not adopted without some hesitation. The point has not been subject to judicial pronouncement. The positioning of the antidumping provisions dealing with origin in Section 269TAC(11), which relates to normal values, is curious. Those provisions are also incongruous when other provisions of the part in the Customs Act that deal with antidumping duty are considered. For instance, under Section 269TAAA, "This Part, so far as it relates to duty that may become payable under Section 8 or 9 of the [Customs Tariff (Anti-Dumping) Act 1975], does not apply to goods that are the produce or manufacture of New Zealand."

This section was introduced in carrying out the 1988 review of ANZCERTA to abolish antidumping duties on goods that have their origin in either of the two countries. Note that the words used are "the produce or manufacture" of New Zealand. These are the words used in Section 151 of the Customs Act, and not the words "country of export" and "country of origin" used in the antidumping provisions. In trying to link Section 269TAAA to the agreements already in place between the two countries concerning rules of origin, the legislators have used a different standard for determining whether or not goods come from New Zealand for antidumping purposes than those applicable to goods from other countries.

5.6. Origin in Countervailing Cases

The Customs Act also empowers the Minister to take countervailing measures against goods that have benefitted from a subsidy, bounty, reduction, or remission of freight or other financial assistance.[87] The relevant provisions of the Customs Act have not been subjected to judicial scrutiny in relation to origin issues. There is a particularly interesting aspect of the provisions that deserves mention in the origin context but that will not be subject to any detailed examination in this chapter.

Section 269TJ permits the Minister to publish notices that have the effect of imposing countervailing duties on goods that have already been exported to Australia and that might in the future be exported to Australia. An oddity appears in the legislative provisions dealing to these two situations. Under Section 269TJ(1), which applies to goods already imported into Australia (in respect of which provisional measures were taken), it appears that the subsidy has to have been paid "in the country of origin or the country of export of the goods." The second provision, Section 269TJ(2), does not stipulate that the payment or grant of the subsidy must be made in a particular place: rather, it

---

87. Customs Act, Section 269TJ.

simply focuses on the effect of any such subsidy on the goods themselves. There is no apparent reason for this difference.

6. Rule of Origin in Other Contexts

6.1.   Trade Descriptions

The Commerce (Trade Descriptions) Act 1905 provides that a person commits an offence if goods to which a "false trade description" is applied are imported by the person into Australia.[88] The importation of such goods is prohibited; and if they are imported, they must be forfeited to the Crown.[89] "Trade description" is defined under Section 3 of the Act as, inter alia, "any description, statement, indication, or suggestion, direct or indirect . . . as to the country or place in or at which the goods were made or produced."

The Act states that it is to "be incorporated and read as one with the Customs Act."[90] Whether this entails the application of Section 151 for the purposes of determining the falsity or otherwise of an origin description of goods is uncertain, for at least the following reasons:

– the Customs Service itself does not treat Section 151 as a code of rules of origin, but rather confines it to the area of preferential treatment of imported goods;[91]
– it would be curious if Section 151 of the Customs Act, developed for the purpose of defining eligibility to preferential duties, was transposed into the different context of consumer protection under the Commerce (Trade Descriptions) Act[92];
– Section 151 uses the words "produce or manufacture," whereas Section 3 of the Commerce (Trade Descriptions) Act uses the words "made or produced."

In an early Australian case concerning an allegedly untrue statement about the origin of certain goods, it was held that it was not false to claim that the

---

88.   Commerce (Trade Descriptions) Act 1905, Section 9(1).

89.   Ibid., Section 11.

90.   Ibid., Section 2.

91.   *See supra* note 31.

92.   Cf. Cooper, CUSTOMS & EXCISE LAW ¶ 2410.

Australian State of Victoria was the place of origin of a billiard table when the components for the billiard table were of imported and Victorian origin.[93]

6.2. Valuation

Origin is not relevant to the valuation provisions of the Customs Act: place of export is relevant. Place of export, for valuation purposes, involves concepts of contractual arrangements, containerization, and the manner of transportation, all different considerations to those used in determining the origin of goods.[94]

6.3. Prohibited Imports

Under the Customs (Prohibited Imports) Regulations, the origin of goods is (currently) relevant for certain goods from South Africa[95] and all goods from Iraq.[96] The applicable regulations prohibit the importation of the relevant goods from South Africa or Iraq, and also the relevant goods of South Africa or Iraqi origin from any other country. No discrete origin rules are set out in the regulations: the authorities should either apply the ordinary or natural meaning of the words used or, with regard to the parent Act to the regulations, perhaps resort to Section 151 of the Customs Act.

7. Conclusions and Recommendations

The Australian Law Reform Commission (ALRC), in its three volume report *Customs and Excise*, makes no recommendation for the introduction of rules of origin into the Customs Act,[97] nor does it postulate about the appropriate selection or range of selections available for such rules to be introduced. The ALRC's focus was directed towards preference and not the more general concept of origin. At one point in the report the ALRC states:

---

93. *Stephens v. Alcock* 28 VLR 93 (1902).

94. *See* the discussion of *Re Midland Metals Overseas Limited and the Collector of Customs, supra* note 77, and *Midland Metals Overseas Limited v. Comptroller-General of Customs, supra* note 76, in § 5.3.

95. Regulation 4Q(2) and Eighth Schedule.

96. Regulation 4QA(2).

97. *See* note 32.

When establishing whether goods are the "produce or manufacture" of a country for the purpose of determining whether a preferential duty rate applies, the origin of goods is not necessarily relevant. Government's policy on the matter is often based on obligations assumed under international treaties. The criteria by which [preferential rules] determine whether preference applies vary from Preference Country to Preference Country, and the fact that certain goods are the produce or manufacture of a particular country does not mean that similar goods meeting the same criteria in respect of another country are necessarily the produce or manufacture of that other country.[98]

But the failure of the ALRC[99] to address these issues does not represent the level of interest of the Australian government. It is understood that the Department of Industry, Technology and Commerce is privately seeking submissions from selected individuals and peak industry bodies in relation to the review of origin rules proposed in the 1988 ANZCERTA review. The options for change proposed by the Department include the implementation of substantial transformation tests to determine New Zealand preference eligibility, rather than the factory or works cost proportion currently in force.

The increasing cost of materials imported into Australia's South Pacific neighbors, as compared to the region's low labor costs, will also lead to new pressures for change in Australia's preferential rules. A lowering of the value requirements will expose the system to more borderline cases and cases considered by the authorities to be unmeritorious if advantages are sought by developed countries. There will be more focus on the substance of what is being done in relation to goods, and tests of transformation might need to be incorporated if factory or works costs are adjusted.

While ANZCERTA and Australia's other treaty commitments might prove to be a catalyst for a change in preference origin rules in Australia, it is likely that Australia's antidumping regime will present new challenges for the Australian authorities that will demand dynamic responses. The current mood is to make antidumping regulation more effective in the interests of safeguarding the justified interests of the Australian industry. That mood is likely to lead to closer scrutiny of so-called country hopping, and the use of the "fast track" investigation power of the authorities when that practice undermines dumping relief in place.

---

98. ALRC Report No. 60, at 368.

99. In fairness, this was due to the enormity of the task before the ALRC and not due to any calculated disinterests of the ALRC, which, in the *Customs and Excise* report and its other reports, provides a wealth of legal research and reform proposals in many areas.

The authors have a short list of recommendations. The details about the rules selected are matters for domestic policy and international consensus, and the recommendations describe principles and issues for discussion rather than the content of the rules themselves.

The policies underpinning preference on the one hand and antidumping on the other are diametrically opposed in many respects: it is too much to expect that a single set of rules of origin could span the gulf between them.

If only for statistical purposes, a set of rules of origin should be introduced in Australia that covers nonpreference and nonantidumping situations.

The relevant legislation, and the Australian authorities administering the legislation, must strive for certainty in any rules and their application that are introduced, and the issues of tracing; what constitutes *materials*; and the significance of a process or processes of production must be addressed.

APPENDIX 1

AUSTRALIAN CUSTOMS ACT 1901, SECTION 151

When goods treated as the produce or manufacture of a country

151. (1) This section does not apply when ascertaining whether goods are the produce or manufacture of Australia for the purposes of this Act.

(2) Goods are not the produce or manufacture of a country for the purposes of this Act unless they are such produce or manufacture under this section.

(3) Notwithstanding subsections (5), (6) and (7), goods are not the produce or manufacture of New Zealand for the purposes of this Act unless:

    (a) they have been shipped to Australia from New Zealand; and

    (b) either:

        (i) they have not been transhipped; or

        (ii) the Collector is satisfied that, when they were shipped from New Zealand, their intended destination was Australia.

(4) Notwithstanding subsections (5), (6) and (12), goods are not the produce or manufacture of Canada for the purposes of this Act unless:

    (a) they have been shipped to Australia from Canada; and

    (b) either:

        (i) they have not been transhipped; or

        (ii) the Collector is satisfied that, when they were shipped from Canada, their intended destination was Australia.

(5) For the purposes of this Act, goods are the produce of a country if they are its unmanufactured raw products.

(6) For the purposes of the Act, goods are the manufacture of a country, being New Zealand, Papua New Guinea, Canada or a country that is not a Preference Country, if they were wholly manufactured in the country from one or more of:

    (a) unmanufactured raw products;

    (b) material wholly manufactured in one or both of Australia and the country; and

    (c) materials imported into the country that the Comptroller has determined, by notice in writing published in the

Gazette, to be manufactured raw materials of the country.

(7) For the purposes of this Act, goods are the manufacture of New Zealand if:

(a)   the last process in their manufacture was performed in New Zealand; and

(b)   not less than 50%, or, where the goods are in a class in respect of which the Comptroller has determined, by notice in writing published in the Gazette, that another percentage is appropriate, that other percentage, of their factory or works cost is represented by the value of labour or materials, or of labour and materials, of New Zealand or of Australia and New Zealand.

(8) For the purposes of this Act, goods are the manufacture of a country, being Papua New Guinea or a Forum Island Country, if:

(a)   the last process in their manufacture was performed in the country; and

(b)   not less than 50%, or, where the goods are in a class in respect of which the Comptroller has determined, by notice in writing published in the Gazette, that a lesser percentage is appropriate, that lesser percentage, of their factory or works cost is represented by the value of labour or materials, or of labour and materials, of one or more of Australia, Papua New Guinea and Forum Island Countries.

(9) For the purposes of this Act, goods are the manufacture of a country, being Papua New Guinea or a Forum Island Country, if:

(a)   the last process in their manufacture was performed in the country;

(b)   they were partly manufactured from materials the produce of New Zealand, being materials:

(i)   any quantity of which could lawfully be imported into Australia; and

(ii)   that, if so imported, the duty of Customs in respect of which ascertained in accordance with sections 22, 24, 26 and 27 of the Customs Tariff Act 1987 would be "Free";

(c)   not less than 50%, or, where the goods are in a class in respect of which the Comptroller has determined, by notice in writing published in the Gazette, that a lesser percentage is appropriate, that lesser percentage, of their factory or works cost is represented by the value of labour or materials, or of labour and materials, of one or more of Australia, New Zealand, Papua New Guinea and Forum Island Countries; and

(d)   not less than 25% of their factory or works cost is represented by the value of labour or materials, or of labour and materials, of one or more of Papua New Guinea and Forum Island Countries.

(10) For the purposes of this Act, goods are the manufacture of a country, being a Developing Country, if:

(a)   the last process in their manufacture was performed in the country; and

(b)   not less than 50% of their factory or works cost is represented by the value of labour or materials, or of labour and materials, of one or more of Australia, Papua New Guinea, Forum Island Countries and Developing Countries.

(11) For the purposes of this Act, goods are the manufacture of a Developing Country, but not of any particular Developing Country, if:

(a)   the last process in their manufacture was performed in Papua New Guinea or a Forum Island Country;

(b)   they are not the manufacture of Papua New Guinea or a Forum Island Country under subsection (8) or (9); and

(c)   not less than 50% of their factory or works cost is represented by the value of labour of materials, or of labour and materials, of one or more of Australia, Papua New Guinea, Forum Island Countries and Developing Countries.

(12) Subject to subsection (12A), for the purposes of this Act, goods are the manufacture of a country, being Canada or a country that is not a Preference Country, if:

(a)   the last process in their manufacture was performed in the country; and

(b)   not less than 75%, or, where the goods are of a kind not commercially manufactured in Australia, 25%, of their factory or works cost is represented by the value of labour or materials, or of labour and materials, of the country or of Australia and the country.

(12A)In its application to Christmas Island, Cocos (Keeling)

Islands and to Norfolk Island, subsection (12) shall have effect as if the reference to 75% in paragraph (b) of that subsection were a reference to 50%.

(13) For the purposes of this Act, the Comptroller may, by notice in writing published in the Gazette:

    (a)   specify the manner in which the factory or works cost of goods is to be determined; and

    (b)   specify the manner in which the value of labour, the value of materials or the value of labour and materials is to be determined.

(14) For the purposes of subsection (12), the Comptroller may, by notice in writing published in the Gazette, determine that the goods, or goods in a class, specified in the notice shall be deemed to be goods of a kind not commercially manufactured in Australia.

(14A) A determination under paragraph (7)(b) or subsection (13) may:

    (a)   make provision for the purposes of:

        (i)   Part XVB only; or

        (ii)   this Act (other than Part XBV): or

    (b)   make different provision for the purposes of Part XVB.

(14B) Subsection (14A) does not limit by implication the application of subsection 33(3A) of the Acts Interpretation Act 1901 in relation to this section.

(15) In this section, "Forum Island Country", "Developing Country" and "Preference Country" have the same meanings as they have in the Customs Tariff Act 1987 and, for the purposes of this section, a place that, for the purposes of that Act, is to be treated as a Developing Country shall be taken to be a country that is a Developing Country and a Preference Country.

APPENDIX 2

FORUM ISLAND COUNTRIES

Cook Island
Fiji
Kiribati
Marshall Islands, Republic of
Micronesia, Federated States of
Nauru

Niue
Solomon Islands
Tonga
Tuvalu
Vanuatu
Western Samoa

DEVELOPING COUNTRIES

DIVISION 1

Countries that are Developing Countries

Afghanistan
Albania
Algeria
Angola
Antigua and Barbuda
Argentina
Bahamas
Barbados
Bahrain
Bangladesh
Belize
Benin
Bhutan
Bolivia
Botswana
Brazil
Brunei Darussalam
Bulgaria
Burkina Faso
Burundi
Cambodia
Cameroon
Cape Verde
Central African Republic
Chad
Chile

China, People's Republic of
Colombia
Comoros
Congo
Costa Rica
Cote d'Ivore
Cuba
Cyprus
Djibouti
Dominica
Dominican Republic
Ecuador
Egypt
El Salvador
Equatorial Guinea
Ethiopia
Gabon
Gambia
Ghana
Grenada
Guatemala
Guinea
Guinea-Bissau
Guyana
Haiti
Honduras

Hungary
India
Indonesia
Iran
Iraq
Israel
Jamaica
Jordan
Kenya
Korea, Democratic People's
Korea, Republic of
Kuwait
Lao People's Democratic Rep.
Lebanon
Lesotho
Liberia
Libyan Arab Jamahiriya
Madagascar
Malaysia
Malawi
Maldives
Mali
Malta
Mauritania
Mauritius
Mexico
Mongolia
Morocco
Mozambique
Myanmar, Union of
Nepal
Nicaragua
Niger
Nigeria
Oman
Pakistan
Panama
Paraguay
Zambia

Peru
Philippines
Poland
Qatar
Romania
Rwanda
St. Christopher and Nevis
St. Lucia
St. Vincent and the Grenadines
Sao Tome and Principe
Republic of Saudi Arabia
Senegal
Seychelles
Sierra Leone
Singapore
Somalia
Sri Lanka
Sudan
Surinam
Swaziland
Syrian Arab Republic
Tanzania, United Republic of
Thailand
Togo
Trinidad and Tobago
Tunisia
Turkey
Uganda
United Arab Emirates (Abu
  Dhabi, Dubai, Sharjah,
  Ajman, Umm al Qaiwain,
  Fugairah, Ras al Khaimah)
Uruguay
Venezuela
Vietnam, Socialist Republic of
Yemen, Republic of
Yugoslavia
Zaire
Zimbabwe

DIVISION 2

Places treated as Developing Countries

American Samoa
Anguilla
Bermuda
British Indian Ocean Territory
British Virgin Islands
Cayman Islands
Falkland Islands and Dependencies
French Polynesia
Gibraltar
Guam
Hong Kong
Johnston Island

Macao
Mariana Islands

Midway Islands
Montserrat
Netherlands Antilles
New Caledonia
Palau
Pitcairn Island
St. Helena
St. Pierre and Miquelon
Taiwan Province
Tokelau Islands
Turks and Caicos Islands
Virgin Islands of the United States
Wake Island
Wallis and Futuna Islands

CHAPTER 5

Canadian Rules of Origin

Richard S. Gottlieb

1. Introduction

The determination of the country of origin of goods imported into Canada is relevant for a number of purposes. These include

1. the determination of tariff treatment (rates of customs duty vary within a tariff classification depending on tariff treatment);
2. the determination of whether or not imported goods are subject to antidumping or countervailing duties or safeguard measures;
3. the determination of whether or not the importation of goods is conditional on the issuance of an import permit; and
4. finally, the application of various laws on the marking, packaging, and labelling of goods.

This chapter addresses these points in turn.

2. Rules of Origin Pertaining to Tariff Treatment

The rules of origin, as they pertain to tariff treatment, are spelled out in the Customs Tariff[1] and its regulations.[2]

There are eight tariff regimes that apply to goods imported into Canada. These are

1. the General Tariff (GT);
2. the MFN Tariff;
3. the General Preferential Tariff (GPT);
4. the Least Developed Developing Countries (LDDC) Tariff;
5. the Commonwealth Caribbean Countries (CARIBCAN) Tariff;
6. the British Preferential Tariff (BPT);

---

1. R.S. 1985, C.41 (3d Suppl.) (CT).

2. § 13(2) CT.

7.   the Australia and New Zealand (A&NZ) Tariff; and
8.   the United States Tariff (UST).

All but the GT are preferential.

2.1.   Criteria Used to Determine Country of Origin

In general, save for the UST, the factors that are taken into account in determining the country of origin include

1.   the value and origin of materials and component parts used in the manufacture of the imported goods
2.   the relative proportions of expenses incurred within the beneficiary countries plus a reasonable profit in respect to the total value of the finished good, and
3.   the routing of the shipment.

Determination of the UST may also depend on the criterion of change in tariff heading.

2.2.   Value and Origin of Materials and Component Parts Used in the Manufacture

Goods originate in a country if the whole[3] or a specified portion[4] of the value of the goods is produced in that country.

3.   The General Tariff[5]

The Canadian government may subject any or all goods of a particular country that does not benefit from preferred tariff regimes to the GT. General Tariff treatment may also be applied to goods originating in a country that is the beneficiary of a more favorable tariff treatment but that fail to meet the conditions of that treatment.

The duty rate that applies to all imported goods under the GT is 35 percent of the value for duty.

---

3.   § 13(1) CT.

4.   § 13(2) CT.

5.   § 46 CT.

4. Preferential Rules of Origin

4.1. The Most-Favored-Nation Tariff[6]

The most commonly applied tariff regime is the MFN Tariff. It is extended to all signatories to the GATT and to any country that has unilaterally agreed to extend to Canada rates as favorable as that country extends to other countries. It applies to goods originating in these countries unless a more preferential tariff treatment is specifically granted to some or all of the products of such countries.[7] Most-Favored-Nation treatment may be removed and the less beneficial GT may be applied to some or all of the goods of designated countries.[8] The following sections discuss the rules of origin that apply to MFN treatment.[9]

4.1.1. Cost Criteria

At least 50 percent of the cost of production of the imported goods must be incurred by the industry of one or more countries that are beneficiaries of the MFN Tariff or by the industry of Canada. The cost of production includes cost of materials (exclusive of duties and taxes), labor, and factory overhead. The gross profit of the manufacturer or exporter, export packing expenses, royalties, transportation, and insurance costs to the point of direct shipment to Canada, customs duties, and any other costs or charges arising after the completion of the manufacture of the goods are not to be included in the calculation of cost of production.

4.1.2. Place of Finishing

The imported goods must have been finished in a country that is a beneficiary of the MFN Tariff in the form in which they are imported into Canada.

---

6. §§ 22-25 CT.

7. § 23(1)(a) CT.

8. § 23(1)(c) CT.

9. British Preferential Tariff and Most-Favoured-Nation Tariff Rules of Origin Regulations, SOR/78-315, 2 March 1978 as amended by SOR/88-76 and SOR/89-52.

4.1.3.   Shipment Conditions

4.1.3.1.   General Rule: Direct Shipment

The goods must be shipped directly to Canada, with or without transhipment, from a country that is a beneficiary of that tariff.

Goods are shipped directly to Canada from another country when the goods are conveyed to Canada from that other country on a through bill of lading to a consignee in Canada.[10] Note that the through bill of lading need not originate in the country of export but, rather, may originate in any country that is a beneficiary of the MFN Tariff.

4.1.3.2.   Exception: Transhipment[11]

Exceptionally, transhipment through any intermediate country is permitted provided that the goods

1.   remain under customs transit control in the intermediate country;
2.   do not undergo any operation in the intermediate country other than unloading, reloading, splitting up of the load, or operations required to keep the goods in good condition;
3.   do not enter into trade or consumption in the intermediate country; or
4.   do not remain in temporary storage in the intermediate country beyond a prescribed period (currently six months).

The term *transhipment* is not defined. However, the transfer of goods from one vehicle or craft to another is considered by the Department of National Revenue, Customs and Excise (DNR) to be transhipment. Stopover by means of carriage at a port in a country other than the country of transport or in Canada is no longer considered, by the DNR, to constitute transhipment.

4.2.   The General Preferential Tariff[12]

This tariff treatment is afforded to goods of designated developing countries. The duty rates that apply are generally lower than those that prevail under the MFN Tariff.

---

10.   § 17 CT.

11.   § 18 CT.

12.   § 35 to 41 CT.

4.2.1. Extension of General Preferential Tariff Benefit[13]

The government may extend the benefit of the GPT to any or all goods that originate in a country that is a beneficiary of the BPT or MFN Tariff where, in its opinion, that country is a developing country.

4.2.2. Rules of Origin That Apply to General Preferential Tariff Treatment[14]

4.2.2.1. Value Criteria

The value of the materials, parts, or products originating outside the country or in an undetermined location and used in the manufacture or production of the goods amounts to no more than 40 percent of the exfactory price of the goods as packed for shipment to Canada. In calculating the value of the materials, parts, or produce originating outside the beneficiary country or of undetermined origin, any materials, parts, or produce used in the manufacture or production of the goods originating from any other GPT country or from Canada and any packing required for the transportation of the goods not including packing in which the goods are ordinarily sold for consumption in the beneficiary country are deemed to have originated in the beneficiary country.

The exfactory price is the total value of:

materials,

component parts,

factory overhead,

labor,

any other reasonable cost incurred during normal manufacturing process (e.g., duties and taxes paid on imported materials and not refunded when exported), and

reasonable profit.

Any costs incurred subsequent to the goods leaving the factory (e.g., freight, loading, temporary storage) are not included in the exfactory cost.

---

13. § 36(1) and 36(2) CT.

14. § 35(1) CT and General Preferential Tariff and Least Developed Developing Countries Rules of Origin Regulations, CRC, Vol. V, ch. 528, at 3641, as amended by SOR/79-568, SOR/83-78, SOR/84-655, SOR/88-76 and SOR/89-52.

4.2.2.2. Place of Finishing

The imported goods must have been finished in a country that is a beneficiary of the GPT Tariff in the form in which they are imported into Canada.[15]

4.2.2.3. Shipment Conditions

4.2.2.3.1. Direct Shipment[16]

The goods must be shipped directly to Canada with or without transhipment from a producing country that is a beneficiary of the GPT on a through bill of lading from the beneficiary country in which they were certified and consigned to a consignee in a specified port in Canada.

4.2.2.3.2. Transhipment

Transhipment is permitted under certain conditions.[17] For example, the transhipment of goods of Mexican origin is permitted through the United States under certain conditions.[18] The transhipment of goods of Peoples' Republic of China origin is permitted through Hong Kong under certain conditions.[19]

4.2.3. Withdrawal of General Preferential Tariff Benefit[20]

The government may withdraw the benefit of the GPT from any or all the goods that originate in a beneficiary country.[21] This generally occurs when the duty benefit is considered to be harmful to Canadian industry. Thus, some commodities in sensitive industries do not presently qualify for GPT benefit.

---

15. § 3 of the Guidelines to GPT and LDDC Regulations.

16. § 40(b) CT.

17. § 41 and Guideline 10 of GPT and LDDC Regulations.

18. Mexico Direct Shipment Condition Exemption Order, 30 June 1988, SOR/88-349.

19. China Direct Shipment Condition Exemption Order, 7 February 1985, SOR/85-156 as amended by SOR/88-76.

20. General Preferential Tariff Withdrawal Order, SOR/88-70, SOR/89-84 and SOR/90-197.

21. § 36(1)(b) CT.

In the case of the withdrawal of GPT benefits, the government indicates whether MFN or BPT will apply in its stead.[22] Likewise the application of GPT benefits may be reinstated if the minister of finance recommends.

4.3. Least Developed Developing Countries Tariff[23]

4.3.1. Extension of Least Developed Developing Countries Tariff Benefits

The government may designate as an LDDC any country that is a beneficiary of the GPT and extend the benefit of free rates of customs duty to any or all goods that originate in that country and for which there are GPT rates of customs duty in effect.

4.3.2. Withdrawal of Least Developed Developing Countries Tariff Benefits

The government may withdraw the benefit of free rates of customs duty from any or all goods that originate in a country that is a beneficiary of the LDDC.[24] In such case, the government must indicate those goods to which the benefit of the GPT will apply.[25]

4.3.3. Rules of Origin That Apply to Least Developed Developing Countries Tariff Treatment

Conditions of qualification are similar to those described above for the GPT, with one exception. For the purposes of the LDDC Tariff, goods originate if the value of the materials, component parts, or products originating in a non LDDC and used in the manufacture of the goods amounts to no more than 60 percent of the exfactory price of the goods as packed for shipment to Canada.

---

22. § 36(2)(c) CT.

23. § 38(1) and (2) CT.

24. § 38(2)(b) CT.

25. § 38(2)(c) CT.

4.4. The Commonwealth Caribbean Countries Tariff[26]

4.4.1. Extension of Commonwealth Caribbean Countries Tariff Treatment[27]

The government designates those countries whose goods will benefit from duty free CARIBCAN treatment.

4.4.2. Withdrawal of Commonwealth Caribbean Countries Tariff Benefit[28]

The government may withdraw the benefit of free rates of customs duty from any or all goods of any or all CARIBCAN countries and make those goods subject to the tariff treatment that would apply to those goods if they were not entitled to free rates of customs duty.

4.4.3. Rules of Origin That Apply to Commonwealth Caribbean Countries Tariff Treatment[29]

The rules applying to CARIBCAN qualification are similar to those for the GPT and LDDC Tariff, with the following exceptions:

1. To satisfy the conditions of CARIBCAN, the goods must have proof of origin, be entitled to the benefit of free rates of duty, and meet direct shipment requirements.
2. To be eligible for duty-free tariff treatment, at least 60 percent of the exfactory price must originate in one or more beneficiary countries or Canada.
3. Certain goods, such as the goods of Chapters 50-65 of the Schedule of the Customs Tariff are excluded from the benefits of the CARIBCAN Tariff treatment.

---

26. § 53 to 58 CT.

27. § 53 CT.

28. § 54(1)(a) and (2)(b) CT.

29. Caribbean Rules of Origin regulations, SOR/87-290, as amended by SOR/88-76 and SOR/89-52.

4.5.   The British Preferential Tariff[30]

4.5.1.   Extension of British Preferential Tariff Benefit

The government may extend the benefit of the BPT to any or all goods that originate in a country that is a beneficiary of the MFN Tariff.[31]

4.5.2.   Withdrawal of British Preferential Tariff Benefit[32]

The government may withdraw the benefit of the BPT from any or all goods that originate in a BPT country. In such a case, it must indicate the goods to which the benefit of the MFN Tariff or the GT, as the case may be, extends.[33]

4.5.3.   Rules of Origin That Apply to British Preferential Tariff Treatment

4.5.3.1.   Value Criterion

Not less than 50 percent of the cost of the production of the goods must be produced by the industry of one or more countries whose goods have been extended the benefits of the BPT. In calculating the costs of production, the elements that are included and excluded are the same as those that pertain to the MFN Tariff treatment.

4.5.3.2.   Place of Finishing

The goods must be finished in a BPT country in the form in which they were imported into Canada.

---

30.   § 26-32 CT.

31.   § 27(1)(a) CT.

32.   § 27(1)(b) CT.

33.   § 27(2)(c) CT.

4.5.3.3. Shipment Conditions

4.5.3.3.1. Direct Shipment

Save for certain exceptions, the goods must be shipped directly, without transhipment, on a through bill of lading from a country whose goods are entitled to BPT treatment, from any other country that is the beneficiary of a more favorable tariff treatment, or from an other country as designated by Order in Council.[34]

4.5.3.3.2. Permissible Transhipment

Imported goods for which BPT treatment is claimed are exempt from the transhipment prohibition when the goods are shipped through a BPT beneficiary country or British country or are transhipped owing to circumstances beyond the control of the importer, namely

1. a strike or lockout at the Canadian port of consignment;
2. damages to the conveyance, rendering a shipment without transhipment impossible; or
3. any other circumstances rendering a direct shipment without transhipment impossible.[35]

Generally, goods subject to BPT treatment benefit from lower rates of duty than goods qualifying for MFN treatment and, save for some exceptions, are subject to higher rates of duty than goods that qualify for GPT treatment.

4.6. The Australia and New Zealand Tariff[36]

Goods that originate in Australia or New Zealand are entitled to the BPT rates of customs duty, if any, or the special rates of customs duty for Australia and New Zealand, if any, set out with respect to specific goods. The following sections discuss the rules of origin that apply to Australia and New Zealand.[37]

---

34. § 29(b) CT.

35. British Preferential Tariff Direct Shipment Without Transshipment Exemption Order, SOR/88-78 as amended by SOR/89-183.

36. §§ 47-49 (New Zealand); §§ 50-52 (Australia).

37. New Zealand and Australia Rules of Origin Regulations P.C. 1983-18, 13 January 1983, as amended by SOR/88-76.

4.6.1. Value Criteria

Not less than 50 percent of the cost of the production of the goods must be produced by the industry of New Zealand or Canada in the case of New Zealand or in Australia or Canada in the case of Australia. The manner of calculating the cost of production is the same as that which is employed in determining the origin of goods that may be entitled to MFN treatment.

4.6.2. Finishing Requirements

The goods must be finished in New Zealand or Australia in the form in which they are imported into Canada.

4.6.3. Shipment Conditions[38]

Qualifying goods must be shipped directly to Canada from the beneficiary country unless they are subject to permissible forms of transhipment.

4.7. Documentation Required to Claim Preferential Tariff Treatment

4.7.1. Invoice

A separate invoice for goods for which favored tariff treatment is claimed must be presented.

4.7.2. Certificate of Origin

To claim entitlement to the GPT, CARIBCAN Tariff, or LDDC Tariff treatment for goods imported into Canada, the importer must present, as proof of origin, a Certificate of Origin.

4.7.3. Proof of Origin

Importers of goods for which claims are made for GPT, BPT, MFN Tariff, GT, or A&NZ Tariff treatments must present to the DNR evidence of proof of origin.

---

38.   § 48(c), 49, 51(c), and 52 CT.

4.8.   United States Tariff[39]

Under the Canada-U.S. FTA, goods exported from one country to the other that meet the rules of origin in the FTA (FTA goods) qualify for the preferential FTA duty rates.

4.8.1.   Imported Goods

Imported goods are entitled to the UST treatment only if
1.   proof of origin of the goods is given in accordance with the CA;
2.   the goods are FTA goods; and
3.   the goods are shipped directly to Canada from the United States (certain forms of transhipment through third countries are allowed).[40]

4.8.2.   Rules of Origin That Apply to Free Trade Agreement Tariff Treatment

The following are entitled to FTA Tariff Treatment:
1.   goods wholly obtained or produced (e.g., harvested or extracted) in the territory of Canada or the United States (the United States includes Puerto Rico)
2.   goods produced in the territory of Canada or the United States wholly from the goods described in paragraph 1
3.   goods manufactured in Canada or the United States containing non-FTA material, provided that such material has been transformed to the extent required by the rules of origin. (In certain cases a North American value criterion must also be met in addition to minimum transformation.)
4.   certain goods that contain a minimum of 50 percent North American value
5.   accessories, spare parts, and tools in quantities and of a value customary for the FTA goods, if exported with the FTA goods.

We will study the latter three in greater detail.

---

39.   § 25.1-25.3 CT; United States Tariff Rules of Origin Regulations, 30 December 1988, SOR/89-49.

40.   § 25.2(6) CT.

4.8.3. Goods Deemed to Originate by Virtue of Sufficient Transformation

Canadian or U.S. manufactured goods containing non-FTA material must meet the following conditions to qualify as FTA goods:

1. The difference between the tariff classification of the non-FTA material and the tariff classification of the processed good must meet or exceed the change in tariff classification required by the specific rules of origin that apply to the manufactured good
2. The processing must have occurred in Canada, the United States, or both, and the manufactured goods must not have subsequently undergone any processing in a third country.

Non-FTA materials cannot be sufficiently transformed (1) by simple packaging or dilution with another substance or (2) by any process that is performed solely to circumvent the rules of origin.

The rules of origin do not only operate at the Canada-U.S. border. If non-FTA materials are used in the manufacture of a subcomponent or submaterial for use in the final manufactured goods, the intermediate good will be considered to originate in Canada or the United States if the rules of origin that apply to it are met (FTA intermediate good).

The entire value (as defined) of FTA intermediate goods is considered to be North American value when determining whether any value criteria that apply to manufactured goods incorporating the intermediate goods have been met.

4.8.4. North American Value Criteria in Addition to Transformation Criteria

A number of products, such as electronic goods, automobiles, chemicals, footwear, and certain machinery are subjected to a North American value test in addition to tariff classification change requirements. The value of FTA materials, plus the "direct cost of processing" performed in the United States or Canada, must constitute not less than 50 percent (70 percent for some chemicals) of the "value of the goods when exported."

For ease of reference, the "value of FTA materials" plus the "direct cost of processing" will be referred to as "North American value."

The North American value criteria may be considered in terms of the following formula:

$$\frac{A + B}{C} \geq 50\%$$

A = the direct cost of processing or assembling in the United States or Canada

B = the value of FTA materials (including non-FTA material used in FTA intermediate good)

C = the value of the goods when exported = A + B + the value of non-FTA materials not used in intermediate goods meeting the rules of origin

4.8.4.1.   Direct Cost of Processing

The direct cost of processing or assembling in the United States or Canada is defined as including "all costs that are directly incurred in, or that can be reasonably allocated to, the production of the good." The following amounts are not included:

1. general business expenses such as executive, financial, sales, advertising, marketing, accounting, legal, and insurance
2. import and export brokerage charges;
3. communication charges including telephone and mail
4. export packing costs
5. royalty payments for distribution or sales rights to the goods
6. all costs related to real property used by nonmanufacturing personnel including rent, mortgage interest, depreciation, insurance maintenance, and taxes
7. profit.

4.8.4.2.   Value of Free Trade Agreement Materials

The value of FTA materials in respect of the exported goods is defined as including

1. the price paid for FTA materials;
2. the price paid for non-FTA materials used in FTA intermediate goods manufactured by the producer of the exported goods; and
3. the following costs related to the above:
    a. freight, insurance, packing and other costs incurred in transporting the above materials to the premises of the producer of the exported goods

b. customs duty, sales taxes, and brokerage fees for the above materials

c. the cost of the waste or spoilage of the above materials, less scrap value

d. the value, apportioned as appropriate, of the following goods and services in respect of the above materials and supplied directly or indirectly by the producer of the exported goods free of charge at reduced cost for use in connection with the production of the above materials, to the extent that the value has not been included in the price actually paid or payable:

  i. materials, components, parts, and similar items incorporated in the above materials

  ii. tools, dies, molds, and similar items used in the production of the above materials

  iii. materials consumed in the production of the above materials

  iv. engineering, development, artwork, design work, plans, and sketches necessary for the production of the above materials and undertaken elsewhere than the country into which the materials were imported.

4.8.4.3. Price Paid

The price paid by a producer for materials is defined to be the actual price paid or payable by a producer when materials are purchased in an arm's length transaction or, in any other case, the price at which the producer would ordinarily have purchased the materials in an arm's length transaction at the time when and the place from which the materials were shipped to the producer. A transaction between related persons is not an arm's length transaction unless the relationship between those persons did not affect the price paid or payable.

4.8.4.4. Value of Non-Free Trade Agreement Materials Not Used in Intermediate Free Trade Agreement Goods

The value of this component of the North American value criteria formula is calculated in a manner similar to the calculation of the value of FTA materials.

4.8.4.5. Determining the Origin of Intermediate Goods and Purchased Materials

The calculation of whether a finished exported good satisfies the North American value criteria has been outlined above.

The same procedure is employed when determining whether intermediate goods and purchased materials are FTA goods.

4.8.5. Origin Determined Solely by a North American Value Criteria

Manufactured goods that do not meet the sufficient transformation criteria in the Rules of Origin for the following reasons are deemed to be FTA goods if 50 percent or more of the value of the goods when exported is represented by the direct cost of Canadian or U.S. processing and the value of FTA materials in the following cases:

1. The goods were assembled from unassembled third country components, imported together, that were classified as if they were the assembled goods
2. One or more third country parts were classified in the same six-digit tariff subheading that applies to the manufactured good.

Goods qualifying under the 50 percent North American Value rule cannot have undergone any processing or further assembly in a third country subsequent to their processing or assembly in Canada or the United States.

4.9. Determination of Origin and the Appeal Mechanism

Until 1988, there was no mechanism in place by which the authorities could redetermine the origin of imported goods as declared by the exporter or importer. Nor was there any review possible of the minister's decision on the tariff that applied by reason of the origin of the goods.[41]

In practice, investigations of origin were conducted informally and determinations were made by administrative dictate. There are no recorded cases reflecting efforts on either side to litigate these issues. Therefore, there are no precedents indicating how the various provisions of the Customs Tariff (CT) or the regulations should be interpreted.

With the adoption of the FTA, the authorities amended the CT adding details on the furnishing of proof of origin.[42] A formal mechanism was also established for the determination of origin.

---

41. § 3(5) CT.

42. § 35.1(1) CT.

4.9.1. Determination of Origin[43]

The origin of imported goods for customs duty purposes may be determined by a customs officer before, or within thirty days after, they are formally imported.

If no such determination was made, it is deemed to have been made thirty days after the date of accounting in accordance with any representations made at that time for the origin of the goods by the person accounting for their origin.[44]

4.9.2. Redetermination of Origin[45] of Non-U.S. Goods

A determination of origin is final unless, in the case of goods other than goods imported from the United States, a redetermination of the origin of the imported goods is made by the Minister of National Revenue within two years after deemed determination.

4.9.3. Redetermination of Origin of Goods Exported from the United States

For goods imported from the United States, there is an elaborate appeal mechanism set out, with the final decision ultimately in the hands of the Deputy Minister of National Revenue, Customs and Excise (the deputy minister).[46]

4.9.4. Appeal to the Canadian International Trade Tribunal[47]

Any person dissatisfied with a decision of the deputy minister may appeal to the Canadian International Trade Tribunal (CITT).

---

43.   § 57.1 of the Customs Act (CA) and 13 CT.

44.   § 57.2(2) CA.

45.   § 57.2(3) CA.

46.   § 64 CA.

47.   § 67(1) CA (Customs Memorandum D11-6-1).

4.9.5. Appeal to the Federal Court of Canada

Finally, the decision of the CITT may, with the leave of a judge of the Federal Court of Canada, be appealed to that court on a question of law.

4.9.6. Correction of Obvious Error

For goods imported from the United States, a tariff and values administrator may, on his or her own initiative, redetermine the origin of goods imported from the United States within ninety days after a determination or an appraisal is made. This provides a mechanism by which the decision issued by a commodity specialist may be corrected when both the officer and the importer agree about an obvious error in the origin of the imported goods. Redetermination may also be initiated by the deputy minister for similar reasons.

To the best of our knowledge, there have been no reported administrative or judicial decisions concerning origin issues.

5. Rules of Origin in the Context of Antidumping or Countervailing Duty Proceedings

Canadian antidumping and countervailing duty law is contained in the Special Import Measures Act (SIMA).[48]

SIMA refers to country of origin in few places. However, as we shall see, the legislation lends itself to considering country of origin or country of export as relevant for antidumping and countervailing duty purposes.

A superficial reading of the SIMA gives the impression that it is the activities in the country of export that determine whether or not the exported goods are dumped or subsidized.

5.1. Investigation of Dumping and Subsidization

Throughout the SIMA, reference is made to the country of export. Thus, when the deputy minister initiates an investigation, he or she "shall cause notice of the investigation . . . to be given to the exporter . . . the government of the country of export".[49] Other notices specified in the SIMA are to the same effect. What is the country of export? As we shall see, it is often the country of origin. We will examine the role the country of origin plays in the SIMA.

---

48. 1984 SC Ch. 25.

49. § 34(a)(i) SIMA.

5.2.   Country of Origin in Subsidy Cases

Country of export is defined[50] as meaning "in the case of subsidized goods, the country in which the subsidy originated." This is usually the country of origin whether the goods are shipped directly or indirectly to Canada, but not necessarily. Thus, *subsidy* is defined as including any financial or commercial benefit accruing to persons engaged in the

> production, manufacture, growth, processing, purchase, distribution, transportation, sale, export or import of goods, as a result of any scheme, program, practice or thing done, provided or implemented by the government of a country other than Canada.[51]

The limiting factor is the requirement that material injury be caused by goods like those produced in Canada.[52]

However, where the goods investigated are described, for example, as "color television receiving sets and component parts thereof, including picture tubes, tuners, chassis, etc.," and the components are produced in two subsidizing countries, there are two subject countries, each of which is a country of export as defined above. Depending on production, shipment, and other circumstances, it is conceivable that neither country is the country of origin or the country of export of the finished product, as these phrases are commonly known.[53]

That more than one subject country may be contemplated by SIMA is confirmed by the provision that a subsidy does not include the amount of duty or internal tax imposed on goods by the government of the country of origin or country of export from which the goods, because of their exportation from the country of export or country of origin, have been exempted or have been or will be relieved by means of refund or drawback.[54]

---

50.   § 21(1) SIMA (Definition of Country of Export).

51.   § 2(1) SIMA (Definition of Subsidy).

52.   § 2(1) SIMA (Definition of Material Injury).

53.   In the remarks that follow, the goods that are alleged to be dumped or subsidized are referred to as the subject goods; the countries of origin or export are referred to as the subject country.

54.   § 2(1) SIMA (Definition of Subsidy).

5.3. Country of Origin in Antidumping Cases

Country of export is defined to mean, in the case of dumped goods, the country from which the goods were shipped directly to Canada or, if the goods have not been shipped directly to Canada, the country from which the goods would be shipped directly to Canada under normal conditions of trade.[55]

Like in the case of subsidized goods, in the above example of color televisions and components, the subject countries could be the country in which each dumped component was produced as well as that where the goods were finished — thus resulting in many subject countries of origin and many subject countries of export "directly or indirectly" to Canada.

An example of how this can work in practice is exemplified by the case of "Hydraulic Turbines" from Japan and China.[56] The subject goods were described as "Hydraulic Turbines or Original Equipment Components Thereof, as Well as Spare Parts and Replacement Runners, for Use in the Generation of Electric Power Including all Embedded, Stationary, and Rotating Components, Whether or Not Imported Separately, but Excluding Governor Control Actuators and Turbine Inlet Valves, Originating in or Exported from Japan, or Originating in or Exported from The People's Republic of China and Introduced into The Commerce of Canada by or on Behalf of a Manufacturer, Producer, Vendor or Exporter in Japan." The principal targets were Japanese producers of hydraulic turbines. However, since a major component was produced in the People's Republic of China, it was also made a subject country.

5.3.1. Country of Origin or Export in the Case of Transhipment

The above definition of *country of origin* is not very helpful, even in the case of goods that are fully produced in one country but shipped through another country before coming to Canada. It is difficult to discern what was contemplated when the legislator stated that it includes "the country from which the goods would be shipped directly to Canada *under normal conditions of trade.*"

If the goods are shipped directly to Canada from the place of production, the country of export and the country of origin would be the same. However, where the goods pass through one or more countries before coming to Canada, then more than one country may be a subject country (i.e., the country of

---

55.   § 2(1) SIMA (Definition of Country of Export).

56.   ADT-9-84.

origin and the country of export).[57]

Determinations of dumping (i.e., based on the establishment of normal values and export prices) depend on events transpiring in the country of export.[58] Thus, normal values are established on the basis of the price of like goods when sold by the exporter to purchasers in the country of export.[59] This definition may contemplate the country of origin or the country through which goods are exported if they are shipped indirectly to Canada. The determination of normal value on the basis of the cost of production plus an amount for administrative, selling and all other costs and profit[60] visualizes the country where the goods were produced (nor necessarily by the exporter or in the country of export). To further confuse matters, however, the regulations[61] speak of determining profits on the basis of those earned by the exporter on sales of like or similar goods in the country of export.

Finally, the establishment of normal values on the basis of the price of "like goods sold by the exporter to importers in any country other than Canada"[62] visualizes sales from either the country of origin or country of export.

Let us look at the transhipment situation. The country from which the goods are shipped directly to Canada (the intermediate country) may be held to be the country of export unless the following conditions are met:[63]

1. The bill of lading for the transportation of the goods from the place of original shipment shows the ultimate destination of the goods to be a specified port in Canada,

2. The goods have not been entered for consumption or for warehouse or have not remained for any purpose other than transhipment in any intermediate country,

3. The original bill of lading or a copy of it is filed with the deputy minister.

---

57.   This follows from the definition of *country of export* in § 2(1) of SIMA and from § 30 of SIMA to be discussed below.

58.   See §§ 15 ff. SIMA.

59.   § 15(c) SIMA.

60.   § 19(b) SIMA.

61.   § 11 SIMA regulations, SOR/84-927 and SOR/89-63.

62.   § 19(a) SIMA.

63.   § 30(1) SIMA; § 25 SIMA Regulations.

However, if these conditions are met, "the normal value and export price will be determined as if the goods were shipped directly to Canada from the country of origin."

It is difficult to determine how the export price should be calculated when the goods are sold to a purchaser in the intermediate country (A) who resells it to the Canadian importer (B). When goods are sold to A at a price of X (as opposed to being merely transhipped by the original producer) and A, in turn, resells the goods to B at a price of Y, which price prevails? Section 30(2) of the SIMA suggests that it is X. However, the SIMA visualizes the determination of "the export price of goods sold to an importer in Canada."[64] Thus, arguably, Y would be the export price.

This is probably a more realistic approach since § 30(2)(b) of the SIMA contemplates thwarting the effort to acquire lower "normal values" by shipping the goods through another country. While it is to be expected that the normal values would, thus, be based on events in the country of origin, it is also normal that the export price (which determines the basis on which goods are introduced into the commerce of Canada) would be, precisely, the price to the Canadian importer.

Having said this, it should be pointed out that it is DNR policy to calculate the export price of goods shipped to Canada on an exfactory basis, notwithstanding intervening sales. This policy is of doubtful validity. While § 30(2)(b) of the SIMA seems to suggest that it is also the export price that must be determined in the country of origin, the clear wording of § 24 of the SIMA suggests otherwise.[65]

When the conditions outlined in § 25 of the SIMA regulations are not met, it is the policy of the DNR to attempt to establish normal values and export prices in the intermediate country in the case of indirect shipment even if it is a nonsubject country. There are three possible outcomes of indirect shipment to Canada.

5.3.1.1. Where the Normal Values in the Intermediate Country Are Lower Than Those in the Country of Origin

Where any goods

(a) are or are to be shipped indirectly to Canada from the country of origin through one or more other countries, and

(b) would, but for this section, have a normal value as computed under

---

64. § 24 SIMA.

65. It is suggested that §30 of SIMA is limited to cases in which there is no intervening sale between the vendor in the country of origin and the Canadian importer.

sections 15 to 23 that is less than the normal value would be if the country of export were the country of origin,

the normal value and export price of the goods shall, notwithstanding any other provision of this Act, be determined as if the goods were or were to be shipped directly to Canada from the country of origin.[66]

These provisions were designed, evidently, to prevent companies from attempting to secure low normal values by shipping goods from a country with relatively high costs of production and selling prices through one with relatively low ones.

5.3.1.2. Where the Normal Values in the Intermediate Country Are Higher Than Those in the Country of Origin

Where the normal values in the intermediate country are higher than those in the country of origin, the normal values in the intermediate country apply — even if the country is not a subject country.

Thus, the policy of DNR in the case of indirect shipment is to determine normal values at the higher of those prevailing in the country of origin or the country of export.

5.3.1.3. Where Normal Values Cannot be Established in the Intermediate Country

If the intermediate country is a nonsubject country, it is usually impossible to secure the cooperation of manufacturers (if there are any) or traders regarding costs of production and selling prices in the intermediate country. In that case, the normal values are arbitrarily established by ministerial specification.[67] As a matter of practice, these normal values are usually substantially higher than those prevailing in the country of origin, resulting in the imposition of substantial antidumping duties.[68]

---

66. § 30(2) SIMA.

67. § 29(1) SIMA.

68. An example of this arose in connection with a recent antidumping case involving footwear originating in Brazil transhipped through the United States. Normal values were based on selling prices in the United States. It is submitted that there is no legal basis for this approach. It is also illogical. If goods have normal values based on conditions of manufacture and sale in the country of origin, why should some of them be subject to higher normal values because they happen to land in a high-value intermediate country?

5.3.2. Designation of Subject Country or Countries by Reference to Country of Origin or Country of Export

In view of the difficulty in interpreting *country of origin* or *country of export*, and to cover all possible eventualities, complainants often consider it prudent to describe the subject goods as originating in or exported from a particular country.

5.3.2.1. Problems Arising from Designating the Country of Origin Alone

Referring to the country of origin alone creates difficulty whenever
1. the country of origin is unknown
2. the dumping does not emanate from the country of origin
3. the material injury is not being caused by exports from the country of origin but rather the dumping and material injury is caused by activities of the exporter(s) in the intermediate country.[69]

Another difficulty is that the term *country of origin* is, itself, ambiguous. Does it mean the country from which the goods are originally exported? Or, does it mean the country of origin as determined pursuant to the rules used to determine the country of origin for tariff purposes as detailed in § 2 and its subsections? If it is the latter, the complainant may encounter difficulties in attempting to secure the information necessary to identify the country of origin.

Generally, the DNR disregards the tariff rules of origin in antidumping and countervailing duty cases.[70]

In view of the above, it is considered essential to refer to the country from which the goods originate or the country of export.

---

69. It is unfortunate that producers in countries from which goods originate may get caught up in antidumping proceedings due to the acts of a customer or customers in third countries who chose to injuriously dump the goods into Canada.

70. However, on occasion, the DNR, at least implicitly, has raised this issue for goods assembled in third countries. Thus, the DNR has, on occasion, attempted to assess antidumping duty when major components were shipped from a subject country to a nonsubject country, assembled there and exported to Canada. In the case of color television receiving sets originating in or exported from Japan, ADT-4-75, some effort was made to subject color television receiving sets produced by U.S.-based sister companies of Japanese producers to antidumping duty on the basis that the DNR considered that there was insufficient U.S. content to justify considering these goods as being of U.S. origin. This issue has not yet been tested.

5.3.2.2. Problems Arising from Designating Country of Export Alone

The identification of the country of export obviated the need to inquire into the origin of the goods. However, it would not be effectual to merely identify the country of export. If, in fact, the injurious dumping is caused by goods that are exported from a particular country (whether or not produced there), it would be a simple matter to change the country of export and circumvent antidumping control.

Referring to the country in which the goods originate in addition to the country of export attempts to solve that problem.

5.3.3. Country of Origin and the Issue of Component Parts

5.3.3.1. Where the Description of the Subject Goods Does Not Include Component Parts

Where the subject goods are being imported in knocked down condition or in kit form, or could be so imported, it is often possible to circumvent antidumping control.

If the Harmonized System (HS) rules of Tariff Classification applied to antidumping matters, imported kits would be considered equivalent to the finished product. However, this is not the case under the SIMA, which requires, at least theoretically, that the imported goods be like the goods produced in Canada.

Material injury is defined as being injury to "the production in Canada of like goods."[71] The test to meet to be considered a producer is less stringent than for a manufacturer. Simple assembly has been considered sufficient to characterize someone as a manufacturer, or at least a producer.

In the case of *Harry D. Shields Limited* v. *Deputy Minister*,[72] the importer took the position that it was a manufacturer of bicycles although it was importing all components of the bicycles and merely assembling the bicycles in Canada. The DNR took the position that assembly was not manufacturing.

In maintaining the importer's appeal, the Tariff Board decided that if products are manufactured through an assembly process and that is the standard in the trade, then assembly is equivalent to manufacturing.

Likewise, the Tariff Board has held a party to be a manufacturer even though the production process consisted of bolting two components together

---

71.   § 2(3) SIMA.

72.   2 C.E.R. 1 (Tariff Board Appeal No. 1489).

and attaching a few wires to produce a generating set.[73]

In the case of *Gruen Watch Company et al.* v. *The A.G. of Canada*,[74] the court held that "the Plaintiff by importing the movements and placing them in watch cases . . . were *producers* of watches."[75]

The test under the CT which required that the importer be a manufacturer of bicycles, is more stringent than that in SIMA, which speaks about producers and not manufacturers.

Thus, in the case of *"Single Row Tapered Roller Bearings and Parts thereof from Japan,"*[76] the complainant, Canadian Timken Limited, imported the cups and the cones and only performed a simple assembly in Canada. Nonetheless, it was considered a producer in Canada having the status to claim antidumping protection.

In the case of *"Color Television Receiving Sets from Japan,"*[77] the tribunal considered as producers Canadian companies, particularly those with Japanese affiliations that imported substantially complete chassis from abroad and assembled the color television in Canada.

In considering imported goods, therefore, this notion works in favor of circumvention through assembly in Canada.

5.3.3.2. Condition of Goods at the Time of Importation

In cases of tariff classification and customs valuation, imported goods are to be classified and valued as they exist at the time of importation. The SIMA is considered to be a law relating to the customs[78] (i.e., *in pari materia*). Thus, the notions applying to tariff classification and customs valuation apply here.

In *DMNR* v. *MacMillan & Bloedel (Apberni) Ltd.*,[79] it was held that imported goods must be classified in their form at the time of importation.

---

73. *Kipp Kelly Ltd.* v. *DMNR* 7 T.B.R. 102 (Appeal No. 1479).

74. 4 D.T.C. 784 (Ont. S.C.).

75. Ibid. (emphasis added).

76. ADT 8-75.

77. *Supra* note 68.

78. § 2(8) SIMA.

79. S.C.R. 366 (S.C.C. 1965).

In the case of *Triton Industries Inc.* v. *DMNR*,[80] it was concluded that the date of the entry of imports is the date on which the value for duty must be determined.

Likewise, the SIMA requires that antidumping duty is to be levied, collected, and paid on the imported goods of the same description as the goods to which the CITT's finding applies.

There is no reference in any of this legislation (save for end use tariff items) to circumstances after importation.

In certain cases where the description of the subject goods has not included component parts, the DNR has attempted — with varying degrees of success — to collect antidumping duties on goods imported in kit form on the basis that the imported goods were in reality finished goods since they required minor assembly in Canada. Often, the DNR adopts internal minimum Canadian content guidelines.[81] These practices are of doubtful legal validity. Thus, if simple assembly is equivalent to production, it seems that goods cannot be produced in two places. At the time of importation the goods are either a bicycle or not, for example.

If the bicycle is assembled or produced in Canada, it cannot be a bicycle at the time of importation. Also, from a purely definitional point of view, if the imported components constitute the finished product, why can they not function? If the television components are a television when they come to Canada, why is it that it does not play? Why does it only play after it is produced in Canada?

5.3.3.3. Description of Goods as Including All or Certain Imported Components

Where the subject goods are or could be imported in knocked down condition, the complainant will usually describe the subject goods generically and add the phrase "and component parts thereof" designating certain specific major components. Otherwise, if the subject goods are merely referred to as "color televisions," for example, the importer could circumvent an injury finding by importing components for assembly in Canada.

When the subject finished goods are described as including their components, then you have two classes of subject goods originating in or exported from a subject country, that is, components and finished goods.

In the premises, the countries of origin or export may differ.

---

80.   Tariff Board Appeal No. 1454, 4 February 1980.

81.   Content requirements that do not appear in the legislation are irrelevant. Harry D. Shields, *supra* note 72.

While the practice of including all or certain components in the description of subject goods is understandable, it leads to problems of (1) determining the country of origin or export of the goods and (2) meeting the statutory requirements of relating the dumping of goods to material injury to Canadian production of goods like those found to have been dumped.

In effect, when an enterprise produces the finished goods in Canada, even from dumped components, it is as much a Canadian producer of the subject goods as the complainant. Let us look at how the CITT has dealt with these matters.

In the *Hydraulic Turbines*[82] case, the subject goods were hydraulic turbines or original equipment components, as well as spare parts and replacement runners, for use in the generation of electrical power, including all imbedded, stationary and rotating components, whether or not imported separately.

The Anti-Dumping Tribunal (tribunal), predecessor to the CITT, found that the dumping of the subject goods, excluding replacement runners, had caused material injury.

Dealing with the parts issue, the tribunal said:

It may be noted at once that a hydraulic turbine is never imported as such, but because of its huge size, is invariably shipped to the construction site in its component parts, with delivery spread over a considerable period of time. The words "or original equipment components thereof" constitute the relevant part of the description. The words which then follow "as well as spare parts and replacement runners" are those which created the difficulty. *"Spare parts" are distinguishable from replacement runners as they form part of the bid price by the original equipment manufacturer and no question arises as to the appropriateness of their inclusion in the class. Replacement runners, however, are in no way in consideration in the contract award for a turbine.* They will be required thirty or forty years later. In fact, because of the turbine design considerations, the probability is that the original equipment supplier, if still around, will get this award.[83]

In effect, the tribunal decided that spare parts are included in the class of goods subject to antidumping duty if they form part of the bid price for a contract. On the other hand, components that are not considered in the award of a contract (e.g., for service and repair) are not included in the class of

---

82. *Supra* note 57.

83. Ibid, at 10 (emphasis added).

goods. It is also the practice of the DNR to limit subject parts to original equipment manufacturer (oem) parts and not replacement and repair parts.

If the component part is an object of commerce in its own right, it may be the object of a finding of material injury if the dumping causes material injury to the production in Canada of such component parts.

In the case of *Photo Albums with Self-Adhesive Leaves and Component Parts thereof Originating in Japan and the Republic of Korea*,[84] the tribunal found that the photo albums with self-adhesive leaves had caused injury. The leaves were considered separate articles of commerce available to the ultimate consumer and were analyzed on the basis of serving a market independent of photo albums with leaves. The tribunal found that the dumping of leaves had not caused material injury. However, ten years later, in the matter of *Photo Albums with Self-Adhesive Leaves, Originating in or Exported from Hong Kong and the United States of America and Self-adhesive Leaves, Originating in or Exported from Hong Kong, the United States of America and the Republic of Korea*,[85] the CITT found material injury both for albums and leaves. In the case of the leaves, the Tribunal noted that the availability of self-adhesive leaves from the subject countries at dumped prices had caused the complainant, a Canadian album and leaf producer, to lose substantial sales of the separate leaves to the importer, who was also a Canadian album producer.

Further, since the leaves represented a significant portion of the cost of the completed album, the purchase of low-priced leaves had allowed the importer to undercut the complainant on a price basis on the sale of the finished albums.

5.3.4.   Upstream Dumping

In the case of "Slide Fasteners or Zippers and Parts thereof,"[86] the tribunal found that both the zippers and parts thereof had caused injury. The issue arose whether, when the preliminary determination includes components or parts of a product, each component or part is to be considered as an article of commerce and a case made to establish injury to the production in Canada of that component or part.[87]

---

84.   ADT-4-74.

85.   CIT-18-84, 9 C.E.R. 108 (1985).

86.   ADT-1-74.

87.   Ibid, at 10.

The tribunal stated that "the proposition did not *hold in this case.*"[88] It held that the deputy minister had been careful to state that the parts, which he determined to be dumped, were articles so advanced in manufacture that they were components of slide fasteners. Even though the parts could be sold separately, the tribunal refused to ignore the fact that all Japanese exports of the parts were being sold to its Canadian subsidiary and that these components, said to be dumped by the deputy minister, were being assembled in Canada for distribution in Canada as finished zippers at prices that reflected the dumped prices of the components.

In the *Bicycles*[89] case, the subject goods were "bicycles, assembled or unassembled, and bicycle frames, forks, steel handle bars and wheels." The tribunal found that the dumping of bicycles had caused material injury. With respect to the components, the tribunal found that the volume of imports was not such that it had caused past or present injury but found that there was a likelihood of such injury should the dumping of the components not be inhibited by the application of antidumping duties.

The tribunal set out the rule as follows:

It would be an exorbitant task, indeed, to expect the manufacturers to advance evidence of material injury to the production of specific bicycle components. The usual criteria for establishing material injury, such as loss of market share, reduced profitability, diminished employment, idle capacity, etc., lose their relevance when components are considered independently of the completed article. It is true that the Deputy Minister has investigated the importations of these bicycle components, has found them to be dumped, and has identified them in his preliminary determination, but the Tribunal does not believe that a separate inquiry into material injury is required in respect of each and every component identified. It may be stated, as a general rule, *that where it is found that dumping of an article has caused, is causing and is likely to cause material injury, then, in all likelihood, where there is production in Canada of the major components of that article, continued dumping of those components will also cause material injury.* This rule must find its application where, in the opinion of the Tribunal, the purpose and effectiveness of antidumping measures levied against a complete article would otherwise be frustrated, as the Tribunal believes it to be the case where the feasibility *of*

---

88. Ibid. (emphasis added).

89. ADT-11-77.

simple assembly has been demonstrated.[90]

In the case of *Paint Brushes*,[91] the subject goods were paint brushes using natural hog bristle as the filament material, and the components thereof known as heads. The preliminary determination of dumping by the deputy minister covered both paint brushes and their components known as heads. The tribunal concluded that the dumping of the paint brushes had caused injury. In the case of heads, the tribunal concluded that there was no past or present injury due to the absence of importation but there was a likelihood of injury to the production in Canada of like goods.

Citing its previous decision in the bicycle case,[92] the tribunal said:

The head is a major component of a paint brush in terms of value. It can easily be imported separately from the handle should circumstances establish the advantage of such action. *Consequently, there is the likelihood of injury occurring to the production in Canada of brush heads, and, certainly in terms of reduced employment and underutilization of production capacity to the production of completed paint brushes, should the dumping of heads be permitted to take place.*[93]

5.3.5. Downstream Dumping

However, the tribunal did not stop there. In respect of heads, it stated:

There is no evidence of the production in Canada of component heads for sale. All production of heads is for the purpose of manufacturing paint brushes , and it follows that if the dumping of paint brushes has caused and is causing material injury to the production in Canada of paint brushes, it did automatically cause and is causing material injury to the production in Canada of the heads, which are integral components of paint brushes. A similar rationale leads to the conclusion that the likelihood of material injury attributable to continued dumping of paint brushes would likely cause material injury to the production in Canada of heads.[94]

---

90. Ibid., at 24 (emphasis added).

91. ADT-6-84.

92. *Supra* note 89.

93. *Supra* note 91, at 7 (emphasis added).

94. Ibid. (emphasis added).

Thus, the CITT may find that the dumping of a major component causes material injury to the production in Canada of the finished good. While this is more likely to be the case where there is Canadian production of the components,[95] it is not a condition sine qua non. Thus, it is possible that the tribunal may similarly find that the dumping of components is injurious to the production of a finished product in Canada even when the component is not produced in Canada.

5.3.6. Like Goods and Causality Issues Relating to Component Part Designations

The proposition that the dumping of components can cause material injury to the production in Canada of the finished article is of questionable legal justification on the basis of the like goods argument (i.e., a Canadian producer of components can complain that dumped components are causing injury to the production in Canada of like goods — domestically produced components). However, Canadian producers of finished goods cannot claim that dumped components are causing injury to finished products that are not like goods.

In *Steam Traps, Pipeline Strainers, Automatic Drain Traps for Compressed Air Service, Thermostatic Air Vents and Air Eliminators including parts, Screens and Repair Kits pertaining thereto, produced by or on behalf of Sarco Co. Inc., Allentown, Penn., U.S.A.;*[96] the tribunal stated:

It appears to the tribunal that the question of whether goods are "like" is to be determined by market considerations. Do they compete directly with one another? Are the same consumers sought? Do they fulfill the same need? Can they be substituted one for the other?

In the light of the foregoing, how can it be argued that the parts are "like goods" to the finished product?

---

95.   See, for example, the case of *Hair Accessories, and Component Parts and Packaging Materials* ADT-2-74 in which the tribunal found that the subject goods were not causing material injury to the production in Canada of like goods.

The complainants were importers of the components and to a lesser degree, finished hair accessories.

The Tribunal stated, "All of the complainants were importers of components, and to a lesser degree, of finished hair accessories. This has its significance in considering whether the production in Canada of hair accessories, as represented by the six Canadian producers, has been, or is being, or is likely to be materially injured." Ibid. at 7.

96.   ADT-10-76.

In the *Hair Accessories* case,[97] the class of goods, hair accessories, included the following component parts:

hair rollers, roller fasteners, hair pins and bobby pins, clips, curlers, hair brushes, combs of all kinds, barrettes, ponytail holders, software (shower caps, slumber caps, hair nets and wave nets, rain bonnets, turbans, etc.)

As the tribunal so succinctly put it, "What the Tribunal is required to look into is the question of material injury to the production in Canada of 'like goods' . . . It is obvious that hair brushes are not "like goods" to combs, or bobby pins to shower caps."[98]

In this connection, it is interesting to examine the decision of the tribunal in the case of Certain *Power Conversion Systems and Rectifiers Imported From, Supplied by or Otherwise Introduced into the Commerce of Canada by, or on Behalf of, Jeumont-Schneider (France), Fuji Electric Co. Ltd. or Toshiba Corporation (Japan).*[99]

The subject goods being described as a system, consisted of a combination of goods and services, some Canadian and some foreign. Even the complainant, Canadian General Electric (CGE) included substantial foreign content in its system. In making a finding of no material injury in respect of Jeumont-Schneider, the tribunal noted that the CGE bid included substantial French content. Indeed, the bidder was a Joint Venture between CGE and Alsthom, a French company. The tribunal stated:

Setting aside for the moment the question of the likelihood of material injury arising from continued dumping, the Tribunal had some concern whether, given the definition of the subject goods, there is a question at all of considering past or present injury caused to C.G.E., as a Canadian producer. The subject goods are described as "power conversion systems" and "rectifiers". Had the joint venture obtained the award, the rectifier as such and the parts of the power conversion system would have been of French supply, not Canadian. Insofar as the concept of past or present injury is considered, one would, at the very least, have to exclude from such a finding all those components to be supplied by Alsthom, which fall within the definition and comprise some 30 per cent of all subject goods

---

97. *Supra* note 95.

98. Ibid., at 38.

99. ADT-13-84.

to be supplied, as set out in C.G.E.'s confidential exhibit A-12.[100]

It further stated:

Given the fact that the award was for a turn-key contract for the construction of an operating substation in which the supply of the subject goods constituted about half only of the value of the contract to the joint venture; given the fact that, had the joint venture obtained the award, a considerable portion of the subject goods would not have been produced in Canada in any event; and given the considerations already discussed as to the importance of French content and the apparent preference of the owner to deal with Jeumont-Schneider, the Tribunal is unable to conclude that the dumping found caused material injury to the complainant.[101]

The inclusion of component parts in the definition of subject goods creates situations which, it is submitted, distort the operations and purposes of SIMA. Also, it causes confusion as to the country of origin (or export) of the subject goods. Thus, if the competition is coming from finished goods, the investigation of foreign components exported to Canada for assembly is uncalled for. If the finished product is considered to be the subject good, the country of origin is Canada. A determination of dumping in respect of components allows the tribunal to make a finding of material injury caused to the production in Canada by other goods produced in Canada. Let us visualize two situations: one in which the complainant-producer is not an importer of components; the other in which the complainant-producer is an importer of components, but not from the subject country.

In the first case, by finding material injury, the tribunal is supporting one Canadian producer of the finished product against another, merely because the latter imports components as well as the finished product. This is due to the distortion of the notion of like goods.

In the second case, the tribunal is asked to support one foreign country's producers of components to the detriment of another country's producers of components. Also, this approach muddies the distinction between domestically produced and foreign produced goods.

Thus, for example, if the Canadian industry consisted of assemblers of computers using U.S. components and an antidumping complaint is launched against computers and parts of them imported from or originating in Japan, an injury finding could conceivably trap Canadian producers of computers

---

100. Ibid., at 13.

101. Ibid.

using Japanese components in favor of Canadian producers of computers using U.S. components. It is doubtful that Canadian antidumping legislation was designed for that purpose.[102]

An example of the ridiculous extremes to which this can lead appears from the *Hyundai* case.[103]In that case, the complainants, General Motors of Canada Limited and Ford Motor Company of Canada, filed an antidumping complaint against the following goods:

Cars (Including those in a Semi-knocked Condition), With or Without Options Such as Automatic Transmissions, Produced by or on Behalf of Hyundai Motor Company, Seoul, Republic of Korea, or by Companies With Which it is Associated, and Originating in or Exported From The Republic of Korea.

The selection of the target, Hyundai Motor Company instead of Korea, was carefully designed to exclude Daewoo and Kia Motors, being Korean automobile producers exporting cars to the complainants.

Furthermore, counsel for Hyundai argued that by attacking the importation of components, what the complainants were seeking was not the support of production in Canada of cars (since most of the Canadian production was exported to the United States and, furthermore, used substantial foreign parts) but rather the support of their production of automobiles in the United States since most of the cars sold by the complainants in Canada were manufactured in the United States. When antidumping protection is sought to support one group of foreign factories against another group of foreign factories, questions arise not only whether the statute's objectives are being achieved but also about the relevancy of these proceedings. Also, the complainants were seeking to reduce or eliminate competition from Hyundai Automobile Canada Inc., a Canadian subsidiary of Hyundai Motor Corporation and a prospective Canadian producer of cars. There are also obvious antitrust implications to these approaches.

Note that the tribunal was mindful of this problem many years before when, in making a finding of material injury for photo albums and leaves, it

---

102. It is suggested that a proper complaint against imported components must be filed by Canadian producers of those components. So if Canadian television producers use foreign dumped picture tubes instead of domestic picture tubes and there is no Canadian picture tube industry, how can the dumping of picture tubes be injurious to Canadian production of picture tubes? Indeed, it is potentially beneficial to Canadian producers of televisions. If such a producer sources less competitive picture tubes elsewhere, how does it relate its injury to dumping?

103. CIT-13-87.

noted:

> During the hearing, the complainant stressed that he was quite willing to sell bulk leaves to album manufacturers at reasonable prices, allowing them to manufacture covers and sell complete albums at a profit. The Tribunal is satisfied that the complainant has shown good faith in this regard and has no intention to squeeze its manufacturing competitors in Canada out of the market.[104]

5.3.7. Absence of Designation of Country of Export or Origin in Dumping and Countervailing Duty Proceedings

In a number of cases, neither the country of export nor the country of origin is mentioned in the class of goods. Rather, it is a particular producer, exporter, or importer who is targeted, sometimes indicating its head office.

Thus, in the case of *Hair Accessories*, and components parts and packaging materials,[105] the goods were further identified as being "exported to Canada by H. Goodman and Sons Incorporated, Kearny, New Jersey, United States of America." In that case, a substantial portion of the components originated in various Asian countries.

In the case of *Power Conversion Systems*,[106] the goods were described, inter alia, as being "imported from, supplied by or otherwise introduced into the commerce of Canada by, or on behalf of, Jeumont-Schneider (Champagne-Sur'Seine, France)."

A preliminary objection was made on the basis that the tribunal had no jurisdiction to make a finding of injury with respect to any of the subject goods to be supplied by Jeumont-Schneider that were not produced in France. In denying the objection, the tribunal stated:

> It is the dumping activity of the importers/exporters with which the Tribunal is concerned and which it may brand as materially injurious to Canadian production. If, in any particular case, specific goods are claimed not to fall within the description of the goods caught by an affirmative finding of material injury, the importers/exporters have their recourse in

---

104. *See supra* note 84, at 115.

105. ADT-2-74.

106. *Supra* note 99.

another forum.[107]

These and similar cases[108] lend themselves to potentially controlling the worldwide exports to Canada of particular goods by particular companies. It has often been said, tritely or facetiously, that countries do not dump, individuals do. If so, is there any need to designate a country of origin or export in any case?

In certain cases the description of the subject goods also includes the phrase "introduced in the commerce of Canada by."[109] Here again, the country of origin of the subject goods could very well be Canada.

5.3.8. Investigations or Findings Irrespective of Lack of Exports

In Canada, determinations of dumping and findings of material injury have been made even though the goods were never exported to Canada or even manufactured. These are so-called tender cases, involving capital goods. In these cases, the country of origin (or export) is that where the goods could have been produced.[110]

Thus, in the case of *Electric Generators originating in or exported from Italy*,[111] the Italian producer, Ansaldo, s.p.a., tendered to supply the subject goods to a Canadian utility. The tender was never accepted. Nonetheless, the deputy minister found that the tender had been made at dumped prices.

The exporter moved to quash the preliminary determination on the basis that the tender did not constitute a sale as contemplated by the Anti-Dumping Act.[112] The Federal Court, Trial Division[113] dismissed the application on the basis that an irrevocable tender was an "agreement to sell." This was affirmed on appeal by the Federal Court of Appeal.[114]

---

107. Ibid., at 8.

108. *See Steam Traps*, *supra* note 96.

109. *See, e.g. Power Conversion Systems*, *supra* note 104.

110. If the target is described as a particular commercial entity, then an injury finding can be made against goods potentially originating in or exported from any country.

111. ADT-8-83.

112. § 2(1) (defined sale as including an agreement to sell).

113. *Ansaldo s.p.a.* v. *DMNR et al.*, 6 C.E.R. 334, Court No. T-1226-83 (2 June 1983).

114. 11 C.E.R. 289.

Subsequently, the tribunal found material injury on the basis that, in one case, the Canadian producer was obliged to revise his prices downward to meet the Ansaldo price and that, in the second case, anticipating a low bid by Ansaldo, the Canadian producer tendered (and secured the contract) at an unprofitably low price.

An extension of the notion of material injury being caused or likely to be caused in Canada due to potential imports from a particular country appears from the case of *subsidized Grain Corn originating in or exported from the U.S.A.*[115]

In the case in question, it was acknowledged that exports of grain corn to Canada from the United States were declining from year to year. However, U.S. subsidies created downward pressure to U.S. corn prices on the Chicago Grain Exchange and Canadian prices were thereby adversely affected. The argument, which was sustained by the CITT (by a two-to-one majority) and ultimately by the Supreme Court of Canada, was that it sufficed that a foreign subsidy caused material injury (in the form of price suppression) to the production in Canada of like goods *irrespective of whether goods in the country of origin were actually exported to Canada*. While in the final analysis the tribunal covered this leap in logic by stating that there was a likelihood of injury due to the fact that massive quantities of corn could be exported to Canada but for reduction by Canadian producers of their prices, the decision stands as an example of how far the notion of identifying and punishing designated foreign entities can go.

The majority of the tribunal ruled that the CITT should look at "potential" as well as "actual" exports. The rationale was expressed in this way:

Both the Special Import Measures Act and the GATT Subsidies Code exist for the express purpose of dealing with unfairly traded goods which cause or threaten injury. Necessarily, their provisions must be interpreted, not in the abstract, but within the context of the environment within which they apply, namely, international trade. Since the economic and commercial realities of international trade dictate that price be met or market share lost, the majority of the panel is persuaded to adopt the broader interpretation of "subsidized imports", that is, that cognizance be taken of potential or likely imports in the determination of material injury. To do otherwise, in the view of the majority of the panel, would be to frustrate the purpose of the system.[116]

---

115. CIT-7-86, C.E.R. 1 (1987).

116. Ibid., at 22.

In the view of the majority, without the application of countervailing duty, the Canadian producers would have been obliged to reduce their prices to unprofitable levels to avoid substantial influx into Canada of U.S. corn.

In a strong dissent, Mr. Bissonnette, a member of the CITT, relying on the GATT Subsidies and Countervailing Duty Code and EEC Council Regulation No. 2176/84, found that injurious imports were a precondition to countervailing duty relief. He stated:

In the case of the European Economic Community, the GATT obligations are embodied in Council Regulation No. 2176/84 relating to dumping and subsidization. I find that here again the injurious effects of subsidization must be transmitted through actual imports. The intention is crystal clear. "A determination of injury shall be made only if the dumped or *subsidized imports* are, *through the effects of* dumping or *subsidization*, causing injury, etc.", and criteria similar to those of the GATT are then spelt out.[117]

. . .

There are many provisions in SIMA relating to the procedures of investigation and determination which only make sense in the context of a presence in Canada of subsidized imports. The investigation by Revenue Canada could not get off the ground without imports.[118]

6. Country of Origin in Safeguard Proceedings

Canadian safeguard proceedings arise mainly out of the operation of the Export and Import Permits Act (EIPA).[119] Under the EIPA, the government may establish the Import Control List and place any article on it whose importation it deems necessary to control.[120] In the case of a number of goods, the government also designates the subject country.

---

117. Article 4, Council Regulation (EEC) no. 2176/84 of 23 July 1984: "A determination of injury shall be made only if the dumped or subsidized imports are, through the effects of dumping or subsidization, causing injury, i.e., causing or threatening to cause material injury to an established Community industry, or materially retarding the establishment of such an industry. Injuries caused by other factors, such as volume and prices of imports which are not dumped or subsidized, or contraction in demand, which, individually or in combination, also adversely affect the Community industry must not be attributed to the dumped or subsidized imports."

118. Ibid., at 39 (emphasis added).

119. R.S., C. E-17.

120. Ibid., § 5.

The limitations can also be "voluntary" on the part of certain exporting countries. In the latter case, such countries usually allocate a license to their own producers enabling the latter to export to Canada.

In either case, neither the EIPA nor its regulations[121] indicate whether the limitation relates to goods exported from or originating in a country. Also, there are no rules of origin established in respect of specific countries.

Nonetheless, the Regulations requires that the applicant for a permit specify, inter alia, the country of origin of the goods and the country "from which the goods are imported".

A reasonable case can be made that the requirement of information relating to country of origin is statistical only and bears no relationship to the requirements of the Export and Import Permits Act. The rationale is derived from a reading of the words of the Export and Import Permits Act which deals with imports and the lack of reference to (either a country of export or) country of origin on the Import Control List itself.

Furthermore, since the EIPA is mainly concerned with setting global quantitative limits to the importation of certain goods, the country of origin — even if it could be determined in fact or by reference to tariff rules of origin — would be irrelevant. When a voluntary restraint agreement is entered into with specific exporting countries, our law and practice leaves the discretion of issuing licenses entirely in the hands of such countries. Presumably, such countries will ensure that the goods to be thus exported will meet its own content or origin rules.

Certain import quotas are country specific. In these cases, there is a continuing threat of circumvention. It is the practice of the Department of External Affairs, which administers the EIPA, to consider the country from which the finished goods were originally shipped to be that for which the quota shall be applied.[122]

7. Country of Origin in Marking or Labelling Legislation

The Marking of Imported Goods Order[123] contains a schedule of goods that, if imported into Canada, must be legibly marked, stamped, branded, or labeled

---

121. Import Permits Regulations, SOR/79-5, as amended.

122. In a recent case involving Korean textiles (under quota), transhipped through Japan (a nonquota country), criminal proceedings were initiated against importers on the grounds of illegal circumvention of restraints against Korean textiles.

123. P.C. 1963-1775.

to indicate the country of origin. Under the regulations,[124] the country of origin is the country where the goods were substantially manufactured.

7.1. Rules of Origin in the Context of Procurement in Canada

There are numerous federal and provincial government programs and policies designed to favor Canadian produced goods as opposed to foreign-produced goods. Other programs and policies give preference based on the degree of Canadian content in a product or system.

When preference is based on the degree of local content, each purchaser has its own guidelines on what is considered to be local content and how this criterion is to be evaluated, weighted, etc. As can be appreciated, the rules tend to be murky and lend themselves to considerable discretionary action and political manipulation.

8. Conclusion

Rules of origin should not, per se, constitute tariff or nontariff barriers to trade. This occurs when the rules are vague, imprecise, or contradictory, leaving too much room for administrative abuse and fostering costly litigation.

8.1. Tariff Rules of Origin

By and large, save for the UST, the rules of origin have stood the test of time reasonably well. The UST is of recent vintage and the most complex of all the tariff systems rules. Already, considerable difficulty is being experienced with the substantial transformation rules as well as with the definitions applying to the content requirements.

The FTA rules of origin were designed by the United States of America to avoid "back door" importation, at favorable tariff rates, of non-FTA goods from Canada into the United States.

Thus, the FTA rules require that non-FTA materials or component parts undergo change of tariff classification en route to a beneficiary country. Rules spelling out the extent to which change of tariff classification must occur are set out in elaborate rules set out for each class of goods. These transformation rules discriminate against non-FTA goods. The discrimination is exacerbated by adding minimum FTA value criteria for a wide range of goods and situations.

Amongst situations that frequently arise and that require a minimum of 50

---

124. Ibid, § 3(i).

percent FTA content are those in which the non-FTA input (as a part item) and the finished product carry the same tariff item.

Thus, the FTA rules of origin are highly discriminatory against non-FTA inputs.[125] The administration of the FTA rules of origin, particularly by the U.S. Customs officials, has been stringent. As can be appreciated by an examination of the rules, they contain many imprecisions, lending themselves to administrative harassment. One well publicized instance of this is the recent investigation of exports by Honda Canada of Canadian-produced cars.

These rules will be clarified somewhat if and when the North American Free Trade Agreement (NAFTA) signed by Canada, the United States and Mexico is adopted by the legislatures of those governments. However, the NAFTA rules, if anything, exacerbate the discrimination against *non-territorial* inputs. Thus, NAFTA content for automobiles will increase, in stages, from 50 percent to 55 percent and then 62.5 percent as opposed to the present 50 percent content requirement in the FTA.

8.2. Special Import Measures Act Rules of Origin

In the case of SIMA, vague notions of country of export and country of origin coupled with a creative administrative practice has caused much uncertainty and has hampered exports to Canada. The examples cited above are by no means exhaustive. Accordingly, it is suggested that reform is required to clarify and define more precisely. But this reform cannot be done in a vacuum. Efforts at the international level to codify standard rules of origin, at least in trade related areas, should be encouraged. However, the proposed GATT Agreement on Rules of Origin promises to create as many problems as it solves. The proposed rules (no doubt imposed by the United States) embody the problems referred to above in connection with the FTA rules of origin. In an antidumping context, they will raise many questions on subject goods and subject countries. For example, if a major component is shipped from country A to country B to be made up into a finished good exported to country C and a complaint of injurious dumping is filed for the finished product, which is the country of origin or export if there is insufficient transformation in country B?

Finally, it is suggested that it makes little sense to establish rules of origin guidelines without, at the same time, revamping those sections of the Anti-Dumping Code and the Subsidies and Countervailing Duty Code relating to issues such as upstream or downstream dumping or subsidization, causality, and like goods. All these elements overlap to such a degree that an abstract

---

125. Compounding the problem is the removal of drawback on non-FTA inputs effective 1 January 1994 thus further discouraging the use of third country inputs.

set of rules of origin would create more difficulties than it solves. Accordingly, we suggest that rules of origin be developed at the international level concurrently with appropriate modifications to the GATT codes.

8.3.   Safeguard Actions

Due to considerable uncertainty in the law, the authorities must develop clear guidelines on whether *country of origin* or *country of export* will govern, define the meaning to be given to the selected phrase, and set out precise rules of origin.

8.4.   Procurement Rules of Origin

It is unrealistic to expect uniformity or clarity in an area fraught with political expediency. It is hoped that our international trading rules will minimize and precisely circumscribe the occasions of permissible local preference.

CHAPTER 6

Japanese Rules of Origin

Professor Norio Komuro

1. Introduction

Japan's rules of origin consist of three kinds of nonpreferential rules and preferential rules for the GSP.

With regard to nonpreferential rules of origin, three agencies administer each rule of origin within the framework of the relevant law. Whereas the Ministry of Finance-Customs Services and the Ministry of International Trade and Industry (MITI) apply each rule of origin for trade law purposes, Japan's Fair Trade Commission (FTC) applies its own rules of origin for competition law purposes. However, it should be noted that those rules of origin, although partially different according to purpose, have neither drawn the attention of other trading countries in the context of trade friction nor given rise to disputes before administrative or judicial institutions in Japan.

The GSP rules of origin are based on principles typically different from nonpreferential rules to pursue the GSP's purposes and are stricter than nonpreferential rules. They have played a vital role for trading companies, but their significance has been partially diminished by reason of the progressive reduction of nonpreferential customs tariffs.

Keeping in mind such general features, we will examine the framework (use, procedure) and substantive rules relating to Japan's rules of origin.

2. General Overview

Irrespective of the nonpreferential or preferential area, two basic origin criteria, the wholly produced criterion and the substantial transformation

---

1. The author would like to thank Edwin Vermulst, Paul Waer, and Madelein Perrick for their helpful comments on previous drafts of this chapter. However, the author is solely responsible for the contents.

criterion, are applied.[1] However, the tests to determine whether substantial transformation takes place are different for each area.[2]

In the nonpreferential area, Customs rules of origin are based mainly on a change of tariff classification test and subsidiarily on a processing test for specified products, whereas MITI and the FTC use a processing test. Nonpreferential rules do not use value-added tests.

In the preferential area, four tests apply: change of tariff classification tests, processing tests, value-added tests, and mixed tests, which are more rigid than nonpreferential tests.

3. Nonpreferential Rules of Origin

Japan's nonpreferential rules of origin can be divided into three groups: Customs rules of origin for customs law purposes, MITI's rules of origin for trade control purposes, and the FTC's rules of origin for competition law purposes.

3.1. Customs Rules of Origin

3.1.1. Use and Procedure

Customs rules of origin are used for several objectives: the determination of customs tariff, the control of false origin marking, import statistics, and certification of origin.

---

1. Japan has however entered a reservation regarding the substantial transformation criterion in accepting Annex D.1 Concerning Rules of Origin in the Kyoto Convention. The reason for the reservation is that under the GSP scheme, "products which have been produced in two or more countries in the specified region [i.e. the ASEAN region] shall be regarded as products wholly produced in the country where the final processing has been carried out." In other words, under the GSP's cumulation rule, the country of origin is the exporting ASEAN country where the final processing is carried out, if the substantial transformation occurs within the territories of the ASEAN. Accordingly, Japan's reservation does not mean that Japan denies the substantial transformation criterion. Article 22-7 of Cabinet Order for Enforcement of the Temporary Tariff Measures Law explicitly refers to the substantial transformation principle as the origin criterion for the GSP.

2. Customs Co-operation Council's publication (column "Japan" in "Compendium Rules of Origin"; "Recueil des Règles d'origine des marchandises") says that "the rules of origin for goods to which the MFN tariff rates should be applied are almost identical to the rules for GSP treatment," but this description is an error. As explained later, Japan's nonpreferential rules of origin and the GSP's rules of origin differ considerably in substantial transformation tests.

3.1.1.1.   Use

3.1.1.1.1.   Determination of Customs Tariff

Historically speaking, Customs rules of origin were adopted when Japan joined the GATT (September 1955) in view of the necessity of applying MFN tariffs to imported products.

Under customs law, the nonpreferential customs tariff varies depending on the country of origin as well as relations between MFN tariff and national tariffs, which consist of a general tariff applied continuously and a temporary tariff fixed annually. Goods originating in a GATT contracting party are entitled to the MFN tariff if it is lower than the national temporary tariff (which is in most cases lower than the national general tariff and precedes the latter) but are subject to the national tariff if the MFN tariff is higher than the national tariff. Therefore, customs rules of origin have been expected to play a certain role in the application of customs tariffs.

However, those rules have recently become of little importance in the framework of the determination of customs tariff.

First, goods to which the MFN tariff applies have decreased in number, because the national temporary tariff has become lower than the MFN tariff with regard to many products through a series of tariff lowering measures taken to open the domestic market and narrow Japan's trade surplus.

Second, as temporary tariffs that apply to a majority of imported goods (including all machinery products belonging to Chap. 84-92 of HS Code) have been reduced to zero as a result of 1990 tariff lowering measures,[3] it is now unnecessary to strictly determine the country of origin on the basis of origin rules. In short, the customs tariff is in the majority of cases the same (zero or low tariff) irrespective of the country of origin. This explains why Customs rules of origin are in practice not so important for customs tariff purposes. Nevertheless, an importer who falsely declares country of origin is

---

3.   According to the 1991 Customs Tariff Schedules of Japan published by the Japan Tariff Association, there are two categories of goods to which the GATT tariff applies: goods for which the GATT tariff is lower than the temporary tariff (e.g., Veneer sheets and sheets for plywood of rosewood, ebony wood, etc. [4408.90.100]; pallets and other load boards [4415.20]; certain wood articles [4421.90.099]) and goods for which the GATT tariff is lower than the general tariff and for which the temporary tariff is not fixed (e.g., certain waterproof footwear [6401.10.090], certain other footwear [6402.20]).

Among machinery or industrial products [Chaps. 84-92], goods for which the temporary tariff is not zero are limited to six products: insulated electric wire or cable [8544], carbon electrodes [8545], tanks or other armoured fighting vehicles [8710], spectacle frames [9003], sunglasses [9004], and watch bands or bracelets [9113]. With regard to those products, a temporary tariff still applies since it is lower than the GATT tariff.

liable for "imprisonment at forced labor of not more than one year or a fine of not more than one hundred thousand yen, or . . . both."[4]

3.1.1.1.2. Control of False Origin Marking

Customs rules of origin are rather used to control false origin marking, which is voluntarily affixed to imported goods (under Japanese law, contrary to the U.S. system, origin marking is not required, but if marking voluntarily affixed to the goods is false or misleading, it is subject to control).

If imported goods "show, directly or indirectly, a false marking of origin or carry any indication of origin which may lead to misconception," Customs will not give an import permit to them and shall cause an importer to choose between obliterating or correcting the false marking or reshipping the goods within a time limit fixed by the Director-General of Customs after immediate notification under Art. 71 of Customs Law.[5]

Customs applies its rules of origin to judge whether an origin marking affixed to imported goods is false or misleading.

Besides these uses, Customs rules of origin are used either by Customs to make import statistics or by chambers of commerce to issue certificates of origin for exported goods.

3.1.1.2.   Procedure

3.1.1.2.1. Procedure Pertaining to Adoption of Rules

The Ministry of Finance has adopted Customs rules of origin in the form of an administrative circular. Under Japanese customs law, it has general powers to adopt circulars that are addressed to subordinate organs (Customs Service) or their officials with an aim to ensuring uniform interpretation of customs law. However, those circulars may in theory be subject to judicial review in a private action against Customs measures based on them, if they happen to conflict with the law.

3.1.1.2.2. Procedure Pertaining to Implementation of Rules

With regard to Customs measures such as the determination of customs tariff and false marking control, any party may file a protest before Customs if he

---

4.   Art. 113 bis of Customs Law.

5.   Art. 71 of Customs Law is the national implementation of the Madrid Convention 1891 on the prevention of false or misleading origin marking

or she is not satisfied with the measures. The time limit for filing a protest shall not be longer than two months from the day immediately following the day when measures are known. This protest may be followed by an appeal to the Minister of Finance, who shall consult the Customs Dissatisfaction Review Committee established in the Ministry of Finance for investigation and deliberation. Decisions of the Minister of Finance may, however, be subject to judicial review for annulment by a district court, whose judgments may in turn be appealed to a high court. The Supreme Court may grant petitions to review judgments of the high court.

It should be noted, however, that Customs measures may not be rendered void by the court of justice because of conflicts with Customs rules of origin, since Customs rules of origin, being embodied in administrative circular, do not have the character of law or governmental regulation (cabinet order, ministerial ordinance); consequently administrative measures taken in contravention of Customs rules of origin are still legal as far as they comply with the law or regulations.

3.1.2.   Substantive Rules

Customs rules of origin have been provided for in two ministerial Circulars for Customs Law: General Circular 68-3-4 and Particular Circular 71. The former is intended to implement Art. 68 of Customs Law on import documents, and the latter to implement Art. 71 of Customs Law on false marking control.

3.1.2.1.   Origin Rules of General Circular 68-3-4

3.1.2.1.1.   Origin Criteria

According to General Circular 68-3-4, the origin of imported goods is determined according to the "wholly-produced" criterion and the "substantial transformation" criterion. The former applies to natural products (mineral products, agricultural products, live animals, etc.) entirely obtained in a given country. The latter applies to products in the manufacturing process of which two or more countries have been involved. In the case of those products, the country of origin should be "the country where the process bringing about the substantial transformation and conferring a new property was carried out in the last place."

The substantial transformation criterion is expressed by change of tariff heading test, positive processing test and minimal operations test.[6]

3.1.2.1.2. Change of Tariff Heading Test

If a change of tariff heading (HS's four digits) occurs between a finished product and nonoriginating materials or parts and components as a result of processing or working operations, the country of processing is in principle regarded as the country of origin, as the substantial transformation has taken place there.

Especially with regard to products produced or assembled from various nonoriginating materials or parts, (i.e. important materials conferring properties to the final product and unimportant materials), an inquiry is made into a change of tariff heading between the product and important imported materials.

3.1.2.1.3. Positive Processing Test

Concerning specified products, the following processing operations confer origin, even if they do not give rise to a change of tariff heading between final products and nonoriginating materials. A list of those processing operations is called the "positive list" in that they confer origin in spite of the absence of a tariff heading change:

-   grinding and grading of the raw materials for natural abrasives
-   refining operations that change or specify the use for sugars, oils and fats, waxes, or chemical products
-   manufacture with chemical change for chemical products (Chaps. 28-38), plastics, rubbers, and articles thereof (Chaps. 39-40)
-   processing such as coloring, dyeing, mercerization, resinification, and embossment for leather, yarn, and woven fabrics
-   manufacture of thrown yarn from single yarn
-   manufacture of yarn from fibers, manufacture of fabrics from yarn, and manufacture of clothes from fabrics for fabricated asbestos fibers (6812), glass fibers (7019), and articles thereof (6812, 7019)

---

6. Japanese rules of origin have introduced the third original criterion for exposed photographic or cinematographic films (3704, 3705, 3706), which is not provided for in the Kyoto Convention (Annex D.1. Concerning Rules of Origin). Its country of origin shall be the national country of the photographer, but not the country of photographing where the film has been substantially transformed through exposure.

- processing of worked products from unworked materials for pearls, diamonds, precious or semi-precious stones, and synthetic precious stones
- manufacture of alloys from materials
- manufacture of unwrought metal from metal waste
- manufacture of metal foil from metal plates, sheets, or strip
- manufacture of ingot, wire, and bars for precious metals (Chap. 71) and certain base metals (copper, nickel, aluminium, lead, zinc, and tine)
- manufacture of final articles from worked materials that belong to the same tariff heading as final articles for animal carving articles such as articles of ivory or coral (9601) as well as vegetable or mineral carving article such as amber articles (9602)

3.1.2.1.4. Minimal Operations Test

In contrast to the positive list, minimal operations listed below do not confer origin, even if they give rise to a change of tariff heading:[7]
- selection, sorting, and repacking
- marking or labelling
- packing in a bottle, a package, or other recipients
- making a set
- simple cutting
- freezing, drying, brining or other similar operations for the purpose of transportation or preservation
- simple mixing
- simple assembly of parts
- operations consisting of these operations
- rolling flat photographic films that are not exposed

Mention should be made of the following administrative interpretation with regard to "simple assembly of parts":[8]
- Simple assembly means the assembly of parts and components "through simple operations such as simple fastenings (screws, bolts, nuts, etc.) rivetting or welding."

---

7. Operations such as selection, marking, labelling, or packing do not, indeed, bring about a change of tariff heading. But, the following operations do: manufacturing travel sets (9605) or sets consisting of woven fabric and yarn (6308); manufacturing wood (4007) or veneer sheets (4008) by cutting; freezing, drying, or brining of meat, fish, or vegetables; manufacturing certain industrial products by assembly.

8. Particular Circular 71.

- Even if such simple assembly "brings about significant effects on property or performance of the goods in question," it does not confer origin.

This interpretation would permit to distinguish between complicated assembly (e.g., sophisticated assembly processes requiring high technology) and simple assembly and to consider that the former confers origin through a change of tariff heading whereas the latter does not irrespective of its effects on property of the goods.

3.1.2.2. Origin Marking Rules of Particular Circular 71

While General Circular 68-3-4 is used for any purpose (the determination of customs tariff, false marking control, import statistics, certification of origin), Particular Circular 71 is used only for false marking control purposes with imported goods. This Particular Circular was adopted by the Director of Import Affairs in 1974 and functions as a *lex specialis* vis-à-vis General Circular 68-3-4 among Customs rules of origin.

Under Particular Circular 71, simple assembly does not include "assembly operations which bring about significant effects on property or performance of the goods in question" for the false marking control purposes. For example, the assembly of electric calculators or watches does not constitute a simple assembly for false marking control purposes. With regard to those assembled products, a voluntary marking should show that they are "assembled in" a given country.

This circular sharply differs from General Circular 68-3-4 on the concept of simple assembly operations.

In General Circular 68-3-4, simple assembly such as certain watch assembly is considered ab initio as insubstantial. Consequently if watches are assembled of Japanese parts in a foreign country and are reimported to Japan, they would be marked "Made in Japan" under General Circular 68-3-4, because assembly operations do not confer origin and therefore those watches are regarded as originating in the country where the parts were manufactured (i.e., Japan). However this kind of marking would cause consumers to misunderstand that those watches were manufactured in Japan from Japanese parts. Particular Circular 71 has been adopted to prevent such a misleading marking, which would be permitted under General Circular 68-3-4. Consequently, the watches would bear the marking "assembled in" a given country, rather than "made in Japan."

3.1.3. Implementation of Rules

3.1.3.1. Determination of Country of Origin for Customs Tariff Purposes

As previously pointed out, Customs rules of origin provided for in General Circular 68-3-4 are of little importance for customs tariff purposes. Accordingly Customs determines the country of origin of imported goods on the basis of relevant documents or evidence (invoice, certificate of origin, bill of lading, etc.), which are listed in General Circular 68-3-6. This method has not given rise to any controversy, as the customs tariff is generally zero or low independently of the country of origin.[9]

3.1.3.2. Determination of Country of Origin for Marking Control Purposes

Customs rules of origin are much more important for marking control purposes than for customs tariff purposes.

Customs administers rules of origin for false marking control from the viewpoint of consumer protection. For example, for products such as

---

9.   Customs practice as to the determination of the origin of integrated circuits is worth noting. Customs has confirmed the origin of integrated circuits mainly by means of an invoice or bill of lading as follows: U.S. origin for integrated circuits assembled in Mexico from chips diffused in the United States, NIEC origin for integrated circuits assembled in an NIEC country from chips diffused in Japan, etc. This practice seems at first sight contradictory, because in the former case the country where diffusion takes place is regarded as the country of origin, whereas in the latter case the country where assembly takes place is regarded as the country of origin. Nevertheless, according to the following informal interpretation of the authorities, administrative practice conforms to Customs rules.

Under the Customs change of tariff heading test, the origin of integrated circuits would be the country where the diffusion process has been carried out, since this process brings about a change of tariff heading between "mirror polished wafers" not yet diffused (3818) and chips (8542.11.100 or 8542.19.100). On the contrary, the assembly process (bonding, molding, lead forming, and testing) does not bring about a change of tariff heading between chips used for assembly and monolithic integrated circuits (8542.11). Consequently, the case of U.S. origin integrated circuits, clearly complies with Customs rules. However the cases of NIEC origin integrated circuits also conforms to Customs rules. In this case, where the manufacturing process cannot be identified by evidential documents at the time of importation, Customs has confirmed the country of origin by means of the invoice or other similar documents (bill of lading, etc.) on the basis of General Circular 68-3-6. Consequently, Customs has regarded the integrated circuits country of origin not as the country where assembly takes place as such but the country of origin mentioned on the invoice (i.e., the exporting country). Anyway, the determination of the country of the origin of integrated circuits is not likely to give rise to polemics because of the zero duty.

integrated circuits and floppy disks, that are assembled in Newly Industrializing Economy Countries (NIEC) (Taiwan, Singapore, etc.) from Japanese parts (integrated circuit chips and magnetic disks used for floppy disk) and reimported to Japan, Customs accepts an origin marking to the effect that parts are "made in Japan" and a final product is "assembled in" an NIEC,[10] because such a marking prevents consumers from misunderstanding that the products were wholly made in a given country (the NIEC or Japan). This Customs position conforms not only to Customs special marking rules (Particular Circular 71) but also to the FTC's position to which we will refer later.

3.1.4.　Problems

There are two kinds of problems with regard to Customs rules of origin; internal problems and external problems.

As for internal problems, it is evident that Customs rules of origin have formal and substantive shortcomings. As they have taken the form of an administrative circular, Customs is not bound by them (i.e., Customs measures taken in conflict with such a circular are still legal if those measures conform to Customs Law). Therefore interested parties cannot legally rely on them. From the substantive viewpoint, Customs rules of origin, inter alia a change of tariff heading test, do not permit the determination of the origin of industrial goods produced through complicated processes in several countries.[11]

10.　Such a marking for integrated circuits is considered flexible, because it permits Japanese firms to reexport those integrated circuits assembled in an NIEC to any country without necessitating additional costs of export formalities. Although the rules of origin for integrated circuits differ between the European Community (diffusion country principle) and the U.S. Customs Service (assembly country principle), it is not necessary to change the marking accordingly.

11.　A change of tariff heading test would produce unequal results regarding the origin of complicated assembled products. Complicated assembly operations would bring about a change of tariff heading for products that are assembled from different tariff heading parts (e.g., printers of HS Code 8471 assembled from components of HS Code 8473). But the same operations would not bring about a change of tariff headings to products assembled from the same tariff heading parts (e.g., copiers of HS Code 9009 assembled from components of HS Code 9009.90). In this regard the judgments *Überseehandel* and *Cousin* of the European Court of Justice have rightly said that it is not sufficient to seek criteria for defining origin in the tariff classification of processed products, the common customs tariff not having been conceived for purposes of the determination of origin. See chapter 3, § 3.3.1.; Norio Komuro, *Rules of Origin and Japanese firms* (Tokyo: Japan Machinery Exporters' Association, 1993).

Besides those problems, external problems are brought about mainly as a result of the GATT Uruguay Round. Japan has vigorously called for an international harmonization of origin rules — which at the moment are different according to country — and has undertaken to prepare proposals for this harmonization taking account of shortcomings of its own rules of origin as well as trading partners' abuses in applying rules of origin.

3.2. The Ministry of International Trade and Industry Rules of Origin

3.2.1. Use and Procedure

The Ministry of International Trade and Industry rules of origin are intended to control import and export under two laws: the Foreign Exchange and Foreign Trade Control Law (the Foreign Exchange Control Law) and the Export and Import Transactions Law (the Transactions Law).

3.2.1.1. Use

3.2.1.1.1. Import Control Under the Foreign Exchange Control Law

Art. 52 of the Foreign Exchange Control Law (1949) provides: "In order to ensure sound development of foreign trade and national economy, any person desiring to effect imports may be required to obtain approval thereof as provided for by Cabinet Order."

To implement this provision, the Import Control Order of the cabinet has introduced three kinds of import control systems (i.e. the import quota system, the import approval system, and confirmation systems) and empowered MITI to publish items for each system in its Import Notice. Actual import control systems are provided for in the Import Notice of 1992 as follows.

Import quota system: The import quota system, under which an importer is required to obtain an import quota allocated by MITI so that the importation that is in principle prohibited may be admitted within the limit of the quota, applies to the following items irrespective of the country of origin:

- nonliberalized items, which consist of items to which quantitative restrictions apply deemed to be justified by provisions of the GATT (Arts. 17, 20, and 21) and residual restriction items
- species of wild fauna and flora threatened with extinction, which are listed in Appendix I of the Washington Convention
- substances destroying the ozone layer, which are listed in the Montreal Protocol

Import approval system: The import approval system, under which an importer is required to obtain import approval from MITI, applies to the following items originating in or shipped from specified countries:
  Items intended for the protection of domestic industries i.e. (1) raw silk (including those which will be used as raw silk by unsewing) originating in or shipped from 14 countries (China, Taiwan, Rep. of Korea, Hong Kong, India, Vietnam, North Korea, Brazil, France, Italy, United Kingdom, Greece, Bulgaria, Romania), (2) silk yarn (including fabrics of silk and other fibre mixture which will be used as silk yarn by unsewing) originating in or shipped from 141 countries (China, Taiwan, Rep. of Korea, Hong Kong, 12 EC countries, U.S.A. etc), (3) woven fabrics of silk originating in China, Korea, Taiwan and Japan but indirectly imported via third country (including those which are woven in China or Japan and then dyed, resined, embossed or processed by other similar methods outside of China) and (4) silk products such as silk bedlinen which are used as woven fabrics of silk by unsewing and originate in China and Japan (including those which are woven in China or Japan and then sewed or processed outside of China and Japan)
  Import prohibited items intended for complying with international conventions to which Japan is a contracting party, i.e. (1) species of wild fauna and flora (including their processed products) listed in Appendix II which originate in or are shipped from non-member countries of Washington Convention (excluding non-member countries with quasi-management authority); species listed in Appendix III, which originate in Appendix III countries and are shipped from non-member countries, (2) whales and their preparations originating in or shipped from non-member countries of International Whaling Convention.
  Import prohibited items intended for conforming to international rules or United Nations' resolutions, i.e. (1) salmon and trout or preparations originating in or shipped from Taiwan, which are caught by Taiwanese ships in violation of the principle of mother river country, (2) all items originating in or shipped from Iraq and Yugoslavia, which are mentioned in United Nations' resolutions on economic sanctions.
Confirmation systems: The confirmation systems are not intended for the direct control of imports but for complementing import approval systems or complying with international conventions. They consist of MITI's confirmation systems under which MITI confirms certain documents prior to customs clearance and Customs confirmation systems under which Customs simply confirms concerned documents at the moment of customs clearance.
  MITI's confirmation systems apply inter alia to the following items originating in or shipped from specified countries:

- items intended for complementing import approval systems i.e. (1) woven fabrics of silk originating in or shipped from countries other than China, Korea, Taiwan, EC, U.S.A. and Switzerland (e.g. Asian NIES countries such as Hong Kong), (2) silk manufactures for Japanese traditional dress originating in or shipped from China, Korea or Taiwan
- items intended for complying with international conventions, i.e. (1) species of wild fauna and flora (including their processed products) listed in Appendix II or III of Washington Convention the exportation of which is prohibited by certain originating countries; live animals listed in Appendix II or III, (2) whales and their preparations originating in or shipped from member countries of International Whaling Convention

Under the customs confirmation systems, Customs confirms the following documents with regard to items originating in or shipped from certain countries:

- an invoice on which the Korea Export Association of Textiles has stamped its export visa to administer Japano-Korean governmental VER (Voluntary Export Restraints) agreements with regard to the direct import of woven fabrics of silk from Korea
- a document on which Taiwan Textile Federation has stamped its export visa to administer the unilateral private VER with regard to the direct import of woven fabrics of silk from Taiwan
- a certificate of origin issued by an official organization of the country of origin with regard to woven fabrics of silk imported from the EC, Switzerland and U.S.A. as well as silk manufactures for Japanese traditional dress imported from countries other than China, Korea and Taiwan
- an original export permit or re-export certificate with regard to species of wild fauna and flora (including their processed products) listed in Appendix II or III of Washington Convention which are not subject to MITI's confirmation systems and are shipped from member countries (and non-member countries with Quasi-Management Authorities) of Washington Convention

Import control for silk related items and wild fauna and flora: As shown above, the country of origin is typically relevant in the context of import control of silk related items and wild fauna and flora (See Appendix 2 of this chapter).

As for silk related items, the import control covers all items from raw materials to downstream products (woven fabrics of silk, silk manufactures)[12] and is so exhaustive, especially with respect to woven fabrics of silk originating in three major countries (China, Korea, Taiwan), that direct import,[13] and indirect import, or third-country processing are subject to MITI's approval or Customs confirmation.

The same applies to import control of wild fauna and flora. Apart from species listed in Appendix 1 that are subject to import quota independently of the country of origin, species and their processed products listed in Appendix 2 or 3 and originating in certain countries (member countries of Washington Convention, originating member countries, nonmember countries) are subject to MITI's approval or confirmation or Customs confirmation.

---

12. Raw silk has been Japan's traditional and competitive export item. However with the increase of imports of low-cost raw silk from China, Korea, and Brazil, Japan adopted in 1974 the State's Exclusive Importing System of Raw Silk to protect its domestic sericultural industry. The introduction of import control over raw silk has immediately brought about the exhaustive import control of silk yarn and downstream products, because the protection of raw material has caused the following chain-reaction: (1) the circumvention of control through imports of thrown yarn (used as a substitute of raw silk) and the necessity of import control over silk yarn, (2) the price increase of domestic raw material and the necessity of import control over low-cost downstream products (woven fabrics of silk, silk manufactures), (3) the circumvention of import control over downstream products through the indirect import or third-country processing and the necessity of anticircumvention measures. The history of import control over silk-related items gives us a good lesson to the effect that the protection of domestic raw material gives rise to the integral protection embracing all downstream products and accelerates the decline of domestic industry. According to the Draft GATT Agreement on Textiles, restrictions on silk-related items (classified as non-MFA items) shall be brought into conformity with the GATT within one year following the entry into force of the Agreement or phased out progressively within ten years, whereas restrictions on MFA items (cotton, wool, man-made fiber textiles, etc.) shall be progressively eliminated under certain conditions.

It should be noted that Japan has not adopted import quotas within the framework of MFA and that the Japanese-American Textiles Arrangments (1974-1992) concern the export quota of MFA items from Japan to the United States under Article 4 of MFA (on restrictions established by bilateral agreements).

13. Methods for controlling the direct import of silk fabrics originating in three major countries differ according to the originating country. On the one hand, the direct import of Korean or Taiwanese products is controlled principally by exporting countries within the annual quota fixed by governmental or private VER and subsidiarily by Customs confirmation procedures. On the other hand, the direct import of Chinese fabrics is controlled by different systems. See note 14.

3.2.1.1.2. Import Control Under Transactions Law

While the import control under Foreign Exchange Control Law constitutes purely governmental measures, the import control under Transactions Law functions rather as a complement to import cartels that are concluded either by importers or by the importers' association with the approval of MITI.

Under Article 30 of Transactions Law, MITI may take the import control to totally or partially extend import cartels between insiders to outsiders — in other words, to keep all importers (including outsiders) under MITI's control — if it considers import cartels insufficient to secure the sound development of import trade. In practice, MITI has used this kind of import control only for Chinese silk fabrics to complement import cartels concluded by Japan Textiles Importers' Association. Consequently, the direct import of Chinese silk fabrics is controlled under Transactions Law,[14] whereas the indirect import is controlled under Foreign Exchange Control Law — Import Control Order.

3.2.1.1.3. Export Control Under Transactions Law and Foreign Exchange Control Law

The Ministry of International Trade and Industry may control inter alia the exportation of products affixed with false or misleading origin markings under two relevant laws.

Under the Transactions Law, if exported goods, whether domestic or foreign imported, are affixed with a false origin marking, exportation is prohibited because it constitutes "unfair export transactions" under the Export and Import Transactions Law of 1952. The Ministry may not only warn the exporter in question but also impose an export ban within one year if the violation is regarded as considerably impairing the international reputation of domestic exporters.

Under the Foreign Exchange Control Law, if foreign products with misleading origin marking (e.g., "Made in Japan") are exported after having temporarily been landed in Japan (but not imported to Japan), MITI may prohibit the exportation by refusing to issue an export permit and impose

---

14. More precisely, the annual quota for direct import is fixed by governmental VER agreements. And the Importers' Association administers approval procedures with powers delegated by MITI.

sanctions in the case of an exportation without ministerial approval under the Foreign Exchange Control Law and its implementing acts.[15]

3.2.1.2. Procedure

3.2.1.2.1. Procedure Pertaining to the Adoption of Rules

The Ministry of International Trade and Industry has adopted and published two kinds of rules of origin for import control under the Foreign Exchange Control Law and the Import Control Order: general rules in MITI's Circular and special rules in the Import Notice. But MITI does not publish rules of origin for export control under the Transactions Law, which were adopted in the form of an internal document.

3.2.1.2.2. Procedure Pertaining to Implementation of Rules

The Ministry of International Trade and Industry implements rules of origin when taking import control measures (e.g., an import ban of Chinese silk fabrics indirectly imported) under the Foreign Exchange Control Law and the Import Control Order.

If a protest is filed against MITI's measures or a request for reinvestigation is submitted with regard to them, MITI grants interested parties the opportunity for a public hearing by serving them with a notice a reasonable time in advance. At the public hearing, any interested parties shall be given an opportunity to adduce evidence and express opinions on the issues. No legal action may be commenced seeking for the reversal of MITI's measures until a ruling on the demurral or a decision on the request for reinvestigation has been made.

The same applies to export control measures under the Foreign Exchange Control Law.

The Ministry of International Trade and Industry also implements rules of origin when taking export control measures i.e. warning and sanctions with regard to exported products with false origin marking under the Transactions Law.

The Ministry of International Trade and Industry's sanctions may be protested before this authority and then subject to judicial review for annulment in exactly the same manner as Customs measures. However, there have been no cases in which MITI's sanctions were protested.

---

15. *See* Art. 48, para. 3 of Law, Art. 2 of Ministerial Order of Export Transactions; MITI's Communication No. 482 (November 1987).

3.2.2. Substantive Rules

3.2.2.1. Rules of Origin for Import Control

The Ministry of International Trade and Industry's rules of origin for import control consist of general rules for all items and special rules for certain important items.

3.2.2.1.1. General Rules of Origin

According to general rules of origin laid down in MITI's "Circular on interpretation of the country of origin,"[16] the country of origin for import control is defined as follows:

- the country where goods in question are produced, manufactured or processed (excluding the country where minimal operations such as selection or repacking are carried out);
- the country of origin of the principal part with regard to goods composed of two or more parts which respectively originate in different countries.

Those definitions are too simple to permit interested parties to identify the origin of certain industrial goods. However it does not matter in practice, because a majority of items originating in specified countries and subject to import control are wholly produced goods (and their preparations) and the origin of certain important items can be clearly identified by special rules of origin.

3.2.2.1.2. Special Rules of Origin

The Ministry of International Trade and Industry's special rules of origin for important items such as woven fabrics of silk and processed products of wild fauna and flora are specially designed to prevent circumvention and considerably differ from Customs rules of origin.

While Customs rules of origin provide that processing operations such as coloring, dyeing, resinification, mercerization, or embossment confer origin to any woven fabrics, MITI has decided that weaving operations (i.e., manufacture of fabrics from yarn) confer origin to silk fabrics. Consequently, under MITI's rules of origin, silk fabrics woven in China are regarded as

---

16. Circular of 16 February 1959, amended on 4 June 1981.

originating in China and subject to import control over Chinese fabrics, even if they undergo processing operations in a third country (e.g., Hong Kong). The Ministry of International Trade and Industry considered that those special rules of origin were indispensable to prevent the circumvention of import control through the third country processing and thereby to achieve the Foreign Exchange Control Law's objective of securing "the sound development of the foreign trade and the national economy."

As previously explained, certain processed products of wild fauna and flora (e.g., certain crocodile skin handbags) are subject to MITI's confirmation system, if they are listed in Appendix II or III of Washington Convention and are designated as export prohibited items by originating countries of wild fauna or flora. With regard to those processed products, MITI applies special rules of origin according to which the country of origin for processed products of wild fauna or flora is not the country where such products were processed but the country where the wild fauna or flora in question were captured or caught.[17]

Those rules are deemed to be crucial to attain the Washington Convention's objective of protecting certain species of wild fauna or flora.

3.2.2.2.   Rules of Origin for Export Control

3.2.2.2.1. Rules of Origin for Export Control Under the Transactions Law

The Ministry of International Trade and Industry (Export Direction) has in 1979 adopted rules of origin in the form of an internal document (not published) for the purpose of controlling exported products affixed with false origin markings under the Transactions Law.

Those rules of origin follow the general lines of Customs rules of origin in that they prescribe for the substantial transformation criterion, several processing tests similar to Customs rules and exactly the same minimal processing tests as for Customs rules. But as they provide for no more than processing tests for specified products[18] and do not explicitly refer to change

---

17.   Accordingly, a crocodile-skin handbag processed in a European country from a crocodile captured in a southern American country is regarded as originating in the latter country and should be subject to MITI's confirmation as far as the latter country prohibits the exportation of crocodiles in question or their processed products.

18.   Almost the same processing tests as Customs rules are laid down for natural abrasives; sugars, oils, fats, waxes, chemical products, leather, yarn, or woven fabrics; thrown yarn; unwrought metal; or metallic plate.

of tariff heading tests, it is not clear what tests apply to determine the origin of a number of industrial products.

3.2.2.2.2. Rules of Origin for Export Control Under the Foreign Exchange Control Law

The Ministry of International Trade and Industry does not adopt special rules of origin for the purpose of controlling misleading origin markings under the Foreign Exchange Control Law.

It is worthwhile to note that those misleading markings mean a marking "Made in Japan" or other similar representations affixed to foreign goods that are temporarily landed and reexported without being imported into Japan; accordingly, MITI's controls are limited to rare circumstances.

3.2.3. Implementation of Rules

3.2.3.1. Implementation of Rules for Import Control

3.2.3.1.1. Import Control of Woven Fabrics of Silk

When implementing rules of origin for silk fabrics, MITI has discovered two categories of circumvention of import control over silk fabrics originating in major producing countries.

The first is the circumvention through indirect import of silk fabrics in issue via a third country (e.g., indirect import of Chinese silk fabrics via Hong Kong, Macao, Singapore, Philippines, etc.); such fabrics were accompanied with false certificates of origin.[19]

The second is the circumvention through third country processings. Some cases were reported where Chinese silk fabrics had undergone dyeing operations in Hong Kong to circumvent import control and had been restored to the original state in Japan. With the introduction of anticircumvention measures against third country processings in 1978, imports of Chinese silk

---

19. In the Chinese silk fabrics case (Tokyo District Court, judgment of 29 January 1982), Chinese silk textiles had been imported into Japan either via the Philippines or via Spain (in reality via Hong Kong) in 1980. The Tokyo District Court declared that the concerned parties who had indirectly imported silk fabrics without obtaining import approval were liable for a penalty in accordance with the relevant provisions of the Foreign Exchange Control Law, Customs Law, and Criminal Law.

fabrics processed in Asian countries have de facto been prohibited[20] and consequently have disappeared.

3.2.3.1.2. Import Control of Species of Wild Fauna and Flora

The Ministry of International Trade and Industry applies rules or origin in import approval and confirmation procedures and communicates with originating countries and exporting countries to identify the origin of concerned species or processed products.

Customs too intervenes in import control by confirmation procedures and has discovered many false certificates of origin and export permits.

3.2.3.2. Implementation of Rules for Export Control

3.2.3.2.1. Control of False Origin Markings Under the Transactions Law

There is only one case in which a false marking affixed to exported goods has been unmasked and sanctioned under the Transactions Law.[21] In this case, a marking "Made in Japan" had been affixed in Japan to exported goods (automobile engine parts), that were manufactured in Korea from Korean materials and therefore regarded as originating in Korea.

No cases are reported where difficulties have occurred in implementing origin rules.[22]

---

20.   All Chinese silk fabrics processed in third countries are not prohibited.   For example, Chinese silk fabrics dyed for neckties or scarves in Italy are imported into Japan without being subject to import control, because it is practically impossible to identify their real origin at the moment of customs clearance and processing operations in Europe have brought about considerable value added.

21.   Tôtosangyo Co. Ltd. case (MITI's sanction of 20 July 1990). In this case, a false marking "made in Japan" had been affixed to NIEC products that were imported to Japan and reexported to thirty-two foreign countries. This was because goods could be sold at a high price when the marking "Made in Japan" was affixed to NIEC products. The MITI imposed an export ban of six months to the firm in question under the Export and Import Transactions Law.   At the same time Customs imposed a fine because of a false export declaration under Article 113 bis of Customs Law, whose sanctions apply not only to false import declaration but also to false export declaration.

22.   One could think of difficult cases in which Japanese rules applied to exported goods and the importing country's rules applied to imported goods are different. In those cases, the same origin marking may be considered false in the exporting country and correct in the importing country or the other way around. To avoid such a dilemma, it would be necessary

3.2.3.2.2. Control of Misleading Origin Markings Under the Foreign Exchange Control Law

The Ministry of International Trade and Industry has not yet imposed sanctions on misleading origin markings affixed to foreign products temporarily landed. It would be practically difficult to discover such cases considering limited circumstances where such misleading markings occur.

3.2.4. Problems

Problems relating to Customs rules of origin (internal and external problems) apply mutatis mutandis to MITI's rules of origin.

First, MITI's rules of origin do not escape internal problems, since they have formal and substantive defects. The rules of origin for import control laid down in the administrative circular (and import notice) are insufficient to serve as a legal basis for interested parties, while the rules of origin for export control, although laid down in the internal document, are not published. The former differ from Customs rules with regard to certain items, whereas the latter are not clear for a majority of products.

Second, MITI's rules of origin encounter external problems posed by the GATT Uruguay Round. According to the Draft GATT Agreement on rules of origin (Dunkel Paper), the GATT contracting parties are required, after international harmonization works of national rules of origin, to apply harmonized rules of origin equally for all nonpreferential purposes, administer them in a consistent and uniform manner, and publish them in conformity with the principle on the publication of trade regulations. Those obligations would oblige MITI to abandon its anticircumvention oriented rules of origin and to publish its new rules.

3.3. Other Nonpreferential Rules of Origin

We later refer to other non-preferential rules of origin such as the FTC's rules of origin (§ 6.1.) and rules in the context of trade policy instruments (§ 5).

4. Preferential Rules of Origin

Japanese preferential rules of origin are limited to origin rules for the GSP which Japan established under the Temporary Tariff Measures Law in August 1971 in the light of UNCTAD discussions.

---

for the authorities to apply their rules of origin taking into consideration the importing country's rules of origin.

4.1. The Generalized System of Preferences Rules of Origin

The Generalized System of Preferences' rules of origin are administered only within the framework of Japan's GSP, which aims to provide goods originating in certain developing countries with tariff preferences and thereby contribute to the industrialization and economic development of these countries.

4.1.1. Framework and Procedure

4.1.1.1. Framework

Japan's GSP scheme can be summarized as follows:

There are 129 (including 36 LDDC) and 25 preference-receiving countries and territories respectively (See Appendix 3 of this chapter). As for GSP product coverage and GSP tariffs, the system is typically different for agricultural-fishery products and mining-industrial products. For the former, the GSP applies to only 77 items (positive list) of HS four digit, and GSP tariffs are reduced 10-100 percent from MFN tariffs (i.e., free of duty in the case of 100 percent reduction). For the latter, the GSP applies to any items other than the twenty-seven excluded HS four-digit items on the negative list and GSP tariffs are zero with the exception of 67 selected products (SPs), items for which tariffs are reduced by 50 percent from MFN rates. The application of the GSP tariff is administered by a ceiling system (a limit in the application in terms of value or volume) for 145 categories (450 HS headings) of mining-industrial products. Moreover, safeguard mechanisms (escape clauses) permit Japan to suspend preferential treatment in the case of increasing imports irrespective of agricultural-fishery or mining-industrial products. For LDDCs, they enjoy special treatment for all products covered by the scheme; duty-free entry even for SP items and an escape-clause system for certain mining-industrial products instead of a ceiling system.[23]

---

23. Japan's GSP schemes are elaborated taking into account the impact on domestic producers. Products for which domestic producers are not competitive compared with developing countries' producers are either excluded from GSP coverage (case of agricultural products other than positive list, case of twenty-four industrial items among twenty-seven negative list; leather, plywood, textiles, shoes, watch bands, or bracelets; etc.) or subject to reduced tariffs in place of free duty (case of sixty-seven SP items). Safeguard mechanisms apply to any products as far as domestic industry suffers an injury caused by an increasing imports and certain conditions are satisfied. Under ceiling systems preferential treatment is automatically suspended independently of the effect of imports on domestic industry, if a ceiling is exceeded. See JASTPRO (Japan Association for Simplification of International Trade Procedures), *Getting the Best Benefits of Japan's GSP; Exporter's Manual*, (Tokyo;

Noted that GSP coverage has de facto been reduced as a result of recent tariff lowering measures.[24] As nonpreferential tariffs (temporary tariffs) have been lowered to zero for most products, the number of products to which the GSP tariff is applied has sharply decreased. Consequently, the GSP's rules of origin are still very important for products for which the temporary tariff is not lowered to zero (e.g., many agricultural-fishery products, several mining products, six HS four-digit industrial products [Chaps. 84-92], seven HS four-digit arms [Chap. 93], and twenty-four miscellaneous HS four-digit products [Chaps. 94-96]).[25]

4.1.1.2.   Procedure

4.1.1.2.1. Procedure for the Adoption of Rules

The GSP's rules of origin have been provided for in the Cabinet Order and Ministerial Order for Enforcement of the Temporary Tariff Measures Law that outlines the GSP schemes.[26] These orders are annually reviewed with necessary modifications.

4.1.1.2.2. Procedure for the Implementation of Rules

In implementing the GSP's rules of origin, Customs makes a response, which is effective for a year, to any inquiry made by any interested party on the application of GSP tariffs under a prior response system.[27] Customs definitive measures for the application of GSP tariffs may be subject to administrative and judicial control in the same manner as the above-mentioned Customs measures for the application of nonpreferential tariffs.

The Association; 1988); The Ministry of Foreign Affairs, *Japan's GSP* (1991/92); Komuro, *supra* note 11.

24.   Temporary Tariff Measures Law of 1990.

25.   As far as machinery products (Chaps. 84-92) are concerned, the temporary tariff has been lowered to zero with regard to any products other than six items mentioned before (see note three). The GSP tariff applies only to those six items.

26.   Art. 22-7 to 22-12 of Cabinet Order for Enforcement of the Temporary Tariff Measures Law and Art. 8 to 10 as well as Annex of Ministerial Order for Enforcement of the Temporary Tariff Measures Law (Ministry of Finance).

27.   Art. 7, para. 3 of Customs Law. General Circular 7-16 and 7-17 for Art. 7 of Customs Law.

4.1.2.   Substantive Rules

4.1.2.1.   Basic Principles

The rules of origin for Japan's GSP are based on the following principles.

4.1.2.1.1.   Principle of Origin Criteria

For goods exported from a preference-receiving country to Japan to be eligible for preferential treatment, they should be regarded as originating in that country in conformity with the origin criteria (i.e., the "wholly produced goods" criterion and the "substantial transformation" criterion). The former concerns natural products entirely produced in a given country and the latter refers to goods produced through manufacturing operations in more than two countries.

4.1.2.1.2.   Direct Consignment Principle

When goods that originate in a preference-receiving country are transported to Japan, they should be consigned directly to Japan from the former country, without passing through the territory of a third country.

However, goods are regarded as directly consigned to Japan from the preference-receiving country of exportation and entitled to preferential treatment if they pass through the territory of a third country for transhipment, temporary storage, or exhibitions that are carried out in the bonded area and under customs control of the third country.[28]

4.1.2.1.3.   Preference-Giving Country Content Principle

For preferential treatment eligibility, Japanese materials are considered as originating in a preference-receiving country if they are supplied to the preference-receiving country and used there in the production process of the finished product in question (a so-called "preference-giving country content" principle or "donor country content" principle).[29] Accordingly, a finished

---

28.   Art. 22-12, Cabinet Order for Enforcement of the Temporary Tariff Measures Law.

29.   Developing countries have requested developed countries to introduce the preference-giving country content rule during UNCTAD Working Group conferences of December 1970. But several developed countries have opposed this request. According to them, the rule in question would overlap the existing "outward processing system" (i.e., customs duty reduction rule with regard to domestic raw materials that are exported for

product is regarded as being wholly obtained in the preference-receiving country, even if it is produced only from Japanese materials or only from Japanese materials and the preference-receiving country's materials. In case of a finished product produced from Japanese or the preference-receiving country's materials and any other countries' materials, the country of origin is determined according to the substantial transformation criteria presupposing that Japanese or preference-receiving country's materials are wholly obtained in the latter country.

This rule is applied in nine countries (Japan, Canada, Australia, New Zealand, Czechoslovakia, Bulgaria, Hungary, Poland, and the former USSR), but the Japanese rule is distinct from other countries' rules in two respects.[30]

First, under Japanese law the rule does not apply to sensitive finished products such as animal leathers (4104-4107, 4109), trunks and cases (4202), apparel articles (4303), wickerworks (ex Chapter 46), footwear (6403-6405), textile articles (Section VI), hats (6501), and toys (9501-9503), to protect domestic medium and small enterprises producing like products, although it applies to any finished products under other countries' laws.

Second, only Japan requires special documentary evidence to support a claim under this rule.

---

processing or assembly and reimported in the condition as incorporated in a finished product). Moreover, this new rule would accelerate, they added, vertical trade between a developed country and a specified developing country that provides cheaper labour. Consequently the UNCTAD Working Group could not reach an agreement on this matter and has left to the discretion of a preference-giving country whether to introduce the rule at issue subject to reviewing the effect of this rule on the establishment of vertical trade. UNCTAD, TD/B/AC. 5/WG/ I/14 21 December 1970.

Japan has adopted this preference-giving country content rule for the following reasons.

First, the rule does not overlap entirely with the Japanese outward processing system with regard to reimported domestic materials (Art. 8 of Temporary Tariff Measures Law), because the latter system applies only to articles of apparel (Chap. 62) and machinery (Chaps. 82-92).

Second, the GSP scheme is controlled by ceiling systems in a flexible manner in that an application of preferential treatment to specific industrial products is suspended when a ceiling is exceeded.

Third, if the preference-giving country content rule does not apply to sensitive products, it would be possible to minimize the negative effect of this rule on domestic producers of those products.

However, it is not clear whether Japan has reviewed the effect of the rule on the establishment of vertical trade after its implementation.

30. Digest of Rules of Origin, Generalized System of Preferences, UNCTAD/TAP/133/Rev. 6, July 1990, at 24, 44-48, Appendix V.

4.1.2.1.4. Cumulation Principle

The principle of cumulative origin applies to goods produced within the ASEAN territories. According to this principle, the processes and manufacture performed in any ASEAN countries are cumulated for the purpose of applying the preferential scheme. In other words, the ASEAN as a whole is regarded as one preference-receiving area.

As a result, the following goods are recognized as being produced in ASEAN:

- goods wholly produced in ASEAN, i.e., goods that consist only of materials obtained in the ASEAN countries, materials exported from Japan into the ASEAN countries, or materials of ASEAN countries and Japan
- goods substantially transformed in ASEAN, i.e., goods that consist of materials wholly produced in ASEAN and materials produced in countries other than Japan and ASEAN countries and that have undergone substantial transformation in ASEAN

4.1.2.1.5. Documentary Evidence

Two kinds of documentary evidence must be submitted to Japanese Customs authorities at the time of import declaration for goods to receive preferential tariff treatment. The first relates to the origin of goods and consists of three certificates issued by the authorities of the exporting preference-receiving country: (1) a certificate of origin required for all goods; (2) a certificate of materials imported from Japan, which is indispensable for the application of the preference-giving country content principle; and (3) a cumulative working/processing certificate issued for ASEAN products. The second concerns direct consignment and consists of documents such as a through bill of lading, a certification by the transit country authorities, or any other substantiating documents deemed sufficient.

4.1.2.2. Substantial Transformation Criterion

When more than two countries are involved in the manufacturing process of goods, in other words when goods have been produced in a given preference-receiving country from nonoriginating materials or materials of unknown origin, the finished goods should be considered as originating in this preference-receiving country if those materials have been substantially transformed in that country.

This substantial transformation criterion is expressed by four kinds of tests: a change of tariff classification test, a double processing test, a value-added test, and a mixed test.[31]

4.1.2.2.1. Change of Tariff Classification Test

A change of tariff heading between a finished product and the nonoriginating materials represents a processing sufficient to confer origin on the preference-receiving country. This test applies to many agricultural products and to some industrial products such as inorganic chemicals (Chap. 28), organic chemicals (Chap. 29), and articles of base metal (7323, 7326, 8215, etc.).

4.1.2.2.2. Double Processing Test

For some categories of nonmachinery industrial products, the following doubleprocessing operations confer origin on the preference-receiving country:

- the manufacture of fabrics from staple fibers, i.e., the double processing consisting of the manufacture of yarn from staple fibers and the production of fabrics of yarn;
- the manufacture of clothes from yarn, i.e., double processing consisting of the manufacture of fabrics from yarn and the production of clothes from fabrics;
- the manufacture of stainless steel wire (7223) from ingot, i.e. processing involving a manufacture of bars from ingot and the production of wire from bars.

4.1.2.2.3. Value-Added Tests

Different value-added tests are provided for machinery and similar products (Chaps. 84-92).[32]

45 percent import content test (55 percent value-added test): For products assembled of parts bearing the same tariff heading and parts bearing different tariff heading (e.g., frames for spectacles of tariff heading 9003 assembled of fitting parts [9003.90] and copper plates [7409], the value of the nonoriginating parts must not exceed 45 percent of the value of the finished

---

31.   Art. 9 and Annex of Ministerial Ordinance for Enforcement of the Temporary Tariff Measures.

32.   It is clear that Japanese GSP's rules of origin such as a value-added test are based on the European Community's Yaoundé rules and its GSP rules.

product for the later to obtain origin from a preference-receiving country. More precisely, the value of the different tariff heading parts should not exceed 40 percent of the finished product and the value of the same tariff heading parts must not exceed 5 percent of the product (the 5 percent parts rule). Briefly, a 55 percent value-added test applies in this case.

40 percent import content test (60 percent value-added test): For products assembled of different tariff heading parts only (e.g., insulated wire [8544] manufactured from copper wire [7408], watch bands of precious metal [9113.10] manufactured from silver materials [Chap. 71]), the value of the nonoriginating parts must not exceed 40 percent of the value of the finished product. Therefore a 60 percent added-value test applies to this category of products.

Calculation of import content ratio: The import content ratio should be calculated on the basis of precise data for the numerator and the denominator. The numerator is the customs value of the nonoriginating parts at the time of importation into the preference-receiving country, which is determined under the GATT code on Customs Valuation and includes the cost of transport and insurance and associated costs incurred within the country of importation. The denominator is the FOB price of the finished product exported to Japan, which is fixed in the preference-receiving country's port after the remission of internal taxes and accordingly includes export-country inland freight and related costs (warehousing, loading, forwarding, lighterage, etc.) if they are not included in the exfactory price.

4.1.2.2.4. Mixed Test

Finally, a mixed test of processing operations and value-added is provided for with regard to a number of products. This test appears in three different forms:

1. a test requiring manufacture from different tariff heading materials and less than 40 percent import content (i.e., more than 60 percent value-added) for certain food preparations (1806, 2004, 2005, 2008, etc.)

2. a test requiring manufacture from different tariff heading materials and less than 50 percent import content (i.e., more than 50 percent value-added) for medicaments (3003), odoriferous substances (3302), preparations for use in dentistry (3407), specified chemical products (ex. Chap. 38), umbrellas (6601), brushes (9603), buttons (9606), etc.;

3. a test requiring manufacture from the same tariff heading materials and less than 50 percent import content for cut worked containers and glassware (ex. 7010, ex. 7013).

As clearly shown here, the GSP's rules of origin are much more strict and complicated than nonpreferential rules of origin. The GSP origin rules are stricter than the nonpreferential origin rules in the sense that they impose relatively severe value-added tests and double processing tests, while nonpreferential origin rules have no value-added tests and the processing test requires only one stage of processing. Moreover, the GSP's percentage parts rule in the value-added test may in theory make it difficult for certain producers in preference-receiving country to enjoy preferential treatment.

The GSP's rules of origin are more complicated than nonpreferential rules because of the mixed test and two different value-added tests.

4.1.3.   Implementation of Rules

Problems in the implementation of origin rules have in practice not concerned substantive origin rules but evidentiary rules. According to Customs, there have been several instances where GSP benefits could not apply. The main reason was that a certificate of origin for GSP was not sent to the importer or that the certificate of origin, sent to the importer, was not correct.[33]   No cases are known where the implementation of preferential rules of origin has been contested before Customs or appealed to the court of justice.

4.1.4.   Problems

The internal problem for the GSP's rules of origin is that the current system is unnecessarily complicated. It is therefore desirable that the current complicated system be simplified and rules such as the mixed test and the 5 percent parts rule be reviewed so that the GSP's scheme will not have a negative and unequitable impact on trade and investment.

The external problems for the GSP's rules of origin occur as a result of the GATT Uruguay Round. Under the Draft GATT Agreement on rules of origin,[34] preferential rules of origin (not only the GSP's rules but also free trade areas' rules of origin), unlike nonpreferential rules of origin, have not become the object of harmonization. However, they should be subject to several principles: clear definitions, positive standard principles, prompt origin

---

33.   JASTPRO, *supra* note 23, at 5.

34.   Annex II, Common Declaration with Regard to Preferential Rules of Origin.

assessment, nonretroactivity of new changes, prompt review of administrative measures, and nondisclosure of confidential information.

4.2. Other Preferential Rules of Origin

Whether Japan will enter into a regional agreement such as a free trade area agreement and adopt its rules of origin is unknown. In this regard, relations with NIECs and pacific countries or future plans for an Asia-Pacific Economic Co-operation Conference deserve attention.

5. Rules of Origin in the Context of Trade Policy Instruments

Generally speaking, Japan's trade law lato-sensu divides into three sectors: (1) trade law administered by the Ministry of Finance-Customs and MITI, consisting of customs law and trade policy instruments (antidumping, countervailing, and emergency measures); (2) trade control law administered by MITI; and (3) other related laws. It is necessary to examine whether Customs rules of origin apply to the trade policy instruments and other related laws.

5.1. Antidumping and Countervailing Duties

5.1.1. Antidumping Duties[35]

According to Article 9 of the basic Customs Tariff Law, an antidumping duty may be imposed on goods of a specified exporting country if the goods have been dumped and have caused or threaten to cause material injury to domestic industry. The implementing order, Cabinet order relating to anti-dumping duty of 1980, refers either to "the country exporting the imported goods in question" or to "the country of origin of the imported goods" like the GATT Antidumping Code.

It is therefore difficult to assess whether Japan's antidumping duty may be imposed on goods of the exporting country or the country of origin, in other words whether an antidumping duty may be extended or not from "goods originally found to be dumped and exported from a specified country" to

---

35.   *See* S. Hagiwara, Y. Noguchi, and K. Masui, *Anti-Dumping Laws in Japan*, 24 Journal of World Trade, 35-50 (1990); M. Matsushita, *Comments on Antidumping Law Enforcement in Japan* in Antidumping Law and Practice, J. Jackson and E. Vermulst, eds., (Ann Arbor: University of Michigan Press, 1989) 389-395; Norio Komuro, *Japan's First Antidumping Measures in the Ferro-Silico-Manganese Case*, 27 Journal of World Trade 3, 5-30 (1993).

"goods found to originate in the exporting country but exported from the other country," apart from a question whether automatic extension of an antidumping duty by means of origin rules conflicts or not with the GATT Anti-dumping Code.

Furthermore, as relevant rules remain silent on rules of origin for antidumping duty purposes and as Japanese authorities have neither imposed antidumping duties nor accepted undertakings offered by the exporting industry until in the Ferrosilicon mangan case,[36] it is impossible to predict whether rules of origin are applied or not in the antidumping sector, and if so, which rules of origin may be applied in this sector.

5.1.2.   Countervailing Duties

Article 8 of the Customs Tariff Law and its implementing Cabinet Order of 1980 provide that a countervailing duty may be levied on goods of a specified exporting country if those goods are granted subsidies and have caused or threaten to cause material injury to domestic industry.

In the absence of relevant texts and cases where countervailing duties have been imposed or undertakings have been accepted by the authorities,[37] it would be prudent to consider that it is an open question whether rules of origin are relevant to countervailing measures area.

---

36.   In the Korean cotton yarn case, the petition was withdrawn in 1983 after the Japanese industry has accepted the voluntary export restriction offered by the Korean industry. In the Norwegian-French ferrosilicon case, the Japanese industry withdrew its filing in 1984 as a result of an improvement of the import price and statements by the French and Norwegian Embassies to the effect that those exporting industries would not export to Japan under conditions incompatible with the GATT rules. In the Korean knitwear case, the petition was withdrawn in 1989 following the voluntary export restrictions offered by the Korean industry.   In the Chinese-Norwegian-South African ferrosilicon-mangan case, Japanese authorities have for the first time imposed antidumping duties on Chinese products and accepted price undertakings offered by two Chinese exporters on 29 January 1993. However, this case has not involved an application of rules of origin. *See* Norio Komuro, *Japan's First Antidumping Measures in the Ferro-Silico-Manganese Case*, 27 Journal of World Trade 3, 5-30 (1993).

37.   In the Pakistani cotton yarn case, the petition was withdrawn in 1984 as a result of Pakistan's removal of subsidies and a change of situation in the Japanese spinning industry. In the Brazilian ferrosilicon case, the petition was withdrawn in 1984 following the improvement of the market situation and the Brazilian government response.

5.2. Emergency and Retaliatory Duties

5.2.1. Emergency Duties

Under Article 9 bis of the Customs Tariff Law and its implementing Cabinet Order of 1971, an emergency duty may be levied on specified imported goods irrespective of country of origin (i.e., in a nondiscriminatory manner), if they are imported in such increased quantities that they cause or threaten to cause serious injury to domestic producers of like or directly competitive goods. Accordingly, rules of origin are and should be unnecessary when an emergency duty is imposed.

It would however in theory become necessary to apply rules of origin (probably Customs rules of origin) when, under Article 9 bis paragraph 2, the Minister of Finance takes countermeasures against goods of a country that has adopted safeguard measures vis-à-vis Japanese goods. But Japan has not yet taken countermeasures, although a lot of Japanese products have been subject to safeguard measures of trading partners (inter alia the United States).

5.2.2. Retaliatory Duties

Under Article 7 of the Customs Tariff Law, if a foreign country treats "any vessel or aircraft of Japan or any goods exported from or passing through Japan" less favourably than any products of any other country, the authorities may levy a "retaliatory duty" on certain imported goods originating in the discriminating country. This duty is imposed, in addition to the customs duty, in an amount equal to or less than the customs value of the concerned imported goods.

Apart from a question whether this unilateral retaliation is compatible with the GATT rules, it is not clear whether Customs rules of origin may be applied to levy a retaliatory duty on goods originating in a specified country.

5.3. Government Procurement

Ministerial communications on statistics for government procurement, issued by the Minister of Finance to other ministers in 1983 and 1985, determined the ways to judge the country of origin for goods in government procurement as follows:

- the indication of the country of origin (e.g., Made in USA, product of France) by means of a label, nameplate, carved seal, or weaved mark as well as the indication of the name of the producer or the trade mark

- the indication of the country of origin, the name of the producer, or the trade mark, that are stated in sales contracts or other documents (import invoice, maker's invoice, bill of lading, packing list, etc.)

However, since these communications do not refer to rules of origin, they do not answer what rules of origin apply to government procurement.

6. Rules of Origin in the Context of Competition Law

Among nonpreferential rules of origin, rules in competition law (i.e., the FTC's rules of origin) play a not less important role than rules in trade law.

6.1. The Fair Trade Commission's Rules of Origin

6.1.1. Use and Procedure

Japan's FTC[38] uses its own rules of origin to control a misleading marking within the framework of consumer protection policy.

6.1.1.1. Use

Misleading marking control has been provided for in the special law entitled Act Against Unjustifiable Premiums and Misleading Representations.[39] This

---

38. The Japanese FTC was established by the 1947 Antimonopoly Act to promote free and fair competition. It is composed of a chairman and four commissioners, who are appointed by the prime minister with the consent of both Houses of the Diet and are required to perform their duties independently (Sec. 27-29 of the Act). *See* Mitsuo Matsushita, *Introduction to Japanese Antimonopoly Law* (Tokyo: Yuhikaku, 1990); M. Nakagawa ed., *Antimonopoly Legislation of Japan* (Tokyo: Fair Trade Institute, 1984).

39. Japan's antimonopoly law prohibits "private monopolization, unreasonable restraint of trade and unfair trade practices" along the same line as U.S. Anti-trust law, Sec. 1 of Act concerning prohibition of private monopoly and maintenance of fair trade, Act No. 54 of 14 April 1947. With regard to unfair trade practices, the FTC has designated "deceptive customer inducement" as one category of unfair trade practices and has defined this concept as follows:

Unjustly inducing customers of a competitor to deal with oneself by causing them to misunderstand that the substance of a commodity or service supplied by oneself, or terms of the transaction, or other matters relating to such transaction are much better or more favourable than the actual one or than those of the competitor (para. 8 of FTC Notification No. 15, 18 June 1982).

Act Against Unjustifiable Premiums and Misleading Representations (Act No. 134 of 15 May 1962, Amendment by Act. No. 44 of 30 May 1977) is a special law on deceptive customer inducement (including misleading representations), that supplements the basic Antimonopoly Act of 1947.

act refers to misleading marking, inter alia representations that are likely "to be misunderstood by consumers in general," "to induce customers unjustly and to impede fair competition," and entrusts the FTC with the power to designate types of misleading representations.

The FTC has designated the following two types of misleading representations in its Notification of 1973 on Misleading Representations Concerning Country of Origin of Goods:

1. representations applied to domestically made goods, that make it difficult for general consumers to distinguish the goods as domestically made, e.g., representations comprising the name of a foreign country, a trade mark of a foreign entrepreneur, the literal description made in foreign letters, etc.

2. representations applied to foreign-made goods, that make it difficult for general consumers to distinguish the goods as made in the foreign country in question, e.g., representations comprising the name of any other country than the country of origin of the goods, a trade mark of an entrepreneur in any other country than the country of origin of the goods, the literal description made in Japanese lettering, etc.

Therefore, any false or misleading origin marking has been prohibited from a consumer protection point of view, whether it is affixed to domestic goods or imported goods. In cases of misleading representations including false origin marking, the FTC may order the entrepreneur concerned to cease and desist the act (a cease and desist order) or to take the measures necessary to prevent the resurgence of the act.

6.1.1.2. Procedure

6.1.1.2.1. Procedure Pertaining to the Adoption of Rules

The FTC adopted rules of origin for misleading marking control in the form of an administrative circular in 1973. This circular is entitled Enforcement Detailed Guides on the Definition of Country of Origin in Misleading Representations.

6.1.1.2.2. Procedure Pertaining to the Implementation of Rules

When the FTC issues a cease and desist order for a misleading origin marking on the basis of rules of origin, any person who is prejudiced by the order may request the FT to initiate hearing procedures within thirty days from the day of notification. The FTC may take the final and conclusive decision after hearing procedures.

A suit to quash the FTC's decision should be filed within thirty days from the date on which the decision became effective. Original jurisdiction over the suit lies in the Tokyo High Court, and the court may quash the FTC's decision either because the facts on which the decision is based are not established by substantial evidence or because the decision violates the Constitution or other laws or orders.

Tokyo High Court decisions may be appealed to the Supreme Court.

6.1.2. Substantive Rules

6.1.2.1. Origin Criterion

The FTC's origin criterion seems almost the same as Customs' "substantial transformation" criterion, since, according to the FTC, the country of origin for misleading marking control is defined as a "country in which a treatment or process effecting a substantial change to the substance of the goods is performed" in the Addenda of the FTC Notification of 1973.

However, the FTC's rules of origin do not coincide with Customs rules. The former differs from the latter in tests for the "substantial change" criterion.

6.1.2.2. Tests for Substantial Change Criterion

Unlike Customs, the FTC has not adopted a change of tariff heading test. It has introduced processing operations tests for several categories of products as well as minimal operations tests.

6.1.2.2.1. Processing Operations Tests

Processing operations for specified products are described as follows:

1. food & beverage
   - manufacturing coarse tea for green tea and black tea
   - dilution of beverage as to drinks made by diluting essence on condensed fruit juice for soft drinks including fruit juice drinks
   - grilling or frying for rice cake
2. clothing apparel
   - weaving for the fabrics which are not dyed and those which are dyed before being weaved
   - dyeing for the fabrics which are dyed after being weaved
   - weaving and dyeing for certain silk fabrics for traditional Japanese style clothes that are dyed after being weaved

- embroidery for embroidery lace
- sewing for underwear, pyjamas, outer clothes, hats and caps, and gloves
- knitting for socks
3. personal belongings: binding of upper and bottom leathers by pasting, sewing, or other ways for leather shoes
4. miscellaneous goods
   - the assembly of movements for wrist watches
   - the assembly of movements plus manufacturing of cases or bands in the case of high class watches and special watches such as waterproof watches whose cases and bands comprise substantial value of the watches

It is worthwhile to make two observations.

On the one hand, the FTC's processing operations test (except for the test for watches) substantially corresponds to the Customs test. The majority of those processing operations coincide with the Customs tariff heading test in that they give rise to a change of tariff heading.[40] For dyeing (for fabrics that are dyed after being weaved), it confers origin even in the absence of a change of tariff heading in exactly the same manner as Customs, positive list.

On the other hand, the FTC's rules and Customs rules differ for watches. The former consider the country where movements are assembled as the origin of watches, while the latter refer to the final assembly country for marking control purposes. For high class watches or special watches, the FTC's rules permit the indication of two countries of origin if the assembly of movements and the manufacture of cases or bands are carried out in different countries. It sharply contrasts with Customs rules, which require the identification of one country of origin.

6.1.2.2.2. Minimal Operations Test

The FTC's rules provide for minimal operations insufficient to confer origin, e.g. labelling, marking, packing, sorting, or "simple assembly of parts." The

---

40. See a change of tariff heading between soft drinks (2202) and condensed fruit juice (2009) by reason of dilution, a change between rice flour preparations (1901.20.311) and rice cake (1905.90.311) by grilling and frying, a change between plant parts (1211) and green or black tea (0902) by manufacture of coarse tea (0902), a change between yarn (5006) and silk fabrics (5007) by weaving, a change between parts (6406) and leather shoes (6403) by binding, a change between fabrics (Chaps. 50-55) and embroidery lace (5810), a change between knitted or crocheted fabrics (6002) and gloves (6109) by sewing, and a change between yarn (Chaps. 54-55) and socks (6115) by sewing.

FTC has published the following interpretations of the concept of simple assembly in answering questions posed by an association of department stores:

Operations such as assembly of toys which can simply be carried out by general consumers, assembly of furniture which can be performed by bolts, nuts etc. and reassembly of pieces of furniture which have been disassembled by reasons related to their transportation are regarded as simple assembly; On the contrary, operations such as assembly of room airconditioners and assembly of golf clubs do not constitute simple assembly but are considered to be a substantial change.[41]

6.1.3. Implementation of Rules

The FTC implements its own rules of origin on two occasions: answering questions on origin asked by interested parties and controlling misleading origin marking.

6.1.3.1. The Fair Trade Commission's Answers to Questions on Origin

The FTC has given informal interpretations of origin rules whenever it is asked questions on the country of origin for a given product by interested parties. Having no clear test to determine the origin of any products other than those to which the positive processing tests apply, the FTC has always made case-by-case interpretations on origin for particular products (e.g., floppy disks, integrated circuits, audio cassette tapes, etc.) on the basis of substantial change criteria.[42] It is to be noted that the FTC tries to avoid

---

41.   The FTC's Answer of 3 October 1973. It is not clear whether the FTC in general regards assembly operations of machinery products as a substantial change conferring origin.

42.   As for floppy disk (8523.20) assembled from a magnetic disk (cookie) and mechanical components, the FTC has informally considered that a part of the manufacturing process of coating the magnetic disk, (coating the base film with magnetic paint for the purpose of manufacturing that magnetic disk) constitutes a substantial change in the sense of the FTC's rules of origin. Consequently, with regard to floppy disks that are assembled in NIECs from Japanese magnetic disks and reimported to Japan, the FTC has admitted a marking "magnetic disk: made in Japan, cartridge: assembled in (a foreign country)."

The Ministry of Finance (Customs) has tacitly supported the FTC's interpretation, because it complies with Customs rules of origin. Under a change of tariff heading test, the coating process brings about a change of tariff heading between a base film (3920.62) and a magnetic disk (8523.20), but the assembly process does not because the components (the magnetic disk, mechanics) and the final product belong to the same tariff heading (8523).

conflicts with Customs on the interpretation of origin rules[43] and to formulate an interpretation adapted to the progress of technology.[44]

6.1.3.2. Misleading Marking Control

The FTC has issued several cease and desist orders relating to misleading origin markings. At the outset, the FTC's orders concerned markings by which domestic products were misunderstood as UK or U.S. goods.[45] But the situation has radically changed as the quality of domestic products improved. Recently the FTC's orders have condemned misleading origin markings or the removal of origin markings, that cause consumers to mistake NIEC's products for domestic products.[46] In the traditional silk fabrics case, the FTC regarded silk fabrics weaved in Korea as originating there by reason of weaving operations on the basis of the Enforcement Detailed Guide and

---

43. A typical example is watches. Under the FTC's rules watches are considered as originating in the country of movement assembly, whereas under Customs rules (Particular Circular 71) watches must be affixed with a marking that shows the country of casing (final assembly of all parts including movements and proving). And Customs have generally recommended that interested parties affix a marking that shows the manufacturing country for parts and the final assembly country with regard to products assembled in a foreign country from Japanese parts. The FTC's officials have informally admitted such a marking recommended by Customs.

This consistency between Customs rules and the FTC's practice in Japan contrasts with inconsistency between rules applied by the Customs Service and the Federal Trade Commission in the United States. There are many instances in which two U.S. agencies apply inconsistent rules of marking according to independent statutes.

44. It is true that the assembly of analog watch movements was an important process when the FTC's rules of origin were published. But with the popularization of digital quartz watches, the casing process became important. This fact seems to partially explain the FTC's informal position on marking of watches.

45. The case of domestic sweaters affixed with representations "Bentley England," which caused the products to look like UK products (FTC Order of 29 August 1968), the case of domestic jeans affixed with origin marking "Made in USA" (FTC Orders of 22 March 1972).

46. The case of Korean or Hong Kong clothes from which markings "Made in Korea" or "Made in Hong Kong" have been removed and markings "Made in Japan" or Japanese trade marks have been affixed (FTC orders of 24 December 1987; FTC Order of 17 March 1989) and the case of Taiwanese secondary batteries in which the marking "Made in Taiwan" has been hidden by a label of notice and the product has been put in a package with a representation of Japanese firm (FTC order of 5 August 1992).

thereby held that it was illegal to affix a misleading marking "produced in (Japan)" to those products.[47]

6.1.4. Problems

Just like Customs and MITI's rules of origin, the FTC rules have internal and external problems.

The most important internal problem is that the FTC's rules of origin are not clear. The FTC's relevant documents and practices do not permit the clarification of the "substantial change" criterion, the difference between the FTC's criterion and Customs criterion ("substantial transformation" criterion), and the origin test for particular products. A positive point is that the FTC has tried to avoid contradictions with Customs rules.

The external problem for the FTC's rules of origin is the critical question whether the FTC's rules of origin are to be harmonized following the GATT Uruguay Round. Although the Draft GATT Agreement on rules of origin provides for harmonizing all nonpreferential rules of origin including "origin marking requirements under Art. IX of the GATT," it remains to be seen whether the Japanese and the U.S. FTCs' rules of origin constitute marking rules under GATT Article IX and therefore are to be harmonized.

6.2. Rules of Origin in Other Competition Law Contexts

6.2.1. Unfair Competition Law

Do the FTC's rules apply to other competition laws such as the unfair competition law?

The Act Against Unfair Competition prohibits certain categories of unfair competition, inter alia "affixing false origin representations to goods, their advertisements or transactions documents as well as sale or exportation of goods affixed with false origin representations".[48]

---

47. *Oshima-tsumugi* case, FTC Orders of 9 October 1975 and 16 October 1976. Having been the first case of the application of the FTC Misleading Representations Notifications No. 34, this case has attracted public attention. Oshima is a southern island that is famous for its production of precious silk fabrics called *Oshima-tsumugi*. Oshima can be considered an *appellation d'origine* guaranteeing the quality of products.

48. This act was adopted on 27 March 1934 to implement Art. 10 bis & ter of the Paris Convention for the protection of industrial property (20 March 1883). Art. 10 bis provides that "the countries of the Union are bound to assure to nationals effective protection against unfair competition" and that "any act of competition contrary to honest practices in industrial or commercial matters constitutes an act of unfair competition" including "indications or

If any person is likely to suffer injury relating to his or her transaction interests, that person may request injunctions from the court of justice (i.e. district court in the first instance, the high court in an appeal instance, and the Supreme Court in a final instance). The defendant is liable for damages as far as he or she has made false representations with intention or fault and has thereby impaired the transaction interest of the plaintiff. In short, false representations are controlled mainly through private claims for damages within the framework of the unfair competition law.[49] It is in striking contrast to misleading marking control enforced through the FTC's cease and desist orders.

The court of appeal treated matters of false origin marking for the first time in the Belgium diamond case[50] and held as follows:

> As for products such as diamonds whose commercial value greatly depends on processing, "the country where processing has been carried out is generally regarded as country of origin."; Since it is clear that the diamonds at issue had been processed in Belgium, indications in a leaflet "(diamonds) imported from Belgium" do not constitute false origin representations.

The court's reasoning that processing confers origin to diamonds corresponds to Custom's rules of origin (positive processing test). However, the court has not referred to any legal basis for the origin criteria. It therefore remains unclear what rules of origin (the FTC's rules, Customs rules, or other rules) the court applies in unfair competition law contexts.

---

allegations the use of which in the course of trade is liable to mislead the public as to the nature, the manufacturing process, the characteristics, the suitability for their purpose, or the quality, of the goods." Art. 10 ter provides for measures that the authorities of the Union undertake to repress unfair competition, assure to nationals of other countries of the Union "appropriate legal remedies," and provide measures to permit interested parties to take action in the courts or before the administrative authorities.

49. Japanese law provides for neither consumers' right of action nor administrative control with regard to unfair competition including false representations. However, it provides that any person who commits false representations shall be liable to imprisonment at forced labor for not more than three years or a fine of not more than 500,000 yen and that the juridical person concerned shall be liable to the same fine (Art. 5 and 5 bis of Act). This criminal sanction has been applied to transcribing English lettering "Bradford, England, London" to Japanese suit material. High Court of Tokyo, Judgment of 29 July 1974.

50. High Court of Tokyo, Judgment of 23 May 1978.

6.2.2.   Distribution Law

The Ministry of International Trade and Industry has recently introduced the same rules of origin as Customs rules in the specific distribution law. This measure is closely related to the Japanese-American Structural Impediments Initiative negotiations. As Japan has committed itself to improve the distribution system for the purpose of opening the domestic market, inter alia to ease restrictions on new large-scale retail stores, the law has been adopted, according to which "new opening or expansion of floor space for import sales (up to 1000 square meters) in a large-scale retail store" is exempted from certain procedures (coordination procedures after notification).[51] Consequently, MITI issued in January 1992 special rules of origin for the definition of imported goods, which faithfully follow Customs rules of origin.

7. Conclusion

It cannot be denied that nonpreferential rules of origin have some shortcomings, although they have not been discretionally applied to misuse trade policy instruments such as antidumping or safeguard measures. Nevertheless the government has not amended the existing rules or introduced new rules. The reason is that the harmonization of origin rules following the GATT Uruguay Round would afford the government a major opportunity to replace not only major trading partners' unreasonable rules but also its own defective rules with new harmonized rules.

To this end, the authorities established a Special Committee for International Harmonization of Rules of Origin in the Japan Machinery Exporters' Association in September 1991. This committee coordinates reports presented by thirteen industrial associations. The associations study origin rules for specific products taking into consideration some developed countries' problematic rules and abuses in the application of rules (e.g., the European Community's negative rules and result-oriented origin standards, the United States inconsistent applications of rules, etc.)[52] as well as defects of

---

51.   *See* USTR, *1992 National Trade Estimate Report on Foreign Trade Barriers* 154.

52.   For Japanese government and firms, the EC and U.S. rules of origin have obviously been more controversial than Japanese rules. The European Community has negative rules (e.g., copiers' regulation) as well as a result-oriented rules (e.g., integrated circuits regulation), and EC members have differently applied rules (e.g., the Ricoh California case). The United States has inconsistently applied rules for various policy purposes (e.g., Customs rules for customs tariffs, Department of Commerce's rules for antidumping, Customs marking rules, the FTC's marking rules, rules for government procurement, court decisions, etc.) in violation

Japanese rules and propose rules of origin for industrial products (Chaps. 84-92) to the Japanese government with an aim to contributing to future international negotiations in the CCC and GATT.

According to the special committee, the harmonized rules for machinery products should be based on the following principles:

- The principal origin test must be a change of tariff classification test, since it ensures a legal certainty, objectivity, and predictability in the determination of origin. A change of tariff heading test applies to certain products that are assembled from different tariff heading parts, whereas a change of tariff subheading test applies to certain products that are assembled from the same tariff heading parts;[53]
- If a change of tariff classification test fails to determine the country of origin, the secondary test applies lest goods should lose their origin,
- A value-added test and a processing test may be accepted as supplementary tests. The method of the calculation of value-added should be simple and immune from the fluctuation of exchange rates as far as possible. A processing test requiring the manufacture of key components should be an exceptional test, since it restricts the manufacturing flexibility of producers;
- With respect to substantial transformation, the assembly operations that are not regarded as simple assembly (e.g. operations requiring sophisticated high technology) should confer origin,
- Nonpreferential rules of origin should be less strict than preferential rules of origin. Therefore the automatic application of preferential rules of origin (e.g., the FTA's rules) must be avoided,
- Rules of origin should be flexible in the light of technical improvement and be based on a positive test.

With regard to preferential rules of origin, apart from the question of the simplification of complicated rules, the crucial question is to what extent those rules are subject to GATT disciplines. Considering the impact of rules of origin on trade and investment, it is desirable that not only the FTA's rules but also the GSP's rules be subject to GATT disciplines including the dispute

---

of Art. X, para. 3 of GATT, which requires a uniform application of rules.

53.   See footnote 11. However, a change of tariff sub-heading test exceptionally applies to computers of HS Code 8471.91, which are assembled from different tariff heading parts (e.g. Central Processing Units and Printed Circuit Boards of HS Code 8473) and the same tariff heading units (e.g. Floppy Disk Drives and Hard Disk Drives of HS Code 8471.93).

settlement mechanism, although these preferential regimes constitute an exception to the most favored nation principle (Article 1 of the GATT).

APPENDIX 1:   Customs' Rules of Origin and Related Provisions (Unofficial Translation)

1. General Circular 68-3-4 for Art. 68 of Customs Law, issued by the Ministry of Finance (rules of origin for customs tariff purposes). The country of origin of imported goods shall be determined according to the following provisions in case of applying GATT tariffs.

(1)   Origin of goods is the country where either of the following production, processing or manufacture has been carried out with regard to those goods, which do not however include goods referred to in paragraph (2).

a)   country where goods have wholly been produced

b)   country where the process bringing about the substantial transformation and conferring a new property has been carried out in the last place, in case the production of goods spreads over more than two countries

(2)   With regard to goods bearing tariff headings 3704, 3705 and 3706 (excluding photographic paper, paperboard and textiles of tariff heading 3704), their origin is the country to which a manufacturer of those goods belongs.

(3)   The following goods shall be regarded as having been wholly produced in one country referred to in below.

a)   mineral products extracted from one country (including its continental shelf)

b)   vegetable products harvested in one country

c)   live animals born and raised in one country

d)   products derived from live animals

e)   products of hunting or fishing carried out in one country

f)   products of sea-fishing taken from the high sea by vessels of one country

g) goods obtained on board factory ships only from products referred to in subparagraph f)

h) mineral products extracted in the high sea by vessels or other constructions of one country (excluding products referred to in subparagraph a)

i) waste products which are collected in one country and are only fit for the recovery of raw materials

j) scrap products derived from manufacturing operation in one country derived from manufacturing operations

k) goods which are produced in one country exclusively from goods referred to in subparagraphs a) to j)

(4) The process bringing about the substantial transformation and conferring a new property means either of the following processing or production. It does not however include the processing or production which consists of only the process referred to in paragraph (5).

a) manufacture (including processing) by which tariff heading of goods becomes different from tariff heading of non-originating materials used for manufacture of those goods

b) the following manufacture (including processing), among any other manufacturers using non-originating materials than subparagraph a)
- grinding and grading of the raw materials for natural abrasives
- refining operations which change or specify the use for sugars, oils and fats, waxes or chemical products
- manufacture with chemical change for products belonging to Section 6 or 7 in customs tariff schedule
- processing such as colouring, dyeing, mercerization, resinification and embossment for leather, yarn and woven fabrics
- manufacture of thrown yarn from single yarn
- the following manufacture for products bearing tariff heading 6812 or 7019 in customs tariff schedule
  1. manufacture of yarn from fibers
  2. manufacture of fabrics from yarn
  3. manufacture of clothes from fabrics
- processing of worked products from unworked materials for products bearing tariff heading 7101 to 7104

- manufacture of alloys
- manufacture of unwrought metal from metal waste
- manufacture of metal foil from metal plates, sheets or strip
- manufacture of products belonging to Chap. 71 (only precious metal), Chap. 74 to 76, or Chap. 78 to 81 (only ingot, wire, bars and other goods of the form referred to Chap. 7203, 7205 to 7217, 7228 or 7301 to 7326)
- manufacture of products bearing tariff heading 9601 or 9602 from worked materials bearing the same tariff heading

Note: If, in the case of manufacture using more than two kinds of nonoriginating materials, there are important materials conferring properties to the final product and unimportant materials, and manufacture constitutes paragraph (a) or (b) according to an analysis on the basis of important materials, the manufacture concerned shall be regarded as manufacture referred to in paragraph (a) or (b).

(5) The following process shall not be included in the process bringing about the substantial transformation and conferring a new property.
- selection, sorting and repacking
- marking and labelling
- packing in a bottle, a package or other recipients
- making a set
- simple cutting
- freezing, drying, brining or other similar operations for the purpose of transportation or preservation
- simple mixing
- simple assembly of parts
- operations consisting of above mentioned operations
- rolling flat photographic films which are not exposed.

2. Particular Circular 71 On Treatment of Importation of Goods with False Origin Indication issued by the Director of Import, Ministry of Finance (28 March 1974, Amendment of 6 April 1974): The following criteria have been provided for to ensure clarification and unification of administrations relating to identification of false or misleading origin indications affixed to imported goods under Art. 71 (importation of goods with false origin indication) and Art. 78 (postal matters with false origin indication) of Customs Law. They are expected to apply from April 1, 1974 until further notice.

(1)   concept of origin

In general origin means country or territory where goods have been produced. Criteria provided for in General Circular 68-3-4 (Origin criteria) shall apply for the purpose of determining origin.

A "simple assembly of parts" in General Circular 68-3-4 means the process by which parts for a finished product are assembled through simple assembly operations such as simple fastening (screws, bolts, nuts etc.), rivetting or welding. It however excludes assembly operations which bring about significant effects on property or performance of the goods in question [for false origin marking purposes—supplement by the author]. For example, assembly of electric calculators or watches do not constitute a simple assembly. With regard to those products, a true origin indication should show that they are "assembled in" x (country name etc) and if a name or trade mark as deemed to be Japanese is affixed to goods, the name or trade mark should be described in Japanese lettering.

Note: The preceding provision on the exclusion of certain assembly operations makes it clear that the origin criteria defined in Articles 71 and 78 of Customs Law differ from those defined in General Circular 68-3-4 in application. Note that this provision takes into consideration the purposes of Articles 71 and 78 of Customs Law.

3. Art. 71 of Customs Law (importation of goods with false origin marking)

(1)   No import permit shall be given to any foreign goods showing, directly or indirectly, a false declaration of origin or showing any indication of origin which may lead to misconception.

(2)   With respect to any foreign goods as prescribed in the preceding paragraph, the Director-General of Customs shall immediately notify a person, who has submitted an import declaration, of such false indication of origin or indication of origin which may lead to misconception and shall cause him, at his option, to obliterate or correct those indications or reship those goods within such a time period as may be designated by the Director-General of Customs.

Import Control of Silk Related Items and Wild Fauna and Flora

TABLE 1.   Import control of silk related items under Japan's Import Notice

Items	Originating or Exporting Countries	Import Control	Purpose
Raw silk	14 (including China, Korea, Brazil)	MITI's approval	Secure the state's exclusive importing system Implement bilateral VER with China and Korea
Silk yarn	141 (including China, Korea, U.S., EC)	MITI's approval	Complement the state's exclusive importing system for raw silk Implement bilateral VER with China and Korea
Woven fabrics of silk	China direct import	MITI's approval	Implement bilateral VER
	indirect import or third country processing	MITI's approval	Complement VER and prevent third country circumvention
	Korea direct import	Customs confirmation	Implement bilateral VER
	indirect import	MITI's approval	Complement VER
	Taiwan direct import	Customs confirmation	Implement unilateral VER
	indirect import	MITI's approval	Complement VER

	Japan		
	reimport or third country processing	MITI's approval	Prevent misuse of bond system
	Countries other than China, Korea, Taiwan, EC, U.S.A., and Switzerland (e.g., Asian NIEC)	MITI's confirmation	Prevent indirect import and third country processing with regard to products originating in China, Korea, Taiwan, and Japan
Fabrics of silk and other fiber mixture	China, Korea, etc. use as raw silk or silk	MITI's approval	Prevent circumvention
	yarn by unsewing use without unsewing	MITI's confirmation	Confirm the absence of unsewing
Silk bedlinen	China, Japan use as silk fabrics by unsewing	MITI's approval	Prevent third country circumvention or misuse of bond system
	use without unsewing	MITI's confirmation	Confirm the absence of unsewing
Silk manufactures of kimonos	China, Korea, Taiwan	MITI's confirmation	Investigate the originating country

Note: The import of raw silk and silk yarn is not subject to import control if those raw materials are used in Japan's bonded factories for the manufacture of silk fabrics that are reexported to foreign countries. Accordingly, the reimport of silk fabrics woven in Japan's bonded factories is subject to MITI's approval system. The same applies to bedlinen, that are woven in Japan's bonded factories for reexportation and then reimported to be used as silk fabrics by unsewing.

TABLE 2.   Import Control of Wild Fauna and Flora Under Japan's Import Notice

Items	Originating or Exporting Countries	Import Control
Items of Appendix I	All countries	MITI's quota
Items of Appendix II	Originating in or shipped from non-member countries (excluding countries with quasi- management authority)	MITI's approval
	Originating in member countries that prohibit exportation	MITI's confirmation
	Live animals	MITI's confirmation
	Originating in and shipped from member countries (and nonmember countries with quasi-management authority)	Customs confirmation
Items of Appendix III	Originating in Appendix III countries and shipped from nonmember countries (excluding those with quasi-management authority)	MITI's approval
	Originating in Appendix III countries that prohibit exportation	MITI's confirmation
	Live animals	MITI's confirmation
	Others	Customs confirmation

Note: Appendix I of the Washington Convention includes species threatened with extinction that are or might be affected by trade. The trade of such species for commercial purposes is in principle prohibited and permitted only in exceptional cases. Appendix II includes especially all species that although not necessarily now threatened with extinction might become threatened unless trade in specimens of such species is subject to strict regulation. Appendix III covers all species which that any party identifies as being subject to regulation within its jurisdiction for the purpose of preventing or restricting exploitation, and that need the cooperation of other parties in the control of trade. As for species listed in Appendix II and III, the trade for commercial purposes is permitted under certain conditions (e.g., on condition that they are accompanied with export certificates or certificates of origin).

APPENDIX 3: Japan's Generalized System of Preferences

1. Preference-Receiving Countries

Beneficiaries of preferential treatment are designated by cabinet order from countries or territories requesting preferential treatment, subject to meeting several criteria: economy in the stage of development, membership in UNCTAD, willingness to receive a preference, ability to issue a certificate of origin for GSP, and nondiscrimination against Japan. They number 129 and are classified into the following four groups by the Ministry of Finance (March 1991) [asterisks indicate LDDCs]:

(1) A group (89 of 94 Asian and African countries) : *Afghanistan, Algeria, Angola, Bahrain, *Bangladesh, *Benin, *Botswana, Brunei, *Burkina Faso, *Burundi, *Bhutan, Cambodia, Cameroon, *Cape Verde, *Central African Republic, *Chad, Congo, Egypt, *Equatorial Guinea, *Ethiopia, Fiji, Gabon, *Gambia, Ghana, *Guinea, *Guinea-Bissau, India, Indonesia, Iran, Iraq, Israel, Ivory Coast, Jordan, Kenya, Republic of Korea, Kuwait, *Laos, Lebanon, *Lesotho, Liberia, Libya, Madagascar, *Malawi, Malaysia, *Maldives, *Mali, *Mauritania, Mauritius, Mongolia, Morocco, Mozambique, Union of Myanmar, Nepal, *Nigel, Nigeria, Oman, Pakistan, Papua New Guinea, Philippines, Qatar, *Rwanda, *Sao Tome and Principe, Saudi Arabia, Senegal, Seychelles, *Sierra Leone, Singapore, Solomon Islands, *Somalia, Sri Lanka, *Sudan, Swaziland, Syria, *Tanzania, Thailand, *Togo, Tonga, Tunisia, *Uganda, United Arab Emirates, *Vanuatu, Viet Nam, *Western Samoa, *Yemen, Yugoslavia, Zaire, Zambia, Zimbabwe.

(2) B group (3 of 30 Western European countries): Cyprus, Malta, Turkey

(3) C group (all 33 Central and Southern American countries): Antigua and Barbuda, Argentina, Bahamas, Barbados, Belize, Bolivia, Brazil, Chile, Colombia, Costa Rica, Cuba, Dominica, Dominican Republic, Ecuador,El Salvador, Grenada, Guatemala, Guyana, *Haiti, Honduras, Jamaica, Mexico, Nicaragua, Panama, Paraguay, Peru, St. Christopher and Nevis, St. Lucia, St. Vincent and the Grenadines, Surinam, Trinidad and Tobago, Uruguay, Venezuela.

(4) D group (4 of 9 Eastern European countries): Bulgaria, Hungary, Poland, Romania.

2. Preference-Receiving Territories

Preference-receiving territories number 25: American Samoa, Bermuda, British Anguilla, British Virgin Islands, Canary Island, Cayman Island, Ceuta and Melilla, Cook Islands, Falkland Islands and Dependencies, Gibraltar, Gilbert and Elice Islands, Greenland, Guam, Hong Kong, Macao, Monserrat, Netherlands Antilles, New Caledonia, Niue, St. Helena and Dependencies, Taiwan, Tokelau Islands, Trust Territory of the Pacific Islands, Turks and Caicos Islands, U.S. Virgin Islands.

TABLE 3. **Development of importation of GSP goods**
(100 million Japanese yen)

Fiscal Year	Fiscal Year 1986	percentage	Fiscal Year 1990	percentage
Total amount of imported goods from the world	19,886,732	100	33,745,525	100
A. Total amount of GSP imported goods	9,145,695	47.3	16,311,311	48.3
a. Goods covered by the GSP (a)	1,927,740	9.7	3,260,385	9.7
b. Goods to which the GSP applied (b)	1,105,540	5.6	1,574,354	4.7
(LDDC share)	3,084		21,427	
Ratio of GSP applied (b/a)	57.4%		48.3%	
B. Total amount of GSP agricultural-fishery imported goods	1,685,466	8.5	2,058,411	6.1
a. Goods covered by the GSP (a)	285,907	1.4	376,795	1.1
b. Goods to which the GSP applied (b)	268,191	1.3	341,928	1.0
(LDDC share)	1,463		17,346	
Ratio of GSP applied (b/a)	94.1%		90.7%	
C. Total amount of GSP industrial-mining imported goods	7,730,229	38.9	14,252,900	42.2
a. Goods covered by the GSP (a)	1,642,634	8.3	2,883,590	8.5
b. Goods to which the GSP applied (b)	837,416	4.2	1,232,426	3.7
(LDDC share)	1,585		4,081	
Ratio of GSP applied (b/a)	51.0%		42.7%	

Source: Ministry of Finance.

TABLE 4. Beneficiaries of the GSP in Fiscal Years 1986 and 1990

Fiscal Year 1986		Fiscal Year 1990	
Country/Territory	Percentage	Country/Territory	Percentage
1. Republic of Korea	24.5	1. Republic of Korea	24.1
2. Taiwan	21.2	2. Taiwan	17.1
3. ASEAN countries	18.0	3. ASEAN countries	17.0
Philippines	6.4	Philippines	4.3
Singapore	4.4	Indonesia	4.0
Malaysia	2.4	Thailand	3.4
Thailand	2.4	Malaysia	3.0
Indonesia	2.3	Singapore	2.2
4. China	8.7	4. China	11.3
5. Brazil	4.4	5. Brazil	7.8
6. Saudi Arabia	2.8	6. Venezuela	3.3
7. Mauritania	1.9	7. Morocco	1.5
8. Mexico	1.7	8. Argentina	1.3
9. Hong Kong	1.5	9. Saudi Arabia	1.2
10. Morocco	1.4	10. Mexico	1.2
11. Venezuela	1.3	11. India	1.2
12. Canary Islands	1.2	12. Hong Kong	1.1
13. United Arab	0.9	13. Chile	1.0
Emirates		14. Peru	1.0
14. Romania	0.8	15. United Arab	0.9
15. Peru	0.8	Emirates	
16. Bahamas	0.8	16. Canary Islands	0.9

Source: Ministry of Finance.

Note: The ratio of Brunei, one of the ASEAN countries, is not available.

CHAPTER 7

Rules of Origin in the GATT

Edurne Navarro Varona

1. First Efforts to Find a Common Definition of Origin

1.1. Concern of the General Agreement on Tariffs and Trade About Origin[1]

The General Agreement on Tariffs and Trade[2] includes no specific regulation on origin matters. The Contracting Parties are, so far, free to determine their own rules of origin. However, the question of origin is relevant in relation to various issues regulated in GATT, and the text of the agreement refers to the problem at several points.[3]

Some of the side agreements to GATT also refer to the origin question. In this sense the Agreement on Government Procurement,[4] which establishes in Article II:3 that:

---

1.   *See* John H. Jackson, WORLD TRADE AND THE LAW OF GATT, Ch. 17.8 (1969),; *see also* John H. Jackson and William J. Davey, LEGAL PROBLEMS OF INTERNATIONAL ECONOMIC RELATIONS, Ch. 6.2 (2d ed., 1986).

2.   The agreement is applied by virtue of the Protocol of Provisional Application (and following protocols) of 1947, 55 United Nations Treaty Series 308.

3.   *See* Jackson, *supra* note 1, at 464-469. Art. I, in relation to MFN treatment, refers to "products of territories of other contracting parties," an expression we find in Articles II:1(b),(c); III:2,4; VI:3,4,5,6,(a); XI:1; and XIII:1. However, Article XXIV:8 expressly refers to "originating in," although both expressions have been considered equivalent. Furthermore, Article IX includes some dispositions related to origin marking, and Article VIII concerns certificates of origin as a formality connected to the importation and exportation of goods. In relation to certificates of origin, see *infra* note 14. On marks of origin, see 5th Suppl. BISD 103 (1957) and 7th Suppl. BISD 31 and 117 (1959).

4.   Concluded in the Tokyo Round, GATT 26th Suppl. BISD 33-55 (1980).

The Parties shall not apply rules of origin to products imported for purposes of government procurement covered by this Agreement from other Parties, which are different from the rules of origin applied in the normal course of trade and at the time of importation to imports of the same products from the same Parties.

Already in 1947 in the preparatory work of GATT the draftsmen considered that it was within the competence of each country to stipulate the rules that would determine where goods had their origin.[5] In the absence of any further common determination by the Contracting Parties on how origin should be determined, this liberty has prevailed.

Nevertheless, some attempt was made to find a common definition of origin. The initiative came originally from the International Chamber of Commerce (ICC),[6] and gave rise to some discussion in GATT.[7] The ICC Resolution recommended the adoption by the CONTRACTING PARTIES, of a common definition of nationality of manufactured goods.[8] The question was discussed, and the CONTRACTING PARTIES recommended the gathering of further information on the subject as a first essential step, prior to the adoption of any decision.[9] The Contracting Parties were required to cooperate in furnishing a statement of their principles and practices, on which the secretariat would make a preliminary survey. A guideline suggested the kind of issues that would be considered.[10]

---

5.   U.N. Doc. EPCT/174, at 3 (1947): "it is within the province of each importing member country to determine, in accordance with the provisions of its law, for the purpose of applying the most-favored provision, whether goods do in fact originate in a particular country." Despite the text of the preparatory work, which seems to be limited to MFN purposes, the freedom to determine origin applies to any purpose. Jackson, *supra* note 1, at 468.

6.   The ICC has often recommended initiatives to GATT, and on some occasions its representatives have even participated in GATT discussions as experts. *See* Jackson, *supra* note 1, at 144.

7.   GATT, 1st Suppl. BISD 100 (1953).

8.   GATT, 1st Suppl. BISD 104 (1953).

9.   Ibid.

10.   GATT, 1st Suppl. BISD 104-105 (1953):
REPORT ON THE NATIONALITY OF IMPORTED GOODS
1.   Purposes for which origin is required to be established in various countries at present, e.g.
    (a) Admission at differential rates of duty;

It is interesting to note that the whole approach in this first consideration of a common definition of origin in GATT was characterized by extreme simplicity. The difficulties that appear in the determination of origin,[11] and some of the principles that are still used nowadays[12] were already present, but the kind of analysis that the parties adopted was far too superficial.[13] It is therefore not surprising that no agreement was reached.

Several attitudes could be distinguished in relation to the definition of origin.[14]

   (b) Admission under quantitative restrictions;
   (c) Trade statistics;
   (d) Merchandise marks;
   (e) Other reasons.
  2.   Definition of origin:
   (a) Natural procedure;
   (b) Goods manufactured in one country from national raw materials;
   (c) Goods manufactured in one country from imported raw materials;
   (d) Goods manufactured in more than one country.
  3.   Treatment of goods which have passed through one or more countries on the way to the country of importation as regards:
   (a) Admission at differential rates of duty;
   (b) Admission under quantitative restrictions;
   (c) Trade statistics;
   (d) Merchandise marks.
  4.   Proof of origin:
   (a) Form of certificates or other proof;
   (b) Issuance of certificates;
   (c) Verification of facts by customs authorities of the importing country.
  5.   Conclusions as to international action called for in the light of the review of the subject.

11.   Note, e.g., the invitation that the GATT CONTRACTING PARTIES addressed to the ICC "to initiate a similar enquiry of their members with a view to obtaining a more precise statement of any difficulties met by businessmen due to the absence of a common definition of nationality of imported goods." GATT, 1st Suppl. BISD 105 (1953).

12.   The principle applied in case of the intervention of only one country in the production, or the "substantial transformation" principle. See below.

13.   *See* the model for the "Report on the Nationality of Imported Goods," *supra* note 10.

14.   The question of proof of origin was also discussed, and resulted into the Recommendation of 17 November 1956 (for a previous version, see GATT, 2nd Suppl. BISD 57 (1954)), 5th Suppl. BISD 33 and 102 (1957), in which the CONTRACTING PARTIES recommended that

France, Germany, and Italy proposed to establish both a standard international definition of origin and uniform rules for determining the nationality of imported goods.[15] Such an approach is the closest to the recent efforts taken in the Uruguay Round. The proposal also included the establishment of a list of goods for which no proof of origin would be needed but without further specification on which kind of goods would enjoy such privilege. That idea has not been reproduced in the most recent harmonization proposals and would actually be difficult to justify. The French, German, and Italian Governments also referred to some more administrative aspects, such as the preparation of a standard certificate of origin and the need for an agreement regarding the authorities competent to issue those certificates as well as provisions for the verification of such certificates.[16] It is interesting to note that in the current discussions the question of certificates of origin has not been evoked.

Other governments expressed a more general wish of simplifying the procedures for the determination of the origin of imported goods.[17]

A third group, composed of New Zealand and the United Kingdom, were sceptical about any kind of international definition of origin, since they considered origin as "inescapably bound up with national economic policies, which are unavoidably different in different countries."[18] Such an attitude reflects the common view of the origin determination as an instrument of

---

(a)   Certificates of origin should be required only in cases where they are strictly indispensable.

(b)   In order to avoid delay to traders, governments should authorize a sufficient number of competent offices and bodies to issue certificates of origin and/or the visa certificates issued by traders.

(c)   Differences between the goods accompanied by a certificate of origin and the description in the certificate should not lead to a refusal to allow importation when the differences are due to minor clerical errors such as mistakes in the numbering of sacks, etc.

(d)   When, for any sufficient reason, an importer is unable to produce a certificate of origin at the time of importation, the customs authorities should grant the period of grace necessary to obtain this document, subject to such conditions as they may judge necessary to guarantee the charges which may eventually be payable. Upon the certificate being subsequently produced, the charges which may have been deposited, or the amount paid in excess, should be refunded at the earliest possible moment.

15.   GATT, 2nd Suppl. BISD 54 (1954).

16.   Ibid.

17.   GATT, 2nd Suppl. BISD 54-55 (1954).

18.   GATT, 2nd Suppl. BISD 55 (1954).

economic policy, rather than as a purely technical, objective, and neutral instrument.[19]

But despite the controversy among the members of the Working Party and the opposition of some countries to transmit any proposition to the CONTRACTING PARTIES, the majority succeeded in submitting a text elaborated by a small drafting group based on the text proposed by the French Delegation.[20] The proposal reads as follows:

A. The nationality of goods resulting exclusively from materials and labour of a single country shall be that of the country where the goods were harvested, extracted from the soil, manufactured or otherwise brought into being.

B. The nationality of goods resulting from materials and labour of two or more countries shall be that of the country in which such goods have last undergone a substantial transformation.

C. A substantial transformation shall — inter alia — be considered to have occurred when the processing results in a new individuality being conferred on the goods.

Explanatory Note: Each Contracting Party, on the basis of the above definition, may establish a list of processes which are regarded as conferring on the goods a new individuality, or as otherwise substantially transforming them.[21]

1.2. The Kyoto Convention and the Customs Cooperation Council

Even though the GATT did not manage to impose a general regulation of origin and its Contracting Parties remained free to unilaterally determine their rules of origin, another international institution expressed some interest in the harmonization of the rules of origin. The CCC,[22] which is based in Brussels

---

19. Compare to the inspiration claimed by the new proposal, see *infra*.

20. GATT, 2nd Suppl. BISD 55-56 (1954).

21. GATT, 2nd Suppl. BISD 56 (1954).

22. Created by the Brussels Convention, signed on 15 December 1950. The organization has so far been joined by 111 countries (as of October 1991). Lately countries such as the USSR and Mongolia have become part of the CCC. The CCC is a technical organization, basically involved in assisting its members with customs matters. Most of its members are developing countries, which the CCC often assists in practical customs issues, establishing cooperation programs with developed countries, etc. The CCC has also tried to harmonize national provisions in the customs field, promoting and administering several international

and which gathers custom experts from several countries, encouraged the conclusion of an International Convention on the Simplification and Harmonization of Customs Procedures, known as the Kyoto Convention.[23] Annex D.1 of the Kyoto Convention is dedicated to rules of origin.[24]

The EEC became party to the convention in 1975,[25] and accepted Annex D.1 concerning rules of origin in 1977.[26] Twenty-three countries have also ratified Annex D.1 so far.[27] The United States only partially ratified the convention, excluding the part concerning rules of origin.[28]

The Kyoto Convention applies to all rules of origin, both preferential and nonpreferential.[29]

The introduction refers to the different criteria that apply the determination of origin, analyzing their advantages and disadvantages. Based on this general

---

conventions: the Kyoto Convention, the Harmonized System of Tariff Classification, the Brussels Valuation Convention, and the GATT Valuation Code being the most significant.

23.   The convention was signed at Kyoto on 18 May 1973 and entered into force on 25 September 1974.

24.   It entered into force on 6 December 1977. *See* CCC Kyoto Convention Handbook, (1977). Annex D.1 is also reproduced in EEC O.J. (1977) L 166/3.
We shall occasionally refer to Annex D.1 as the Kyoto Convention, since we will not be dealing with any other parts of the Convention.

25.   Council Decision 75/199/EEC concluding an international convention on the simplification and harmonization of customs procedures and accepting the Annex thereto concerning customs warehouses O.J. (1975) L 100/1.

26.   Council Decision 77/415/EEC accepting on behalf of the Community several Annexes to the international convention on the simplification and harmonization of customs procedures O.J. (1977) L 166/1.

27.   As of November 1991: Australia, Austria, Belgium, Denmark, France, Germany, Hungary, India, Ireland, Israel, Italy, Japan, Kenya, Korea, Luxembourg, Morocco, Netherlands, New Zealand, Portugal, Spain, Switzerland, United Kingdom and Zimbabwe.

28.   John H. Jackson, THE WORLD TRADING SYSTEM: LAW AND POLICY OF INTERNATIONAL ECONOMIC RELATIONS, 352 n. 41 (1989). U.S. instrument of accession deposited to the CCC on 8 October 1983, entered into force for the U.S. on 28 January 1984. *See* 129 *Congressional Record* S 8803 and 8814 (1983); *see also* 8 *U.S. Import Weekly* 535 (1983).

29.   The Kyoto Convention defines "rules of origin" as "[t]he specific provisions, developed from principles established by national legislation or international agreements ('origin criteria'), applied by a country to determine the origin of goods." Compare with the Proposal of GATT Agreement, *infra*.

analysis, a series of standard practices and recommendations[30] are established for the determination and application of rules of origin.

Some of the rules proposed in the convention are the object of general agreement. Such is the case in relation to goods "wholly obtained" in one country,[31] for example. For the more controversial issues the convention does not always propose a single approach but rather tends to gather the possible alternatives, leaving open to the countries the choice between them. Such is the case, for instance, in relation to the valuation system for the calculation of value added.[32]

In this sense, the convention did not provide a uniform international origin system. Given "the desirability of moving progressively towards harmonization in this field,"[33] its function was instead limited to clarifying certain concepts, such as the different criteria to apply in the determination of origin

---

30. Which we shall refer to as *rules*.

31. Rule 2 provides that:
Goods produced wholly in a given country shall be taken as originating in that country. The following only shall be taken to be produced wholly in a given country:

(a)   mineral products extracted from its soil, from its territorial waters or from its sea-bed;

(b)   vegetable products harvested or gathered in that country;

(c)   live animals born and raised in that country;

(d)   products obtained from live animals in that country;

(e)   products obtained from hunting or fishing conducted in that country;

(f)   products obtained by maritime fishing and other products taken from the sea by a vessel of that country;

(g)   products obtained aboard a factory ship of that country solely from products of the kind covered by paragraph (f) above;

(h)   products extracted from marine soil or subsoil outside that country's territorial waters, provided that the country has sole rights to work that soil or subsoil;

(ij)   scrap and waste from manufacturing and processing operations, and used articles, collected in that country and fit only for the recovery of raw materials;

(k)   goods produced in that country solely from the products referred to in paragraphs (a) to (ij) above.

32.   Rule 5 provides that for the ad valorem percentage rule, the value to be taken into consideration should be: "for the materials imported, the dutiable value at importation or, in the case of materials of undetermined origin, the first ascertainable price paid for them in the territory of the country in which manufacture took place, and for the goods produced, either the ex-works price or the price at exportation, according to the provisions of national legislation."

33.   Introduction to Annex D.1, *supra* note 24.

(substantial transformation, value-added, change in tariff position, etc.),[34] and recommending certain practices and standards.

In relation to accessories, spare parts, and tools for use with a machine, for example, these should be deemed to have the same origin as the machine if they were imported and sold with it, and correspond to its normal equipment.[35]

The only packing to take into account for the determination of the origin of the good are packings in which the goods are ordinarily sold by retail.[36]

The convention also instigated the publication of a compendium that gathered information on the different national rules of origin, under the coordination of the CCC.[37] The contributions to the compendium are submitted directly by the national administrations, and are often general descriptions, insufficient for practical purposes. Furthermore, certain contributions, such as those from the United States and the EEC, have only recently been received.[38] The compendium, although not very detailed, together with the convention itself, will constitute a useful basis for the harmonization process that will result from the Uruguay Round (see § 2). In effect, certain provisions of the convention, such as the criteria applied to define "wholly produced" articles,[39] or the operations that are not to confer origin,[40] are likely to be the basis of the future negotiations.[41]

---

34.   We shall comment in more detail on the specific criteria when discussing the proposal of harmonization in GATT (see § 2.6.2.).

35.   Rule 7 of Annex D.1 *supra* note 24.

36.   Rule 10 of Annex D.1 *supra* note 24.

37.   Customs Co-Operation Council, Compendium of Rules of Origin (June 1986); Amending Supplement No. 1 (March 1988); Amending Supplement No. 2 (June 1990).

38.   These appear in Supplement No. 2 (June 1990).

39.   See *supra* note 31.

40.   Rule 6 of the Convention:
Operations which do not contribute or which contribute to only a small extent to the essential characteristics or properties of the goods, and in particular operations confined to one or more of those listed below, shall not be regarded as constituting substantial manufacturing or processing:
(a)   operations necessary for the preservation of goods during transportation or storage;
(b)   operations to improve the packaging or the marketable quality of the goods or to prepare them for shipment, such as breaking bulk, grouping of packages, sorting and grading, repacking;
(c)   simple assembly operations;

2. New Efforts in the Uruguay Round

If the question of origin has traditionally been a controversial one,[42] the recent evolution in the production patterns have made the problem more acute. The production structure has taken advantage of the transport facilities. Manufacturing plants are being transferred to countries where labor costs are reduced and components from several countries are used in the production, making origin determination more complex. Furthermore, the form taken by certain rules of origin has sometimes turned them into barriers themselves, as they are formulated to provide certain products with specific origin and therefore specific treatment.[43]

This evolution resulted in a series of international discussions at the political level, between the United States and the EEC, the United States fearing, for example, that certain local content requirements in the EEC provisions would disfavor the purchase of American products. Other countries, such as Hong Kong, that saw their products strongly affected by foreign origin regulations also insisted on the need for a common international origin system.[44]

The result was the inclusion of the origin problem in the Uruguay Round agenda, in the framework of the Negotiating Group on Non-Tariff Measures. Proposals from several Contracting Parties were submitted during 1989. An informal drafting group, open to all participants, was established in 1990 and

---

(d)　mixing of goods of different origin, provided that the characteristics of the resulting product are not essentially different from the characteristics of the goods which have been mixed.

41.　In this sense Mr. J. Mark Siegrist, Interview at the CCC, 15 October 1991.

42.　It is not surprising that the first case in the United States that defined the basic approach on the matter, *Anheuser-Busch Brewing Association v. United States*, 207 U.S. 556 (1907), is dated 1907!

43.　In this sense, for example, the much criticized EEC origin rules for photocopiers and integrated circuits. Commission Regulation (EEC) No 288/89 on determining the origin of integrated circuits, O.J. (1989) L 33/23; Commission Regulation (EEC) No 2071/89 on determining the origin of photocopying apparatus, incorporating an optical system or a system of the contact type, O.J. (1989) L 196/24; *see also* Edwin Vermulst and Paul Waer, *European Community Rules of Origin as Commercial Policy Instruments?*, 24:3 Journal of World Trade 55, at 66-67 (June 1990).

44.　On the need for a common system, see also USITC, The Impact of Rules of Origin on U.S. Imports and Exports, Pub. 1695, at ix and 102-7 (1985).

elaborated a draft "Agreement on Rules of Origin,"[45] which continued to undergo certain changes in December 1990.[46]

2.1. Scope of the Harmonization: Preferential and Nonpreferential

The scope that the negotiations on rules of origin should take had been the object of discussion from the beginning of the negotiations. While some countries, such as the United States, proposed a harmonization extended to all rules of origin,[47] others preferred to restrict the discussions to the nonpreferential provisions, excluding all origin rules contained in FTAs, the GSP, etc.[48]

The restrictive approach prevailed, and Article 1(1) of the Origin Agreement expressly excludes rules of origin "related to contractual or autonomous trade regimes leading to the granting of tariff preferences going beyond the application of Article I:1 of the General Agreement."[49]

Preferential rules of origin often reveal the specificity of the agreements in which they are contained, which aim to confer a special treatment to countries with which special links exist (historical, geographical, or merely political). Therefore, Contracting Parties are less likely to accept the intervention of other countries in the determination of such specific regimes.

In this sense, preferential rules of origin applied by a country differ depending on the degree of "preference" it is willing to confer to the beneficiary country. For instance, the United States requires a different percentage of value added in the various preferential systems, so that a lower percentage is required for the countries to which a closer relation exists. In the same way the systems of cumulation vary and allow a more or less flexible

---

45. Ernst-Ulrich Petersmann, "The Uruguay Round Negotiations 1986-1991," in THE NEW GATT ROUND OF MULTILATERAL TRADE NEGOTIATIONS: LEGAL AND ECONOMIC PROBLEMS, Ernst-Ulrich Petersmann & Meinhard Hilf, eds., 536 (2d ed., 1991).

46. The version prior to the December 1990 changes was published, *Text of Draft Rules of Origin Agreement*, Inside U.S. Trade, Special Report, November 9, 1990, at S-14 to S-18. We shall basically refer to the published draft, and expressly indicate when otherwise.

47. Communication from the United States, 27 September 1989. *See* Appendix to N. David Palmeter, *The U.S. Rules of Origin Proposal to GATT: Monotheism or Polytheism?*, 24:2 Journal of World Trade 25, at 34 (April 1990).

48. In this sense, the EEC. For a detailed analysis of preferential rules of origin, see the different national studies elsewhere in this book.

49. *Supra* note 46.

addition of the transformations performed in various countries to determine origin.

Therefore, a harmonization of preferential rules of origin seems rather difficult, given the individuality intrinsic to the preferential rules of origin. An exception to this argument could be found in the case of GSP preferential treatment, which in fact follows a general initiative of the developed countries towards developing countries through the UNCTAD,[50] and therefore to a common approach.[51] In this sense, UNCTAD has been urging worldwide harmonization.[52]

Despite the exclusion of preferential rules of origin from the origin agreement, Annex II has incorporated a "Common Declaration with regard to preferential rules of origin."[53] The "Common Declaration" seems to reach a compromise. In effect, it does not intend to harmonize preferential rules of origin, but simply extends some of the guarantees established for the nonpreferential rules to preferential rules. However, future agreements on preferential rules of origin are not excluded.

It is likely that the signatories to certain preferential agreements decide freely to incorporate into their agreements the origin rules resulting from the harmonization program established for nonpreferential rules. Discussions of this nature seem to have taken place between the United States and Canada in relation to their FTA.[54] The question could be of special interest now that the United States and Canada are discussing the extension of their free trade

---

50.   *See* 72 American Journal of International Law 513.

51.   However it is interesting to note that there are important differences when considering the countries that are conferred such treatment. In this sense, the U.S. excludes all nonmarket economies (which do not even receive MFN treatment) from their GSP program.

52.   UNCTAD, COMPARATIVE ANALYSIS OF THE RULES OF ORIGIN APPLIED BY THE PREFERENCE-GIVING MARKET ECONOMY COUNTRIES, U.N. DOC. TD/B/C.5/WG (VI)/4 (14 March 1977).

53.   *Supra* note 46.

54.   Canada-U.S. Free Trade Agreement, 23 December 1987, 27 International Legal Materials 281 (1988).

area to Mexico.[55] A similar approach could be followed by the European Economic Area formed by the EEC and EFTA.

2.2. Form of the Agreement

The form that the agreement will take is still uncertain and will be decided at the last moment.

2.3. Harmonization

The aim of the Origin Agreement proposed in GATT is certainly quite ambitious. The main objective is to harmonize the existing national rules of origin, to establish an international common system[56] that would alleviate the present problems. Producers, exporters, and importers would be able to refer to a single system of rules of origin for all purposes and all countries that are signatories to the agreement.

However, certain problems are likely to remain, since the scope of the harmonization is somewhat restricted. As we pointed out, it will only apply to nonpreferential rules of origin and therefore does not concern the vast field of preferential agreements. The so called grey area of the VRAs,[57] which actually impose quantitative restrictions, also often include rules of origin, which remain out of the harmonization program. This is especially interesting since VRAs have recently given rise to certain conflicts.[58]

---

55. On NAFTA and the origin rules related to it, see 9 Inside U.S. Trade No 44, at 4-5 (1 November 1991). A system based on change of tariff classification is to be expected, although the most technically complex industries that use multiple components as inputs should be bound by a rule of origin that includes a value-added requirement. Particularly uncertain are the rules to be applied in the car industry, which should avoid the problems that arose in the Canada-US FTA.

56. The harmonization of rules of origin was expressly suggested in the U.S. proposal. See *supra* note 48.

57. On VRAs and their special nature, see John H. Jackson, *The GATT Consistency of Export Restraint Arrangements*, 11 World Economy 485 (1988); Ernst-Ulrich Petersmann, *Grey Area Measures and the Rule of Law*, 22:2 Journal of World Trade 23 (1988).

58. In this sense the Israel-U.S. conflict, in the frame of the U.S.-Israel Free Trade Area, (Implementation Act of 1985, Pub. L. No. 99-47, 99 Stat. 82, *reprinted* in 19 U.S.C.A. §2112 note), that gave place to a Panel decision on June 1991. See 8 International Trade Reporter 1069 (1991); 9 Inside U.S. Trade No. 36 at 13 (6 September 1991). *See also* Sierck, *Rules of Origin: The Emergence of a Technical Customs Issue as a Reflection of International Trade and Investment Policy Concerns in the US, Canada and the EC*, RDAI, No. 8, 1016,

To what extent all the aspects related to nonpreferential rules of origin will be totally harmonized also remains uncertain. A considerable degree of freedom will be left to the countries on certain issues, such as the criteria used for establishing the value added in a certain country (see § 2.3.2.3.).

Another controversial point that might limit the effect of harmonization was the refusal by some countries to apply the same rules of origin for all purposes. The controversy was based essentially on the U.S. and Canadian origin systems, which apply different nonpreferential rules of origin for different purposes.[59] Such differences would be difficult to maintain in a system that aims to totally harmonize rules of origin. On this point EEC legislation offers quite a different approach, since Regulation 802/68[60] and the developing regulations apply, in principle, to all purposes.[61] However, certain changes in the EEC are also likely to result from this "all purpose" approach.

---

at 1018 (1989). Sierck refers to the U.S. Section 1322 of the Omnibus Trade and Competitiveness Act of 1988, Pub. L. 100-418 (amending Section 805 of the Trade and Tariff Act of 1984, 19 U.S.C. 2253), which gives the president large powers to enact measures that relieve the injury caused by import competition. In this context a bill addressing the country of origin of steel products subject to VRAs was passed, giving the president the discretion to consider that steel products melted and poured in a VRA country were included in the VRA quota, even if they suffer a substantial transformation in a non-VRA country. Such a provision implies that the substantial transformation criterion can be simply ignored in these cases, the products being considered as originated in the VRA country for quota purposes. Such an attitude seems to be a reaction to the *Ferrostaal* case, 664 F. Supp. 535 (CIT 1987), in which steel sheet originating in Japan, and subject to the VRA between Japan and the United States, suffered substantial transformations in New Zealand, obtaining New Zealand origin, and could therefore enter the United States without being submitted to the Japanese VRA. It is important to note, though, that the court expressed very clearly that the defendant's argument that substantial transformation rules do not govern country of origin decisions under the arrangement could not be accepted. Ibid., 664 F. Supp. at 542.

59.   On the U.S. approach see chapter 2.

60.   Basic EEC origin provision: Council Regulation (EEC) No 802/68 on the common definition of the concept of origin of goods, O.J. (1968) L 148/1 [EEC Regulation 802/68 or EEC Basic Origin Regulation].

61.   However, it is interesting to note that for antidumping purposes, the basic antidumping regulation establishes the possibility, so far never used, of applying specific provisions for the determination of origin. In effect, Article 13(7) of Council Regulation (EEC) No 2423/88 of 11 July 1988, on protection against dumped or subsidized imports from countries not members of the European Economic Community, O.J. (1984) L 201/1 provides, "In the absence of any special provisions to the contrary adopted when a definitive or provisional anti-dumping or countervailing duty was imposed, the rules on the common definition of the concept of origin and the relevant common implementing provisions shall apply."

Certain aspects, such as marking, that had so far been left to the national regulations of the EEC Member States will also be included in the scope of the Origin Agreement, and be therefore subject to common provisions.[62]

In the last draft of the Origin Agreement, the principle of the application of the same rules for all purposes was finally postponed until the final period (see § 2.3.1.2.), and removed from the provisions applicable during the transitional period. Therefore countries such as the United States and Canada obtained a measure of delay to accommodate their present system to the "one single rule for all purposes" that will inspire the harmonized provisions.

Finally, it is obvious that the administration of the rules will be left to the national customs. Therefore there is always a risk that the interpretation and application of the harmonized rules differs from country to country. In this sense, the precedent of the EEC common rules of origin is a good example. In effect, the implementation of the rules of origin by the EEC Member States has often differed, the question being then referred to the Origin Committee,[63] where a common solution to the problem was developed. To what extent such a mechanism can be reproduced in the GATT sphere is still uncertain. In this sense, an interesting example is the GATT Customs Valuation Code.[64] This established international rules for the determination of customs value, and instigated a system that enabled the Contracting Parties to discuss conflicting issues, in a similar way to that proposed in the origin field.[65]

---

62. It is interesting to note that, the marking of imported products not being compulsory in all Member States, the question had not been the object of inclusion in the scope of the EEC Origin Basic Regulation. In this context, certain countries, such as the United Kingdom, were not eager to accommodate their provisions to international decisions in a field they consider bound to the consumer protection policy. However, for the United States, having important marking origin regulations, it would have been difficult to leave this matter out of the scope of the Origin Agreement.

63. Composed by representatives of the Member States and a Chairman from the Commission. Article 12 of EEC Regulation 802/68, *supra* note 60. For a detailed analysis of the role and functioning of the Origin Committee, see the chapter 3.

64. Agreement on Implementation of Article VII of the General Agreement on Tariffs and Trade (Customs Valuation Code), 26th Supp. BISD 116-150 (1980).

65. Actually several dispositions contained in the Origin Agreement seem to have been directly "inspired" by the Valuation Code.

2.3.1.   A Two-Step Approach

The agreement establishes two distinctive periods in the harmonization progress. Initially, some discussions took place in relation to the procedure that was to be followed. A two-step approach similar to the one included in the final draft of the agreement already appeared in the U.S. proposal.[66] The United States suggested that first the CCC establish reports on rules of origin on the basis of which the GATT Contracting Parties would negotiate the harmonization of such rules.[67] The EEC proposal approached the problem in a slightly different way. For the EEC it was essential to first agree in the GATT framework on the general principles that would influence the whole process and only then refer the question to the CCC, which would deal with the technical aspects concerning the interpretation of the origin rules.

The final result seems a blend of both attitudes. As proposed by the United States, the CCC will prepare the basic reports on the basis of which the GATT Contracting Parties will reach a final agreement. But, as proposed by the EEC, the basic principles that are to influence the harmonization procedure are set out in the text of the agreement, on which the CCC will base its work.

These basic principles are not as important in the final version of the agreement as they were initially. Previous drafts of the agreement had dedicated a specific article to each principle.

2.3.1.1.   Transitional Period

During the transitional period, the Technical Committee on Rules of Origin (see § 2.4.2.), in cooperation with the Committee on Rules of Origin (see § 2.4.1.), will elaborate a proposal of harmonization. On the basis of this work the CONTRACTING PARTIES will elaborate an annex, part of the agreement, and will establish the time-frame for its entry into force. The transitional period will last three years, starting as soon as possible after the Uruguay Round.

During the transitional period some of the formal guarantees related to the issue and application of rules of origin provided for in the agreement, will already apply.

---

66.   U.S. Proposal, see supra note 46.

67.   Ibid.

2.3.1.1.1. Clear, Published, and Nonretroactive Rules

The principle of *clarity* implies that rules of origin should be objective, understandable, and predictable and that requirements imposed in the rules of origin should be clearly defined

- in cases where the criterion of change of tariff classification is applied, such a rule of origin, and any exceptions to the rule, must clearly specify the sub-headings or headings within the tariff nomenclature which are addressed by the rule;
- in cases where the ad valorem percentage criterion is applied, the method for calculating this percentage shall also be indicated in the rules of origin;
- in cases where the criterion of manufacturing or processing operation is prescribed, the operation which confers origin on the good concerned shall be precisely specified.[68]

Furthermore, laws, regulations, and judicial and administrative rulings of general application are to be *published*. The publicity obligation is specially relevant to the extent that it applies not only to general provisions but to customs decisions issued for specific cases as well (see § 2.3.1.1.3.).

If the rules were to suffer modifications, or new rules be introduced, they would *not* be applied *retroactively*. Moreover, they should be published at least sixty days before their entry into force, to enable interested parties to become acquainted with the new provisions. However, if exceptional circumstances arise or threaten to arise for a contracting party, the modified or new rule shall only be published as soon as possible.[69] Needless to say, this provision only applies during the provisional period, after which all new rules should result from a common review carried by the committee and the Technical Committee, especially "where the rules need to be made more operational or need to be updated to take into account new production processes as affected by any technological change."[70]

---

68. Origin Agreement, see *supra* note 46.

69. Newest version of the Origin Agreement, not yet published. Previous versions did not mention a sixty day limit.

70. *Supra* note 46.

2.3.1.1.2. Negative Rules

Negative rules of origin shall be avoided already during the transitional period.[71] They will only be acceptable in exceptional cases, as clarification of positive rules, or where a positive determination of origin is not necessary.

Negative rules of origin have been used by the EEC for products such as vermouth[72] and photocopiers.[73] The use of such negative definitions has traditionally been criticized, since they are often addressed to particular purposes and situations. In this sense, for example, the EEC photocopier origin rule was criticized for being oriented basically to avoid conferring U.S. origin to photocopiers produced by Japanese firms in the United States, so that antidumping duties imposed on Japanese photocopiers would apply to the photocopiers transformed in the United States.[74] Such use of rules of origin would not be acceptable under the terms of the Origin Agreement, which explicitly establishes that "notwithstanding the measure or instrument of commercial policy to which they are linked, their rules of origin are not used as instruments to pursue trade objectives directly or indirectly."[75]

Moreover, negative rules of origin provide only a partial solution to the determination of origin, since they only establish the conditions that do *not* confer origin but remain silent about how origin should be conferred.

2.3.1.1.3. Origin Assessment

One of the most important provisions introduced by the Origin Agreement is the possibility conferred to an exporter, importer, or any person with a justifiable cause, to request from the national administration an assessment of the origin they would accord to a product. This opens the possibility of knowing in advance what origin is to be conferred to a product, before trade

---

71. Introduced by the U.S. proposal, *supra* note 47, Part III(a).

72. Regulation (EEC) 315/71 on determining the origin of basic wines intended for the preparation of vermouth, and the origin of vermouth, O.J. (1971) L 36/10. Article 1 establishes that processing operations carried out on wines for the preparation of basic wines intended for the making of vermouth shall *not* confer on the basic wines thus obtained the origin of the country in which those operations took place.

73. Regulation (EEC) 2071/89 on determining the origin of photocopying apparatus, incorporating an optical system or a system of the contact type, O.J. (1989) L 196/24.

74. It is interesting to note that certain Member States were opposed to this approach. *See* European Report, No. 1513, at 10 (15 July 1989).

75. *See supra* note 46.

is started, and therefore provides some guarantees on the conditions to which goods will be subject when imported. Such assessments were already common practice in certain countries, such as the United States (see chapter 2), and start being used in the EEC. In the EEC, where the principles for origin decisions are taken by the Origin Committee,[76] the problem for individuals has often been how to bring the committee to consider the question. In effect, no direct access to particulars was contemplated, and the question therefore had to be raised either by a Member State or by the Commission.[77] Furthermore, no guarantee was provided about the delay taken by such a consultation.

The Origin Agreement sets a time limit for the authorities to provide the assessment. This should be issued as soon as possible, but in no case later than 150 days since the request was introduced, provided that all necessary elements have been submitted. However, during the first year from entry into effect, the 150 days limit will not apply (on the conditions that will apply after the transitional period see infra § 2.3.1.2.). The assessment will remain valid for three years, provided that the conditions remain comparable,[78] and that no judicial review is the object of a decision contrary to the assessment.

Interestingly enough, assessments will be made publicly available,[79] which will give a more exact idea of the line of interpretation of the rules by the national administrations. In the EEC, the question who shall be charged with issuing the origin assessments remains open. So far, the Member States customs services have expressed their opinions when required by individuals and have only referred the question to the Origin Committee when an important doubt or question of interpretation of the common provisions arose. In practice, important differences could be found in the attitude of the Member States, so that while some usually considered themselves self-sufficient and were reluctant to transfer the question to the common forum, others (basically new Member States) were more likely to directly refer the question to the Origin Committee, which would issue a decision that guaranteed a common approach for all Member States.

In the light of the new Origin Agreement, such a system is likely to be kept, leaving it up to the countries to decide whether or not to unilaterally opt for a specific origin question or to refer the problem to the committee.

---

76. *See* Article 13 of EEC Regulation 802/68, *supra* note 60, and chapter 3 for further detail.

77. Ibid.

78. The interpretation of to what extent the changes are sufficient to invalidate the previous assessment might in practice be controversial.

79. Provided all confidential data is kept secret.

However, it seems from the agreement that individuals should also be entitled to obtain a decision directly from the Origin Committee, this being the basic body charged with interpreting the EEC origin provisions. It should be noted that, in practice, as the Committee functions nowadays, it is unlikely to respect the strict time constraints set in the agreement.[80] Furthermore, the Commission's department for origin matters,[81] which plays an important role in the preparation of the discussions to be carried in the committee, seems to have a quite reduced staff, likely to be insufficient to attend to the demand of origin assessments that is to be expected.

2.3.1.1.4. Judicial Review

Any administrative action taken in relation to the determination of origin shall be reviewable promptly by judicial, arbitral, or administrative tribunals or procedures, independent of the authority issuing the determination.[82] Such a procedural guarantee is certainly important, but insufficient. It guarantees the challenge of decisions that implement rules of origin, but not the rules themselves.

Such is the case in the EEC, where rules of origin cannot be directly challenged.[83] In effect, Article 173(2) of the EEC Treaty provides action only against decisions addressed to the person challenging the decision, or against decisions or regulations that, even though addressed to another person, are of direct and individual concern to the claimant. Nevertheless, in the past, indirect formulas have allowed the challenge of certain origin provisions, through the preliminary questions referred by national judges to the Court of Justice.[84]

In the EEC a further problem arises in relation to the informal interpretative decisions taken by the Origin Committee in relation to specific

---

80.   The committee meets, in principle, once a month.

81.   Directorate General XXI, Directorate B-2.

82.   Origin Agreement, *see* supra note 46.

83.   Vermulst and Waer, *supra* note 43, at 64.

84.   Article 177 EEC Treaty. Such was the case in the *Yoshida* cases, in which the provision to determine the origin of zippers issued by the Commission was considered inadequate by the Court of Justice. *Yoshida Nederland B.V. v. Kamer van Koophandel en Fabrieken voor Friesland,* (1979) ECR 115, Case 34/78; *Yoshida GmbH. v. Industrie- und Handelskammer Kassel,* (1979) ECR 151 Case 114/78. *See also Brother International GmbH v. Hauptzollamt Giessen,* (1989) ECR 4253, Case 26/88.

goods. These are not usually published, although some can be found in the Customs Compendium published by the Commission.[85] The same problem arises for the memoranda and telexes sent by the Commission to the Member States authorities recommending certain interpretations.[86]

2.3.1.2. Final Period

The entry into effect of the Agreement on Rules of Origin will almost immediately follow the finalization of the Uruguay Round, although the ratification process of the agreement by the contracting parties will probably take up to a year.[87] The harmonization negotiations, which are expected to start right after the conclusion of the Agreement, are planned to last three years.[88] The final result of the harmonization work will be incorporated as an Annex to the Agreement.[89]

The principles already introduced during the transitional period will basically continue to be applied. Only two principles will be introduced after the transitional period: equal application of rules to all purposes and the application of the "wholly obtained" and "last substantial transformation" criteria.

2.3.2. Criteria

The harmonization work will be conducted systematically, by product sector, as represented in the Harmonized Tariff System.

When only one country intervenes in the production of the good, origin will be conferred where the goods have been *wholly obtained*. A common definition of what is to be considered as being "wholly obtained in one country" shall be established in the first three months of the harmonization

---

85. Compendium of Community Customs Legislation, VII/A/19-20 (1989) (in relation to radio and televisions receivers) VII/A/23 (in relation to corned beef); VII/A/37 (in relation to sterilized medical instruments).

86. See *Brother Industries v. Commission*, (1987) ECR 3757, Case 229/86. Vermulst and Waer, *supra* note 43, at 64.

87. Interview with Mr. J. Mark Siegrist, CCC, 15 October 1991.

88. Origin Agreement, *supra* note 46.

89. Ibid.

program.[90] For such purposes the already quite elaborate principles set in the Kyoto Convention[91] will probably be used as a model. Furthermore, the definition of "wholly obtained" in most national legislation is based on similar principles. Nevertheless, certain aspects, such as the criteria that apply to extractions from territorial waters and seabed,[92] or scrap,[93] might become controversial.

When several countries are involved in the production of the product, origin will be conferred in the country where the *last substantial transformation* has been carried out.

2.3.2.1. Last Substantial Transformation

The substantial transformation criterion has been traditionally applied in the nonpreferential rules of origin in the EEC[94] and for both preferential and nonpreferential systems in the US (see chapter 2). The Kyoto Convention also referred to it,[95] and it will become the basic principle in the Origin Agreement harmonization program.[96]

---

90.   In this same period a definition of what are "minimal operations or processes" that do not by themselves confer origin to a product shall also be established. For a definition found in the Kyoto Convention, see *supra*.

91.   *See supra* note 31.

92.   *See* Forrester, *EEC Customs Law: Rules of Origin and Preferential Duty Treatment*, European Law Review 167, at 178 (1980). The limits of the territorial waters and seabed is an international law controversy issue in itself.

93.   A good example of the controversies that arise in this field can be found in *Commission v. Belgium*, Case C-2/90, Judgment of 9 July 1992, not yet reported. *See* Peter v. Wilnowsky, *"Abfall und freier Warenverkehr: Bestandsaufnahme nach dem EuGH-Urteil zum wallonisher Einführverbot"*, Europa Recht, 414 (1992).

94.   Article 5 of Regulation 802/68, *supra* note 60.

95.   Rule 3 of Annex D.1, *supra* note 24.

96.   It is interesting to note that as set in the final draft of the Origin Agreement (not yet published), the substantial transformation criterion will only have to be applied when the harmonization program is completed. The previous version of the agreement (see *supra* note 46) had considered imposing the substantial transformation criterion already during the transitional period.

The substantial transformation shall be an operation or transformation of such an importance that the foreign products can be considered as "integrated in the economy" of the country where they are performed.[97]

This principle presents the advantage of being flexible, applicable to any good and kind of transformation. However, it is often too vague and requires further interpretation. In this sense, for example, the EEC requires that the transformation be not only substantial but also economically justified, carried out in an undertaking equipped for the purpose, and resulting in the manufacture of a new product or representing an important stage of manufacture.[98]

The question was addressed in the Kyoto Convention, which proposed several criteria that could be applied, alternatively or cumulatively, to determine when a product had been substantially transformed. The criteria mentioned were change in tariff headings, lists of specific operations that do or do not confer origin, and ad valorem percentage rules.[99]

The same criteria have been used in the Origin Agreement, although in this case an order of preference is established.[100] When possible, the change in tariff position shall determine origin. Only when this criterion is inadequate or insufficient will other criteria apply, in a supplementary or exclusive manner. The alternative criteria are, as it was the case in the Kyoto Convention, specific operations and ad valorem percentage (for a more detailed analysis of these criteria, see below).

It must be noted that the Origin Agreement refers to the *last* substantial transformation, following Article 5 of the EEC Basic Origin Regulation.[101] Among several significant operations, the last, and not the most significant, should confer origin. Such an approach favors certainty, since if a certain substantial transformation is performed in a country, origin shall be conferred in that country whatever previous transformations the good has suffered. It also simplifies the determination of origin, which will disregard all previous operations.

However, the implementation of the principle does not always maintain its initial intention. In effect, the last substantial transformation principle is often further developed by rules that, to some extent, seem to contradict its original

---

97.   Claude Jacquemart, *La Nouvelle Douane Europeenne*, 127 (1974).

98.   Article 5 Regulation 802/68, *supra* note 60.

99.   Rule 3, Note 1 of Annex D.1, *supra* note 24.

100. *See* Part IV of the Origin Agreement, *supra* note 46.

101. The Kyoto Convention did not refer to the *last* substantial transformation.

intention. Such is the case, for example, when a specific transformation (or a list of transformations) is considered to determine origin. In effect, it would seem that a specific transformation criterion would take into consideration the *most* important process in the manufacturing chain and would therefore be contrary to the last process requirement.[102]

2.3.2.2.   Change in Tariff Position

This criterion has already been used in the EEC preferential agreements[103] and in certain nonpreferential provisions.[104] These base origin on change of tariff position. However, for some goods change in tariff position is not sufficient to confer origin, specific transformations or added value being required. Moreover, for certain products even if no change in tariff position takes place origin will be conferred if certain transformations or a sufficient value has been added in a country.

A similar system has been applied in the Canada-U.S. FTA,[105] and is being discussed as the basis for the NAFTA that would extend to Mexico.[106] The application of this criterion in the FTA brought the U.S. to propose the change in tariff position as the basis of the International Harmonization of Rules of Origin in GATT.[107]

This criterion presents the advantage of being objective and precise. However, to the extent that the tariff classification has been elaborated for purposes other than origin determination, its adequacy for origin purposes has often been questioned.[108] In effect the criterion can be quite rigid in certain

---

102.   *See* Note of Paulette Vander Schueren on Case 26/88 *Brother International GmbH v. Hauptzollamt Giessen*, 27 C.M.L. Rev. 341, at 349 (1990).

103.   The EEC preferential agreements follow a similar structure. For an analysis see chapter 3, and for a complete list of the agreements see Annex 2 to chapter 3.

104.   Regulations for the determination of origin of ceramics, O.J. (1973) L 206/32, O.J. (1990) L 347/10; grape juice, O.J. L 206/33 (1973), O.J. (1990) L 276/13; and textiles, O.J. (1978) L 101/7, O.J. (1991) L 130/18 and 28.

105.   Article 301.2 and Annex 301.2 of the Canada-U.S. FTA, *supra* note 54.

106.   *See supra* note 55.

107.   *See* U.S. Proposal, *supra* note 47.

108.   For a critical approach see N. David Palmeter, *The FTA Rules of Origin and the Rule of Law*, Paper presented to The Seventh Annual Judicial Conference of the U.S. Court of Appeals for the Federal Circuit, 24 May 1989. Palmeter fears that origin rules based on

cases, but the complement with the other criteria can compensate for the inconvenience.

2.3.2.3. Value Added

The value-added criterion determines the origin of a product on the basis of the value that has been added by the manufacturing or transformation processes undergone in a country or by the materials or components used in manufacturing or producing the goods. When this added value equals or exceeds a specific percentage, origin is conferred.

The value-added criterion has been praised for its simplicity and precision. However, the variety of methods of calculation that can be applied and the relative flexibility of certain data (profit margins, the calculation of certain costs such as overheads, the fluctuation of market prices and currencies, etc.) can lead to a certain confusion and have given place to criticism as well. Furthermore, in borderline cases, it might seem quite arbitrary that on the basis of a small percentage, the product is assigned one or another origin.[109]

Especially controversial when facing a harmonization of the rules of origin is the method of calculation, which has so far been the object of diverse approaches in different countries and, in many respects, remains unclear. To a certain extent, the GATT Customs Valuation Code has established common rules for valuation.[110] Article 1 sets the transaction value, that is, the price actually paid or payable for the goods, as the basic value to take into account. This basic criterion can be subject to certain adjustments as established in Article 8. Especially problematic is the case in which the seller and the purchaser are "related persons."[111] If the price is influenced by their

---

the tariff change position could bring an bureaucratization of the rules of origin, which could lead to the regulations coming under political control, leaving them out of the control of the courts.

109. Reference to such disadvantages is also found in the Kyoto Convention, Annex D.1, Point B, *supra* note 24.

110. Agreement on Implementation of Article VII of the GATT [GATT Valuation Code], GATT, 26th Suppl. BISD (1980). Ratified by twenty-eight countries as of June 1989, among them Australia, Canada, the EEC, Japan and the United States.

111. Article 15 of the GATT Valuation Code establishes:
4. For the purposes of this Agreement, persons shall be deemed to be related only if:
(a)   they are officers or directors of one another's businesses;
(b)   they are legally recognized partners in business;
(c)   they are employer and employee;

relationship, a variety of alternative criteria can apply: transaction value of identical goods,[112] transaction value of similar goods,[113] deductive value,[114] or computed value.[115] However, there is always the possibility of proving that the price does not suffer from such a relationship.[116] To prove it, the same alternative criteria for the transaction value of the good apply.[117]

The possibility of applying such different criteria limits the valuation harmonization. In effect, the EEC traditionally uses the deductive value approach, while the U.S. tends to apply the constituted value system. Such a difference can lead to quite divergent conclusions in the same circumstances.

Other variables add uncertainty, such as the currency or exchange rate considered; the estimation of factors such as "royalties"; or the way of considering the components of the final product as single parts or dividing them in subparts, subsubparts, etc.

The problem of royalties, for example, has also been analyzed in the context of the GATT Valuation Code. Article 8(1)(c) establishes that the following should be added to the price paid for the goods:

royalties and licence fees related to the goods being valued that the buyer must pay, either directly or indirectly, as a condition of sale of the goods

---

(d) any person directly or indirectly owns, controls or holds 5 per cent or more of the outstanding voting stock or shares of both of them;
(e) one of them directly or indirectly controls the other;
(f) both of them are directly or indirectly controlled by a third person;
(g) together they directly or indirectly control a third person; or
(h) they are members of the same family.
5. Persons who are associated in business with one another in that one is the sole agent, sole distributor or sole concessionaire, however described, of the other shall be deemed to be related for the purposes of this Agreement if they fall within the criteria of paragraph 4.

112. Article 2 of the GATT Valuation Code.

113. Article 3 of the GATT Valuation Code.

114. Article 5 of the GATT Valuation Code.

115. Article 6 of the GATT Valuation Code.

116. Article 1(2)(b) of the GATT Valuation Code.

117. Article 1(2)(b) of the GATT Valuation Code.

being valued, to the extent that such royalties and fees are not included in the price actually paid or payable.[118]

All these are questions in which the national administrations often still lack a coherent attitude. In relation to the EEC, for example, Advocate- General Van Gerven in the *Brother* case, referred to two possibilities when considering an economic criterion: one based on the costs of the production, in terms of materials and labor; the other in terms of prices, both of the final product and of the components used in the production.[119]

It is therefore uncertain whether an effort will be made in the harmonization process to establish common principles on these questions, or if they would be left to national administrations to resolve. Realistically, the last approach would be more likely. In this sense, the provisions for the transitional period establish that "costs not directly related to manufacturing or processing may be included for the purposes of the application of an ad valorem percentage criterion."[120]

Certain disparities in the interpretations are therefore to be expected, with the degree of contradiction that may result. In effect, the different approaches might very well lead to conferring different origin to the same product depending on how the value calculations are performed. Nevertheless, since the value added criterion is going to occupy a secondary role, the conflicts can be reduced. Furthermore, the harmonization of rules of origin does not impose

---

118. For an exhaustive analysis of the question, see Saul L. Sherman Hinrich Glashoff, *Customs Valuation: Commentary on the GATT Customs Valuation Code,* 272 ff. (1988).

119. *Brother International GmbH v. Hauptzollamt Giessen,* (1989) ECR 4260, 4268 Case 26/88. Given the confusion that often arises between both criteria, we shall reproduce the argument of the Advocate General in full: "The criterion of 'work done and material expenditure' is an accountancy approach in terms of cost. The 'added value', that is to say the value added by the processor, refers to the difference between the sale price of the finished product and the purchase price of the raw material, energy and, if necessary, rent and so forth. Theoretically the latter criterion differs from the first in two respects: apart from payment for labour, it also includes capital and real property costs, two production factors which are missing in the calculation of the 'work done and material expenditure' and it is based on the market prices arising from the interplay of supply and demand. In practice those differences are of little importance: the first difference is slight and foreseeable (and may be replaced by a flat rate), no doubt in view of the relative importance of the production factors as part of the total cost or the added value of the final product; the second difference is purely theoretical in many cases and certainly in the present case, for there is no sufficiently wide and transparent market for the various separate (Brother) components for electronic typewriters. In the absence of such a market it is necessary to have recourse to the approach based on cost."

120. Origin Agreement, see *supra* 46.

on the countries the determination of one or another origin. Certain disparities in the application might prevail. In the last instance, the interpretative role of the Technical Committee can solve such conflicting situations.

So far, in the EEC the criterion generally applied to determine the value of the finished product for origin purposes has been that of the exworks price.[121]

A further difference in relation to value, in relation to which no agreement was reached by the GATT Code, is that of the CIF versus FOB (free on board) basis.[122] Most countries consider prices on a CIF basis, while Australia

---

121. See the indications provided by the Origin Committee for the implementation of the Commission Regulation (EEC) No 2632/70 on determining the origin of radio and television receivers, O.J. (1970) L 279/35, in Compendium of Community Customs Regulation, Vol. 2, p. VII-A-20 (1988):

1.   To calculate the percentage . . . account should be taken of the increase in value resulting from assembly, finishing and control operations and, if it applies, the incorporation of parts originating in the country concerned or in the Community — wherever the operations in question were carried out — including the profit made and the general costs borne in the country or in the Community as a result of the said operations.

2.   . . . the Community origin of apparatus manufactured by firms in the EEC and intended for export may be determined in accordance with the following detailed rules:

(a)   in order to calculate whether the value acquired in the Community as a result of assembly operations and, if it applies, the use of parts originating in the Community accounts for at least 45% of the ex-works invoice price of the apparatus, an overall calculation shall be made covering the whole of the production exported to third countries by each firm concerned in the specific period, which may not exceed one year.

(b)   in making this calculation it shall be admitted, given the relative homogeneity within the Community of the industry in question, that the cost of assembly, finishing and control plus profit and general costs are to be estimated as representing an aggregate of 40% of the ex-works invoice price of radio receivers and 35% of the ex-works invoice price of television receivers.

If the actual sum of the above factors represents a higher percentage than those indicated, this higher percentage shall be taken into account, provided that the party concerned can produce evidence to justify it.

3.   The "parts" referred to in the Regulation are to be understood to be all the components, of whatever nature, used in the manufacture of the apparatus in question.

Although no specific indication is given for the value to be taken into account in case of goods produced in third countries, the same "ex-works invoice price" seems to apply.

122. Article 8(2) of the Valuation Code leaves the question open:

In framing its legislation, each Party shall provide for the inclusion in or the exclusion from the customs value, in whole or in part, of the following

(a)   the cost of transport of the imported goods to the port of importation;

and the United States have traditionally considered prices on a FOB basis.[123] The U.S. practice is due to the traditional effort to avoid discrimination between the various states.[124]

2.3.2.4. Specific operations

The determination of a list of operations that confer (or do not confer — on negative rules of origin, see § 2.3.1.1.2.) origin, also referred to as a technical criterion, shall also be used to define when a substantial transformation has taken place. The operations taken into account shall be those that confer on the good its basic characteristics and will obviously be different for each good.

This criterion offers the advantage of being clear and precise and enables the use of parameters adapted to each good. It is objective[125] and guarantees a certain coherence. However, the establishment of the different criteria for each product can become burdensome. Furthermore, the differences between the diverse models of each product and the technological evolution to which certain goods are subject might complicate the task.[126]

In the EEC, for example, most Regulations interpreting Article 5 of the Basic Origin Regulation have applied this system.[127] Furthermore, certain

---

(b)   loading, unloading and handling charges associated with the transport of the imported goods to the port or place of importation; and

(c)   the cost of insurance.

123. Sherman and Glashoff, *supra* note 118, at 54.

124. Jackson and Davey, *supra* note 1, at 384, quoting the U.S. Tariff Commission, Customs Valuation, Report to Senate Comm. on Finance, 93d Cong., 1st Sess. 83-86 (Comm. Print 1973): "On a c.i.f. basis, however, identical goods from the same source could be valued differently, depending upon the location of the U.S. port of entry. F.o.b. valuation, therefore, does not favor one state over another or one port over another, since, whatever the valuation may be, it is assessed uniformly throughout the United States."

125. However, see the criticism on the photocopiers and integrated circuit EEC Regulations, supra note 44.

126. Such difficulties arose, for example, when the EEC Origin Committee intended to establish a rule of origin for printed circuit boards, combining specific transformations (essentially the engraving and stuffing of the board) and a value-added criterion. Finally, no origin rule was adopted.

127. Regulations on goods produced from eggs, O.J. (1969) L 83/15, O.J. (1990) L 276/14; essential spare parts, O.J. (1970) L 7/6; vermouth, O.J. (1971) L 36/10; meat and offals, O.J. (1971) L 104/12; woven textiles, O.J. (1971) L 113/13, O.J. (1991) L 130/18);

preferential agreements have included lists of specific transformations as a complement to the basic change of tariff position criterion.[128]

2.4. Institutions

Two institutions will be established to perform the harmonization planned by the agreement. They will continue to play an important role once the harmonization process has been completed, to guarantee a uniform interpretation of the agreement. They shall also be charged with updating the provisions for new production processes and other technological changes.[129]

The nature and function of both institutions are similar to those of the institutions created in the frame of the Customs Code to which we have already referred.[130] Therefore, the experience provided in the valuation context might be interesting when approaching the new origin framework.[131]

2.4.1. Committee on Rules of Origin

The committee will be composed of the representatives from each of the contracting parties. It will meet as often as necessary and at least once a year. It will consult and direct the Technical Committee (see § 4.2.2.).

The Agreement does not specify how the decisions in the committee ought to be reached and how the voting system will be. However, a decision-making method based on consensus would be difficult to apply if the three-year limit set in the agreement to reach a harmonized system is to be respected.[132] Therefore, a majority voting system that considers the contracting parties present at the time of the voting would seem more likely to be adopted. A majority voting method is likely to imply the dissatisfaction of certain

---

knitwear, O.J. (1977) L 164/16, O.J. (1991) L 130/18 and 28; slide fasteners, O.J. (1977) L 242/5; ball bearings, O.J. (1978) L 210/49, O.J. (1990) L 356/30; integrated circuits, O.J. (1989) L 33/23; photocopiers, O.J. (1989) L 196/24.

128. EEC preferential agreements (*supra* note 103) and the Canada-U.S. FTA (*supra* note 55), for example.

129. Express reference is made to this situation within the agreement, in the article relative to "Review."

130. Article 18 of the GATT Valuation Code and Annex II to it, *see supra* note 110.

131. In this sense, for example, see the value of the decisions taken by the Technical Committee, § 2.4.2.

132. Interview with Mr. J. Mark Siegrist, *supra* note 41.

contracting parties on some points, which would raise the problem of reservations being introduced. Whether such reservations would be acceptable in the frame of the Origin Agreement is still uncertain yet cannot be totally excluded.[133] However, reservations would seem contrary to the general objectives of the agreement, which include a global agreement, especially in relation to controversial goods.

2.4.2.   Technical Committee on Rules of Origin

The Technical Committee will be established under the auspices of the CCC. It will be charged with the technical work related to origin rules, initially during the progress of the harmonization and later during the implementation of the agreement.[134]

In relation to the value of the decisions taken by the Technical Committee, it is interesting to consider the experience registered in the Valuation Code, which establishes that "the different views expressed in the relevant discussions" of the Valuation Technical Committee will be recorded.[135] Such decisions have therefore been considered as useful guides to interpretation but not directly binding and, in case of contradiction, as not superseding national law.[136] Whether such a situation will be reproduced in the Origin Technical Committee will basically depend on the voting method to be adopted by the Technical Committee. If the decisions are to be consensual, they will not be binding; but if a majority vote applies, decisions are likely to be binding. The

---

133. Although the nature of Annex D.1 on Rules of Origin to the Kyoto Convention was quite different to the GATT Agreement, it is interesting to note that several countries (among them the EEC and Australia, for instance) included reservations as they ratified the Annex. See other chapters 3 and 4.

134. As established in Annex I to the Agreement, *supra* note 46:
The on-going responsibilities of the Technical Committee shall include the following:
(a)   at the request of any member of the Technical Committee, to examine specific technical problems arising in the day-to-day administration of the rules of origin of contracting parties and to give advisory opinions on appropriate solutions based upon the facts presented;
(b)   to furnish and advise on any matters concerning the origin determination of goods as may be requested by any contracting party or the Committee;
(c)   to prepare and circulate periodic reports on the technical aspects of the operation and status of this agreement; and
(d)   to review annually the technical aspects of the implementation and operation of this agreement.

135. Par. 21, Annex II, GATT Valuation Code, *supra* note 110.

136. In this sense Sherman and Glashoff, *supra* note 118, at 57.

question is left open by the Origin Agreement, which delegates to the Technical Committee the determination of the procedure and the election of a chairperson. The Valuation Code opted for a consensual vote, so that only in case of unanimity are the opinions issued by the Technical Committee binding. However, also in the context of the CCC, the Harmonized System Committee decides by vote rather than by consensus.

In relation to the voting system, another important point on which the Agreement remains unclear is that of the EEC position. In the GATT Valuation Code and the Harmonized System Committees the EEC acts as a single entity, and the same approach is likely to be kept in the origin context.[137] The EEC would therefore have a single vote for all twelve Member States. The position of the EEC could thus be considerably weakened. The question has received some attention in the broader context of GATT, of which the EEC is not a formal member.[138] In effect, the twelve EEC Member States continue to be contracting parties to the GATT, although a tradition of unanimous voting has been established and the EEC has concluded as Community Agreements, without additional direct acceptance by the Member States, most trade agreements negotiated within GATT since 1970, among which are the agreements of 1979 on the interpretation and application of Articles VI, VII, XVI, and XXIII of GATT.[139]

Every contracting party to the agreement will have the possibility of participating in the Technical Committee, although the countries who are likely to be most heavily involved in the process of harmonization and implementation of the agreement are those which nowadays have already included complex origin provisions in their regulations (basically the EEC and the United States), and those affected by these (Japan, Hong Kong, Taiwan, etc.). Members of the CCC that are not parties to the Origin Agreement may attend the Technical Committee as observers.

Especially noteworthy is the possibility open to the industry (trade organizations such as chambers of commerce, etc.) to take part in the negotiations of the Technical Committee as observers. The role of the industry may be very important, specially during the harmonization negotiations. In effect, the industry can be of great help in defining the criteria that will

---

137. Interview with Mr. Siegrist, *supra* note 41.

138. On the participation of the EEC in GATT, see Ernst-Ulrich Petersmann, "The EEC as a GATT Member — Legal Conflicts Between GATT Law and European Community Law," in THE EUROPEAN COMMUNITY AND GATT, Meinhard Hilf, Francis G. Jacobs and Ernst-Ulrich Petersmann, eds., 23, at 32-39. For a proposal on a new formula of membership of the EEC, see John H. Jackson, *Restructuring the Gatt System*, 5 (1990).

139. Petersmann, *supra* note 138, at 37-38.

determine the origin of specific goods. In fact, various national customs authorities have already started contacting their local industries to receive their views on the future origin harmonization.

2.5. Dispute Settlement

Despite the harmonization of origin rules that is to be established among the signatory countries of the Origin Agreement, problems might arise in the interpretation and implementation of the rules. Such conflicts could be discussed multilaterally in the committees instituted by the agreement. In case no agreement is reached, the agreement has established dispute settlement provisions that, referring to Articles XXII[140] and XIII[141] of GATT, may be

---

140. GATT Article XXII:
1. Each contracting party shall accord sympathetic consideration to, and shall afford adequate opportunity for consultation regarding, such representations as may be made by another contracting party with respect to any matter affecting the operation of this Agreement.
2. The CONTRACTING PARTIES may, at the request of a contracting party, consult with any contracting party or parties in respect of any matter for which it has not been possible to find a satisfactory solution through consultation under paragraph 1.

141. GATT Article XXIII:
1. If any contracting party should consider that any benefit accruing to it directly or indirectly under this Agreement is being nullified or impaired or that the attainment of any objective of the Agreement is being impeded as the result of
(a)   the failure of another contracting party to carry out its obligations under this Agreement, or
(b)   the application by another contracting party of any measure, whether or not it conflicts with the provisions of this Agreement, or
(c)   the existence of any other situation,
the contracting party may, with a view to the satisfactory adjustment of the matter, make written representations or proposals to the other contracting party or parties which it considers to be concerned. Any contracting party thus approached shall give sympathetic consideration to the representations or proposals made to it.
2. If no satisfactory adjustment is effected between the contracting parties concerned within a reasonable time, or if the difficulty is of the type described in paragraph 1(c) of this Article, the matter may be referred to the CONTRACTING PARTIES. The CONTRACTING PARTIES shall promptly investigate any matter so referred to them and shall make appropriate recommendations to the contracting parties which they consider to be concerned, or give a ruling on the matter, as appropriate. The CONTRACTING PARTIES may consult with contracting parties, with the Economic and Social Council of the United Nations and with any appropriate inter-governmental organization in cases where they consider such consultation necessary. If the CONTRACTING PARTIES consider the circumstances are serious enough to justify such action, they may authorize a contracting party or parties to suspend the application to any other contracting party or parties of such concessions or other obligations under this Agreement as they determine

used to resolve the conflict.[142] These provisions will apply as improved and modified in the Uruguay Round.[143]

Through this formula, which refers directly to the GATT provisions, the Origin Agreement has avoided the introduction of a double dispute settlement procedure, as has been done in other side agreements.[144]

Although the conflicts shall basically arise once the harmonization program is completed, it is interesting to note that the dispute settlement provisions will already apply during the transitional period.

Such provisions will provide a legal structure for the resolution of international conflicts in origin matters. So far, certain provisions, such as Article 10 of the Kyoto Convention, provided for a dispute settlement procedure,[145] but this procedure has never been used.

---

to be appropriate in the circumstances. If the application to any contracting party of any concession or other obligation is in fact suspended, that contracting party shall then be free, not later than sixty days after such action is taken, to give written notice to the Executive Secretary to the CONTRACTING PARTIES of its intention to withdraw from this Agreement and such withdrawal shall take effect upon the sixtieth day on which such notice is received by him.

142. Generally on GATT dispute settlement, see Jackson, *supra* note 28, at 91 f.; Ivo Van Bael, *The GATT Dispute Settlement Procedure*, 22:4 Journal of World Trade 67 (1988); William J. Davey, *Dispute-settlement in GATT*, 11 Fordham International Law Journal 51 (1987).

143. On the new "Improvements to the GATT Dispute Settlement Rules and Procedures," GATT document L/6489 (adopted on 12 April 1989), see Eric Canal-Forgues and Rudolf Ostriahansky, *New Developments in the GATT Dispute Settlement Procedures*, 24:2 Journal of World Trade 67 (April 1990); Ernst-Ulrich Petersmann, "The GATT Dispute Settlement System and the Uruguay Round Negotiations on its Reform", in LEGAL ISSUES IN INTERNATIONAL TRADE, P. Sarcevic and H. van Houtte, eds., 53 (1990).

144. Such had been the case in the Antidumping Code, for example, in which Article 15 introduced a dispute settlement provision slightly different from GATT Article XXIII. On the problems that such a double regulation implied, see Ernst-Ulrich Petersmann, *GATT Dispute Settlement Proceedings in the Field of Antidumping Law*, 28 Common Market Law Review 69, 86 (1991).

145. Article 10 of the Kyoto Convention, of 18 May 1973, O.J. L 100 (1975) 1:
1. Any dispute between two or more Contracting Parties concerning the interpretation or application of this Convention shall so far as possible be settled by negotiation between them.
2. Any dispute which is not settled by negotiation shall be referred by the Contracting Parties in dispute to the Permanent Technical Committee which shall thereupon consider the dispute and make recommendations for its settlement.
3. If the Permanent Technical Committee is unable to settle the dispute, it shall refer the matter to the Council, which shall make recommendations in accordance with

The EEC has instituted a regional Origin Committee that solves the conflicts between its Member States.[146] A committee formed by representatives of the EEC and the EFTA countries also discusses the problems that arise in applying the EFTA-EEC agreements rules of origin.[147] However, these committees are essentially consultation fora in which decisions are basically taken by consensus. In the EEC, for example, the real conflicts are referred to the European Court of Justice. Other preferential agreements, such as those concluded by the United States with Israel and Canada,[148] also provide dispute settlement provisions, these being more close to the model generally used in GATT. In the framework of the Israel-US FTA a Panel decision was recently issued, in which rules of origin were discussed.[149]

In all these dispute settlement systems, and again in the Origin Agreement provisions, only Contracting Parties have access to the dispute settlement system. Individuals will only be able to put forward their cause in the national courts (on the specific procedure in the EEC, see § 2.3.1.1.4.). At the international level, the claim will depend on the willingness of the government to introduce a dispute. Individuals are denied all direct action.

3. Conclusion

The overall conclusion to be drawn from the Agreement is positive. A series of improvements are introduced, some of them even before the harmonization of the rules is reached. Certain formal guarantees will be provided, such as the publicity of the rules and the possibility of challenging them in court. Even more important is the chance of obtaining, with a brief delay, an assessment of the origin that would be accorded to a product. All these factors shall notably clarify the different national origin systems.

Article III(e) of the Convention establishing the Council.

4. The Contracting Parties in dispute may agree in advance to accept the recommendations of the Permanent Technical Committee or Council as binding.

146. *Supra* note 63.

147. Protocol 3 concerning the definition of the concept of "originating products" and methods of administrative cooperation of the following agreements: Agreement between the European Economic Community and Austria, O.J. (1972) L 300/38; Sweden, O.J. (1972) L 300/131; Switzerland, O.J. (1972) L 300/224; Iceland, O.J. (1972) L 301/106; Norway, O.J. (1973) L 171/45; and Finland, O.J. (1973) L 328/49.

148. Canada-U.S. FTA, *supra* note 55; Israel-U.S. FTA, *supra* note 58.

149. The decision has not yet been published. See *supra* note 58.

Once the harmonization of the content of the rules is completed, a simplification of the determination of origin will be added to the formal guarantees. All contracting parties will apply the same rules, based on technical and clear criteria (essentially change of tariff classification and, exceptionally, value added and specific transformations lists). Furthermore, these rules will be used for all purposes, getting rid of the present confusion and conflict raised by the existence of diverse rules for different purposes. Only in the preferential rules of origin is the harmonization still pending, and it seems unlikely to be reached in the near future. The inclusion of a Common Declaration accompanying the Origin Agreement refers only to some of the principles established for the nonpreferential rules of origin but without making their application compulsory. Furthermore, the grey area of the VRA shall remain excluded even from the scope of the application of the Common Declaration.

However, these advantages are reserved for the countries party to the agreement.[150] No universal origin system will be established,[151] although the largest part of the international trade community is expected to be bound by the new provisions.

A further problem in establishing a harmonized system is the risk of differences in the implementation of the rules by the different national administrations. In effect, the harmonization proposed in the agreement might not always be detailed enough concerning certain points to guarantee a uniform implementation, as we mentioned when discussing the value added criterion (see § 2.3.2.3.). Occasionally, this could result in several countries determining different origin for the same product. For example, a product undergoing transformations in, or including materials from, both countries A and B, could be considered as having origin in A by country X, while having origin in B by country Y, depending on how X and Y implemented the rules established in the Agreement. In such cases the discussions in the committees instituted by the agreement and, if necessary, the dispute settlement provisions could resolve such differences. However, it is unclear how efficient these will be.

---

150. It is still uncertain how the Uruguay Round will be concluded, but it is likely to result in a single package to be accepted as a whole. In that case, most GATT Contracting Parties (over a hundred countries) would subscribe to the Origin Agreement.

151. It is interesting to note the absence from GATT of countries such as Taiwan, often involved in origin matters. However, the access of Taiwan to GATT is being currently negotiated.

An important issue not addressed by the agreement is that of circumvention. The EEC Basic Origin Regulation refers to circumvention explicitly in Article 6:

Any process or work in respect of which it is established, or in respect of which the facts as ascertained justify the presumption, that its sole object was to circumvent the provisions applicable in the Community or the Member States to goods from specific countries shall in no case be considered, under Article 5, as conferring on the goods thus produced the origin of the country where it is carried out.[152]

Certain bilateral agreements contain similar provisions.[153] However the Origin Agreement has remained silent on this point. In the antidumping provisions, the issue has also received some attention, especially in relation to the EEC "Screwdriver" provision, issued to avoid imported goods sanctioned with antidumping duties not paying such duties due to the fact they were produced in assembly plants within the Community.[154] The GATT Panel of March 1990, which condemned the EEC provision has left the question open for the time being.[155]

Another problem remaining unresolved by the Origin Agreement is that of rules of origin for services. The agreement reduces its scope to goods, and most of the criteria that it contains would not apply to services. However, the discussions on origin that have so far been limited to goods will soon have to consider the determination of the origin of services as well. If the discussions that are taking place within GATT for the liberalization of services are successful, the problem of whether a service is from a country entitled to MFN, for example, shall be raised. But even at a regional level, certain

---

152. EEC Regulation 802/68, *supra* note 60.

153. Article 301.3.c) of the Canada-U.S. FTA (*see supra* note 54) establishes that origin shall not be conferred by "any process or work in respect of which it is established, or in respect of which the facts as ascertained clearly justify the presumption, that the sole object was to circumvent the provisions of this Chapter."

154. Article 13(10) of Regulation 2423/88, O.J. (1988) L 209/1. For a detailed comment, see Edwin Vermulst and Paul Waer, *Anti Circumvention Rules in Anti-Dumping Procedures: Interface or Short-Circuit for the Management of Interdependence?*, 11 Michigan Journal of International Law 1119, 1157 ff. (1990). Specifically on rules of origin see also Vermulst and Waer, *supra* note 43, at 83 ff.

155. For further detail, see Vermulst and Waer, supra note 154, at 1177 ff.

agreements concern not only goods but services.[156] In these cases, the question of the origin of services is also likely to appear. With the liberalization of services, a new dimension of the origin question appears. This shall hopefully be solved in the light of the experience in goods rules of origin.

156. The EEC is without any doubt the more relevant example (articles 59-66 EEC Treaty). Other agreements are also interesting models: Israel-U.S. Free Trade Agreement, Declaration on Trade in Services, 24 International Legal Materials 653, 679 (May 1985); Canada-U.S. Free Trade Agreement, Chapter 14, *supra* note 54; Protocol on Trade in services to the Australia New Zealand Trade Agreement on Closer Economic Relations-Trade Agreement (ANZCERTA), signed on 18 August 1988, entered into force on 1 January 1989, amending the Closer Economic Relations-Trade Agreement of 1983, published by the Australian Department of Foreign Affairs and Trade, Australian Government Publishing Service, Canberra, Treaty Series 1988, No. 20.

CHAPTER 8   **Comments by Experts**

The End of Innocence

Ian S. Forrester

The progenitors of this book are to be commended for taking the initiative, and pursuing that initiative, through the arduous burdens and delays of editorship to completion. The topic of rules of origin has fluctuated in importance in Community legal practice over the past twenty years. I wish to consider the reasons for those fluctuations, to commend greater frankness and realism when examining the Community's record, and to submit that the controversy over whether rules of origin are being "abused" is really misplaced and that in truth such controversy is the natural consequence of using inadequate instruments to make painfully difficult decisions in the application of protective trade policy measures.

In the 1970s, the major preoccupation of those who followed Community rules of origin was preferential rules of origin. Preferential trade between the Community of nine Member States and the EFTA countries was established by the various association agreements concluded in 1972 and 1973, under which, at the end of a transitional period, duty-free status was granted to all industrial products originating in the EEC or the several EFTA countries. Considerable effort was devoted to arranging investment patterns to avoid customs duties on shipments from, for example, Portugal to France. Legal and accounting skills were deployed in ensuring that traffic patterns such as Portugal-Norway-EEC were duty free despite the incorporation of significant levels of U.S. or Japanese content at the first two stages. Although the penalties for being wrong could be momentarily severe (unpaid duty, interest, arrears of duty, financial penalties of astonishing ferocity in the case of France and mild or moderate severity in the case of other Member States with a less brutal customs regime), the rules and the benefits accorded by satisfying them were reasonably clear.

Queen's Counsel at the Scots Bar; Member of the New York Bar; Visiting Professor in European Law, University of Glasgow; Chairman of the European Trade Law Association; practises law in Brussels.

The topic of nonpreferential rules of origin attracted relatively little attention from practicing lawyers and generated little political controversy. These halcyon conditions reflected the fact that EC antidumping policy was only an embryonic possibility and that the Community's external competence was less significant in reality than in theory. Putting it differently, Member States controlled their external trade relations much more than today and needed relatively limited recourse to Community powers to protect themselves.

However, by the 1980s, the main preoccupation of trade lawyers was not the availability of duty preferences, but the basic problems of achieving or preventing access to the Community marketplace. A principal factor underlying this phenomenon was anxiety about the size and intractability of the Japanese trade surplus. As informal national techniques for hindering imports were gradually eliminated, and as the principles of free circulation were more consistently respected, only Community-legal mechanisms for blocking or restraining unwelcome imports could be counted on (save in those Member States where Community law was disregarded).

Customs duties seemed of little use for protective purposes. European Community customs duties, following the reductions effected in successive rounds of multilateral tariff cutting, are now on average around 4% ad valorem. Thus they are usually no significant barrier to imports into the Community. By contrast, the emergence of antidumping measures as a regularly invoked element in the Community's external relations policy, the major changes in what conduct would be deemed to constitute dumping, and the absence of exhaustive judicial verification of the validity in legal terms of these changes did constitute a major obstacle to penetrating the Community market; these developments marked the end of the Community's trade policy innocence.

The steps leading from 1975 when EC antidumping procedures were almost unknown and, if conducted, would have followed methods that corresponded to laypeople's concepts of what constituted dumping and how to deal with it to 1985 when EC antidumping procedures were frequent, profoundly acrimonious, and controversial are described in *EEC Trade Law and the United States*[1] as well as in many other works. One of the difficulties in deciding what goods should be reachable by antidumping matters is that there is a deep ambivalence in whether antidumping measures are intended to correct excessively cheap imports from a particular country or to chastise unfair exporters.

---

1.   I. Forrester, EEC Trade Law and the United States, 469 Fordham Corporate Law Institute (1988).

An antidumping procedure is in practice directed against individual enterprises. It involves what amounts to an accusation of unfair or abusive conduct against specific parties, on whom specific penalties in the form of antidumping duties may be imposed. They must be investigated and defended. They are of course entitled to be treated fairly in procedural terms even if the underlying legislation inevitably contains elements of unfairness. Antidumping officials thus have to balance the world of trade policy negotiated in Geneva between states and the behaviour of an individual company and the marketplace in which it operates.

Only one term, *dumping*, is available to connote two different phenomena: wilful predatory or preemptive pricing intended to injure foreign industry and a situation where there is no particular intent to injure but where after a comparison of the relevant prices and costs and exchange rates, a margin of dumping is found. Complaints almost always allege wilfulness or at least recklessness. Exporters almost always deny intent to injure and assert their commitment to fair trade. Investigators pay little attention to the (of course unverifiable) question of intention. It is unfortunate that the term dumping is so emotionally charged, but it is the only one available to describe a whole range of financial and economic circumstances.

It is not the purpose of this comment to argue that antidumping measures should be abolished. On the contrary, their availability is probably a kind of safety valve, an alternative to more widespread trading hostilities. Confining the process to clearly identified categories of goods from identified sources is a desirable means of limiting the scope of a process that is certainly crude and often not completely rational, either in terms of fairness or accounting. However, since dumping is officially defined as unfair trade, there is a natural temptation to chastise unfairness wherever it may be found, from whatever country it comes. If antidumping duties are applied to the exports of "Tanaka K.K." of Osaka, this implies that the exports of that company have been priced at an unfairly low price. Community industry will ask why the same conclusion should not be drawn as to the identical goods made by "Tanaka New York Inc."? The same group makes the same goods and sells them at the same low price in the Community: surely there must be something that can be done? Once more we see the difficulty in deciding whether antidumping duties are trade policy measures, to correct by a neutral tax a trade distortion, or penalties.

Logic and commonsense might suggest to us that if a group disrupts trade in the Community with cheap exports, the geographic base for such activities should make no difference to the Community's capacity to take remedial action. But the GATT Anti-dumping Code makes it clear that duties may be imposed only on imports of goods from a particular country or countries and may not be imposed by reference to the identity of the dumper. Rules of origin are the mechanism that allows the Community legally to hit exports to the Community by the same dumping group but exported from another country. Putting it differently, they are the mechanism that can serve to immunize products coming from Canada against EC antidumping duties (or other protective measures) applicable to physically identical products from Singapore. If the goods made in Canada, from Singaporean and other components, originate in Canada, they should not be subject to duties on Singaporean products.

Unfortunately, the Community's rules of origin were not designed with this application in mind. Indeed, the concept of a single origin is ill-adapted to modern times; due to the globalization and interdependence of the world industry, it is often unrealistic to attribute a single origin to a product in the manufacture of which two or more countries have contributed. Dumping is also often a slippery and unsuitable concept for today's business world with its growing internationalism. Companies based in America have factories in Japan and Europe. Japanese companies have joint ventures with European companies who complain about them in dumping cases. European companies depend on components supplied by the alleged dumpers. American companies have production facilities in Korea, Japan, and Europe. Dumping measures, it is submitted, are based on outdated assumptions of defenders of a clearly defined territory and penetration by aggressors. It is difficult to tell whether an American-based multinational with its European headquarters in Sweden, a factory in France, and an affiliate in Japan is friend or foe according to traditional concepts when considering a possible dumping case. Despite these ambivalences and despite a much more critical attitude to the wisdom of antidumping measures, there is growing support for the suggestion that tighter origin and antidumping rules should be adopted.

Let us now look at the rules that are used to make such important distinctions. Council Regulation 802/68 establishes criteria that Member State customs officers shall follow in determining origin where no specific rules of origin apply to the particular import. Article 5 of Regulation 802/68 provides that a product should be deemed to originate

in the country in which the last substantial process or operation that is economically justified was performed, having been carried out in an undertaking equipped for the purpose, and resulting in the manufacture of a new product or representing an important stage of manufacture.

That Article contains a number of elements: (1) substantial nature of the operation; (2) economic justification; (3) adequacy of the equipped nature of the place of manufacture; and (4) (i) new product or (ii) important stage in the manufacturing process. The text is written as if these tests are cumulative (with the alternative under 4 (i) and 4 (ii). But good sense would suggest that any one individually ought to be enough to associate the product significantly with the exporting economy. It would seem absurd to argue that a substantial operation was not economically justified, or that even although economically justified, the place of manufacture was inadequately equipped. The explanation of the strange text lies in the fact that the rule when first formulated was a pastiche of several Member States' different rules. These were pressed into one rule that was not altogether internally consistent.

It would seem difficult to argue that a photocopier made in a large and well-equipped factory from a large number of small parts did not originate there. But such was the determination of the Commission's services to declare Ricoh's exports of photocopiers from California to the Community as susceptible to the same antidumping regime as Ricoh's exports of photocopiers from Japan that a regulation with this intended effect was adopted.[2] (As things turned out, some Member States in effect declined to apply the new rule.) Ricoh's difficulties owed much to the fact that a Ricoh official imprudently announced that the establishment of its U.S. factory was influenced by the imposition of duties on direct exports from Japan. Thus the Commission's services might well have felt the need to do something to bring an evader within the net of sanctions. It seems intellectually very difficult, however, to reconcile this with Article 5, which attributes origin to the place of last substantial processing.

The most natural reading of the words of Article 5 of Regulation 802/68 is; Where did the last process occur? Was that process substantial? However, this reading has been modified significantly to read; Of the various processes that occurred, which was the most substantial? The rule for semiconductors in effect puts the test slightly differently: Of the various not insubstantial processes that occurred, were the later operations significantly less important than the earlier operations? The "significantly less important" test of Regulation 288/89 on the origin of integrated circuits asserts that the complex, sophisticated and costly process of assembly is

so significantly less important than diffusion that they cannot individually or collectively constitute a substantial operation and thus cannot meet the requirement of being the last substantial operation in the manufacture of integrated circuits . . . .[3]

---

2. Commission Regulation (EEC) No. 2071/89 of 12 July 1989, O.J. (1989) L 196 at 24.

3. O.J. (1989) L 33 at 23.

I do not argue that it is unreasonable to decide the origin of a photocopier by reference to where its lens rather than its drum is manufactured, or to decide that where a semiconductor die is diffused is more important than where the integrated circuit is completed and tested. A trade policy case could certainly be made for such a conclusion. But it seems difficult to reconcile such a conclusion with the words of the basic EEC origin regulation.

It is understandable that origin officials were reluctant to express themselves about the originating status of goods made in newly established factories in the Community or in third countries. They were being asked to decide whether such goods might be hit with protective measures, and the tools at their disposal to make that decision were manifestly inadequate. Regulation 802/68 was drafted in another era. Using liberal origin rules in deciding whether to apply or not to apply a protective trade policy measure could not be other than controversial and politically sensitive. It could not be nonpolitical. It might be unfair for the officials to be accused of being influenced by political considerations, but their decisions are inevitably politically sensitive. The significance of the decision is too politically heavy. Either a trade policy objective of the Community will be thwarted, or the 1960s notion of origin will be ignored twenty years later.

That said, it would be wrong to imply that difficult or sensitive origin questions were regularly resolved in favor of the imposition of duties and against the interests of the exporting group. For example, in the case of Mita Hong Kong, an elaborate investigation was conducted of the premises at which assembly and subassembly operations were carried out, and it was concluded that the machines made in Hong Kong did indeed originate there and were not liable to be hit with EC antidumping duties.

It is therefore submitted that the Community's nonpreferential rules of origin cannot be examined in a vacuum. The decisions about what goods to hit with antidumping duties are reached after a lengthy and careful procedure, in which broad economic issues are debated as well as technical issues. It could not be expected that the mushrooming of new factories in other countries to manufacture identical goods to the "dumped" goods would have occurred without any Community reaction.

It cannot be argued that nonpreferential rules of origin are interpreted and applied now as they were ten years ago. This outcome is not surprising though it might be regretted. Thus rules of origin, like antidumping measures, lost their innocence as the Community's trade policy came of age in the late 1980s.

Rules of origin have also been debated in a quite different context in past years, in the field of free circulation. It is well-known that Italy has maintained in force GATT-valid and EEC-legal quotas on Japanese cars, motorcycles, and other products. Article 115 of the EEC Treaty permits a

Member State to obtain from the Commission authorization to support such quotas on direct imports from third countries by exclusions from Community treatment at internal frontiers. Otherwise, Japanese origin cars could enter Germany quota free, then enter Italy by virtue of free circulation. Questions frequently arose whether vehicles assembled in Europe with Japanese components under Japanese or partly Japanese auspices should be regarded as Japanese (and therefore liable to be included in the Italian quota) or non-Japanese. The test was not whether they originated in the Community, but rather whether they originated in Japan.

In the case of the Honda Accord car and the Scoopy motorcycle, Commission origin experts carefully investigated the technical processes, the value added, and other relevant factors. They concluded that the vehicles should not be regarded as originating in Japan, and the Italian government did not obstruct their importation. In this case, the system worked well. A challenge was made, an investigation was conducted, a legal conclusion was reached, and a trading pattern developed in consequence.

By contrast, in the case of the Nissan Bluebird car, the French Republic sought to argue that cars made in the North of England by a subsidiary of the Japan-based Nissan group were Japanese and were therefore ineligible for importation into France. The French posture was, in terms of Community law, total nonsense. The quota announced by President Giscard d'Estaing at the Paris Motor Show in 1979, whereby Japanese cars imported into France could not exceed 3 percent of new car registrations in France, was no secret. Yet its existence was never revealed (admitted might be more accurate) in any official text. The French authorities refrained from stating publicly what they were in practice doing. By this means the French authorities were able to maintain a flagrant infringement of Community law for more than a decade.

The EC Commission was well aware of the quota, received frequent complaints about it, and conveyed displeasure to the French authorities on numerous occasions, but the measures were never formally challenged before the Court of Justice of the European Communities. This was, it is submitted, a grave breach of the Commission's duty to uphold and enforce the treaty. The reason for the failure to act was, of course, a fear of the political consequences. If France were to be judicially held to account for its conduct, a crisis could erupt.

In any event, during the late 1980s, the French quota came into conflict with the establishment in the United Kingdom of car factories producing vehicles bearing Japanese marques. During 1987 and 1988, there were protracted exchanges of correspondence about the status of the Nissan Bluebird between U.K. officials and ministers, Commissioners and Commission officials, and French officials and ministers. The French justification for blocking such imports was that they did not originate in the

United Kingdom and that in any event the absence of a clear Community rule of origin was lamentable. This justification was baseless for two reasons: First, the French quota was illegal under Article 113 and its provisions on the Common Commercial Policy of the Community. Second, the cars were in free circulation and eligible for free movement, regardless of whatever Japanese content they might have had.

The regrettable silence of the Commission when faced with these misrepresentations caused confusion and uncertainty in the minds of private citizens. Commission representatives said nothing and by their silence compounded the heresy that the eligibility of the cars in free circulation depended on how much value had been added in their production in the Community. The fundamental principle of free movement of goods was misrepresented by the press and politicians as giving entitlement to free circulation within the Community only to goods with EC origin.[4]

In the end, all sides were able to claim a victory. The U.K. authorities were reassured that the cars would be admitted, and the French authorities continued with their idiosyncratic treatment of direct imports of vehicles from Japan. The episode reflects no credit on the political leadership of the Commission: When the Community rule is perfectly clear and is clearly flouted but is not challenged, it is evident that the enforcement of the law is colored by political considerations. If we choose to condemn the illogicalities of how technically outmoded rules of origin are applied in the context of highly sensitive trade tensions, we should also condemn the failure for political reasons to enforce the law.

One final observation is not controversial. Clearer rules of origin can be applied more predictably and neutrally. In 1985, the USITC in *The Impact of Rules of Origin on U.S. Imports and Exports* recorded that companies had reported losing large volumes of sales because of the application of rules of origin and very large expenses in dealing with the administrative costs they create. The estimates of the costs "ranged from negligible costs to several million dollars, with most of them in the $30,000 to $100,000 range."[5] The Community's rules certainly contributed to these burdens. It would be desirable to adopt clearer and less flexible rules, appropriate to the trade policy age in which, for better or for worse, we now live.

---

4.   *See, e.g.*, Montagnon, *Financial Times*, 30 September 1988; and Dawkins and Done, *Financial Times* 1 October 1988.

5.   USITC, The Impact of Rules of Origin on U.S. *Imports and Exports* 78 (1985).

SECTION 2 # Rules of Origin from a Policy Perspective

Gary N. Horlick and Michael A. Meyer

Rules of origin are usually the stepchildren of other discriminatory devices.[1] If MFN tariffs were the only regulation of trade, there would be no logical need for rules of origin except to satisfy the need of economic analysts (and some politicians) for country-by-country trade statistics[2] and to maintain the last bastion of economic nationalism, country of origin marking (one can remember when "Made in Japan" was a disincentive for customers).

Since the origin of origin rules is in commercial policy programs, logically each such program could well have its own rules of origin to be interpreted in accordance with the purpose of the program (i.e., a protectionist rule for Steel VRAs and a liberal rule for the GSP).[3] The practice, as ably described in Palmeter's review of U.S. cases, has been confusion and a tendency (subject to substantial variation) toward restrictive standards for all programs,[4]

O'Melveny & Myers, Washington, D.C.

1.   As Steele and Moulis point out (chapter 4, § 1.1.), without preferences or discrimination, origin becomes commercially irrelevant. As in so many other areas of trade policy, a discriminatory rule (in this case, different rules for closely related products) often signals a trade-distorting motive (see, e.g., the discussion by Waer in chapter 3 § 3).

2.   For such statistical series to be consistent, presumably one would need consistent rules of origin used in all reporting countries.

3.   Waer reports that the contracting parties to the CCC considered that rules of origin are commercial policy rather than Customs law, which would imply some tailoring of rules of origin to specific commercial trade policy purposes. See chapter 3, citing an interview with Mr. Gervais Farines, of the CCC.

4.   As Waer notes (chapter 3, § 4.3.1.), the EC Court of Justice in the *S.R. Industries* case permitted stricter rules of origin for preferential programs than for normal customs tariff purposes. This reaction might be consistent with the observation by Robert Baldwin in his elegant essay on "The Inefficacy of Trade Policy" that, once a distortion to trade is erected, traders will try to find some way around it. Baldwin, *The Inefficacy of Trade Policy*, 150 Essays in Int'l Fin. 5 (1982). In a domestic context, this practice is frequently considered to

including preferential ones (e.g., the dicta in the U.S. court decisions in the *Madison Galleries* case discussed by Palmeter in chapter 2, § 4.2.1.1.).

One result of the inconsistent results in rules of origin decisions in the U.S. was a counterreaction within the Customs Service, which seized its opportunity in the 1987 U.S.-Canada FTA negotiations to replace the vague "substantial transformation" standard (and the intense politicization of certain rule of origin decisions in the 1980s) with the change of tariff heading (CTH) concept from the Kyoto Convention.[5] The CTH concept was an appealing idea because it "permits the precise and objective formulation of the conditions determining origin,"[6] but was vulnerable to charges that, for some tariff items, it is very easy to change tariff headings even when there is very little change in the product. As a result, several of the Kyoto Convention alternatives were used in the FTA. First, it tightened the CTH rules, so that, for example, many of the U.S.-Canada FTA changes of origin require a change in two-digit chapter to ensure that there is really a "substantial transformation" (*quaere* whether changing technology will outrun changes in the HTS).[7]

Another solution, used with a few products, was to require the use of specified processes in addition to CTH. This solution poses its own origin problem (assuming that agreement can be reached on which process gives essential character). For example, defining the origin of an airplane as the country where its engine is added, merely begs the question of how to define the origin of the engine[8] (which might well have many components imported from third countries[9]). The Kyoto Convention recognized the difficulty of

---

be good business planning, while in international trade it is transmuted into circumvention, evasion, or worse.

5. International Convention on the Simplification and Harmonization of Customs Procedures, Annex D.1.A, 18 May 1973, S. Treaty Doc. No. 23, 97th Cong., 2d Sess. (1982) [Kyoto Convention].

6. *Ibid.*

7. U.S. Canada Free Trade Agreement, Annex 301.2, 2 January 1988, U.S.T.____, T.I.A.S. No.____, reprinted in 27 I.L.M. 281 (1988) (U.S.-Canada FTA).

8. As Navarro points out (chapter 7), technological evolution and differences among models also render the use of specified processes a poor choice if stability and certainty are the goals. Perhaps the new origin institutions under a new GATT Rules of Origin Agreement can alleviate this problem.

9. The Australian experience with gold chains and batteries, described by Steele and Moulis (chapter 4, § 4.2.2.) shows the two conflicting answers.

creating lists of manufacturing processes that would have to be "constantly updated to keep them abreast of technical developments and economic condition."[10]

Finally, the solution most instinctively reached for by politicians is to require a certain amount of value added. A value-added requirement is easy enough for the larger party to impose in one-way preferential programs (such as the GSP, the CBI, and, in effect, the U.S.-Israel FTA), but it is not so easy to use in a truly two-way trading relationship (such as the U.S.-Canada FTA) since the politicians on one side of the border who insist on a high percentage value-added origin to limit the scope of imports that receive the benefits of the preferential arrangement will sometimes be condemning their own producers to an undesirable rule if those producers wish to export to the other country. Nevertheless, value-added requirements show up in many tariff items for the U.S.-Canada FTA, including many of the most important ones (e.g., automobiles).[11]

The experience under the U.S.-Canada FTA showed another, more practical problem with a 50 percent value-added test — for many small and medium-size businesses, potential savings from FTA duty reduction were more than outweighed by the paperwork cost of documenting the value added (a cost not present with a pure CTH approach).[12] Consequently, going into the NAFTA negotiations, U.S. Customs became increasingly aware that, whatever the political attraction of a 50 percent value-added rule, it is frequently more trouble than it is worth.

Future bilateral and multilateral negotiations will raise another problem of a value-added rule. As definitions of value-added become more restrictive, (e.g., contrast the definition of value-added under the 1965 U.S.-Canada Autopact legislation,[13] with the value-added definition under the U.S.-Canada

---

10. Kyoto Convention, Annex D.1.A.

11. *See* U.S.-Canada FTA Chapters 3 and 10.

12. Since the primary FTA rule of origin required 100 percent FTA origin ("wholly manufactured"), even one trivial, non-FTA component could trigger a massive paperwork burden (if the assembled product had a value-added requirement — even if the requirement were easily met). The Australian *de minimis* rule (see chapter 4, § 2.3.2.) is a more practical approach (and likely to be adopted in NAFTA).

13. Under the Autopact, value-added included the aggregate cost of the following: locally produced parts and materials; transportation; insurance; iron, steel, and aluminium content of parts poured locally; wages for direct and indirect labor; light, heat, power, and water; worker's compensation and unemployment insurance; taxes on land and buildings; fire and other insurance; rent, maintenance and repairs of buildings; nonpermanent plant equipment; R&D; SGA expenses, depreciation in production machinery; and a capital

FTA[14]) a country with relatively low labor costs will have a harder time adding value than a country with higher wage rates.[15] This problem creates a tension between the political imperative of imposing high value-added requirements and the practical problems of imposing impossible administrative burdens on U.S. exporters (to qualify for foreign preferences)[16] in addition to the difficulties for developing-country exporters in reaching high value-added requirements with lower labor costs.

The jury is still out on the rules of origin issue, as the 20 December 1991 draft GATT Agreement on Rules of Origin seems to show a mild preference for CTH, while leaving open the door to specific processes or value-added requirements.[17] The Draft Agreement provides a three-step process for harmonizing rules of origin. First, a Technical Committee must identify all goods that are wholly obtained in one country and define minimal operations that do not confer origin.[18] Second, the Committee must examine the use of

---

allowance. *See* Tariff Item 950 Regulations, § 2, Canada Privy Council, Memo D49-30 (18 January 1965).

14. The U.S.-Canada FTA limits value added to the value of materials originating within the FTA country plus the direct costs of processing or assembly. U.S.-Canada FTA, Chapter 3, Article 304. The value of materials originating within the FTA country includes locally produced materials, transportation costs, duties, taxes, brokerage fees, and scrap. The direct cost of processing or assembling covers all labor costs, inspection and testing, energy, fuel, dies, depreciation and maintenance of equipment, development, design and engineering, rent, mortgage interest, depreciation on buildings, and royalty licensing. *Ibid.*

15. In addition, to the extent that the FTA requires high value added within the FTA area, the FTA in effect becomes a preferential sourcing rule with considerable potential for trade diversion.

16. These burdens include expanded recordkeeping, complex accounting requirements (e.g., tracking the changes in percentage of value of origin caused by exchange rate fluctuations), and the quasi-mystical problems typified by the question of "roll up" — is one seeking the origin of the imported product, the origin of its components, or the origin of the raw materials of the components?

The added burden on Customs authorities — already burdened by sharp increases in trade flows and proliferation of commercial regimes — caused by a value-added rule should also not be ignored. This becomes of particular concern as tariff cuts reduce the margin of preference to a point where administrative costs to comply with rules of origin can exceed that margin (Chapter 3).

17. Draft Final Act Embodying the Results of Uruguay Round of Multilateral Trade Negotiations, Agreement on Rules of Origin, MTN.TNC/W/FA/D (20 December 1991) (Draft Agreement).

18. Draft Agreement, Article 9.2 (c) (i).

CTH to define origin for specific products or product sectors and elaborate on the minimum change within the nomenclature that meets the substantial transformation criterion.[19] Finally, for products or sectors where CTH insufficiently expresses substantial transformation, the Technical Committee "shall consider . . . the use, in a supplementary or exclusive manner, of other requirements, including ad valorem percentages and/or manufacturing or processing operations when developing rules of origin."[20]

The draft Agreement's preference for CTH, although mild, is apparent in that the supplementary or exclusive use of other requirements (i.e., value-added or further processing) is only considered for those products where the exclusive use of CTH is first deemed insufficient. That is to say, after the Technical Committee has applied CTH wherever possible, then it may turn to other standards for harmonizing rules of origin.

One particular problem apparent from the Draft Agreement is the treatment of antidumping and countervailing duty cases. Article 1.2 provides that the Rules of Origin Code applies to antidumping and countervailing duty cases, but footnote 2 provides that "it is understood that this provision is without prejudice to those determinations made for purposes of defining 'domestic industry' or 'like products of domestic industry' or similar terms wherever they apply."[21]

The footnote would seem to exempt from the Draft Agreement a loosely defined set of terms often used in antidumping cases. While the disciplines on rules of origin would apply to defining which imports would be subject to antidumping or countervailing duties investigations, the rules would not apply to the definition of the "domestic" product that is allegedly injured by the imports. Therefore, a product that might not be considered of U.S. origin under the harmonized rules still could be considered a U.S. domestic like product in an antidumping or countervailing duty investigation.

The exception for antidumping cases opens up an interesting new frontier in discrimination. Since dumping can be found on almost any imported product (the U.S. found dumping on 95 percent of all cases investigated in the first half of the 1980s — when the dollar was overvalued)[22] and finding the requisite injury need not be a barrier in most countries, a rule of origin that excludes only antidumping issues would require nonprotectionist or

---

19. Draft Agreement, Article 9.2 (c) (ii).

20. Draft Agreement, Article 9.2 (c) (iii).

21. Draft Agreement, Article 1.2, note 2.

22. J. Bovard, FAIR TRADE FRAUD 1 n. 1 (1991).

nondiscriminatory rules of origin for all purposes except the one (antidumping) that could be best used to protectionist effect. This misuse of rules of origin will be exacerbated if, as Navarro surmises (chapter 7, § 2.3.), "grey area" measures — often born out of dumping charges — are excluded from the new Draft Agreement.

Probably the most important aspect of the Draft Agreement, once it is completed (i.e., several years from now, once the CCC completes the work on a harmonized system of rules as envisioned by the Draft Agreement), will be the incorporation, through Article 8, of the binding GATT procedures for dispute resolution envisioned in the draft text on dispute resolution.[23] It is likely that such procedures would have had a healthy effect on the political rule of origin decisions of the United States and the EC in the 1980s, whether by GATT review of national decisions or by an intimidating effect on national decisions that would make GATT review unnecessary.

---

23. Draft Final Act Embodying the Results of the Uruguay Round of Multilateral Trade Negotiations, Understanding on Rules and Procedures Governing the Settlement of Disputes under Articles XXII and XXIII of the General Agreement on Tariffs and Trade, MTN.TNC/W/FA/S (20 December 1991).

Rules of Origin: Commentary

Professor Jeffrey Waincymer

The country-specific chapters in this book highlight the diverse and technical nature of rules of origin as they apply in the world trading system. Traditionally, little attention has been given to the analysis and reform of such rules, either by economists, lawyers, or trade negotiators. These rules have tended to be viewed as mere matters of domestic fine detail within the trade system developed at the international level. Over time, the fallacy and danger of this attitude has become more and more evident. Rules of origin clearly have important resource allocation ramifications. They can be used as discriminatory barriers to trade. Ambiguity and complexity add to the dead weight costs of doing business and undermine the benefits that would otherwise flow from international trade.

As the international trading community has come to realize the importance of this area of the law, attempts have been made to begin the process of analysis and reform. The draft text emanating from the Uruguay Round of GATT talks is the latest and most far reaching example of this trend. Yet there are many problems still to be considered and foundational issues that are likely to be overlooked in the rush to try and finalize the round as a whole. The attempt to develop rules of origin in the world trading system shows a particular problem for any single international economic organization trying to develop rules that are equitable, efficient, and simple. First, as indicated above, rules of origin have been traditionally seen as matters of administration. Thus, in spite of their importance to tariff issues debated and negotiated under the GATT system, the development and reform of the rules themselves was left in the past to the more technical forum of the CCC. That body is responsible for some excellent work, yet it must be remembered that dividing tariff negotiations and rule development between two quite distinct bodies is highly artificial and fraught with danger.

Yet it is not only technical matters that are sometimes bypassed in GATT

Faculty of Law, Deakin University, Melbourne, Australia.

negotiations. At the other extreme, any sensible attempt to develop an efficient definition must look carefully at the economics of competing options. For quite different reasons, direct economic analysis has largely been outside the normal field of GATT negotiations although the Secretariat does much valuable work. The failure of the negotiators to address key economic issues is partly explained because GATT contains contracting parties with quite diverse economic philosophies, but also because negotiators tend to have more of a diplomatic orientation and do not approach problems in the manner of theoretical economists. Regardless of the reasons for this historical position, it is certainly unfortunate. Given that the aim of GATT is to promote the liberalization of trade and to develop equitable and efficient rules that foster international trading relationships, the key definitions within those rules must similarly be equitable and efficient.

Until quite recently, little effort has been made to try and analyze rules of origin from this perspective. Instead the concern has tended to be to seek some harmonization of the rules to remove uncertainty and appearances of bias. These are certainly important aspects of these rules, but in the view of this writer, they are subordinate to the efficiency arguments that economics would postulate. Changes in trading patterns have made the economic impact of rules of origin more important. Historically, products tended to be manufactured within one country with few foreign inputs other than raw materials. Modern manufacturing practices see multinational corporations, who, it must be remembered, are responsible for a significant and growing percentage of world trade, break up the manufacturing process and use components manufactured in different parts of the world to maximize economies of scale. The growth of knowledge-based industries and developments in transport, allied to the freer movement of capital and labor, and the inclusion of many more third world countries in international intellectual property protection conventions, all serve to accelerate this trend. Kingston draws attention to the ironical fact that unduly restrictive origin rules can have unexpected domestic consequences if they encourage foreigners to set up local manufacturing, which could then put local producers out of business. Table 1 of Kingston's paper also shows that whichever rule is used, it will not apply with equal economic impact to different types of goods. This in turn could bias production decisions away from certain types of goods. Simple economic analysis will, as a result, highlight the problems without providing simple solutions. It is against the background of these economic issues that we need to evaluate the recent GATT initiatives.

Rules of Origin Under GATT

On the historical side, Navarro's paper points out the failure of the original GATT Agreement to give any direction on origin matters. The agreement itself has not even prevented discriminatory rules of origin. Article I, which provides for MFN treatment, has not prevented a varied array of rules of origin, many of which are specifically aimed at fostering discrimination and protection. Many of these practices shelter behind other discriminatory elements of the GATT Agreement even though the whole philosophy of the agreement would not, on any expansive interpretation, condone an origin regime that had different rules for some countries for protectionist reasons. A more technical argument under Article I is that these would not breach the Agreement as the nondiscrimination norm only applies once you have determined what are "products of territories of other contracting parties." Discriminatory rules that relate to such products might therefore be argued to not technically offend against Article I. One would hope that such a casuistic approach would be unlikely to survive the analysis of a modern GATT Panel. Yet many important issues are never brought before Panels. Reform of the law is always more desirable through direct analysis and negotiation. It is certainly appropriate to consider these issues as part of the comprehensive Uruguay Round review.

Early work within the GATT also showed the important dual issues of first devising an appropriate theoretical formula and secondly, ensuring that it is administratively workable. Where the latter is concerned, attention needs to be given to methods of examining, licencing, and verification. Navarro has described the background and content of the Kyoto Convention, which sought to deal with the major administrative aspects of Customs law harmonization. While that convention was an important first step, much was left open, partly because administrative issues tend to be seen as domestic matters regardless of the impact they have on the rules agreed to at the international level. Customs administrators are then less likely to see them as matters requiring international consensus and harmonization. For example, like the GATT Valuation Code, the Kyoto Convention outlines and identifies different acceptable methods of determining origin of goods. Unlike the Valuation Code, however, it does not rank these in any agreed hierarchy. In essence, it brought together the leading alternatives and excluded any less reasonable methodologies.

The Kyoto Convention provided a number of options and gave considerable discretion to domestic governments but did little to foster uniform and nondiscriminatory rules of origin. Thus the contracting parties to the GATT resolved to seek further reforms as part of the Uruguay Round negotiations. While those negotiations were far from finalized at the time of this writing, certain limitations were already evident. It is particularly unfortunate that the Uruguay Round negotiations appear to be excluding preferential rules of origin. As preferential trade continues to grow and cause increasing tension with the GATT principle of nondiscrimination, it makes no theoretical sense to exclude origin rules in such agreements. Navarro also points to the equally important problem of determining the origin of services, a matter not addressed as yet in the GATT negotiations.

The Uruguay Round Proposals

The origin agreement proposes that last substantial transformation be the test. It goes on to describe and expand on various criteria for determining when this occurs. As is so often the case with complex matters of commercial regulation, it is not easy to develop rules that are equally equitable, efficient and simple. Looking at the last substantial transformation rather than the most substantial transformation clearly simplifies the process. It does, however, leave open significant interpretational, administrative, and circumvention issues. Concentrating on the last process encourages multinationals to organize production in particular ways to gain duty-free access to targeted markets, including free trade areas. This reaction has in turn led to some highly protectionist responses. Where it is allowed, it would tend to divert trade from more efficient suppliers. It encourages resources to be allocated to gain duty benefits and not because of any economic factors. Where it is not allowed, the protectionist responses are often Draconian, as the Japanese motor car industry has found out.

An approach that looks at specific defined operations to determine origin, while simple to apply, is most difficult to develop fairly and efficiently. To leave it to individual governments to draw up the lists merely allows for protectionist measures and disharmony. Australia has followed the value added approach to determine the origin of a product. This criterion, which has the illusion of precision, simply does not behave in this way, at least in the absence of very specific rules and an elaborate bureaucratic structure. As has long been documented,[1] a value-added approach raises many complex accounting questions. Should value be determined on the basis of fixed costs or should it include variable costs? How should variable cost be calculated? To what extent should general overheads be included in relation to specific products? How should capital expenses be amortized? What level of profit margin should be used? How are differential inflation and currency rates to be dealt with? How should the calculation be made when the foreign supplier

---

1. *See, e.g.*, Kyoto Convention Annex D.1. Point B.

will not provide relevant details, given that neither the importer nor the customs bureaucrat has any power to compel the presentation of evidence? To what extent is value added a reasonable criterion, given that prices and values will differ depending on the market conditions in the particular country? In particular, labor prices often vary considerably. Navarro (chapter 7) also points to the Valuation Code rules dealing with related party transactions. Similar issues can arise with an origin agreement. Are figures to be accepted in all related party transactions? If not, what tests should apply to distinguish between acceptable and unacceptable figures?

If all these accounting questions are left to national administrations to resolve, with the potential for conflict and disharmony that this implies, Navarro's suggestion that the Technical Committee under an origin agreement might solve such conflicting situations seems overly optimistic, both in practical terms and as a matter of the interpretation of international rules having domestic force. It is also not clear why he asserts that if majority voting applies in the Technical Committee, decisions are likely to be binding. These questions will surely be determined by the approach of each individual country's legal system to the domestic application of international treaties. In the case of Australia for example, an international treaty has no domestic effect until legislation has been enacted. Thus, it is quite the opposite of the position in the European Community. To speak of these decisions as being "binding," confuses the role of the bureaucracy and the role of the courts. Given that the CCC is essentially staffed by customs officials of the various countries, one could easily expect that decisions made within its committees will be applied in the first instance by bureaucrats. In that sense there is a binding element to them. But if those decisions are challenged, courts in nearly all jurisdictions will use traditional methods of statutory interpretation to apply their own country's domestic legislation. A different approach might apply in a GATT panel decision on a similar issue, but in most instances origin disputes are merely domestic legal disputes.

A Critique of the Current Approach

In the view of this writer, the general approach to developing and improving rules of origin is flawed. The primary norm of the GATT system is nondiscrimination. If all tariffs were nondiscriminatory, rules of origin would be irrelevant. It is only where there are specific exemptions from the nondiscriminatory norm that rules of origin become necessary. Those exceptions are carefully circumscribed in the GATT Agreement and the codes that emanate under it, or alternatively, are simply illegal derogations from GATT as in the case of the inappropriately named Voluntary Restraint Agreements. Where legal derogations are concerned, the limitations on these have either expressed or strongly implied policy bases. As a result, the rules of origin that relate to those derogations should surely reflect those policy bases. As an example, an origin rule that aims to impose a political sanction on a country might justifiably have a lower percentage value markup than for normal tariff purposes. Rules of origin that relate to customs unions should be consistent with the economic theory that sees customs unions as desirable where they are trade enhancing but not where they are trade diverting. Where preferential agreements are concerned, Kingston (chapter 1) rightly points out that far from making the origin rules consistent with the basis for exempting preferences from nondiscriminatory treatment, the rules are too often designed to take back with one hand the preference given in the other. Making the rules more rigid as the level of preference diminishes in the face of overall reductions in tariff rates is surely not protected by Article XXIV.

Even if this criticism is accepted, it does not make design issues much easier. Because origin rules primarily relate to what tariff rates should apply and because those tariff rates relate to appropriate levels of protection for domestic industry, an essential character or tariff item-based test has much to be said for it. Yet considering the appropriate rule from the perspective of the domestic industry to be protected, such a test ignores the wider macroeconomic issues about resource allocation throughout the national and international community.

Comment was previously made that reform in this area raises circumvention and avoidance issues as well as economic and administrative matters. For example, the question whether a last substantial transformation in a free trade area should be accepted or not when motivated by a desire to minimize duty raises the whole question of the purpose behind particular manufacturing decisions. Navarro (chapter 7) refers to "screwdriver provisions" in a number of countries' antidumping laws. Unlike most countries' domestic taxation laws, GATT agreements and domestic import and export laws do not contain anti-avoidance provisions. Nor have courts developed common law doctrines such as the business purpose test in the United States, simulation rules in the European Community, and fiscal nullity in the United Kingdom, all common to taxation lawyers. Because GATT is an international organization, its ability to come up with viable and fair means of combatting circumvention initiatives can be seriously questioned. What appears to be avoidance to one contracting party, is merely freedom of investment to another. Common-law antiavoidance responses of judges in domestic legal systems would be seen as far too activist for a GATT Panel. Yet the failure to address these issues does not mean that the problem does not exist. Quite the contrary, as GATT evolves as a more sophisticated legal institution, it is inevitably forced to face these issues, simply because traders and governments become more and more sophisticated in their attempts to bypass GATT's normative prescriptions.

The following comments address some of the particular points made by the key authors in this work. Kingston (chapter 1) argues that there can be a conflict between general economic considerations of comparative advantage and the use of origin rules to reinforce unfair trade laws such as countervailing measures. While this conflict is apparent in cases such as the European Court's judgment involving electronic typewriters from Taiwan that he refers to, it is surely not inevitable. Antidumping and countervailing rules, if appropriately drafted, could look at the subcomponents and see if they, as an element of the final product, are subsidized or dumped. If the final product value is less than the normal value in the exporting country only because production has shifted to take advantage of assembly in a country with comparative advantage in labor intensive activities, no economist would see this as unfair. The "screwdriver" cases in the antidumping field merely show that the drafters of the Antidumping Code did not give sufficient attention to circumvention transactions. Provisions being negotiated in the Uruguay Round seek to address these issues, although the problem is unfortunately presumed without being analyzed afresh.

While Kingston rightly points out the bias against accepting assembly in low-labor-cost countries as affecting origin, it is too much to expect domestic governments, at least in this recessionary climate, to subscribe to trade laws that allow comparative advantage to be fully exploited. In any event, comparative advantage in the labor area relates to labor productivity and not merely cost. Many low cost countries also have low levels of productivity through lack of education, technology, and capital equipment. Thus much of the domestic hype and concern is misguided.

Lessons from the Australian Experience

Value-added provisions that allow the cumulation of the value with value in the importing country can mean that insignificant activities in the export country may be shielded from duty. For example, if 45 percent of Australian raw materials by value of the final product had 49 percent value added in Taiwan with 6 percent assembly in New Zealand, the goods could be treated as duty free under the Australia-New Zealand Closer Economic Relations Trade Agreement. The distortionary potential is apparent.

Steele and Moulis, in their chapter on the Australian experience (chapter 4), refer to a group of cases that dealt with legislative provisions that combined a value added rule with an additional requirement that the last process of manufacture be in the relevant country. They point to the growing and unfortunate practice in Australian commercial law of delegating to the bureaucracy the power to direct how certain general requirements are to be determined. In the Australian context, this involved the determination of the way factory and works cost and value of labor and materials are to be determined. Their chapter shows the inevitable ambiguities that arise under such provisions but also shows that the same bureaucracy that was charged with litigating under the provisions saw fit to modify the gazetted material in the hope of overcoming an adverse decision in a case that they had fought and lost. Notwithstanding this amendment, the tribunal in the next case still held against the comptroller and considered that the modification to the rules went beyond the powers conferred on the comptroller under the act. It is easy to criticize this saga on the basis that the legislative provisions were too uncertain and that it is undesirable to give the losing litigant the power to modify the rules for future cases. There is a more important concern, however. In the cases referred to, it was absolutely clear that far more than the relevant percent by way of value content of the finished product originated in the preference country. The fact that the bureaucrat took exception to this factual situation presumably arose from a concern over the fact that the value of the materials far outweighed the value of the processing itself. Yet to take exception to this implies some policy goal wholly inconsistent with a value-added test. Thus, in the view of this writer, the comptroller's response not only was beyond the powers given to him in the act but fundamentally contradicted the policy underlying the act.

Steele and Moulis also quite rightly point to the effective legislative modification by the Federal Court in the *Eveready* case.[2] Because the legislation required the origin and materials to be considered as a preliminary matter and because no separate indication was given on how this was to be determined, the court effectively used a substantial transformation test without any specific legislative direction to do so.

Conclusion

It is certainly a significant development that the GATT negotiators have sought to directly address a topic previously thought to be a mere technical matter. Even basic analysis makes it obvious that rules of origin will have important resource allocation effects and can, if unchecked, constitute intended or unintended barriers to trade. The same analysis shows that none of the developed alternate approaches to determining origin can possibly operate in a neutral fashion. Whichever rule is chosen, some distortion must inevitably arise. The question is then to decide which distortions are acceptable and why. As rules of origin are only required when there are departures from the central

---

2.　*Re Eveready Australia Pty Ltd and The Collector of Customs*, No. G521 of 1991 (4 March 1992) (unreported).

norm of nondiscrimination in GATT, the rules to be applied in each of those areas should be consistent with the policy underlying that departure and should not be any more distortive than necessary. While attempts to harmonize and simplify rules of origin will have clear welfare benefits, the prime lesson to be learned from the reform exercises, both past and present, is the ongoing need to redress the growth of discriminatory practices that have evolved either because of or in spite of the GATT trading system. While contributors such as Kingston (chapter 1) are right in asserting that harmonized and certain rules at least have some benefit in the absence of an ability to develop economically neutral rules, books such as this one should not be shy to remind GATT negotiators that fundamental issues have been largely left unattended.

EC Rules of Origin from an Official's Point of View

Dr. Jochen Matthies

1. Introduction

Origin means the economic nationality of a product. Origin rules determine, where needed, the origin of a particular imported or exported item. They are necessary in order:

- to operate preferential tariff provisions;
- to enforce commercial policy measures (quantitative restrictions) and to apply commercial policy instruments (antidumping measures); and
- to identify origin in connection with a variety of other legislative areas (European Development Fund projects and, to a certain extent, public procurement).

Community rules of origin are divided into two categories: preferential and nonpreferential origin rules.

2. Preferential Origin Rules

2.1. Application of Preferential Origin Rules

Preferential origin rules apply with regard to tariff preferences. These rules are negotiated between the EC and partner countries in the context of preferential agreements (with EFTA, ACP, Mediterranean countries, Hungary, and, let us not forget, Poland, the Czech and Slovak Republics, Bulgaria and Rumania) and are set out as part of those agreements in the form of Origin Protocols.

Head of Division, Directorate-General for Customs and Indirect Taxation, Commission of the European Community, Brussels. The opinions expressed are those of the author and do not necessarily represent those of the EC Commission.

There are, however, cases in which the Community grants a preferential tariff arrangement autonomously. This is, for example, the case for the Generalized System of Preferences and Overseas Countries and Territories.

In preferential arrangements, industrial and certain agricultural products benefit from duty-free or duty-reduced entry into the Community, providing that they originate in preferential countries. The rules of origin determine when a product originates in a particular country and thereby whether it may benefit from preferences. Preferences are not only granted unilaterally by the Community. In some cases they are reciprocal, but not necessarily symmetrical (EFTA, Israel, Cyprus, Malta).

2.2. Purpose of Preferential Origin

The existence of the preferential rules of origin is explained notably by the fact that the benefit of preferential tariff arrangements must be limited to preferential partner countries. The rules of origin should therefore prevent nonpreferential third countries from deflecting trade through these partner countries in order to obtain for themselves preferential access to Community markets.

Furthermore, the preferential rules of origin determine the scope of tariff preferences. If rules of origin are liberal, the possibility to import duty-free is made much easier. Preferential rules of origin are not identical. They depend on the economic development, the geographical situation and political relations between the beneficiaries and the Community.

2.3. Common Principles

However, there are principles which apply equally to all preferential partners:

2.3.1. Sufficient Working and Processing

Preferential rules provide that "*sufficient* working or processing" must occur in the preferential country for a product to obtain its origin. In principle, working or processing is considered sufficient if it entails a change in tariff heading of all the components.

However, the tariff structure, which was not designed for origin purposes, and the objectives of the preferential arrangement in question have made it necessary to complement, or derogate from, this general principle for a great number of products and to provide (in a list) that:

–   in certain cases, a simple change of tariff heading alone is not sufficient to confer origin, but additional specific working or processing, defined product-by-product, and/or a certain percentage of value added is also necessary;

- in other cases, certain working or processing operations, equally specified product-by-product, possibly combined with a value added criterion, are considered as sufficient even if they do not entail a change of tariff heading.

2.3.2. Cumulation

The possibility of cumulation is provided for in a number of origin Protocols.

2.3.3. Direct Transport

The consignments must be transported directly from the beneficiary country to the Community. They can be transhipped through a third country, but in this case they need a so-called "manipulation certificate" from the customs authorities declaring that they have neither entered into commerce nor have undergone operations in that country other than those intended to keep them in good condition.

2.3.4. Documentary Proof of Origin

The consignments must be accompanied by documentary proof of origin (Form A or EUR 1), in some cases issued by Customs or in other cases by Governmental bodies.

2.4. Differences in the Preferential Origin Regimes

Differences in the origin regimes in particular concern *cumulation*:
- Bilateral cumulation for EC/Mediterranean relations (products *originating* in the Community do not need sufficient working or processing in the beneficiary country: Mediterranean countries);
- Full cumulation (operations *carried out* in preferential zones are considered to be carried out in the beneficiary country: European Economic Area, EC/ACP relations);
- Diagonal cumulation (products originating in one preferential zone do not need sufficient working or processing in another preferential zone: EC/Poland, EC/Hungary, EC/Czech Republic, EC/Slovak Republic);
- For GSP countries regional cumulation (ASEAN, ANDEAN) is allowed. A donor country (bilateral cumulation with the EC) content system is envisaged for the near future.

Further differences concern:
- General tolerance 0 - 10%;
- Possibility of alternative percentage rules;

- exporter himself can issue documentary proof of origin (so-called *invoice declaration*) for some countries;
- no draw-back rule.

The origin rules for preferential purposes have the character of individual conditions for preferences, whilst nonpreferential origin rules are based on the last substantial transformation which are not subject to negotiations. This explains why the EC did not wish for its preferential origin rules to be harmonized.

3. Nonpreferential Origin Rules

3.1.   Application of the Nonpreferential Origin Rules

3.1.1.   General

The nonpreferential origin rules are linked to the application of commercial policy measures and instruments, (for example: quantitative restrictions, measures under Regulation (EEC) No 288/82 of 5 February 1982 on common rules for imports,[1] and self restraint agreements with third countries, as in the textile sector and antidumping instruments). Unlike the United States, the EC applies the customs duties consolidated in the GATT for imports from third countries regardless of their origin (the preferential rates have been dealt with above). The EC grants the Most Favoured Nation principle to all countries.

These rules are also used for trade statistics and for a variety of other purposes (e.g., European Development Fund, public procurement). Equally, they are applicable to exports to third countries in so far as these do not fall within a preferential tariff arrangement.

3.1.2.   Origin Rules in the Context of Antidumping Instruments against Goods Produced or Assembled in the Community[2]

Nonpreferential origin rules have considerable relevance in the context of recent legislation on the prevention of circumvention of antidumping duty. This legislation aims to avoid a situation where, instead of importing a product subject to antidumping duty, a firm related to the producer of the finished product liable to antidumping duty imports individual parts of this

---

1.   O.J. (1982) L 35/1.

2.   Article 13(10) of Council Regulation (EEC) No 2423 of 11 July 1988 on protection against dumped or subsidized imports from countries not members of the European Economic Community. Published in O.J. (1988) L 209/1.

machine and uses them in the manufacture or assembly of a product in the Community, thus avoiding the antidumping duty.

In this case, antidumping duty will be chargeable where more than 60% of all parts or materials used in assembly originate in the dumping country. In other words, if 40% or more of all parts originate in any country other than the dumping one, no antidumping duty is liable.

It should be noted that in the legislation described above, the concept of the 40-60 % ration is not derived from origin rules. The origin rules, in this context, only apply in order to establish which of the parts originate in the dumping country and consequently to determine which parts fall under the "60% category" and which fall under the "40% category."

3.2. Nature of Nonpreferential Origin Rules

The nonpreferential origin rules are themselves of a nonpolitical, neutral and technical nature, and the legal approach to their interpretation is further guaranteed by the possibility of control and review by the European Court of Justice in each individual case. Furthermore, these rules must be balanced and unbiased in nature, since the same rules serve for imports into the Community and for certificates of origin for EC exporters (EC certificates of origin are frequently required in contracts between EC manufacturers and third country purchasers, and are often necessary to encash letters of credit in such cases).

3.3. Kyoto Convention

The Community applies the principles of Origin Annex D1 to the Kyoto Convention (1973), an international customs simplification and harmonization instrument. This Convention lays down the concept of last *substantial* operation, to which I will return later. As far as the Community is concerned, this concept was already established in Regulation 802/68,[3] and was then used as a basis for the Kyoto Convention for the purpose of worldwide application.

3.4. Further Qualifying Criteria

Article 5 of Regulation No 802/68 furthermore requires that the operation which confers origin must

–   be economically justified;
–   be carried out in an undertaking equipped for the purpose;

---

3.   Council Regulation (EEC) No 802/68 on the common definition of the concept of the origin of goods, O.J. (1968) L 148/165 which also establishes an Origin committee for administrating the Regulation.

– result in the manufacture of a new product or represent an important stage of manufacture.

3.5. Details Concerning the Criterion of the "Last Substantial Working or Processing"

The last substantial operation criterion establishes the country of origin of a given product where two or more countries are involved.[4] It can be applied in several ways:

– it can be a technical test determined on a case-by-case basis. A product has undergone a last substantial operation when it has properties which it did not possess before that process took place. A significant qualitative change in its characteristics is thus necessary;[5]

– in cases where assembly is principally concerned, the importance of the operation has to be judged in the context of the totality of those operations necessary for manufacture of the complete product.[6] The European Court of Justice has ruled that it may be a simple assembly (no origin), or an assembly which is more than simple, but not substantial (no origin), or an assembly (origin) that constitutes the decisive stage of manufacture which determines the final destination of the used components and which gives to the product its specific qualitative character.[7]

For example, in Germany, the national court (*Finanzgericht Kassel*) has decided that the assembly of electronic typewriters is a simple operation which does not confer origin, even if the PCBs are stuffed in the country of assembly;

– The Community has decided that, in the case of integrated circuits, diffusion confers origin.[8] The EC was not looking for the most substantial but for the last substantial transformation. However, the last substantial operation constitutes in this case the most substantial

---

4.   Article 5 of Regulation (EEC) No 802/68.

5.   *Zentralgenossenschaft des Fleischergewerbes v. Hauptzollamt Bochum* Case 93/83 (1984) ECR 1095.

6.   Ricoh Case (Commission Regulation (EEC) No 2071/89 of 11 July 1989 on determining the origin of photocopying apparatus, incorporating an optical system or a system of the contact type, O.J. (1989) L 196/24).

7.   *Brother International GmbH v. Hauptzollamt Giessen* Case 26/88 (1989) ECR 4253

8.   Commission Regulation (EEC) No 288/89 of 3 February 1989 on determining the origin of integrated circuits, O.J. (1989) L 33/23

transformation which, in some legal circles, has led to confusion;
- The Community has furthermore decided that the assembly of photocopiers and the manufacture of harness, drums, rollers and side-plates is not enough to confer origin.[9] The Community has applied a negative rule, since an individual case had to be decided where the result of the examination was that the operations of the company were not substantial;
- For ball bearings the assembly preceded by heat treatment, grinding and polishing of inner circles confers origin;[10]
- Furthermore, due to the complexity of assembly cases (such as for radios, TV, and tape recorders) the last substantial operation can be interpreted as implying an added-value criterion.[11] This value-added approach is expressly allowed for in the Kyoto Convention and by the European Court.

4. Procedural Aspects Concerning Nonpreferential Rules of Origin

4.1. Responsibilities of Member States

The application of nonpreferential origin rules normally falls within the competence of the customs administrations of the Member States, since no Community customs administration exists.

In the past, equal treatment of imports with regard to customs clearance in the Community has been one prominent feature of the Customs Union. With the completion of the Internal Market, this principle must be respected even more strictly.

4.2. The Role of the Committee on Origin

The Committee on Origin has to ensure that Community law on origin will be applied in a uniform matter. The Committee was set up in accordance

---

9. Supra, fn. 6.

10. Commission Regulation (EEC) No 1836/78 of 27 July 1978 concerning the determination of the origin of ball, roller or needle roller bearings, O.J. (1978) L 210/49 (amended by the Commission in Commission Regulation (EEC) No 3672/90 of 18 December 1990 on determining the origin of ball, roller or needle roller bearings, O.J. (1990) L 356/30).

11. Commission Regulation (EEC) No 2632/70 of 23 December 1970 on determining the origin of radio and television receivers, O.J. (1970) L 279/35; Commission Regulation (EEC) No 861/71 of 27 April 1971 on determining the origin of tape recorders, O.J. (1971) L 95/11.

with Article 12 of the basic Origin Regulation No. 802/68 to examine all questions related to the Regulation. It is chaired by the Commission (usually by the Head of the Origin Division of the Commission) and consists of representatives of the Member States (usually from the ministries competent for economic affairs, accompanied by customs service officials). The Committee meets, on average, about every six weeks for half a week.

4.3. The Procedure of the Committee on Origin

The procedure of the Committee is as follows:

4.3.1. Referral of a Case to the Committee

Cases are usually referred to the Committee at the request of a Member State (since it is most often Member State customs officials confronted with a particular case who will seek guidance). They may also be referred by an importer who complains about the application of rules of origin by the customs service of a Member State.

An importer may also address the Committee if he has a doubt about the origin status of a product to be manufactured or imported in the future. However, while a system of binding information does not yet exist, this is envisaged in the draft text of the GATT agreement on origin.

The Commission may also take the initiative to refer a case to the Committee (in particular in antidumping cases).

4.3.2. Preparation of the Decision

The Origin Division of the Commission carries out its own fact-finding on the case, and then submits a report to the Committee together with a reasoned proposal for a decision. At this fact-finding stage, other services inside the Commission are consulted and an on-the-spot investigation of the production procedures concerned may be carried out (as in the case of Ricoh and Mita).

4.3.3. Informal Procedure

If the Committee agrees unanimously with the Commission proposal, it is applied at once, without further action ("Informal Procedure"). Most decisions of the Committee are of this nature. They are recorded in the minutes of the Committee (Mita case).

4.3.4.   Formal Decision

If a qualified majority of the Committee agrees with the Commission proposal, it is implemented through a Commission Regulation, published in the Official Journal.

If a qualified majority in favour of the Commission proposal is not achieved, the Commission must present a proposal (which theoretically would be a modification of its original proposal) to the Council, which must take a decision by qualified majority within three months. If the Council does not act, the Commission proposal is adopted as a Commission Regulation (Ricoh case).

4.3.5.   Other

However, origin rules may also be applied directly without an informal or formal decision (Brother case).

4.4.   Judicial Review

Decisions of Member State customs authorities can be challenged by the importer before the Court of Justice of the European Communities. The matter has first to be taken to a national court, which will submit the question concerning interpretation of Community origin law before the European Court (preliminary rulings in accordance with Article 177 of the EEC Treaty).

The same procedure applies in cases where the importer is affected by a Community Regulation interpreting a rule of origin.

The importer has no right to challenge a Community Regulation if he is not directly affected by a claim for payment.

5.   Comments   on   the   International   Harmonization   of Nonpreferential Rules of Origin

5.1.   The Role of the Community

Very early on in the Uruguay Round, the Community was among those who considered that the worldwide harmonization of rules of origin would be in the interest of manufacturers, traders, exporters, importers and the public administration.   It was therefore most satisfied when, after months of negotiations, the draft text of a GATT agreement on rules of origin was established which was acceptable to all participating contracting partners. This draft agreement will be part of the package consisting of all files which are subject to the Uruguay Round.

5.2.   Content of the GATT Draft Agreement

Disciplines governing the application of rules of origin, procedural arrangements on notification, review, consultation and dispute settlement have been established.

One important part of the agreement is the harmonization of the rules of origin for the individual products. This will be one of the most ambitious and difficult international operations in customs legislation to be undertaken in recent years. Though the Uruguay Round has not yet been terminated, the Community has already studied the problem and has been discussing possible positions in the area of agriculture.

5.3.   Starting Point of the EC Deliberations on Harmonization of the Industrial Sector

The most important and complex area will be the industrial sector where, above all, the substantial transformation has to be determined for each individual product. I cannot say which position the Community will take in the negotiations in the Customs Cooperation Council and in the GATT. However, it is certain that the Community will start from the criteria set out in the draft GATT agreement. Thus the Commission will examine the question of whether a change of tariff heading can be considered as the substantial transformation.

In so doing, the Commission will insist that the harmonization will not become a political football. A biased, opportunistic approach would be the kiss of death to the rules of origin, since such a harmonization would make rules of origin useless. The harmonization must lead to coherent, uniform, impartial rules which can serve all purposes. They should not be used as instruments of commercial policy and create restrictive, distorting or disruptive effects on international trade. They must, on the other hand, be applicable to enforce measures of commercial policy such as antidumping or quantitative restrictions. If, as a result of harmonization, rules of origin may no longer be used for such purposes, they would in future be disregarded and new instruments, perhaps less impartial, may be invented to enforce measures of commercial policy. The Community will therefore see to it that the harmonization will take into account the objective and technical character of the rules of origin. If measures of commercial policy lead to unwanted effects, they have to be amended, but the rules of origin should not be manipulated according to the requirements of certain commercial scenarios which are welcome today but may have changed tomorrow.

5.4.   Need for Balanced Rules

I should like to remind you that the Community applies rules of origin for both import and export purposes. The Community will therefore strongly plead for balanced, not extreme, rules of origin as a result of the harmonization.

5.5.   One Rule for all Nonpreferential Purposes

Furthermore, the EC emphasizes the need to apply the results of the harmonization to all nonpreferential purposes. The EC would not like to see the harmonized rules of origin being limited to the MFN treatment or origin marking. Such an approach would reduce the benefit of the harmonization for international trade because a great number of Contracting Parties, among them the Community, do not need origin rules for those purposes because their liberal approach in granting MFN treatment to all products regardless of their origin, and because they do not have a general requirement that non-local products must bear an origin marking.

5.6.   Details Concerning Harmonization

As far as details are concerned, I believe that the following points will be of special interest within the harmonization exercise.

5.6.1.   Meaning of the Tariff Heading Change

The change of tariff heading will in many cases either be too strict or not strict enough. The Community already has some experience with the CTH approach, since this is the basic rule in its preferential origin rules. It has turned out that additional rules have been required in this context. In the mechanical goods chapters of the Harmonized System a change of 4 digit HS position means that assembly will confer origin e.g., for:

8407 and 8408	Natural combustion piston engines
8422	Dishwashing machines
8425	Pulley tackle and hoists
8426	Cranes
8427	Forklift trucks
8428	Lifts, escalators, conveyors, teleferics
8456	Machine tools
8469	Typewriters
8470	Calculating machines
8471	Computers

8519	Turntables
8520	Tape recorders
8521	VCRs
8527	Radios
8528	TVs
9009	Photocopiers

It must also be examined whether the assembly of motor cars will confer origin.

If a change of tariff heading were to apply on a 6-digit basis, practically all products falling within the mechanical chapters would obtain origin by assembly. I could imagine that such a situation would not be acceptable to the Community as screwdriver operations, as in the Brother typewriter case, would confer origin. The circumvention of measures of commercial policy would be facilitated too much.

I may mention that the assembly of kits does not change the tariff heading.

5.6.2. Added Value Criterion

The solution could be to add conditions such as an added value criterion. The advantages and disadvantages of such a criterion are well known. The value-added approach has the advantage of being a clear rule, particularly as the calculation of the value-added percentage is made using a rather simple formula (ex-factory price of the finished product minus the customs value of the imported parts). The disadvantages are differences in manufacturing costs between the Community and low-cost countries (a value-added approach works in favour of low-cost component suppliers), inflated profits, manipulated prices, in-house pricing (mother-daughter agreements), currency fluctuation and discounts at the end of the year. You may obtain origin today, but not tomorrow, and next week you could have origin again. However, it should not be overlooked that the important preferential trade between the EC and beneficiary partners to a large extent follows origin rules which are based on added value. The experience of many years demonstrates that such rules are transparent and simple to operate. Major problems have never occurred.

5.6.3. Concern about Divergent Classification

Many companies have already complained about the utilization of tariff headings in the area of nonpreferential rules of origin. They are afraid of divergent classification interpretations. This is not only the experience of the EC Commission, but I believe also of U.S. customs.

5.6.4.   Alternative Percentage Rule

Firms producing complicated products like chemicals and high-tech machinery believe that an alternative percentage rule should be admitted as an alternative to the application of change of tariff heading (plus additional requirements). The Community has preferential origin rules on this basis for the European Economic Area.

5.6.5.   Basis for Added Value Criterion

I personally believe that added value criteria cannot be avoided. The question to be dealt with is whether the U.S. direct manufacturing cost approach or the Community's ex-factory price rule should apply. The EC rules take into account all costs, including overheads and profits. This is simple to operate, though costs may be taken into account which have nothing to do with substantial operations. The U.S. approach of direct cost appears more justified, but its practical application appears very complicated.

5.6.6.   Conclusion

The Community will certainly find answers to these questions. Perhaps the period fixed for the accomplishment of the harmonization programme will turn out to be too ambitious, but the Community is steadfastly determined to make the harmonization exercise a success.

CHAPTER 9

Rules of Origin As Commercial Policy Instruments? — Revisited

Edwin A. Vermulst

. . . Contracting Parties shall ensure that . . . rules of origin shall not themselves create restrictive, distorting, or disruptive effects on international trade.[1]

Mexico now seems willing to accept . . . a crucial provision that any cars assembled in North America would have a 60% regional parts and labour content to qualify for [NAFTA] duty-free treatment — although auto makers may be able to count such costs as executive salaries, employee uniforms, and advertising toward local content.[2]

1. Introduction

The raison d'être for rules of origin is the existence of differentiated[3] restrictions[4] on international trade.[5] Indeed, in a completely open world economy,

---

The author would like to thank John Jackson, Friedl Mazal, Norio Komuro, Gary Horlick, Stefano Inama, John Masswohl, Wim Keizer, Hiroshi and Agnes Imagawa, Martin Rudduck, Paul Waer, Richard Gottlieb, Folkert Graafsma, David Palmeter, Peter Ginman, Teruo Ujiie, Brian Hindley and Marcel van Marion for their helpful comments on previous drafts of this chapter. However, the author is solely responsible for the contents.

1.   Article 2 (b), Agreement on Rules of Origin, Draft Final Act Embodying the Results of the Uruguay Round of Multilateral Trade Negotiations (Dunkel Text, 20 December 1991).

2.   Magnusson, *Building Free Trade Bloc by Bloc*, International Business Week, at 16 (25 May 1992).

3.   The only exception to this might be rules of origin used to support quantitative restrictions. Such quantitative restrictions are not necessarily discriminatory.

4.   An exception to this is the positive discriminatory GSP.

there would not be a demand for rules of origin because it would be immaterial where goods and services originate. Even in a less than open world economy, the prominence of rules of origin would be limited as long as trade-restrictive measures were applied across the board (i.e., on a nondiscriminatory basis).

The expanding importance *c.q.* use of rules of origin seems therefore directly correlated to three factors:

1. the surge in selective contingency protectionist measures
2. the regionalization of the world economy through the creation of trading blocs
3. the establishment of positive discriminatory measures (i.e., the GSP).

Few will contest that origin rules are an indispensable device to support the effectiveness of discriminatory trade regimes.[6] However, over the past decade, rules of origin have taken on a life of their own and arguably have developed into a means *in se* of applying trade-restrictive measures where such restrictions do not necessarily, let alone automatically, follow from the application of other trade law instruments.[7]

Thus, for example, jurisdictions such as the United States and the European Communities have used rules of origin as the legal justification for imposing antidumping duties on third country exports (sometimes retroactively) following findings that merchandise produced in such third countries had not acquired third country origin but continued to have the origin of the country with respect to which antidumping duties were imposed. As such conclusions were drawn without any investigation whether third country exports were dumped and thereby caused injury, the use of rules of origin was effectively extrapolated to construct an independent shortcut for imposing antidumping duties on exports from a third country, although the international legal basis for doing so is ambiguous, to say the least.[8]

---

5. Compare chapter 1, section 2. Rules of origin are also used for the collection of trade statistics. In such a context, however, they have not given rise to any controversy.

6. Although opinions might differ on the necessity or desirability of discriminatory trade regimes.

7. For a different perspective, see chapter 8, section 1, where Forrester takes the more traditional position that the controversy about the abuse of rules of origin is misplaced and that such controversy is rather the result of improper use of trade policy instruments.

8. Vermulst and Waer, *Anti-Diversion Rules in Antidumping Proceedings: Interface or Short-Circuit for the Management of Interdependence?* 11 Michigan Journal of International Law 201 (1990).

While the above perhaps might sound extreme, this author has argued previously[9] that rules of origin not only have the potential of developing into trade policy instruments but will in fact *q.q.* affect on international trade flows. This seems seldom accepted by importing country administrators, who tend to claim that the formulation of rules of origin and the application of such rules to concrete cases are technical exercises in which policy considerations play no role. This makes such administrators an exploitable target for domestic special interests.

All jurisdictions examined in this book distinguish between preferential and nonpreferential rules of origin as far as the origin of goods is concerned. Preferential rules of origin are used to determine whether certain products originate in a preference-receiving country and hence can qualify for preferential treatment. Nonpreferential rules of origin are used for all other purposes.

The jurisdictions analyzed here do not merely have one set of preferential and one set of nonpreferential origin rules but, with the exception of Japan, in fact also have different sets of preferential origin rules. As will be seen in section 4.2., the United States has six different sets of preferential origin rules, the European Community fourteen, Australia five, and Canada six. Clearly, this variety is a major cause for the widely perceived complexity of origin rules.

This concluding comparative chapter follows the template that was provided by the editors to the authors of the country studies: section 2 will provide a general overview of rules of origin; sections 3 and 4 will go into more detail about nonpreferential and preferential rules of origin respectively; section 5 will examine the increasing importance of rules of origin in antidumping proceedings; section 6 will summarize the use of rules of origin in other contexts. Finally, the relatively long section 7 will review the progress made in the draft Agreement[10] on rules of origin and analyze the consequences for the future.

2. General Synopsis of Rules of Origin

To determine the origin of a product, the first question is whether the product is wholly obtained or produced in one country or whether two or more countries have been involved in the manufacture of the product. If a product

---

9. Vermulst and Waer, *European Community Rules of Origin as Commercial Policy Instruments?*, 24:3 Journal of World Trade, 55-121 (1990).

10. It would appear that the rules tentatively agreed on in the Uruguay Round with respect to rules of origin will be embodied in an agreement rather than a code. Comment of Martin Rudduck (23 June 1992).

is wholly obtained or produced in one country, it evidently has the origin of that country and origin in this context has not proven controversial.

However, frequent problems arise if the origin must be determined of a product in the manufacture of which two or more countries have been involved. In such cases, the general concept is that the product will have the origin of the country where the last substantial transformation took place. There are three main methods that are used to ascertain whether substantial transformation occurred:

– an ad valorem percentage rule, often called the percentage criterion test
– a CTH test
– a technical test

The term *process criterion* is sometimes used to describe the latter two methods.[11]

Table 1 provides a schematic overview of the tests used by the five jurisdictions examined in this study.

TABLE 1.   **Tests Used in the United States, the European Community, Australia, Canada and Japan**

Type	U.S.	EC	Australia	Canada	Japan
Non-preferential	Technical test	Technical or percentage	Percentage	Percentage	CTH or technical test
Preferential	Percentage; CTH or percentage for U.S.-Canada FTA	CTH; percentage and/or technical test	Percentage	Percentage; CTH or percentage for U.S.-Canada FTA	CTH; Percentage and/or technical test

---

11.   In UNCTAD circles, the term *process criterion* is used to describe tests that do not use the *percentage criterion*. Thus, the CTH test and the technical test would both be covered by the process criterion. *Compare* Digest of Rules of Origin, UNCTAD/TAP/133/Rev.6, at 6 (1990).

2.1.   Percentage Criterion: Import Content and Domestic Content
Methods; Value-of-Parts Test

The percentage criterion surfaces in three forms. In its first form, as the import content method, it imposes a ceiling on the use of imported parts and materials through a maximum allowable percentage of such parts and materials.

In its second form, as the domestic content test, it requires a minimum percentage of local value-added in the last country in which the product was processed (but see below).

The third form, the value-of-parts test, would examine whether the originating parts reach a certain percentage of the total value of parts. As the value-of-parts test is unusual, it will not be discussed further in this chapter apart from the observation that the test appears rather unfair as it focuses only on parts values and does not take into account assembly costs and overheads in the local production operation. The value-of-parts test is used in the European Community in the product specific origin regulations for radio and television receivers and tape recorders as a subsidiary test when 45 percent value-added (the primary test) is not achieved[12] and in Article 13 (10) of the EC basic Antidumping Regulation.[13]

The percentage criterion directly[14] or indirectly[15] specifies that a certain percentage of value-added in the last production process is necessary to confer originating status; if such a percentage cannot be reached, the last production process does not give origin and origin is given to another country in the case of nonpreferential rules or to no country at all where preferential agreements are concerned.[16]

The percentage criterion, in particular the domestic content variant, requires an analysis of production costs. Before further analyzing the law and practice of the jurisdictions examined in this study, it might be useful to briefly review

---

12.   See chapter 3, sections 3.3.2.5.1.-3.3.2.5.2. The value-of-parts test is also often used by the European Community as one of the elements of mixed tests in preferential trade agreements.

13.   See Vermulst and Waer, *supra* note 8.

14.   "Pure" domestic content test.

15.   Import content test.

16.   If, for example, the last production process is performed in a GSP beneficiary country, but not enough value is added, preferential treatment will be denied without a positive determination about the "real" origin of the merchandise.

production cost items. At this point it should be noted that there are many different methods of qualifying costs of production, and the following breakdown is designed exclusively to facilitate the understanding of the reader of this chapter.[17]

Production costs can be broken down in cost of manufacture and overhead costs. The cost of manufacture, in turn, can be divided into costs of materials, direct labor costs, and manufacturing overheads.

The cost of materials is the purchase price of parts, components, etc. For the application of the percentage criterion, an important distinction exists between originating materials and non-originating materials.

As explained above, the percentage criterion calculates either the maximum allowable import content or the minimum required domestic content. In either case, the question arises at what level imported, non-originating parts ought to be valued (i.e., in ascending order: ex-works, FOB, CIF or into-factory (delivered)).[18] The answer to this question is consequential because each subsequent level leads to a higher price and thereby makes satisfaction of the import versus domestic content test more difficult.

The jurisdictions examined here value non-originating materials at their FOB[19] or CIF[20] value. A CIF valuation base means that all costs incurred from sending the parts from the factory to the importing country border would be treated as non-originating costs and that all post-border costs, such as inland freight in the importing country, customs duties, indirect taxes, etc., would be treated as originating costs. An FOB valuation base would also treat the cost of ocean freight and insurance as originating cost items.

Originating materials are normally valued on an into-factory basis.

Costs of direct labor comprise all the costs of the direct labor that can be identified or associated with the production of the merchandise, such as basic pay, overtime pay, incentive pay, bonuses, shift differentials, employee benefits such as housing, holiday pay, retirement, social security programs, and any other employee-related expenses.

Manufacturing overheads include all expenses incidental to and necessary for the production of the product, such as indirect labor, supervision, depreciation, production royalties, rent, power, maintenance and repairs,

---

17.　It does therefore not purport to be in accordance with any cost accounting standards or generally accepted accounting principles.

18.　The European Community's Article 13 (10) parts test valued non-originating (and originating) parts on an into-factory basis.

19.　United States.

20.　European Community, Australia, Canada, and Japan.

product-related R&D,[21] etc. Manufacturing overheads would normally also include the financing cost related to the production process (as opposed to the financing cost related to the sales process),[22] which typically covers the financing of raw materials and work in progress, the financing of the factory, the production line, etc.

General overhead expenses are often called selling, general, and administrative expenses or SGA. Such SGA expenses cover all other expenses incurred (typically those related to the sales process), for example, salaries of executives, telecommunication expenses, outward freight and insurance, legal and accounting fees, etc. Selling, general, and administrative expenses also cover non-operating expenses (income) such as financing costs related to the sales process and exchange loss (gain).

The addition of all these cost items gives the fully allocated cost; the fully allocated cost plus the profit gives the sales price. The import content can easily be calculated by totalling the FOB or CIF cost of all non-originating materials.

The domestic content can be calculated either by deducting the cost of non-originating materials from the sales price[23] or by adding up all items of local value-added.[24] These two calculation methods would in theory lead to the same result. In practice, however, that is not always the case: certain sets of rules of origin, such as the Canadian and Japanese GSP rules and the European Community's preferential rules to the extent that they rely on percentage criteria, use an import content rule that sets a maximum allowable percentage of imported materials.[25] An import content rule of for example, 40 percent equals a 60 percent domestic content test, and the two calculation methods therefore yield the same result.

However, other sets of rules of origin, such as the U.S. preferential and Australian GSP rules and EC, Australian, and Canadian nonpreferential rules,

---

21. Non-product-related R&D will generally be included in the SGA expenses as general expenses.

22. The financing cost related to the sales process would normally be reported as an SGA expense.

23. This is done under the European Community's and Canada's GSP rules and also under other EC preferential arrangements. See, for example, with respect to ACP, Protocol I of Lomé IV.

24. This is done under the U.S. and Australian GSP rules.

25. *Compare* Consultations on Harmonization and Improvement of the Rules of Origin, Report by the UNCTAD Secretariat, TD/B/C.5/141, at 6 (1992).

rely on a domestic content rule under which a minimum of domestic content must be achieved. In the United States and Australia, not all domestic content is considered relevant for GSP qualification purposes and the two calculation methods will therefore yield different results. The same observation applies regarding Australian and Canadian nonpreferential rules.

TABLE 2.   **Import Content vs. Domestic Content Methods in the U.S., the EC, Australia, Canada and Japan**

Type	U.S.	EC	Australia	Canada	Japan
Nonpreferential	NA	Technical or domestic content	Domestic content	Domestic content	NA
Preferential	Domestic content; CTH or domestic content for U.S.-Canada FTA	Import content	Domestic content	Import content for GSP/ LDDC; domestic content in other cases	Import content

The sales price as such is seldom used as the denominator in percentage criterion tests. Most jurisdictions rather rely on other denominators that require certain adjustments to be made to the sales price. To give a few examples:

The EC uses an ex-works price. The ex-works price is the price of the product at the moment that it leaves the factory; it is equal to the sales price with the exception of post-factory charges if such charges are included in the price. If, for example, the conditions of a certain sale are US$ 100, CIF thirty days, the sales price of $ 100 includes the cost of inland freight in the exporting country, the cost of the ocean or air freight and of the insurance from the manufacturer's premises to the importing country border as well as a thirty-day credit cost borne by the manufacturer. Such costs must then be deducted from the sales price to arrive at the ex-works price.

The Japanese GSP relies in part on the FOB export price. The FOB export price is the ex-works price plus the cost of inland freight and any handling costs incurred in the exporting country.

Thus, the sales price may be, but is not always, identical to the ex-works or the FOB price; it depends on the terms and conditions of sale.

TABLE 3.   Denominators Used to Calculate Percentages in the United States, the European Community, Australia, Canada, and Japan

Type	U.S.	EC	Australia	Canada	Japan
Nonpreferential	NA	Exworks price	Factory cost	Cost of production	NA
Preferential	Appraised value of merchandise as it enters the U.S.	Exworks price	Factory cost	Exfactory price for GSP/ LDDC; cost of production in other cases	FOB export price

It will be clear already from the above that there are many variations between jurisdictions with respect to both the constituent elements (the numerator) and the denominator of the percentage criterion. Furthermore, the allowable import or required domestic percentages are often different, even within each jurisdiction, where they appear to depend on the objective of the law that they are designed to support.

United States preferential *domestic content* calculations include the cost or value of originating materials[26] and direct costs of processing operations, defined as those costs that are either directly incurred in or can be reasonably allocated to the growth, production, manufacture, or assembly of the specific merchandise under consideration. Such costs include

1.   actual labor costs, including fringe benefits, on-the-job training, and the cost of engineering, supervisory, quality control, and similar personnel;

2.   costs of dies, molds, tooling, and depreciation on machinery and equipment that can be allocated to specific merchandise;

---

26.   With the possible benefit of the dual substantial transformation criterion, see chapter 2, section 4.2.1.1. Cost of originating materials includes (1) the manufacturer's actual cost for the materials; (2) the freight, insurance, packing, and all other costs incurred in transporting the materials to the manufacturer's plant, if these are not already included in the manufacturer's actual cost for the materials; (3) the actual cost of waste or spoilage, less the value of the recoverable scrap; and (4) taxes and duties imposed on materials, provided they are not remitted on exportation. If a material is provided to the manufacturer without charge or at less than fair market price, the cost or value is determined by computing the sum of (1) all expenses incurred in the production, manufacture, or assembling of materials including general expenses; (2) an amount for profit; and (3) freight, insurance, packing, and all other costs incurred in transporting the materials to the manufacturer's plant. *See* Digest of Rules of Origin, UNCTAD/TAP/133/Rev.6, at 10 (1990).

3. research, development, design, engineering, and blueprint costs to the extent allocable to the specific merchandise; and
4. the cost of inspecting and testing the specific merchandise.

The U.S. domestic content therefore does not include SGA expenses and profit.[27]

The denominator is the appraised value of the product when it enters the United States. The appraised value is normally determined on the basis of the transaction value, which is the price actually paid or payable by the importer plus, if not included in the price, packing costs incurred by the buyer, selling commissions incurred by the buyer, the value of any assist,[28] any royalties or license fees that are part of the conditions of sale, and the proceeds to the seller of any subsequent resale, disposal, or use of the imported merchandise. Not included are CIF costs, costs or charges incurred after importation and customs duties, and other federal taxes.[29] The denominator therefore is essentially a species of the price at exportation[30] which includes local SGA and profit, although these are not counted as domestic content. The appraised value is determined by the U.S. Customs Service. This means that it will not always be possible for a foreign producer or exporter to determine with certainty in advance whether or not he or she meets the domestic content percentage.

The EC denominator sticks closest to the ex-works price advocated in Recommended Practice 5 of the Kyoto Convention's Annex D.1[31] because

---

27. *See* ibid. Such overhead costs include administrative salaries, casualty and liability insurance, advertising, salesmen's salaries, commissions, and expenses.

28. Assists are items of value (e.g. tools, dies, moulds, etc.). that are provided directly or indirectly by the importer or buyer to the producer at less than full cost or value for use in the production of the imported article. *See* Handbook on Major United States Trade Laws, UNCTAD/TAP/277/Rev.1, at 3 (1989).

29. *See* ibid. at 5-6 (1989).

30. Compare the commentary to Recommended Practice 5 in Annex D.1 of the Kyoto Convention providing that signatories ought to use either the exworks price or the price at exportation. The price at exportation is defined as either the appraised value at importation or the FOB value.

31. Recommended Practice 5 provides that for the calculation of domestic content percentages, imported materials shall be valued at the dutiable value at importation (normally the CIF price) and produced goods shall be valued at the ex-works price or the price at exportation. It is clear that of the countries analyzed in this study, only the United States and Japan use the price at exportation. In fact, the relevant Japanese regulation explicitly refers to a FOB export price (see chapter 6, section 4.1.2.). Although Annex D.1 does not express a preference for the ex-works price over the price at exportation, there would appear to be a

it encompasses, in addition to the costs of materials, direct labor and manufacturing overheads: net SGA,[32] royalties,[33] packing,[34] and profit[35] of the production unit.[36] The European Community's preferential rules of origin often rely on an import content test to supplement the CTH method.[37] In the non-preferential area, the domestic content is in practice often an important factor in the EC informal procedure, especially in assembly cases.[38] As the numerator in the European Community's domestic content

---

certain consensus that the ex-works price is more appropriate. *See, e.g.*, CCC, Permanent Technical Committee, Rules of Origin of Goods, Secretariat Note, 29.215E T7-3231, at 20 (2 November 1982).

32. Net SGA expenses in this chapter means SGA expenses excluding SGA costs incurred after the product left the factory, such as outward inland freight, international transportation and insurance (if the product is sold CIF), customs duties (if the product is sold on a delivered basis), etc.

33. When royalties are payable by the production operation to a parent or related company, the European Community will normally check whether the royalties are reasonable.

34. Compare the Ninth standard *jo*. Recommended Practice 10 in Annex D.1, which taken together would seem to indicate not only that the origin of the packing follows the origin of the product but also that packing should be taken into account in the calculation of domestic content where the goods concerned are ordinarily sold by retail (see chapter 3, section 3.2.2.).

35. The Kyoto Convention refers to the ex-works price, not the ex-works cost and therefore, in the view of this author, clearly establishes that it is concerned with the price, which includes profit. With respect to EC practice, it must be noted that the EC authorities routinely examine whether the profit is reasonable, especially where sales are made between related parties.

36. Compare chapter 3, section 3.2.2. in which Waer concludes on the basis of the Eleventh Standard providing that ". . . no account shall be taken of the origin of the energy, plant, machinery and tools used in the manufacturing . . . of the goods" that ". . . depreciation, lease and rental payments and royalties relating to non-originating plant, machinery and tools should be counted as local value-added."

37. Since the 1988 introduction of the single list, the percentage criterion is no longer used in parallel to the CTH. Thus, under the pre-1988 system, all working and processing in List A had to be performed in addition to the CTH. However, since 1988, CTH is only required for goods covered by an entry in this list if it is explicitly required by the entry.

38. The local domestic content is then calculated by deducting the cost of nonoriginating materials from the exworks price. There is no definition of the exworks price in the nonpreferential area, but under EC preferential rules, the ex-works price is typically defined as the price paid for the product obtained to the manufacturer in whose undertaking the last working or processing is carried out, provided that the price includes the value of the

test is the exact mirror image of the numerator in the European Community's import content test, both methods lead to similar results. For example, a domestic content of 60 percent is identical to an import content of 40 percent in the EC system.

Australian rules of origin predominantly rely on different domestic content percentages that are calculated as a percentage of the factory or works cost (see chapter 4, section 2.3.3.). Domestic content includes the cost of originating materials received into factory (excluding duties and taxes paid or payable in the country of manufacture of the goods in respect of such materials), manufacturing wages, factory overhead expenses, and the cost of inner containers, but excludes SGA expenses and profit.[39] The denominator is composed of the domestic content plus the CIF cost of non-originating materials (excluding duties and taxes paid or payable in the country of manufacture of the goods in respect of such materials).

Canadian nonpreferential and certain preferential[40] rules of origin require a domestic content percentage of 50 percent of the cost of production. The denominator cost of production comprises the cost of originating and non-originating materials (exclusive of duties and taxes) and labor and factory overheads but excludes profit, export packing expenses (as opposed to the packing in which the goods are normally sold for consumption), royalties, transportation and insurance costs to the point of direct shipment to Canada, customs duties, and any other costs or charges arising after the completion of the manufacture of the goods. The domestic content consists of these same items with the exception of the cost of non-originating materials.

The Japanese GSP partly relies on an import content test that is very similar[41] to that of the European Community's preferential origin rules.

Table 4 provides a schematic overview of the elements of domestic content in the five jurisdictions analyzed.

---

originating materials used in manufacture, minus any internal taxes which are, or may be, repaid when the product obtained is exported. *See, e.g.*, Article 3 of Protocol 1 of Lomé IV. The same definition is used in practice to determine nonpreferential origin.

39.   Ibid.

40.   See section 4.2. However, Canada's GSP and LDDC schemes effectively require a domestic content of 60 and 40 percent respectively of the ex factory price. (Technically, Canada's GSP and LDDC schemes are based on the import content rule and require that import content may not be more than 40 and 60 percent respectively.) See further section 4.2.

41.   However, the denominator is the FOB export price and not the ex-works price.

TABLE **4.** **Elements of Domestic Content (Numerator) in the United States, the European Community, Australia, Canada, and Japan**

	U.S.[a]	EC[b]	Australia[c]	Canada[d]	Japan[e]
Originating materials	x	x	x	x	x
Taxes and duties paid on such materials but refunded on export[f]	x	x	x	x	x
Direct labor	x	x	x	x	x
Manufacturing overheads	x	x	x	x	x
Inner containers	x	x	x	x	x
Other packing expenses	x	x	—	—	x
(SGA expenses)					
Royalties[g]	x	x	—	—	x
Transportation[h]	—[i]	—	—	—	—[j]
Insurance	—[k]	—	—	—	—[l]
Customs duties	—	—	—	—	—
Others [net SGA expenses]	—	x	—	—	x
Profit	—	x	—	—	x

Note:

x = included

— = excluded

[a] Preferential.

[b] Nonpreferential (informal procedure) and preferential to supplement CTH.

[c] Preferential and nonpreferential.

[d] Nonpreferential and preferential (with the exception of GSP and LDDC schemes and only as a supplementary test in the U.S.-Canada FTA).

[e] Technically, Japan uses an import content test as a supplementary test to the CTH in its GSP scheme. The domestic content has therefore been constructed by deducting the CIF cost of imported materials from the sales price.

[f] To the extent not refunded on exportation.

[g] If not included in manufacturing overheads.

[h] Including outward inland transportation.

[i] The United States would include inland freight in the exporting country but would not include ocean freight. As inland freight in the exporting country is normally very small, it has been ignored here.

[j] Japan would include inland freight in the exporting country but would not include ocean freight. As inland freight in the exporting country is normally very small, it has been ignored here.

[k] The United States would include insurance in the exporting country but would not include international insurance. As insurance in the exporting country is normally very small, it has been ignored here.

[l] Japan would include insurance in the exporting country but would not include international insurance. As insurance in the exporting country is normally very small, it has been ignored here.

The calculation of the percentage of domestic content then becomes a relatively simple calculation: one adds up the items mentioned above as "included" and the customs value on the importation of non-originating materials to calculate the denominator.[42] The cost items included in the table are then divided by the denominator and multiplied by 100 to calculate the percentage of domestic content. It might be clear from the above that the same facts will lead to different domestic content ratios in the five jurisdictions. Table 5 shows this on the basis of a concrete example:

Ceteris paribus, the EC and Japanese domestic content calculation methods are therefore more liberal than the domestic content calculation methods of the other jurisdictions. They are also the most logical in that they focus on the price of the product as it leaves the factory and therefore count local SGA expenses and profit as domestic content, provided that they are reasonable.

In turn, the Japanese system is slightly more favorable than the EC system. The Japanese denominator is the FOB price rather than the exworks price of the merchandise. Although the denominator is higher, the domestic content will also be higher because the inland freight and insurance in the exporting country are counted as local content. The drawback of using the FOB price is that it provides an unjustified, albeit slight, advantage to companies that are located further from a port. For example, if the port of shipment is Pusan, Korea, the Japanese calculation method will give a company located in Incheon a slight edge over a company located in Taegu because the transportation cost from Incheon to Pusan will be higher than the transportation cost from Taegu to Pusan.

The U.S. method effectively leads to a local cost added that is cut off at the ex-assembly line point. This cost is then divided by the price at exportation, which is jacked up by the inclusion of local SGA expenses and profit. The combination of the two methods deflates domestic content.

Australian and Canadian practice also calculates an ex-assembly line cost but at least divides it by an appropriate denominator, which is established at the same level.

Apart from this lack of uniformity in applying the percentage criterion among jurisdictions, a disadvantage of the percentage criterion is that it penalizes low cost or efficient production operations where labor or assembly costs are lower than in high cost c.q. inefficient facilities.[43] Thus, for

---

42.   In the United States, however, all items mentioned in Table 4 whether or not included in the local domestic content, will be included in the denominator with the exception of SGA expense items such as CIF costs and customs duties in the United States.

43.   See Vermulst and Waer, *supra* note 9.

TABLE 5.   Domestic Content Calculation in the United States, the European Community, Australia, Canada, and Japan

	U.S.	EC[a]	Australia	Canada[b]	Japan[c]
Originating materials	80	80	80	80	80
Taxes and duties paid	5	5	5	5	5
Direct labor	20	20	20	20	20
Manufacturing overheads	20[d]	15	15	15	20[e]
Inner containers	2	2	2	2	2
Other packing expenses	2	2	2[f]	~~2~~	2
(SGA expenses	~~30~~	~~30~~	~~30~~	~~30~~	~~30~~)
Royalties[g]	4	4	4	4	4
Transportation	~~10~~[h]	~~10~~	~~10~~	~~10~~	~~10~~[i]
Insurance	1[j]	~~1~~	~~1~~	~~1~~	~~1~~[k]
Customs duties	0	~~0~~	~~0~~	~~0~~	~~0~~
Net SGA	15	15	~~15~~	~~15~~	15
Profit	~~10~~	10	~~10~~	~~10~~	10
Nonoriginating materials	~~95~~[l]	~~100~~[m]	~~100~~[m]	~~100~~[m]	~~100~~[l]
Denominator	253[n]	253[o]	222[p]	222[q]	253[r]
Domestic content amount	133	153	122	122	153
Domestic content percentage	52.6%	60.5%	55%	55%	60.5%

Note:

[a] Nonpreferential rules.

[b] Not applicable to GSP or LDDC schemes.

[c] Technically, Japan uses an import content test. The domestic content has therefore been constructed by deducting the cost of imported materials from the sales price.

[d] This includes the CIF costs of imported materials.

[e] This includes the CIF costs of imported materials.

[f] "Strike out" has been used to indicate that items are not included in local domestic content.

[g] If not included in manufacturing overheads.

[h] The United States would include inland freight in the exporting country but would not include ocean freight. As inland freight in the exporting country is normally very small, it has been ignored here.

[i] Japan would include inland freight in the exporting country but would not include ocean freight. As inland freight in the exporting country is normally very small, it has been ignored here.

[j] The United States would include insurance in the exporting country but would not include international insurance. As insurance in the exporting country is normally very small, it has been ignored here.

[k] Japan would include insurance in the exporting country but would not include international insurance. As insurance in the exporting country is normally very small, it has been ignored here.
[l] FOB price.
[m] CIF price.
[n] Appraised value of the product when it enters the United States.
[o] Ex-works price.
[p] Factory cost.
[q] Cost of production.
[r] FOB export price. The FOB export price is the same as the European Community's ex works price with the addition of inland freight and insurance in the exporting country. As these tend to be rather small, they have been ignored in the calculation example.

example, it is easier for a color television producer to reach 45 percent domestic content in the European Community than in Thailand. Furthermore, domestic content and import content calculations can change constantly as a result of fluctuations in world market prices for raw materials[44] and in exchange rates. Finally, domestic content calculations provide a certain amount of discretion to administrators[45] and technically would require detailed on-the-spot visits to check the accuracy of data provided.

In general, the import content test seems preferable over the domestic content test because it is easier to apply and leaves the importing country administrators with less discretion.

2.2. Change in Tariff Heading test

The CTH test confers origin if the manufacture results in a product that falls under a — normally four digit — HS number that is different from the

44. This is especially the case with respect to primary commodities whose prices tend to fluctuate widely almost as a matter of course.

45. The Honda dispute under the U.S.-Canada FTA provides good examples of this. A main bone of contention in the dispute between the United States and Canada about cars produced in Canada by Honda is the position of U.S. Customs that North American content includes the amount "paid" for North American materials and that, since Honda produces some of the materials itself in North America, it does not "pay" for them. The value of such materials was therefore not included, although the value of Japanese subparts was. See chapter 2, section 4.2.6.1.1., where Palmeter terms this the "intermediate material" issue. A second issue was whether the cost of die casting and machining qualified as processing costs or as assembling costs. U.S. Customs decided the former and therefore did not count such costs as North American value added. Palmeter's lengthy analysis of the Honda decision concludes that it is an "excellent example of the shortcomings of value added as a standard for determining origin."

numbers under which the non-originating parts or materials fall. The CTH test is the primary test for the European Community's preferential origin rules and for the U.S.-Canada FTA. Japanese nonpreferential rules of origin by and large also use the CTH test.

The advantages of the CTH test are its conceptual simplicity, its ease of application, and its lack of discretion. Furthermore, the adoption by most countries[46] of the HS system means that a similarly applied CTH test[47] normally leads to uniform determinations of origin in such countries. It is therefore convenient that it was decided early on in the Uruguay Round negotiations, at U.S. insistence,[48] that any harmonization of nonpreferential rules of origin delegated to the CCC be principally based on the HS CTH test (see section 7.3).

However, the HS system is primarily designed as a dual-purpose commodity classification and statistics system and might therefore not always be an appropriate basis for conferring originating status. Importing country administrators realized that early on and have recognized two lists of exceptions: (1) a list of products for which a CTH is not sufficient to confer origin but for which origin furthermore depends on a domestic content or import content requirement and/or a requirement that specific manufacturing operations are carried out or materials sourced (obligatory input test) in the country in which the last production process takes place and (2) a list of exceptions with processing operations sufficient to confer origin even if they do not lead to a CTH.

Another drawback of the CTH test is that it requires indepth knowledge of the HS not only on the part of exporting country administrators (not necessarily customs experts) but also on the part of producers and exporters, for both the finished products and the raw materials.[49] This point is often made in UNCTAD discussions about the functioning of the GSP.

---

46. As of 15 May 1992, the HS Code had sixty-six signatories. At least twenty-nine countries use the HS on a de facto basis.

47. This is presently not the case. For example, under the U.S.-Canada FTA, the CTH may vary from a two-digit chapter level change to an eight-digit statistical level change.

48. This is perhaps surprising as the United States "discovered" the existence of the CTH test fairly late and first adopted it only in the U.S.-Canada FTA.

49. Comment Friedl Mazal (21 May 1992).

2.3.   Technical test

The technical test prescribes certain production or sourcing processes that may (positive test) or may not (negative test) confer originating status. The technical test is used in the United States in the nonpreferential and preferential area, in the latter case in combination with a domestic content test, and by the EC in the majority of nonpreferential product specific origin regulations.

The advantage of the technical test is that of the three tests, it is best equipped to deal with the specifics of the situation at hand. However, it is also most easily abused by domestic interests as the U.S. Department of Commerce and EC determinations that the origin of integrated circuits depends on the place of diffusion show. Furthermore, it is extremely complicated to devise all kinds of technical tests for an enormous array of products. Third, it appears difficult to verify the information on specific production processes performed in third countries.[50]

An additional drawback of the negative technical test is that it only delineates those production or sourcing processes that do not confer origin and therefore leaves unanswered whether other production or sourcing processes do. This shortcoming causes obvious uncertainty. The EC product-specific origin regulation for photocopiers (Ricoh rule) (see section 5) is a good example. The Draft Agreement on rules of origin in principle prohibits the use of negative technical tests[51] but immediately makes two exceptions that would still allow negative technical tests (1) as part of a clarification of a positive test or (2) in individual cases in which a positive determination of origin is not necessary. The wording of the second exception would still appear to leave importing country authorities substantial discretion to resort to negative technical tests.

3.   Nonpreferential Rules of Origin

3.1.   Procedure

In the United States, the U.S. Customs Service, an agency under the jurisdiction of the Department of the Treasury, is responsible for the application of most rules of origin (see chapter 2, sections 3.-3.1.2.). Palmeter points out that the Customs Service must make an origin determination on every import at the time of entry as part of the agency's enforcement of the

---

50.   Comment Wim Keizer (22 May 1992).

51.   Article 2 (f), *supra* note 1.

marking law (see chapter 2, section 3.1.1.). Decisions of the Customs Service on protests may be appealed to the CTI.[52]

Under U.S. law, exporters or importers may obtain a prospective ruling from the Customs Service before importation.[53] Such rulings are issued in the form of letters addressed to the parties but may be published in the Customs Bulletin as a Customs Service Decision[54] or in the Federal Register as a Treasury Decision.[55] Palmeter notes that draft Treasury Decisions are published in the Federal Register with a request for comments from interested parties before they are adopted.[56]

A result of the division of powers in the European Community between the EC institutions and the Member States is that an intricate decision-making process exists in which both the EC Commission and Member States officials play an important role (see chapter 3, sections 3.1.-3.1.3.). The EC basic Origin Regulation establishes an Origin Committee consisting of representatives of the Member States with a Commission official, normally the Head of Division of Directorate-General XXI, Directorate B, Division 2, presiding.

As the complicated — and generally lengthy — administrative procedure is described in detail by Waer,[57] suffice it here to point out the distinction between the formal procedure in which, at the end of the day, the Commission plays the predominant role and the informal procedure under which the Member States make decisions by consensus. While the product-specific origin rules that have ensued from the formal procedure have been published in the Official Journal, consensual decisions taken in the informal procedure have not been published.

Although the basic Origin Regulation does not foresee this, in recent years foreign exporters have started to voluntarily submit data to the EC Commission and the Origin Committee with a view to obtaining a clear-cut unanimous ruling from the Committee in the informal procedure before

---

52. Decisions of the CIT may be appealed to the CAFC; judgments of the CAFC may be appealed to the Supreme Court, which decides autonomously whether it will accept the appeal (see chapter 2, section 3.1.).

53. Ibid.

54. If the ruling has a broader interest, ibid.

55. If the ruling involves a significant matter of policy, ibid.

56. Ibid.

57. *See* chapter 3, section 3.1.1. See also Vermulst and Waer *supra* note 9.

shipments start.[58] While time-consuming,[59] this practice has the advantages that administrative decisions on origin tend to be made on a technical depoliticized basis and that an undesirable decision may still be changed if the producer is willing to change production or sourcing strategy.

A company adversely affected by an origin determination of a Member State's administration, the Origin Committee, or the EC Commission may not directly challenge the determination in the European Court of Justice (ECJ) because, in the view of the ECJ, it will not be directly and individually concerned in the sense of Article 173 (2) of the EEC treaty. Rather, such a company must resort to legal action in the Member State(s) (see chapter 3, section 3.1.2.). The national courts may or must refer the matter to the ECJ. This means that a foreign producer who has customs cleared in several EC Member States may be engaged in simultaneous litigation in several Member States, as was the case with Yoshida in 1978 and, still ongoing, with Brother. The EC system with respect to judicial review in origin matters not only is incredibly expensive and time-consuming for affected parties but also may lead to inconsistent judgments by national courts, at least in the first instance.

In Australia, origin determinations are made by the Customs Service (chapter 4, section 3.1.1.). It would appear that in most cases Customs Service decisions on nonpreferential determinations of origin may not be appealed either to the Administrative Appeals Tribunal or to the Federal Court of Australia (chapter 4, section 3.1.2.). It is at present unclear whether an appeal to the High Court of Australia or to a state supreme court would be admissible.

As Canadian tariff law, like the tariff laws of most other jurisdictions, distinguishes between the GT and the MFN tariff (chapter 5, section 2), Gottlieb correctly classifies the MFN tariff as a preferential tariff.[60] For purposes of uniformity, however, we will classify the origin rules pertaining to the MFN tariff as nonpreferential in this comparative chapter.

Rules of origin legislation and regulations fall under the jurisdiction of the Department of Finance and are administered by the DNR in Canada. Until 1988, Canadian "investigations of origin were conducted informally and

---

58. In chapter 3, section 3.1.1. Waer appropriately terms this *producer specific investigations*.

59. Thus, for example, a submission should normally be made for each model. For advanced electronic products with frequent model changes, this implies a continuous process.

60. See chapter 5, section 2. Canada applies its MFN tariff to all countries with the exception of Albania, Libya, Oman, North Korea, and Mongolia.

determinations were made by administrative dictate."[61] This changed with the adoption of the U.S.-Canada FTA: the Customs Tariff was amended and a formal procedure adopted for determinations of origin.

The origin of imported goods may be determined by Canada Customs before or within thirty days after importation.[62] Such a determination is final unless the Minister of the DNR makes a redetermination within two years after importation at the request of the importer (a TVA decision) (see chapter 5, section 4.9.2.). The redetermination may be appealed before the federal court on points of law. Furthermore, on request, the DNR is willing to give a nonbinding origin opinion.[63]

In Japan, rules of origin are adopted by the Ministry of Finance (MOF) in the form of administrative circulars (see chapter 6, section 3.1.1.2.). The rules are applied by Japanese customs. A decision by Japanese customs may be protested within two months. A negative decision on the protest may be appealed to the Minister of Finance. A decision of the latter may be appealed to the court.

A comparison of the country studies indicates that nonpreferential (and preferential) rules of origin are administered by customs authorities (but see sections 5. and 6.) and that the procedural system is most complete and transparent in the United States.[64] In particular, advance publication of draft Treasury Decisions ought to be singled out as a laudable practice that deserves adoption by other jurisdictions. Furthermore, the advance ruling procedure, which would become mandatory if the GATT Agreement on rules of origin were to be adopted, presently exists officially only in the United States. In the European Community, a ruling request is possible in practice. Finally, with the exception of the United States and Japan, satisfactory judicial review of nonpreferential origin determinations appears absent.

---

61. Gottlieb, chapter 5, section 4.9.

62. If no such determination is made, it is deemed to have been made thirty days after importation in accordance with the origin declared by the importer. Paraphrase of Gottlieb, Chapter 5, section 4.9.1.

63. Comment John Masswohl (13 July 1992).

64. On the other hand, U.S. practice, based largely on case law, makes it difficult to derive firm conclusions that might be applied to other similar, but not identical, cases. Comment of Friedl Mazal (21 May 1992); compare section 3.2.

3.2. Substantive law

The basic nonpreferential rule of origin in the United States is substantial transformation (chapter 2, section 3). Substantial transformation has been defined by the U.S. Supreme Court[65] as requiring the emergence from the manufacturing process of "a new and different article with a distinctive name, character or use."[66]

From Palmeter's overview of case law, it would appear that the U.S. non-preferential rules of origin essentially use a technical test to determine whether substantial transformation occurs. This test is applied case by case. Palmeter notices that neither the courts nor the Customs Service have managed to come up with a consistent interpretation of the definition (chapter 2, sections 3.2.1.-3.2.2.3.).

An interesting question in the United States has been whether the policy objective of a statute should have a bearing on the degree of substantial transformation required to confer nonpreferential origin (see chapter 2, section 3.2.2.1. and section 4.2. of this chapter). In other words, should it make a difference for the degree of substantial transformation whether the origin is determined on the basis of the duty drawback provisions, the origin marking statute, MFN tariff rates, VRAs, textile quotas, etc.? In Palmeter's view, neither the administration nor the courts have been able to come up with an unequivocal answer to this question.[67]

Article 5 of the EC basic non-preferential Origin Regulation provides that a product in the manufacture of which two or more countries were involved originates in the country in which

1. the last substantial process or operation,
2. that is economically justified was performed,
3. having been carried out in an undertaking equipped for the purpose and
4. resulting in the manufacture of a new product or representing an important stage of manufacture (see chapter 3, section 3.3.1.1.).

A review of product-specific origin regulations (chapter 3, sections 3.3.2.-3.3.2.11.) and judgments of the ECJ (chapter 3, sections 3.3.1.-3.3.1.7.)

---

65. *Anheuser-Busch Brewing Association v. United States*, 207 U.S. 556 (1907), as quoted in chapter 2, section 1. *jo.* section 3.2.1.

66. Ibid.

67. See also section 7. While the United States in the Uruguay Round proposed uniform rules of origin for preferential and nonpreferential purposes, the European Community proposed uniform rules for all nonpreferential purposes.

reveals that the EC institutions and the Origin Committee prefer the technical test for determining nonpreferential origin. Value-added percentages may be relevant, but only as a subsidiary factor when the technical test does not lead to a conclusive answer.[68] In the European Community, technical tests have sometimes had the effect of protecting domestic producers; the product-specific origin regulations with respect to zippers, integrated circuits, and photocopiers all resulted, advertently or not, in conferring Japanese origin on such products manufactured by Japanese companies in the European Community (zippers and integrated circuits) or in third countries (integrated circuits and photocopiers). The regulation for ball bearings might have had the same outcome, although this is not known to the author.

An informal opinion by the EC Origin Committee issued in connection with the product specific origin rule regarding radio and television receivers furthermore contains the arresting assumption that, for the purpose of applying the 45 percent value-added test, the cost of assembly, finishing and control plus profit and general costs are to be estimated as representing an aggregate of 40 percent of the ex-works invoice price of radio receivers and 35 percent of the ex-works invoice price of television receivers; that is for radios and televisions manufactured in the European Community and intended for export "given the relative homogeneity within the Community of the industry in question" (for the literal text of the opinion, see chapter 3, section 3.3.2.5.1.).

This is convenient for EC producers such as Philips, Grundig, and Thomson, that will have little trouble in reaching 45 percent value-added on the basis of the assumption that assembly costs sensu lato already represent 40 and 35 percent respectively. Foreign producers, on the other hand, wishing to export to the European Community free of trade restrictions such as antidumping duties and Article 115 quotas may not use this assumption but must calculate assembly and related costs on the basis of their actual situation. In low-cost countries such as South Korea, Thailand, Malaysia, Hong Kong, and China, assembly costs are in most cases far below the percentages assumed for the EC industry, and origin therefore effectively depends, at least for televisions, on the origin of the picture tube, which can easily represent 35 percent of the ex-works price.[69]

---

68.   Chapter 3, section 3.3.1.7. Indeed, one could argue that even the product-specific origin regulations for radio and television receivers and tape recorders focus on a technical test by providing as the first test that assembly representing 45 percent value added confers origin.

69.   Color picture tubes are produced in a limited number of countries only, such as Japan, Korea, the European Community, Malaysia, and China.

Australian law stipulates as the general nonpreferential rule (for exceptions, see chapter 4, section 2.2.) that goods are the manufacture of the country where the last process of manufacture occurred, provided that not less than 75 percent of the factory or works cost of the goods is represented by the value of labor or materials or of labor and materials of Australia and that country (see chapter 4, section 3.2.1. and section 2.2.). The 75 percent requirement may be reduced to 25 percent for goods of a kind not produced in Australia (see chapter 4, section 2.2.).

The Australian rule is interesting for several reasons. First, Australia is one of the few jurisdictions examined in this book that primarily relies on a domestic content test for determining nonpreferential origin, and a very high one at that. The manner in which the ACS calculates domestic content (see Table 3) is more restrictive than that of the European Community and as restrictive as the Canadian rule so that the Australian nonpreferential rules of origin are probably the most trade-restrictive of those examined here.

Second, the possible cumulation of third-country and Australian originating materials or the donor country concept,[70] to borrow a GSP phrase, at first sight might appear to alleviate the high domestic content requirement, but it is also a blatant local content notion. And while the donor country concept does not necessarily violate GATT in the context of the GSP,[71] it would certainly appear to run afoul of GATT's national treatment principle on the application of nonpreferential rules of origin.[72] The reason is that the concept stimulates Australian rather than third-country sourcing; it therefore puts Australian industry in a relatively advantageous position.

Finally, the possibility for Australian authorities to decrease the domestic content percentage from 75 to 25 percent in cases in which Australian industry does not produce the merchandise in question is commendable although probably devoid of meaning in practice: when certain products are not manufactured in the importing country, the origin of the imports is unlikely to become a significant issue.

Canada's MFN rules of origin (compare section 3.1.) also rely on a domestic content test but one appreciably lower than its Australian counterpart: at least 50 percent of the cost of producing (as defined in section

---

70. Under the donor country rule, materials sourced in the preference-giving country may be counted as originating materials.

71. The legal basis for the GSP is a 1971 GATT waiver to the MFN obligation of Article I of GATT.

72. While at present rules of origin do not fall within the jurisdiction of GATT, the adoption of the Draft Agreement would necessitate changes in Australian law in this respect.

2.1.) the imported goods must be incurred in the country or countries that benefit from the MFN tariff or in Canada (see chapter 5, section 4.1.1.1.). The donor country concept therefore also surfaces in Canadian nonpreferential origin rules. However, as Canadian law allows unlimited cumulation between MFN countries, the national treatment problem would not appear to arise here.

Japanese nonpreferential rules of origin are based on the CTH test with modifications in the form of a positive list[73] and a negative list of minimal processing operations.[74] Komuro points out (in chapter 6, section 3.1.3.1.) that nonpreferential rules of origin have not given rise to controversy in Japan, presumably because Japan has few discriminatory trade regimes, the enforcement of which depends on rules of origin.

4. Preferential Rules of Origin

The best-known preferential trading regime is the GSP. However, this book shows that all jurisdictions examined here, with the exception of Japan, have concluded a variety of preferential trading agreements, with the European Community leading the pack. In all instances, the preferential trade agreements contain their own sets of origin rules.

Preferential rules of origin are relevant only for determining whether products manufactured in the preference-receiving country qualify for preferential treatment. In other words, they are completely immaterial for determining whether the same products fall within the scope of trade-restrictive measures such as quotas, antidumping duties, etc.

For example, a determination whether compact disc players manufactured in Malaysia qualify for the GSP is made on the basis of the GSP preferential origin rules under which ASEAN-produced materials (for the United States, the European Community, or Japan) or all beneficiary countries' materials (for Australia or Canada) could be cumulated. A determination whether the Malaysian production of the same compact disc players by a Japanese producer constitutes third-country circumvention of antidumping duties imposed on compact disc players originating in Japan, on the other hand, will be made in the European Community and the United States on the basis of the nonpreferential origin rules (in which cumulation is not possible) or in the United States on the basis of the specially enacted third country circumvention provisions.

---

73. Processing operations that confer origin even if they do not result in a CTH.

74. Processing operations that do not confer origin even if they do result in a CTH.

4.1. Procedure

United States procedure for nonpreferential and preferential rules of origin is the same (see chapter 2, section 4.1.).

In the European Community, a distinction must be made between reciprocal or contractual preferential trade agreements, such as EFTA, and unilateral or autonomous preferential trade agreements, such as the GSP (see chapter 3, section 4.1.1.). For the former, origin-related decisions are made in joint committees in which all signatories participate; origin decisions concerning the latter are made by the Commission and the Origin Committee autonomously. With respect to judicial review, the system is the same as that set out in section 3.1. of this chapter.

In Australia (and Canada), an importer may request informal advice from the Customs Service to know in advance whether a certain importation could benefit from preferential treatment (see chapter 6, section 4.1.1.). However, the Customs Service would not consider itself bound by the advice.

A decision by the Customs Service not to accept a claim for preferential treatment may be appealed in three ways, assuming that the duty has been paid under protest. The first avenue is an appeal to the Administrative Appeals Tribunal, a quasi-judicial body (see chapter 6, section 3.1.1.). The scope of review covers manifest errors of fact or patent misconceptions of the law (see chapter 6, section 4.1.1.). Decisions of the Administrative Appeals Tribunal may be appealed to the federal court on points of law. Second, the owner of the goods may bring a direct appeal before the commonwealth or state courts, in which case such courts' review will cover the law and the facts. Third, prerogative writs may be brought in the High Court of Australia or one of the state supreme courts on errors of law.

Canadian law distinguishes between origin disputes arising from the U.S.-Canada FTA and disputes about other preferential origin rules. For the latter, the system is the same as the system described in section 3.1. for nonpreferential origin rules. For U.S.-Canada FTA origin issues, the situation is more complicated. At a first level, the importer may appeal to the Tariff and Values Administrator (TVA) within ninety days of the determination of the Customs Service or within two years if certain criteria are fulfilled. At a second level, the importer may request a further redetermination from the deputy minister of the DNR within ninety days of the TVA's redetermination or within two years under certain conditions. At the third level, the importer may go to the CITT (see chapter 5, section 4.9.4.). Decisions of the CITT may be appealed to the Federal Court of Appeal on questions of law.

In Japan, the institutional framework for the GSP, the only Japanese preferential regime, is similar to that of nonpreferential rules. However,

Japanese customs has an advance ruling procedure under which responses given by customs remain valid for one year.

4.2. Substantive Law

Rather than going into detail about the myriad types of preferential origin rules, Tables 6-10 summarize such rules jurisdiction by jurisdiction.

A fundamental question for the operation of the GSP would appear to be whether GSP rules of origin ought to be stricter than nonpreferential rules of origin[75] (and stricter than those of other preferential trade regimes) (see section 7.1.).

For the United States, the European Community, and Japan, the answer appears to be positive. While U.S. nonpreferential origin rules only require a substantial transformation, the GSP rules require substantial transformation plus a — relatively low — 35 percent domestic content requirement;[76] cumulation possibilities are limited. In Japan, the nonpreferential CTH test is less austere than its preferential equivalents (i.e., double processing, value-added, and mixed tests).[77]

In the European Community, GSP rules of origin are also clearly more stringent than nonpreferential rules of origin, and the ECJ has upheld this difference on the ground that stricter GSP rules

... may ... be necessary to attain the objective of the generalized tariff preferences of ensuring that the preferences benefit only industries which are established in developing countries and which carry out the main manufacturing processes in those countries.[78]

The European Community's 'concern' for the indigenous development of developing countries is somewhat contradicted by its reluctance to accept cumulation among developing countries. In many cases, this implies the denial of GSP benefits for products that comprise materials of two or more developing countries.

---

75. Compare Palmeter's discussion in chapter 2, section 3.2.2.1., *supra*, about the possible linkage between the policy objective of a statute and the degree of substantial transformation required.

76. Of the appraised value.

77. Comment of Norio Komuro (26 May 1992).

78. Case 385/85, *S.R. Industries v. Administration des Douanes*, (1986) ECR 2929, as quoted in chapter 3, section 4.3.1.

TABLE 6.   United States Preferential Origin Rules

Trade Regime	Origin Rule Elements
GSP	– Substantial transformation and local direct cost added of 35% of the appraised value – Dual substantial transformation possible[a] – Full and regional cumulation possible among members of free trade associations[b] – Direct consignment rule
CBI[c]	– Substantial transformation and local direct cost-added of 35% of the appraised value – Dual substantial transformation possible – Unlimited cumulation possible among all CBI beneficiaries – Limited donor country benefit[d] – Direct shipment from any CBI beneficiary possible
Insular possessions[e]	– Local direct cost added of 30% of the appraised value for articles eligible for CBI preferences – Local direct cost added of 50% of the appraised value for other articles – Unlimited donor country benefit
Freely associated states[f]	– Local direct cost added of 35% of the appraised value – Direct shipment rule
U.S.-Israel FTA	– Local direct cost added of 35% of the appraised value – Dual substantial transformation possible – Limited donor country benefit[g] – Direct shipment rule
U.S.-Canada FTA	– CTH rule[h] and/or 50% domestic content test – Donor country benefit in case of domestic content test

Source: Chapter 2, sections 4.2.1.1.-4.2.1.6.; Digest of the Rules of Origin, UNCTAD/TAP/133/Rev. 6 (1990).

Note:
[a] If an imported raw material is itself substantially transformed in the developing country into an intermediate article that is itself a new and different article, that intermediate article has 100 percent developing country origin. Paraphrase of chapter 2, § 4.2.1.1. This dual transformation possibility is quite logical and would appear to be followed by the other jurisdictions too (see, e.g., chapter 3, § 4.2.1.2. and Consultations on Harmonization and Improvement of the Rules of Origin, Report by the UNCTAD Secretariat, TD/B/C.5/141, at 5 (1992)).
[b] The United States accepts cumulation from the following free trade associations: ANDEAN (Cartagena Agreement — Bolivia, Colombia, Ecuador, Peru, Venezuela), ASEAN (Indonesia,

Malaysia, Thailand Philippines) with the exception of Brunei Darussalam and Singapore, and CARICOM (Caribbean Common Market — Antigua and Barbuda, Barbados, Belize, Dominica, Grenada, Guiana, Jamaica, Montserrat, Saint Christopher-Nevis, Saint Lucia, Saint Vincent and the Grenadines, and Trinidad and Tobago).

ᶜ Twenty-seven Central American and Caribbean Nations.

ᵈ Up to 15 percent of the value of U.S. raw materials imported and substantially transformed in a CBI country may be included in the 35 percent domestic content (see chapter 2, § 4.2.1.2.).

ᵉ Guam, Wake Island, Midway Islands, Kingman Reef, Johnston Island, American Samoa, and Commonwealth of the Northern Mariana Islands.

ᶠ Marshall Islands, Federated States of Micronesia.

ᵍ Up to 15 percent of the value of U.S. raw materials imported and substantially transformed in Israel may be included in the 35 percent domestic content (see chapter 2, § 4.2.1.2.).

ʰ Palmeter, in chapter 2, § 4.2.1.6. points out that the change may vary from a two-digit chapter level change to an eight-digit national tariff line change.

Another interesting example of the restricted character of the European Community's GSP origin rules is the requirement for many electronic products such as microphones, and audio and video equipment that all transistors be originating products.[79] Ostensibly designed to prevent the use of too many Japanese transistors, the rule in practice often results in denial of GSP benefits because many transistors are made only in Japan. Nor does the rule help the EC transistor industry because the European Community does not presently recognize the donor country concept and does therefore not stimulate the use of European Community-originating transistors. It can be noted that the transistor rule has disappeared from most of the European Community's other preferential sets of rules of origin (see also section 7).

In view of the strict requirements and the complexity of the EC scheme, it is hardly surprising that the utilization rate of the European Community's GSP is apparently as low as 21 percent![80]

---

79. *See* Commission Regulation (EEC) No. 693/88 of 4 March 1998 on the definition of the concept of originating products for purposes of the application of tariff preferences granted by the European Economic Community in respect of certain products from developing countries, O.J. (1988) L 77/1.

80. As noted by Waer, in chapter 3, section 4.4. with footnote reference. Komuro, in chapter 6, Annex 3.2., observes that the Japanese GSP utilization ratio was 57.4 percent in 1986 and 48.3 percent in 1990. Keizer (letter of 22 May 1992) states that the European Community's GSP utilization rate is actually closer to 50 percent and mentions as possible reasons for the discrepancy between the figures (1) the ACP treatment and (2) the quota system for sensitive products.

TABLE 7. **European Community Preferential Origin Rules**

Trade Regime	Origin Rule Elements
GSP	– Sufficient working or processing, expressed as CTH test,[a] technical test or import content test[b] – Partial and regional cumulation among certain regional groupings[c] – No donor country benefit – Direct consignment rule
EFTA[d]	Same except – Donor country benefit – Cumulation among EFTA countries under certain conditions
ACP countries[e]	Same except – Donor country benefit – Regional cumulation possible – Direct shipment from ACP countries
Mashreq[f]	Same except – Donor country benefit – No cumulation
Maghreb[g]	Same except – Donor country benefit – Regional cumulation possible
Cyprus	Same except – Donor country benefit
Israel	Same except – Donor country benefit
Malta	Same except – Donor country benefit
Slovenia, Croatia, Bosnia-Hercegovina, Macedonia (and Montenegro)[h]	Same except – Donor country benefit
OCTs[i]	Same except – Donor country benefit – Regional cumulation possible
Faroe Islands	Same except – Donor country benefit
Ceuta, Melilla, and Canary Islands[j]	Same except – Donor country benefit – Regional cumulation possible
Territories occupied by Israel	Same except – Donor country benefit
Hungary, Poland, and Czechoslovakia	Same except – Donor country benefit – Regional cumulation possible

Source: Chapter 3, sections 4.1. - 4.4.; Digest of the Rules of Origin, UNCTAD/TAP/133/Rev. 6 (1990).

Note:

[a] Imported materials, parts, or components are considered to have undergone sufficient working or processing when the product obtained is classified in an HS heading at the four-digit level that is different from those in which all nonoriginating materials, parts or components used in the process are classified *see* Digest of the Rules of Origin, at 6.

[b] See chapter 3, § 4.2.1., where Waer also observes that value-added percentages may differ depending on the product and may sometimes be combined with, for example, a value-of-parts test, the obligatory use of certain inputs, or both. The EC value-added tests in the GSP context use the maximum import content method.

[c] The European Community in theory accepts cumulation from the following free trade associations: ANDEAN (Cartagena Agreement — Bolivia, Colombia, Ecuador, Peru, Venezuela), *see* O.J. (1983) L 372/63; ASEAN (Brunei, Indonesia, Malaysia, Thailand, Philippines, Singapore), *see* O.J. (1983) L 372/57; and CACM (Central American Common Market — Costa Rica, El Salvador, Guatemala, Honduras, Nicaragua), see O.J. (1983) L 372/60. However, in practice, only ASEAN and ANDEAN cumulation is accepted, and this only since 1989 and 1992, respectively. The reason why cumulation among the CACM members is not accepted is that this bloc apparently has not yet complied with the administrative cooperation requirements laid down in Articles 6, 7, and 8 of the relevant Commission Regulation.

[d] Austria, Sweden, Switzerland, Iceland, Norway, Finland, and Liechtenstein.

[e] For more detail, see Inama, Handbook on Lomé IV Convention, UNCTAD/ITP/61 (1991).

[f] Syria, Jordan, Lebanon, and Egypt.

[g] Tunisia, Morocco, and Algeria.

[h] Montenegro's position at the moment of writing was still under consideration.

[i] For more detail, see Inama, *supra* note e.

[j] The Canary Islands are presently part of the customs territory of the European Community. The preferential treatment applies only with respect to agricultural products.

TABLE 8.   Australian Preferential Origin Rules

Trade Regime	Origin Rule Elements
GSP	– Last process – 50% factory or works cost – Full and global cumulation among GSP beneficiaries – Donor country benefit – No direct shipment rule
CANATA	– 75% factory or works cost – Direct shipment rule
Australia-Papua New Guinea	– Last process – 50% factory or works cost – Donor country benefit
SPARTECA	– Last process – 50% factory or works cost – Donor country benefit
ANZCERTA	– Last process – 50% factory or works cost – Donor country benefit – Direct shipment rule

Source: Chapter 4, sections 2.1.-2.1.6.; Digest of the Rules of Origin, UNCTAD/TAP/133/Rev. 6 (1990).

Although Australian and Canadian GSP rules of origin require domestic content ratios of 50[81] and 60[82] percent respectively, the unlimited cumulation and donor country content possibilities in both schemes would appear to make up for this. The liberal Australian and Canadian rules should serve as an example for U.S., EC, and Japanese practice as there does not appear to be any logical basis for restrictive cumulation rules and, indeed, the latter arguably frustrate GSP objectives.[83]

81.   Of the factory cost.

82.   Of the ex-factory price.

83.   *Compare* Consultations on Harmonization and Improvement of the Rules of Origin, Report by the UNCTAD Secretariat, TD/B/C.5/141, at 21, 22 (1992).

TABLE **9.** **Canadian Preferential Origin Rules**

Trade Regime	Origin Rule Elements
GPT[a]	Value of imported parts and materials from nonbeneficiary countries may not exceed 40% of the exfactory price[b] Full and global cumulation among GPT beneficiaries Donor country benefit Finishing in beneficiary Direct shipment rule
LDDC[c]	Same except Value of imported parts and materials from non-LDDC countries may not exceed 60% of the exfactory price[d] Unlimited cumulation among LDDC beneficiaries
CARIBCAN[e]	Same except Cumulation among CARIBCAN countries
BPT	50% cost of production Cumulation among beneficiaries Finishing in beneficiary Direct shipment rule (transhipment through nonCommonwealth port is not allowed)
A & NZ	50% cost of production Donor country benefit Finishing in beneficiary Direct shipment rule Cumulation is not possible
U.S.-Canada FTA	CTH rule,[f] 50% domestic content test, or both Donor country benefit in case of domestic content test

Source: Chapter 5, sections 4.3.-4.8.; Digest of the Rules of Origin, UNCTAD/TAP/133/Rev. 6 (1990).

Note:

[a]   General Preferential Tariff (= GSP).

[b]   The exfactory price may include overhead expenses, royalties and profit to the extent that they are reasonable. This is therefore different from the cost-of-production test used under the other Canadian preferential rules.

[c]   LDDC Tariff.

[d]   Digest of Rules of Origin, at 9.

[e]   CARIBCAN Tariff

[f]   Palmeter, in chapter 2, § 4.2.1.6. points out that the change may vary from a two-digit chapter level change to an eight-digit statistical level change.

TABLE **10.**   **Japanese Preferential Origin Rules**

Trade Regime	Origin Rule Elements
GSP	Value of imported parts and materials may not exceed 40% or 45% of the FOB price; CTH test; double processing test or mixed test Partial and regional cumulation for ASEAN countries Donor country benefit Direct shipment rule

Source: chapter 6, section 4.1.2.

5.   Rules of Origin in the Context of Antidumping Proceedings

Practically all the authors in this volume note that the increased use of antidumping measures has had repercussions for the formulation c.q. the application of rules of origin and — directly or indirectly — has largely been responsible for the present controversy about the use of origin rules as commercial policy instruments.[84]   This is perhaps not surprising with the emergence of the antidumping law as the single most important trade policy instrument of the 1980s and 1990s.[85]

The reason is first of all that antidumping proceedings are normally initiated against and antidumping duties imposed on products originating in a certain country, although the GATT-basis for this practice is uncertain.[86] This practice requires the importing country authorities in charge of the administration of the antidumping law to make judgments about the origin of the products that are under investigation or that are subject to antidumping duties.

Second, antidumping complaints must be brought by the importing country industry producing the like product. In an increasing number of antidumping proceedings, foreign producers and their importers question whether the production processes carried out by the domestic industry in the importing country actually are sufficient to confer origin on the merchandise produced.

Third, a number of circumvention problems are solved through the use of rules of origin.

---

84.   See also Vermulst and Waer, *supra* note 8, and Vermulst and Waer, *supra* note 9.

85.   See John H. Jackson and Edwin A. Vermulst, eds., ANTIDUMPING LAW AND PRACTICE: A COMPARATIVE STUDY, (ANN ARBOR: THE UNIVERSITY OF MICHIGAN PRESS, 1989).

86.   For a detailed analysis of the GATT framework, see Vermulst and Waer, *supra* note 8 and Vermulst, Waer, *supra* note 9.

Most countries investigated in this study use a double, if not triple, standard: on the one hand, most administrators of the antidumping law take the position that antidumping duties ought to be imposed on products originating in a foreign country. On the other hand, these same administrators are reluctant to use rules of origin in order to determine whether importing country complainant producers actually qualify as a domestic industry. (Yet another, third, test is used to determine whether importing country producers related to the foreign producers with respect to whom antidumping duties were imposed are circumventing the antidumping duties.)

This two-headed snake approach is condoned by the draft GATT Agreement on rules of origin which provides in Article 1:2 that the agreement applies to antidumping proceedings but then immediately makes an exception in footnote 2 stipulating that the article is without prejudice to determinations made for the purpose of defining the domestic industry.[87] In the United States, as in the European Community, cases are brought against and residual duties imposed on products originating in a specified country. The Department of Commerce is in charge of the enforcement of antidumping duties and U.S. Courts have held that Commerce — for antidumping law enforcement issues — has the authority to make origin determinations that may differ from those issued by the Customs Service and the Treasury Department. Thus, while for Department of Treasury purposes the origin of semiconductors depends on the locus of assembly and testing, for Commerce Department antidumping purposes the origin depends on the diffusion process.[88] To make matters more complicated, to determine whether importing country or third country circumvention occurs, the Commerce Department would examine whether the difference between the value of the completed product and the components or materials from the country subject to the duty is small. Palmeter appropriately terms this the "heads-we-win, tails-you-lose" factor (see chapter 2, section 5.).

As far as the definition of the domestic industry is concerned, it may be noted that the Commerce Department has dismissed a small number of

---

87.   Draft Agreement *supra* note 1. Compare chapter 8 section 2.

88.   Surprisingly, when the European Community was in the process of adopting a product specific rule for semiconductors that focused on diffusion, it encountered vociferous opposition from the United States, although the U.S. Commerce Department had previously adopted the same rule for antidumping purposes: at least the EC rule was consistent for all trade policy purposes.

antidumping petitions, including the controversial *Brother* case, on the ground that they were filed not by producers, but by assemblers.[89]

In the European Community, third-country circumvention is judged on the basis of the nonpreferential origin rules (for more detail, see chapter 3, section 5.1.2.). In 1986, for example, the Commission terminated an antidumping proceeding initiated against the Taiwanese production operations of the Japanese producer Brother on the ground that the typewriters produced in Taiwan had not acquired Taiwanese origin;[90] as a result, the EC Member States applied antidumping duties (retroactively). At the moment of this writing, six years later, Brother is still involved in litigation in at least two EC Member States.[91] More recently, in a case involving compact disc players from Malaysia and Singapore, the Commission is again suggesting that antidumping duties be applied retroactively on the basis that locally produced CDPs did not obtain local origin, but rather had Japanese origin.

Importing country circumvention, on the other hand, was appraised in the European Community on the basis of a 60/40 percent value-of-parts test from 1987 to 1989 until a GATT panel ruled in 1990 that the application of the EC test was GATT illegal. More or less simultaneously, the EC Commission in a number of cases, notably *Photocopiers*,[92] decided to include EC producers in the definition of the domestic industry not on the basis of origin rules or the parts test but rather on vague grounds such as the producers' intentions to increase local value-added or their long-term commitment to investment and employment in the Community.

The Photocopiers proceeding offers a good illustration of the confusing EC tests: in the course of the administrative proceeding, serious questions were raised about the (lack of) local sourcing of the main EC complainant Rank Xerox. However, Rank Xerox promised to increase local sourcing and was therefore included in the definition of the EC industry. After the conclusion of the proceeding, a parts investigation was opened against the Japanese producers' manufacturing operations in the European Community in which the existence of circumvention was determined on the basis of the 60/40 percent value-of-parts test; Rank Xerox, which had links with the Japanese producer

---

89. *See also, e.g.*, Latchet Hook Kits from the United Kingdom, 45 Fed. Reg. 81,241 (1980) (dismissal petition).

90. Typewriters from Taiwan, O.J. (1986) L 140/52 (termination).

91. The Netherlands and Germany. It would appear that litigation in the United Kingdom was recently stopped with Brother agreeing to pay a certain amount of antidumping duties. Comment of Wim Keizer (22 May 1992).

92. Photocopiers from Japan, O.J. (1987) L 54/22.

Fuji Xerox, was excluded from the investigation. Mita's and Ricoh's production operations in Hong Kong and California respectively were also investigated, but this time by Directorate-General XXI of the EC Commission, which used the nonpreferential origin rules to effectively determine whether Mita and Ricoh were circumventing the antidumping duties imposed with respect to Japan. In the case of Ricoh, the Commission issued a regulation that held that assembly accompanied by the manufacture of the harness, drum, rollers, side plates, roller bearings, screws, and nuts (i.e., the production processes performed by Ricoh in California at that time) in any event did not confer origin.[93] This regulation was the main reason for the United States[94] and Japan to insist in the Uruguay Round negotiations that negative origin rules should not be allowed under the Draft Agreement.

The EC antidumping proceeding concerning SCTVs from Hong Kong (see chapter 3, section 5.1.1.) offers a good illustration of the type of problems that can arise as a result of antidumping duties being imposed on countries of origin and would seem to have perplexed even the EC Commission: the Commission admitted in so many words that its investigation revealed that the SCTVs produced in Hong Kong did not have Hong Kong origin, but then proceeded to impose antidumping duties on the Hong Kong producers with the caveat that Member States' "customs authorities . . . may determine an origin which differs from that which is declared" (read, may impose the residual antidumping duty applicable to South Korea if the SCTVs are in fact of Korean origin or may impose no duty at all if, for example, the SCTVs have Japanese, Malaysian, or EC[95] origin). Waer (in chapter 3, section 5.1.1.) correctly points out that the case "effectively is a story of certain Hong Kong producers cooperating in the wrong procedure." One might add, and of the Commission imposing nonsensical antidumping duties.

In Australia, rules of origin thus far do not appear to have given rise to great controversy in connection with antidumping measures. This seems the result of the following factors:

---

93. Commission Regulation (EEC) No. 2071/89 of 11 July 1989 on determining the origin of photocopying apparatus, incorporating an optical system or of the contact type, O.J. (1989) L 196/24.

94. The United States presumably saw further Japanese investment in the United States jeopardized.

95. If the Hong Kong producers were to use EC-originating color picture tubes, the SCTVs would arguably have EC origin on the basis of the subsidiary 35 percent value-of-parts test.

-   Importing country circumvention is unlikely because of the small market, isolated position, and labor conditions of Australia (see chapter 4, section 5.1.).
-   The starting point for dumping margin calculations is the country of export as opposed to the country of origin.[96]
-   Australia has imposed company-based antidumping duties[97] when industrial products were concerned.[98]

The second and third factor combined would seem to indicate that duties are typically imposed on merchandise exported from country X by producer x. If producer x then sets up a joint venture plant x/y in and starts exporting from country Y, presumably the ACS would require a new complaint against the merchandise exported by company x/y from country Y.

In contrast, the Canadian authorities have been confronted with globalization problems in a multitude of cases, perhaps because of Canada's proximity to the United States, and Gottlieb gives a very comprehensive overview of the problems faced and solutions found by the Canadian authorities in chapter 5, section 5.1.-5.3.7.

With respect to the definition of the domestic industry, the Canadian authorities would appear to adopt the most elastic attitude of the jurisdictions examined here by holding repeatedly that mere assembly is sufficient for a producer to qualify as (part of) the domestic industry (see the examples in chapter 5, section 5.3.3.1.).

Importing country circumvention does not appear to have been a major problem in Canada, presumably because of the widespread practice of Canadian industry to file cases not only against finished products, but also against parts and components.[99]

---

96.   See chapter 4, section 5.3. Where the country of export and the country of origin differ, it may be decided by the Minister to base normal value on prices or costs in the country of origin. This happened only once (see chapter 4, footnote 79). In Xlpe cable, the ACS terminated an antidumping proceeding initiated against Xlpe cable allegedly exported from Singapore on the ground that the product was not exported from Singapore but from Korea.

97.   Country-based duties are imposed in Australia essentially where the products under investigation are commodities or where the goods are exported from nonmarket economies (see chapter 4, section 5.4).

98.   See chapter 4, section 5.4. Multicountry sourcing is more likely in the case of industrial products.

99.   This raises certain unique problems with respect to the injury determination (see chapter 5, sections 5.3.3.3.-5.3.6.).

With respect to third-country circumvention, Gottlieb (in chapter 5, section 5.3.2.1.) cites one instance of the DNR attempting to assess antidumping duties on third country production on the ground that the value-added in the third country (the United States) was insufficient and the products therefore continued to have Japanese origin.

Finally, it appears that Canadian antidumping law provides the Canadian industry with substantial discretion to sculpt the targets of the proceeding and that cases may be initiated against products originating in, exported from, originating in or exported from, produced by or on behalf of company x, imported from, supplied by or otherwise introduced into the commerce of Canada by or on behalf of company y, etc. While this possibility to focus on specific companies at first sight may seem bizarre and certainly subject to abuse, Gottlieb pointedly draws our attention to the other side of the coin: "[c]ountries do not dump; individuals do." (see chapter 5, section 5.3.7.). This elementary truth has indeed been almost forgotten under the residual duty practice of the United States and the European Community.

Japan has adopted antidumping measures only once thus far, but rules of origin did not play a role of importance in that case (see Komuro, chapter 6, section 5.1.1.)

6. Rules of Origin in Other Contexts

Rules of origin also play a role in the application of marking, labelling, and false or misleading advertising laws; duty drawback provisions; government procurement; process patents; countervailing duty and safeguard proceedings; quantitative restrictions; prohibited imports; trade embargoes; and services.

In all these areas, they can stir controversy and have on occasion done so (see chapter 2, section 6., chapter 3, sections 5.2.-5.4., chapter 4, section 6., Chapter 5, sections 6.-7., and chapter 6, section 6.). One need only think of the Nissan Bluebird dispute in the European Community which is discussed in detail in other parts of this book (see chapter 3, section 6. and chapter 8, section 1.).

The French position in the Nissan dispute and initial dubious interpretations by the EC Commission of Article 13 (10) of the basic Antidumping Regulation[100] have created the misunderstanding that a certain amount of local content[101] is needed for EC plants to export to other parts of the EC *c.q.* to avoid importing country circumvention. Suffice it here that the French position was utterly illegal under EC law, first because the French quota on

---

100. With respect to the conditions for the acceptance of "parts" undertakings.

101. The French argued for 80 percent in the case of Nissan.

Japanese cars was illegal and second because once products are in free circulation in the EC, as was the case with the Nissan cars produced in the United Kingdom, Community origin is irrelevant.

Komuro pays extensive attention (chapter 6, section 6.) to the Japanese FTC's application of rules of origin in the context of origin marking laws and raises the interesting question whether Japanese and U.S. Federal Trade Commission origin marking requirements fall under the purview of the Draft Agreement on rules of origin. He tentatively concludes that the answer depends on whether such requirements constitute origin marking requirements within the meaning of Article IX of GATT.

7. Conclusions and Recommendations in the Light of the Draft Agreement

Until a few years ago, rules of origin were an obscure area of law in which legal processes were by and large absent and government officials agreed in *in camera* sessions on both policy formulation and policy implementation. Discussions about rules of origin were felt to be a government affair in which private companies, let alone foreign companies, had no standing. The lack of interest was fuelled by the widespread perception of rules of origin as technical rules applied by technicians on the basis of technical considerations. This conceivably explains why the GATT drafters did not deem it worthwhile to include provisions on rules of origin and rather leave it

> . . . within the province of each importing member country to determine, in accordance with the provisions of its law, for the purpose of applying the most-favoured-nation provision [and for other GATT purposes, EAV], whether goods do in fact originate in a particular country.[102]

While some lackadaisical efforts were made in a variety of fora[103] to agree on certain common principles in the period from 1947 to 1989,[104]

---

102. JACKSON, WORLD TRADE AND THE LAW OF GATT 468 (1969).

103. Such as UNCTAD, the OECD, the CCC and GATT. For more detail, see The Impact of Rules of Origin on U.S. Imports and Exports, Report to the President on Investigation No. 332-192 Under Section 332 of the Tariff Act of 1930, USITC, at 70-72 (1985).

104. In fact, in 1922 the League of Nations had already adopted a convention on the simplification of customs procedures that contained provisions on rules of origin.

none of these were particularly successful. For a variety of reasons,[105] not least of all the realization that certain recent formulations and interpretations of origin rules by the European Community[106] and the United States were politically motivated and had trade-restrictive or -distortive ramifications, a number of countries agreed fairly late in the Uruguay Round that an agreement on rules of origin would be worthwhile and consensus on a concept Agreement[107] was reached surprisingly fast. The Draft Agreement provisions are analyzed in chapter 7, section 2. The remainder of this chapter therefore focuses on some of the salient issues raised by authors in this book and reviews to what extent the Draft Agreement satisfactorily addresses such points.

7.1. The Policies of Rules of Origin

Should rules of origin be different depending on the policy objective of the law that they support? This is a fundamental issue that touches the core of the discussion whether rules of origin merely support other trade discriminatory measures or in fact qualify as discriminatory measures themselves and therefore can be used as trade policy instruments. Palmeter discusses this issue in detail with respect to nonpreferential U.S. rules of origin (see chapter 2, section 3.2.2.1.), although it is relevant to all jurisdictions and to the administration of both nonpreferential and preferential rules of origin.

To analyze this issue, it might be useful to distinguish between policy formulation and policy implementation of rules of origin.

At the policy formulation level, all jurisdictions examined here substantively distinguish between preferential and nonpreferential origin determinations and, with the exception of Japan, also differentiate among preferential trading regimes. Regarding the latter, the rationale appears to be that more relaxed rules of origin might be appropriate for those preference-receiving countries with respect to whom the preference-giving jurisdiction has closer economic or political ties. Thus, for example, the EC rules of origin that apply to ACP countries and OCTs allow donor country benefit and full global cumulation possibilities among preference-receiving countries while under the European Community's GSP rules of origin only partial regional

---

105. See Vermulst and Waer, *supra* note 8, at 55-57.

106. *Compare* Hindley, *Foreign Direct Investment: The Effects of Rules of Origin* (1990).

107. *Supra* note 2.

cumulation is possible. Clearly, the result is that the same origin rule is easier to satisfy for an ACP country or an OCT than for a GSP beneficiary. This type of differential treatment could be classified as methodological discrimination.

Another example, this time of what one might call discriminatory severity of the rules themselves: under the EC GSP rule of origin for televisions, (1) the value of all the materials used may not exceed 40 percent of the ex-works price of the television (import content test), (2) materials classified within heading No. 8529 may be used only up to a value of 5 percent of the ex-works price of the television (obligatory input test), (3) the value of non-originating materials used may not exceed the value of the originating materials used (value-of-parts test), and (4) all transistors of heading No. 8541 must be originating products (obligatory input test). In contrast, the ACP rule of origin for televisions only requires (1) that the value of the materials used does not exceed 40 percent of the ex-works price of the television and (2) that the value of all the non-originating materials used does not exceed the value of the originating materials used. Thus, a Zaire producer may use as many Japanese or EC[108] transistors as it wants, but if a Bangladesh producer uses even one, it loses any possibility to claim GSP benefits: *quod licet ACP, non licet GSP*.

Such methodological discriminations and disparities in the stringency of the rules at the policy formulation level amount to an implicit recognition by administering authorities that rules of origin may and in fact do have trade-distortive effects.

They also show the hypocrisy behind policy statements in some jurisdictions that (certain types of) preferential origin rules are designed to help genuine local development: a foreign investor would have to source more local materials in Bangladesh than in Zaire and, mutatis mutandis, would therefore chose Zaire over Bangladesh to set up a plant. If anything, the rules are an expression of nepotism fashioned to foster foreign investment in certain countries rather than others.

The nonneutrality of nonpreferential rules of origin at the policy implementation level is most clear in the United States, where administrative determinations and a number of court judgments indicate that the degree of substantial transformation may differ depending on the policy purpose of the underlying statute.[109] While nonpreferential origin rules in the European Community are the same for all policy purposes, it cannot be denied that

---

108. Donor country benefit!

109. With respect to origin for antidumping purposes, see the separate discussion in sections 7.7. and 7.8.

certain product-specific origin regulations such as the ones on zippers, integrated circuits, and photocopiers, benefitted EC industry and worked to the disadvantage of Japanese producers. In both the United States and the European Community, the potential for trade-restrictive interpretations of nonpreferential rules of origin seems closely connected to the blurry "substantial transformation" respectively "last substantial process" criterion.

The Draft Agreement on rules of origin provides that, at least at the end of the three year transitional period, signatories should use the same rules of origin for all purposes and therefore provides a conclusive answer to the still ongoing U.S. discussion in the nonpreferential area.[110] The successful harmonization of nonpreferential origin rules in the CCC (see sections 7.2.-7.3) will furthermore presumably lead to the abolition of the opaque U.S. and EC standards and replace them with the CTH test, at least as the general rule.

Unfortunately, the Draft Agreement itself starts from the fallacious perception that the drafting of rules of origin is a technical matter.[111] This is likely to give rise to profound problems in the CCC negotiations on harmonization.

Furthermore, the Agreement will not be applied to preferential rules of origin. While opinions differ regarding the desirability and, indeed, the possibility of bringing preferential rules of origin within the ambit of the Draft Agreement,[112] it cannot be contested that the epidemic and expanding establishment of preferential trading blocs creates a major loophole in the applicability of the relevant Draft Agreement provision. The Common Declaration[113] clearly will not close this gap.

In the view of this author, it is regrettable that the chance has been missed to bring some uniformity in the formulation of preferential origin rules (see sections 7.5.-7.6. for more detail). Such rules are effectively used at the policy formulation level to pursue trade, investment, and sourcing policies,

---

110. Article 3 (a), *supra* note 1. This provision would appear to target the United States and arguably would prohibit the U.S. Customs Service and the Commerce Department from adopting differing rules of origin. Although, with regard to Japan's rules of origin, a discrepancy between Custom's rules and MITI's rules for import control of *silk woven fabrics* from China exists, this has not given rise to any controversy at international levels. See chapter 6, section 3.2.2.1.2.

111. Comment Friedl Mazal (21 May 1992).

112. Navarro, see chapter 7, section 2.1., for example, argues that "a harmonization of preferential rules of origin seems rather difficult, given the individuality intrinsic to the preferential rules of origin."

113. Annex II to the Draft Agreement, *supra* note 1.

particularly in the European Community and the United States, in manners that distort an efficient globalization.

In summary, at the policy formulation level, all jurisdictions examined in this book use rules of origin to pursue policy purposes, and the Draft Agreement is unlikely to solve this. At the policy implementation level, the vague definitions in U.S. and EC non-preferential origin rules have led to trade-restrictive or -distortive interpretations. However, the adoption of the Draft Agreement and subsequent successful CCC harmonization can prevent this from occurring in the future.

7.2.   Harmonization of Nonpreferential Origin Rules in the Customs Cooperation Council

It has been agreed in the Draft Agreement that nonpreferential rules of origin will be harmonized in the CCC in Brussels. Fully harmonized rules of origin present an enormous benefit for transnational enterprises, which typically would set up low-end production facilities in low-cost developing countries and high-end production facilities in high-cost developed countries and export from such production bases to the rest of the world (globalized production philosophy). Rational advance sourcing and production planning would allow such transnationals to simultaneously comply with different countries' nonpreferential rules of origin.

It should be noted, however, that the present time schedule, which foresees completion of the harmonization efforts at the end of a three-year period seems highly unrealistic and is unlikely to be met, not in the least because of the diminutive staff and meagre resources of the CCC.

7.3.   Change in Tariff Heading as the Basis for Harmonization

The Draft Agreement stipulates that harmonization negotiations in the CCC will use the HS CTH test to the extent possible.[114] However, experience with the U.S.-Canada FTA origin rules, Japanese nonpreferential origin rules and the EC's preferential origin rules, all three of which also predominantly use the CTH test, makes exclusive reliance on the CTH approach unlikely. Combination with a technical test, a percentage criterion, or both, in many instances will be unavoidable.

It is important for developing/low-cost countries to realize before the negotiations in the CCC start that both tests have a great potential for protectionist applications and that major trading units such as the United

---

114. Article 9 (2) (ii), *supra* note 2.

States, the European Community and Japan[115] are in the process of preparing for the negotiations; they have, for example, already asked domestic industries for their recommendations on the contents of possible harmonization rules. Developing/low-cost countries should prepare for the harmonization negotiations well in advance not to be presented with faits accomplis in the negotiating process.

7.4. Harmonization of Percentage Criterion Calculation Methods

This study has shown enormous differences between jurisdictions with respect to (1) the numerator and (2) the denominator to be used in calculating percentage criteria and (3) the maximum allowable percentage of nonoriginating parts and materials (import content test) or the minimum percentage of domestic content (domestic content test).[116] Clearly, any CCC attempts at harmonization that partly rely on the use of percentage criteria will be undermined by a failure to harmonize underlying calculation methods. The CCC negotiations ought to take this into account.[117]

In section 2.1., I argued that EC and Japanese domestic content and import content calculation methods seem most logical and appear to follow Kyoto Convention recommendations most closely; EC and Japanese rules might therefore serve as a basis for harmonization.

7.5. Harmonization of the General System of Preferences?

Preference-receiving countries have been pointing out since 1970, i.e. almost since the inception of the GSP, that the lack of GSP harmonization is a "major (and also inadvertent) barrier to GSP trade."[118] However, while such countries have been pressing for increased harmonization of GSP origin rules

---

115. See the extensive discussion in chapter 6, section 7. about efforts currently being undertaken in Japan.

116. In 1982, the CCC already made a proposal to use a uniform 50 percent maximum. See CCC, Permanent Technical Committee, Rules of Origin of Goods, Secretariat Note, 29.215E T7-3231 (2 November 1982). However, this proposal was never acted on.

117. Article 9 (2) (iii) of the Draft Agreement, *supra* note 1 merely provides that if the ad valorem criterion is prescribed, the method of calculating this percentage shall also be indicated in the rules of origin.

118. Consultations on Harmonization and Improvement of the Rules of Origin, Report by the UNCTAD Secretariat, TD/B/C.5/141, at 1 (1992).

for more than two decades now, the present study[119] shows that, as of 1993, marked differences exist between donor countries' implementation of the GSP system.

Fundamental issues such as broad (Australia, Canada) or narrow (United States, European Community, Japan) cumulation, (non)acceptance of the donor country principle and more (United States, European Community, Japan) or less (Australia, Canada) strict origin requirements for GSP qualification would appear to have a direct bearing on the possible utilization rates by beneficiary countries. With respect to the GSP, the devil lies in the details, and methodological and substantive details are arguably used by donor countries to covertly protect sensitive products by means of unrealistically high origin requirements. With respect to methodology, the United States, the European Community, and Japan ought to rethink their limited cumulation possibilities, which clearly affect inter-developing country integration.[120]

An obvious forum for the harmonization of GSP rules is the UNCTAD, the force behind the establishment of the GSP and the institution where discussions about the efficacy of and improvements in GSP schemes take place almost continuously.

A recent UNCTAD Secretariat Report,[121] distinguishes between limited harmonization (i.e., harmonization of existing differences within and between the various versions of the process criterion and the percentage criterion, and full harmonization (i.e., an additional choice for either the process criterion or the percentage criterion by all preference-giving countries).

The report tentatively concludes that a percentage criterion based upon import content is preferable because of "its simplicity and straightforwardness"[122] and might therefore form the best foundation for full harmonization.

One might wonder whether this conclusion is sufficiently thought through. First of all, the import content percentage criterion will necessarily leave importing country administrators discretion on how to value imported parts' prices where such parts are sourced from related suppliers. Second, at least

---

119. *See also* Consultations on Harmonization and Improvement of the Rules of Origin, Report by the UNCTAD Secretariat, TD/B/C.5/141 (1992).

120. Compare the 1990 UNCTAD Report, Report of the Special Committee on Preferences, on its Seventeenth Session, UNCTAD, TD/B/1263, at para 26 (1990), which recommends that the United States and the European Community accept the donor country concept and unlimited cumulation among GSP beneficiaries.

121. *Supra* note 199, at 1.

122. Ibid.

at present, there is no uniformity among preference-giving jurisdictions with regard to the appropriate valuation level of imported parts (FOB or CIF) and the denominator to be used in calculating the percentage. Effective harmonization would require consensus on these points also. Third, as the European Community is unlikely to ever give up its CTH test and the United States might not be as reluctant as it was a few years ago to accept a process criterion, from a realistic point of view, harmonization might be achieved more quickly if a choice was made for the process criterion.

Finally, and perhaps most importantly, in view of the choice for the harmonization of nonpreferential origin rules on the basis of the CTH test and the adoption by most countries now of the Harmonized System, it might be better to have any GSP harmonization take place on the basis of the same method; UNCTAD could then not only profit from the work undertaken in the CCC but also from the different balance of power in the CCC under which conflicting interests between the United States, the European Community, and Japan perhaps form a better guarantee for fair rules than GSP rules of origin unilaterally decided on by preference-giving countries.

Indeed, if donor countries could be persuaded to use the same CTH test for nonpreferential and GSP purposes, it would appear to be a significant victory for preference-receiving countries as it would mean an implied reversal of present U.S., EC and Japanese policy that GSP rules of origin ought to be more exacting than nonpreferential rules.

7.6. Different Rules of Origin for Free Trade Areas?

Contrary to the autonomous character of the GSP, free trade areas are contractual. This nature implies that the specifics of the contract, including applicable rules of origin, are negotiated among the members.[123] Because of differing economic interests, it seems almost unavoidable that the relevant rules of origin are highly individualistic and patterned after the economic interests of the members and of the bloc as such.

Article XXIV:4 of GATT recognizes as a matter of principle the "desirability of increasing freedom of trade by the development, through voluntary agreements, of closer integration between the economies of the countries parties to such agreements." Other parts of Article XXIV impose various obligations that customs unions and free trade areas need to comply with.[124] In particular, duties and other regulations of commerce of the regional bloc should not be higher or more restrictive vis-à-vis third countries

---

123. For an illustration, see the citation at the beginning of this chapter.

124. For a detailed description, see JACKSON, *supra* note 102, at 575-625.

than those previously existing at the various countries' levels. The philosophy of Article XXIV is therefore to create trade yet to avoid the diversion of trade.[125]

With respect to preferential rules of origin negotiated as part of an FTA or customs union package, the question therefore is whether such rules divert trade to the disadvantage of nonmembers. Arguably, very stringent rules of origin lead to trade deflection (see the example in the foreword) because members of the bloc need to use more domestic content to qualify for preferential treatment and therefore will use less parts and materials imported from third countries.[126] The donor country concept will yield a similar result because bloc members have an incentive to use parts and materials originating in the bloc. Lax rules of origin, on the other hand, while probably leading to less trade diversion, raise major free rider problems.

In the view of the author, the simplest and least internationally-controversial solution would be to use identical nonpreferential and preferential rules. However, vehement EC opposition to this idea in the Uruguay Round negotiations would appear to preclude this for the decade to come.

7.7.   Rules of Origin to Assess the Circumvention of Antidumping Duties?

A controversial question is whether rules of origin ought to have a place in determining whether the circumvention of antidumping duties takes place. Theoretically at least, one could argue that if importing country or third-country manufacturing is carried out under such conditions that the locally-produced merchandise obtains originating status, it should not be subjected to antidumping duties, unless a full investigation shows that either the parts or the third country exports are dumped and have thereby caused injury to the relevant importing country industry.

Palmeter takes this position (in chapter 2, section 7) by arguing that rules of origin and not specially adopted anticircumvention rules ought to be the basis for determining whether circumvention takes place.

---

125. JACKSON, THE WORLD TRADING SYSTEM 141 (1989).

126. This assumes that the benefits of the preferential agreement are worthwhile enough to comply with the qualification rules. The relatively low level of customs duties these days casts some doubts on this assumption.

This author has previously[127] argued the opposite on the ground that anticircumvention duties are such an extreme measure (because they violate the basic Article VI GATT rule that antidumping duties may be imposed only following findings of dumping and resulting injury)[128] that origin rules, drafted for other purposes, are not an appropriate yardstick. The draft GATT Anti-Dumping Code of 20 December 1991 takes a cryptic approach.[129] It contains a specific importing country anticircumvention provision that clearly would provide the exclusive avenue for determining whether importing country circumvention occurs.[130] With respect to third-country circumvention, however, the draft only contains a mechanism for imposing antidumping duties retroactively once third country circumvention has been determined to exist and findings of dumping and resulting injury have been reached. Already this formulation is giving rise to controversy in Geneva with the European Community taking the position that the draft code would allow the continuation of the EC practice of judging third-country circumvention on the basis of the application of nonpreferential origin rules and other countries making a *lex specialis* argument that retroactivity would be the only resort available to importing country authorities.

7.8.   Rules of Origin to Define the Domestic Industry in Antidumping Proceedings?

The European Community and other main users of antidumping laws have been reluctant to subject the domestic industry to rules of origin tests,[131] a glaring incongruity that is now unfortunately condoned by the Draft Origin Agreement (see section 5.). The domestic industry is therefore likely to continue to be defined on the basis of soft criteria tat offer more openings for political rather than technical input.

---

127. Vermulst and Waer *supra* note 8.

128. Article VI, in turn, is an exception to the tariff bindings and MFN principles, so it must be interpreted narrowly.

129. The draft code is part of the Dunkel package, *supra* note 2.

130. Quaere whether importing country industries can still bring complaints against parts.

131. Vermulst, The Antidumping Systems of Australia, Canada, the EEC and the USA: Have Antidumping Laws Become a Problem in International Trade?" 425-467, at 455, in John H. Jackson and Edwin A. Vermulst, eds., ANTIDUMPING LAW AND PRACTICE: A COMPARATIVE STUDY, (ANN ARBOR: THE UNIVERSITY OF MICHIGAN PRESS, 1989).

7.9.   Procedural Improvements

One of the most interesting innovations of the Draft Agreement and the Common Declaration is the advance ruling procedure (see chapter 7, section 2.3.1.1.3.). At present, all five jurisdictions examined in this book are to varying degrees willing to provide advance information on origin if so requested. However, the process is time-consuming (European Community), not binding (Australia, Canada), and murky (all five jurisdictions). The fairly detailed requirements of the Draft Agreement, including a 150-day time limit for the administering authorities and a publication requirement,[132] will compel the establishment of a ruling procedure in all jurisdictions examined in this book with respect to both nonpreferential and preferential[133] rules of origin.

Such a procedure should, in the view of this author, be a layered one, with a possibility for interested parties to make their views known before a final decision is made, as is the case in the United States with draft Treasury Decisions (see section 3.1.). Clearly, interested parties should also have procedural rights, notably rights of confidential treatment of business proprietary information submitted[134] and of access to the nonconfidential file, and rights to be heard and to obtain an explanation of the essential facts and considerations underlying a proposed ruling as well as the opportunity to comment on them before the adoption. It furthermore ought to be possible for interested parties to directly appeal to the appropriate court from adverse administrative determinations.

On the basis of the above observations, the procedure could become as shown in Figure 1 (page 470).

A special problem in the European Community might be whether administrative and judicial remedies ought to be available at the Member State or the EC level. In the view of this author, the centralization of both at the EC level would be preferable to avoid inconsistencies and save time.

---

132. Technically, the draft Agreement would only require the authorities to make rulings publicly available. However, effective implementation of this requirement would appear to necessitate publication in the jurisdictions' official gazettes.

133. See the Common Declaration, *supra* note 2.

134. Compare Article 2 (k) and 3 (i) of the Draft Agreement, *supra* note 2.

7.10. Power-Oriented or Rule-Oriented Framework?[135]

The establishment of an adversarial legal process to decide on origin with procedural safeguards for interested parties amounts to a long-due recognition of the fundamental character of determinations on rules of origin as decisions on conflicting interests.

Such decisions will always affect investment and sourcing strategies and international trade flows, and it is therefore important that they are harmonized and imperative that they are transparent, depoliticized, and predictable.

With respect to nonpreferential rules of origin, the international community has taken the first step on the road to a rule-oriented system with respect to policy formulation[136] and implementation.

Preferential rules of origin, on the other hand, will continue to generate stumbling blocks to rational allocations of resources as long as harmonization within each jurisdiction and among jurisdictions is not achieved and importing country administrators are free to continue to mete out justice à la carte, at least at the policy formulation level.

---

135. The distinction comes from Jackson, *The Crumbling Institutions of the Liberal Trade System*, 12:2 Journal of World Trade Law, 93-106 (1978).

136. However, the exclusion of preferential origin rules from the harmonization process leaves jurisdictions significant elbow room to continue to pursue policy objectives.

FIGURE **1.**   **Flow Chart of a Possible Ruling Procedure**

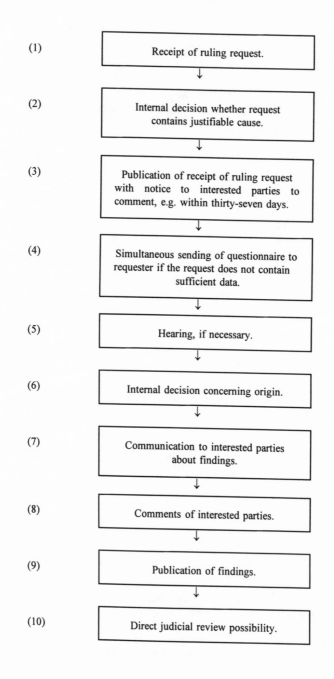

(1)   Receipt of ruling request.

(2)   Internal decision whether request contains justifiable cause.

(3)   Publication of receipt of ruling request with notice to interested parties to comment, e.g. within thirty-seven days.

(4)   Simultaneous sending of questionnaire to requester if the request does not contain sufficient data.

(5)   Hearing, if necessary.

(6)   Internal decision concerning origin.

(7)   Communication to interested parties about findings.

(8)   Comments of interested parties.

(9)   Publication of findings.

(10) Direct judicial review possibility.

Selected Bibliography

Australia

Books, Articles and Government Documents

Australian Customs Service, *Australian Customs Service Manual* (Public Edition).

Cooper, Customs and Excise Law (Sydney: Legal Books, 1984).

Steele, *"The Australian Anti-Dumping System,"* in Antidumping Law and Practice — A Comparative Study, Jackson and Vermulst, eds., (New York, London, Toronto, Sydney, Tokyo: Harvester Wheatsheaf, 1990), 223-286.

Court Decisions

Mitchell v. Curlewis, xv. ALT 143 (1893).

Stephens v. Alcock, 28 VLR 93 (1902).

Irving v. Munro & Sons Ltd., 46 CLR 279 (1931).

Peanut Board v. Rockhampton Harbour Board, 48 CLR 266 (1933).

Prestcold (Central) Limited v. Minister of Labour, 1 All ER 69 (1969).

Re Rubis and the Collector of Customs, 5 ALN N558 (1984).

Marine Power Australia Pty Limited & Anor v. Comptroller-General of Customs & Ors, 89 ALR 561 (1989).

Re Gaylor Jewellery Sales Pty Limited and the Collector of Customs, 12 AAR 86 (1990).

Wellington City Council v. Attorney General, 2 NZLR 281 (1990).

Re Eveready and the Collector of Customs,(No N89/906) (15 April 1991) unreported.

Re Midland Metals Overseas Limited and Collector of Customs, No V90/518 (29 April 1991) unreported.

Midland Metals Overseas Limited v. Comptroller-General of Customs, No G245 of 1991 (26 June 1991) unreported.

Eveready Australia Pty Limited v. Collector of Customs, No. G229 of 1991 (Federal Court of Australia 28 August 1991) (unreported).

Canada

Court Decisions

Ansaldo s.p.a. v. DMNR et al., 6 C.E.R. 334.

DMNR v. MacMillan & Bloedel (Apberni) Ltd. S.C.R. 366 (S.C.C., 1965).

Gruen Watch Company et al. v. The A.G. of Canada, 4 D.T.C. 784 (Ont.S.C.).

Harry D. Shields Limited v. Deputy Minister, 2 C.E.R. 1 (Tariff Board Appeal No. 1489).

Photo Albums with Self-Adhesive Leaves, Originating in or Exported from Hong Kong and the United States of America and Self-adhesive Leaves, Originating in or Exported from Hong Kong, the United States of America and the Republic of Korea, CIT-18-84, 9 C.E.R. 108 (1985).

Kipp Kelly Ltd. v. DMNR, 7 T.B.R. 102 (Appeal No. 1479).

Triton Industries Inc. v. DMNR, (Tariff Board Appeal No. 1454, 4 February, 1980).

The European Communities

Books and Articles

COMPENDIUM OF COMMUNITY CUSTOMS LEGISLATION (1989)

Forrester, EEC Customs Law: Rules of Origin and Preferential Duty Treatment, European Law Review 167 (Part I), 257 (Part II) (1980).

Herin, Rules of Origin and Differences Between Tariff Levels in EFTA and in the EC, Occasional Paper No. 13, European Free Trade Association, 10 February 1986.

Kapteyn, Verloren Van Themaat, INTRODUCTION TO THE LAW OF THE EUROPEAN COMMUNITIES, (Ed. Gormley 2nd ed., 1989).

Langhammer and Sapir, ECONOMIC IMPACT OF GENERALIZED TARIFF PREFERENCES (1987).

Vermulst and Waer, *European Community Rules of Origin as Commercial Policy Instruments?*, 24 Journal of World Trade No.3 55 (June 1990).

Vermulst and Waer, *Anti Circumvention Rules in Anti-Dumping Procedures: Interface or Short-Circuit for the Management of Interdependence?*, 11 Michigan Journal of International Law 1119, 1157 ff. (1990).

Waer and Vermulst, *De toepassing van algemene oorsprongsregels in de Europese Gemeenschap: Een probleemschets naar aanleiding van het Brother-arrest*, 7 S.E.W. 435 (1990).

Court Decisions

(49/76) Gesellschaft für Überseehandel v. Handelskammer Kassel, (1977) ECR 41.

(34/78) Yoshida Nederland B.V. v. Kamer van Koophandel en Frabrieken voor Friesland, (1979) ECR 115.

(114/78) Yoshida GmbH. v. Industrie- und Handelskammer Kassel, (1979) ECR 151.

(827/79) Administrazione delle Finanze v. Ciro Acampora, (1980) ECR 3731.

(162/82) Criminal proceedings against Paul Cousin and Others, (1983) ECR 1101.

(93/83) Zentralgenossenschaft des Fleischergewerbes e.G. v. Hauptzollamt Bochum, (1984) ECR 1095.

(218/83) Les rapides Savoyards Sàrl and others v. Directeur Général des Douanes et Droits Indirects, (1984) ECR 3105.

(385/85) S.R. Industries v. Administration des douanes, (1986) ECR 2929.

(229/86) Brother Industries Limited et al. v. Commission (1987) ECR 3757.

(26/88) Brother International GmbH v. Hauptzollamt Giessen, (1989) ECR 4253.

Japan

Books, Articles, and Related Documents

CCC, column "Japan" in "Compendium Rules of Origin" JASTPRO, *Getting the Best Benefits of Japan's GSP; Exporter's manual* (1988)

JASTPRO, *Alphabetical Commodity Index of Japan's GSP* (July 1991)

The Ministry of Foreign Affairs, (1991/92) Japan's GSP.

Japan Tariff Association, *Japan - Law and Regulations concerning Customs Duties and Customs Procedures (Rev. 2)*, (Tokyo: The Association 1990).

Fair Trade Institute, *Antimonopoly Legislation of Japan* (Tokyo: The Institute, 1984)

Norio Komuro, *Handbook on Rules of Origin* Tokyo:JMEA (1990), *Rules of Origin and Japanese firms* Tokyo: JMEA 1992.

Administrative or Judicial Decisions

Bentley England case., FTC Order of 29 August 1968.

Jeans case, FTC Orders of 22 March 1972.

Japanese suit materials with English lettering case., High Court of Tokyo Judgment of 29 July 1974.

Traditional silk fabrics (Oshima-tsumugi) case., FTC Orders of 9 October 1975 and 16 October 1976.
Belgian diamond case, High Court of Tokyo Judgment of 23 May 1978.
Chinese silk fabrics case, Tokyo District Court Judgment of 29 January 1982
Korean or Hong-Kong clothes cases, FTC Orders of 24 December 1987 and FTC Order of 17 March 1989.
Tôtosangyo Co. Ltd. case., MITI's sanction of 20 July 1990.

United States

Articles and Government Documents

Dearden and Palmeter, eds., FREE TRADE LAW REPORTER (CCH International).

Giesse and Lewin, *The Multifiber Arrangement: Temporary Protection Run Amuck*, 19 Law & Policy in International Business 51 (1987).

Palmeter, *Rules of Origin or Rules of Restriction? A Commentary on a New Form of Protectionism*, 11 Fordham International Law Journal 1 (1987).

Palmeter, *The Canada-U.S. FTA Rule of Origin and a Multilateral Agreement*, 16 International Business Lawyer No.11, 513 (1988).

Palmeter, "The FTA Rules of Origin: Boon or Boondoggle?" in LIVING WITH FREE TRADE: CANADA, THE FREE TRADE AGREEMENT AND THE GATT Dearden, Hart and Seger eds. (Ottawa Institute for Research and Public Policy, 1989).

Palmeter, "The FTA Rules of Origin and the Rule of Law", Proceedings of the Seventh Judicial Conference of the United States Court of Appeals for the Federal Circuit, 128 F.R.D. 500 (1990).

Palmeter, *The U.S. Rules of Origin Proposal to GATT: Monotheism or Polytheism?*, 24 Journal of World Trade No.2, 25 (1990).

Pomeranz, *Toward a New International Order in Government Procurement*, 11 Law & Policy in International Business 1263 (1979).

Simpson, *Reforming Rules of Origin*, Journal of Commerce, 4 October 1988, at 12A. US International Trade Commission, THE IMPACT OF RULES OF ORIGIN ON U.S. IMPORTS AND EXPORTS, Pub. No. 1695 (1985).

Court Decisions

Hartranft v. Wiegmann, 121 U.S. 609.
Tidewater Oil Company v. United States, 171 U.S. 210 (1897).
Anheuser-Busch Brewing Assn. v. United States, 207 U.S. 556 (1907).
United States v. Gibson-Thomsen Co., 27 C.C.P.A. 267 (1940).
United States v. International Paint Co., 35 C.C.P.A. 87 (1948).

Burstrom v. United States, 44 C.C.P.A. 27 (1956).

Amity Fabrics, Inc. v. United States, 43 Cust. Ct. 64 (1959).

Midwood Indus., Inc. v. United States, 64 Cust. Ct. 499 (1970).

Royal Bead Novelty Co. v. United States, 342 F. Supp. 1394 (1972).

Dolliff & Co., Inc. v. United States, 455 F. Supp. 618 81 Cust. Ct. 1, (1978).

United States v. Murray, 621 F.2d 1163 (1st Cir.), *cert den.*, 449 U.S. 837 (1980).

Texas Instruments, Inc. v. United States, 681 F.2d 778 (Fed. Cir. 1982).

Guardian Indus. Corp. v. United States, 3 Ct. Int'l Trade 9 (1982).

Uniroyal, Inc. v. United States, 542 F. Supp. 1026 (Ct. Int'l Trade 1982), *aff'd*, 702 F.2d 1022 (Fed. Cir. 1983).

Belcrest Linens v. United States, 741 F 2d 1368.

Torrington Co. v. United States, 764 F.2d 1563 (Fed. Cir. 1985).

National Juice Products Assn. v. United States, 628 F. Supp. 978 (Ct. Int'l Trade 1986).

Yuri Fashions, 632 F. Supp. 41 (Ct. Int'l Trade 1986).

Coastal States Marketing Inc. v. United States, 646 F. Supp. 255 (Ct. Int'l Trade 1986), *aff'd*, 812 F.2d 860 (Fed. Cir. 1987).

Ferrostaal Metals Corp. v. United States, 664 F. Supp. 535 (Ct. Int'l Trade 1987).

Madison Galleries, Ltd. v. United States, 688 F. Supp. 1544 (Ct Int'l Trade 1988).

Superior Wire, A Div. of Superior Products Co. v. U.S., 669 F. Supp. 472 (Ct. Int'l Trade 1987).

Timex Corp. v. United States, 691 F. Supp. 1445 (Ct. Int'l Trade 1988*)*.

Ashdown U.S.A. v. United States, 696 F. Supp. 661 (Ct. Int'l Trade 1988).

Koru North America v. United States, 701 F. Supp. 229 (Ct. Int'l Trade 1988).

Superior Wire v. United States, 867 F.2d 1409 (Fed. Cir. 1989).

American NTN Bearing Mfg. Corp. v. United States, 739 F. Supp. 1555 (Ct Int'l Trade 1990).

Norcal/Crosetti Foods, Inc. v. United States, 758 F. Supp. 729 (Ct. Int'l Trade 1991).

Contributors

Main Authors

Jacques H. J. Bourgeois: Former Principal Legal Advisor of the EC Commission; Partner, Baker and McKenzie, Brussels; Professor at the College of Europe, Bruges, Belgium.

Richard Gottlieb: Partner, Gottlieb & Pearson, Montreal, Canada.

Ivan Kingston: Partner, Malmgren, Golt, Kingston and Co. Ltd, London; LL.B., London School of Economics; Director, Putnam, Hayes and Bartlett Inc., USA.

Professor Norio Komuro: Associated Professor, National Defense Academy, Japan.

Daniel Moulis: Barrister and Solicitor, Freehill Hollingdale and Page, Canberra; LL.B., Sydney, 1983.

Edurne Navarro Varona: Lic. Jur., Barcelona, 1988; Lic. Spec., European Law, Brussels, 1989; LL.M./S.J.D., Michigan, 1991; Associate, Boden, De Bandt, De Brauw, Jeantet, Lagerlöf & Uría, Brussels.

N. David Palmeter: Partner, Mudge Rose Guthrie Alexander and Ferdon, Washington, D.C.; A.B., Syracuse, 1960; J.D., Chicago, 1963; Chairman, Trade and Customs Law Subcommittee, Antitrust and Trade Law Committee, International Bar Association.

H. Keith C. Steele: Partner, Freehill, Hollingdale and Page, Sydney; B.A., Cantab, 1972; M.A., Cantab, 1976; Barrister and Solicitor; Chairman, Customs Law Committee, Law Council of Australia; Honorary Consultant to the Australian Law Reform Commisssion Reference on Customs Legislation.

Edwin A. Vermulst: Partner, Akin, Gump, Strauss, Hauer, Feld & Dassesse, Brussels; LL.M., Utrecht, 1983; LL.M./S.J.D., Michigan, 1984, 1986.

Paul Waer: Member of the Brussels Bar. Lic. Jur., Antwerp, 1981; LL.M., Hitotsubashi, 1985; LL.M., Harvard, 1987.

Commentators

Ian Forrester: Partner, Forrester, Norall and Sutton, Brussels.

Gary Horlick: Partner, O'Melveny and Myers, Washington, D.C.

Dr. Jochen Matthies: Head of Division, Directorate-General for Customs and Indirect Taxation, Commission of the European Community, Brussels.

Michael A. Meyer: O'Melveny and Myers, Washington, D.C.

Jeff Waincymer: Professor, School of Law, Deakin University, Melbourne.

Index